National Infrastructure Planning Handbook 2016

National Infrastructure Planning Handbook 2016

General Editor

Michael Humphries QC
Barrister, Francis Taylor Building

Assistant Editors

James Pereira QC
Barrister, Francis Taylor Building

Hereward Phillpot QC
Barrister, Francis Taylor Building

Contributors

Douglas Edwards QC
Barrister, Francis Taylor Building

Gregory Jones QC
Barrister, Francis Taylor Building

Alexander Booth QC
Barrister, Francis Taylor Building

Richard Honey
Barrister, Francis Taylor Building

Mark Westmoreland Smith
Barrister, Francis Taylor Building

Rebecca Clutten
Barrister, Francis Taylor Building

Isabella Tafur
Barrister, Francis Taylor Building

Guest Contributors

Cain Ormondroyd
Barrister, Francis Taylor Building

Ned Westaway
Barrister, Francis Taylor Building

Sarah Merritt
Solicitor, Pinsent Masons LLP

Emma Cottam
Solicitor, Pinsent Masons LLP

Bloomsbury Professional

Bloomsbury Professional Ltd, Maxwelton House, 41–43 Boltro Road, Haywards Heath, West Sussex, RH16 1BJ

Bloomsbury Professional is an imprint of Bloomsbury Publishing plc

A CIP Catalogue record for this book is available from the British Library.

ISBN 978 1 78043 851 1

Typeset by Phoenix Photosetting, Chatham, Kent
Printed and bound in Great Britain by CPI Group (UK) Ltd, Croydon, CR0 4YY

Preface

As I write this, the UK has recently voted for Brexit in the EU Referendum; the former Prime Minister, David Cameron, has resigned; a new Prime Minister, Theresa May, is just being installed; and, to cap it all, the England football team is without a manager! What all this means for infrastructure planning in England and Wales, it is simply too early to say with any degree of confidence. My instincts, however, tell me that the timely consenting and delivery of nationally significant infrastructure projects will become more important than ever.

Those instincts are, perhaps, reinforced by the recent arrival of the (still shadow) National Infrastructure Commission ('NIC'), under the leadership of Lord Adonis, and the undoubted interest that this has generated in long-term strategic thinking about our infrastructure needs. The NIC has already produced a number of studies and the proposals for a new National Infrastructure Assessment with a 2050 time horizon are clearly welcome. Already it is clear that the NIC will play an important role in the UK's post-Brexit prosperity.

In the midst of all this, I hope that the *National Infrastructure Planning Handbook 2016* has a role to play in promoting best practice for all those involved in the consenting of nationally significant infrastructure projects. The success of the 2015 edition of this work has encouraged the publishers, Bloomsbury, to bring out an updated and expanded version and I hope that this edition is as well received as the last.

Since the last edition there have been some changes to the line up of those involved. Greg Jones QC and Douglas Edwards QC have asked to step down as Assistant Editors due to the pressure of their other professional engagements. I am grateful, however, for all their work on the Handbook and hope that they will be able to remain involved. Cain Ormondroyd and Ned Westaway, both from ftb, have become new Guest Contributors. The other members of my excellent team at ftb continue to be involved as before and I am extremely grateful, as ever, to all of them.

I must, of course, thank the in-house editorial team at Bloomsbury, Jane Bradford and Leanne Barrett, who work tirelessly on the Handbook and who (mostly) manage to keep me to their exacting time schedule.

Finally, I must thank my wife Juliet for putting up with me despite my frequent absences during weekends and holidays when I have been working on the text for this Handbook; thanks, sweetheart!

Michael Humphries QC
Francis Taylor Building
July 2016

Contents

Contributors

General Editor

Michael Humphries QC

Barrister, Francis Taylor Building

Michael Humphries specialises in all aspects of property development law, but is particularly well known for his major infrastructure planning and compulsory purchase work, where he has acted in relation to some of the largest and most important projects in recent years. Michael has promoted and advised on a large number of nationally significant infrastructure projects under the Planning Act 2008, including the Preesall Underground Gas Storage project, the Thames Tideway Tunnel project, the A30 Improvement project and the Hinkley Point Connection project. Michael has also promoted major infrastructure schemes under the Transport and Works Act 1992, the Town and Country Planning Act 1990, the Electricity Act 1989, the Highways Act 1980, the Gas Act 1965, and the Pipelines Act 1962.

In *Chambers & Partners 2016* Michael was identified as one of the six 'star individuals' at the Planning Bar. He was both *Chambers & Partners* and *Legal 500* planning silk of the year in 2013 and also appeared in *Planning Magazine's* 'Power 100' list as one of the most influential people in the UK planning system. In 2013 Michael was appointed a Visiting Fellow in the University of Cambridge Land Economy Department where he delivers an annual lecture on infrastructure planning. The *Planning Magazine* survey 2016 ranked Michael as the highest rated barrister for infrastructure work.

Published comments about Michael have been consistently complimentary and include: 'increasingly *the* name in large infrastructure projects' (*Chambers & Partners 2013*); 'He is a brilliant advocate whose analysis of legal points cannot be faulted. He is a pleasure to work with however much pressure he is put under' (*Chambers & Partners 2014*); 'Renowned for his expertise in infrastructure law', 'An extremely intelligent operator, with laser-like focus on the issues' (*Chambers & Partners 2015*); and 'Universally admired as one of the top planning silks in London' and 'He is the best infrastructure QC there is' (*Chambers & Partners 2016*).

Michael helped to found the National Infrastructure Planning Association (NIPA) and is its current Treasurer.

Michael was appointed Queen's Counsel in 2003.

Assistant Editors

James Pereira QC

Barrister, Francis Taylor Building

James specialises in planning, environmental, local government and administrative law, compulsory purchase and compensation, and has considerable experience in national infrastructure planning. James promoted both the Galloper Offshore Windfarm project and the Willington cross-country gas pipeline project.

Before taking silk James was in the highest rank of junior barristers in both environmental law and planning law in the *Legal 500 2012* and *Chambers & Partners 2012*, who list him as one of only four 'star individuals' at the junior planning bar. He was also ranked as a leading junior in Administrative Law in both directories. *Chambers & Partners 2015* says that 'He's just got it all – he's approachable, easy to work with, very bright, knows his stuff and clients like him' and *Chambers & Partners 2016* says he is 'Frequently described as a rising star of the planning bar'.

James was appointed Queen's Counsel in 2014.

Hereward Phillpot QC

Barrister, Francis Taylor Building

Hereward has an extensive practice in nationally significant infrastructure planning and has promoted a number of major nationally significant infrastructure projects including the Hinkley Point C nuclear power station, the East Anglia One and Navitus Bay offshore wind farms, Thames Tideway Tunnel and the National Grid Carbon Capture and Storage scheme.

Hereward was named 'Junior Barrister of the Year' in environment and planning by *Chambers & Partners 2012*, which also ranks him as one of only four 'star Individuals' in the field of planning. The *Planning Magazine* survey 2016 identified Hereward as second highest rated barrister for infrastructure work.

Published comments about Hereward include: 'He is our go-to barrister. He is very efficient, really gets to the problem quickly, is very good at thinking around the issues, gives clear advice and guidance, and is just a really nice guy to work with. He's definitely our number-one choice' *(Chambers and Partners 2015*) and 'Highly praised new silk who has acted in a number of nationally significant infrastructure cases' (*Chambers and Partners 2016*).

Hereward was appointed Queen's Counsel in 2015.

Contributors

Douglas Edwards QC

Barrister, Francis Taylor Building

Douglas Edwards practises in the fields of planning, compulsory purchase environment, administrative and local government, highway law and property law. He also has particular expertise in the law relating to common land and greens. He appears regularly for both appellants and local planning and other authorities at inquiries and in the courts. Douglas has advised on a number of nationally significant infrastructure schemes, including the A30 Improvement project.

Chambers & Partners 2015 described Douglas as 'Efficient and commercial in his approach' and 'Very capable, approachable and able to assimilate complex technical issues quickly' and *Chambers & Partners 2016* says that 'He is very astute as to what developers need and what the desired outcomes are'.

Douglas was appointed Queen's Counsel in 2010.

Gregory Jones QC

Barrister, Francis Taylor Building

Gregory has considerable experience in the fields of administrative law including judicial review and statutory challenges, town planning, compulsory purchase, environmental law, EU law and public procurement, education and local government law. Regularly appearing in both public inquiries and the higher courts, Gregory acts on behalf of developers, local planning authorities and third parties.

Gregory has advised on a number of nationally significant infrastructure projects and successfully promoted the Able Marine Energy Park project.

Legal 500 2015 describes Gregory as 'A superb advocate' and *Chambers & Partners 2015* states that Gregory 'gets to grips with complex intellectual issues very quickly and is '[a]n authority on environmental impact assessment, habitats directives and wider planning and environment issues. He is also renowned for his expertise in matters involving CPOs. A likeable, quick-thinking advocate who is always fun to work with and who shows a deep understanding of the implications of EU environmental law on the UK planning system' and that 'He has a very calm and reassuring approach, and his expertise in environmental impact assessment matters is invaluable.' *Chambers and Partners 2016* says that he is 'Universally admired for his advocacy skills and work on high-profile matters'.

Gregory was appointed Queen's Counsel in 2011.

Alexander Booth QC

Barrister, Francis Taylor Building

Alex Booth has huge expertise in planning, compulsory purchase and environmental law. He regularly appears at Public Inquiries, in the Upper Tribunal (Lands Chamber) and in the High Court, and has also appeared in both the Court of Appeal and the Supreme Court.

He has wide experience of infrastructure development generally, and of nationally significant infrastructure projects promoted pursuant to the 2008 Act in particular. As regards the latter, he promoted the Rookery South Resource Recovery Facility on behalf of Covanta, and acted on behalf of Associated British Ports to oppose the Able Marine Energy Park promoted on the south bank of the Humber Estuary. He also acted for Thames Water in the legal challenges to the Thames Tideway Tunnel development consent. Other experience includes the promotion of LNG pipelines in South Wales on behalf of National Grid, opposing the expansion of Coventry Airport and advising statutory undertakers regarding the laying of high voltage electricity cabling in Central London, required in connection with Crossrail.

Published comments on Alex include: 'He continues to act on a number of infrastructure and general planning matters' and that 'He is very good on his feet. The way he deals with the issues as they arise in cross examination is impressive' *(Chambers and Partners 2016).*

Alex was appointed Queen's Counsel in 2016

Richard Honey

Barrister, Francis Taylor Building

Richard Honey practises as a barrister in public and environmental law, with particular specialisms in judicial review and statutory High Court challenges, infrastructure projects, and compulsory purchase and compensation.

Richard's infrastructure experience includes schemes under the Transport and Works Act and the Electricity Act, and parliamentary work including appearances before the Crossrail and HS2 Bill committees for various objectors. Recent infrastructure work includes the Olympics, Thameslink, Crossrail, highway schemes, wind farms and airports (Stansted, Southend, Lydd). Richard advised Natural England on the examinations into Hinkley Point C nuclear power station and the Able Marine Energy Park.

Richard is ranked as a leading barrister by *Chambers & Partners* for planning and environmental law and was also ranked in the top 12 highest rated junior planning barristers in the 2016 *Planning Magazine* survey. *Chambers and Partners 2016* says of Richard that he 'Regularly features in complex infrastructure, planning and compulsory purchase cases' and that he 'has a phenomenal capacity for getting through matters and a very, very strong eye for detail'.

Mark Westmoreland Smith

Barrister, Francis Taylor Building

Mark has particular experience in infrastructure planning and has recently been working on development consent orders for electrical infrastructure, power stations, ports, waste management facilities as well as roads.

In the *Planning Magazine* survey 2016 Mark was ranked as one of the top five junior planning barristers.

Mark has been described as 'a tenacious advocate', 'rapidly scaling the ranks', 'particularly well regarded', having 'a bright future' and 'practical, experienced, down to earth and always gives clear advice' (*Chambers & Partners*). *Chambers and Partners 2016* says that he 'Focuses on development consent order and infrastructure work' and that he 'is approachable, highly competent and knowledgeable, and gives a good strategic lead'.

He is a member of the National Infrastructure Planning Association, the Compulsory Purchase Association and is a former Assistant Secretary to the Planning and Environmental Bar Association.

Rebecca Clutten

Barrister, Francis Taylor Building

Rebecca Clutten was called to the Bar in 2008 and is currently ranked second in the top planning juniors under 35 (*Planning Magazine* Survey, 2016), having been rated consistently highly since joining ftb in 2010.

Rebecca has substantial experience in infrastructure planning, having advised and appeared for promoters of DCOs and Transport and Works Act Orders at the application and examination stages, both being led and in her own right. Recent experience includes promoting the Walney Extension Offshore windfarm for DONG Energy. Her experience also includes Parliamentary work, and she recently appeared before the House of Commons Select Committee on High Speed 2. Rebecca's practice extends to include general town planning matters and compulsory purchase and compensation. Her clients include major utilities providers, developers and local authorities, as well as private individuals.

Chambers and Partners 2016 says that 'She is very, very good and down-to-earth and detailed'.

Rebecca is a member of the National Infrastructure Planning Association and is an elected member of the committees of the Planning and Environmental Bar Association and the Compulsory Purchase Association.

Isabella Tafur

Barrister, Francis Taylor Building

Isabella has gained considerable experience of national infrastructure planning through her involvement in a number of DCO applications.

She has worked for National Grid in relation to its application for development consent for an innovative carbon capture and storage project, as well as for the promoters of the Walney Extension offshore windfarm application in the Irish Sea, the A30 trunk road improvement in Cornwall and the Able Marine Energy Park on the Humber estuary. In these cases she has been involved in the preparation and review of documents both prior to, and after the submission of the application. She has attended preliminary meetings and issue specific hearings and prepared written submissions during the examination period.

Isabella was one of the six highest rated planning juniors under 35 in the Planning Magazine survey 2016.

Guest Contributors

Cain Ormondroyd

Barrister, Francis Taylor Building

Cain undertakes a wide range of planning work, including in relation to infrastructure, and he is particularly known for his environmental law practice.

Cain is an experience Court advocate and is a member of the Attorney General's 'B Panel' of Counsel. He often appears in the High Court on behalf of the Secretary of State for Communities and Local Government and the Secretary of State for the Home Department. He is frequently instructed by HMRC. Cain has also worked with Friends of the Earth, the Environmental Law Foundation and other public interest groups in relation to environmental law issues.

Ned Westaway

Barrister, Francis Taylor Building

Ned has considerable experience of major planning and infrastructure cases both under the Planning Act 2008 and preceding legislation. He appeared at examinations into the Able Marine Energy Park on the Humber Estuary, the Thames Tideway Tunnel in London and the Navitus Bay Wind Farm, where he presented the successful objection on behalf of Natural England. He also has an active High Court practice and is on the Attorney General's Panel of London counsel.

Ned is consistently ranked as a leading barrister in planning and environmental law; *Chambers and Partners 2016* comments that 'he has a very, very good, sharp mind and adopts a very thorough approach to his preparation of cases' and *Chambers and Partners 2015* says that 'he's excellent ... very calm and articulate, very quick on his feet, and thinks strategically'. He is currently ranked as the leading barrister under the age of 35 (*Planning Magazine*, 2016). *Who's Who Legal* 2016 lists him as a leading junior for environment law who is 'extremely active' in the sector.

Ned is a member of PEBA, a trustee of the United Kingdom Environmental Law Association and a visiting researcher at UCL's Centre for Law and the Environment.

Sarah Merritt

Solicitor, Pinsent Masons LLP

Sarah is a senior associate at Pinsent Masons LLP, specialising in major infrastructure planning and regulatory matters.

Sarah advises utility companies, distribution network operators, developers, local authorities and government agencies on a variety of matters, both national and international. Sarah's practice focuses on the energy and natural resources, waste and infrastructure sectors. She has experience of advising on obtaining regulatory consents for nationally significant infrastructure projects, including development consent orders under the Planning Act 2008, planning permission under the Town and Country Planning Act 1990, Electricity Act 1989 consents and nuclear site licences. These projects include biomass, nuclear and gas-fired power stations, energy from waste facilities, electricity distribution infrastructure, proposals for a nuclear waste repository, non-nuclear waste facilities and road schemes.

Emma Cottam

Solicitor, Pinsent Masons LLP

Emma is a Solicitor in the Planning & Environment and Energy & Infrastructure team based in the Pinsent Masons' London office. Emma has experience in consenting major infrastructure projects in England and Wales and has advised on a number of energy schemes at various stages in the Planning Act 2008 process.

Table of Cases

D

E

F

G

H

I

K

L

M

S

T

W

Table of Statutes

Table of Statutory Instruments

Part 1

The Examining Authority and the Secretary of State

The Major Applications and Plans Directorate of the Planning Inspectorate

Written by: Richard Honey, ftb
Edited by: Michael Humphries QC, ftb

On 1 April 2012 the Planning Inspectorate (also known as PINS) became responsible for operating the planning process for nationally significant infrastructure projects. Before that date applications for nationally significant infrastructure projects were handled by the Infrastructure Planning Commission (IPC). The IPC was, however, abolished under the Localism Act 2011 and its functions transferred to the Inspectorate. The Major Applications and Plans Directorate (MAPD) now discharges the former functions of the IPC. MAPD is a department within the Planning Inspectorate that was formed in March 2013 following an internal reorganisation of the Planning Inspectorate that saw the merger of the National Infrastructure Directorate and the Development Plans Directorate.

MAPD has responsibility for the administration of major applications under the Planning Act 2008, local plans and the measures for major planning applications under the Growth and Infrastructure Act 2013 where developers opt to apply direct to the Inspectorate.

MAPD handles major applications and discharges many of the procedural functions of the Secretary of State under the Planning Act 2008, the Infrastructure Planning (Applications: Prescribed Forms and Procedure) Regulations 2009 and the Infrastructure Planning (Examination Procedure) Rules 2010. This includes the pre-application process, submission of an application, acceptance, pre-examination, examination and reporting.

The Secretary of State has established a formal framework of delegation, delegating nationally significant infrastructure projects actions to the Inspectorate's Chief Executive, who in turn has sub-delegated functions to the Director of Major Applications and Plans and the Chief Planning Inspector (as reported in the Inspectorate's 2012/13 annual report and accounts).

MAPD is based at Temple Quay House in Bristol. It currently has a staff of around 70, including both salaried and non-salaried inspectors. The current Director of Major Applications and Plans is Mark Southgate, a chartered town planner with over 20 years' experience. Prior to his appointment he was Director of Casework and Plans at the Inspectorate.

The Planning Inspectorate's 2015/16 annual report and accounts (p 82) shows that the Inspectorate received over £4.1m in fee income for national infrastructure work, against an operating cost of over £6.8m.

Further information about the MAP and the Planning Inspectorate can be found at: http://infrastructure.planningportal.gov.uk.

MAP works with the Consents Service Unit (CSU). The CSU was launched in April 2013 to help provide a 'one-stop-shop' approach to non-planning consents for nationally significant infrastructure projects that are required in addition to any development consent order. The purpose of the CSU is to improve the coordination between the developer, relevant consenting bodies and the Inspectorate, to seek to make the overall consenting process more efficient. The CSU published a 'Prospectus for Developers' that sets out the unit's objectives.

During 2012 the Major Infrastructure and Environment Unit (MIEU) was established within Defra to work on matters relating to the Habitats and Wild Birds Directives and infrastructure projects. MIEU was set up to support progress on individual infrastructure projects and improve processes for infrastructure projects by:

- playing a key early risk management role to identify issues associated with the Habitats and Wild Birds Directives for projects
- ensuring collaboration between all parties to support resolution of issues as necessary
- introducing and overseeing a new process for agreeing evidence requirements
- providing greater clarity to developers on requirements

Further information on MIEU can be found at: http://www.defra.gov.uk/habitats-review/implementation/infrastructure-projects/.

The Appointment and Composition of the Examining Authority

Written by: Isabella Tafur, ftb
Edited by: Michael Humphries QC, ftb

Introduction

Pursuant to section 86 of the Planning Act 2008 (PA 2008), the Examining Authority is defined as either a Panel or a single appointed person appointed by the Secretary of State to examine an application for a development consent order. It is for the Secretary of State to determine whether the application should be handled by a Panel (under Chapter 2 of PA 2008) or by a single appointed person (under Chapter 3 of PA 2008). That decision will be made after an application has been accepted by the Secretary of State and a certificate has been received from the applicant confirming that it has complied with the notice and publicity requirements contained in PA 2008, s 56 (and, where applicable, a notice of the persons interested in land to which a compulsory acquisition request relates) (PA 2008, s 61).

Rule 2(1) of the Infrastructure Planning (Examination Procedure) Rules 2010 (as amended) ('the 2010 Rules') defines the Examining Authority as follows:

> '(a) the Panel or single appointed person appointed under section 62 (appointment of members, and lead member, of a Panel) or section 79 (appointment of a single appointed person), and may include one or more members of the Panel allocated a function of the Panel in accordance with section 76 (allocation within Panel or Panel's functions); or
>
> (b) the Secretary of State, in respect of those matters which are the subject of a direction by the Secretary of State under section 95A(2).'

Section 95A was inserted into the PA 2008 by the Localism Act 2011. It enables the Secretary of State to direct that representations of a type specified in his direction may only be made to persons of a specified description (rather than being made in public). It applies where part or all of the examination procedure will take the form of a meeting or hearing and the Secretary of State is satisfied that the making of oral representations at such a meeting or hearing would be likely to result in the disclosure of information as to defence or national security, and that public disclosure of that information would be contrary to the national interest.

Criteria for determining how an application should be handled

PA 2008, s 61 requires the Secretary of State to publish the criteria that are to be applied in determining whether an application is to be handled by a Panel or a single appointed person. The criteria are currently set out in paragraphs 12–14 of DCLG's 'Guidance for the examination of applications for development consent, (March 2015). The main criteria which the Secretary of State will consider are: (a) the complexity of the case; and (b) the level of public interest in the outcome (paragraph 12). When looking at the complexity of the case the Secretary of State will consider whether the application raises novel issues for development, raises complex legal or technical considerations, proposes associated development which would require consideration of policy contained in more than a single National Policy Statement (NPS), or involves analysis of policy issues because, for example, there is no relevant NPS. In considering the level of public interest the Secretary of State will have particular regard to the likelihood of the examination requiring hearings so that parties can make oral representations about the application. So, for example, of the 15 applications which had been, or were being, examined by the end of 2012, seven were handled by Panels.[1] All of those Panels were made up of three members, with the exception of the Hinkley Point C nuclear generating station application, where a fourth member was subsequently appointed. The remaining eight applications were handled by single appointed persons[2].

Transfer of the application from a single appointed person to a Panel

Where the Secretary of State has appointed a single appointed person to examine the application, he may at any time decide that the application should be handled by a Panel instead (s 62). He must publish the criteria to be applied when making such a decision. DCLG's consultation Guidance explains that the Secretary of State will be able to transfer the application to a Panel if he considers the application is more complex than the original assessment indicated and that it requires a wider range of expertise (paragraph 14). The Guidance does not, however, suggest that the Secretary of State can make a decision to transfer the application to a Panel on the basis that it has generated a greater level of public interest than originally anticipated.

Where an application is transferred from a single appointed person to a Panel, the single appointed person may be appointed as a member of that Panel, and may also be appointed as chair of the Panel (s 71). Where such a transfer is effected, it will not always be necessary for the examination procedure to start again. Pursuant to s 71 the Panel may, so far as it thinks appropriate, decide to treat things done by or in relation to the appointed person on the application as done by or in relation to the Panel. In these circumstances it will be the duty of the lead member to ensure that the members of the Panel have the necessary knowledge of the proceedings which took place under the appointed person.

Notifying the parties

The Secretary of State must, before the preliminary meeting, notify all those who have been notified of the accepted application that the Examining Authority has

1 Rookery South; Hinkley Point Power Station; Galloper Offshore Windfarm; Preesall Saltfield Underground Gas Storage; Able Marine Energy Park; Triton Knoll Offshore Windfarm; and Roosecote Biomass Power Station (which was subsequently withdrawn by the applicant).

2 North Doncaster Chord; Ipswich Chord; Kentish Flats Extension; Brechfa Forest Wind Farm; Heysham to M6 Link Road; East Northants Resource Management Facility; Port Blythe New Biomass Plant; M1 Junction 10a Grade Separation.

been appointed, and give details of who has been appointed (r 4 of the 2010 Rules). Where the Secretary of State had originally appointed a single appointed person and subsequently decides that the Examining Authority should be a Panel, he must notify all interested parties of this decision. He must also notify interested parties of any change in the membership of the Panel or appointment of any replacement appointed person, or any direction made under PA 2008, s 95A.

Appointment and replacement of Panels and single appointed persons

The Panel procedure is set out in Chapter 2 of the PA 2008, and the single appointed person procedure in Chapter 3 of the PA 2008.

Section 65 of the PA 2008 provides that where the Examining Authority comprises a panel, it must be made up of a minimum of three and a maximum of five persons, with one of those members (the 'lead member') appointed as chair. Where a panel of three has been appointed, and one ceases to act, another panel member must therefore be appointed (s. 68(3) PA 2008).

Section 27 of the Infrastructure Act 2015 allows for a panel of two persons to be appointed, and accordingly removes the obligation to appoint an additional panel member if one person in a panel of three has to cease to act. As a consequential change, s 27(4) extends the principle of majority voting (with the lead member having the casting vote) to two person panels. At the time of writing (June 2016), however, the amendments introduced by s 27 have not come into force.

A Panel may, instead of undertaking a part of the examination, allocate the undertaking of that part to one or more of its members (PA 2008, s 76). Where it makes such an allocation, anything which is required or authorised to be done by the Panel under Chapter 4 of the PA 2008 in connection with the allocated part of the examination, may be done by or to the member(s) concerned. The findings and conclusions of the member(s) concerned in respect of the matters allocated will be taken to be those of the Panel as a whole, provided the Panel so agreed at the time of making the allocation (or before the allocation was made). Where there is an allocation to two or more members, the making of a decision by the members concerned requires the agreement of all of them. Procedural powers conferred on the Panel for the purposes of its examination of the application can be exercised by the Panel itself and by any one or more of its members (unless the Panel has decided to restrict or prohibit the exercise of procedural powers other than by the Panel itself) (PA 2008, s 77).

Members of the Panel and single appointed persons can resign their positions by giving notice in writing to the Secretary of State, and they can also be removed by the Secretary of State if he is satisfied that they are unable, unwilling or unfit to perform their duties (sections 66 and 80).

In a Panel, the lead member can be removed from that office without being removed from the Panel altogether. In such circumstances the Secretary of State must appoint another lead member (either from amongst the other members of the Panel or be appointing a new member) (PA 2008, s 69). New members may be appointed by the Secretary of State at any time after the initial appointment of the members (provided the total number does not exceed five), and he must do so if the membership of the Panel falls below three (PA 2008, s 68). He cannot, however, use this power to appoint new members where the Panel ceases to have any members (PA 2008, s 72(5)).

If the Panel ceases to have any members at all, a new Panel must be constituted (PA 2008, s 72). Where a new Panel is constituted, it may decide to treat things done by or in relation to the previous Panel (or treated by the previous Panel as being done by or in relation to that Panel, under PA 2008, s 71(3)) as done by or in relation to the new Panel. The lead member will be responsible for ensuring that the members have the necessary knowledge of the proceedings up until the reconstitution of the Panel.

PA 2008, s 73 makes it clear that the Panel's continuing identity is not affected by any change in its membership; the Panel coming to have only two members or a single member; any change in the lead member; or a vacancy in the office of lead member.

Where a person ceases to be the single appointed person, the Secretary of State must make a new appointment (PA 2008, s 82). Where this happens the new single appointed person may, so far as may be appropriate, decide to treat things done by or in relation to any previous single appointed person as done by or in relation to the new single appointed person (PA 2008, s 82(2)). Where he does so, the single appointed person is under a duty to acquire the necessary knowledge of the previous proceedings on the application.

The functions of the Examining Authority

Regardless of whether it is a Panel or a single appointed person, the functions of the Examining Authority are to: (1) examine the application; and (2) make a report to the Secretary of State on the application setting out: (i) its findings and conclusions in respect of the application; and (ii) its recommendation as to the decision to be made on the application. Its functions must be carried out in accordance with Chapter 4 of the PA 2008 (Examination of applications under Chapter 2 or 3 of PA 2008).

Where the Examining Authority is a Panel, the making of a decision requires the agreement of a majority of its members. The lead member has a casting vote, in the event that the vote is tied.

Appointment of assessors and advisors

Pursuant to PA 2008, s 100, the Secretary of State may, at the request of the Examining Authority, appoint a person to act as an assessor to assist the Examining Authority in its examination of the application. The Secretary of State may only appoint an assessor if it appears to him that the person has the expertise that makes him suitable to provide assistance to the Examining Authority.

The Secretary of State may also appoint, at the request of the Examining Authority, a barrister, solicitor or advocate to provide legal assistance to the Examining Authority in connection with its examination of the application, including carrying out any oral questioning at a hearing on behalf of the Examining Authority.

The role of assessors and legal advisors is to assist the Examining Authority, but those persons do not form part of the Examining Authority.

Where an assessor or a barrister, solicitor or advocate is appointed, the Examining Authority must notify all interested parties of the name of the assessor and/or the details of the legal advisor and, in the case of an assessor, must notify the parties of the particular matters on which the assessor is to assist the Examining Authority (rr 11 and 12 of the 2010 Rules).

DCLG's Guidance explains (paragraphs 66–69) that in most cases the appointment of an assessor is likely to take place at the pre-examination stage, because the initial assessment of the application would usually have identified to the Examining Authority the issues that required further examination with the assistance of an assessor.

DCLG's Guidance also explains (paragraph 70) that the Examining Authority may sometimes need to appoint a professional advocate to ensure evidence is 'tested in the most effective and revealing way'.

The Role of the Examining Authority

Written by: Isabella Tafur, ftb
Edited by: Michael Humphries QC, ftb

Introduction

Once the Secretary of State has appointed either a single appointed person or a Panel as the Examining Authority (see Article 3.2.2 for further details on the appointment and composition of the Examining Authority) its role in relation to the application for development consent is governed by the PA 2008, ss 74–77 and 83.

One of the principal changes introduced by the Localism Act 2011 is that all decisions on development consent applications are now made by the Secretary of State. The role of the Examining Authority is, therefore, limited to examining the application and reporting to the relevant Secretary of State.

Panel

Where the Examining Authority is a Panel, its role is set out in PA 2008, ss 74–77. It must examine the application and prepare a report for the Secretary of State, setting out its findings and conclusions in respect of the application, and its recommendation as to the decision to be made (PA 2008, s 74).

Decisions made by the Panel require the agreement of a majority of its members, and the lead member has a casting vote in the event of a tied vote (PA 2008, s 75). However, the Panel may choose to allocate parts of the examination to one or more members of the Panel (PA 2008, s 76). Where they do so, the findings or conclusions of that member (or those members) will be taken to be the findings and conclusions of the Panel in relation to the allocated matter. If a matter has been allocated to two or more members of the Panel, their decision on that matter requires their unanimous agreement.

Single appointed person

Where the Examining Authority is a single appointed person, its role in relation to the application is governed by PA 2008, s 83. Its functions mirror those set out in s 74 in relation to a Panel: it is to examine the application and prepare a report to the relevant Secretary of State setting out its findings and conclusions in respect of the application and its recommendation as to the decision to be made.

Examination of the application

The functions of the Examining Authority must be carried out in accordance with Chapter 4 of the PA 2008, which governs the manner in which an application should be examined (see PA 2008, ss 74(3) and 83(3)). The Infrastructure Planning (Examination Procedure) Rules 2010 also contain provisions relating to the examination of applications. Later articles consider the 'examination' process in detail.

The Legal Status of the Secretary of State in Litigation

Written by: Richard Honey, ftb
Edited by: Michael Humphries QC, ftb

Although any Secretary of State or other Minister acts formally on behalf of the Crown, it is important to understand the legal distinction between the Queen and her Ministers. Whilst the Crown retains certain prerogatives and indeed public immunity in litigation (subject to the Crown Proceedings Act 1947), Parliament will normally confer administrative powers and duties on 'the Secretary of State' or 'the Minister' and no such prerogatives or immunity attach to such a Minister acting on the Crown's behalf. This greatly assists the operation of administrative law as it means that all legal remedies are potentially available against a Minister.

It is a well-established principle of constitutional law that powers given to Ministers are normally exercised not by the Ministers themselves but by their officers and, further, that a Minister is not obliged to take an action himself but can act through an officer. In *R v Secretary of State for the Home Department, ex p Oladehinde* [1991] 1 AC 254 at 300–B Lord Griffiths held that 'It is obvious that the Secretary of State cannot personally take every decision … The decision must be taken by a person of suitable seniority in the [Department] for whom the [Secretary of State] accepts responsibility. This devolution of responsibility was recognised as a practical necessity in the administration of government by the Court of Appeal in *Carltona Ltd v Works Commissioners* [1943] 2 All ER 560 and has become known as the *Carltona* principle.' Thus it can be said that an act of a duly authorised civil servant is an act of the Minister and, furthermore, that the Minister is legally responsible for the acts of such a civil servant taken in the Minister's name.

It also needs to be recognised that the titles and functions of Ministers and their departments are frequently changed. This is usually effected under the Ministers of the Crown Act 1975. This Act allows the Queen, by Order in Council, to transfer the functions of Ministers and, furthermore, to make changes in departments of the office of Secretary of State. In this regard, such Order in Council may also make a Secretary of State a 'corporation sole' and transfer property etc to a named Secretary of State.

It is in this context that the PA 2008 confers various powers and duties on 'the Secretary of State'. The Act does not, however, identify the particular 'Secretary of State' to which any particular power or duty relates. It is clear, however, from Schedule 1 to the Interpretation Act 1978 that references to 'the Secretary of State' should be taken to mean 'one of Her Majesty's Principal Secretaries of State'. Thus the powers and duties of the Secretary of State are in theory conferred on all the Secretaries of State in existence at the time. This arises because, constitutionally, there is only a single office of Secretary of State although that office may be performed by a number of named Secretaries of State as determined by the Queen in Council.

In practice, however, an application for development consent under the Planning Act 2008 is determined by whichever Secretary of State, or Secretaries of State, have responsibility for the field of activity in relation to which the application relates. Thus, the Secretary of State for Transport in practice determines applications for consent for transport projects. This would include road, rail and port projects. Similarly, the Secretary of State for Energy and Climate Change makes decisions on energy infrastructure applications.

There may be other roles for a Secretary of State in the DCO process. For example, the power in PA 2008, s 127 (statutory undertakers' land) would be exercised by the Secretary of State who is responsible for the particular affected statutory undertaker's activity (for example, the Secretary of State for Environment, Food and Rural Affairs in relation to a water company).

Legal challenges relating to applications for orders granting development consent are to be brought by judicial review under PA 2008, s 118. In litigation connected with an application for a development consent order, it will be the Secretary of State responsible for the decision on that application who would, in practice, be the defendant in any judicial review proceedings. So, for example, the Secretary of State for Energy and Climate Change was the defendant in the judicial review challenges to the decisions on the Hinkley Point C generating station application and the Preesall underground gas storage facility application, as it was that Secretary of State who had taken the decisions challenged.

In practice, it is usual for the Treasury Solicitor's Department (TSol) to act on behalf of a Secretary of State in litigation. The TSol website states that the Litigation Group within TSol acts for over 800 different clients spread across 180 Government Departments and public bodies and that they handle over 20,000 cases each year in a wide range of courts and tribunals. The TSol operates from its headquarters at: Treasury Solicitor's Department, One Kemble Street, London, WC2B 4TS (www.tsol.gov.uk).

Part 2

National Policy Statements

General Procedural Requirements for Designation of an NPS

Written by James Pereira QC, ftb
Edited by Michael Humphries QC, ftb

Introduction

A National Policy Statement (NPS) is a statement issued by the Secretary of State that sets out national policy in relation to one or more type of development falling within s 14 of the PA 2008. NPSs are formally 'designated' by the relevant Secretary of State PA 2008, s 5(1) and (2)). In determining an application for development consent, there is a statutory obligation upon the Secretary of State to determine the application in accordance with any relevant NPS, unless certain specified circumstances apply (PA 2008, s 104). NPSs are, therefore, key policy documents within the PA 2008 regime.

Certain important procedural steps must be undertaken before an NPS can be designated. Broadly speaking, these steps relate to publicity and consultation, parliamentary scrutiny and consideration of sustainability (generally, PA 2008, ss 5–10). The High Court has made clear that the procedural requirements that precede the designation of an NPS mean that changes in circumstances relating to the strategic need for a particular type of project should properly be raised by way of a request to the Secretary of State to modify the NPS, rather than as a factor justifying departure from that NPS in any given case: see *R (Thames Blue Green Economy Limited) v Secretary of State* [2015] EWCA Civ 876 (a decision on a judicial review permission application).

The procedural steps are outlined in this section. Reference should be made to the provisions of the Act for the detail.

Publicity and Consultation

Prior to the designation of an NPS, or a proposed amendment to an NPS, certain publicity requirements must be met (PA 2008, s 5(4) and (7)). In relation to a 'proposal' to designate an NPS or an amendment to an NPS (s 7(3)), the PA 2008 gives the Secretary of State a discretion to carry out such consultation and arrange for such publicity as the Secretary of State thinks appropriate, subject to certain mandatory requirements being met (PA 2008, s 7(2), (4) and (5)). The Secretary of State must, however, have regard to the responses to such consultation and publicity when deciding whether to proceed with such a 'proposal' (PA 2008, s 7(6)).

Formal consultation is mandatory in relation to such persons and descriptions of persons as may be prescribed (PA 2008, s 7(4)).

In relation to publicity, the Secretary of State must ensure that 'appropriate steps' are taken to publicise the 'proposal' where it identifies one or more locations as suitable or potentially suitable for a specified description of development (PA 2008, s 7(5)). When deciding what publicity is appropriate for these purposes, PA 2008, s 8 requires the Secretary of State to consult the relevant local authorities on the publicity requirements (see PA 2008, s 8(1)–(5) for identification of which local authorities need to be consulted).

The publicity requirements may be satisfied in relation to modified versions of an earlier proposed policy statement, where the Secretary of State thinks that the modifications do not materially affect the policy as set out in the 'earlier proposal' which itself complied with the relevant publicity requirements (see PA 2008, s 6A(1)–(3), to which reference should be made).

Parliamentary scrutiny

A proposed NPS, or amendment to an NPS, must be laid before Parliament (PA 2008, s 9(2)). Before doing so, the Secretary of State must specify the relevant period within which either House of Parliament may make a resolution with regard to the proposal, or a committee of either House may make a recommendation with regard to the proposal (PA 2008, s 6B(4), (6) and (7)). The Secretary of State must lay before Parliament his response to any resolution or recommendation: PA 2008, s 6B(4) and (5).

Following these steps, the proposed policy or amendment to policy can be laid before Parliament, though the formal step of laying the policy before Parliament may need to be repeated in certain circumstances (PA 2008, s 6B(8) and (9)). Section 6A(4) contains provision relevant to changes made to the proposed policy after it has been laid before Parliament.

Sustainability

No policy statement can be designated an NPS unless it has first been subject to a sustainability appraisal (PA 2008, s 5(3)). This requirement is intended to satisfy the obligation to carry out Strategic Environmental Assessment pursuant to the SEA Directive 2001/42/EC. A sustainability appraisal that fails to satisfy the requirements of the SEA Directive will be liable to challenge under PA 2008, s 13.

When designating or reviewing an NPS the Secretary of State must also exercise his functions with the objective of contributing to the achievement of sustainable development, in particular with regard to the desirability of mitigating and adopting to climate change and achieving good design (PA 2008, s 10).

Designation as an NPS

Once the consultation and publicity requirements in PA 2008, s 7 have been met, and the parliamentary requirements in PA 2008, s 9 have been discharged, the policy statement can be designated an NPS provided that the statement has been approved by resolution of the House of Commons after being laid before Parliament under PA 2008, s 9(8) and before the end of the 'consideration period', or the 'consideration period' for the statement has expired without the House of Commons resolving during that period that the statement should not be proceeded with (PA 2008, s 5(4)).

The 'consideration period' is defined under PA 2008, s 5(4A) as the period 21 sitting days beginning with the first sitting day after the day on which the statement is laid before Parliament under s 9(8). This period may itself be extended by 21 sitting days or less, and extended more than once, subject to certain procedural requirements (PA 2008, s 6B).

Review and amendment of an NPS

The Secretary of State must review all or part of an NPS where he considers it appropriate to do so (PA 2008, s 6(1) and (2)).

In deciding whether to do so, the Secretary of State must have regard to whether there has been a significant change in circumstances on the basis of which the relevant policy or part of the policy was decided; whether that change was anticipated at the time; and whether, if the change had been anticipated, any of the relevant policy would have been materially different (PA 2008, s 6(3) and (4)).

A review may result in the NPS being amended, withdrawn or left as it is (PA 2008, s 6(5)).

PA 2008 s 6(6) provides that a sustainability appraisal must be carried out before an NPS is amended. The same requirement could be argued to apply to a decision to withdraw an NPS: see by analogy *Cala Homes v Secretary of State* [2010] EWHC 2866 (Admin) (decision to revoke Regional Spatial Strategies unlawful unless preceded by SEA).

Amendments to an NPS are subject to similar requirements for consultation, publicity and Parliamentary scrutiny, as apply to an NPS itself (PA 2008, s 6(7), referring to PA 2008, ss 7 and 9).

NPSs and the Requirement for Environmental Assessment

Written by Rebecca Clutten
Edited by Michael Humphries QC

The nature and effect of NPSs

National Policy Statements ('NPSs') are the statutory planning policy statements for nationally significant infrastructure projects in England and Wales. By virtue of s 104 of PA 2008, wherever there is an extant NPS,[1] the Secretary of State must when determining an application for a DCO have regard to *inter alia* that relevant NPS.[2]

Although there are other specified documents and matters to which the Secretary of State must have regard, PA 2008 goes on to provide that, save in specified circumstances (that is, where the circumstances set out in sub-ss (4)–(8) apply), DCO applications must be decided in accordance with the relevant NPS.

The NPS therefore has a comparable status in the decision making process to the statutory development plan in the determination of applications for planning permission under the Town and Country Planning regime, in that it sets the framework for *inter alia* the nature and scale of development that may be brought forward.[3]

The need for an assessment of sustainability

As a consequence of their setting of the parameters for development that can be brought forward (and in some cases, such as nuclear, the locations in which development may be brought forward), the NPSs have a significant role to play in determining the nature and scale of environmental, social and economic effects that will in due course occur as a result of such development.

In order to ensure that the policies contained within the NPSs are appropriate in environmental terms, it is therefore vitally important that they be subject to environmental assessment prior to their taking effect upon designation.

The procedure for the preparation and designation of NPSs contained in s 5 of PA 2008 makes provision for precisely this. Section 5(3) states that, 'Before designating a statement as a national policy statement for the purposes of this Act the Secretary of State must carry out an appraisal of the sustainability of the policy set out in the statement'.

The same requirement applies where the Secretary of State proposes to amend an existing NPS: see s 6(6) of PA 2008.

1 PA 2008, s 104(1).
2 PA 2008, s 104(2).
3 Cf Planning and Compulsory Purchase Act 2004, s 38(6).

What is required by way of sustainability appraisal?

No guidance is given in PA 2008, or any related documents, as to precisely what is required as part of an 'appraisal of the sustainability of the policy set out in the statement'.

It is nonetheless clear that, as a minimum, it needs to contain all the information that would be required of a strategic environmental assessment ('SEA') carried out pursuant to the Environmental Assessment of Plans and Programmes Regulations 2004 (as amended) ('the SEA Regulations'), which implement the requirements of European Directive 2001/42/EC on the assessment of the effects of certain plans and programmes on the environment ('the SEA Directive').

This is because, quite independently of any requirement of PA 2008 to carry out a sustainability appraisal, a NPS would be a 'plan or programme' for the purposes of the SEA Regulations, which—

> '(a) is prepared for agriculture, forestry, fisheries, energy, industry, transport, waste management, water management, telecommunications, tourism, town and country planning or land use, and
>
> (b) sets the framework for future development consent of projects listed in Annex I or II to Council Directive 85/337/EEC on the assessment of the effects of certain public and private projects on the environment as amended by Council Directive 97/11/EC [the Environmental Impact Assessment Directive])'.[4]

The substantive requirements of the SEA Regulations are set out in Part 3 of the same, with reg 12 requiring the preparation of an environmental report that:

> 'describe[s] and evaluate[s] the likely significant effects on the environment of—[5]
>
> (a) implementing the plan or programme; and
>
> (b) reasonable alternatives taking into account the objectives and the geographical scope of the plan or programme'.

As in the case of environmental impact assessment ('EIA') of development control projects, the report prepared need only to include such of the information referred to in Sch 2 to the SEA Regulations as may reasonably be required, taking account of (a) current knowledge and methods of assessment; (b) the contents and level of detail in the plan or programme; and (c) the stage of the plan or programme in the decision-making process. The authority may in the case of SEA also consider the extent to which certain matters are more appropriately assessed at different levels in that process in order to avoid duplication of the assessment (reg 12(2)).

4 Annex I or II projects are those projects that are respectively subject to the mandatory carrying out of environmental impact assessment ('EIA'), or exceed specified thresholds and are likely to have significant effects on the environment that require necessitate the carrying out of EIA: reg 5. NB reg 6 is irrelevant as no preparatory act relating to a NPS could have occurred before 21 July 2004, NPSs not coming into existence until the commencement of PA 2008.

5 Available at http://planningguidance.communities.gov.uk/.

By virtue of reg 13, there is a requirement for consultation upon that environmental report, together with the draft plan or programme to which it relates (sub-s (1)). The consultation must last for a specified period 'of such length as will ensure that the consultation bodies and the public consultees are given an effective opportunity to express their opinion on the relevant documents' (sub-s (4)). Regulation 13(2) contains detailed requirements as to how the consultation exercise is to be carried out.

The 'consultation bodies' are defined in reg 4 of the SEA Regulations, and include agencies such as Historic England, Natural England and the Environment Agency and, in appropriate cases, the Scottish Ministers/National Assembly for Wales. 'Public consultees' are those whom the authority preparing the plan 'are affected or likely to be affected by, or have an interest in the decisions involved in the assessment and adoption of the plan or programme concerned' (reg 13(2)(b)).

Consultations must also extend to other EU Member States if it is considered that the plan or programme is likely to have significant effects on the environment of that other Member State: reg 14(1).

Although not of direct application to appraisals carried out pursuant to PA 2008, the Government's online National Planning Practice Guidance does contain useful guidance on sustainability appraisals and SEA in the context of the local plan preparation process, including a SEA checklist, much of which will apply by analogy.[6]

The need for Habitats Regulations Assessment (HRA)

In addition to the requirement for sustainability appraisal or SEA, the preparation of NPSs will also necessitate the carrying out of an Appropriate Assessment ('AA') for the purposes of the Conservation of Habitats and Species Regulations 2010 ('the Habitats Regulations'), article 61 of which provides that,

> '(1) A competent authority, before deciding to undertake, or give any consent, permission or other authorisation for, a plan or project which—
>
> (a) is likely to have a significant effect on a European site or a European offshore marine site[7] (either alone or in combination with other plans or projects), and
>
> (b) is not directly connected with or necessary to the management of that site,
>
> must make an appropriate assessment of the implications for that site in view of that site's conservation objectives'.

As in the case of SEA, consultation on the AA is required. First, with the 'appropriate nature conservation body' to whose responses 'regard must be had', and second, with the public, though only if the competent authority[8] considers it appropriate.[9]

6 At the time of writing, the relevant title was 'Strategic environmental assessment and sustainability appraisal', reference ID 11-001-20140306.

7 As defined in reg 8, including *inter alia* special areas of conservation and sites of community importance.

8 Defined in reg 7.

9 Regulation 61(3) and (4)

By virtue of reg 61(6), the competent authority may agree to the plan or project only after having ascertained that it will not adversely affect the integrity of the European site or the European offshore marine site (as the case may be). This requirement is qualified by the power of the competent authority to show,[10] in cases where an adverse effect on integrity will occur, that there are imperative reasons of overriding public interest ('IROPI') justifying adoption of the plan or project in any event.

It follows from the above that, in the absence of an IROPI justification, a draft NPS could not be designated in circumstances where it had been demonstrated that its provisions would affect the integrity of the European site or the European offshore marine site.

10 Regulations 61(5) and 62.

Context for the Identification of need in National Policy Statements

Written by: Rebecca Clutten, ftb
Edited by: Michael Humphries QC, ftb

Introduction

The Government's stated aim in *Planning for a sustainable future*, the White Paper that preceded the PA 2008, was to create a system for determining applications for nationally significant infrastructure projects that was 'timely, efficient and predictable'.

One of the perceived major obstacles to bringing forward such projects was the absence of clear policy frameworks for all types of nationally significant infrastructure. This resulted in a lack of certainty for promoters and communities, and significant time being spent at public inquiries debating high-level issues including need.

In order to address this problem, the Government proposed the introduction of the national policy statements ('NPSs'), which would 'set out the national need for infrastructure and explain how this fits with other policies such as those relating to economic development, international competitiveness, climate change, energy conservation/efficiency and protection of the historic and natural environment'.

NPSs were subsequently introduced through Part 2 of the PA 2008.

The legislative framework relating to the identification of need

Need in NPSs

The legislative basis for NPSs is found in Part 2 of the PA 2008. By virtue of the PA 2008, s 5, the Secretary of State has power to designate a statement that sets national policy in respect of one or more specified descriptions of development.

PA 2008, s 5(5)(a) specifically provides that the Secretary of State may, in particular,

> 'set out, in relation to a specified description of development, the amount, type or size of development of that description which is appropriate nationally or for a specified area'.

PA 2008, s 5(5)(c) empowers the Secretary of State to set out in the NPS 'the relative weight to be given to specified criteria'.

PA 2008, s 5(1) and (5) taken together therefore permit the Secretary of State to identify through NPSs both the need for national infrastructure, and the weight to be attached to that need.

How need is taken into account in determining applications for development consent

The primary provision identifying how national policy on need is to be taken into account when determining applications for development consent is section 104 of the PA 2008. Section 104 requires that, where there is a designated NPS having effect in relation to development of the description to which the application relates, the Secretary of State must in deciding the application:

- Have regard to that NPS (PA 2008, s 104(2)); and
- Determine the application in accordance with it, unless one of the situations identified in PA 2008, s 104(4)–(8) apply (PA 2008, s 104(3)).

The effect of PA 2008, s 104 is therefore to require the Secretary of State to have regard to the national policy position on need, including the weight that it has been determined should to be attached to it, and to determine the application so as to accord with that policy position (including by attaching any prescribed weight to the need for that type of development), save in one of the cases identified in PA 2008, s 104(4)–(8).

Also noteworthy are PA 2008, ss 87 and 106. PA 2008, s 106 entitles the Secretary of State, when determining an application for development consent, to disregard any representations made to him or her relating to the merits of a policy set out in a NPS. PA 2008, s 87 makes similar provision for the Examining Authority.

As a result of these enactments, where the need for infrastructure (and any weight to be attached to the same) has been identified in a NPS, promoters of, and objectors to, schemes will, in effect, be precluded from taking issue with the need as identified.

Designated National Policy Statements

A number of NPSs have now been designated under PA 2008, s 5, as follows:

- Overarching National Policy Statement for Energy (EN-1) (DECC July 2011);
- National Policy Statement for Fossil Fuel Electricity Generating Infrastructure (EN-2) (DECC July 2011);
- National Policy Statement for Renewable Energy Infrastructure (EN-3) (DECC July 2011);
- National Policy Statement for Gas Supply Infrastructure and Gas and Oil Pipelines (EN-4) (DECC July 2011);
- National Policy Statement for Electricity Networks Infrastructure (EN-5) (DECC July 2011);
- National Policy Statement for Nuclear Power Generation (2 volumes) (EN-6) (DECC July 2011);
- National Policy Statement for Ports (DfT January 2012)

- National Policy Statement for Waste Water: A framework document for planning decisions on nationally significant waste water infrastructure (Defra March 2012); and
- National Policy Statement for Hazardous Waste: A framework document for planning decisions on nationally significant hazardous waste infrastructure (Defra June 2013).
- National Policy Statement for National Networks (DfT January 2015).

Other NPSs are anticipated in relation to:

- Aviation (DfT); and
- Water Supply (Defra).

The Identification of need in the Energy National Policy Statements

Written by: Rebecca Clutton, ftb
Edited by: Michael Humphries QC, ftb

Introduction

DECC has designated the following NPSs under the PA 2008, s 5 in relation to Energy Infrastructure:

- Overarching National Policy Statement for Energy (EN-1) (DECC July 2011);
- National Policy Statement for Fossil Fuel Electricity Generating Infrastructure (EN-2) (DECC July 2011);
- National Policy Statement for Renewable Energy Infrastructure (EN-3) (DECC July 2011)
- National Policy Statement for Gas Supply Infrastructure and Gas and Oil Pipelines (EN-4) (DECC July 2011);
- National Policy Statement for Electricity Networks Infrastructure (EN-5) (DECC July 2011); and
- National Policy Statement for Nuclear Power Generation (2 volumes) (EN-6) (DECC July 2011).

The Overarching Energy NPS (EN-1) together with the relevant technology-specific NPSs (EN2 – EN-6) are intended to set out national policy for energy infrastructure, including that on national need.

Applicants are informed in EN-1 that they should 'ensure that their applications, and any accompanying supporting documents, are consistent with the instructions and guidance in this NPS, the relevant technology NPS and any other NPSs that are relevant to the application in question' (paragraph 1.1.3).

EN-1: Overarching Energy

EN-1 first sets out the overarching need for energy infrastructure. The Government emphasises that significant new infrastructure will be required not only to meet and secure energy demands in the right location, but also to contribute to the mitigation of climate change (paragraph 2.1.2). The security of supply will be dependent upon factors including having sufficient electricity capacity to meet demand at all times, and having available energy from a diverse mix of technologies (paragraph 2.2.20). Developers are thereby encouraged to bring forward applications for a wide range of energy infrastructure projects.

EN-1 also sets out, in Chapter 3, the Government's position on need in relation to each of the energy infrastructure types for which there is a technology-specific NPS. A summary of the need for each is given below.

Need for electricity infrastructure NSIPs

Adopting prudent assumptions as to likely levels of electricity demand, the Government considers that the UK will need at least 113GW of total generating capacity by 2025, some 28GW over and above current capacity. 59GW is anticipated to come from new-build electricity infrastructure. Of that 59GW, 33GW is to come from renewable sources (to meet committed targets), with the remaining 26GW (of which 8GW is already under construction) coming from elsewhere, in a mix to be determined by industry. The Government is supportive of nuclear contributions that that remaining 18GW (paragraph 3.3.22).

Need for renewables NSIPs

There is an urgent need for large-scale renewable generation (from sources including onshore and offshore wind, biomass, energy from waste and wave and tidal power), in order to meet the target of sourcing 15% of energy from renewables by 2020, and to facilitate de-carbonisation of the power sector by 2030 (section 3.4).

Need for nuclear electricity generation

Nuclear power is one of the key elements of the Government's de-carbonisation strategy, being capable of large-scale deployment and the least expensive source of low-carbon energy (paragraphs 3.5.7–3.5.8). It is also needed to ensure energy security, as uranium prices are less subject to fluctuation than gas and other fossil fuels. The Government therefore seeks the early construction and operation of new stations, in any case before 2025 (paragraph 3.5.9).

Need for fossil fuel generation

Fossil fuel generating stations are more flexible than many renewable technologies (which produce energy intermittently) and are considered to remain necessary in order to ensure security of energy supply (paragraphs 3.6.2–3.6.3).

A reduction of emissions from this kind of infrastructure is, however, needed in order to meet carbon reduction targets. The Government considers that carbon capture and storage ('CCS') offers a potential means of achieving such reductions. The Government is therefore seeking to support four commercial-scale demonstration projects for the full CCS chain, and the IPC is directed to take account of the importance placed on these projects in considering applications for CCS projects and infrastructure (paragraphs 3.6.4–3.6.5).

Pending demonstration of the viability of CCS, combustion power stations (300MW or greater) will however need to be carbon-capture ready (i.e. CCS will be adoptable at a later stage) and coal-fired stations will need to demonstrate CCS on up to 300MW of capacity (paragraph 3.6.6).

The need for these CCR fossil fuel stations, and the CCS demonstration projects, is regarded as urgent, as existing capacity will go offline by the end of 2015 (paragraph 3.6.8).

Need for electricity networks infrastructure

The urgent need for additional transmission infrastructure reflects the 'similar' urgent need for new generating capacity to be provided (paragraph 3.7.7). It is recognised that much new generating capacity (particularly wind farms) will be sited in locations where there is little or no existing electricity infrastructure, and it will have to be provided (paragraph 3.7.1).

Need also arises as a result of increasing demands for electricity, which will require a sufficiently robust network to prevent interruptions. A sufficiently robust network will be achieved through making existing infrastructure 'evolve and adapt' and through expansion of the network through new lines (paragraph 3.7.2). The scale of need can be appreciated through consideration of the increases in generation and net electricity flows to 2020 set out in EN-1 (paragraph 3.7.6). Whilst there is an urgent need for transmission and distribution infrastructure generally, it is considered that there is a particular need for new lines of 132kV upwards (paragraph 3.7.10).

The IPC is directed to consider need as demonstrated if it: (a) represents an 'efficient and economical means' of connecting a new generating station; or is (b) reinforcing the network. The cost/benefit of achieving these aims (eg by overhead line or underground cable) and alternatives must however be considered before consent is granted (paragraph 3.7.10).

Need for gas NSIPs

Gas infrastructure will continue to be required to meet both domestic (household and industrial) needs, including peaks in demand, and export demand (paragraphs 3.8.2 and 3.8.7). The Government's current assessment is that in order to ensure security of supply, without consumer price risks, additional infrastructure, over and above that which is existing and under-construction, is needed (paragraph 3.8.8).

Particular emphasis is placed on the need for gas (gaseous and liquid) import and storage infrastructure, as the UK's gas production and reserves decline (paragraph 3.8.9). Decisions as to the nature, location, capacity and specification of gas infrastructure are, however, commercial ones for the industry (paragraphs 3.8.13 and 3.8.20).

Need for oil NSIPs

The Government considers that the need for oil products will continue to increase in the short-medium term as a result of transport sector dependency, notwithstanding a predicted fall in petrol consumption (paragraph 3.9.2). The need to ensure the security of this supply, and protect against excessive costs, means that new infrastructure for the importation, production, storage and distribution is required (paragraph 3.9.3).

There is a particular focus on the need for pipeline infrastructure, and works associated with the same, the 'significant need' for which the IPC is to take as its starting point in considering applications coming forward (paragraphs 3.9.6–3.9.8).

As a result of the identified need for energy infrastructure, the IPC (now the Examining Authority and/or Secretary of State, but referred to as the IPC for consistency with the original text) is directed to start its consideration of applications with a 'presumption in favour of granting consent to applications for energy NSIPs', the application of such presumption being subject to any more specific and relevant policies set out in the technology-specific NPSs which 'clearly indicate that consent should be refused', and to section 104 of the 2008 Act (paragraph 4.1.2). Need is also a factor which the IPC is directed to take into account in its consideration of where the balance of favour lies on any given application (paragraph 4.1.3).

The weight to be attached to the need for energy infrastructure of all types is also set out in EN-1. Such weight should be 'substantial' but 'proportionate to the anticipated extent of a project's actual contribution to satisfying the need for a particular type of infrastructure' (paragraph 3.2.3).

As in other, non-energy NPSs, the section of EN-1 dealing with Assessment Principles sets out a number of specific policies which require the IPC to weigh in the balance the benefits of the proposed development, which expressly include the stated need for the same (including national need), against various harms which might arise.

These harms include, after mitigation, likely harm to the notified special interest features of a Site of Special Scientific Interest ('SSSI'), in which case the benefits including need should 'clearly outweigh' the harm if consent is to be granted (paragraph 5.3.11). They also include harm to species or sites of principal conservation importance, ancient woodland (by reason of loss or deterioration), and dynamic shorelines (by reason of impacts on sediment flow or other coastal processes) in which case the benefits would need simply to 'outweigh' the harm (paragraphs 5.3.17, 5.3.14 and 5.5.11 respectively).

In the case of designated sites, consent should be granted on sites with national designations (such as Areas of Outstanding Natural Beauty) only in 'exceptional circumstances', where development has been shown to be in the public interest, including by reference to the need for it (paragraph 5.9.9). Regional and local designations should not be used to refuse consent without more (paragraph 5.3.13), and where local landscape impacts arise, the IPC is required to consider whether any adverse impacts are 'so damaging' as to outweigh the benefits, including the need for development of that type (paragraph 5.9.15).

Need is also a factor in decisions as to whether or not to grant consent for development proposals on existing open space, sports and recreational buildings and land. Such proposals should not be consented unless, amongst other things, the decision-maker determines that the benefits of the project (including need) outweigh the potential loss of such facilities (paragraph 5.10.14).

Finally, because of the need for energy infrastructure, the Government's policy is that the IPC is entitled to give little weight to 'speculative assertions of [adverse] socioeconomic impacts [arising from energy development] not supported by evidence' (paragraph 5.12.7).

Whilst no specific reference is made to the weight attaching to the need for the proposed infrastructure, the presumption in favour of consent, and repeated reference to it as benefit of the proposals that must be weighed in the balance, it is clear enough that the weight attached to need by decision-makers is likely to be substantial.

EN-2 – EN-6: the technology-specific energy NPSs

EN-2 - EN-5 inclusive are the technology specific NPSs for energy, providing detailed policy for each of the different kinds of energy infrastructure within the 2008 Act regime.

The majority of the technology-specific energy NPSs do not contain a discrete chapter addressing the need for energy deriving from the technology with which those documents are concerned. EN-2 – EN-6 inclusive (Fossil fuels, Renewables, Gas, Electricity Networks and Nuclear respectively) each cross-refer back to the need identified in Chapter 1.3 of EN-1.

In each case, the need for the energy infrastructure identified in EN-1 is also then reiterated and the IPC is directed, when determining applications for development consent, to 'act on the basis that the need for the infrastructure covered by this NPS [ie the technology-specific NPS in which the statement appears] has been demonstrated' (2.1.2).

A number of the technology-specific NPSs do provide either further commentary on the need that had been identified in EN-1 (for example, emphasising the role a particular technology has to play), or further guidance as to how the need for particular energy infrastructure is to be taken into account by the Secretary of State where particular issues (for example, environmental impacts) arise on any given application. These policies are identified, by NPS, below. NPSs not referred to do not contain any such comment or guidance.

EN-3: Renewable Energy Infrastructure

In addition to the cross-reference to EN-1, EN-3 sets out the principles guiding assessments of applications for each specific type of renewable energy infrastructure covered by the NPS (Biomass and Waste Combustion, Offshore Wind, and Onshore Wind).

There are just two technology-specific references to the need for energy infrastructure. First is the reference, made in Chapter 2.5, to the increasingly important role that energy from waste is anticipated to play in meeting the UK's energy needs.

Second is the reference to balancing the need for offshore wind infrastructure with the impact that the presence of that infrastructure has on recreational craft. It is stated that the IPC should be satisfied that offshore wind schemes have been designed to minimise impacts on such craft. However, in cases where adverse impacts are identified, and no reasonable mitigation is feasible, the IPC is required, 'in view of the level of need for energy infrastructure', to 'weigh the harm caused with the benefits of the scheme', instead of simply refusing the scheme on the basis of that residual harm (paragraph 2.6.166).

EN-4: Gas Supply Infrastructure and Gas and Oil Pipelines

In addition to the cross-reference to EN-1, and in spite of the emphasis on low-carbon energy resources, the continued importance of, and need for, gas and oil energy infrastructure is made clear at the outset of EN-4, which states:

'The efficient import, storage and transmission of natural gas and oil products is crucial to meeting our energy needs during the transition to a low carbon economy. We cannot achieve national objectives relating to security of supply without enabling investment in new infrastructure' (paragraph 1.1.1).

EN-5: Electricity Networks Infrastructure

In addition to the cross-reference to EN-1, EN-5 also emphasises the continued need for electricity networks infrastructure, notwithstanding the emphasis on low carbon resources. It states that:

'The new electricity generating infrastructure that the UK needs to move to a low carbon economy while maintaining security of supply will be heavily dependent on the availability of a fit for purpose and robust electricity network. That network will need to be able to support a more complex system of supply and demand than currently and cope with generation occurring in more diverse locations' (paragraph 1.1.1).

Chapter 2.3 of EN-5 gives specific guidance on circumstances in which the need for electricity infrastructure will have to be weighed in the balance against other factors. It addresses the general assessment principles for electricity networks, and states *inter alia* that, in view of the need for planning to take a holistic approach to the impacts of energy infrastructure development, applications for new generating stations and related infrastructure should, wherever reasonably be possible, be contained in a single application (paragraph 2.3.1).

Where this is not possible or appropriate, and an application for network infrastructure is brought forward in isolation, the IPC will have to have regard to both the need for the network infrastructure identified in EN-1 and the indirect, secondary and cumulative effects that the proposed development is likely to have, and be satisfied that there are no obvious reasons why the necessary approvals for the other element are likely to be refused (paragraph 2.3.3).

Chapter 2.3 goes on to identify two circumstances in which the IPC might consider it appropriate to consider a network infrastructure-only application. One is the situation where 'the project is based on reasonably anticipated future requirements' (also paragraph 2.3.3). It therefore appears that promoters of network infrastructure-only schemes may be required to demonstrate a more specific need for their project, over and above the general need for electricity network infrastructure, which the IPC is directed in Chapter 2.1 to treat as established.

EN-6: Nuclear Power Generation

Whilst EN-6 cross-refers to EN-1, it also contains additional policy relating to need, including the need for early deployment of nuclear technology, if policy ambitions in relation to the de-carbonisation of the energy industry are to be met (paragraphs 2.1.1–2.1.2).

EN-6 provides that the number of sites identified gives the IPC sufficient flexibility to meet that need, but also to refuse consent on any of those sites, if it considers it appropriate to do so (paragraph 2.4.4). This tends to suggest that the level of national need for nuclear power is not as great as the output from eight stations.

EN-6 also addresses the relationship between the stated urgent need for nuclear power stations to come forward, and the consideration of alternatives. The guiding principle for the IPC in the consideration of alternatives is,

'Whether there is a realistic prospect of the proposed alternative being able to generate a comparable amount of low carbon electricity on a comparable timescale' (paragraph 2.5.2).

This guiding principle applies to both alternative sites and alternative proposals (paragraph 2.5.1).

In relation to flood risk assessments, the IPC is advised that part of the Exception Test applying to developments in flood risk zones does not apply to new nuclear development, in view of *inter alia* the need for that development to come forward (paragraph 3.6.13). It appears that, in view of the continued application of the Exception Test in relation to other development, the need for nuclear development is considered particularly pressing, though it is acknowledged that the policy may also be recognising the greater physical constraints upon the provision of new nuclear facilities (such as the need to be near the sea).

The Identification of need in the Non-energy National Policy Statements

Written by: Rebecca Clutton, ftb
Edited by: Michael Humphries QC, ftb

Introduction

Defra and DfT have designated the following NPSs under section 5 of the Planning Act 2008 (PA 2008) in relation to non-Energy Infrastructure:

- National Policy Statement for Ports (DfT January 2012)
- National Policy Statement for Waste Water: A framework document for planning decisions on nationally significant waste water infrastructure (Defra March 2012);
- National Policy Statement for Hazardous Waste: A framework document for planning decisions on nationally significant hazardous waste infrastructure (Defra June 2013); and
- National Policy Statement for National Networks (DfT January 2015).

In addition DfT has also produced an interim policy document entitled 'Strategic Rail Freight Interchange Policy Guidance' (DfT November 2011) that it proposes will be replaced by the National road and rail networks NPS.

Other NPSs are anticipated in relation to:

- Aviation (DfT); and
- Water Supply (Defra).

Ports NPS

The need for new ports infrastructure is set out in Chapter 3 of the Ports NPS, in particular in Chapters 3.4 and 3.5.

The headline in relation to need is that there is a 'compelling need for substantial additional port capacity' in all areas, over the 20–30 year period from 2012 (paragraph 3.4.16). This is based on a number of factors including:

- Demand forecasting, which at 2007 indicated a need for substantial increases in capacity for containers and ro-ro traffic (182% and 101% respectively), and 4% in non-unitised traffic (paragraphs 3.4.2–3.4.3).
- The need to support the offshore wind industry, both in respect of the shipment of parts, and in respect of installation, operation and maintenance facilities (paragraph 3.4.5).

- The need to provide sufficient capacity to facilitate genuine choice and competition for ports users. This may mean capacity in excess of forecast demand. Such capacity also contributes to the resilience of the UK's ports infrastructure (paragraphs 3.4.13–3.4.15).
- To meet growth in the coastal shipping sector, as an alternative to inland freight (paragraph 3.4.14).

There is no specific policy on where such growth should be located. The Government recognises the merit in the provision of a wide range of facilities at a wide range of locations, such as will enable changing market demands and shipping patterns to be met (paragraph 3.4.11).

As for energy infrastructure, the need described is considered to be of a level and urgency that the IPC should 'start with a presumption in favour of granting consent to applications for ports development', subject to PA 2008, s 104 and any other, more specific policies within the NPSs, which 'clearly indicate' that consent should be refused (paragraph 3.5.2).

There are also number of specific policies identified within the Assessment Principles set out in the Ports NPS which require the IPC to weigh in the balance benefits of proposed development, which expressly include the stated need (including national need), against various harms which might arise. The approach is broadly reflective of that taken in relation to energy, and the situations contemplated include where there would, after mitigation, be harm to a SSSI interest or other sites of principal conservation importance, in which case the benefits would need to 'clearly outweigh' the harm (paragraph 5.1.12 and footnote 37, and paragraph 5.5.18), or where open space, sports and recreation facilities would be lost, save where they are surplus to requirements (paragraph 5.13.13).

The impact of national, regional and local land designations, and whether these are capable of outweighing the identified need, is also addressed. Current policy is that regional and local designations should not, of themselves, be a reason for refusing consent (paragraph 5.1.14). In the case of land subject to national designations (National Parks, AONB and the Broads), the IPC is guided that it may grant consent for development in these areas in exceptional circumstances, which expressly include the need for the development (paragraph 5.11.8).

In respect of harm to ancient woodlands (by loss or deterioration) and dynamic shorelines (through impact on sediment flows or coastal processes), permission should only be granted where the benefits, again including national and local need, outweigh those adverse impacts (paragraphs 5.1.15 and 5.1.39 respectively).

Waste Water NPS

The need for new waste water infrastructure is set out in Chapter 2 of the waste water NPS. Policy objectives and demand drivers are set out in sections 2.2 and 2.3. The waste water infrastructure considered to meet that need is set out in section 2.6.

It remains Government policy to reduce the need for waste water capacity, through reductions in water use, increasing use of sustainable drainage systems, separation of surface and waste water sewers, and through decentralisation of waste water treatment infrastructure (i.e. encouraging more local treatment) (section 2.4). However, even with these measures in place, more and better waste water infrastructure will be required to:

- meet the requirements of European and domestic legislation in relation to water body management, waste water and freshwater (paragraphs 2.3.1–2.3.4);
- adapt to the increased pressure on infrastructure resulting from climate change generated events, such as intense rainfall events and reduced river flows (paragraphs 2.3.5–2.3.7);
- meet the additional capacity requirements generated by the expected increase in population growth (paragraph 2.3.8) and also the increase in urbanisation (and corresponding reduction in permeable surfaces) (paragraph 2.3.9); and
- to ensure that existing, dated infrastructure remains fit for purpose or is replaced (paragraph 2.3.10)

Waste water infrastructure projects and improvements required to meet legislative and environmental objectives (which typically overlap) are currently identified by the Environment Agency ('EA') in their National Environment Plan (NEP), which is subject to confirmation by the Secretary of State, and which is scrutinised by OFWAT through water undertakers' business plans (paragraphs 2.5.1–2.5.2).

The NEP currently identifies two projects for which there is a need: improvements at Deephams Sewage Treatment Works ('STW') and the Thames Tideway Tunnel (section 2.6). The need for these, and other projects included in the NEP and said by the EA to be necessary for environmental reasons, is considered to be established (paragraphs 2.5.3-2.5.4).

The urgent need for such infrastructure means that the decision-maker should start with a presumption in favour of granting consent to applications for waste water NSIPs, subject to any more specific and relevant policies in the NPS that 'clearly indicate that consent should be refused', and the requirements of the Planning Act 2008 (paragraph 3.1.2). Further, need is a particular factor which must be taken into account when weighing the benefits and adverse impacts of any proposed NSIP (paragraph 3.1.3).

As for the other NPSs, the Assessment Principles require the decision-maker to weigh in the balance benefits of proposed development, which expressly include the stated need (including national need), against various harms that might arise. These include where there would, after mitigation, be likely to be harm to a SSSI's notified special interest features, to sites or species of principal conservation importance, or ancient woodland, in which case the benefits would need to 'clearly outweigh' the harm (paragraphs 4.5.10, 4.5.13 and 4.5.16).

The impact of national, regional and local land designations, and whether these are capable of outweighing the identified need, is also addressed. Current policy is that regional and local designations should not, of themselves, be a reason for refusing consent (paragraph 4.5.12). In the case of land subject to national designations (National Parks, AONB and the Broads), development should be demonstrated to be in the public interest and consideration of such applications should include an assessment of, amongst other things, 'the need for the development, including in terms of any national considerations [covering both national need and impacts upon the national economy] and the impact of consenting, or not consenting it, upon the local economy' (paragraph 4.7.8).

Need is also a factor in decisions as to whether or not to grant consent for development proposals on existing open space, sports and recreational buildings and land. Such proposals should not be consented unless, amongst other things, the decision-maker determines that the benefits of the project (including need) outweigh the potential loss of such facilities (paragraph 4.8.13).

The need for waste water infrastructure is also a factor which has resulted in a policy that the Secretary of State may reasonably conclude that:

> 'speculative assertions of [adverse] socioeconomic impacts [arising from waste water development] not supported by evidence should be given little weight' (paragraph 4.15.10).

Hazardous Waste NPS

The need for new hazardous waste infrastructure is set out in Chapter 3 of the Hazardous Waste NPS, in particular in sections 3.2 and 3.5.

The headline in relation to need is that there is a need for a 'small number of large facilities' for nationally significant hazardous waste, to deal with a range of hazardous waste arisings (paragraphs 3.3.7 and 3.4.1).

The need for increasing numbers of hazardous waste facilities is a result of:

- the trend toward increased hazardous waste arisings (deriving from both the continuing demand for consumer goods producing such waste, as well as from more waste being classified as hazardous) (section 3.2); and
- the need to meet European and domestic legislative requirements in relation to disposal of waste, in particular the requirements of the Waste Framework Directive (2008/98/EC) for pushing waste up the waste hierarchy (ie improved levels of recycling and re-use) (paragraphs 1.5.3, 3.2.3–3.2.6 and 3.3.5) and for national self-sufficiency in terms of capacity to dispose of hazardous waste (paragraph 3.3.3–3.3.4).

The need for a large number of small facilities arises because of the economies of scale which operate in the waste disposal sector, and in order to avoid cumulative impacts which might be generated by the operation of multiple, smaller sites (paragraph 3.3.6). The author notes that smaller facilities may still come forward through the Town and Country Planning regime.

The Government has not sought to identify particular technologies which should be used, or to identify locations for development, it being considered ill-advised to be too prescriptive when technologies are evolving (paragraph 3.4.1), and because it considers the industry best placed to know where facilities should be located (paragraph 2.4.2). This provides significant flexibility to applicants for hazardous waste developments, as compared to applicants for some other NSIPs.

Broad types of facilities required are however identified, drawing on the 2007 Strategy for Hazardous Waste Management in England (paragraph 3.3.6). The types of facility for which there is an identified need are:

- Waste electrical and electronic equipment plants – a small number of larger facilities (paragraph 3.4.3);
- Oil regeneration plants – a requirement of at least one new plant already existing at July 2011 (paragraph 3.4.3);
- Treatment plants for air pollution control residues;
- Facilities to treat oily washes and oily sludges;
- Bioremediation/soil washing facilities;
- Ship recycling facilities (which covers oil and gas platform recycling) – a mixture of new facilities with capacity to manage both above and below 30,000t of ship(s) pa within the next 10 years (paragraph 3.4.12); and
- Hazardous waste landfill sites.

The Examining Authority is directed to examine applications for facilities falling within these categories on the basis that the need for them has been demonstrated (paragraph 3.4.14). Moreover, there is a presumption in favour of granting consent for applications for such facilities where they clearly meet the need for infrastructure identified in the NPS (paragraph 4.1.2). This presumption is subject, as in other NPSs, to the other policies of the Hazardous Waste NSP and also PA 2008, s 104. The need for types of hazardous waste facilities not included on the above list is to be considered on a case-by-case basis, following consultation by the applicant with Defra (paragraph 3.4.1).

The Assessment Principles require the decision-maker to weigh in the balance benefits of proposed development, which expressly include the stated need (including national need), against various harms that might arise. These include where there would, after mitigation, be harm to species or sites of principal conservation importance, or ancient woodland, in which case the benefits would need to 'clearly outweigh' the harm (paragraphs 5.3.14 and 5.3.17).

The impact of national, regional and local land designations, and whether these are capable of outweighing the identified need, is also addressed. Current policy is that regional and local designations should not, of themselves, be a reason for refusing consent (paragraph 5.1.13).

In the case of land subject to national designations (National Parks, AONB and the Broads), development should be demonstrated to be in the public interest and consideration of such applications should include an assessment of, amongst other things, 'the need for the development, including in terms of any national considerations [covering both national need and impacts upon the national economy] and the impact of consenting, or not consenting it, upon the local economy' (paragraph 5.9.7).

The need for hazardous waste infrastructure is also a factor that has led the Government to include guidance that the Secretary of State may reasonably conclude that:

'speculative assertions of [adverse] socioeconomic impacts [arising from hazardous waste development] not supported by evidence should be given little weight'.

National Networks NPS

The need for development on national road and rail networks is set out in section two of the National Networks NPS (NN NPS).

The NN NPS makes it clear (para 2.1) that the national road and rail networks that connect cities, regions and international gateways play a significant part in supporting economic growth, as well as existing economic activity and productivity and in facilitating passenger, business and leisure journeys across the country. Well-connected and high-performing networks with sufficiency capacity are vital to meet the country's long-term needs and support a prosperous economy.

In that context it is then made clear (para 2.2) that there is a critical need to improve the national networks to address road congestion and crowding on the railways to provide safe, expeditious and resilient networks that better support social and economic activity; and to provide a transport network that is capable of stimulating and supporting economic growth. Improvements may also be required to address the impact of the national networks on quality of life and environmental factors.

The NN NPS then sets out specific guidance on

- paras 2.12–227 – the need for development of the national road network, including options for addressing road need (Table 1);
- para 2.28–2.41 – the need for development of the national rail network; and
- paras 2.42–2.56 – the need for development of strategic rail freight interchanges.

The Status and Role of NPSs within the Planning Act 2008 Regime

Written by: Rebecca Clutten, ftb
Edited by: Michael Humphries QC, ftb

Introduction

National Policy Statements ('NPSs') are the statutory planning policy statements for nationally significant infrastructure projects in England and Wales. They derive from PA 2008, Part 2.

This article explains the status that NPSs have within the PA 2008 regime. Any references to NPSs herein are references to NPSs which have been designated in accordance with PA 2008, s 5. Further information on the requirements for designation can be found in other parts of this Service.

PA 2008, s 104: the primacy of the NPS

The primary effect of NPSs is set out in PA 2008, s 104 (decisions in cases where national policy statement applies).

PA 2008, s 104 will apply in respect of any application for a development consent order (DCO) for development in relation to which there is an extant NPS: see PA 2008, s 104(1). Where section 104 applies, the Secretary of State must, when determining an application for a DCO, have regard to *inter alia* that relevant NPS: see PA 2008, s 104(2). Although there are other specified documents and matters to which the Secretary of State must have regard, the PA 2008 goes on to provide that, save in specified circumstances (that is, where the circumstances set out in PA 2008, s 104(4)–(8) apply), the DCO application must be decided in accordance with the relevant NPS.

The NPS therefore has a comparable status in the decision making process to the statutory development plan in the determination of applications for planning permission under the Town and Country Planning regime. It is important to note, however, that Planning and Compulsory Purchase Act 2004, s 38(6) which requires planning applications to be determined in accordance with the development plan unless other material considerations indicate otherwise, does not apply to applications for development consent under the PA 2008. There is, therefore, no conflict between the requirements of the two regimes.

The circumstances in which an application for a DCO can be determined otherwise than in accordance with the relevant NPS are as follows (PA 2008, s 104(4)–(8)):

- the SoS is satisfied that to do so would lead to the UK being in breach of any of its international obligations;
- the SoS is satisfied that to do so would lead to him being in breach of any duty imposed on him by or under any enactment;

- the SoS is satisfied that to do so would be unlawful by virtue of any enactment;
- the SoS is satisfied that the benefits of doing so would outweigh the adverse impacts; and
- the SoS is satisfied that to do so would meet any prescribed condition for determining an application otherwise than in accordance with the relevant NPS.

At the time of writing, there are no prescribed conditions as referred to in the last exception.

Again, a comparison can be drawn between these exceptions to the primacy of the NPSs, and in particular the exception at PA 2008, s 104(7) (benefits outweigh adverse impacts), and the ability for applications for planning permission under the Town and Country Planning regime to be determined other than in accordance with the development plan where 'material considerations indicate otherwise'.

In light of the primacy afforded to NPSs, it is vital that applicants explain in detail how their proposals relate to and comply with the NPS and, insofar as that is not so, make the case for consent being granted in any event by reference to the exceptions identified. For a decision in which the Examining Authority and Secretary of State did not consider that an NSIP was in accordance with the NPS see the *Preesall* underground gas storage report and decision.

Thus promoters will need to consider carefully and establish that:

- the NSIP is 'in accordance with' any material NPS; and
- the exceptions in PA 2008, s 104(4)–(8) to not outweigh the policy support in the NSIP and the benefits of the project.

Section 106: restricted challenge to NPS policy

A further effect of the NPSs is set out in PA 2008, s 106, which provides that in determining an application for a DCO the Secretary of State may disregard representations which he considers 'relate to the merits of policy set out in a national policy statement': see PA 2008, s 106. In this regard, clearly, the Examining Authority and Secretary of State must act with *Wednesbury* reasonableness. The practical effect of this is preclude challenges to the merits of a national policy other than through the NPS consultation process, or at the Secretary of State's discretion.

A similar provision is contained in PA 2008, s 94(8), which allows the Examining Authority to refuse to allow representations at any hearings relating to a DCO application where it considers those representations to relate to the merits of a policy contained in a NPS. Again this power must be exercised reasonably.

Suspension

Effect of suspension of the NPS

It is possible for the Secretary of State to suspend the operation of all or part of an NPS if an unexpected change in circumstances arises that would have led to the policy in the NPS being materially different had that change of circumstances been anticipated at the time: see PA 2008, s 11.

Where such suspension occurs the designation of all or part of the NPS (as the case may be) is treated as withdrawn and, until such time as designation is reinstated, the NPS will not be treated as extant and relevant for the purposes of the duty to determine in accordance with the NPS (PA 2008, s 104) nor, indeed, to the blight provisions referred to further below.

Suspension of the determination of an application

If the SoS considers that a NPS should be suspended and reviewed as a result of an unexpected change in circumstances, and that such review should take place before any given application for a DCO is determined, he has a further power to direct that the examination of the application (if not already completed) be suspended pending that review: see PA 2008, s 108.

NPSs can therefore be a potential source of delay for applicants in the DCO process.

A cause of statutory blight

Amendments to the Town and Country Planning Act 1990 brought about by the PA 2008 also mean that land which is 'in a location identified in a national policy statement as suitable (or potentially suitable) for a specified description of development' is now 'blighted land' for the purposes of the submission by an affected party of a statutory blight notice pursuant to s 150 of and Sch 13 to the TCPA 1990. A new s 165A of the TCPA 1990 gives the Secretary of State power to compulsorily acquire such blighted land where a statutory blight notice is served.

Legal Challenges to National Policy Statements

Written by: Rebecca Clutten, ftb
Edited by: Michael Humphries QC, ftb

Introduction

Section 13 of the Planning Act 2008 ('PA 2008') prescribes the means by which legal challenges to National Policy Statements ('NPSs') can be brought, and restricts the time period within which prospective claimants have to lodge their claims.

This article provides information on:

- the circumstances in which PA 2008, s 13 applies;
- the effect of PA 2008, s 13 upon: the mode by which challenges to NPSs and decisions related to them can be brought, the time limit applicable to such challenges, and the date from which time runs in each case;
- the effect of a legal challenge on the status of a NPS; and
- challenges brought to date.

When does PA 2008, s 13 apply?

Broadly speaking, PA 2008, s 13 applies where a person seeks either to challenge a NPS or a decision of the relevant Secretary of State ('SoS') relating to a NPS.

PA 2008, s 13, however, identifies six specific circumstances where a challenge may be brought. Thus a court may entertain proceedings questioning:

- a NPS or anything done, or omitted to be done, by the SoS in the course of preparing a NPS (PA 2008, s 13(1));
- a decision of the SoS not to carry out a review of all or part of a NPS pursuant to PA 2008, s 6 (PA 2008, s 13(2));
- a decision of the SoS to carry out a review of all or part of a NPS pursuant to PA 2008, s 6 (PA 2008, s 13(3));
- anything done, or omitted to be done, by the SoS in the course of carrying out a review of all or part of a NPS pursuant to PA 2008, s 6 (PA 2008, s 13(4));
- anything done by the SoS under PA 2008, s 6(5) after completing a review of all or part of a NPS (that is, amending or doing nothing to an NPS, or withdrawing its designation) (PA 2008, s 13(5)); and
- questioning a decision of the SoS as to whether or not to suspend the operation of all or part of a NPS under PA 2008, s 11 (PA 2008, s 13(6)).

Whilst it is envisaged that that the six circumstances described cover all decisions relating to the designation and subsequent review of NPSs, PA 2008, s 13 is not phrased in such a way as to preclude challenges to other decisions relating to NPSs, should they arise. It contains no drafting comparable to, for example, section 284 of the Town and Country Planning Act 1990 (as amended), precluding any challenge to the validity of development plans etc, except as provided for in that Part.

It is considered that, in the event that a claimant wished to challenge a decision of the SoS relating to a NPS, but which did not fall within any of the six circumstances referred to in PA 2008, s 13(1)–(6) inclusive, that decision would be treated in the same way as any other decision of a Minister not subject to any statutory provision relating to challenge, that is, ordinary judicial review principles and procedure would apply.

The effect of PA 2008, s 13

Where it applies, PA 2008, s 13 has three main effects:

- it requires a person wishing to bring a challenge to do so by way of judicial review;
- it imposes a time limit of six weeks, within which any application for judicial review must be lodged; and
- it identifies the day from which that time limit runs in each circumstance described.

Challenge by way of judicial review only

The requirement that any challenge to a NPS be brought by way of judicial review has a number of implications for prospective claimants. It requires them to have standing to bring a claim (presently, a 'sufficient interest'), to obtain the permission of the court to bring a claim, and it limits them to challenging the decision on traditional judicial review grounds (i.e. broadly, irrationality, illegality and procedural impropriety). In other words, there is no direct opportunity to challenge the merit of Government policy in an NPS, as opposed to the legality of such policy.

Furthermore, PA 2008, s 106 provides that, when determining applications for development consent for Nationally Significant Infrastructure Projects, the Secretary of State is entitled to disregard any representations he or she receives relating to the merits of policy set out in a NPS. A similar power to disregard applies to the Examining Authority (section 87).

When read together with PA 2008, s 106, the effect of PA 2008, s 13 is, therefore, to preclude the public at large from challenging the merits of planning policy that has been set at national level, other than through the instigation of the review procedure provided for by PA 2008, s 6.

Date from which time runs

Readers are referred to s 13 (as amended by the Criminal Justice and Courts Act 2015) for details of the date from which the six week time limit runs in each given circumstance (see PA 2008, s 13(1)–(6) inclusive).

It should be noted that in the section as originally enacted, time ran from the day beginning with the date on which the NPS was designated. The words 'beginning with' in PA 2008, s 13 contrasted with the word 'from' which is used in r 54.5 of the Civil Procedure Rules (CPR) for judicial review challenges generally. In the case of the similarly worded time limit in s 118 this led to two challenges to the Thames Tideway Tunnel DCO being held to be made out of time when the applicants calculated the six weeks from the day after publication of the DCO and their applications for judicial review were dismissed: see *R (oao Blue Green London Plan and LB Southwark) v Secretary of State for Environment Food and Rural Affairs* [2015] EWHC 495 (Admin).

Following the decision in these challenges the wording of s 13, in relation to challenges to NPSs, was amended so as to provide that a challenge by way of judicial review must be made within the period of six weeks 'beginning with *the day after*' (emphasis added) the designation of the NPS.

For example: if a NPS was designated and published on 5 January (the circumstance identified in PA 2008, s 13(1)), the first day of the six weeks would be 6 January, and the time for challenge would expire on 17 February.

Accuracy is vital bearing in mind the inability of the court to extend the time limit in cases of error (see below).

The time limit of six weeks is set by statute

The time limit of six weeks for challenges to is one set by statute (ie by the terms of s 13 and not by the Civil Procedure Rules) and thus it is important to note that the court has no power or discretion to extend it: see *Mucelli v Government of Albania* [2009] 1 WLR 276

Effect of a challenge

The filing of a claim for judicial review of a NPS has no impact upon its status. The NPS remains extant and valid for the duration of any challenge.

In principle it seems possible that, in appropriate circumstances, the court might exercise its discretion grant to a claimant injunctive relief, preventing decisions being taken in accordance with a NPS the subject matter of a current application for judicial review.

Such a course of action would require the court to balance the harm caused by any policy vacuum that would be created, with any harm caused by determining an application for development consent in accordance with a potentially flawed or unlawful policy. The outcome of any such balancing exercise would represent a judgment on the facts of the given case.

Challenges to date

At January 2015, ten of the twelve currently proposed NPSs had been designated and published; the most recent (the National Networks NPS) on 14 January 2015. These designations resulted in just one application for permission to apply for a judicial review.

The application, made by Greenpeace in August 2011, related to the designation of the Nuclear Power NPS ('the Nuclear NPS'). In short, Greenpeace alleged that, in designating the Nuclear NPS at that time, the Government had acted prematurely and had failed to take into account the implications of the nuclear disaster at Fukushima, Japan, which had occurred earlier that year.

Permission was refused in December 2011. Although his reasons for refusing permission have not been published, it was reported in the legal press that Ouseley J considered that the matters upon which Greenpeace argued further evidence was required before a decision could be taken on potentially suitable sites through the NPS – flood risk, off-site electricity supply and on-site emergency controls – were matters upon which evidence would be considered by the (then) Infrastructure Planning Commission and the Office of Nuclear Regulation when determining whether development consent and/or an operating license should be granted at any site for which an application ultimately came forward.

Part 3

Nationally Significant Infrastructure Projects

General Characteristics of an NSIP

Written by: Alex Booth, ftb
Edited by: Michael Humphries QC, ftb

Nature of Development

There is no single, over-arching definition of a 'nationally significant infrastructure project' ('NSIP') contained in PA 2008. The closest that the legislation comes to providing such definition is at PA 2008, s 14, of which subsection 14(1) provides a list of 16 types of development which may potentially comprise a NSIP.

The spectrum of development identified in PA 2008, s 14(1) is diverse. It ranges from highways and harbours to reservoirs and railway infrastructure. Further, whilst the list provided at PA 2008, s 14(1) is expressed in exhaustive terms, the 2008 Act confers on the Secretary of State an express power both to add new types of development to that list, and to remove existing ones from it: see PA 2008, s 14(3).

When seeking to understand the scope of development which may currently be classified as an NSIP, one can at least note that the various developments cited all fall within one of five categories, namely: energy, transport, water, waste water and waste. Indeed, even the Secretary of State's power to identify a new form of development as comprising an NSIP is subject to this same restriction, since only development falling within these five categories of infrastructure may be newly classified as an NSIP.

Currently, the 16 types of NSIP project identified in PA 2008 comprise:

- generating stations (PA 2008, s 15);
- electric lines (PA 2008, s 16);
- underground gas storage facilities (PA 2008, s 17);
- LNG facilities (PA 2008, s 18);
- gas reception facilities (PA 2008, s 19);
- gas transported pipelines (PA 2008, s 20);
- other pipelines (PA 2008, s 21);
- highways (PA 2008, s 22);
- airports (PA 2008, s 23);
- harbour facilities (PA 2008, s 24);
- railways (PA 2008, s 25);
- rail freight interchanges (PA 2008, s 26);
- dams and reservoirs (PA 2008, s 27);
- transfer of water resources (PA 2008, s 28);

- waste water treatment plans (PA 2008, s 29); and
- hazardous waste facilities (PA 2008, s 30).

In addition, The Infrastructure Planning (Waste Water Transfer and Storage) Order 2012, made under PA 2008, s 14(3), extended the 16 types of NSIP project to include a further type being, infrastructure for the transfer and storage of waste water with a capacity of over 350,000 cubic metres.

Note also, that the effect of s 26 of the Growth and Infrastructure Act 2013 was to amend PA 2008, s 35 to allow the Secretary of State to direct that certain business and commercial projects be treated as development for which development consent is required.

Scale of Development

Whilst only development relating to the five categories identified may comprise an NSIP, it goes without saying that not all development within those categories will do so. The question of whether a development will comprise an NSIP turns largely on the scale of development in question. That is to say, it is only in circumstances where the development comprises infrastructure of a particular scale that the consenting procedure of the 2008 Act will be engaged.

As to whether development is of sufficient scale to merit classification as an NSIP, it is necessary to consider whichever is applicable of the various statutory thresholds contained in ss 15–30 of the PA 2008 (and, indeed, the Waste Water Transfer and Storage Order, as above). These provisions, which are the subject of separate articles in this Service, provide in respect of each of the various (now) 17 types of development, a threshold couched in terms of scale or capacity that is used to determine whether or not the development proposed must be regarded as an NSIP or not.

Although all NSIPs are, by definition, 'nationally significant' it would not be right to conclude that they will all necessarily comprise development on a 'grand' scale; indeed, this has been one of the issues that taxed Government and practitioners alike in the early years of the new regime. An obvious example relates to 'electric lines'. The definition in PA 2006, s 16, as originally drafted, was such that an electric line of 132 kilovolts and above was 'nationally significant' even if it only comprised a single tower and span. The thresholds in s 16 were amended by The Planning Act 2008 (Nationally Significant Infrastructure Projects) (Electric Lines) Order 2013 to exclude, for example, a project where the length of the line (when installed) will be less than two kilometres in length. Other changes to the original thresholds may be anticipated over time as the new regime beds down.

A further threshold issue relates to 'extensions'. Many of the types of NSIP in PA 2008, ss 15–30 are defined by a threshold that relates to both 'construction' or 'extension' of a project. By way of example, the construction or extension of a generating station is an NSIP where its capacity is more than 50 megawatts. This may, however, appear a relatively modest 'extension' to an existing (say) 1,500 megawatt combined cycle gas turbine generating station (circa 3%). Again, this may be an issue that the Government will need to tackle as the regime matures.

Highway Related Development

Written by: James Pereira QC, ftb
Edited by: Michael Humphries QC, ftb

Introduction

Section 14(1)(h) of the PA 2008 includes within the list of NSIPs the category 'highway related development'. However, it is only highway related development that satisfies the relevant criteria set out in PA 2008, s 22 that will require a DCO. It is important to note that section 22, as originally enacted, was replaced with a new PA 2008, s 22 with effect from 24 July 2013. The new PA 2008, s 22 was introduced by article 3 of the Highway and Railway (Nationally Significant Infrastructure Project) Order 2013 ('the 2013 Order'). The replacement PA 2008, s 22 was introduced because of concerns that the thresholds in the original version were too low, so that the PA 2008 procedures were being imposed upon highway related development that was not truly of national significance. In addition, it was recognised that the original version of PA 2008, s 22 lacked clarity, which was giving rise to uncertainty as to whether a DCO was required and hence delays in progressing important infrastructure proposals (see, generally, the Government's consultation documents on the draft 2013 Order, 'Nationally significant road and railway schemes: changes to the Planning Act 2008 definitions' (DoT, 18 December 2012 (the consultation) and 3 June 2013 (the response to consultation)).

The current PA 2008, s 22 seeks to overcome these concerns by providing clearer criteria, including size thresholds, which must be satisfied before highway related development will require a DCO.

Construction, alteration and improvement of highways: definitions

For highway related development to require a DCO it must comprise one of three categories of development, and meet certain criteria applicable to each of the three categories. The categories are the construction, alteration and improvement of the highway. Relevant definitions are found in PA 2008, s 235(1).

The term 'highway' is defined in PA 2008, s 235(1) as having the same meaning as it has under section 328 of the Highways Act 1980. By PA 2008, s 328(1), 'highway' means the whole or part of any highway other than a ferry or a waterway. By PA 2008, s 328(2), where a highway passes over a bridge or through a tunnel, that bridge or tunnel is to be taken as part of the highway.

It will be noted that the definition of highway is tautologous, since it includes the word 'highway' within the definition. It is relevant to consider the common law definition of highway. At common law, a highway is 'a way over which there exists a public right of passage, that is to say a right for all of Her Majesty's subjects at all seasons of the year freely and at their will to pass and re-pass without let or hindrance' (*ex p Lewis* (1888) 21 QBD 191 at 197). This definition will be of relevance under the PA 2008.

The term 'Highway Authority' is defined under PA 2008, s 235 as having the same meaning as it has under sections 1 to 3 of the Highways Act 1980. Sections 1 to 3 set out in detail the different highway authorities that may exist in law and the highways to which they relate. Reference should be made to those sections of the Highways Act 1980 in relation to the facts of any particular case. Only general guidance can be given here. Generally, though not always, a Unitary Authority will be the highway authority for roads within its area, a county council of a district will be the highway authority for roads within its county area, Transport for London is the highway authority for certain roads within London, and the Secretary of State will be the highway authority for certain major roads, such as motorways and trunk roads.

The term 'construction' is not given a specific definition (in this context) under section 235(1). It should therefore be given its ordinary meaning. So 'construction' would usually be concerned with the physical making or laying out of a new highway.

The term 'alteration' is defined under PA 2008, s 235 as including stopping up, diverting, improving, raising or lowering the highway. The definition is not, however, exhaustive and other kinds of works to an existing highway, which can properly be termed an alteration to that highway, are likely to fall within this expression.

The term 'improvement' in relation to a highway is defined under section 235 as having the same meaning as it has under the Highways Act 1980. Section 329(1) of the Highways Act 1980 defines 'improvement' as 'The doing of any act under powers conferred by part V of this Act, and includes the erection, maintenance, alteration and removal of traffic signs, and the freeing of a highway or road-ferry from tolls.'

Part V of the Highways Act 1980 sets out specific acts that are deemed to be highway improvements. There is a general power of improvement given by section 62(2) of the Highways Act 1980 in respect of highways maintainable by the highway authority carrying out the improvements. This power is then subject to specific kinds of improvement that are excluded from the general power and for which specific powers must be found. The specific powers are set out in the rest of part V of the Highways Act 1980.

It is important to note that highway improvements which are carried out by a highway authority within the boundaries of a road may be exempt from the definition of development under section 55 of the Town and Country Planning Act 1990. The exemption does not apply where they are likely to have significant adverse environmental effects: see section 55(2)(b) of the Town and Country Planning Act 1990. This proviso seeks to give effect to obligations arising out of the Environmental Impact Assessment Directive.

Relevant criteria for the construction, alteration or improvement of highways

PA 2008, s 22 contains detailed criteria in relation to each of the three categories of highway related development. Reference should be made to its provisions in relation to any particular case. The text below considers certain issues that arise on the wording of the section.

The location of the highway and the requirement for the Secretary of State to be the highway authority

None of the three categories of development (construction, alteration or improvement of a highway) will require a DCO unless the highway falls entirely within England and the Secretary of State is or will be (in the case of a newly constructed highway) the highway authority for the highway: see PA 2008, s 22(2)(a) and (b), (3)(a) and (b), and (5)(a) and (b).

A question arises as to whether this criterion is satisfied by highway related development where the Secretary of State is or will be the highway authority for part only of the highway. The drafting of PA 2008, s 22 does not clearly identify whether such a highway will be caught by PA 2008, s 22 or not. However, since the definition of highway includes the whole or part of any highway (see section 328(1) of the Highways Act 1980), this criterion can be read as being met where the Secretary of State is or will be the highway authority for at least part of the highway as constructed, altered or improved.

The application of size thresholds to development consisting of the construction and alteration of highways

The construction or alteration of a highway will not be highway related development falling within PA 2008, s 14(1)(h) unless the area of development is greater than the relevant limit set out under PA 2008, s 22(4) (PA 2008, s 22(2)(c) and (3)(c)).

The limits under PA 2008, s 22(4) are as follows:

(a) in relation to the construction or alteration of a motorway, is 15 hectares;

(b) in relation to the construction or alteration of a highway, other than a motorway, where the speed limit for any class of vehicle is expected to be 50 miles per hour or greater, is 12.5 hectares; and

(c) in relation to the construction or alteration of any other highway is 7.5 hectares.

The 'area of development' is then defined under PA 2008, s 22(9) as follows:

(a) in relation to construction of a highway, it means the land on which the highway is to be constructed and any adjoining land expected to be used in connection with its construction;

(b) in relation to alteration of a highway, it means the land on which the part of the highway to be altered is situated and any adjoining land expected to be used in connection with its alteration.

In relation to the definition of 'area of development', a number of points arise.

First, 'in connection with [the] construction' of the highway is not defined in the PA 2008. The words should therefore be given their natural meaning. The land to be included is therefore land that the developer expects to use in connection with the works of construction or alteration (as the case may be), rather than land which may be needed for other development that is part of the scheme, such as associated development. The land to be included would normally comprise construction and works compounds and the like. This approach is supported by the fact that the size thresholds were based upon the size of the works areas required to construct or alter a single junction on the various categories of road that make up the Secretary of State's network (see page 6 of the Government's response to the consultation on the changes proposed in the draft 2013 Order (June 2013)).

Secondly, to be included within the 'area of development' such land must be 'expected to be used' in connection with the construction and also be 'adjoining' the highway. The legislation therefore expects that all land that the developer expects to use in connection with the construction or alteration will be included within the application for the DCO (since otherwise the thresholds could be circumvented). However, the use of the word 'adjoining' suggests that construction compounds which are remote from the land on which the highway is to be constructed are not to be included in the calculation of the threshold.

Thirdly, what approach should be taken in cases where part but not all of the highway being constructed or altered is (or will) be a highway for which the Secretary of State is (or will) be the highway authority. In such a case, should the area of development only include those works areas expected to be used in connection with the Secretary of State's part of the highway, or should it include works areas expected to be used in connection with the construction or alteration of the entire highway? The position is unclear. However, it may be thought that limiting the area of development to that expected to be used in connection with the Secretary of State's highway was more in keeping with the underlying objective of the changes to PA 2008, s 22, and with the basis upon which the sizes of the thresholds were chosen.

The need for significant environmental effects for development consisting of the improvement of a highway

In addition to the criteria already referred to, the improvement of a highway will not be highway related development falling within PA 2008, s 14(1)(h) unless the improvement is likely to have a significant effect on the environment (PA 2008, s 22(5)). This should be read as having the same meaning as the equivalent term under the Environmental Impact Assessment Regulations and Directive. For guidance on the approach to be taken to the assessment of whether development has significant environmental effects, see *R (Loader) v Secretary of State* [2012] EWCA Civ 869.

Alteration of a highway that is necessary as a result of development with planning permission

In certain circumstances the alteration of a highway is necessary as a result of a development that already has the benefit of a grant of planning permission. Such alterations will not be highway related development falling within PA 2008, s 14(1)(h) if the developer has asked for the alteration to be made to the highway: see PA 2008, s 22(7). Note however that the alteration must be 'necessary' as a result of the development that has planning permission. This would appear to be an objective test. It would not be satisfied where the alteration were merely desirable.

Effect of requirement for development consent on certain statutory orders under the Highways Act 1980 and New Roads and Street Works Act 1991

PA 2008, s 33(4) provides a list of statutory orders under the Highways Act 1980 and the New Roads and Street Works Act 1991 that may neither be made nor confirmed in relation to a highway or in connection with its construction, improvement or alteration, where development consent is required for that construction, improvement or alteration. Reference should be made to PA 2008, s 33(4) for the list of orders in question.

Limited exemption from the requirement for Development Consent where certain statutory orders under the Highways Act 1980 or the New Roads and Street Works Act 1991 have already been made

However, where an order listed under PA 2008, s 33(4) has *already* been made, the construction, improvement or alteration of the highway may be exempt from the requirement for development consent by reason of either PA 2008, s 22(6) or 22(8). Reference should be made to the detailed wording of those provisions in relation to any particular case.

Associated development

Some highway related development may include associated development. The Guidance on associated development applications for major infrastructure projects (DCLG, April 2013), lists the following as examples:

- replacement roadside facilities where this becomes necessary due to the elimination of an existing facility by highway improvement;
- infrastructure associated with cycle/pedestrian access;
- off-site landscaping, habitat creation and other environmental works;
- off-site drainage works;
- alteration/diversion/stopping up of local roads, accesses and other rights of way; and
- off-site diversion of statutory undertakers' equipment

The Infrastructure Planning Commission's Interim Guidance Advice 134/10 included as examples of associated development Motorway Service Areas, Rest Areas and Truck Stops. Associated development may therefore include reasonably significant forms of development.

Note that some highways works will comprise associated development for other kinds of NSIPs. The Guidance on associated development applications for major infrastructure projects (DCLG, April 2013), lists access arrangements and demand management measures as examples.

National Policy Statement for National Networks

In December 2014 the Department for Transport designated the National Policy Statement for National Networks ('the NN NPS') setting out national policy for certain transport infrastructure, including the national road network. The NN NPS provides the policy framework within which 'highway related development' falling within ss 14(1)(h) and 22 will be considered under s 104 of the PA 2008. The NN NPS outlines 'wider Government policy' on national network (including such issues as road tolling and charging), sets out 'assessment principles' on a range of issues and explains the approach to be taken to the consideration of 'generic impacts' (such as biodiversity and the historic environment).

Construction or Alteration of a Railway

Written by Alexander Booth QC, ftb
Edited by Michael Humphries QC, ftb

Introduction

This article is concerned with PA 2008, ss 14(1)(k) and 25. The former provides that works for the 'construction or alteration of a railway' may comprise an NSIP, and the latter sets out the statutory thresholds that determine whether the construction or alteration of a particular rail project will comprise an NSIP. This category of NSIP is distinct from the construction of a rail freight interchange, provision for which is made by PA 2008, ss 14(1)(l) and 26. In this regard PA 2008, s 25(3) expressly excludes development falling within s 14(1)(k) to the extent that the railway the subject of the works does or will form part of such a freight interchange.

There have been a number of DCOs granted in respect of 'Rail NSIPs', all of which have entailed the 'construction' of a railway. These include:

- The Ipswich Rail Chord (SI 2012/2284),
- The North Doncaster Rail Chord (SI 2012/2635),
- The Redditch Branch Enhancement Scheme (SI 2013/2809)
- The Norton Bridge Area Improvements Scheme (SI 2014/909)

In passing, it is perhaps worth noting that this clutch of DCOs were all granted prior to the designation of the relevant NPS; the National Policy Statement for National Networks was published in draft in 2013, before being designated in December 2014.

A further point to note, is that significant changes were made to PA 2008, s 25 by the Highways and Railway (Nationally Significant Infrastructure Project) Order 2013 (SI 2013/1883), which introduced additional requirements that any railway scheme must now meet in order to classify as an NSIP (see in particular PA 2008, s 25(1)(ba) and (2)(ba). Significantly in this regard, works of construction or alteration must now include the laying of a continuous stretch of track measuring 2km or more. One project consented by means of a DCO prior to the making of the 2013 Order would now no longer fall within the statutory definition of a 'Rail NSIP'; in the case of the Ipswich Rail Chord, the relevant length of track did not exceed 1.5km.

'Construction' versus 'Alteration'

PA 2008, s 14(1(k) embraces both the 'construction' and 'alteration' of a railway. The Act provides definitions of both these terms (PA 2008, s 235), but neither definition applies to rail related infrastructure. Thus the words must be given their natural meaning.

Statutory Requirements for NSIP classification

General Observations

The statutory requirements in respect of proposals to 'construct' a railway are all but identical to those relating to the 'alteration' of one. In summary, it is necessary:

(a) that the works (whether of construction or alteration) be undertaken wholly in England;

(b) that the railway (i.e. that part newly altered or constructed) be part of a network operated by an approved operator; and

(c) that the works (whether of construction or alteration) not comprise permitted development.

Further, and following the 2013 Order, it is necessary also that the newly altered or constructed stretch of railway includes a length of track that is both:

(a) of more than 2 kilometres continuous length, and

(b) not located on land which previously comprised the operational land of a railway undertaker.

It is important to note the distinction between how these two sets of requirements take effect. The former are, at least arguably, absolute requirements. That is, it would appear necessary that the entirety of the length of railway undergoing alteration or construction satisfy the requirements as to location (ie that it be located 'wholly in England') and operation (ie that it '*be part of a network operated by an approved operator*'), and that none of the works comprising the NSIP amount to permitted development. Such interpretation of the legislation would appear to follow from the decision in *R (on the application of Gate on behalf of Transport Solutions for Lancaster and Morecambe) v Secretary of State for Transport* [2013] EWHC 2937. Notwithstanding that the development at issue in that case comprised a highway scheme (the M6-Heysham Link), the reasoning of Turner J regarding the wording of PA 2008, s 14 applies equally to railway development as to road. In particular, in *Gate* the Court emphasised that s 14(1) provides that an NSIP is a project which '*consists*' of (as opposed to 'includes') the various categories of development there identified. On this basis, and given that PA 2008, s 25(1) and (2) stipulate that development will fall within the terms of s 14(1) (k) 'only' if the criteria as to location / operation / permitted development are met, it would appear that the requirements must be satisfied by the entirety of the NSIP.

This position can be contrasted with the requirements imposed by the 2013 Order, both of which may be satisfied by part of the length of the railway undergoing alteration or construction. In such circumstances there is no necessity for the entirety of the railway to meet those requirements.

Networks and Approved Operators

As noted above, in order for development to comprise an NSIP, the track the subject of the works must form part of a network operated by an approved operator. The term 'approved operator' is defined by PA 2008, s 25(4)–(6), whilst s 25(7) provides that the term 'network' should have the definition contained in the Railways Act 1993, s 83(1). This identifies a network as:

(a) any railway line, or combination of two or more railway lines, and

(b) any installations associated with any of the track comprised in that line or those lines

which constitute a system of track and installations used for and in connection with the support, guidance and operation of trains.

Very often there will be no difficulty as regards these particular requirements, since the majority of Rail NSIPs will be likely to comprise track constructed either by an operator (such as Network Rail) for the purpose of extending / improving its network, or by the developer of some other significant project (presumably to provide access in connection with that project's construction or operation) with the intention that it be passed to an operator as part of its network.

However, there may be circumstances where significant stretches of track are constructed as 'private' railways in the context of large infrastructure projects. Where track is not intended to be made over to an operator as part of its network, such a railway – however extensive – will fall outside the definition of an NSIP; although it may be 'associated development'.

Operational Land

The requirement as to operational land summarised above is subject to qualification, in that what the statute actually requires is that the land:

(a) must not comprise operational land of railway undertaker immediately prior to the construction/alteration works.

Alternatively to the extent that it does comprise such operational land, the land

(b) must have been acquired for the purpose of the particular construction or alteration works in question.

In this context, PA 2008, s 25(7) stipulates that the term 'operational land' will have the meaning provided for by the Town and Country Planning Act 1990. The relevant provision of the TCPA 1990 is s 263, subject to the qualification provided by s 234.

Permitted Development

A railway development will not comprise an NSIP in circumstances where part or all of it comprises 'permitted development'. In this context the relevant permission is that granted pursuant to Class A of Part 8 of Schedule 2 to the Town and Country Planning (General Permitted Development) Order 2015 (SI 2015/596), which provision authorises the carrying out of development by railway undertakers on their operational land where such development is required in connection with the movement of traffic by rail.

However, paragraph A.1(a) of Class A excludes from the scope of the permission any development which comprises '*the construction of a railway*'. Further, and more broadly, Article 3 of the 2015 Order engages to exclude development requiring environmental impact assessment. Thus the majority of railway works that would fall to be classed as an NSIP are unlikely to be excluded from the PA 2008 regime because they are 'permitted development'.

Development to be consented

NSIP

The definition of the term 'railway' in the PA 2008 Act borrows from the Transport and Works Act 1992, s 67(1); see PA 2008, s 235. That provision defines a 'railway' as a system of transport employing parallel rails which:

(a) provides support and guidance for vehicles carried on flanged wheels, and

(b) forms a track which either is of a gauge of at least 350 millimetres or crosses a carriageway (whether or not on the same level), but

(c) does not include a tramway.

Having regard to this definition, it would appear that the PA 2008 does not intend that the definition of a Rail NSIP should embrace the construction of items such as 'station' development; platforms, ticket offices and similar; again, this may be subject to consideration of whether any such development may be 'associated development'. Rather, it appears to intend that the NSIP itself comprise only the infrastructure along which (rail) traffic will pass. This would of course include rails, sleepers and ballast, but also includes matters such as the embankments and cuttings in/on which such infrastructure sits.

Such relatively narrow approach is consistent with that adopted in respect of the DCOs issued to date. In this regard, by way of example, the Redditch DCO confined the scope of the NSIP (Work No.1) to what might broadly be termed 'the railway line', being the infrastructure along which trains would travel, with all other matters comprising 'associated development'. Such 'associated development' included the 'construction of a new station platform …' (Work No.2), and the 'construction of a new footbridge to connect from the existing platform…' (Work No.3).

In this context, one might have expected signalling equipment/infrastructure to form part of the 'system of transport' comprising the railway, and thus the NSIP. However in the Redditch DCO 'signal equipment buildings' (Work Nos 6 and 7) and other '*signalling works*' were consented only as 'associated development'.

Notwithstanding what is said above, it would appear that the system does admit of some flexibility. In this regard the Ipswich Chord DCO included within the terms of the NSIP not only works to embankments but also the construction and reconstruction of bridges; similarly the Doncaster Rail Chord NSIP included the construction of temporary haul roads. Perhaps the broadest approach to what may comprised part of the NSIP is that adopted in the Norton Bridge Area Improvements DCO, which included not only the line itself, but also:

'...all associated items that comprise a railway including track, cess drainage, combined troughing and walking route, overhead line electrification... signalling, telecommunications and cutting or embankment earthworks, maintenance access track, crest drainage ... and boundary fencing'.

Associated Development

A narrow interpretation as to the extent of the NSIP is consistent with what is said in the guidance provided by DCLG as to 'associated development'. In this regard the relevant guidance (the 2013 publication 'Planning Act 2008 – Guidance on associated development applications for major infrastructure projects') identifies in Annex B development that may constitute 'associated development' connected with a 'Rail NSIP'. Examples of such development include:

- the construction of new railway stations, and improvements, alterations and extensions to existing stations (new footbridges, platforms extensions, ticket halls;
- the construction/alteration of maintenance depots and marshalling yards; and
- the provision of pressure relief or ventilation shafts (and access to them)

The DCOs granted to date have delivered a myriad of items as Associated Development; these have included matters such as

- the construction of bridges (both vehicular and pedestrian);
- the diversion of other infrastructure (roads and pipelines); and
- the diversion of other linear features (footpaths and rivers).

Contiguity of Development

There is no requirement that the scheme of proposed works comprise a contiguous 'whole'. The closest the PA 2008 comes in this regard are the equivalent stipulations in s 25(1)(b) and (2)(b) that the stretch of track the subject of the construction / alteration be part of a network operated by an approved operator (see above).

However, it would appear that so long as the railway that is subject to the works undertaken (whether of construction or alteration) forms part of such a network, it may form part of the same NSIP. This may be of some significance in circumstances where a party is seeking to carry out various works in various different locations that are not geographically proximate. In such a scenario it would arguably be sufficient if only one of those works satisfied the requirements regarding length of track and operational land – imposed by PA 2008, s 25(1)(ba) and (2)(ba) – in order for all the remainder to comprise part of an NSIP.

Policy

As noted above, the National Networks NPS was designated in December 2014. The document provides detailed guidance not only in respect of Rail NSIPs promoted pursuant to PA 2008, s 14(1)(k), but also highways and rail freight interchange development.

The guidance is extensive, and those promoting or objecting to applications seeking development consent for the construction / alteration of railways will of course need to consider it in detail so as to ascertain whether a proposal is compliant with the NPS for the purposes of the presumption contained in PA 2008, s 104(3). However, by way of generality it should be noted that the National Networks NPS contains a strong presumption in favour of railway related development, both in terms of freight and in terms of passenger traffic, where that development will improve the performance of the rail network. In this regard the following paragraphs are worthy of particular note:

- 'The Government has … concluded that at a strategic level there is a compelling need for development of the national networks – both as individual network and as an integrated system. The Examining Authority and the Secretary of State should therefore start their assessment of applications for infrastructure covered by this NPS on that basis' (paragraph 2.10)
- 'Rail transport has a crucial role to play in delivering significant reductions in pollution and congestion …' (paragraph 2.35)
- 'The Government has therefore concluded that at a strategic level there is a compelling need for development of the national rail network …' (paragraph 2.36)
- 'Modal shift from road and aviation to rail can help reduce transport's carbon emissions, as well as providing wider transport and economic benefits. For these reasons, the Government seeks to accommodate an increase in rail travel and rail freight where it is practical and affordable by providing for extra capacity' (paragraph 2.40).

Thus, to the extent that proposed development may have some adverse impact – in terms of planning considerations such as heritage and visual impact – any such impacts must be assessed in policy context that is supportive as a matter of principle. Clearly however, such policy support in no way excuses rail related development from compliance with the many and onerous requirements relating to 'environmental impact assessment' and, where necessary, 'appropriate assessment.'

Construction and Alteration of a Rail Freight Interchange

Written by James Pereira QC, ftb
Edited by Michael Humphries QC, ftb

Introduction

Under PA 2008, s 26, the construction and alteration of a rail freight interchange ('RFI') will be an NSIP, provided that the thresholds and criteria in the legislation are met. The policy guidance on RFIs is found within the NPS for National Networks (December 2014).

The requirements of PA 2008, s 26 are considered below.

What is a rail freight interchange?

There is no definition of an RFI in the legislation. The NPS for National Networks (December 2014) explains at paragraph 2.43 that:

> 'Rail freight interchanges (RFI) enable freight to be transferred between transport modes, thus allowing rail to be used to best effect to undertake the long-haul primary trunk journey, with other modes (usually road) providing the secondary (final delivery) leg of the journey.'

In fact, the NPS uses the term 'strategic rail freight interchange' ('SRFI') to describe rail freight interchanges that qualify as NSIPs (see paragraph 1.1 of the NPS). So although the term 'strategic' is not used in the legislation, it is clear that the NPS in referring to SRFIs is referring to the same development as RFIs that meet the thresholds and criteria to be NSIPs under the PA 2008.

Paragraph 2.44 explains that:

> The aim of a strategic rail freight interchange (SRFI) is to optimise the use of rail in the freight journey by maximising rail trunk haul and minimising some elements of the secondary distribution leg by road, through co-location of other distribution and freight activities. SRFIs are a key element in reducing the cost to users of moving freight by rail and are important in facilitating the transfer of freight from road to rail, thereby reducing trip mileage of freight movements on both the national and local road networks.

Footnote 42 of the NPS states as follows:

> 'A strategic rail freight interchange (SRFI) is a large multi-purpose rail freight interchange and distribution centre linked into both the rail and trunk road system. It has rail-served warehousing and container handling facilities and may also include manufacturing and processing activities.'

In the light of the NPS, it appears that the essence of an SRFI is that it provides facilities for the reciprocal transfer of goods to and from the rail network, to and from other modes of transport. The extent to which other uses such as manufacturing and processing activities might be included within an SRFI application is discussed later in this section.

Threshold requirements and other criteria

To qualify as an NSIP, the proposed new RFI must, when constructed, be *'expected to'* meet each of the conditions set out in PA 2008, s 26(3)–(7). These are that it must:

- Be in England (PA 2008, s 26(3)(a));
- Be part of a railway network in England (PA 2008, s 26(5));
- Be on land of at least 60ha in area (PA 2008, s 26(3)(b));
- Be capable of handling consignments of goods from more than one consignor and to more than one consignee (PA 2008, s 26(4)(a));
- Be capable of handling at least four good trains per day (PA 2008, s 26(4)(b)). Goods train is defined as a train (excluding any locomotive) that consists of rolling stock designed to carry goods (PA 2008, s 26(9)); and
- Include warehouses to which goods can be delivered from the railway network in England either directly or by means of another form of transport (s26(6)).

RFIs that form part of a military establishment are expressly excluded from the regime (PA 2008, s 26(7)). A military establishment is defined as an establishment intended for use for naval, military or air force purposes or for the purposes of the Department of the Secretary of State responsible for defence (PA 2008, s 26(9)).

The terms 'network', 'rolling stock' and 'train' are given the same meaning as under the Railways Act 1993, s 83(1) (PA 2008, s 26(9)).

Alterations to an RFI

Alterations to an RFI will qualify as an NSIP where the same criteria are expected to be met following the alteration, save that the land area criteria applied to an alteration is that it must increase by at least 60 ha the land on which the RFI is situated (PA 2008, s 26(2)).

The inclusion of other uses within an RFI application

It is in the nature of RFIs that other uses, such as processing and manufacturing uses, may find it advantageous to locate within an RFI site. This is because the SRFI will facilitate the receiving of raw materials and dispatching new products by rail or road. While footnote 42 in the NPS (quoted above) suggests that processing and manufacturing uses can be found on an SRFI, such uses are likely to be an end in themselves, and so are unlikely to qualify as associated development under the PA 2008.

In the East Midlands Gateway Rail Freight Interchange and Highway Order 2016, the accommodation of other primary uses was allowed for through the drafting of the Order.

Regulation 5(2) of the Order provided as follows:

> 'It does not constitute a breach of the terms of this Order, if, following the coming into force of this Order, any development, or any part of a development, is carried out or used within the Order limits under planning permission granted under the 1990 Act.'

This provision was recognized by the Examining Authority as providing flexibility to accommodate the commercial requirements of future occupiers who could not be known at the time, and to provide flexibility to accommodate future uses that would fall outside the PA 2008 but which could be granted planning permission (Examining Authority's report, paragraphs 7.1.18 and 7.1.21).

DCOs granted for RFIs and alterations to RFIs

DCOs granted under this section include:

- The East Midlands Gateway Rail Freight Interchange and Highway Order 2016 (granting development consent for a new rail freight interchange and highway infrastructure at Castle Donnington, Leicestershire).
- The Daventry International Rail Freight Interchange Alteration Order 2014 (granting development consent to expand the existing Daventry International Rail Freight Interchange Terminal).

Construction or Alteration of a Hazardous Waste Facility

Written by: Mark Westmoreland Smith, ftb
Edited by: Michael Humphries QC, ftb

Introduction

Section 14 of the PA 2008 identifies those 'types' of project that are 'nationally significant infrastructure projects' ('NSIPs') for the purposes of the PA 2008 regime; subject to the thresholds set by PA 2008, ss 15–30. PA 2008, s 14(1)(q) states that a project consisting of 'the construction or alteration of a hazardous waste facility' is an NSIP; this is subject to the thresholds set out in PA 2008, s 30.

This article considers the scope and effect of these provisions.

Commencement

Section 14(1)(p) came into effect on 26 November 2008 for the purposes of making orders (other than development consent orders) regulations or rules relating to its exercise, but for all other purposes that section and s 30 came into effect on 1 October 2011.

Thresholds and geographical issues

The effect of PA 2008, ss 14(1)(p) and 30 together is that:

- The 'construction' of a hazardous waste facility is a nationally significant infrastructure project where:
    - The facility (when constructed) will be in England;
    - The main purpose of the facility is expected to be the final disposal or recovery of hazardous waste; and
    - It is expected to have the capacity of, in the case of the disposal of hazardous waste by landfill or in a deep storage facility, more than 100,000 tonnes per year and, in any other case, more than 30,000 tonnes per year; and
- The 'alteration' of a hazardous waste facility is a nationally significant infrastructure project where:
    - The facility is in England;
    - The main purpose of the facility is expected to be the final disposal or recovery of hazardous waste; and

- The alteration is expected to have the effect, in the case of the disposal of hazardous waste by landfill or in a deep storage facility, to increase by more than 100,000 tonnes per year the capacity of the facility and, in any other case, to increase the capacity of the facility by more than 30,000 tonnes per year (irrespective of whether the capacity of the original facility exceeded the thresholds).

PA 2008, s 14(1)(q) relates, therefore, to hazardous waste facilities in England only. In Scotland, Wales and Northern Ireland, planning consents for all hazardous waste projects are devolved to the Scottish Government, Welsh Government and Northern Ireland Executive respectively.

Development consent for development that is 'associated' with the construction or alteration of a hazardous waste facility within PA 2008, s 14(1)(q) (ie 'associated development' under PA 2008, s 115) is also restricted to England.

It is worth noting that the thresholds for both 'construction' and 'alteration' are set by reference to the 'capacity' or 'increased capacity' of the facility, and not its intended or likely throughput; this is important.

Where a proposed hazardous waste development in England does fall below the thresholds in s 30, the applicant may request the Secretary of State to issue a s 35 Direction to the effect that the project should be treated as an NSIP such that an application for development consent could be considered under the PA 2008 regime.

Definitions within PA 2008, s 30

PA 2008, s 30 contains a number of defined terms, some of which are defined in other legislation.

PA 2008, s 30(5) defines the terms:

- 'disposal',
- 'hazardous waste', and
- 'recovery'

by reference to the Hazardous Waste (England and Wales) Regulations 2005 and, in particular, regulation 5 of those regulations.

Regulation 5(2) defines 'disposal' to mean 'any operation which is not recovery even where the operation has as a secondary consequence the reclamation of substances or energy (Annex I of the Waste Directive sets out a non-exhaustive list of disposal operations)'.

Regulation 5(2) defines 'recovery' to mean 'any operation the principal result of which is waste serving a useful purpose by replacing other materials which would otherwise have been used to fulfil a particular function, or waste being prepared to fulfil that function, in the plant or in the wider economy (Annex II of the Waste Directive sets out a non-exhaustive list of recovery operations)'.

In both cases 'the Waste Directive' means Directive 2008/98/EC of the European Parliament and of the Council on waste.

Regulation 5(2) defines 'hazardous waste' by reference to regulation 6, which states that

> 'Subject to regulation 9, a waste is a hazardous waste if it is—
>
> (a) listed as a hazardous waste in the List of Wastes;
>
> (b) listed in regulations made under section 62A(1) of the 1990 Act; or
>
> (c) a specific batch of waste which is determined pursuant to regulation 8 to be a hazardous
>
> waste, and the term 'hazardous' and cognate expressions shall be construed accordingly.'

Regulation 9 identifies specific waste to be treated as non-hazardous and the term 'List of Wastes' is refined in regulation 4.

Essentially, 'hazardous waste' is waste that contains one or more hazardous properties that may cause harm to human health or the environment. It does not include waste classified as radioactive waste under the Environmental Permitting (England and Wales) Regulations 2010 (except in the limited circumstances where such waste does not require a permit because it falls under an exemption provision), such that facilities for the disposal or recovery of radioactive waste do not fall to be considered as an NSIP under PA 2008, s 14(1)(p) and 30.

Note, however, the National Policy Statement for Hazardous Waste (June 2013) (see below and paragraph 2.2.1 of the NPS) states that proposals for hazardous waste facilities that handle a relatively small proportion of low level radioactive waste ('LLW') alongside hazardous waste may fall within the scope of the NPS and PA 2008, ss 14(1)(p) and 30.

The term 'Deep storage facility' in PA 2008, s 30 is defined by sub-s (6) to mean a facility for the storage of waste underground in a deep geological cavity.

The National Policy Statement for Hazardous Waste

The National Policy Statement for Hazardous Waste was published in June 2013 and will be used by the Secretary of State as the 'primary basis' for decision on development consent applications for hazardous waste infrastructure falling within the 2008 Act regime in England (para 1.1.1).

The NPS sets out a summary of the Government's policy on Hazardous Waste, the main objectives of which are (section 2.1 summary):

- To protect human health and the environment – stringent legislative controls are in place to control the management of waste with hazardous properties;
- Implementation of the waste hierarchy – to produce less hazardous waste, using it as a resource where possible and only disposing of it as a last resort;
- Self-sufficiency and proximity – to ensure that sufficient disposal facilities are provided in the country as a whole to match expected arisings of all hazardous wastes, except those produced in very small quantities, and to enable hazardous waste to be disposed of in one of the nearest appropriate installations;

- Climate change – to minimise greenhouse gas emissions and maximise opportunities for climate change adaptation and resilience.

The NPS concludes that a small number of large facilities (ie with a capacity above the NSIP thresholds) are likely to be needed to meet the expected increase in arisings in hazardous waste (para 3.3.7 and see section 3.1 Summary of Need).

Having set out Government policy on hazardous waste (Part 2) and the need for large scale hazardous waste infrastructure (Part 3), the NPS then sets out in detail:

- the Assessment Principles for hazardous waste infrastructure (Part 4), and
- the Generic Impacts to be considered by the Planning Inspectorate when examining an application for hazardous waste infrastructure (Part 5).

The King's Cliffe application

To date there has been a single application under PA 2008, ss 14(1)(p) and 30 for the alteration of existing and the construction of new facilities for the recovery and disposal of hazardous waste and disposal of low level radioactive waste at the East Northants Resource Management Facility, Stamford Road, Northamptonshire, known as 'King's Cliffe'.

During the examination itself and at the time the Examining Authority came to report (22 April 2013), only the draft NPS (July 2011) was available. As a result the Examining Authority's Report was based on the approach set down in PA 2008, s 105 ('Decisions in cases where no national policy statement has effect'). The NPS was, however, adopted on 6 June 2013 about five weeks before the Secretary of State's decision letter (11 July 2013). The Secretary of State, therefore, determined the application under PA 2008, s 104 ('decisions in cases where national policy statement has effect'). He did not, however, consider the changes between the draft and the final versions of the NPS significant enough to warrant further consultation.

A further interesting feature of this case was a jurisdictional point. As can be seen from the description of development above, that the application included the disposal of low level (radioactive) waste ('LLW'). Given that the definition of hazardous waste does not include radioactive waste, the Examining Authority asked the applicant (Augean) to set out how LLW fell within PA 2008, ss 14(1)(p) and 30.

Paragraphs 2.2.4-2.2.7 of the Examining Authority's Report states as follows:

> 'LLW is not included in the definition of hazardous waste specified in section 30(5) of PA 2008 and I therefore asked Augean to provide a legal submission setting out why, and on what basis, it considered it appropriate to include the disposal of low level waste in the draft DCO when this is not hazardous waste as defined in PA 2008. In its response Augean referred to section 115 of PA 2008.20 This states in subsection (1) that "development consent may be granted for development which is (a) development for which development consent is required: and (b) associated development." Augean considered that disposal of LLW in the hazardous landfill facility can fall within either of these categories. Section 31 states that "consent under this Act (development consent) is required for development to the extent that

> the development is or forms part of a nationally significant infrastructure project." In Augean's view use of the words "forms part of" demonstrates that the development does not itself have to constitute an NSIP but also that the development can form part of an NSIP. In addition section 30 which defines hazardous waste NSIPs states that "the main purpose of the facility is expected to be the final disposal or recovery of hazardous waste." Augean argued that the facility would continue to be an NSIP notwithstanding that activities subsidiary to the main purpose of disposal of hazardous waste are carried on. Such subsidiary activities could for example include the disposal of other appropriate waste types.
>
> Augean concluded on this point that "It is considered that Sections 30 and 31 of the Act allow for the disposal of LLW in the hazardous landfill facility NSIP provided that it is subsidiary/subordinate to the main purpose of the NSIP which requires development consent. It is therefore development for which development consent is required and it is correct to characterise it as integral."
>
> Augean considered whether the disposal of LLW might also be regarded as associated development and be included in the DCO on that basis. Drawing on revised guidance on associated development put out for consultation by DCLG in April 2012 Augean concluded that the Secretary of State would have sufficient flexibility to make his decision on a case by case basis and that"'the disposal of LLW would fit well within the tenor of the proposed amended core principles."
>
> The draft DCO submitted by Augean with the application does not identify LLW as associated development and in this report I have considered it as an integral part of the development for which consent is sought not as associated development. Consideration is given later in this report to whether the inclusion of LLW as part of the waste to be disposed of at the site has any implications in terms of this proposed development remaining an NSIP.'

On this issue the Examining authority concluded at paragraph 5.134 that

> 'A hazardous waste facility is classified as an NSIP if, inter alia, "the main purpose of the facility is expected to be the final disposal or recovery of hazardous waste" (s30(1)(b) PA 2008). That leaves scope for some other activity to form part of the facility. In my view it is reasonable, as considered earlier at paragraphs 2.24 to 2.27, for disposal of LLW to be included as part of the proposed development for which development consent is being sought as long as that does not prevent the NSIP from being used for it "main purpose".'

The Secretary of State considered this issue and agreed with the Examining Authority's conclusion (para 24). A total limit on the amount of LLW was imposed, however, to ensure that the disposal of hazardous waste remains the main purpose of the NSIP.

Part 4

Requirement for Development Consent

When Development Consent is Required

Written by: Mark Westmoreland Smith, ftb
Edited by: Michael Humphries QC, ftb

Introduction

Although brief, Part 4 of the PA 2008 is pivotal to the entire regime, as it sets out when development consent is required. It is this Part of the PA 2008 that also ensures various other consents are not required for NSIPs, which was one of the principal objectives behind the new regime. As a result, there is much cross-referencing to other Acts in order to dis-apply the need for consents other than development consent for NSIPs. This makes the navigation of this Part somewhat difficult.

The requirement for development consent

PA 2008, s 31 is the key provision and provides as follows:

> 'Consent under this Act ('development consent') is required for development to the extent that the development is or forms part of a nationally significant infrastructure project.'

Two concepts require consideration, being:

- 'development', and
- 'is or forms part of a nationally significant infrastructure project'.

'Development'

PA 2008, s 32 defines the term 'development' for the purposes of the PA 2008. It provides that, subject to PA 2008, s.32(2) and (3), 'development' has the same meaning as in Town and Country Planning Act 1990 ('TCPA1990').

'Development' is defined by s 55 of the TCPA1990 as being 'the carrying out of building, engineering, mining or other operations in, on, over or under land, or the making of any material change in the use of any buildings or other land', subject to further definitions and exclusions set out in that section.

The construction or alteration of nationally significant infrastructure projects will almost always involve some form of operational development (ie building, engineering, mining or other operations) and so clearly fall within the PA 2008, s 32 definition for the purposes of the PA 2008. Perhaps less clear, however, is that development comprising a 'material change of use' and for that reason the Act provides some clarification in s 32.

The effect of PA 2008, s 55(2) is that:

- the conversion of a generating station with a view to it using crude liquid petroleum, a petroleum product or natural gas as a fuel source (s 32(2)(a));
- starting to use a cavity or strata for the underground storage of gas (s 32(2)(b)); and
- an increase in the permitted use of an airport (s 32(2)(c));

are all treated as a 'material change of use' and therefore fall within the meaning of 'development' for the purposes of the development consent regime. This clarification is helpful.

The conversion of generating stations

The effect of the provision relating to generating stations makes clear that the conversion of such a station with a view to its using certain fossil fuel types is a material change of use and, therefore, 'development' for the purposes of the PA 2008. Interestingly, the conversion of such a station to the use of non-fossil biofuels is not so brought within the definition of development; although such a conversion could still require consent under s 36 of the Electricity Act 1989 depending on the particular circumstances.

Until June 2013, the provision relating to the conversion of generating stations to the use of certain fossil fuels had to be understood in the context of s 14 of the Energy Act 1976 under which the Secretary of State was able to control the fuelling of new or converted power stations. However, s 14 has been repealed by the s 18 of the Growth and Infrastructure Act 2013 (effective June 25, 2013). Section 14 of the 1976 Act implemented EU Directive 75/404/EEC on the restriction on the use of natural gas in power stations and Directive 75/405/EEC concerning the restriction on the use of petroleum products in power stations. Both Directives have since been repealed (EC/75/404 in 1991 and EC/75/405 in 1997) and the policy objectives behind s 14 (arising in response to market conditions for gas and petroleum products in the 1970s) no longer exist.

Although the conversion of a generating station to the use of certain fossil fuel is a material change of use, and therefore 'development for the purposes of the PA 2008, such development will only be an NSIP requiring development consent, however, if the 'construction' or 'extension' of that generating station exceeds the thresholds in PA 2008, s 15.

Thus the conversion of a generating station to the use of fossil fuels that was *not* (i) the construction or extension of a generating station in England or Wales with a capacity of more than 50MW, or (ii) the construction or extension of an offshore generating station of more than 100MW, would not be an NSIP for the purposes of the PA 2008 and would not, therefore, require development consent.

The use of natural porous strata for underground gas storage

There are broadly two forms of underground gas storage development being (i) the creation of gas storage caverns in underground salt deposits by solution mining, and (ii) the use of natural porous strata (eg depleted gas production fields). The first of these clearly involves 'operational' development, whilst the second may simply amount to a change of use. What PA 2008, s 32(2)(b) makes clear, however, is that such a change of use is a 'material' change of use for the purposes of the PA 2008 regime.

Again, although such a use of porous natural strata may amount to a 'material change of use' and therefore comprise 'development' for the purposes of the PA 2008, it will only be an NSIP requiring development to the extent that such development 'is starting to use underground gas storage facilities' in England or Wales above the relevant 'working capacity' or 'maximum flow rate' threshold in PA 2008, s 17.

Increase in permitted use of an airport

Clearly operational development comprising the 'construction' or 'alteration' of an airport will be an NSIP, subject to the thresholds in PA 2008, s 23. The effect of s 32(2)(c), however, is to make an increase in the permitted use of an airport a 'material change of use'. Such a change of use could, potentially, involve no operational development, but still be an NSIP by virtue of s 23(1)(1)(c) and (7).

PA 2008, s 23(1)(c) relates to 'an increase in the permitted use of an airport in a case within subsection (7)'; which sets an annual passenger or air transport movement threshold. The words in s 23(1)(c) reflect those in s 32(2)(c). The important words here are 'permitted use'. The term 'permitted' is defined in s 32(4) and s 23(9) are meaning permitted by planning permission or development consent. At present no airport has been permitted by development consent and so, for all practical purposes, this means permitted by planning permission.

More important, however, is that, currently, very few UK airports have a level of 'use' – in terms of annual passenger numbers or air transport movements – that is controlled by the terms of any planning permission. Heathrow and Stansted airports do have planning conditions limiting the use of the airport, but most do not. Thus the application of the 'material change of use' in PA 2008, s 32(2)(c) may be of relatively limited scope.

PA 2008, s 32(3) further clarifies the meaning of 'development' for the purpose of the PA 2008 by making it clear that the following is development (to the extent that they would not be otherwise):

- Works for the demolition of a listed building or its alteration or extension in a manner which would affect its character as a building of special architectural or historic interest;
- Demolition of a building in a conservation area;
- Works resulting in the demolition or destruction of or any damage to a scheduled monument;
- Works for the purpose of removing or repairing a scheduled monument or any part of it;
- Works for the purpose of making any alterations or additions to a scheduled monument; and
- Flooding or tipping operations on land in, on or under which there is a scheduled monument.

In short, this provision ensures that the development consent regime is aligned with the Planning (Listed Buildings and Conservation Areas) Act 1990 and the Ancient Monuments and Archaeological Areas Act 1979. Where development consent is required for development, PA 2008, s 33(1)(f), (g), (i) and (j) then removes the requirements for consent under those other Acts and thereby removes the need for multiple consents for the same development.

'Is or forms part of a nationally significant infrastructure project'

Development consent is only required for development under PA 2008, s 31 to the extent that it is, or forms part of, a nationally significant infrastructure project. The determination of what is, or forms part of, an NSIP needs to be considered by reference to s 14 in combination with the thresholds in ss 15–30.

Section 31 required development consent for two broad types of development, being;

- development that is an NSIP; and
- development that forms part of an NSIP.

Different issues arise in relation to each.

Development that is an NSIP

A consideration of PA 2008, ss 14 and 15–30 reveal three aspects that need to be considered, namely:

- an action;
- a type of project; and
- a relevant threshold.

The various types of project identified in PA 2008, ss 14 and 15–30 are usually preceded by what might be described as an 'action'; for example, the 'construction or extension' of a generating station, or the 'construction or alteration' of a waste water treatment plant. Even those types of development that do not have an associated 'action' in the various sub-categories within s 14(1), and there are four of them, still have such 'actions' in their corresponding threshold section (ie ss15–30). So, for example, s 14(1)(h) is simply 'highway-related development', but s 20 makes it clear that the NSIP must be the 'construction', 'improvement' or 'alteration' of a highway.

PINS has made it clear that it will expect an applicant to specify, to use the example above, whether PA 2008, s 20 development is the 'construction', 'improvement' or 'alteration' of a highway; that is, to specify what 'action' is engaged. It is worth noting that an 'action', so called, is not the same as the limb of operational development, in that, extending the example, the 'construction', 'improvement' or 'alteration' of a highway may all be classified as 'engineering operations'.

The various terms to describe what this article has referred to as an 'action' are often derived from the predecessor legislation and are, no doubt, maintained as development below the relevant threshold would still be determined under that predecessor legislation. Thus PA 2008, ss 14(1)(b) and 16 refer to the 'installation' of an electric line above ground, echoing the language in s 37 of the Electricity Act 1989.

The next aspect to consider is the 'type of project' identified in PA 2008, ss 14 and 15–30. In some cases the threshold section does further define the type of development, but often it doesn't. So, for example, s 18(3) defines what is meant by an 'LNG facility', but s 24 does not define the term 'harbour facility'.

Even where a type of project is further defined, however, there still seems to be considerable scope as to what is properly described as being, for example, a 'hazardous waste facility': see the Examining Authority's Report (paras 2.24-2.27 and 5.134) and Secretary of State's decision (para 24) on the East Northants Resource Management Facility (aka 'King's Cliffe') DCO application.

This raises wider the issue as to whether development normally constructed together with a particular form of infrastructure (for example, a generating station) can properly be described as being 'part of' that type of development', as opposed to 'associated development' within PA 2008, s 115. This issue is particularly relevant in Wales where, subject to the exception in s 115(4), a development consent order cannot include 'associated development'. In this regard the Examining Authority's comments in its report into the Brechfa Forest West wind farm DCO application are interesting (see paras 4.139-4.146).

The final aspect to consider is the relevant threshold. For the most part these are quantitative and set by reference to an aspect of the scale or capacity of the particular development. These thresholds are considered in more detail in other parts of this work.

Development that forms part of an NSIP

Clearly many of the above considerations relate to development that forms 'part of' an NSIP, but additional points are also potentially relevant.

Clearly, a development may form 'part of' an NSIP because it is a phase of a larger project. Thus, for example, an early phase of an offshore generating station that was itself below the threshold in s 15(3), would nevertheless require development consent under s 31 if it was 'part of' a larger offshore generating station that was above that threshold. The words 'part of' in this context is clearly intended to prevent the 'salami slicing' of projects to bring them under a relevant threshold.

Issues do then arise as to whether a development below the relevant threshold would be within the PA 2008 regime if it was an early phase of a much larger project that was not expected to be promoted for some years. In other words, when does a phase of a project become a separate project? At the moment no clear guidance exists and the issue will have to be approached on its own facts, if and when it arises.

Secretary of State's Direction that Project of National Significance

Written by Mark Westmoreland Smith, ftb
Edited by Michael Humphries QC, ftb

Introduction

Under PA 2008, s 35 a project which falls outside of the relevant thresholds for NSIPs may, nonetheless, be treated as a NSIP on a direction from the Secretary of State. It was a section that was little used until it was significantly amended by the Localism Act 2011. It has again been amended by the Growth and Infrastructure Act 2013, which has further widened its scope.

The original PA 2008, s 35

PA 2008, s 35 as originally enacted permitted the Secretary of State to direct that a project, which met certain conditions, was to be treated as an application for development consent for specified purposes or generally.

The conditions were that:

- the Secretary of State thought that the project was of national significance, either by itself or when considered with one or more other projects or proposed projects in the same field;
- an application for a consent or authorisation listed in PA 2008, s 33(1) or (2) had been made, which includes planning permission, listed building consent, consent under the Transport and Works Act 1992;
- the project was in one of the following fields: energy, transport, water, waste water or waste; and
- the project was located in England, in waters adjacent to England (up to the seaward limits of the territorial sea) or, in the case of a project for the carrying out of works in the field of energy, a Renewable Energy Zone (except where any part of the Renewable Energy Zone was under the jurisdiction of Scottish Ministers).

If such a direction was made the relevant authority to which the application had been made had to refer the application to the Commission (as it was then) rather than deal with it itself.

Shortcomings

As originally enacted, the section only provided a power to direct that a project be treated as an NSIP where an application for that project had already been made. That was a significant restraint on the utility of the provision. For example, the Thames Tideway Tunnel did not fall within any type of development within PA 2008, s 14.

To have sought a direction under the original version of PA 2008, s 35 would have involved not a single planning application, but planning applications to 14 different local authorities. This would have been a huge undertaking that would have led to the project's pre-application procedures being undertaken under the Town and Country Planning Act 1990 and its consideration and determination under the PA 2008. In fact, Thames Water was able to avoid this issue because under PA 2008, s 14(3) the Government made an Order creating a new type of s 14 development, being 'waste water storage and transfer tunnel'.

Initial amendments: Localism Act 2011

The first amendments to PA 2008, s 35 were made by s 132 of the Localism Act 2011. It amended PA 2008, s 35 to allow the Secretary of State to direct that a development is to be treated as requiring development consent under the 2008 Act before any application has been made on receipt of a 'qualifying request'.

'Qualifying request'

A 'qualifying request' is one which is made in writing, which specifies the development to which it relates and explains why the conditions in PA 2008, s 35(2)(a) and (b) are met in relation to the proposed development (respectively that it is a project in the field of energy, transport, water, waste water or waste or is a business or commercial project of a prescribed description and will meet the territorial requirements (ie it is in England or waters adjacent or is an energy project in a Renewable Energy Zone (except those administered by the Scottish Ministers)) (see PA 2008, s 35ZA(11) for the definition of 'qualifying request').

Timetable

A new PA 2008, s 35A was also inserted into the 2008 Act which provides a timetable for dealing with requests for the Secretary of State to direct that a project is to be determined under the PA 2008.

PA 2008, s 35A provides that the Secretary of State must make a decision within 28 days of the date the qualifying request is made, unless the Secretary of State asks for further information (before 28 day period ends) from the person who made the qualifying request, in which case the Secretary of State must make a decision within 28 days of the information being provided if the person to whom the request for further information provides it within 14 days (PA 2008, s 35A(4)). There appears to be a lacuna in the timetable in that if a request for further information is made and the person to whom the request is made fails to provide it within 14 days then there is no deadline by which the Secretary of State must made his determination on the qualifying request.

PA 2008, s 35ZA

PA 2008, s 35ZA was also inserted by the Localism Act 2011. The original PA 2008, s35 had included procedural provisions but the Localism Act 2011 amendments carved these out into a new separate section. However, PA 2008, s 35ZA as inserted by the Localism Act 2011 has been replaced by a new PA 2008, s 35ZA by virtue of the Growth and Infrastructure Act 2013, s 26. Consequently, the procedural aspects of the direction regime are addressed below following introduction of the Growth and Infrastructure Act 2013 amendments.

Conclusion on the Localism Act changes

These were significant changes: now there is no cost associated with up front applications under other consent regimes before a project can be directed to be treated as a NSIP. The changes brought about by the Localism Act came into force on 1 April 2012. Prior to that date, no direction had been made under section 35; a period of some three and half years.

Shortly after the amendments came into effect, on 1 June 2012, the Mayor of London made the first application for a direction under PA 2008, s 35 in relation to the Silvertown Tunnel – a proposed new road tunnel under the River Thames – which did not meet the NSIP thresholds. The tunnel will link Silvertown and Greenwich and is designed to relieve congestion at the Blackwell Tunnel by providing an alternate route. On 26 June 2012 the Secretary of State for Transport directed that the project would be determined under the 2008 Act. The reasons included that London is an important for national economic growth; congestion is expected to increase if no action is taken; congestion at the existing Blackwall Tunnel is having a direct impact on the strategic road network; and the project was comparable to other NSIPs.

Just as interesting were the reasons for the application from the Mayor of London. The Mayor of London was keen to bring the project within the ambit of the 2008 Act due to the short and visible timescales of the process and the ability to streamline consents. In short, the 2008 Act regimes increased the likelihood of the tunnel opening on time.

Further amendments: Growth and Infrastructure Act 2013

As set out above, further amendments to PA 2008, s 35 were made under the Growth and Infrastructure Act 2013, s 26 of which replaced s 35 as it was then and inserted a new s 35ZA.

The substituted PA 2008, s 35 expands the scope of those projects that can be directed to be NSIPs and enables the Secretary of State to direct that certain commercial and business development fall under the 2008 Act. A separate article addresses 'Commercial and Business Development' considers this issue in greater detail.

Procedure

The new PA 2008, s 35ZA sets out a number of procedural points.

Limitations

First, it limits the power to give a direction in relation to projects in the field of energy, transport, water, waste water or waste to circumstances where there has been no prior application for planning permission or, indeed, any other consent mentioned in PA 2008, s 33. This is precisely the inverse of the way in which section 35 originally enacted.

Secondly, with regards to commercial and business projects, PA 2008, s 35ZA(2) makes it clear that a s 35 direction in respect of such development may only be made in response to a 'qualifying request' made by:

- a person who proposes to carry out the development to which the request relates;
- a person who has applied, or proposes to apply, for planning permission, or various other consents in PA 2008, s 33(1) or (2); or
- a person who, if a PA 2008, s 35 direction is made, proposed to apply for development consent in respect of the proposed development.

It is clear, therefore, that for business and commercial projects, a 'qualifying request' may be made not only by someone who has already applied for planning permission for development (by contrast to projects in the fields of energy, transport, water, waste water or waste), but also by someone proposing to apply for such permission.

In practice, the need to draft a development consent order, and provide certain other documents that would normally accompany an application for development consent, will mean that there will be considerable time and procedural advantages in making a 'qualifying request' before making a planning application and, if a PA 2008, s 35 direction is made, proceeding under the PA 2008 regime from the outset. Any other approach is likely to waste considerable resources.

Determining a 'qualifying request'

In considering whether to make a PA 2008, s 35 direction, the Secretary of State can:

- direct an authority to whom an application for planning permission (or other PA 2008, s 33 consent) for the relevant project has been or is proposed to be made – that is, 'a relevant authority' as defined by PA 2008, s 35ZA(11) – to take no further action in relation to the application, or proposed application, until the Secretary of State has decided whether to give the direction (PA 2008, s 35ZA(7)); and
- require a relevant authority to provide any information required for the purpose of enabling the Secretary of State to decide whether to and in what terms give a direction under PA 2008, s 35 (PA 2008, s35ZA(8)).

Making a PA 2008, s 35 direction

The Secretary of State must give reasons for a decision to grant a direction (PA 2008, s 35ZA(10)). Interestingly, there is no statutory requirement for providing reasons in relation to a refusal of a 'qualifying request'. However, it is suggested that the Secretary of State would be well advised to provide reasoning in relation to all determinations of 'qualifying requests', whatever the outcome.

If a PA 2008, s 35 direction is made, then the Secretary of State may:

- if an application for planning permission (or other PA 2008, s 33 consent) has been made, direct that that application is be treated as an application for development consent; and
- if a person proposes to make an application for planning permission (or other PA 2008, s 33 consent or authorisation), direct that the proposed application be treated as a proposed application for development consent (PA 2008, s 35ZA(3)).

A relevant authority must refer the application, or proposed application, to the Secretary of State instead of dealing with it themselves once a direction has been made (PA 2008, s 35ZA(6)).

Ability to modify the PA 2008 and other acts

Whilst PA 2008, s 35ZA(5) provides that a PA 2008, s 35 direction may provide that specified provisions of the PA 2008, or any other Act, shall have effect in relation to an application with any specified modifications or be treated as having been complied with, the Secretary of State is likely to use this power sparingly for fear of creating some procedural unfairness and, therefore, potential target for challenge. Developers considering making a 'qualifying request' would be well advised, therefore, to anticipate having to comply with the pre-application and application requirements of the PA 2008 regime.

Directions to date

In addition to the Silvertown Tunnel, by June 2016 the following directions had been made:

- Norwich Northern Distributor Road, Transport, Norfolk County Council, 9 August 2013:
  - Reasons given by the Secretary of State: it would provide a direct connection to and from an international airport to the Trans-European Network-Transport and the Strategic Road Network, it would aid national growth by supporting over 135ha of proposed employment growth and improved connections to/ from the Great Yarmouth Enterprise Zone which supports the offshore energy industry.
- Triton Knoll Offshore Windfarm, Energy (grid connection infrastructure), RWE Npower Renewables Limited, 14 November 2014:
  - Reasons: need to deliver the electricity from the windfarm into the national grid, benefits of being determined by the same decision maker as the wind farm and benefits of having the entire connection being examined under the same consent regime and removing the need for Marine Management Organisation and local planning authority consents.

- London Paramount, Commercial and business, London Resort Companies Holdings, 9 May 2014:
  - Reasons: significant economic impact, important in driving growth in the economy, an impact wider than a single local authority area and physical size also relevant.
- The International Advanced Manufacturing Park, Commercial and business, Sunderland City Council and South Tyneside Council, 15 September 2015:
  - Reasons: significant economic impact, important in driving growth in the economy, an impact wider than a single local authority area and physical size also relevant.

Commercial and Business Development

Written by: Michael Humphries QC, ftb

Introduction

Whilst the Planning Act 2008 (PA 2008) was originally conceived as a means of improving the process for delivering major infrastructure projects, its success has attracted the attention of those seeking to provide the same benefits for other forms of development and, in particular, major business and commercial development.

The PA 2008 regime has a number of features that may be attractive to major business and commercial developers including:

- a (largely) single consenting regime;
- a single application across local authority area boundaries;
- determination by the Secretary of State;
- fixed timetables; and
- the ability for private developers to promote the compulsory purchase of land.

Whilst some of these benefits may be available to developers with the support of a host local planning authority, such support is not always forthcoming. In consequence, during 2012 the Government decided to extend the PA 2008 regime to include business and commercial projects.

The timetable for the amendments

On 6 December 2012 the Government announced, by written Ministerial statement, a series of reforms to the PA 2008, including a commitment to extend the development consent regime to business and commercial projects.

On 22 November 2012 a consultation paper was published seeking views on the form of any extension of the PA 2008 to business and commercial development.

On 23 April 2013 the Growth and Infrastructure Act 2013 was enacted giving effect to the Government's proposals as refined following consultation. Section 26 of the 2013 Act made amendments to the PA 2008 by substituting PA 2008, s 35 with a replacement s 35 and inserting a new PA 2008, s 35ZA.

The Infrastructure Planning (Business or Commercial Projects) Regulations 2013 (SI 2013/3221) ('the BCP Regs') were made on 17 December 2013 and came into force the following day. It was the coming into force of the BCP Regs that effectively 'switched on' the PA 2008 regime for business and commercial development.

On 29 October 2013 DCLG deposited in the libraries of House of Commons and the House of Lords a 'Policy Statement' entitled 'Extension of the nationally significant infrastructure planning regime to business and commercial projects'. This is, currently, the only DCLG guidance on the operation of the new business and commercial regime.

The new PA 2008, ss 35, 35ZA

PA 2008, s 35 gives the Secretary of State power to give a direction for development to be treated as development for which development consent is required, inter alia, if the development is or forms part of 'a business or commercial project (or proposed project) of a prescribed description', will be in England or English waters, and the Secretary of State thinks that the project is of 'national significance' either by itself or when considered with one or more other business or commercial projects (or proposed projects) (see PA 2008, s 35(2)).

PA 2008, s 35ZA sets out various procedural matters in relation to directions given by PA 2008, s 35. Most importantly, for business and commercial projects, PA 2008, s 35ZA(2) make it clear that a PA 2008, s 35 direction in respect of such development may only be made in response to a 'qualifying request' made by:

- a person who proposes to carry out the development to which the request relates;
- a person who has applied, or proposes to apply, for planning permission (or various other consents in PA 2008, s 33(1) or (2); or
- a person who, is a PA 2008, s 35 direction is made, proposed to apply for development consent in respect of the proposed development.

This is important as it is clear that a 'qualifying request' may be made not only by someone who has already applied for planning permission for development, but also by someone proposing to apply for such permission. In practice, the need to draft a development consent order, and provide certain other documents that would normally accompany an application for development consent, will mean that there will be considerable time and procedural advantages in making a 'qualifying request' before making a planning application and, if a PA 2008, s 35 direction is made, proceeding under the PA 2008 regime from the outset.

If a PA 2008, s 35 direction is made, then PA 2008, s 35ZA(3) makes it clear that the Secretary of State may:

- if an application for planning permission (or other PA 2008, s 33(1), (2) consent) has been made, direct that that application be treated as an application for development consent;
- if a person proposes to make an application for planning permission (or other PA 2008, s 33(1), (2) consent), direct that the proposed application be treated as a proposed application for development consent.

Geographical scope of the provisions

As stated above, the new business and commercial provisions in section 35 only apply to development in England and English waters; not to development in Wales. This reflects the devolution settlement in Wales.

It is also worth noting that if all or part of the business or commercial development is in London, the Secretary of State will only make a section 35 direction with the consent of the Mayor of London (see PA 2008, s 35(4)). It is also clear that that consent should be obtained before making any 'qualifying request' to the Secretary of State (see the DCGL 'Policy Statement').

Types of business and commercial development

As stated above, PA 2008, s 35(2) provides that a 'qualifying request' may only be made in respect of 'a business or commercial project (or proposed project) of a prescribed description' (PA 2008, s 35(2)(a)(ii)). It is the BCP Regs that 'prescribe' the descriptions of development in respect of which a direction may be made.

Regulation 2 provides that the descriptions of business and commercial project (or proposed project) in regulation 2(2) are 'prescribed' for the purposes of PA 2008, s 35(2)(a)(ii).

Regulation 2(2)(a) states that a project must be of a description that 'consists wholly or mainly' (emphasis added) of development within SI 2013/3221, reg 2(2)(a)(i) or (ii). Thus it is clear that development forming part of a project falling within the prescribed description can be authorised, if it meets the other requirements in sections 35 and 35ZA.

Regulation 2(2)(a)(i) identifies development comprising the 'construction of buildings or facilities' for the purposes of one or more of the matters in the Schedule to SI 2013/3221. The Schedule identifies the following matters:

- Office use
- Research and development of products and processes
- An industrial process or processes
  - [see the definition of 'industrial process' in reg 1(2)]
- Storage or distribution of goods
- Conferences
- Exhibitions
- Sport
- Leisure
- Tourism

Regulation 2(2)(a)(ii) identifies a further form of development, being the winning and working of minerals in, on or under land. The term 'minerals' for these purposes is defined in SI 2013/3221, reg 1(2), but there is a specific exception for the winning or working of 'peat, coal, oil or gas' (see SI 2013/3221, reg 2(2)(b)(i)). So, for example, 'fracking' would not currently fall within SI 2013/3221, reg 2(2)(a)(ii) and would not, therefore, be development of a prescribed description for the purposes of a PA 2008, s 35 direction.

Establishing national significance

The DCLG consultation on business and commercial development included numerical 'thresholds' for the scale of such development if it was to a regarded as nationally significant. Such thresholds reflected the approach adopted for nationally significant infrastructure projects within PA 2008, ss 15–31.

In the event, the BCP Regs not have numerical thresholds to indicate national significance, but leave this as a matter of judgement for the Secretary of State on a case-by-case basis.

The DCLG 'Policy Statement', however, does set out the Secretary of State's intended approach to the issue of national significance, as follows:

> 'In considering whether a project is of national significance, the Secretary of State will consider all relevant matters, including:
>
> - whether a project is likely to have a significant economic impact, or is important for driving growth in the economy;
> - whether a project has an impact across an area wider than a single local authority area;
> - whether a project is of a substantial physical size – further details are set out below; or
> - whether a project is important to the delivery of a nationally significant infrastructure project or other significant development.
>
> The Secretary of State will reach a decision on any request on the basis of the information provided by developer. The Secretary of State will also consider any matter which the Secretary of State considers relevant to whether a direction should be made. This will include:
>
> - whether a project is likely to require multiple consents or authorisations, and which, in consequence, would benefit from the single authorisation process offered by the nationally significant infrastructure regime;
> - whether the project is related to a nationally significant infrastructure project being brought forward at the same time and therefore would benefit from the scheme being considered as a single application through the PA 2008 regime.
>
> Each request will be considered on its own merits, but the Secretary of State would expect those developers who are thinking of asking for a direction to bear in mind the following.
>
> Although size in itself will not be the determining factor in whether a project is nationally significant or not, the Secretary of State would not normally expect to receive requests for directions in relation to projects that are not of a substantial size. For example, the Secretary of State would not normally expect to receive requests for construction projects where the gross internal floorspace to be created by the project is less than 40,000m2; for leisure, tourism and sports facilities where the area to be developed is less than 100 hectares; or for sports stadia where the seating capacity is less than 40,000 seats.

> For minerals projects, the Secretary of State would not normally expect to receive requests for projects unless they involve the extraction of a strategically important industrial mineral, or extraction of a mineral on a significant scale, for example where the surface or underground area was over 150 hectares.'

As stated above, this is currently the only guidance on the operation of the regime in relation to business and commercial projects.

Exclusions from the new provisions

As identified above, the winning or working of 'peat, coal, oil or gas' is expressly excluded from the descriptions of business or commercial projects prescribed for the purposes of PA 2008, s 35(2)(a)(ii) (see the BCP Regs, reg 2(2)(b)(i)).

A rather more significant exclusion, however, for many business or commercial projects is the exclusion of 'the construction of one or more dwellings' (see the BCP Regs, reg 2(2)(b)(ii)). This follows the provisions of PA 2008, 35(5) which makes it clear that regulations made under PA 2008, s 35(2)(a)(ii) may not prescribe a description of project which includes the construction of one or more dwellings. It also reflects the approach taken in the PA 2008 generally towards 'associated development', which may not include the construction of one or more dwellings (see PA 2008, s 115(2)(b)).

Thus a mixed-use business, commercial and residential development could not be the subject-matter of a PA 2008, s 35 direction and brought under the PA 2008 regime. In such circumstances any direction could only be made in respect of the business and commercial element.

National Policy Statements

It seems reasonable clear that DCLG does not intend, certainly for the foreseeable future, to publish a National Policy Statement (NPS) for business and commercial development. In reality such development is likely to be far too varied in character to be easily susceptible to a single NPS establishing need and identifying potential impacts.

A consequence of this, however, is that business and commercial projects promoted through the PA 2008 regime will not benefits from presumption in PA 2008, s 104(3) of the Act, but will have to be considered under PA 2008, s 105.

In deciding an application where there is no NPS, PA 2008, s 105(2) requires the Secretary of State to have regard to:

> '(a) any local impact report (within the meaning given by section 60(3)) submitted to the [Secretary of State] before the deadline specified in a notice under section 60(2),
>
> (b) any matters prescribed in relation to development of the description to which the application relates, [none have been prescribed] and
>
> (c) any other matters which the Secretary of State thinks are both important and relevant to the Secretary of State's decision.'

Opting-in to the PA 2008 regime

It is important to recognise that the effect of the substituted PA 2008, s 35 and new s 35ZA is not to require the prescribed forms of business and commercial development to be dealt with under the PA 2008 regime, but simply to give the promoters of such development the opportunity to make a 'qualifying request' to be brought within the regime by a PA 2008, s 35 direction.

Before making such a 'qualifying request' promoters will have to consider a number of tactical issues including;

- the effects on their prospect of success;
- whether they would have needed to apply to more than one local planning authority;
- the likely timescales for achieving development consent;
- the potential effect on relations with the local planning authority and other stakeholders;
- the need for land assembly; and
- the need for other consents.

Making a 'qualifying request' – procedure

A 'qualifying request' must both specify the development to which it relates and explain why the requirements of PA 2008, s 35(2) are met (see PA 2008, s 35ZA(11)).

The decision-maker for business and commercial development applications is the Secretary of State for Communities and Local Government and it is, therefore, to that Secretary of State that any 'qualifying request' should be made. Further information should be available via the National Planning Casework Unit at npcu@communities.gsi.gov.uk (enquiry line – 0303 444 8050).

To enable the Secretary of State to make a decision within the statutory deadline of 28 days (PA 2008, s 35A), developers should provide the following with each request:

- details about the nature of the project including its size;
- the relevant local planning authority or authorities; confirmation that the project falls within the prescribed description;
- and reasons why the Secretary of State should consider the project of national significance.

Applicants should also have regard to the BCP Regs and ensure that their project meets the requirements set out within them.

Preparing an application for development consent following a PA 2008, s 35 direction

Whilst PA 2008, s 35ZA(5) provides that a PA 2008, s 35 direction may provide that specified provisions of the PA 2008, or any other Act, shall have effect in relation to an application with any specified modifications or, indeed, be treated as having been complied with, the Secretary of State is likely to use this power sparingly for fear of creating some procedural unfairness and, therefore, potential target for challenge.

Developers considering making a 'qualifying request' would be well advised, therefore, to anticipate having to comply with the pre-application and application requirements of the PA 2008 regime. These are covered in other articles and in the materials within this work.

PA 2008, s 35 directions for business and commercial development

Business and commercial schemes have now started to come forward under the PA 2008 regime and on 9 May 2014 the Secretary of State for Communities and Local Government made the first s 35 direction for business and commercial development in respect of the London Paramount project in Kent. Since then, on 15 September 2015, a further s 35 direction for business and commercial has been made in respect of the International Advanced Manufacturing Plant project in Sunderland.

Part 5

Pre-application Procedures

Legal Requirements for the Statement of Community Consultation

Written by: Rebecca Clutten, ftb
Edited by: Michael Humphries QC, ftb

Introduction

The Planning Act 2008 ('PA 2008') places prospective applicants for development consent under an obligation to consult the local community about their proposals. Before any such consultation takes place, however, applicants are required to prepare a statement 'setting out how the applicant proposes to consult, about the proposed application, people living in the vicinity of the land': see PA 2008, s 47(1). This document is known as a Statement of Community Consultation ('SOCC').

Once a SOCC is prepared, the applicant is under a statutory duty to both publicise the document in the manner specified in PA 2008 and carry out its consultation in accordance with the proposals identified in it: see PA 2008, s 47(7)

This article provides information on:

- the preparation of the SOCC;
- consulting in accordance with the SOCC; and
- revisions to the SOCC.

Preparing the SOCC

The content of the SOCC

Save insofar as relates to environmental information (considered further below), there are no specific requirements as to the information the SOCC is to contain. Typically, however, SOCCs which have been submitted with accepted applications include details of:

- the project, including its scale and the positive and negative benefits which might arise;
- how consultation is to be carried out, in terms of the methods of consultation to be employed, any phasing of consultation, and provisional periods allowed for responses;
- the information to be provided to consultees (at each stage for phased consultations);
- who it is proposed to consult; and
- how feedback is to be captured and recorded.

The former (now withdrawn) PINS Advice Note 16: The developer's pre-application duties (April 2012) (pages 4–5) also suggested that an SOCC should include details of PINS role as examining authority; that attention be drawn to any relevant National Policy Statements (NPSs) and their status; and for details of any other consultations taking place in the area to be noted (to demonstrate that the applicant has had regard to the need to avoid 'consultation fatigue' when programming its own consultation process).

As to the methods of consultation that are to be set out in an SOCC, the DCLG Guidance on the pre-application process (March 2015) states that:

> 'Guidance on Community Engagement for Onshore Wind Developments' provides useful non statutory guidance on approaches to assist developers and local communities in considering how best to engage with one another. This guidance should be read alongside 'Guidance on Community Benefits for Onshore Wind' which promotes good practice and sets out principles and expectations for developers, local authorities and communities. Both sets of guidance may be of benefit to pre-application consultation for other types of *developments*.' (emphasis added)

In relation to environmental information, reg 10 of the Infrastructure Planning (Environmental Impact Assessment) Regulations 2009 requires that the SOCC contain:

- a statement as to whether the development for which the applicant proposes to make an application is EIA development; and
- if that development is EIA development, how the applicant intends to publicise and consult on the preliminary environmental information ('PEI').

Although a previous version of PINS Advice Note 15 contained a statement suggesting that the PEI must be available at the time the preparation of the SOCC is consulted on (on which, see further below), that advice has now been withdrawn and the Inspectorate has confirmed, in its Register of Advice, that the level of environmental information to be made available is a matter for the applicant. The level of information provided must, however, be enough to enable meaningful consultation. In practice, this means that a local authority must have sufficient information about the environmental impacts of the project to be able properly to advise who should be consulted: see the PINS Register of Advice, Response to Marcus Bate of Pinsent Masons dated 12 December 2011 and Response to Ben Wallace of ESBI Investments dated 26 January 2012.

Consultation on the draft SOCC

The proposed content of the SOCC must itself be consulted upon. Applicants are required to contact all those local authorities in whose area the land subject of the proposed application falls to ascertain their views as to what the statement should contain: see PA 2008, s 47(2) referring to s 43(1).

Some NSIPs may have impacts that extend beyond the boundaries of the authority in which the land upon which the project proposed is situated. In such cases, applicants are well advised to consult with potentially affected parties in those extended areas, and DCLG Guidance suggests that the intention to consult people in a wider area should be made clear in the SOCC: see paragraph 36 of the DCLG Guidance on the pre-application process (March 2015). If such extended consultation is to be undertaken, it is also advisable for the applicant to include any authorities for those areas in its consultation on the content of the SOCC, notwithstanding the absence of a statutory obligation to do so.

In order to canvass the relevant local authorities' views on the SOCC, the applicant must send to them *'the consultation documents'*. There are no statutory requirements as to the contents of the consultation documents and they are simply defined in, s 47(4) as 'the documents supplied to the local authority by the applicant for the purpose of consulting the local authority under subsection (2)'. In practice, however, applicants usually send to the relevant local authorities a draft SOCC and sample consultation materials, along with details of the aspects of it upon which the local authorities' views are sought.

DCLG Guidance on the pre-application process (March 2015) identifies (paragraph 39) various aspects of the content upon which applicants should seek local authority input. These include but need not be limited to:

- the size and coverage of the proposed consultation exercise;
- the appropriateness of the techniques proposed, including electronic techniques;
- the design and format of consultation materials;
- the issues to be covered in the consultation materials;
- suggested times and locations for public consultation events;
- local bodies and representative groups who should be consulted; and
- timescales for consultation.

Once it has received 'the consultation materials', a local authority has 28 days within which to respond. Applicants should remind local authorities of the deadline when providing the consultation materials. An applicant has a statutory obligation to 'have regard' to any consultation responses received by the applicant before the expiry of the 28-day deadline (that is, up to and including the 28th day), but consideration of any received after that time will be at the applicant's discretion.

The DCLG has noted that 28 days is a short timescale and suggests that applicants undertake informal 'pre-consultation consultation' to iron out any issues that might arise in advance: see the DCLG Guidance on the pre-application process at paragraph 37.

The obligation to 'have regard' to local authority responses does not mean that an applicant is under an obligation to give effect to any suggestions made, or to address all issues raised. Where an applicant is unable or chooses not to do so, however, the reason for adopting that course of action should be clearly explained in the application documentation.

The Planning Inspectorate may also be able to offer guidance in cases where applicants and local authorities are unable to agree on the consultation process: see the DCLG Guidance on the pre-application process (March 2015) at paragraph 40.

Although local authorities are usually willing to engage with applicants in relation to the SOCC, it is not unheard of for some authorities to fail to respond. In such cases, the applicant must satisfy itself that (and be able to explain in the application document how) its consultation proposals will ensure that all affected and interested parties (including 'hard to reach' and minority groups) have an opportunity to engage with and comment upon the proposals.

Publicising the SOCC

Pursuant to s 47(6) of PA 2008, once an applicant has prepared its SOCC it must:

- make the statement available for inspection by the public 'in a way that is reasonably convenient for people living in the vicinity of the land'; and
- publish in a newspaper circulating in the vicinity of the land a notice stating where and when the SOCC can be inspected.

There is, also, a third obligation in, s 47(6) on applicants to publicise the SOCC in such manner as may be prescribed but, as yet, no publication requirements have been so prescribed.

In respect of the first requirement, there is no existing law or guidance on how an applicant should determine whether a location for inspection is 'reasonably convenient for people living in the vicinity of the land'. What would be 'reasonably convenient' location or locations is perhaps best explored with the local authorities during the consultation SOCC. It is considered that, if an applicant makes its SOCC available in a manner suggested by the relevant local authority or authorities, the Examining Authority is unlikely to find non-compliance with the requirement.

Consulting in accordance with the SOCC

Once plans are finalised and publicised, consultation must be carried out in accordance with the contents of the SOCC: see PA 2008, s 47(7).

There is also a duty, under PA 2008, for applicants to take into account responses received to consultation carried out in accordance with the SOCC.

Before an application is accepted for examination, the Examining Authority will contact the relevant local authorities (ie those who were or should have been consulted on the SOCC) to ask for their views on the adequacy of the consultation carried out in accordance with the SOCC. Local authorities are therefore able to explain whether or not they agreed with the contents of the SOCC and highlight any feedback given which the applicant did not address and, furthermore, state whether they consider consultation to have been carried out in accordance with the SOCC.

Although the ultimate decision as to whether or not an application is to be accepted rests with the Examining Authority, which will take into account a range of factors, it is important to try to ensure that any disagreements between an applicant and relevant local authorities about the adequacy of consultation are resolved prior to submission of the application. It is also important for applicants to be open in their application materials in disclosing any incidents where pre-application consultation has not met any SOCC requirement. This needs to be seen in the context of the somewhat more relaxed requirement in PA 2008, s 55, following amended by the Localism Act 2012, for the Secretary of State to conclude that 'the application … is of a standard that the Secretary of State considers satisfactory'.

Revisions to the SOCC

There is no formal mechanism for revising the SOCC once it has been published. Experience has, however, shown that revisions are sometimes necessary (for example, because there is more or less public interest in the proposals than was anticipated). In such cases, because applicants are in effect producing a new SOCC they would be well advised to undertake the same process as was carried out in relation to the first SOCC.

PINS Advice Note 14: Compiling the consultation report (April 2014) does state (page 4) that where more than one SOCC was prepared for a project, for example where an SOCC was subject to one or more updates, the consultation report should include a narrative about why the SOCC was reviewed and updated.

Best practice indicates that it may be possible to draft an SOCC such that it may not need to be revised to allow for further consultation. The DCLG Guidance on the pre-application process (March 2015) states (para 76) that:

> 'In circumstances where a particular issue has arisen during the pre-application consultation, or where it is localised in nature, it may be appropriate to hold a non-statutory, targeted consultation. A developer' Statement of Community Consultation should be drafted so that it does not preclude this approach.'

General Principles Relating to Consultation

Written by: Richard Honey, ftb
Edited by: Michael Humphries QC, ftb

Introduction

This article focuses on the general common law principles relating to 'consultation' as established through case law. Separate articles will examine the specific legal duties and guidance relating to consultation under the PA 2008.

The duty to consult

There is no general duty to consult. In particular circumstances, however, a duty to consult might arise. In *R (Harrow Community Support Ltd) v Secretary of State for Defence* [2012] EWHC 1921 (Admin) Haddon-Cave J said that 'when decisions will have a specific impact on a definable group, fairness and natural justice may entail a duty to consult with those affected by the decision depending on the context of the decision' (para 28). He went on to say (para 29):

> 'A duty to consult does not arise in all circumstances. If this were so, the business of government would grind to a halt. There are four main circumstances where consultation will be, or may be, required. First, where there is a statutory duty to consult. Second, where there has been a promise to consult. Third, where there has been an established practice of consultation. Fourth, where, in exceptional cases, a failure to consult would lead to conspicuous unfairness. Absent these factors there will no obligation to consult.'

Fundamental rules of proper consultation

Where a duty to consult arises, or where a consultation is voluntarily undertaken, the consultation must be undertaken properly. Lord Woolf MR said in *R v North & East Devon Health Authority, ex parte Coughlan* [2001] QB 213 at paragraph 108 that 'whether or not consultation of interested parties and the public is a legal requirement, if it is embarked upon it must be carried out properly'.

Fair consultation involves giving the persons consulted a fair and proper opportunity to understand fully the matters about which they are being consulted and to express their views, with the person undertaking the consultation thereafter considering those views properly and genuinely (*R v Secretary of State for Trade and Industry, ex p Unison* [1996] ICR 1003).

Four fundamental principles of consultation have been set out by the courts in a number of places and were helpfully summarised by Lord Woolf MR in *Coughlan* at para 108 where he stated that:

> 'To be proper, consultation must be undertaken at a time when proposals are still at a formative stage; it must include sufficient reasons for particular proposals to allow those consulted to give intelligent consideration and an intelligent response; adequate time must be given for this purpose; and the product of consultation must be conscientiously taken into account when the ultimate decision in taken.'

These four fundamental principles will now be examined in a little more detail.

Consultation must be carried out at a time when proposals are still at a formative stage

In relation to the first principle, it has been said that 'the requirement that consultation must be at a time when proposals are at a formative stage can be expressed as a requirement that the decision maker has not pre-determined the issue upon which he goes out to consultation, i.e. that he has an open mind. That said... to have an open mind does not mean an empty mind': see *Royal Brompton and Harefield NHS Foundation Trust v Joint Committee of Primary Care Trusts* [2011] EWHC 2986 (Admin) at para 16.

Consultation requires that there must be a real opportunity for those consulted to make representations to the decision-maker. The decision-maker should keep a 'responsive and open mind' (*R v Warwickshire City Council, ex p Boyden* [1991] COD 31 at p32) and a 'receptive mind' (*R (Partingdale Lane Residents' Association) v Barnet LBC* [2003] EWHC 947 (Admin) at para 45).

It is well-established that there can be consultation on a 'preferred option'. The fact that a provisional view has been taken, or a preferred option identified, does not prevent a consultation exercise being conducted in good faith at a stage when the position is still formative in the sense that no final decision has yet been made. There is no conflict between a person keeping an open mind and consulting on the preferred route; it is permissible to consult on proposals rather than options which are not being proposed: see *R (Bailey) v Brent LBC* [2011] EWHC 2572 (Admin) at para 90.

The consultation must give sufficient reasons for any proposal to allow intelligent consideration and response

In relation to the second rule, Lord Woolf MR said in *Coughlan* at paragraph 112 that the 'obligation is to let those who have a potential interest in the subject matter know in clear terms what the proposal is and exactly why it is under positive consideration, telling them enough (which may be a good deal) to enable them to make an intelligent response'.

A consultation document must present the issues in a way that facilitates an effective response. It must be clear to the general body of respondents. It must present the available information and the options fairly. It has been said that 'the object of requiring fairness is to ensure high standards in decision-making by public bodies, and to enable responses to be made which will best facilitate a sound decision as a result': see *R (Royal Brompton and Harefield NHS Foundation Trust) v Joint Committee of Primary Care Trusts* [2012] EWCA Civ 472 at para 11.

If during a consultation process, prior to the final decision-making, a new factor or new material emerges which is of potential significance to the decision to be made, fairness may demand that the consultees should be given an opportunity to deal with it: see *R (Edwards) v Environment Agency* [2006] EWCA Civ 877 at para 94.

Similarly, if circumstances change, or what is preferred changes, there may be a duty to re-consult. This will not be the case if the change is trivial, but if there is a fundamental difference between the proposals consulted upon and what is to be adopted then there would be a requirement for a fresh consultation: see *R (M) v Croydon LBC* [2013] EWCA Civ 116 at paras 22-23.

In *R (Devon CC) v SSCLG [2010] EWHC* 1456 (Admin) it was held that a change in approach during a consultation was unfair and deprived the affected councils of the opportunity to make their case in the consultation process (para 98). In that case there had been a last minute change of stance with which the consultees had no chance to anticipate and deal (para 81).

Adequate time must be given for consultation and response

In relation to the third rule, case law sets no prescribed time period for consultation although it is clear that 'adequate' time must be given. Consultation periods can be shorter than usual if there are good reasons for the urgency. Conversely, it has been held that a consultation period of one month including Christmas was too short in the circumstances of a particular case (*R (Green) v Gloucestershire CC* [2011] EWHC 2687 (Admin)).

The courts have rejected the argument that 'a decision-maker can routinely pick and choose whom he will consult', holding that 'a fair consultation requires fairness in deciding whom to consult as well as fairness in deciding the subject matter of the consultation and its timing': see *R (Milton Keynes Council) v SSCLG* [2011] EWCA Civ 1575 at para 32.

The product of consultation must be conscientiously taken into account in finalising the proposals

In relation to the fourth rule, the representations should form 'part of the matrix of the decision-making process': see *R v Warwickshire City Council, ex p Boyden* (1991) COD 31 at p32. The burden created by this rule should not be under-estimated. An example is the HS2 judicial review, where it was held that the consultation on blight and compensation was so unfair as to be unlawful because a particular important consultation response was not conscientiously considered (*Buckinghamshire County Council & Ors v Secretary of State for Transport* [2013] EWHC 481 (Admin)).

Unlawful consultations

Fairness is an intrinsic part of consultation: see *R (Edwards) v Environment Agency* [2006] EWCA Civ 877 at paras 90-94 and 102-106. The substantive test of lawfulness is whether a consultation process was so unfair as to be unlawful. The Court will judge on an objective basis whether the process has been so unfair as to be unlawful in all the circumstances: see *R (JL Baird) v Environment Agency* [2011] EWHC 939 (Admin) at para 51.

It has been held that, provided the fundamental requirements of consultation are observed, a decision-making authority has a comparatively wide discretion as to how the process is carried out, bounded only by irrationality (*Wainwright* at para 11). The threshold to be applied was considered by Sullivan J in *R (Greenpeace) v Secretary of State for Trade and Industry* [2007] EWHC 311 (Admin) where he said at paragraph 62:

> 'A consultation exercise which is flawed in one, or even in a number of respects, is not necessarily so procedurally unfair as to be unlawful. With the benefit of hindsight it will almost invariably be possible to suggest ways in which a consultation exercise might have been improved upon. That is most emphatically not the test. It must also be recognised that a decision-maker will usually have a broad discretion as to how a consultation exercise should be carried out.'

If it is alleged that a consultation process is unfair, clear unfairness must be shown (*Royal Brompton* at para 13). 'In reality, a conclusion that a consultation exercise was unlawful on the ground of unfairness will be based upon a finding by the court, not merely that something went wrong, but that something went 'clearly and radically' wrong' (*Greenpeace* at para 63).

It is not necessary to show that the consultation was in general unfair, merely that it was unfair in relation to a group of persons affected (*Royal Brompton* at para 14).

The aspects of alleged unfairness should be reviewed both individually and in aggregate, as an individual aspect of unfairness may seem trivial on its own but when seen with other aspects of unfairness it may acquire greater significance (*Royal Brompton* at para 12).

PA 2008, s 48 Publicity

Written by: Hereward Phillpot QC, ftb
Edited by: Michael Humphries QC, ftb

Publicity requirements

PA 2008, s 48(1) imposes a duty on the applicant to 'publicise the proposed application in the prescribed manner'. The detailed requirements for publicising the application are to be found in the Infrastructure Planning (Applications: Prescribed Forms and Procedure) Regulations 2009 ('the 2009 Regulations').

In addition to the requirements imposed by the 2009 Regulations, PA 2008, s 50(3) imposes a duty on the applicant to have regard to any guidance issued by the Secretary of State about how to comply with those requirements.

Infrastructure Planning (Applications: Prescribed Forms and Procedure) Regulations 2009

Regulation 4 of the 2009 Regulations prescribes the manner in which an applicant must publicise a proposed application.

The notice must be published for at least two successive weeks in one or more local newspapers, once in a national newspaper and once in the London Gazette (if land in Scotland is affected, it must also be published in the Edinburgh Gazette). It must also be published other specialist publications (Lloyd's List and an appropriate fishing trade journal) where the proposal relates to offshore development.

Although the meaning of 'successive weeks' is not defined, it does not appear to mean every day for two weeks. Rather, the notice must be published once a week for two successive weeks. That is reflected in the DCLG Guidance on the pre-application process at paragraph 58, which refers to 'the two required local newspaper advertisements'.

Regulation 4 also identifies what the notice must include, namely:

- the name and address of the applicant;
- a statement that the applicant intends to make an application for development consent to the Secretary of State;
- a statement as to whether the application is EIA development;
- a summary of the main proposals, specifying the location or route of the proposed development;
- a statement that the documents, plans and maps showing the nature and location of the proposed development are available for inspection free of charge at the places (including at least one address in the vicinity of the proposed development) and times set out in the notice;

- the latest date on which those documents, plans and maps will be available for inspection (being a date not earlier than the deadline in sub-paragraph (i));
- whether a charge will be made for copies of any of the documents, plans or maps and the amount of any charge;
- details of how to respond to the publicity; and
- a deadline for receipt of those responses by the applicant, being not less than 28 days following the date when the notice is last published.

Applicants would be well advised to pay close attention to the precise terms of each of these requirements, and to ensure that the notices that they publish satisfy them in all particulars. Inevitably, however, there will be occasions when notices are published which fall short of meeting the precise terms of the requirements. In those circumstances the Secretary of State will need to make a judgment as to whether any departure from the requirements is so significant that the applicant has failed to comply with the requirements of Chapter 2 of Part 5 of the PA 2008. If it is, then the application will not be accepted (s 55(3)(e)).

The degree of force with which an objector could argue that a departure should lead to the application being rejected would be likely to depend in large part on whether an individual or individuals could demonstrate a plausible case that they were substantially prejudiced as a result.

The Thames Tideway Tunnel project provides an example of a project where the section 48 notice involved two inadvertent departures from the requirements, but where this was not judged to be so significant as to justify a decision not to accept the application. In that case the Planning Inspectorate noted in its section 55 checklist that the notice did not explicitly state that the documents, plans and maps showing the nature and location of the proposed development were available free of charge, and did not state whether a charge would be made for copies of those documents. Thames Water had itself drawn attention to these departures in the checklist submitted with the application, and set out its reasons for arguing that they were not material. Whilst some objectors sought to persuade the Planning Inspectorate that this was a significant omission, they did not succeed. The Planning Inspectorate concluded that the omissions did not render the notice a nullity, and that it would be unreasonable to conclude as a result of the omission that the applicant had failed to comply with Chapter 2 of Part 5.

Infrastructure Planning (Environmental Impact Assessment) Regulations 2009

Regulation 11 of the Infrastructure Planning (Environmental Impact Assessment) Regulations 2009 requires that where the proposed application is an application for EIA development, the applicant must, at the same time as publishing the PA 2008, s 48 notice, send a copy of that notice to the consultation bodies and to any person notified to the applicant in accordance with regulation 9(1)(c).

Timing of pre-application publicity

DCLG Guidance

Paragraph 58 of the DCLG's guidance on the pre-application process describes the section 48 publicity as *'an integral part of the local community consultation process'*. It advises that, where possible, the first of the two required local newspaper advertisements should coincide approximately with the beginning of the consultation with communities. However, the guidance also acknowledges that because of the detailed information required for publicity under regulation 4 of the 2009 Regulations (see above) 'aligning publicity with consultation may not always be possible, especially where a multi-stage consultation is intended'.

PINS Guidance

The Planning Inspectorate's (now withdrawn) Advice Note 16 (April 2012) is similarly limited in the advice it offers in relation to the section 48 stage, but it also suggests it would be 'helpful' if the deadline for responses to section 48 publicity are 'as close as possible to deadlines given to landowners and local authorities etc in the s.42 consultation'.

Relationship to pre-application consultation

The DCLG and PINS guidance documents thereby raise, but do not fully resolve, the issue of how the section 48 publicity stage relates to the overall process of pre-application consultation. For smaller and less complex proposals, there may be no difficulty in undertaking pre-application consultation and section 48 publicity at the same time. In larger and more complex cases with multi-stage consultation, however, it may simply be impractical to do that whilst complying with the detailed information requirements set down by regulation 4 of the 2009 Regulations. In such circumstances there does not appear to be any objection in principle to PA 2008, s 48 publicity being undertaken following section 42 and 47 consultation and this was certainly the approach adopted in respect of the Thames Tideway Tunnel project.

Feedback on section 48 publicity

The applicant must have regard to any relevant responses received to section 48 publicity when deciding whether the application that it is actually to make should be in the same terms as the proposed application (s 49(2)).

PA 2008, s 37(3) requires the applicant to submit with his application a consultation report. That report must give details of what has been done in compliance with ss 42, 47 and 48, any relevant responses and the account taken of any relevant responses. This is a useful discipline, because it forces the applicant to engage with the responses it receives at each stage, including what is said in response to s 48 publicity. In writing up the responses, it is important to provide sufficient information so that the reader can understand why changes were or were not made (as the case may be) in response to representations. The Planning Inspectorate can be expected to scrutinise the consultation report with some care to ensure that this has been done carefully and conscientiously.

Taking Consultation into Account

Written by: Hereward Phillpot QC, ftb
Edited by: Michael Humphries QC, ftb

The requirements of PA 2008, s 49

Where an applicant has complied with the duties to consult upon and to publicise the proposed application pursuant to PA 2008, ss 42, 47 and 48, and proposes to go ahead with making an application, PA 2008, s 49(2) imposes a duty to first take account of responses to consultation and publicity.

The terms of the duty are expressed as follows:

> 'The applicant must, when deciding whether the application that the applicant is actually to make should be in the same terms as the proposed application, have regard to any relevant responses.'

'Relevant responses' are defined in PA 2008, s 49(3) as those responses received to consultation and to publicity before the deadlines imposed in each case.

In complying with its duty under PA 2008, s 49, the applicant must have regard to any guidance issued by the Secretary of State about how to comply with the requirements of PA 2008, Pt 5, Ch 2 (PA 2008, s 50(1) and (3)).

Compliance with this duty must be demonstrated to the satisfaction of the Secretary of State at the stage of acceptance: see PA 2008, s 55(3)(e), which provides that the Secretary of State may accept the application only if he concludes that the applicant has complied with the pre-application procedures in PA 2008, Pt 5, Ch 2. The key documents to which the Secretary of State is likely to refer in forming a view about the applicant's compliance or otherwise with the duty under PA 2008, s 49 are those to which he is obliged to have regard pursuant to PA 2008, s 55(4): namely, the Consultation Report received under PA 2008, s 37(3)(c), and any adequacy of consultation representation received from a local authority consultee. PA 2008, s 55(4)(c) also obliges the Secretary of State to have regard to the extent to which the applicant has had regard to any guidance issued under PA 2008, s 50.

DCLG Guidance

The DCLG Guidance 'Planning Act 2008: Guidance on the pre-application process' (March 2015).

Paragraph 18 of the DCLG Guidance lists a series of potentially significant benefits for all parties that can be brought about by the early involvement of local communities, local authorities and statutory consultees. These include allowing members of the public to influence the way projects are developed and how they are integrated into the community, resolving misunderstandings, allowing applicants to obtain important information about the likely impacts of the scheme, enabling potential mitigation measures to be considered and in some cases built into the project, and so on. In order to realise these benefits, however, it is essential that applicants comply with their duty under PA 2008, s 49 and approach the responses received to consultation and publicity with a genuinely open mind. Applicants must be willing to learn from the feedback from consultation and, where it is justified, to adapt their proposals in response.

The DCLG Guidance also rightly emphasises that it is more difficult to make changes to an application once it has been accepted for examination and explains that this is why it is important that issues are made known and explored during pre-application consultation and prior to finalising the application. See also on this issue the DCLG Guidance 'Planning Act 2008: Guidance for the examination of applications for development consent' (March 2015) at paragraphs 109 to 115.

Applicants are advised in the DCLG Guidance 'Planning Act 2008: Guidance on the pre-application process' (March 2015) to ensure that their Consultation Report sets out specifically what the applicant has done in compliance with the requirements of the PA 2008, secondary legislation, the DCLG Guidance and any relevant policies, guidance or advice published by Government or the Planning Inspectorate. The report should also set out how the application has been influenced by relevant responses to consultation, outlining any changes made as a result, and explain why responses advising on major changes to a project were not followed (paragraph 80).

Applicants need not agree to all suggestions made in response to consultation, but they are required to take them into account. In practice, demonstrating that they have done so requires a clear and coherent explanation as to why a particular suggestion has not been adopted. Formulaic or 'standard' responses to points raised by consultees are not sufficient – the response must engage with the issue raised and enable the reader to understand why it is that a particular suggestion was or was not accepted.

Other relevant aspects of the DCLG Guidance are considered below.

PINS Advice Note

PINS Advice Note 14: Compiling the consultation report (April 2012) states (page 2) that a consultation report should draw together:

(a) an account of the statutory consultation, publicity, deadlines set, and community consultation activities undertaken by the applicant at the pre-application stage under PA 2008, ss 42, 47 and 48;

(b) A summary of the relevant responses to the separate strands of consultation; and

(c) The account taken of responses in developing the application from proposed to final form, as required by s 49(2).

The consultation report, therefore, represents the culmination of the three different strands of consultation and publicity set out in s 37. PINS Advice Note 14 stresses (page 2) that 'the primary purpose of the report is to capture and reflect upon all of the responses received from these three distinct pre-application consultee groups and explain how the developer has met its duty (s 49 of the Act) in the preparation of the application to have regard to the views expressed'.

Thus the consultation itself should be carried out in a way that allows the submission of a robust and detailed report at application stage. PINS Advice Note 14 also makes clear that the report can capture non-statutory or 'informal' consultation that takes place outside the requirements of the PA 2008 so that the Secretary of State has a comprehensive picture of all the consultation activity relevant to a particular project.

PINS Advice Note 14 contains detailed guidance on the preparation and content of a consultation report and includes an annex containing a helpful 'Indicative schedule of relevant responses'.

General case law on taking consultation into account

There is a well-developed body of case law that addresses what is necessary to ensure that consultation is adequate, including the requirement for a conscientious and open-minded consideration of relevant matters.

The requirements were neatly summarised in *R v North and East Devon Health Authority, ex parte Coughlan* [2001] 2 QB 213 at para 108:

> 'To be proper, consultation must be undertaken at a time when proposals are still at a formative stage; it must include sufficient reasons for particular proposals to allow those consulted to give intelligent consideration and an intelligent response; adequate time must be given for this purpose; and the product of consultation must be conscientiously taken into account when the ultimate decision is taken'.

The courts have elaborated upon that final requirement, explaining that an applicant must embark upon the consultation process prepared to change course, if persuaded by it to do so (*R v London Borough of Barnet, ex parte B* [1994] ELR 357 at 375C).

The duty to take responses conscientiously into account does not equate to a duty not to make a decision without the prior agreement or consensus of the consultees (*R (Smith) v East Kent Hospital NHS Trust* [2002] EWHC 2640 (Admin)). In other words, there is no obligation to agree with the points made by consultees, but it is necessary to show that they have been properly considered and that the reasons for disagreeing with them are rational and properly articulated.

A practical consideration to keep in mind is that in order to demonstrate that responses have conscientiously been taken into account, sufficient time for that to happen must be allowed between the receipt of the response and the final decision. If a consultation response raises complex technical matters, requiring expert consideration, the applicant will need to have allowed itself time – and obtained any necessary expert input – to be in a position properly to have regard to those matters.

The authorities also serve to underline the importance of adequately capturing the reasons why a particular suggestion made in response to consultation has not been accepted, at the time that the decision is made (in the PA 2008 context this would be in the consultation report). Late reasons proffered for taking a particular decision, particularly if provided in response to a subsequent legal challenge to the adequacy of consultation, will be approached with an appropriate degree of scepticism by the courts and are unlikely to be accepted (see eg *R (Medway Council and others) v Secretary of State for Transport* [2002] EWHC 2516 (Admin); *R (Nash) v Chelsea College of Art and Design* [2001] EWHC 538 (Admin)).

Changing a proposed project in response to consultation

The DCLG Guidance acknowledges (para 70) the tension between consulting early but also having project proposals that are firm enough to enable consultees to comment. The DCLG Guidance seeks to reconcile this tension by making clear (paras 70/71) that:

> '… applicants are encouraged to consider an iterative, phased consultation consisting of two (or more) stages, especially for large projects with long development periods. For example, applicants might wish to consider undertaking non-statutory early consultation at a stage where options are still being considered. This will be helpful in informing proposals and assisting the applicant in establishing a preferred option on which to undertake statutory consultation.
>
> Where an iterative consultation is intended, it may be advisable for applicants to carry out the final stage of consultation with persons who have an interest in the land20 once they have worked up their project proposals in sufficient detail to identify affected land interests.'

The courts have accepted that it is lawful to define the parameters of public consultation so as to exclude an option or options (*R (Medway Council and others) v Secretary of State for Transport* [2002] EWHC 2516 (Admin)).

A number of applicants have successfully adopted this staged approach, whereby the options are consulted upon and then narrowed down through an initial round (or rounds) of informal non-statutory consultation, and then statutory consultation is undertaken on a more firm proposal. National Grid, for example, has developed such an approach informed by its early experiences of the PA 2008 process, which it now adopts for all of its grid connection projects.

The DCLG Guidance (paras 73-75) offers the following advice in relation to the procedural implications of making changes to a proposed project in response to the formal statutory public consultation:

> 'Applicants are not expected to repeat consultation rounds set out in their Statement of Community Consultation unless the project proposals have changed very substantially. However, where proposals change to such a large degree that what is being taken forward is fundamentally different from what was consulted on, further consultation may well be needed. This may be necessary if, for example, new information arises which renders all previous options unworkable or invalid for some reason. When considering the need for additional consultation, applicants should use the degree of change, the effect on the local community and the level of public interest as guiding factors.
>
> Where a proposed application changes to such a large degree that the proposals could be considered a new application, the legitimacy of the consultation already carried out could be questioned. In such cases, applicants should undertake further re-consultation on the new proposals, and should supply consultees with sufficient information to enable them to understand the nature of the change and any likely significant impacts (but not necessarily

> the full suite of consultation documents), and allow at least 28 days for consultees to respond.
>
> If the application only changes to a small degree, or if the change only affects part of the development, then it is not necessary for an applicant to undertake a full re-consultation. Where a proposed application is amended in light of consultation responses then, unless those amendments materially change the application or materially changes its impacts, the amendments themselves should not trigger a need for further consultation. Instead, the applicant should ensure that all affected statutory consultees and local communities are informed of the changes.'

In these respects the Guidance reflects the approach that has been adopted by the courts in considering the need for re-consultation where proposals change (see eg (*R (Smith) v East Kent Hospital NHS Trust* [2002] EWHC 2640 (Admin)).

Ultimately the applicant and its advisors are left to form a judgment as to whether their proposed changes fall on one side of the line or the other. In view of the emphasis placed upon the importance of the pre-application consultation process, and the 'sudden death' nature of the rigorous PA 2008, s 55 acceptance process, applicants tend in practice to be fairly cautious.

Where the judgment is reached that the changes are so significant as to warrant re-consultation, then, as stated above, the DCLG Guidance suggests that consultees should be supplied with sufficient information to enable them to fully understand the nature of the change and any likely significant impacts – but not necessarily the full suite of consultation documents – and allow at least 28 days for consultees to respond (paragraph 74). This approach of a 'targeted' re-consultation can help to reduce the burden on the applicant, and was successfully adopted by Thames Water Utilities Limited in the pre-application consultation process for the Thames Tideway Tunnel proposals.

Where proposed changes made in response to consultation are judged to be more limited and not to require re-consultation, the DCLG Guidance suggests that instead the applicant should ensure that all affected statutory consultees and local communities are informed of the changes (paragraph 75).

Part 6

Information and Surveys

Obtaining Information about Interests in Land

Written by: Douglas Edwards QC, ftb
Edited by: Michael Humphries QC, ftb

Introduction

PA 2008, s 52 comprises a detailed procedure for the obtaining of information concerning the interests held in land affected by a DCO as well as the identity of those who may be entitled to compensation.

In practice, the detailed requirements for pre-application consultation and the requirement in particular to notify the Secretary of State of those affected by proposed compulsory acquisition within a DCO is likely lead to this provision becoming well used.

However, the power to seek such information is limited and is exercisable only following compliance with particular and strict procedural requirements, no doubt at least in part being a recognition of the fact that compelling an individual to disclose information may be considered an infringement of privacy.

PA 2008, s 52 is the subject of PINS Advice Note 4.

The purpose of PA 2008, s 52 and the time at which it may be used

PA 2008, s 52 is available both where a person 'is applying' and where a person 'proposes to apply' for an order granting development consent (s 52(1)). This reflects the purposes of the exercise of the power (s 52(1)), being, to enable to person proposing or promoting a DCO to comply with:

- Chapter 2 of Part 5 of PA 2008 (ie pre-application procedure and in particular the duty under s 44 to consult owners, lessees, tenants and occupiers of land affected by the DCO) or
- Chapter 1 of Part 6 of PA 2008 (eg notification of an accepted application and to those whose interests are to be acquired).

It is likely in practice that it is at the pre-application stage that the power is likely to be of its most use. Since an applicant will generally be expected to have fully identified relevant interests in land to be compulsory acquired it is only exceptionally that the power is likely to fall to be exercised after the DCO application has been made and accepted, possibly where it is known that an interest in land has changed since the original request for information.

The requirement for the Secretary of State's consent

In broad terms, a PA 2008, s 52 notice may require:

- information about landowners or those with an interest in land (s 52(2)), and/or
- information about those who may be able to make a 'relevant claim' (s 52(2A)).

These types of notice are discussed later in this article. In both cases, however, a notice requesting information may not be served without the consent of the Secretary of State.

PINS Advice Note 4 sets out the procedure to be followed and the information required by the Secretary of State where his consent is sought under s 52. The information that should be provided is as follows:

- the contact details of the organisation making the request,
- a demonstration that the request for authorisation is linked to a project requiring development consent,
- a description of the project,
- a table summarising the details of the proposed land for which authorisation for service of a land interests notice is to be sought – a suggested format for the table is annexed to Advice Note 4, and
- a plan (known as Plan A) that shows the land required for or affected by the NSIP – detailed guidance as to the form, scale and colouration of Plan A is given in Advice Note 4.

With regard to the need to demonstrate that the request for authorisation is linked to a project requiring development consent, PINS advice is that:

> 'An explanation should be provided by the developer as to why service of a land interest notice will enable compliance with the pre-application consultation duties or the requirement to notify persons of an accepted application and to give notice to persons interests in land to which a compulsory acquisition request relates. It will be for the developer to seek their own legal advice as to how to best address these matters.'

This advice reflects a recognition that the service of a notice under PA 2008, s 52 on an individual is potentially intrusive and onerous, particularly given the criminal sanctions that apply to non-compliance with such a notice (about which see below). The Secretary of State will need to be satisfied that the service of the notice is therefore genuinely required.

A fee is payable when seeking the consent of the Secretary of State under s 52. The fee is currently set at £1,000 – see regulation 3(1) of the Infrastructure Planning (Fees) Regulations 2010.

PA 2008, s 52 a 'last resort'

There is no statutory requirement to seek any required information voluntarily before making a request under PA 2008, s 52. Advice Note 4 clearly indicates, however, that developers should seek to obtain any required information directly before recourse is had to s 52.

Reference is made in Advice Note 4 to the DCLG Guidance on the Infrastructure Planning (Fees) Regulations 2010, which comments in relation to PA 2008, s 52 (at para 3 of the annex) that 'Applicants are expected to act reasonably, first seeking to obtain relevant information or permission to access land directly before seeking authorisation under these provisions. Specifically, applicants should only submit requests for those aspects of information ... where they consider they have been reasonably refused that information.' The same Guidance at paragraph 6 provides that requests under s 52 should only be made as a *'last resort'*.

Advice Note 4 continues as follows:

> 'It is expected that a developer will demonstrate that all reasonable efforts have been made to obtain information about interests in the land identified in green on Plan A, prior to making the request(s), to satisfy the Secretary of State that the authorisation request(s) are a last resort. It is expected that there will have been an exchange of correspondence and dialogue, wherever possible, between the developer and the proposed recipient(s) in an attempt to obtain information about the interests in land, prior to making the s 52 request(s).'

Advice Note 4 provides detailed guidance as to the form of the correspondence and dialogue that is expected to have taken place. Evidence of such correspondence and dialogue (or efforts to stimulate such a dialogue) should be submitted to the Secretary of State with any request under PA 2008, s 52.

As a matter of policy, therefore, the Secretary of State will wish to see other opportunities to obtain the requisite information exhausted before recourse is had to PA 2008, s 52. Thus a developer should have a detailed strategy in place to obtain the required information before the s 52 procedure is engaged. Moreover, an evidence base should be assembled to demonstrate the implementation of this strategy. It is this evidence base that will need to be provided to the Secretary of State in the event that it ultimately becomes necessary to seek a notice under s 52.

Consultation

There is no statutory duty on an applicant, or on the Secretary of State, to consult with 'affected persons' when making or considering a request under PA 2008, s 52.

However, Advice Note 4 makes it clear that an applicant is required to serve a copy of the PA 2008, s 52 notice request, and all accompanying documents, on all proposed recipients of the notice if it were to be served. The letter accompanying service of the request and information should notify the recipient that he/she may make representations to the Secretary of State within 21 days starting the day after the date of the letter. The applicant will be given an opportunity to respond to any comments received before the Secretary of State makes a decision on the request.

Types of PA 2008, s 52 notice

As stated above, in substance PA 2008, s 52 provides for two types of notice to be served with the Secretary of State's consent.

First, a notice may be served under s 52(2) requiring 'the recipient' to give the name and address of any person the recipient believes is one or more of the following, namely:

- an owner, lessee, tenant (whatever the tenancy period) or occupier of the land;
- a person interested in the land;
- a person having power
  - to sell and convey the land, or
  - to release the land.

It is worth noting that 'the recipient' of the notice does not have to be one of the persons identified in s 52(2). The 'person' on whom a notice may be served under s 52(2) (ie 'the recipient') may be any one of those identified in s 52(3), namely:

- an occupier of the land,
- a person who has an interest in the land as freeholder, mortgagee or lessee,
- a person who directly or indirectly receives rent for the land, and
- a person who, in pursuance of an agreement between that person and a person interested in the land, is authorised to manage or arrange for the letting of it.

Thus a managing agent could be 'the recipient' of a notice in respect of the landowner's interest in the land.

It is also worth noting that the notice may require 'the recipient' to give the applicant in writing 'the name and address' of any of the types of person identified in PA 2008, s 52(2). Thus a notice must be carefully drafted so as to specify the full range of interests in respect of which 'the recipient' may be able to supply 'names' and 'addresses'.

The reference above to a 'person interested in the land' would certainly include those with an 'interest in land' as defined in s1 of the Law of Property Act 1925, in order words, easements and 'profit a prendre' etc, and would appear also to include persons with an equitable interest, such as the interest of a tenant for life under a settlement. The name and address of any mortgagee would also fall within s 52(2).

Secondly, a notice may be served under PA 2008, s 52(2A) requiring 'the recipient' to give the name and address of any person who, 'if the order sought by the application or proposed application were to be made and fully implemented, would or might be entitled':

- as a result of implementing the order,
- as a result of the order having been implemented, or
- as a result of the use of the land once the order has been implemented,

to make a 'relevant claim'.

Again, 'the recipient' of any such notice must be a person identified in s 52(3).

A 'relevant claim' is defined in PA 2008, s 52(14) and comprises a claim under s 10 of the Compulsory Purchase Act 1965 or Part 1 of the Land Compensation Act 1973 or s 152(3) of the 2008 Act. In substance, this provision covers an entitlement to statutory compensation for injurious affection or other harm arising from the carrying out of the proposed development and its operation, where no land is acquired.

A notice served under s 52(2A) must explain the circumstances in which a person would be entitled to compensation as mentioned in that subsection: see s 52(5A).

Clearly any determination as to persons who 'would or might' be entitled to make a relevant claim will involve careful judgments as to potential environmental impacts that will have to be clearly justified in making any application for a s 52 notice under s 52(2A).

The form of notice and period for response

There is no statutory form of a notice to be served under PA 2008, s 52. Section 52(4) does, however, identify certain formal requirements; including drawing the recipient's attention to the fact a criminal sanction arises in cases of non-compliance. These are mandatory requirements for a notice.

The notice must be in writing and must specify the deadline by which a response must be given. That deadline must be not earlier than the end of 14 days beginning with the day on which the notice is served on the recipient (s 52(5)). Provisions for service of noticed under the 2008 Act are set out in PA 2008, ss 229 and 230.

Failure to comply with a notice

A failure to comply with a notice served under PA 2008, s 52, without reasonable excuse, amounts to a criminal offence (s 52(6)), as does the giving of information which is false in a material respect and which, when it was given, the person knew or ought reasonably to have known to be false (ss 152(6) and (7)).

Other statutory powers for obtaining information about interests in land

There are several other statutory provisions by which persons may be compelled to disclose the existence of interests in land. Section 16 of the Local Government (Miscellaneous Provisions) Act 1976 is a well-used example and is available to local authorities in respect of 'a function conferred' on that local authority by any enactment. A similar power is available under s 330 of the Town and Country Planning Act 1990 in the context of functions arising under that Act. Furthermore, for the purposes of compulsory acquisition, s 5A of the Acquisition of Land Act 1981 entitles an 'acquiring authority' to serve a notice to secure 'information about land in relation to which an acquiring authority is entitled to exercise a power of compulsory purchase'.

These powers are, however, related to 'functions' of public authorities under other legislation and it seems questionable that they could be used, even by such authorities, for the purpose of promoting an application for a development consent order.

Rights of Entry under the PA 2008 and other Statutory Powers Granting Rights of Entry

Written by: Douglas Edwards QC, ftb
Edited by: Michael Humphries QC, ftb

Introduction

PA 2008, s 53 introduced, with safeguards, a wide ranging power for those proposing or promoting a DCO to enter private land for the purpose of the carrying out of surveys etc.

As is to be expected, however, that power:

- is limited to surveys required for specified purposes;
- requires ministerial consent; and
- is subject to the payment of compensation.

PINS have published guidance, in the form of Advice Note 5, in respect of section 53.

The power

PA 2008, s 53(1) provides that any person duly authorised in writing by the Secretary of State may, at any reasonable time, enter land

- for the purpose of surveying and taking levels of it, or
- in order to facilitate compliance with the Environmental Impact Assessment Directive (85/337/EEC), the EU Habitats Directive (92/43/EC) or any EU instrument replacing those Directives (s 53(1A)),

in connection with:

- an application for a DCO which has been accepted by the Secretary of State, whether in relation to that land or other land (s 53(1)(a));
- a proposed application for a DCO (S 53(1)(b)), where it appears to the Secretary of State that the proposed applicant is considering 'a distinct project of real substance' (s 52(2)); or
- an order granting development consent that includes provision authorising the compulsory acquisition of that land or of an interest in or a right over it (s 53(1)(c)).

It is clear, therefore, that the power to enter land is exercisable pursuant to PA 2008, s 53 (i) before a DCO application has been made, (ii) when that application has been accepted, and (iii) after the DCO has been granted, albeit only in respect of those aspects of the order which concern compulsory acquisition. It is likely to be in the first of those situations that the power will be of most ultility and, in particular, in the context of the design of the scheme or for the purposes of the preparation of the environmental statement or habitats regulations assessment.

The power to enter land for the purpose of surveying that land under PA 2008, s 53(1) includes a power to search and bore for the purposes of ascertaining the nature of the subsoil or the presence of minerals or other matter in it (s 53(3)). This power may be particularly relevant for projects such as underground gas storage facilities within s 17 of the Planning Act 2008. This power is, however, subject to a requirement to give notice of an intention to search and bore etc (s 53(9)) and the authority of the 'appropriate Minister' (see s 53(11)) is the land in question is held by a statutory undertaker and that undertaker objects on the ground that the works would be 'seriously detrimental' to the carrying on of their undertaking.

The power to enter land to facilitate compliance with the two identified EU Directives (above) includes a power to take, and process, samples of

- air,
- water,
- soil or rock,
- flora,
- bodily excretions, or dead bodies, of non-human creatures, or
- any non-living thing present as a result of human activity.

Thus, and by way of example, samples of contamination on the land could be taken to facilitate compliance with a Directive. Living fauna could not however be taken from the land.

It will be apparent from the above that the power is limited to certain specific purposes. As will be made clear below, in considering whether to grant the power to enter private land under PA 2008, s 53, the Secretary of State requires clear and specific detail of the nature of the surveys etc to be carried out.

The requirement for the Secretary of State's consent

A right to enter private land pursuant to PA 2008, s 53 is subject to the consent of the Secretary of State.

The procedure for applying for consent and the information which the Secretary of State requires for the purposes of such an application is set out in PINS Advice Note 5.

There is no prescribed form of application and an application should, therefore, be made by letter. Advice Note 5 provides that '[PINS] has to be satisfied that the developer has a genuine need to enter on to the land in relation to a distinct project which requires, or has already been granted, development consent. Therefore, as much information as possible should be provided to the IPC'.

Advice Note 5 indicates that the following information should be provided when making an application under s 53:

- contact details;
- information linking the request to a project requiring development consent;
- information to demonstrate that the requirements of s 53(2) are met;
- a description of the project requiring development consent;
- a table summarising the details of the land in respect of which the rights of entry are sought - a suggested format of the table is annexed to Advice note 5;
- evidence that the owner / occupier of the land has been consulted (this is not a legal requirement, but is expected);
- a plan of the land, marked as plan A;
- details of the proposed survey and works;
- any conditions which the developer considers should be attached to the authorisation; and
- evidence to demonstrate reasonable efforts have been made to agree access.

PINS Advice Note 5 gives more detailed guidance in relation to each of these items. A fee is payable by a developer for making an application under s 53 and this should also accompany the application.

What runs though the guidance in Advice Note 5 is a requirement for a detailed and full justification as why entry is genuinely necessary, no doubt in recognition of the conflict with privacy and the right to quiet enjoyment of land which the exercise of the powers of entry may generate.

This is particularly the case in respect of a proposed application for a DCO, where, as stated above, the Secretary of State must be satisfied that 'the developer is considering a distinct project of real substance which genuinely requires entry onto the land'.

Moreover, Advice Note 5 offers clear instruction as to the level of detail required of the proposed surveys etc:

> 'The developer should clearly specify what surveys they intend to carry out, outlining their methodology and providing an explanation as to why the surveys are connected with the proposed / accepted / consented DCO. The developer should demonstrate to [PINS] that these surveys comply with the purpose of the s 53 authorisation request in relation to the project. This may include information about the need to investigate and assess environmental impacts … This and the following information should be provided in relation to each land parcel:
>
> - the scope of the environmental surveys that has been agreed with the relevant regulatory/environmental bodies;
> - survey area, timescale and period, together with an indication of whether or not repetitive visits would be required, and

- any other survey requirements including access into buildings, and night-time surveys.'

As with applications under PA 2008, s 52, there is no express requirement for a developer to exhaust all opportunities by informal means to secure entry onto land for surveys etc, before making an application under s 53. However, Advice Note 5 makes clear that it is the Secretary of State's policy that such applications should be made 'as a last resort' and that he will require clear evidence that 'all reasonable efforts' have been made to obtain entry by negotiation and discussion before resort is had to the powers of compulsion set out in s 53. As such, a developer would be well advised to maintain a documentary record of all correspondence, requests for entry and dialogue that he or she may have had with each landowner before making an application to the Secretary of State under s 53.

The exercise of a power of entry under PA 2008, s 53

A person authorised by the Secretary of State to enter land must serve not less than 14 days' notice of intended entry onto land, where that land is occupied (s 53(4)(b)). Where invasive surveys are to be undertaken under s 53(3) to establish the nature of subsoil and the presence of minerals, then as stated above, the intention to do so must be specified in the notice (s 53(9)). The person entering the land must also produce evidence of the authority to enter and the purpose of entry if requested to do so (s 53(4)(a)), and must comply with any conditions subject to which authorisation of the Secretary of State was given (s 53(4)(c)).

A person who wilfully obstructs a person authorised to enter land under s 53(1) is guilty of an offence (s 53(5)).

Compensation

Where the exercise of a right of entry or the carrying out a survey causes 'damage to land or chattels' compensation may be recovered by the person suffering the damage from the person exercising the right of entry (s 53(7)) and any question of disputed compensation must be referred to and determined by the Upper Tribunal (s 53(8)). It is of note that this right to compensation appears to be limited to physical damage to land or to chattels, and not to any consequential economic loss.

Crown land

By PA 2008, s 54, the right of entry provided for by s 53(1)–(3A) apply to Crown land subject to certain exceptions. Two, in particular, are worthy of note.

First, a person must not enter Crown land unless that person has the permission of (i) a person appearing to be entitled to give such permission, or (ii) the appropriate Crown authority (s 54(2)).

Secondly, the requirements within s 53(4) including the requirement to give 14 days' notice of intended entry onto occupied land, as well as the criminal sanction for obstruction, is disapplied in respect of Crown land.

Other powers to entry for the carrying out of surveys etc

There are other legislative provisions that may be available to applicants, and in particular statutory undertakers, that authorise entry into land to carry out surveys. By way of example, paragraph 10 of Schedule 4 to the Electricity Act 1989 provides the following power to enter land for electricity 'licence holders', that is generating companies, transmission companies and distribution companies holding a licence under s 6 of the 1989 Act:

> '(1) Subject to the following provisions of this paragraph and without prejudice to any other right of entry, a person authorised in writing by a licence holder may, at any reasonable time, enter upon and survey any land for the purpose of ascertaining whether the land would be suitable for use for any purpose connected with the carrying on of the activities which the licence holder is authorised by his licence to carry on.
>
> (2) A person authorised to enter upon any land under this section shall not demand to do so as of right unless—
>
> (a) 14 days' notice of the intended entry has been given to the occupier; and
>
> (b) if required to do so, he has produced evidence of his authority.
>
> (3) The powers conferred by this paragraph shall not be exercisable in relation to land which is covered by a building or will be so covered on the assumption that any planning permission which is in force is acted on.
>
> (4) The power to survey land conferred by this paragraph includes power to search and bore for the purpose of ascertaining the nature of the subsoil; but works may not be carried out on the land for this purpose unless—
>
> (a) notice of the proposed works is included in the notice given under sub-paragraph (2) above; and
>
> (b) where land is held by statutory undertakers who object to the works on the ground that the carrying out of the works would be seriously detrimental to the carrying on of their undertaking, the Secretary of State gives his consent.
>
> (5) Where any person exercises any powers conferred by this paragraph, the licence holder by whom he was authorised shall make good any damage done to the land.
>
> (6) In this paragraph "building" includes any garden, yard, outhouses and appurtenances belonging to or usually enjoyed with a building.'

The Schedule 4 paragraph 10 power is subject to a compensation provision in the following terms (Sch 4 para 11(2)):

> 'Where in the exercise of any power conferred by or under paragraph … 10 above any damage is caused to land or to moveables, any person interested in

> the land or moveables may recover compensation in respect of that damage from the licence holder on whose behalf the power is exercised; and where in consequence of the exercise of such a power a person is disturbed in his enjoyment of any land or moveables he may recover from that licence holder compensation in respect of that disturbance.'

Whilst the Schedule 4 provisions have some similarities with those under s 53 there are clear differences, including:

- the Schedule 4 paragraph 10 power does not require the authorisation of the Secretary of State, but may be exercised on the authority of the 'licence holder';
- the Schedule 4 paragraph 10 power may not be exercised over land covered by a building, as defined; and
- compensation under Schedule 4 paragraph 11 may be recovered in respect of 'damage' to land and moveables and, furthermore, in respect of disturbance to a person's enjoyment of his land.

Electricity 'licence holders' clearly have an alternative procedure to that availably under PA 2008, s 53 for obtaining entry onto land for the purpose of surveys etc. Similar provisions granting rights of entry are available to other statutory undertakers. Promoters will need to consider carefully whether alternative rights may be available and, where they are available, the relative advantages and disadvantages of each.

PA 2008, s 53 Applications – Seeking Rights of Entry on to Third Party Land for Nationally Significant Infrastructure Projects

Written by: Sarah Merritt and Emma Cottam, Pinsent Masons LLP
Edited by: Michael Humphries QC, ftb

Introduction

PA 2008, s 53 allows the Secretary of State to authorise entry on to third party land, at any reasonable time, for specific purposes in the context of a nationally significant infrastructure project. This power does not, however, extend to Crown land, save with the permission of the appropriate Crown authority.

Whilst various statutory undertakers may already have access to similar rights under their enabling legislation – see, for example, the powers of various license holders under the Electricity Act 1989 – not all applicants under the PA 2008 have such pre-existing rights to access third party land without obtaining the consent of the relevant landowners, which in this article shall be taken to include owners, lessees, tenants or occupiers of the land.

PA 2008, s 53 authorisation, therefore, provides certain applicants with an important new power where a landowner objects to a project and would otherwise be able to prejudice the delivery of such a project – either by virtue of refusing entry to those seeking access to survey the land or by seeking a 'ransom' fee for allowing such access.

Since the PA 2008 came into force, only a handful of projects have applied for and/or been granted a s 53 authorisation; these include the Yorkshire and Humber CCS Cross Country Pipeline, the Wrexham Energy Centre, and the Dogger Bank Teeside A&B wind energy development, amongst others. This article therefore explores the legal parameters of, the procedures for and the timing of these rare (but commercially vital) applications.

PA 2008, s 53 – the legal parameters

PA 2008, s 53 allows an applicant to request authorisation from the Secretary of State for a right of entry to gain access onto land for the purposes of:

- **surveying** – including the power to 'search and bore for the purpose of ascertaining the nature of the subsoil or the presence of minerals or other matter in it' (Planning Act 2008, s 53(3);
- **taking levels or samples** from water, air, soil or rock, flora, bodily excretions, or dead bodies, of non-human creatures, or any non-living thing present as a result of human action; or

- **facilitating compliance with relevant environmental directives** – such as the Environmental Impact Assessment Directive or Habitats Directive.

An applicant can only be granted authorisation for a right of entry if it is in connection with:

- a proposed application for a DCO;
- an application for a DCO which has been **accepted** for examination by the Secretary of State, or
- a DCO (which includes a provision authorising the compulsory acquisition of that land or of an interest or right over it) which has been **granted**.

The key point about a PA 2008, s 53 authorisation is that it is a criminal offence for a person to wilfully obstruct a person exercising a power granted by a s 53 authorisation (see s 53(5)).

The application process for PA 2008, s 53 authorisation

The process for applying for access to land under PA 2008, s 53 is (deliberately) relatively onerous. Any application under s 53 is considered by the Planning Inspectorate ('PINS') to be very much a last resort, although an applicant does not need to wait until a landowner is no longer prepared to negotiate in good faith before initiating the s 53 procedure as such negotiations could go on almost indefinitely. It is clear, however, that a history of negotiations with the relevant landowner(s) needs to have taken place prior to submission of the application and an applicant will need to have had regard to the legislation and the detailed guidance provided in PINS Advice Note 5 (October 2013) and the Department for Communities and Local Government's Guidance: *Planning Act 2008: The Infrastructure Planning (Fees) Regulations 2010* (the 'DCLG Guidance').

There is no set format for a PA 2008, s 53 application; however applicants will need to complete the table and checklist that accompany Advice Note 5 and provide certain plans – including a plan showing: the proposed development; any land controlled by the applicant; and the land over which rights of entry are sought. In addition, applicants are encouraged to notify PINS of an intention to submit an application at least four weeks in advance of submission. It is suggested that applicants will need to consider submitting a suite of documents to make up a PA 2008, s 53 application, all under cover of a letter that demonstrates compliance with the legislation and relevant guidance.

Importantly, there is no prescribed timeframe for the Secretary of State to make a decision on an application under PA 2008, s 53; however experience suggests that section 53 applications are likely to be determined within three months of submission.

For a PA 2008, s 53 application to be successful in the case of a project where a DCO application has not been accepted by PINS or a DCO granted, the applicant must demonstrate that they are 'considering a distinct project of real substance genuinely requiring entry onto the land' (s 53(2)(a)). Evidence of this might include non-statutory or statutory consultation, submission of a Scoping Report to PINS or notification of a project on the PINS website.

Through its suite of PA 2008, s 53 application documents, an applicant will need to provide detailed information about:

- the proposed project/the reference number of the accepted application/a copy of the DCO granted (as appropriate);
- the land over which access rights are being sought and details of those interested in that land;
- what surveys and works the applicant proposes will be required on the relevant land;
- a history of the negotiations that have taken place with the relevant landowner(s) and confirmation as to why an application under Planning Act 2008, s 53 is being made (effectively, why it is an application of last resort and that access has been unreasonably refused);
- confirmation that the relevant landowner(s) have been notified of the application;
- confirmation of payment of the relevant fee(s) (PINS normally requires a fee for each land parcel – as such a single project may require a suite of Planning Act 2008, s 53 applications all bundled together depending on the number of land parcels requiring access); and
- detailed information on matters including the proposed conditions to attach to any authorisation and confirmation as whether there are any issues involved under particular habitats and species legislation.

PA 2008, s 53: the timing

Considering the timing of any PA 2008, s 53 application at a very early stage in the life of a nationally significant infrastructure project is key. Environmental surveys may have very specific windows of time within which the consultant team can carry them out. As such, an applicant will need to factor in negotiation time and time to prepare, submit and for the Secretary of State to determine a s 53 application in order to know what its 'cut-off' date for agreeing access voluntarily may be.

It is worth noting that appropriate Ministerial authority is required if any statutory undertaker is a relevant landowner and objects to the proposed works on the grounds that the proposed works would be 'seriously detrimental' to its undertaking.

PA 2008, s 53 – a balancing Act?

Essentially, any application under PA 2008, s 53 is a justification for the Secretary of State to authorise an interference with a landowner's enjoyment of their land. As such, an applicant needs to make clear that the balance has tipped in favour of an interference being justified (ie that it is lawful, proportionate and in the public interest). This will involve several elements including:

- Detailing the consultation that has taken place with the landowner(s). The DCLG Guidance states that that 'applicant[s] are expected to act reasonably, first seeking to obtain relevant information or permission to access land directly before seeking authorisation under these provisions. Specifically, applicants should only submit requests … where they consider they have been unreasonably refused that information or access'. A rough 'rule of thumb' is that several months' worth of negotiations should have taken place – with this being evidenced in a supporting Schedule of Correspondence that will form part of the Planning Act 2008, s 53 application.

- Negotiating/discussing the conditions that may be attached to any Planning Act 2008, s 53 authorisation. The conditions (pursuant to s 53(4)(c)) act to limit the applicant's interference with the land. Conditions may include: restricting the time period in which the applicant is authorised to enter the land; limiting the right to of the applicant to gain entry on to the land to working days only; restricting the hours in which the applicant is authorised to enter on to the land, and also prohibiting the applicant from restricting landowner/ occupier access.
- It is worth noting that recent caselaw makes clear that a Planning Act 2008, s 53 authorisation is not a taking of the land, but an application for an authorisation to carry out surveys on the land under a set of conditions which ensures that any damage caused is remedied.

PA 2008, s 53 – considerations once authorisation has been granted

Once a PA 2008, s 53 authorisation has been granted, an applicant will need to be mindful of the potential for affected landowners to judicially review the Secretary of State's decision (at least one of the granted s 53 authorisations has been so challenged, albeit unsuccessfully). This too should be factored into an applicant's overall project programme.

The PA 2008 makes clear (see s 53(4)) that an applicant must when seeking to exercise its powers:

- If required, produce evidence of the person's authority and their purpose of entry;
- Provide 14 days' notice of intended entry where land is occupied; and
- Comply with the conditions of the s 53 authorisation.

In the event that an applicant seeks to use the power to conduct intrusive surveys, this must also be specified in the notice. Indeed, it is worth noting that a landowner can claim (see s 53(7)) for any damage to land or chattels caused in the exercise of the authorisation to enter/survey granted by PA 2008, s 53.

Conclusion

PA 2008, s 53 provides a crucial, commercial lifeline to nationally significant infrastructure projects being promoted by applicants who do not possess statutory powers of entry on to third party land. Any application for an authorisation needs to be thought about early on in the pre-submission programme for a project. An application will be a detailed suite of documents, evidencing a history of unsuccessful negotiations with landowners. Whilst it is a time-consuming process to go through, there are several projects currently before PINS that would arguably not have progressed to the submission stage without this rarely used but vital provision of the PA 2008.

Part 7

Making an Application

Application Documentation

Written by: Isabella Tafur, ftb
Edited by: Michael Humphries QC, ftb

Introduction

An application for development consent must satisfy the requirements of PA 2008, s 37 and reg 5 of the Infrastructure Planning (Applications: Prescribed Forms and Procedure) Regulations 2009 ('the 2009 Regulations'). Regulation 6 deals with the particular requirements for specific types of project, and is explored further in Article 10.2.3. In addition, national policy statements (NPSs) for particular types of infrastructure may also require applicants to supply other specified information as part of the application.

DCLG has produced Guidance on DCO application documents ('Nationally significant infrastructure projects - Application form guidance') and the Planning Inspectorate (PINS) Advice Note 6 ('Preparation and Submission of application documents') also deals with such documents.

The application form

The application must specify the development to which it relates (PA 2008, s 37(3)(a)) and be made in the prescribed form (PA 2008, s 37(3)(b)), which is currently set out at Sch 2 to the 2009 Regulations. Section 2 of the DCLG Guidance (paragraphs 10–48) set out detailed guidance on completing the numbered boxes in the prescribed application form.

The application form requires the applicant to provide a brief explanation of why the application falls within the development consent regime, and a brief non-technical summary of the development proposal and of the location or route of the development (with reference to appropriate plans).

The form also requires the applicant to indicate (with appropriate references) whether any associated development is included in the application and to give references for certain documents, including the consultation report, copies of newspaper notices, the draft order and explanatory memorandum, and the land and works plan.

Where relevant, references must also be given to a number of other documents, such as the environmental statement and, if the application seeks authorisation for compulsory acquisition the statement of reasons, funding statement and book of reference (which comply with reg 7 of the 2009 Regulations).

The DCLG Guidance (paragraph 7) encourages applicants to avoid using complex or technical terminology in the application form. PINS requires three paper copies of the full application to be submitted along with six electronic copies (on DVDs or memory sticks) (PINS Advice Note 6). Electronic documents should not exceed 50MB and each paper copy should be provided to PINS as an individual package.

The consultation report

The application must be accompanied by the consultation report (PA 2008, s 37(3)(c)), which explains what has been done in compliance with PA 2008, ss 42 (duty to consult), 47 (duty to consult local community) and 48 (duty to publicise) in relation to the application, gives details of any relevant responses (defined in s 49(3)) and of the account taken of the relevant responses. Later articles consider the pre-application consultation requirements of the PA 2008.

Prescribed documents and information

Pursuant to PA 2008, s 37(3)(d) the application must also be accompanied by documents and information of a prescribed description. Regulation 5(2) of the 2009 Regulations sets out what constitutes the prescribed documentation and information. It requires an application to be accompanied by the following:

(a) An environmental statement and any scoping or screening or scoping opinions and directions (where applicable);

(b) The draft proposed order;

(c) An explanatory memorandum explaining the purpose and effect of the provisions in the draft order;

(d) A book of reference (where applicable) which complies with the requirements in reg 7 of the 2009 Regulations;

(e) A copy of any flood risk assessment;

(f) A statement dealing with whether the proposal engages one or more of the matters set out in s 79(1) of the Environmental Protection Act 1990 (statutory nuisances), and if so, how the applicant proposes to mitigate or limit them;

(g) A report identifying any European site to which reg 48 of the Conservation (Natural Habitats &c) Regulations 1994 applies or any Ramsar site, which may be affected by the proposed development, together with sufficient information that will enable the Secretary of State to made an appropriate assessment of the implications for the site, if required by regulation 48(1);

It should be noted that this provision appears to contain a drafting error (or a failure to amend), in that it refers to the 1994 Conservation Regulations, which were repealed (in England and Wales) by the Conservation of Habitats and Special Regulations 2010, SI 2010/490. The result is that there does not appear to be a specific requirement, in England or Wales, to identify sites to which the Conservation of Habitats Regulations 2010 apply, or to provide information enabling the Secretary of State to carry out an appropriate assessment (under reg 61 of the 2010 Regulations). However, the intention of the provision is clearly to require the identification and provision of relevant information in relation to European sites and applications should (where relevant) provide this information regardless of the apparent error in reg 5(2)(g);

(h) A statement of reasons and a statement indicating how an order containing the authorisation of compulsory acquisition is proposed to be funded (where the proposed order would authorise the compulsory acquisition of land or an interest in or right over land);

The DCLG Guidance explains that the statement of reasons must set out why the compulsory acquisition is necessary to enable to proposed development to proceed, and that the funding statement must contain sufficient information to enable the Secretary of State to be satisfied that, if such powers are granted, the proposed development is likely to be undertaken and not prevented due to difficulties in obtaining the requisite funding;

(i) A land plan identifying:

 (i) the land required for, or proposed by the development;

 (ii) any land over which it is proposed to exercise powers of compulsory acquisition or any right to use land (where applicable);

 (iii) any land over which it is proposed to extinguish easements, servitude and other private rights; and

 (iv) where the land includes special category land and replacement land, that land;

(j) A works plan showing, in relation to existing features:

 (i) the proposed location or (for a linear scheme) the proposed route and alignment of the development and works; and

 (ii) the limits within which the development and works may be carried out and any limits of deviation provided for in the draft order;

(k) A plan identifying any new or altered means of access, stopping up of streets or roads or any diversions, extinguishments or creation of rights of way or public rights of navigation (where applicable);

(l) A plan with accompanying information identifying (where applicable) –

 (i) any statutory or non-statutory sites or features of nature conservation such as sites of geological or landscape importance;

 (ii) habitats of protected species, important habitats or other diversity features; and

 (iii) water bodies in a river basin management plan,

 together with an assessment of any effects on such sites, features, habitats or bodies likely to be caused by the proposed development;

(m) A plan (where applicable) with accompanying information identifying any statutory or non-statutory sites or features in the historic environment, including scheduled monuments, World Heritage sites, listed buildings and other historic structures, archaeological sites and registered battlefields, together with an assessment of any effects on such sites, features or structures likely to be caused by the proposed development;

(n) A plan with accompanying information identifying any Crown land (where applicable);

(o) Any other plans, drawings and sections necessary to describe the proposals for which development consent is sought, showing details of design, external appearance, and the preferred layout of buildings or structures, drainage, surface water management, means of vehicular and pedestrian access, any car parking to be provided, and means of landscaping;

(p) Any of the documents prescribed by reg 6 (Matters prescribed in relation to applications for specific types of projects) which are relevant to the particular project;

(q) Any other documents considered necessary to support the application; and

(r) If requested by the Secretary of State, three paper copies of the application form and supporting documents and plans.

Regulation 5(3) provides that any plans, drawings or sections required to be provided must be no larger than A0 in size, must be drawn to an identified scale (not smaller than 1:2500) and, in the case of plans, must show north. Where a plan comprises three or more separate sheets, a key plan must also be provided, showing the relationship between the different sheets (reg 5(4)).

Order and format of application documents

PINS Advice Note 6 deals with the order and format of documents submitted with the application. It explains that prior to the submission of an application, applicants will be provided, on request, with a structured electronic application index for arranging the application documents. The application index should identify all documents submitted with the application.

The order in which the documents should be organised is set out in Appendix 1 to Advice Note 6. For more detailed guidance, regard should be had to that Appendix, but in summary, the order of the documents should be as follows:

- Application form;
- Plans/drawings/sections;
- Draft development consent order;
- Compulsory acquisition information;
- Reports/statements;
- Environmental impact assessment and habitat regulations information;
- Photographs;
- Other media;
- Additional information for specific types of infrastructure;
- Other documents.

Summaries

Each document submitted to PINS should include a summary of the key issues contained within the document, which should be no longer than 1,500 words, or 10% of the original document size. Summaries should clearly and accurately highlight the main points and direct the reader to the evidence on which they are based.

References

Each document and plan submitted with the application should be referenced with the following:

- The scheme name;
- A document or plan title;
- A document or plan reference number;
- The appropriate reg 5(2) paragraph number to which the document relates;
- The date of production of the document or plan;
- The author;
- A chronological note of any revisions made to the document or plan, including the revised document or plan.

Pagination, paragraph numbers and font

PINS also sets out the following guidance in Advice Note 6:

- Each application document must be paginated and paragraphs must be numbered.
- The paragraphs within appendices should also be numbered.
- Written document should, as far as is possible, be printed on both sides of the page in order to reduce the overall bulk of the application.
- Unless it is no more than two pages of A4 paper, each document should also contain a table of contents setting out chapter and topic headings.
- The main body of text in reports should have a minimum font size of 12 pt, using a clear and recognisable font such as Arial or Verdana.

Video and audio information

Video and audio information should not be submitted, except in exceptional cases. The PINS advice encourages applicants to consult with PINS before submitting such information.

Photographs

Any photographs should be correctly labelled, annotated and dated, and the location at which the photographs were taken should be identified on a map. The type of lens used to take the photograph must also be specified (e.g. wide angle).

Glossary, bibliography and links to other documents

A glossary should be included for each written document in order to provide clarification of meaning for all readers, including the general public.

Larger documents, such as the environmental statement, should include a clearly references bibliography. Any links to relevant documents (such as an NPS or development plan) should be made to the specific passage or policy rather than just to the document.

Plans

Each plan must be clearly labelled in the bottom right hand corner with 'title page' information. A list of revisions should be produced to make it easy to identify the latest version of the plan.

The scale used for each plan, drawing or section should ensure that each clearly and accurately portrays the proposals and a scale bar should be included on each plan to prevent any ambiguity when dimensions or distances are measure. Key dimensions and measurements should be notated on each plan, drawing or section. Where sequenced drawings are provided (eg for a linear scheme) a key plan and sequence notation should also be provided.

Appendices

The PINS Advice recognises that appendices are useful for setting out factual, technical and other material upon which the main body of information is based in an ordered and readily identifiable form.

Appendices must be referenced and indexed and divided by section dividers. The relevance of the appendices must be clearly explained in the document to which they relate.

Fees

At the time the application is made, the applicant must pay the correct fee to PINS. The fee is currently £4,500 (reg 5 of the Infrastructure Planning (Fees) Regulations 2010).

Checklist

Appendix 2 to Advice Note 6 contains a checklist to assist decision-makers in determining whether or not to accept an application for examination.

It may be useful for applicants to refer to the checklist in preparing their applications for submission, to ensure that all requirements have been satisfied. Indeed, many applicants submit a copy of the completed checklist with their application.

This checklist is also a useful tool for applicants, as it forces them to review whether procedural requirements that will be considered in determining whether to accept an application have been correctly completed.

Assistance from the Planning Inspectorate

PINS Advice Note 6 encourages an applicant to submit its draft application, DCO and supporting documents to PINS whilst it carries out its consultation and works up detailed proposals, so that any quality control issues can be identified before the application is submitted. This approach will enable PINS to provide (non-binding) feedback as to whether the documents are likely to be of the requisite standard and cover sufficient material, and give the applicant an opportunity to remedy any shortcomings before formal submission of the application.

Applications for a DCO: Formalities

Written by: James Pereira QC, ftb
Edited by: Michael Humphries QC, ftb

Introduction

In order to help applicants to ensure that they comply with the formal requirements of an application, the Planning Inspectorate has published Advice Note Six, 'Preparation and submission of application documents'. The Advice Note is accompanied by an Application Checklist that applicants are encouraged to use to assist with ensuring that the formal contents of the application meet the statutory requirements for acceptance of an application. It is this advice that forms the subject-matter of this article.

Other parts of this work consider the substantive requirements of section 37 (applications for orders granting development consent).

Statutory requirements

PA 2008, s 55 is concerned with the acceptance of applications for DCOs. PA 2008, s 55(3)(f) provides that one of the matters about which the Secretary of State must satisfy himself before accepting an application for a DCO is that:

> '... the application (including accompaniments) is of a standard that the Secretary of State considers satisfactory.'

Section 55(5A) of the PA 2008 provides as follows:

> 'The Secretary of State when deciding whether the Secretary of State may reach the conclusion in subsection (3)(f) must have regard to the extent to which –
>
> a) the application complies with the requirements in section 37(3) (form and contents of application) and any standards set under section 37(5), and
>
> b) any applicable guidance given under section 37(4) has been followed in relation to the application.'

Therefore, quite apart from the other matters set out in PA 2008, s 55, the Secretary of State has a general discretion not to accept an application if the form and content (as opposed to the merits) of the application is not satisfactory in some way. Given the scale and complex nature of NSIPs, together with the focus on written examination under the PA 2008, the power to 'not accept' an application for being of an inadequate standard is necessary and understandable.

Statutory guidance

Paragraph 11 of the DCLG Application form guidance (June 2013) advises as follows:

> 'Applicants are required to submit full application in both electronic and hard copy formats. The applicant should discuss with the Inspectorate the appropriate format for the submission of application documents, for example electronic index, number of electronic and paper copies required, etc.'

Applicants are therefore advised to seek advice from the Planning Inspectorate as to the form and content of applications.

The Planning Inspectorate's guidance

The Planning Inspectorate's guidance on the form and content of applications is found in Advice Note Six: Preparation and submission of application documents. The Advice Note has no statutory status, but compliance with it will increase the likelihood that the application for a DCO achieves the requisite standard for acceptance. Readers are referred to the full text of the advice. An overview is given here, emphasising some key points. Note that applicants are encouraged to submit their application documents in draft while carrying out their consultation and working up detailed proposals, in order to obtain informal advice from the Inspectorate on the content of the application in advance of its formal submission.

Standard application form

The development consent application form is a prescribed form and it must be used to make the application. Statutory guidance on the application form is found in the DCLG Application form guidance (June 2013).

Copies of the application

Applicants are required to submit their full application in both electronic (six copies) and hard copy (three copies) format. Further copies may be sought of the application or of particular documents. Copies of the full application must be made available to all persons notified of the accepted application. The Advice Note gives details of the address and times for submission of an application.

Ordering the application documents

Appendix 1 of Advice Note Six sets out an index and file structure for documents, which can be applied to both electronic and hard copies. This provides a suggested order of information submitted with the application. The advice note states that if any prescribed document type is included within another document, the applicant should make clear in which document it is located and provide a precise reference to it.

Applicants are encouraged to request from the Planning Inspectorate an electronic copy of its application index to ensure that the application is presented in a manner compatible with the Inspectorate's electronic system. File sizes should be kept to a maximum of 50MB each to allow for uploading onto the National Infrastructure Portal.

Appendix 2 of Advice Note Six provides further guidance on the use of the structured electronic application index.

Documents and summaries

Each submitted document should include a summary not exceeding 1,500 words or 10% of the original document size. Summaries should clearly and accurately highlight the main points and direct the reader to the evidence on which they are based. They should not introduce any new material not covered in the main document.

Applicants are encouraged to use appendices to set out in an ordered and readily identifiable form the factual, technical and other material upon which the main body of information is based.

Referencing and heading of plans, documents and photographs

Advice Note Six gives guidance on the referencing of such documents, including (for photos) the need for a photo location plan and details of the type of lens used.

Format of documents

Advice Note Six gives detailed guidance on the format and presentation of documents, including, for example, the use of headings, font size and type, the use of contents and glossaries, double sided printing and so on.

Scale of plans and drawings

Advice Note Six contains general guidance on the scale of plans, drawings and sections. The guidance recognises that the most appropriate scale will depend upon the particular application, and applicants are encouraged to discuss this with the Planning Inspectorate.

Data protection and privacy

Applicants are asked to be mindful of the inclusion of personal data relating to individuals in the documents they submit, in particular the Consultation Report. Advice Note Six advises that the Planning Inspectorate will follow the protocols set down by the Information Commissioner's Office, and that it will redact personal details prior to publication.

Applications in Wales

Particular guidance is given in relation to compliance with the Welsh Language Act 1993.

GIS shapefile

Applicants are requested to provide a GIS shapefile of the land over which authorisation is sought within the application. The Advice Note sets out guidance on what is expected. The shapefile is requested to be submitted at least 2 weeks before the formal submission of the application.

Application fees

The application fee must be paid at the same time the application is made. Further fees are charged at different stages in an application's consideration. Advice Note Six refers to The Infrastructure Planning (Fees) Regulations 2010 (as amended) where details of the fees payable are set out.

Application acceptance checklist

Appendix 3 of Advice Note Six contains an application acceptance checklist. This comprises a checklist based upon the criteria in PA 2008, s 55, which the Planning Inspectorate will use to check compliance with s 55. Applicants are therefore encouraged to refer to the checklist when preparing their application. Note, however, that the Advice Note expressly provides that compliance with the checklist will not be a guarantee that the application will be accepted.

Prescribed Matters for Certain Types of Project

Written by Rebecca Clutten
Edited by Michael Humphries QC

All applications for development consent must satisfy the requirements of s 37 of the Planning Act and reg 5 of the Infrastructure Planning (Applications: Prescribed Forms and Procedure) Regulations 2009 (as amended).

For some projects, however, reg 6 of the 2009 Regulations requires the production of additional, technology-specific documents. This article identifies those requirements and, where appropriate, gives or identifies guidance in respect of their production.

Technologies with additional prescribed matters

As set out above, reg 6 of the 2009 Regulations identifies certain types of project in respect of which additional information is prescribed. At the time of writing (May 2016), the technologies subject to additional prescribed matters were as follows:

(a) Onshore and offshore generating stations;

(b) Highway related development;

(c) Construction or alteration of a railway;

(d) Construction or alteration of harbour facilities;

(e) Construction of a pipeline;

(f) Construction of a hazardous waste facility; and

(g) Construction of a dam or reservoir.

The requirements relating to each project type are set out in turn below.

Onshore generating stations

Regulation 6(1)(a)(i) of the 2009 Regulations requires that an application for an onshore generating station (other than a gas fuelled generating station) be accompanied by a statement setting out who will be responsible for designing and building the connection to the electricity grid.

In the case of gas fuelled generating stations, the requirement set by reg 6(1)(a)(ii) is for a statement setting out who will be responsible for designing and building the gas pipeline connection to the proposed station.

This information is typically provided in a document entitled 'Grid Connection Statement' or 'Gas Connection Statement', as the case may be. Examples can be found on the Planning Inspectorate's website in the documentation accompanying previously consented generating facilities.

Offshore generating stations

Where an application is for an offshore generating station, reg 6(1)(b) requires that the applicant provide: (i) details of the proposed route and method of installation for any cable; and (ii) a statement as to whether applications will be made for safety zones.[1]

This information is typically provided in two discrete documents, often called the 'Safety Zone Statement' and the 'Grid Connection and Cable Statement', respectively. Examples can be found on the Planning Inspectorate's website in the documentation accompanying previously consented offshore windfarms.

Construction or alteration of a railway

Regulation 6(2) requires that applications for the construction or alteration of a railway must be accompanied by section drawings 'accompanied by suitable horizontal and vertical scales, [and] which show, by reference to Ordnance Survey or Chart datum' the following:

(a) The levels of proposed works, including in particular 'and where relevant':

  (i) ground levels;

  (ii) the height of every proposed bridge, viaduct, aqueduct, embankment and elevated guideway;

  (iii) the depth of every proposed cutting and tunnel;

  (iv) the levels of the bed of any tidal waters or inland waterway in which it is proposed that any works should be situated;

  (v) the height of every structure or device (including a cable, but not catenary and related equipment) intended to be erected above, on or below the surface of, or on or beneath the bed of tidal waters or an inland waterway; and

  (vi) drainage outfall details for highways;

(b) a cross section of every intended tunnel and any altered gradient of a carriageway or a way forming part of a guided transport system on either side of every level crossing, bridge, tunnel or underpass which would carry the carriageway or way or through which it would pass.

The drawings should also comply with the guidance for application documentation set out in the PINS Advice Note 6 at pages 7–8, which suggests that drawings should:

(a) be no larger than A0 size;

(b) show North;

(c) be drawn to an identified scale no smaller than 1:2,500 (for onshore development);

1 Safety zones are exclusion zones around offshore generating structures, designed to ensure the safety of those coming into proximity to them, both in the construction and operation phases of a project.

(d) include a scale bar; and

(e) be annotated to show key dimensions and measurements.

Although the reference to drawings being required only 'where relevant' makes clear that some prescribed drawings can be omitted, to avoid delays in acceptance, applicants would be well advised to ensure that, insofar as certain drawings have been omitted, a clear explanation of the reason for any such omissions is given in the application material.

Construction or alteration of harbour facilities

By virtue of reg 6(3), applications for the construction or alteration of harbour facilities must be accompanied by a statement setting out why the making of the development consent order is desirable, in one of two respects:

(a) in the interests of securing the improvement, maintenance or management of the harbour in an efficient and economical manner; or

(b) facilitating the efficient and economic transport of goods or passengers by sea or in the interests of the recreational use of sea-going ships.

Although the two interests are described disjunctively, making clear that it is not necessary for an application to promote both, if a project is in fact desirable in both respects, then there is no reason why an applicant should not set out in the statement how both interests are served by its proposal.

In harbour facility applications the prescribed information can acceptably be included within the Planning Statement: see, for example, the York Potash Harbour Facility application.

Construction of a pipeline

Regulation 6(4) requires that applications for the construction of a pipeline are accompanied by details of the following:

(a) the name of the proposed pipeline;

(b) the owner of the proposed pipeline;

(c) the start and end point of the proposed pipeline;

(d) the length of the proposed pipeline in kilometres;

(e) the external diameter in millimetres of the proposed pipeline;

(f) what will be conveyed by the proposed pipeline; and

(g) whether the grant of any rights in land or consents to road or river crossing works are required and if so whether they can be obtained by agreement.

It is suggested that each of these matters (with the possible exception of (a) and (b)) would necessarily be covered by any description of the project that was fit for purpose. However, in the applications made to date, this information has typically been provided in a separate 'Regulation 6' or 'Additional Information' document.

Construction of a hazardous waste facility

Pursuant to reg 6(5), applications for the construction or alteration of a hazardous waste facility must be accompanied by a statement detailing the proposed purpose of the facility and an estimate of the annual capacity of the plant for the final disposal or recovery of hazardous waste.

As in the case of the matters prescribed in respect of pipeline applications, it is suggested that these matters would necessarily be covered by any description of the project that was fit for purpose.

Construction of a dam or reservoir

By virtue of Reg 6(6), applications for the construction of a dam or reservoir must be accompanied by a statement setting out what, if any, recreational amenities will be made available.

Inclusion of the prescribed information within the application form

Where reg 6 applies, DCLG's Planning Act 2008 Application form guidance states, at paragraph 40, that a brief description of the information being submitted should be stated within Box 22 of the development consent application form, with any more detailed information being set out in an accompanying document, appropriately referenced.

Paragraph 40 further explains that, where this information is contained within other documents already cited on the application form, then those documents should be identified in Box 22, rather than duplicating the information within additional documents.

The PINS Advice Note 6 on preparation and submission of application documents also includes, at Appendix 1, details of the suggested order in which documentation is submitted with an application. That document indicates that documentation required pursuant to reg 6 should follow after the Environmental Statement, any photographs and other media. This recommendation assumes, however, that the prescribed information is not already included within any other category of document, in which case the advice against duplication ought to be followed.

National Policy Statements

In addition to the legislative requirements placed on applicants by section 37 of PA 2008 and regs 5 and 6 of the 2009 Regulations, it should be recalled that the National Policy Statements (NPSs) also specify further information that the Secretary of State will expect to see included within their applications. Although the requirements contained in NPSs are not 'prescribed', and as such, beyond the scope of this article, applicants should be aware that DCLG's Planning Act 2008 Application form guidance makes clear, at paragraph 4, that a failure to include this information *may* lead to the Secretary of State refusing to accept an application.

Part 8

Contents of a Development Consent Order

Defining the Nationally Significant Infrastructure Project

Written by: Alex Booth, ftb
Edited by: Michael Humphries QC, ftb

Introduction

There is no single, over-arching definition of a 'nationally significant infrastructure project' ('NSIP') contained in the PA 2008. The closest that the legislation comes to providing such definition is at PA 2008, s 14, of which subsection 14(1) provides a list of 16 'types of project' that may potentially comprise an NSIP.

The spectrum of development identified in subsection 14(1) is diverse. It ranges from highways and harbours to reservoirs and railway infrastructure. However, when seeking to understand the scope of development that may currently be classified as an NSIP, one can at least note that the various forms of development all fall within one of five 'fields'; namely energy, transport, water, waste water and waste. Thus each of the 16 'types of project' falls within one of the five 'fields'.

The purpose of this article is to look firstly at what types of project are capable of amounting to an NSIP, before turning to consider the precise extent of development that is capable of being so regarded.

Types of project

PA 2008, s 14 (as amended) identifies the following 'types of project' as being nationally significant infrastructure projects, subject to the 'thresholds' identified in PA 2008, ss 15–30:

- Energy
  - Generating stations (s 15)
  - Electric lines (s 16)
  - Underground gas storage facilities (s 17)
  - LNG facilities (s 18)
  - Gas reception facilities (s 19)
  - Gas transported pipe-lines (s 20)
  - Other pipe-lines (s 21)
- Transport
  - Highways (s 22)
  - Airports (s 23)

  - Harbour facilities (s 24)
  - Railways (s 25)
  - Rail freight interchanges (s 26)
- Water
  - Dams and reservoirs (s 27)
  - Transfer of water resources (s 28)
- Waste Water
  - Waste water treatment plants (s 29)
  - Infrastructure for the transfer or storage of waste water (s 29)
- Waste
  - Hazardous waste facilities (s 30)

These thresholds determine the scale of development that is deemed to be nationally significant and, therefore, within the ambit of the PA 2008. Thus the pre-existing consenting regimes still apply to projects below the relevant thresholds.

It is important to note that the PA 2008 has not been 'switched on' for all the types of project listed in s 14. The provisions relating to energy and transport types of project came into force on 1 March 2010. The provision relating to water types of project have still not been brought into force. The provisions relating to waste water treatment plants came into force on 6 April 2011. The provisions relating to infrastructure for the transfer or storage of waste water were introduced by the Infrastructure Planning (Waste Water Transfer and Storage) Order 2012 and came into force on 23 June 2013. The provisions relating to waste were brought into force on 1 October 2011.

Statutory power to include/exclude development

It is important to note that whilst the list provided at PA 2008, s 14(1) is expressed in exhaustive terms, the PA 2008 confers on the Secretary of State an express power both to add new types of development to that list and to remove existing ones from it (see s 14(3)). However, the power of the Secretary of State to amend the types of project that may be an NSIP is not without restriction. Only development connected with the five 'fields' of infrastructure project already identified (ie energy, transport, water, waste water and waste) may be added (s 14(5)(a) and (6)); furthermore the development must be one to be carried out entirely in England, its territorial waters, or a Renewable Energy Zone (except one where the Scottish Ministers have functions) (s 14(5)(b) and (7)). There is no corresponding power to add a new type of NSIP in Wales.

So far the PA 2008, s 14(3) power has only been exercised once; that being is relation to waste water infrastructure. The Infrastructure Planning (Waste Water Transfer and Storage) Order 2012 amended s 14 to create a new type of NSIP consisting of 'infrastructure for the transfer or storage of waste water' (amendment to s 14(1)(o)). The Order also created a 'threshold' for this new type of project by amending s 29 and made a 'supplementary provision' relating to compliance with pre-application requirements under the Act and certain regulations.

Thresholds

When a particular development is of a type identified in PA 2008, s 14, the issue as to whether such development comprises an NSIP for the purposes of the PA 2008 turns on the application of the 'threshold criteria' set out in sections 15-30. These criteria are, therefore, of critical importance in determining whether development requires development consent pursuant to the PA 2008 or is to be authorised under some other consenting regime.

The individual thresholds for particular types of project are considered in other articles. What follows are some general points on the approach to thresholds.

Development forming part of an NSIP

The PA 2008 is designed to prevent a developer from artificially defining a project so as to fall below a relevant threshold; thereby avoiding the need to obtain development consent. PA 2008, s 31 states that 'Consent under this Act ('development consent') is required for development to the extent that the development is *or forms part of* a nationally significant infrastructure project' (emphasis added). As discussed above, whether a project is a nationally significant infrastructure project will depend both on the type of project and its relevant threshold. Clearly the words 'or forms part of' are intended to deal with the situation where a developer proposes to bring a project forward in phases with each phase falling below the relevant threshold, but the whole project falling above the relevant threshold. In such circumstances development consent would be required for each phase, as each would form 'part of' an NSIP.

This does raise the issue of what is meant by a 'project' in PA 2008, s 14. Whilst the term is familiar from European environmental law, it is not defined as such within the PA 2008. Much, however, hangs on the proper definition of the term. Clearly it might be possible to bring a development within the PA 2008 regime by claiming that it was an early phase of a much larger project or, alternatively, remove it from the regime by claiming that each phase was an entirely independent project.

The pragmatic solution to this issue may simply be that in most cases the thresholds are so low that nearly all developments within a particular type will be classed as nationally significant and there will be little opportunity for a coherent development below the threshold to be brought forward.

Identity of the applicant

For most types of project the relevant threshold is defined by reference to the scale or capacity of the proposed development. For some, however, it is the identity of the infrastructure provider that it critical. For example, PA 2008, s 20 makes the construction of a pipe-line an NSIP, subject to certain thresholds, where is it is to be constructed by a 'gas transporter'. That term is defined by s 235 as having the same meaning as in Part 1 of the Gas Act 1986. A pipe-line to be constructed other than by a gas transporter, however, is a different type of project and subject to different thresholds under PA 2008, s 21. This distinction would have implications for other provisions within the Act, such as s 156(3).

It is also worth noting that whilst PA 2008, s 22(2)(a) relates to a highway for which the Secretary of State will be highway authority, the applicant for such a highway project may be someone other than the Secretary of State. Clearly, however, such a project could only be promoted with the consent of the Secretary of State. Where the applicant is a highway authority PINS is likely to want to see an agreement under s 6 of the Highways Act 1980 (delegation of functions in relation to trunk roads).

The activity constituting the development

Each of the thresholds also has a term or terms describing the 'activity' that constitutes the development requiring development consent. In many cases this is simply 'construction or extension' – as in 'construction or extension of a generating station' (PA 2008, s 15) – but in other cases alternative terms are used, such as 'improvement', alteration' or 'installation'. These terms often reflect the language of the predecessor consenting regime, which will still apply to development below the relevant threshold. Thus PA 2008, s 16 relates to the 'installation' of an electric line above ground; reflecting the language of section 37 of the Electricity Act 1989.

As underground gas storage may take place in a depleted natural gas field, which is not constructed but is naturally occurring, PA 2008, s 17 makes it clear that the development would be 'starting to use' such a facility (s 17(2)(b)).

In each case it will be important to understand the relevant language and, where there is a choice of 'activity' – for example, the 'construction', 'improvement' or 'alteration' of a highway under PA 2008, s 22 – it will be important for the DCO and its supporting documents to be clear on what 'activity' and, therefore, what threshold applies.

Construction or alteration

In most instances it will be clear whether development is the 'construction' or 'alteration' of a project. However, there may be circumstances where the distinction is not so clear. At what point does the 'alteration' of (say) a gas reception facility under section 19 become so extensive that it is really the 'construction' of a new gas reception facility. Such questions will usually be a matter of fact and degree, but the issue may be an important one.

Taking the above example of a gas reception facility – 'construction' has a threshold of a maximum flow rate of 4.5 million standard cubic metres per day, whereas 'alteration' has a threshold of an 'increase' of 4.5 million standard cubic metres per day. Thus if a gas reception facility with an existing capacity of 3 mscm per day is completely rebuilt in phases with an ultimate capacity of 6 mscm per day, is such development an NSIP or not? The answer may be that if the gas reception facility continued to operate at full capacity throughout the rebuilding that is an alteration, but if it closed down and was rebuilt that is the construction of a new facility.

Extent of an NSIP

Whilst it may often prove straightforward to determine that certain parts of a development comprise an NSIP, or part of an NSIP, this will not always be the case. Specifically, it may be less than obvious whether development comprises part of the NSIP, or is simply 'associated development' within the meaning of PA 2008, s 115.

The PA 2008 draws a clear distinction between an NSIP for which development consent is required, and 'associated development' that may be included in a development consent order but doesn't have to be. PA 2008, s 115 recognises that these are two elements of development are distinct, one from the another, whilst at the same time making clear that a development consent order may be granted in respect of both.

Other articles deal with 'associated development' and 'associated development in Wales', but the issue of what in the NSIP and what is associated development is particularly pressing in Wales where, subject to a limited exception in relation to underground gas storage projects (see PA 2008, s 115(4)), associated development may not be included in a development consent order.

In England a number of confirmed DCOs do not draw a distinction between those parts of the project that are NSIP and those parts that are not, but others do. There does not appear to be any legal requirement to specify what part of a proposed development is NSIP and what part is not, so long as it is clear that at least some part of the proposed development is an NSIP or part of an NSIP; in other words, as long as it is clear that the proposed development does properly fall within the PA 2008 regime. There may be perfectly valid reasons for not wanting to specify what is NSIP and what is associated development, although as a matter of policy PINS does encourage applicants to make the distinction clear in Schedule 1 to any draft DCO.

Associated Development in England

Written by: Alex Booth, ftb
Edited by: Michael Humphries QC, ftb

Introduction

A development consent order may be granted not only in respect of development for which development consent is required (PA 2008, s 115(1)(a)) – that is, development which is or forms part of a nationally significant infrastructure project ('NSIP') as defined in PA 2008, ss 14-30 – but also in respect of certain other development known as 'associated development' ('AD') (PA 2008, s 115(1)(b)).

As to what comprises AD, PA 2008 itself provides only limited guidance. The term is defined as referring to development which is 'associated' with an NSIP (s 115(2)(a)), but which does not comprise construction/extension of one or more dwellings (s 115(2)(b). In *R (on the application of Innovia Cellophane Ltd) v Infrastructure Planning Commission* [2011] EWHC 2883 the High Court made clear that this exclusion on dwellings did not extend to temporary accommodation for workers.

Associated development can include development in England and in waters adjacent to England (s 115(3)). It can also include development in the field of energy in a Renewable Energy Zone, but not part of any Renewable Energy Zone in relation to which the Scottish Ministers have functions (s 115(3)). Associated development may not include development in Scotland or waters adjacent to Scotland. In Wales, an application for development consent may not include AD, save in respect of surface works, boreholes and pipes associated with underground gas storage by a gas transporter in natural porous strata (s 115(4)).

The remainder of this article is concerned with associated in England and waters adjacent to England; the position in Wales is the subject of a separate article in the Service.

DCLG Guidance on associated development

In the DCLG Guidance on associated development (2013) the Secretary of State will decide on a case by case basis whether development is 'associated development'. The Secretary of State does, however, set out (paragraph 5) certain 'core principles' that will be applied in making any such decision:

- The definition of associated development (in PA 2008, s 115) *requires a direct relationship* between associated development and the principal development. Associated development should therefore either support the construction or operation of the principal development, or help address its impacts.
- Associated development *should not be an aim in itself* but should be subordinate to the principal development.

- Development *should not be treated as associated development* if it is *only necessary as a source of additional revenue* for the applicant, in order to cross-subsidise the cost of the principal development. This does not mean that the applicant cannot cross-subsidise, but if part of a proposal is only necessary as a means of cross-subsidising the principal development then that part should not be treated as associated development.
- Associated development *should be proportionate to the nature and scale of the principal development.* However, this core principle should not be read as excluding associated infrastructure development (such as a network connection) that is on a larger scale than is necessary to serve the principal development if that associated infrastructure provides capacity that is likely to be required for another proposed major infrastructure project. When deciding whether it is appropriate for infrastructure which is on a larger scale than is necessary to serve a project to be treated as associated development, each application will have to be assessed on its own merits. For example, the Secretary of State will have regard to all relevant matters including whether a future application is proposed to be made by the same or related developer as the current application, the degree of physical proximity of the proposed application to the current application, and the time period in which a future application is proposed to be submitted. [*emphasis added*]

This last point about development being associated with a future application is interesting and is further elaborated in footnote 3 in the DCLG Guidance as follows:

> '… in the case of an application for an offshore generating station, the Secretary of State may consider it appropriate for a degree of overcapacity to be provided in respect of the associated transmission infrastructure, so that the impacts of one or more other planned future projects which could make use of that infrastructure would be reduced by taking advantage of it. Applications that include elements designed for the basis of overcapacity would be expected to demonstrate the need for the overcapacity as well as fully assessing the environmental effects.'

Thus the four core principles in paragraph 5 of the DCLG Guidance are:

- there must be a 'direct' relationship between the NSIP and the AD;
- the AD should not be an aim in itself;
- the AD should not be included only to cross-subsidise the NSIP; and
- the AD should be 'proportionate' to the 'nature and scale' of the NSIP.

Some issues

What is beginning to emerge, however, is that there may not always be clear line between that development which properly forms part of the NSIP itself and that which is AD. For example, are the internal roads within a proposed generating station site part of the NSIP or simply AD? This might not matter in England, where any AD can be included in an application for development consent, but it matters greatly in Wales where such AD would have to be applied for by planning application. Indeed, even in England the distinction may matters as the Planning Inspectorate has started to request applicants to make clear in their DCO schedules what parts of the 'authorised development' are NSIP and what parts AD. In this regard it is interesting to note that whilst some approved DCOs have made this distinction, others have not. Whilst there does not appear to be any legal authority for the Planning Inspectorate's position on this point, it does appear to be developing as a policy position.

It is apparent, therefore, that some tension may exist between what is part of the NSIP and what is AD. Indeed, that tension may pull in different directions in England and in Wales. In England, there may be a tendency to restrict the scope of the NSIP and enlarge that of AD. That would allow a developer to amend or supplement the AD by subsequent applications for planning permission; an avenue not available to development that is or forms part of an NSIP: see PA 2008, s 31. In Wales, by contrast, where AD is only available in the very limited circumstances of certain underground gas storage projects, there may be a tendency to widen the definition of the NSIP to include as much development as possible. Such a result is undoubtedly an unintended consequence of the Welsh devolution settlement, but is unwelcome nevertheless.

The DCLG Guidance on associated development (2013) does encourage applicants to include AD in a single application for development consent under the PA 2008, rather than applying for it via other routes (paragraph 8). That has clear merit in allowing the Examining Authority and Secretary of State to determine an application for the entire project and all its environmental effects; although such a solution is not, for the most part, available in Wales.

Examples of associated development

The DCLG Guidance on associated development (2013) sets out various examples of associated development, being (a) examples of general types of associated development (Annex A) and examples of associated development specific to individual types of major infrastructure projects (Annex B).

However, the guidance identifies three important caveats to the examples provided, being:

- the annexes are not intended to be exhaustive;
- the annexes should not be read as a statement that the development in them should be treated as associated development as a matter of course; 'these lists should be read together with the core principles'; and
- the annexes should not be treated as an indication that the development in them is not an NSIP or an integral part of an NSIP for which development consent is required.

The annexes are, however, a useful starting point from which the core principles can be applied on a case by case basis as suggested by the Secretary of State.

Associated Development in Wales

Written by: Alex Booth, ftb
Edited by: Michael Humphries QC, ftb

Introduction

As compared to the situation in England, which was described in an earlier article, the position regarding what may lawfully comprise 'associated development' ('AD') in Wales is significantly more restricted.

As is the case with England, statutory definition of development in Wales for which a development consent order may be granted is set out in PA 2008, s 115. However, the detail as to what can be considered AD in the two jurisdictions is governed by two different sub-sections; the relevant provisions for England being a combination of sub-ss 115(2) and (3), with those for Wales being sub-ss 115(2) and (4).

This article should be read together with the more general article on 'associated development' in England.

The Limits on 'associated development' in Wales

The criteria for including 'associated development' in an application for development consent in Wales are threefold:

- the first element of the restriction is locational, in that any such development must be '*carried out wholly in Wales*' (PA 2008, s 115(4)(a));
- the second element describes the nature of the development, which is confined to *'the carrying out or construction of surface work, boreholes or pipes'* (PA 2008, s 115(4)(b)); and
- the third element is that the NSIP with which the AD is associated must be development within s 17(3), that is, *'facilities for the storage of gas underground in natural porous strata'* (PA 2008, s 115(4)(c)) – thus an application for development consent for an NSIP comprising the storage of gas underground in cavities (see PA 2008, s 17(6)) would not be able to include AD in Wales. Furthermore the gas storage facility would still have to have to comply with the threshold in s 17(4).

DCLG Guidance on associated development

In the DCLG Guidance on associated development (2013) the Secretary of State will decide on a case by case basis whether development is 'associated development'. The Secretary of State does, however, set out (paragraph 5) certain 'core principles' that will be applied in making any such decision.

Those core principles are discussed in some detail in the article on associated development in England, but in broad terms they can be summarised as follows:

- There must be a 'direct' relationship between the NSIP and the AD;
- The AD should not be an aim in itself;
- The AD should not be included only to cross-subsidise the NSIP; and
- The AD should be 'proportionate' to the 'nature and scale' of the NSIP.

The DCLG Guidance on associated development (2013) also sets out various examples of associated development, being: (a) examples of general types of associated development (Annex A); and (b) examples of associated development specific to individual types of major infrastructure projects (Annex B).

Some issues

As discussed in the context of the article on associated development in England, the distinction between the NSIP itself and AD does create some tensions in the definition of these terms, particularly in Wales.

These tensions came to the fore in the examination of the Brechfa Forest West wind farm application in Wales, where Carmarthenshire County Council ('CCC') argued that certain elements of the proposed wind farm (for example, an access roads) were not within the definition of a generating station and therefore not part of the NSIP. This would have meant, in Wales, that they could not be included in an application for development consent.

The Examining Authority considered this jurisdictional issue in the context of the 2009 version of the DCLG Guidance on associated development, which was current at the time. The key passage in that guidance stated (paragraph 10) that 'Development should not be treated as associated development if it is actually an integral part of the NSIP'.

The Examining Authority reported its consideration on this issue as follows:

> **'Scope of proposed works**
>
> 4.139 The proposed authorized project is described in Schedule1 Part 1 of the draft DCO. It includes provision for an access track, a borrow pit and an electricity sub-station.
>
> 4.140 CCC noted in its relevant representation that in Wales consent cannot be given within the DCO for works which are associated development (RREP2 LA). While the legislation is a little more complex than this, CCC's interpretation in respect of this project, an onshore electricity generating station, appears sound. CCC referred to guidance issued by the Department for Communities and Local Government (DCLG) (Guidance on Associated Development, Applications to the Infrastructure Planning Commission, DCLG, September, 2009). This included as examples of associated development some work items included within the applicant's schedule of works for which development consent is sought. CCC requested that I consider whether the application included elements of work that should be considered to be associated development, and thus not be included within the DCO.

4.141 I asked CCC whether they wished to offer any comments to inform this consideration. CCC raised the issue of the proposed site access, but offered no assessment as to whether this, or other elements of the proposed development, might be more properly identified as associated development, rather than seen as integral to the project (REP2 LA).

4.142 Examples included in Annex A of DCLG's guidance, which are of potential relevance to this application, include vehicular access arrangements and sub-stations. In assessing this I have also given consideration to the borrow pit which might, in appropriate circumstances, be properly identified as associated.

4.143 I note a number of points on this issue before addressing the substance:

- The DCLG guidance is not directly applicable to this project; a DCO consenting an electricity generating station in Wales cannot include associated development.
- Nevertheless, some of the analysis in the guidance is relevant.
- The list of examples in the guidance is clearly identified as types of development which 'may qualify as associated development', with the list acknowledged to be neither exhaustive nor prescriptive.
- The guidance advises that development should not be treated as associated development if it is an integral part of the NSIP.

4.144 Given that this is an electricity generating station in Wales the key consideration is whether the individual elements of work can properly be seen as integral to the development of this project.

4.145 The applicant addressed this issue directly in the explanatory memorandum to the draft DCO, submitted as part of the initial application (APP4, paras 2.12 et seq). This argued that all works items for which consent is sought are integral to the development. I find the arguments convincing. In particular, I note the consideration of the definition of a generating station in the explanatory memorandum, and that none of the works identified have a purpose other than the construction and/or operation of the wind farm. The sub-station sits within the site boundary and is required for the production of electricity. The borrow pit is also within the site boundary, and has no wider function than providing material for the construction of the wind farm. The access track is required to connect the main site to the highway network for construction, maintenance and in due course removal.

4.146 I conclude that each of the elements identified in the draft DCO forms an integral part of the proposed development.'

The Secretary of State endorsed that conclusion and all elements of the generating station (including the access road etc) were granted development consent. Interestingly, the key passage from the 2009 DCLG Guidance that the Examining Authority relied on – 'Development should not be treated as associated development if it is actually an integral part of the NSIP' – was omitted from the latest 2013 version on the DCLG Guidance on associated development. It is not absolutely clear, therefore, to what extend Brechfa represents the correct approach under the latest guidance.

Cable Ducts for Future Projects

Written by Hereward Phillpot QC
Edited by Michael Humphries QC

Introduction

This article concerns a specific issue that has arisen in relation to energy infrastructure projects, but has potential implications for other nationally significant infrastructure projects (NSIPs) because it concerns the approach to the question of what is 'associated development' (AD) under PA 2008, s 115.

The specific issue arises in circumstances where it is likely that future NSIP projects will need to lay electricity transmission cables along the same route proposed to be used for such cabling as part of an application for a development consent order (DCO). There are obvious practical advantages of installing the ducting for all of the cabling (that needed now, and that needed in the future) at the same time. As and when the future projects come to be implemented, all that would then be needed is the relatively quick and straightforward operation of pulling the cables through the ducts. Such an approach presents significant advantages both to the developer and those who might be affected by the works.

For the developer there is a saving in time and money, with one set of works to install the ducts rather than repeated works, and no need to either negotiate several sets of agreements or seek multiple orders for powers of compulsory acquisition. The process of implementing the future projects will also be quicker and easier.

Those who are affected by the works (particularly those who own or occupy the relevant land) are not subject to repeated disturbance by the developer's contractors, and productive use of the land can therefore be resumed and continued uninterrupted once the initial works are complete. The environmental effects arising from the more substantial engineering works involved in installing the ducts (traffic, noise, dust etc) only occur once, rather than repeatedly over a number of years.

In practical terms, it is therefore eminently desirable.

The issue is whether it is lawful and appropriate to include such works (and the powers of compulsory acquisition needed to implement them) in a DCO.

The legal issue

In order for such works to be included in a DCO, it must be shown that they are AD, and thus fall within PA 2008, s 115.

AD is defined by PA 2008, s 115(2) as development which is associated with the principal development (ie the NSIP for which development consent is required). In the case of an application for a DCO, the principal development will be the NSIP for which development consent is being sought at that time (as opposed to any potential future NSIP). Thus the additional ducting can only lawfully be approved if it is found to be 'associated with' the NSIP which is the subject of the application.

Guidance

DCLG has published *Guidance on associated development applications for major infrastructure projects* (April 2013) (the AD Guidance)

Paragraph 5 of the AD Guidance states that it is for the Secretary of State to decide on a case by case basis whether or not development should be treated as AD, and that in making the decision he will take into account four 'core principles'. Of particular relevance here are the following:

- Core principle (i) is that there must be a 'direct relationship' between the AD and the NSIP, and the AD should 'either support the construction or operation of the principal development, or help address its impacts'.
- Core principle (iv) is that the AD should be proportionate to the nature and scale of the NSIP. However, it is made clear that '… this core principle should not be read as excluding associated infrastructure development (such as a network connection) that is on a larger scale than is necessary to serve the principal development if that associated infrastructure provides capacity that is likely to be required for another proposed major infrastructure project'.
  - A footnote gives the following example: '… in the case of an application for an offshore generating station, the Secretary of State may consider it appropriate for a degree of overcapacity to be provided in respect of the associated transmission infrastructure, so that the impacts of one or more other planned future projects which could make use of that infrastructure would be reduced by taking advantage of it. Applications that include elements designed for the basis of overcapacity would be expected to demonstrate the need for the overcapacity as well as fully assessing the environmental effects.'
  - It is said that in assessing whether overcapacity should be treated as AD, the Secretary of State will have regard to all relevant matters including whether a future application is proposed to be made by the same or related developer as the current application, the degree of physical proximity of the proposed application to the current application, and the time period in which a future application is proposed to be submitted.

Thus the AD Guidance explicitly contemplates an application for a DCO including a degree of 'overcapacity' in the associated transmission infrastructure, but it does not make clear whether the provision of separate additional ducting would constitute 'overcapacity' or the legal basis for concluding that such development was 'associated with' the NSIP for which development consent was being sought. That was left to the decision-making process.

The East Anglia One decision

The first application to tackle this issue was the East Anglia One Offshore Windfarm (EA One), submitted in November 2012 and determined in June 2014. As the name suggests, this was the first in what was intended to be a series of four applications for Offshore Generating Stations (the other three being referred to as EA Two, Three and

Four) in the North Sea off the coast of Suffolk. An application in relation to EA Three was subsequently submitted in November 2015.

The AD for which development consent was sought in 2012 included not only the onshore transmission infrastructure for the EA One Windfarm, but also the laying of cable ducts for EA Three and Four alongside the ducts and cables for EA One.

One of the main controversial issues in the examination was whether this additional ducting was properly to be regarded as AD, and whether powers of compulsory acquisition should be granted to allow that part of the development to be implemented. The controversy was not as a result of any significant local objection to this aspect of the development. On the contrary, it had been included within the application in large part as a response to views expressed by local residents and businesses, and the local authority. The high profile given to the issue was as a result of the Examining authority quite properly approaching the matter on an inquisitorial basis and wanting to be satisfied that this was both lawful and justified.

The legal argument successfully employed on behalf of the promoter was that the additional ducting was properly treated as being associated with the EA One NSIP because it would help to address its *cumulative* impacts. These impacts included those likely to occur as result of the future works that would be associated with the EA Three and Four projects.

Thus the Examining authority was able to conclude that the ducts could properly be regarded as AD applying the first of the core principles from the AD Guidance set out above (see paragraph 4.16 of the Examining authority's report).

By reference to the concept of 'overcapacity' in the AD Guidance, it was concluded that there is '… no distinction, in principle, between providing extra cable capacity, and providing additional duct capacity' (paragraph 5.41 of the Examining authority's report).

In addition, the Examining authority was satisfied that the factors identified in the fourth core principle pointed towards a conclusion that the ducts were AD:

> 'The development consent applications for east Anglia Three and Four would either be submitted by the same or by a related developer. A high degree of physical proximity would exist between the schemes. The onshore cable ducts to accommodate East Anglia Three and Four would be laid along the same route as the onshore cables for East Anglia One to connect to their respective converter stations adjacent to the East Anglia One converter station at Bramford. It is anticipated that the applications for development consent for East Anglia Three and Four would be made within a reasonable timescale. In particular at the ISH [HE-31] it was made clear that studies were well-advanced for the future wind farms' (paragraph 4.13 of the Examining authority's report).

Ultimately, the Examining authority endorsed the promoter's submission that '… this is a paradigm case of the type of overcapacity provision that properly qualifies as associated development' (paragraph 5.46 of the Examining authority's report).

A requirement was imposed to secure the simultaneous installation of the ducts and cables (save in specified circumstances), thus ensuring that the advantages relied upon to justify the inclusion of the additional ducting in the DCO would be realised in practice.

Those conclusions cleared the way for the authorisation of the necessary powers of compulsory acquisition to be granted on the basis that the additional ducting was therefore 'development to which the development consent relates' and therefore section 122(2)(a) was engaged (see paragraph 5.116 of the Examining authority's report).

The Secretary of State endorsed both the conclusions and the reasoning of the Examining authority on these points (see paragraphs 4.4 and 4.74 of the decision letter dated 17 June 2014).

Conclusion

Although the issue has not yet been tested before the courts, the carefully reasoned decision in the EA One case seems likely to provide a reliable precedent for other promoters. It was, however, properly described as a 'paradigm case' because its facts were so clearly aligned with the AD Guidance. There will no doubt be other cases where the facts are less clear cut, and where the limits of this approach will fall to be tested.

DCO Model Provisions

Written by: Michael Humphries QC, ftb

Introduction

Regulation 5(2)(b) of the Infrastructure Planning (Applications: Prescribed Forms and Procedure) Regulations 2009, SI 2009/2264 ('the Applications Regulations') requires that an application for an order granting development consent must be accompanied by 'the draft proposed order'.

It needs to be stressed that the drafting of a 'draft proposed order' is a very technical legal exercise and, as PINS Advice Note 13 makes clear, 'Developers are strongly urged to take appropriate legal advice at all stages in the preparation and examination of a draft DCO'.'

This article will examine the role of 'model provisions' in the drafting of a 'draft proposed order'.

The status of model provisions

PA 2008, s 38(1) (as originally enacted) allowed the Secretary of State by order to prescribe 'model provisions' for incorporation in a draft order accompanying an application for an order granting development consent. Furthermore, s 38(2) required the then IPC to 'have regard' to any such prescribed model provisions, although it was made clear (s 38(3)) that it was not mandatory for provisions included in a draft order to be in the prescribed form.

The Secretary of State exercised the power under Planning Act 2008, s 38 in prescribing the Infrastructure Planning (Model Provisions) (England and Wales) Order 2009, SI 2009/2265. ('the Model Provisions Order').

The Explanatory Memorandum to the Model Provisions Order states (paragraph 7.8) that the order was 'intended to assist the applicant in preparing the draft proposed order, and to enable common issues across all or most applications to be addressed in a consistent manner'. The Government had consulted on a draft version of the order in 2009 and in the Explanatory Memorandum reported (paragraph 8.11) that 'The predominant view of respondents was that the model provisions were helpful, and would assist applicants when they come to formulate an application to the IPC'.

Despite this seeming endorsement of the role of model provisions, the Localism Act 2011 repealed PA 2008, s 38 with effect from 1 April 2012. Paragraph 1.2.9 of 'Statutory Instrument Practice' (November 2006) published by the Office of Public Sector Information observes that 'If an enabling Act, or the enabling section of it, is repealed, instruments made under it will lapse unless they are saved, i.e. continued in effect.' The Model Provisions Order does not appear to have been 'saved' and so should formally be regarded as having lapsed.

Despite this, it remains clear that PINS still wishes to be informed of any departures from the model provisions. Current guidance in PINS Advice Note 13 is as follows:

> 'Model provisions were intended as a guide for developers in drafting orders, rather than a rigid structure, but aided consistency, and assisted developers to draft a comprehensive set of lawful provisions.
>
> In the absence of relevant guidance published by DCLG, it would be helpful for the Planning Inspectorate to receive a track-change draft of the DCO showing any departures from the model provisions. The Planning Inspectorate would wish to receive such a track-change draft of the DCO both at the pre-application stage and with the formal submission of the application for development consent.' (emphasis added)

Interestingly, Examining Authorities will also often ask parties to a DCO Issue Specific hearing why a model provision should be followed. It is clear, therefore, that for the moment at least the Model Provisions Order will continue to play a role in the Planning Act 2008 regime.

For this reason, this article will continue to describe, in broad terms, the structure of the Model Provisions Order

The structure of the Model Provisions Order

The Model Provisions Order contains four schedules comprising:

- General model provisions;
- Model provisions for railways;
- Model provisions for harbours; and
- Model provisions in respect of requirements.

The Explanatory Memorandum to the Model Provisions Order states (paragraph 7.9) that 'The model provisions Order is constructed in such a way that promoters of nationally significant infrastructure projects only need look to the Schedule which is relevant to the infrastructure type.'

As will be seen in the text below, for most DCOs this statement goes too far and those drafting a DCO are likely to have to look beyond the schedule relevant to any particular infrastructure type.

In that context, however, it is worth noting that the DCLG 'Application Form Guidance' (September 2008) states (paragraph 20) that the Explanatory Memorandum for a DCO 'should also clearly explain if and why any provisions in the draft order diverge from the model provisions in the Infrastructure Planning (Model Provisions) Order 2009'.

General model provisions

During consultation on the draft Model Provisions Order, some respondents requested that DCLG produce bespoke model provisions for each infrastructure type within sections 15-30 of the 2008 Act. Whilst the Explanatory Memorandum to the Model Provisions Order make it clear that DCLG considered doing this, it goes on to make clear (paragraph 8.12) that 'we found it impossible to fulfil all such requests, as many infrastructure types would only require 'general' model provisions, or would need provisions that are so specific to the project in question that model provisions would not assist.'

Having referred to the model provisions for railways and harbours, the Explanatory Memorandum to the Model Provisions Order states (paragraph 7.10), therefore, that:

> 'We have not set out a complete set of model provisions for other NSIP types, since promoters of such projects are likely to need provisions which are bespoke to that project. However, Schedule 1 sets out a series of model provisions which may be relevant to a large number of infrastructure projects, which cover a number of issues common to large construction projects, such as the compulsory acquisition of land and stopping up of streets. In all cases, individual applicants will need to decide if they need to modify the model provisions for the purposes of their own draft development consent orders.'

Schedule 1 is not, therefore, put forward as a complete list of provisions likely to be relevant to all projects, but is clearly a menu of model provisions that may be relevant to any particular project and from which a promoter can select and, as appropriate, adapt and supplement DCO provisions.

Model provisions for railways

The Explanatory Memorandum to the Model Provisions Order states (paragraph 7.9) that:

> 'Schedule 2 sets out a complete set of model provisions to be used in nationally significant infrastructure projects (NSIP) relating to railways, and is based largely on the contents of the existing Transport and Works (Model Clauses for Railways and Tramways) Order 2006 (SI 2006/1954).'

Again, early experience seems to suggest that, far from regarding the Schedule 2 model provisions as a 'complete set', promoters are adapting and supplementing them.

The Doncaster and Ipswich Chord DCOs provide a helpful precedent for drafting detailed provisions in a rail DCO.

Model provisions for harbours

The Explanatory Memorandum to the Model Provisions Order further states (paragraph 7.9) that:

Schedule 3 sets out a complete set of model provisions to be used in NSIP harbour projects, and is based on provisions stemming either from the Transport and Works (Model Clauses for Railways and Tramways) Order 2006, SI 2006/1954 or from one or more Harbour Revision Orders or Harbour Empowerment Orders.'

Again, as with Schedule, 2 above, early experience seems to suggest that, promoters are adapting and supplementing the Schedule 3 model provisions. Indeed, Part 2 of the Hinkley Point C (Nuclear Generating Station) Order 2013 is an example of a highly adapted use of some of the Schedule 3 model provisions.

Model provisions in respect of requirements

The Explanatory Memorandum to the Model Provisions Order further states (paragraph 7.11) that:

> 'The model provisions Order also includes (at Schedule 4) a series of model 'requirements' (akin to planning conditions under existing regimes). We expect that applicants will include what they consider to be suitable requirements, in the draft proposed order they submit along with their application.'

Whilst the 'model provisions in respect of requirements' cover a broad range of issues, they will almost certainly need to be amended and supplemented to meet the needs of any particular project.

Guidance has not yet been published on the drafting of DCO requirements. In essence, however, the requirements in a DCO will be similar to the conditions attached to a grant of planning permission and so the advice in circular 11/95 may be of some assistance.

The predecessor regimes as a basis for precedent

The Explanatory Memorandum to the Model Provisions Order appears to acknowledge, not surprisingly, that even the Model Provisions Order itself has borrowed from previous model clauses and, indeed, from actual clauses in orders made by the Secretary of State. This is helpful as in early DCO examinations the then Commissioners were often reluctant to recognise the value of draft DCO provisions adapted from other regimes. More recently, however, PINS appears to have accepted the assistance that may be derived from other regimes. PINS Advice Note 13 states that:

> 'Provisions used in 'predecessor' regimes such as for Transport and Works Act Orders or Harbour Empowerment Orders may be helpful in the drafting of a DCO. Developers should satisfy themselves that the inclusion of particular wording is appropriate and relevant in all the circumstances of a given project. The relevant precedent and the rationale for including the particular wording of a provision will need to be set out and justified in the explanatory memorandum.'

There seems little doubt that provisions from previous orders, whether made under the Planning Act 2008 or otherwise, will continue to be a useful source of precedent in drafting DCO provisions. What is clear, however, is that PINS will expect the Explanatory Memorandum for any such draft DCO to set out and justify the proposed wording. Indeed, recent experience in examinations tends to indicate that Inspectors will not only seek an explanation for any departure from a model provision, but also, on occasion, an explanation for compliance with a model provision.

Drafting conventions for statutory instruments

If the 'draft proposed order' makes provision for: (a) the making of byelaws; (b) the creation of offences; (c) the application, modification or exclusion of a statutory provision; or (d) the making of amendments, repeals or revocations of statutory provisions of local application, then that 'draft proposed order' must be contained in a statutory instrument: see PA 2008, s 117(4). Experience so far with applications for development consent has shown that most DCOs will indeed need to 'apply, modify or exclude' statutory provisions and will, therefore, have to be made in the form of a statutory instrument.

An 'SI template' is available on the Office of Public Sector Information (OPSI) website, together with an 'SI template user manual'.

The Office of Parliamentary Counsel (OPC) has published 'Drafting Guidance' (August 2015) for the drafting of legislation that sets out a number of general drafting principles as well has detailed drafting guidance. Although this guidance is designed for members of OPC in the drafting of Bills, it is also clearly helpful for those drafting statutory instruments.

Conclusions

Although the Model Provisions Order has formally lapsed, it is clear that PINS continues to regard the model provisions as a helpful template and applicants need to be prepared, therefore, to justify departures from those provisions. As more DCOs are made, however, an expanding data base of acceptable provisions, for each NSIP type, will become available and, in these circumstances, it may be that the current standing of the model provisions will begin to fade.

Modern Drafting Conventions

Written by Michael Humphries QC

Introduction

Inspectors at DCO drafting Issue Specific Hearings have started to require promoters to adopt 'modern' drafting conventions for the wording of development consent orders. This has been reinforced by PINS Advice Note 15 (October 2014) on Drafting Development Consent Orders, which gives the following advice (para 2.1):

> "DCOs must follow the statutory drafting conventions for SIs. Guidance is publicly available from OPSI and should be followed by applicants. In particular applicants should:
>
> - provide footnotes in relation to statutory provisions referred to in the SI to provide the user of the SI with information about relevant amendments or extensions to, or applications of, enactments mentioned in the instrument;
> - use gender-neutral drafting (for example avoiding the use of 'he' or 'she' to refer to the Secretary of State or other persons, unless referring to a particular living individual);
> - provide an adequate preamble with recitation of powers;
> - avoid use of the words 'shall' or 'will' (because of ambiguity over whether they are an imperative or a statement of future intention); and
> - avoid archaisms (for example 'therewith', 'aforesaid')."

The reference to 'OPSI' is to the Office of Public Sector Information documents Statutory Instrument Practice (2006) ('the SI Practice') and SI Practice Circulars. Since PINS Advice Note 15 was published, the Drafting Techniques Group of the Office of Parliamentary Counsel has produced new guidance in 'Office of Parliamentary Counsel – Drafting Guidance' (August 2015) ('the Drafting Guidance').

This article identifies and discusses some of the advice in the SI Practice and the Drafting Guidance that may be particularly relevant to DCOs. This article does not seek to summarise all the points made, or include all of the examples given, in the SI Practice and the Drafting Guidance and it is also supplemented, where appropriate, with the author's own experience and views on good practice in 'modern' drafting.

The SI Practice

Paragraph 2.15.4 of the SI Practice states that:

> "Following an exchange of correspondence during 2005 between the Joint Committee on Statutory Instruments and the Minister for the Cabinet Office, it was accepted that there was a need to modernise the style of

drafting in Statutory Instruments. Drafters are now expected to consider the entire text critically with a view to making it as easy as possible to read. At times complexity may be unavoidable because sufficient precision to give effect to the intended policy cannot be achieved otherwise. But that does not justify excessively long or complex sentences or use of surplus material, obsolete or archaic language, or unnecessarily formal terminology purely to follow precedent."

SI Practice Appendix I

The SI Practice then refers (para 2.15.5) to specific guidance intended to help drafters avoid particular pitfalls that was issued to departments on 19 September 2005 as SIP Circular No.4 (05) and which is reproduced at Appendix I to the SI Practice ('SI Practice Appendix I').

The SI Practice Appendix I makes the following points concerning 'modern' drafting:

Preambles

The SI Practice makes it clear that there is no need for the indication that the maker of the SI 'hereby' makes it. 'The Secretary of State ... makes the following [Order/ Regulations/Rules/Scheme]' is sufficient.

The full powers exercised when an instrument is made should be quoted specifically in the preamble; consequently, the use of the phrase 'and in exercise of all other powers enabling [her/him/them] in that behalf' within the recital of powers ought to be unnecessary. Where the enabling power and prerogative action are clearly inter-dependent then the phrase remains appropriate to cover the prerogative action, but that is very rare and, if something is needed, 'in that behalf' should be replaced by more contemporary words such as 'to do so'.

Reducing length and complexity of sentences - encouraged in relation to operative parts of statutory instruments - is equally applicable to preambles. The SI Practice Appendix I give a number of hypothetical examples of points relating to preambles that are aimed at establishing a general approach rather than a standard format. These examples are not repeated here.

Operative provisions

The SI Practice Appendix I suggests that drafters do not use indications in references to provisions of a statutory instrument such as 'above', 'below' or 'of this Order' except for specific references to avoid ambiguity; similarly drafters should avoid using general provisions such as 'any reference in this Order to a numbered Schedule shall be taken to be a reference to the Schedule so numbered in this Order'. However if a new provision is inserted by amendment into an instrument that contains those types of expression it is desirable to follow the usage already in the instrument.

Expressions such as 'the said', 'hereafter', 'herein, 'therein' and 'therewith' sound antiquated. Drafters should aim to avoid them unless there is no alternative to achieve precision. Similarly Latin expressions should be avoided unless they are the only means of describing a recognised technical term such as 'bona vacantia'. For example, the use of 'mutatis mutandis' to apply a rule to different circumstances is better avoided. In such a case an expression such as 'with any necessary modifications' should be used or, if that gives rise to uncertainty, the application of the rule to those circumstances should be set out expressly. Similarly, it is generally possible to translate 'ex parte' by 'without giving notice to the [other party]'.

Long sentences should be avoided where possible. Sub-clauses beginning 'provided that' or 'save that' should also be avoided. Indeed, sentences containing numerous propositions qualified by a saving or proviso are particularly to be avoided, as it will often be unclear whether the qualification covers one, some or all of them.

Finally, on the desirability of avoiding unnecessary complexity, it should be stressed that if too many propositions are crammed together unintended effects may arise and, again, this should be avoided.

The Drafting Guidance

The Drafting Guidance relates to the drafting of Bills, rather than to Statutory Instruments, but gives more detailed and practical guidance on 'modern' drafting conventions.

This section of this article follows the broad structure of the Drafting Guidance but, again, simply identifies and adapts some points that may be particularly relevant to those drafting DCOs.

Telling the story

The Drafting Guidance makes a number of points about 'telling the story' including:

- *Find a logical order and structure* – the material in a DCO should be set out in a logical order, so that later propositions build on earlier ones. Re-ordering material can also help in reducing the need for extensive cross-referencing throughout the document.
- *Get to the point* – get to the point as quickly as you can. Ideally the opening part of an article will contain the main proposition or at least give the reader some idea of what the article is about.
- *Keep propositions short* – clarity is helped by the use of short sentences and it is usually best to stick to one idea per sentence. That said, there may be occasions with complex propositions where it is better to have a long sentence rather than a series of short sentences that then have to be put together again to make sense of the idea.
- *The medium is not the message* – a DCO should not draw more attention to its structure and mechanics than it needs to.
- *Tone* – the story must be told in a moderate level tone. The Drafting Guidance makes it clear that 'Legislation should speak firmly but not shout'.

Syntax

In relation to 'syntax' the Drafting Guidance includes the following advice:

- *Sentence structure* – Sentences should be simply and logically constructed. The classic structure is 'subject – verb – object'. If possible, avoid inserting words between the subject and the main verb.
- *Positive and negative* – Positive is often easier to understand than negative. Thus 'speak after the tone' is better than 'do not speak until you hear the tone'. Having said that, a prohibition may be better expressed in the negative; for example, 'do not walk on the grass'.
- *Active and passive* – The active voice is usually more readily understood than the passive. So, 'The relevant planning authority must give notice' is better than 'Notice must be given by the relevant planning authority'. An exception to this may be where the agent is unimportant, universal or unknown. Thus 'If a notice is given to the relevant planning authority …' is acceptable.
- *Verbs and nouns* – A verb is easier to understand than a noun; so prefer 'A person may apply' to 'A person may make an application'.
- '*Shall'* – Policy within the Office of Parliamentary Council is to avoid the use of the legislative 'shall', unless the context requires it (for example, inserting amending text into a DCO that already uses 'shall'). The fundamental objection to the use of the word 'shall' appears to be that it is imprecise and ambiguous, having different shades of meaning as a requirement to do something. Drafters should use the word 'must', if that is the particular meaning intended.

Vocabulary

Again, the Drafting Guidance has some helpful advice on good drafting:

- Which words to choose? – The Drafting Guidance urges those drafting to write in modern, standard English using vocabulary that reflects ordinary general usage. Thus avoid archaic language and other words or phrases that may give rise to difficulty. Equally, drafting should not be at the vanguard of linguistic development. The Drafting Guidance points specifically to the advice of Sir Earnest Gowers in 'The Complete Plain Words' on 'how best to convey our meaning without ambiguity and without giving unnecessary trouble to our readers':
  - Use no more words than necessary;
  - Use the most familiar words; and
  - Use precise and concrete words rather than vague and abstract words.
- Use no more words than necessary – Drafters should prefer the single word to the 'roundabout phrase'; so, for example, consider using 'to' rather than 'for the purpose of' and using 'by' or 'under' rather than 'in accordance with'.

- Use the most familiar words – Do not use words that are not in modern standard English; so avoid 'hereafter' or 'thereby'. Also seek to avoid jargon, whether legal jargon or policy jargon, although technical legal expressions may sometimes be necessary
- Use precise and concrete words – Drafters often intend words to have a broad meaning, such as 'affect' or 'in relation to', but is a more precise word can be used it is likely to get the meaning across more clearly.

Gender neutrality

There are two parts to gender neutral drafting being:

- Avoiding gender-specific pronouns (such as 'he') for a person who may be male or female; and
- Avoid nouns that appear to assume that a man or woman will perform a particular role (eg chairman).

Drafters should consider the following techniques for avoiding gender-specific pronouns:

- *Change the pronoun* – For example, consider making the noun plural and using the word 'they'.
- *Repeat the noun* – If the noun is 'person' then consider repeating the word 'person' rather than using 'he' or 'she' in subsequent references. If there is a long compound noun (eg 'a person guilty of an offence') consider using a defined term ('the offender').
- *Rephrase to avoid the need for a pronoun or noun* – Consider using the passive voice (despite earlier warnings); so use 'explaining why the requirement has not been discharged' rather than 'explaining why he has not discharged the requirement'. Also consider using 'who' instead of 'if he'; so 'a person who commits an offence' rather than 'if he commits an offence'; indeed, try generally to use impersonal constructions. Consider substituting 'the' or 'that' for a personal pronoun; thus 'the default' rather then 'his default'. It may also be possible to omit the pronoun altogether as in 'circumstances that justify doing so' as opposed to 'circumstances that justify his doing so'. Indeed, it may be possible to omit the phrase with the pronoun; thus 'the Secretary of State may' rather than 'the Secretary of State may, if he thinks fit'.

Drafters should also avoid gender-specific nouns such as 'chairman'. The word 'chair' is now widely used, as are other gender-neutral expressions such as 'convenor' or 'president'. Some gender-specific words are now falling out of use so that 'manager' would commonly be understood to refer to a man or woman and is, therefore, acceptable, as the term 'manageress' is increasingly redundant.

Numbers and dates

Cardinal numbers

The Drafting Guidance advises, as follows:

- Figures (ie numerals) should be used for all numbers above 10.
- Figures should also be used for numbers up to and including 10 that relate to sums of money, ages, units of measurement or in quasi-mathematical contexts.
- In other context, whether numbers up to and including 10 are spelt out or expressed as figures should depend on what seems more natural or appropriate in the context.
- Drafters should mixing words and figures for things of the same kind.

Ordinal numbers

Drafters should adopt the following advice:

- Ordinal numbers above 10th should <u>not</u> be spelt out.
- Whether ordinal numbers from 1st to 10th are spelt out should be decided in the light of what seems more natural.

Percentages

Drafters should use '%' rather then 'per cent'.

Dates

Numbers should be used *without* the endings –st, -nd, -rd and -th; thus 1 January 2016, not 1st January 2016.

Headings

Headings should give the reader an indication of the contents of that part of the DCO, individual article or schedule. Drafters should try to ensure that headings do not go into a second line. Headings should allow the reader to understand the overall structure of the DCO from just looking at the headings in the contents sheet.

Articles

Drafters should try to avoid articles having more than ten paragraphs, although this is a matter of judgement and will depend on context, including whether it would be inappropriate to break the article into two.

Within an article, the starting point is that each sentence in a paragraph (ie the sub-part of an article) should be a separate numbered provision, although there is no absolute rule against two sentences.

There are particular rules in the Drafting Guidance for formulae, method statements and tables that are less likely to be needed in DCOs and so are not summarised here.

Conjunctions between paragraphs

'And' and 'or'

Ensure that it is clear whether paragraphs are intended to operate cumulatively, or instead as alternatives.

Often it will be sufficient to put the appropriate conjunction at the end of the penultimate paragraph and rely on the implication (in the absence of a contrary indication) that each of the preceding paragraphs is separated by the same conjunction.

However, this makes the reader wait until then to know whether the paragraphs are cumulative or alternative and may be unhelpful with a long list of paragraphs.

Do not mix conjunctions, ie put different conjunctions at the ends of different paragraphs in the same provision.

'Or'

'Or' can have an inclusive and an exclusive sense: so 'A or B' can mean 'A or B or both' or 'A or B but not both'. Reed Dickerson *Fundamentals of Legal Drafting* (Aspen Publishers, 1965) suggests that: 'Observation of legal usage suggests that in most cases 'or' is used in the inclusive rather than the exclusive sense'. This construction may be reinforced, or alternatively excluded, by the context.

The Drafting Guidance suggests that it may be tempting to omit 'or' from provisions in order to avoid any suggestion of exclusivity and perhaps to make it clear from the opening words what is intended. But where it is obvious from the context that the provisions would be read in an inclusive sense, it may be better from the point of view of clarity or consistency across the statute book to follow normal English and use 'or'.

Sometimes it will be desirable to spell out that both of two alternatives are a permissible option. For example, a provision allowing the imposition merely of a 'fine or a term of imprisonment' might be construed in favour of a defendant so as to exclude the imposition of both. So if both may be wanted, it is probably best to say so.

'And'

Similar issues can arise with 'and'. If, in the example above, the court were given power to order a fine and a term of imprisonment, would it have to do both? Again, though, the context will probably supply the answer.

Neither 'and' nor 'or'

It is possible to avoid a single conjunction by making it clear in the opening words whether the paragraphs are cumulative or alternative. Thus 'The undertaker must submit to the relevant planning authority [all] [at least one] of the following documents …'. This can be heavy-handed, however, in simple propositions when 'and' or 'or' may be better.

Cross-references

Within an article it may be unnecessary to cross-refer to other parts of that article, as meaning may be clear from the order of the paragraphs or from the context or words used generally. Thus:

'(1) An undertaker shall apply to the relevant planning authority to ...

(2) Any such application must ...'

Needing to make forward references (ie to a concept not yet introduced) may indicate that the overall order of the provisions is not quite right. Again, this is not a hard and fast rule and forward sign-posting may be helpful.

The Drafting Guidance indicates that, on the whole, drafters should not use the words 'above' or 'below', although this may be necessary to achieve certainty.

Definitions

Definitions are broadly of four kinds, being:

- Definitions of major concepts without which the reader would not be able to understand parts of the DCO. For example, ''authorised development' means the development and associated development described in Part 1 of Schedule 1 ...'.
- Definitions adopted for the sake of drafting convenience. For example, ''the 2008 Act' means the Planning Act 2008 ...'.
- Definitions of words or expressions that will be understood in general terms, but which require a degree of certainty or clarity. For example, ''business day' means a day other than a Saturday or Sunday or a public holiday in England'.
- Definitions making, for convenience or clarity, a minor adjustment to what a word or expression might otherwise mean. For example, ''building' includes and building, structure or erection or any part of a building, structure or erection ...'.

Where a defined word or expression appears only once in a DCO, it should be defined in the article or schedule where it is used.

Where a word or expression is used more than once in a DCO then:

- If it is used in the body of the DCO, the word or expression should be defined in an 'interpretation' article early in the DCO (nearly always article 2);
- If it is used only in a particular schedule (this most frequently applies to the requirements schedule) then the word or expression should be defined in an 'interpretation' paragraph early in that schedule (often paragraphs 1 or 2).

Bodies corporate

Statutory corporations and other bodies corporate should be treated as singular, rather than plural. Thus 'The Environment Agency has ...', *not* 'The Environment Agency have ...'.

Periods of time

The objective when drafting in relation to periods of time is to make it easy for the reader to understand when the period starts, the duration of the period and when the period ends. This is important because periods of time will often relate to the right to make an application or to enter an appeal.

Start of period

The expression 'beginning with [an event]' indicates that time runs from the date of that event. By contrast, the words 'from' and 'after' an event will usually be taken to mean that time runs from the day following the event. Because of the potential ambiguity with the words 'after' and 'from' it may be better to use the expression 'beginning with'. These terms were discussed in the context of the (then) wording of s 118 of the PA 2008 in *R (oao Blue Green London Plan) v Secretary of State for the Environment and Rural Affairs* [2015] EWHC 495.

The period

The expression, 'a period of [XX] days' is often used, but the words 'a period of' do not really add anything and '[XX] days' may be sufficient.

It is sometimes necessary to use the expression 'working days' in order to exclude weekends and public holidays, in which case it is good practice to define the expression.

End of period

The expression 'before the end of [a period] beginning with [a date]' would allow an action to be taken at any time up to the end of the specified period, including before the period began. By contrast, the expression 'within [a period] from [a date]' would limit the taking of the action to the period specified. Often there expressions will be the same in practice, but this will not always be the case.

Words and phrases

The Drafting Guidance gives specific advice about 'modern' drafting conventions for a number of words or phrases commonly used in legislation. This advice has been adopted here with some adaptations to make it more relevant to the drafting of DCOs.

'affect'

The 'nothing in provision A affects provision B' formula is useful if you do not know all the effects that A might have on B, or where those effects would be too numerous to mention. But if you can identify what effect it is you have in mind, being specific may help the reader (so, for example, 'A does not limit B).

'any'

Beware of a proliferation of the use of 'any'. In many cases 'a' or 'an' is just as good.

'Any' can be ambiguous. For example, 'The relevant planning authority must consult any parish council within which construction activities will be undertaken.' Does this mean any 'one' parish council or 'all' parish councils?

'Any' may, of course, be useful to emphasise that something is of universal application or without qualification (but consider whether emphasis is really needed).

'apart from'

For 'apart from', in the phrase 'apart from this section', consider 'but for' or 'leaving aside'.

However, the awkwardness here is not so much the words themselves as the task they impose on the reader - that of working out what the situation would be without the provision in question. It might be more helpful to expand on the thought and say what you have in mind.

'description'

This can seem rather vague and abstract; for example, 'development of a description specified in …'. Drafters might like to consider 'kind', 'class' or 'category' (or even 'sort'?).

'function'

Draft on the basis that the natural meaning of 'function' covers powers and duties. In *Hazell v Hammersmith and Fulham London Borough Council* [1992] 2 AC 1 Lord Templeman said that the word 'functions' in s 111 of the Local Government Act 1972 embraced: 'all the duties and powers of a local authority; the sum total of the activities Parliament has entrusted to it'.

A definition to the effect that 'functions' includes powers and duties is generally unnecessary and unhelpful. If something further is needed, consider whether it is possible to get the point across more clearly.

'provide'

Where a DCO 'provides' for something it effects or gives rise to that thing in law. So for example, a DCO may give an undertaker power to enter an agreement with a street authority that will 'provide for the dedication of any new street as a public highway …'. The term is very useful because it does not require that the DCO should create it in any particular way. Sometimes 'make' or 'create' will allow for the same flexibility.

However, consider in any given case whether it is possible to be more precise. Will the DCO 'enable', 'authorise', 'require', 'set out', 'stipulate' a particular result? A more immediate word may also be less legalistic.

'provision'

The word 'provisions' in a DCO may be a useful expression to refer to articles and schedules generally without having to specify which, although sometimes the word could be omitted without changing meaning.

Used in the expression 'make provision', the word is a useful generic phrase for what legislation does, but in some circumstances it can be legalistic and off-putting. It may be worth thinking about what the DCO actually does in the case you are concerned about: does it 'regulate', 'authorise', 'require'?

It may be possible to avoid the word 'provision' completely. So rather than 'This Part of this Schedule makes further provision about …', it might be better to say 'This Part of this Schedule contains more about …'.

'pursuant to'/'in pursuance of'

Where one thing follows directly from another, with no intervening cause or condition, 'pursuant to' can often be rendered as 'under'. Thus '… the provision of further information pursuant to paragraph …' could simply be '… the provision of further information under paragraph …'. The expression '… in accordance with' may also be appropriate in certain circumstances, as may 'as required by' or 'as authorised by'. In other cases 'because of' may work.

The same points may be made in relation to 'in pursuance of'.

'in relation to'/'in respect of'/'with respect to'/'as respects'

These phrases are all extremely useful, and sometimes essential, in that they do not require one to specify any particular relationship. 'In respect of' has been said to have 'the widest possible meaning of any expression intended to convey some connection or relation': see *Albon v Naza Motor Trading* [2007] EWHC 9 (Ch) at 27.

It is though tempting to use them in circumstances where a more precise relationship could be specified. In some circumstances 'in the case of', 'for', 'about', 'to' or 'as to' will do as well.

'subject to'

'Subject to' is not a very precise way of describing a relationship between two propositions. For example, this article 'is subject to' another article may not be easily understood and it may be better to describe the relationship between the two articles.

If you can't conveniently describe the relationship, 'subject to' can sometimes be avoided. A signpost such as '(but see section x)' is suggested by the Drafting Guidance as possibly serve to alerting the reader to the fact that there are qualifications without sounding as legalistic.

The relationship between the provisions may be particularly hard to follow if 'subject to' is at the beginning of the sentence. It may be better to start with the main proposition and then indicate that there is a qualification, perhaps in a second sentence.

'Subject to' is also not necessarily helpful if you cannot identify the provisions you are talking about. 'Subject to what follows' should be avoided unless it is abundantly obvious from the context exactly which of the following provisions are being referred to. Where there is any doubt, specify exactly which provisions you mean (or express the relationship in some other way).

It may be possible to dispense with 'subject to' altogether, especially if the qualifying proposition is close to the proposition it qualifies - in which case the reader may be expected to grasp the relationship between the two without extra help.

'Such'

Avoid 'such' where possible. Often 'the' or 'a' will do just as well or the word can be omitted altogether. Thus '... at such locations within the Order limits as the undertaker reasonably requires' may be drafted as '... at the locations within the Order limits as the undertaker reasonably requires'.

'supplemental'/'supplementary'

There is no obvious difference in meaning between 'supplementary' and 'supplemental'. The Drafting Guidance says that drafters should prefer 'supplementary', as perhaps the more usual formulation.

'by virtue of'

Where a relationship is direct, there may be alternatives to the rather archaic 'by virtue of'.

Sometimes 'by' on its own is enough. Where one thing authorises or requires another, 'under' may be possible. Where one thing causes another, or makes it possible, try 'as a result of' or 'because of'.

That said, 'by virtue of' can be particularly useful for indirect relationships. For example, '... a power conferred by this Order may be exercised despite a provision made by, or by virtue of, a specified enactment ...'.

'where'/'if'

'Where' is useful for stating a case or a set of circumstances in which a later proposition applies. 'If' is used for stating a contingency.

So 'where' may be better for cases which inevitably will occur, 'if' for conditions which may or may not be satisfied.

There is, however, of course no clear-cut distinction and, in some cases, it may depend on the perspective from which you are looking at the situation.

'without prejudice'

Consider what the 'prejudice' might be and focus on that. So in the phrase 'Without prejudice to the generality of article 13 …', if the fear is that the new provision might limit what article 13 says, perhaps used the drafting 'Without limiting article 13 …'. If the fear is that the new provision might *affect* or *change* the way another provision operates, perhaps say that (but see *affect* above).

A phrase beginning without 'without prejudice to…' can often be recast so as to start with the main proposition and then say how it relates to the other one.

Another way of avoiding 'without prejudice' is by 'in particular'. Thus rather than, '(b) without prejudice to the generality of (a) above, the undertaker may …', it may be possible to draft in the form, '(b) in particular the undertaker may …'.

Conclusions

This article is intended to give an overview of 'modern' drafting conventions drawing on the Office of Public Sector Information documents Statutory Instrument Practice (2006) and the Drafting Techniques Group of the Office of Parliamentary Counsel guidance in 'Office of Parliamentary Counsel – Drafting Guidance' (August 2015).

Other reference works exist on modern drafting conventions, including Michele Asprey's *Plain Language for Lawyers* (The Federation Press).

Clearly, as more DCOs go through the examination process drafting experience is continuing to develop and drafters will need to consider and adopt emerging best practice.

Limits of Deviation

Written by Richard Honey
Edited by Michael Humphries QC

Purpose of limits of deviation

Limits of Deviation (LODs) were first utilised in private Acts of Parliament and are still used in modern hybrid Acts that authorise particular infrastructure projects. In hybrid Acts, LODs are the limits within which lateral deviation in the construction of the works are allowed. Plans typically show the centre line of a linear work, such as a railway, and then show limits either side within which the powers to construct the work may be exercised.

LODs enable flexibility to deal with problems encountered during construction, such as engineering limitations or adverse ground conditions, as well as the inevitable differences that arise between what is shown on the plan and what is constructed in practice. Without this flexibility, there would be a risk that the works could not be constructed in practice, as they would be confined to the precise positions shown on the plans. The works can be constructed anywhere within the LOD.

In DCOs, the concept of the LOD needs to be distinguished from: (a) the 'Order limits', being the land shown on the works plans within which the authorised development may be carried out; and (b) the 'Order land', being the land shown on the land plans within which land may be acquired and which is identified in the Book of Reference. For the most part the powers granted under a DCO will be exercisable only within the Order limits, although there are cases where powers have been granted that could in principle be exercised outside a scheme's Order limits.

LODs, by contrast, have the function of setting a limit on where the authorised development, or more particularly an individual Work forming part of the authorised development, may be carried out. LOD are now used for most schemes, not only linear schemes such as railways or power lines, in order to provide the flexibility that most promoters want and many promoters need.

Horizontal and vertical limits of deviation

Horizontal limits of deviation are shown on the plans. Some DCOs, such as the Preesall Underground Gas Storage Facility Order 2015, only include horizontal or lateral limits of deviation, as shown on the plans.

Vertical limits of deviation tend to be defined in textual terms within the relevant article in the DCO, being a certain height above or below the level shown on a scaled section, although sometimes the vertical LOD is itself indicated on the section. It is often the case for major development works that a specific maximum height limit is set. This is especially relevant for the purposes of environmental impact assessment, in order to provide a 'Rochdale envelope' for assessment.

Downward vertical LODs are often unlimited. An unlimited downward vertical LOD will not usually have any environmental impact, but there will be cases where digging down could be problematic in some locations, as it might for example interfere with groundwater flows or buried archaeology. In such cases a limit on downward vertical deviation in some locations may be warranted.

Relevant statutory provisions

The PA 2008 does not have much to say about LODs. The phrase is mentioned in only a couple of places, where amendments are made to other legislation dealing with blight (see PA 2008, ss 175–176).

The Infrastructure Planning (Applications: Prescribed Forms and Procedure) Regulations 2009 provide in reg 5(2) that applications for DCOs must be accompanied by a works plan showing the proposed location or, for a linear scheme, the proposed route and alignment of the development and works, and the limits within which the development and works may be carried out and any limits of deviation provided for in the draft order.

Approach to drafting limits of deviation

It is in individual DCOs that the provisions on LOD are to be found. For example, the National Grid (Hinkley Point C Connection Project) Order 2016 defines the limits of deviation in Art 5. That article provides that in carrying out the authorised development the undertaker may:

(a) deviate laterally from the lines or situations of the authorised development shown on the Works Plans within the limits of deviation relating to a Work shown on those plans; and

(b) deviate vertically from the levels of the authorised development shown on the sections:

  (i) to any extent upwards not exceeding 4m in respect of the overhead lines;

  (ii) to any extent upwards not exceeding 10% of the maximum height in respect of structures such as substations and bridges; and

  (iii) to any extent downwards as may be found to be necessary or convenient.

Art 5 also provides specific limits for particular pylons. For example, in relation to one pylon it is provided that it must not deviate laterally in one direction at all from the position shown on the plans. This form of asymmetric LOD may be relevant in providing protection for a particular environmental receptor.

Art 3(2) provides that the authorised development must be constructed and installed in the lines and situations shown on the Works Plans listed in Schedule 2 and in accordance with the levels shown on the sections, subject to the limits of deviation in Art 5. There are also protective provisions in Art 51 that provide, for land at Bristol Port, that the lateral limits of deviation are confined to a maximum of 5m. Again, this form of non-standard LOD may be relevant in overcoming a particular issue.

The Network Rail (Tinsley Chord) Order 2015 is similar. Art 6 provides that in constructing or maintaining any of the scheduled works, the promoter may: (a) deviate laterally from the lines or situations shown on the works and land plan to the extent of the limits of deviation for that work; and (b) deviate vertically from the levels shown on the sections: (i) to any extent not exceeding 3m upwards; or (ii) to any extent downwards as may be found to be necessary or convenient. Art 6(2) contains a clarification that the points of commencement and termination of the works may deviate laterally.

Interestingly, in Art 13 of the Tinsley Chord Order the power to acquire land compulsorily is described as applying to 'land within the limits of deviation', rather than to 'the Order land', which is not a defined term. Furthermore, the term 'the Order limits' is defined as meaning 'any limits of deviation and any additional limits of land to be acquired or used which are shown on the works and land plan'. This Order, perhaps helpfully in the case of the particular project, thereby elides the concepts of the land to which the order powers relate with the LODs for particular works and the identification of the land to which the powers of compulsory purchase relate.

Variations in approach to drafting limits of deviation

LODs vary between orders, as can be seen. The upwards vertical LOD in the Able Marine Energy Park Development Consent Order 2014 and the Network Rail (Ipswich Chord) Order 2012 were, for example, 1m. The latter DCO also included a provision in Art 7(2) preventing any deviation which would reduce the headroom or clearance beneath any proposed bridge - or diminish the width of any walkway, staircase, flight of steps, carriageway, tunnel, footpath or cycleway - by more than 200mm from its dimension as shown on the design drawings. The M1 Junction 10a (Grade Separation) Order 2013 limited upward vertical deviation to 1.5m.

There are a variety of other variations, some examples of which are as follows.

The Norfolk County Council (Norwich Northern Distributor Road (A1067 to A47(T))) Order 2015 contained in Art 5 a table specifying different upwards vertical, downwards vertical and lateral limits of deviation for different works or groups of works. Permissible vertical deviation range from zero to 1m.

Article 3 of the Swansea Bay Tidal Generating Station Order 2015 provided that in constructing or maintaining the authorised development, the undertaker may: (a) deviate laterally from the lines or situations shown on the works plans within the limits of deviation, subject to maximum dimensions set out in a schedule; and (b) deviate vertically from the levels shown on works plans for specific works to any extent downwards as may be found necessary or convenient. In the schedule, a table provided maximum heights and dimensions for structures including the seawall, turbine housing, buildings and cranes.

Article 4 of the East Midlands Gateway Rail Freight Interchange and Highway Order 2016 contained provisions described as 'parameters of authorised development' rather than LOD. It provided that the authorised development is to be carried out within the parameters shown and described on the parameters plans, but went on to say that in carrying out the authorised development the undertaker may deviate laterally to the extent of LOD shown on the plans and vertically to 1.5m, save for some specific works which had 1.5m upwards and 2.5m downwards limits.

The North Blyth Biomass Power Station Order 2013 contained limits of lateral deviation shown on the plans for certain works but no textual provisions for limits other than a provision in Art 3(3) saying that the undertaker may deviate laterally from the lines or situations shown on the works plan within the limits of deviation.

Wind farms

The National Policy Statement for Renewable Energy Infrastructure (EN-3) supports micrositing for wind turbines and encourages the 'granting consents that allow for micrositing to be undertaken within a specified tolerance', to allow 'changes to be made to the precise location of infrastructure during the construction phase so that account can be taken of unforeseen circumstances' (para 2.6.146). The precise siting of turbines could influence effects on interests such as bats, peat resources, habitats, watercourses and the like.

For onshore wind, the NPS says (para 2.7.24) that:

> 'Whilst it is for the applicant to specify the level of tolerance they are seeking, a tolerance of between 30m and 50m of elements of the required infrastructure is typical. However, there may be some circumstances where the IPC considers that the micrositing tolerance requested by the applicant is too great, and that on the evidence of the EIA and its own assessment of the proposal, that it is necessary to restrict either the overall tolerance for the scheme or the tolerance of specific elements of the proposal. When making this judgement, the IPC should take into account the reason for the applicant having requested the micrositing'.

The Clocaenog Forest Wind Farm Order 2014, for example, contains a power (Art 6) for individual turbines to deviate laterally within LOD. There were separate restrictions in the Order that prevented turbines from being constructed within 50m of forest edges and watercourses. These provisions were intended to protect bats and also avoid run off into the watercourse (see report, 20 August 2015, para 6.0.22). Comparable provisions, including a limitation in relation to watercourses, were included in the Brechfa Forest West Wind Farm Order 2013.

Environmental impacts

The A19/A1058 Coast Road (Junction Improvement) Development Consent Order 2016 contained in Art 5 not only a limit on vertical deviation of a maximum of 0.5m upwards and 1m downwards, but also had the proviso that any deviation was only permitted if it is unlikely to give rise to any materially new or materially different environmental effects from those assessed in the environmental report.

The Thorpe Marsh Gas Pipeline Order 2016 contains limits of deviation in Art 6, which are defined laterally by limits shown on the plans and for vertical deviation are, with some specific exceptions, between 1.2m and 20m below the surface of the ground. Art 6(a) provides that certain works can deviate 'vertically only to the maximum extent assessed in the environmental statement' (see also report, 7 December 2015, para 9.2.23).

These provisions illustrate a tension between the natural desire of promoters to include a degree of flexibility in Orders to allow for design development and the equally natural desire of the Planning Inspectorate to ensure that the project, including its LODs, have been properly environmentally assessed.

Clearly LODs are an important element of the parameters against which a project will undergo environmental impact assessment. The draft order, including plans, and the environmental assessment must be consistent. It will often be important to assess the reasonable worst case impacts of the authorised works being undertaken anywhere within their LODs, although in practice works will often be sited to avoid the worst impacts of the development.

Justification for the limits of deviation

Limits of deviation are not mandatory under the PA 2008. It is however usually a good idea to include limits of deviation. If they are to be included, as with other provisions of a DCO, they should be justified. The explanatory memorandum should explain why they are required, at least in general terms.

The Inspectorate has said that whether the deviation sought is acceptable is 'really a question of impacts, mitigation and merits which it will be for the ExA to take a view on' (register of advice, 18 April 2011, North Blyth Biomass).

It is good practice for applicants to produce reports to set out the rationale and justification for the LOD selected. This was done for example on the Willington C Gas Pipeline project, as an appendix to the environmental statement. The Willington C Gas Pipeline Order 2014 contained in Art 7 limits of deviation both laterally (by limits of deviation shown on the plans, 30m either side of the centre line) and vertically. The vertical deviation was defined generally as between 1.1m and 70m below the surface of the ground, but there was an upper limit of 2.8m in one location and specific height limits set out in a schedule for certain works.

A promoter will have to show that the limits of deviation are necessary and proportionate, especially if they are at the upper end of what is in practice adopted in DCOs. Examining Authorities have raised questions about LOD previously, during examination, including for example on the Thames Tideway Tunnel project and the National Grid North London Reinforcement project.

For schemes that are non-linear and involve little engineering work, there may be little justification for significant LOD. It is notable that the former Infrastructure Planning (Model Provisions) (England and Wales) Order 2009 included limits of deviation in the model provisions for railways but not the general model provisions. This may, however, simply indicate that for non-linear projects flexibility in the siting and scale of development can also be achieved through the use of parameter plans forming a 'Rochdale Envelope' for environmental impact assessment: see PINS Advice Note 9 – Rochdale Envelope.

In practice, how wide LODs will need to be is significantly influence by how far advanced the design of the project is and how much has been done by way of site investigation and the like. It is advisable to err on the side of caution when setting LOD to allow flexibility to deal with the unexpected.

Use of the Works

Written by Richard Honey
Edited by Michael Humphries QC

The need for statutory authority

Authority is required not only for the construction of an infrastructure project but also for its use. Such authority can be express or implied from the statute that authorises the project. Some promoters may be authorised to operate a development, once constructed, under other legislation.

There will be a defence of statutory authority to a claim in nuisance where a statute authorises the user of land in a way that will inevitably involve a nuisance, even if every reasonable precaution is taken (see eg *Barr v Biffa* [2013] QB 455).

It was said by Lord Wilberforce in *Allen v Gulf Oil Refining* [1981] AC 1001 that 'where Parliament by express direction or by necessary implication has authorised the construction and use of an undertaking or works, that carries with it an authority to do what is authorised with immunity from any action based on nuisance'. The Act in that case provided 'authority to construct and operate a refinery upon the lands to be acquired'.

Dissenting in *Allen*, Lord Keith noted the approach of Lord Esher MR in *Altrincham Union Assessment Committee v Cheshire Lines Committee* (1885) 15 QBD 597 (at 603) to the construction of private legislation, 'which is obtained by persons for their own benefit', as being to 'construe more strictly provisions which they allege to be in their favour', 'because the persons who obtain a private Act ought to take care that it is so worded that that which they desire to obtain for themselves is plainly stated in it'.

In *Manchester Ship Canal v United Utilities* [2014] 1 WLR 2576, Lord Sumption said (para 2):

> 'A statutory right to commit what would otherwise be a tort may of course be implied. But since this necessarily involves an interference with the rights of others, the test has always been restrictive. The implication must be more than convenient or reasonable. It must be necessary. As a general rule, this will involve showing either that the existence of the power is necessarily implicit in the express terms of the statute, or else that the statutory purpose cannot be effectually achieved without the implication. In particular a right to commit what would otherwise be a tort may be implied if a statutory power is incapable of being exercised or a statutory duty is incapable of being performed without doing the act in question'.

Relevant provisions in the PA 2008

PA 2008, s 157 deals with the use of buildings in respect of which development consent is granted by a DCO. It provides that if development consent is granted for development that includes the erection, extension, alteration or re-erection of a building, the order granting consent may specify the purposes for which the building is authorised to be used. It goes on to provide that, if no purpose is so specified, the consent is taken to authorise the use of the building for the purpose for which it is designed.

Section 157 echoes the provision in the Town and Country Planning Act 1990, s 75 in relation to which there has been some case law (eg *Barnett v Secretary of State for Communities and Local Government* [2009] EWCA Civ 476). It should be noted that there is no equivalent provision for the use of works other than buildings.

There are some provisions of the PA 2008 which govern what DCOs can contain in relation to the operation or use of certain projects: operation of generating stations (PA 2008, s 140), keeping electric lines installed above ground (PA 2008, s 141), and use of underground gas storage facilities (PA 2008, s 142). Note also that PA 2008, s 194 and Sch 9 also amend various other Acts to insert a power to override easements and other rights in relation to the use of land.

PA 2008, s 158, which provides statutory authority for carrying out development and doing anything else authorised by a DCO, is considered elsewhere in this work, as is PA 2008, s 152 which makes provision for compensation for the carrying out of the works.

Guidance on drafting DCOs

It will normally be the provisions of the DCO itself that confer the powers to use the works. PINS Advice Note 13 (April 2012) says that 'the description of the proposed development together with the provisions of the DCO (including requirements) will determine what is authorised to be carried out'. The advice note goes on to make the point that 'it is the responsibility of developers (not the Planning Inspectorate) to ensure that the draft order applied for would provide them with all the necessary powers and authorisations to implement and use their scheme'. As the document notes, 'clarity and precision in the description and drafting of the provisions can, for example, prevent future uncertainty over whether development and other activities are carried out within the terms of the order'.

The general model provisions in the former Infrastructure Planning (Model Provisions) (England and Wales) Order 2009 contained a grant of development consent in Art 2 together with a right in Art 3 to maintain the authorised project. This would probably have encompassed authority to use the works for the purpose for which they were authorised to be constructed under the DCO. In practice, many individual DCOs take a more explicit approach. The approach taken in relation to a range of different projects is considered below.

Gas storage

The Preesall Underground Gas Storage Facility Order 2015 contains in Art 3(1) the grant of consent not only for the carrying out of the development but also 'to use the authorised development for the purpose for which it is designed including use of the cavities to be created for the underground storage of gas'. This reflects the PA 2008, s 120 and Sch 5, para 7 that expressly identifies 'The use of underground gas storage facilities' as a matter that may be included in a DCO as relating to, or to matters ancillary to, the development for which development consent is granted. Article 4 also includes the right to maintain the authorised development.

Rail freight interchange

The East Midlands Gateway Rail Freight Interchange and Highway Order 2016 includes the grant of development consent for carrying out the authorised development (Art 3) and the power to maintain (Art 6) but also includes in Art 5(1): 'the undertaker and any persons authorised by the undertaker may operate and use that part of the authorised development comprised in Works Nos 1 to 6 inclusive for the purposes of a rail freight terminal and warehousing and any purposes ancillary to those purposes'.

Harbour facilities

Article 11 of the Able Marine Energy Park Development Consent Order 2014 provides that 'the undertaker may from time to time within the area of jurisdiction provide and operate such harbour facilities, together with works ancillary to those facilities, as may be necessary or convenient for the construction of the authorised development or the operation of the undertaking'.

Rail

For rail projects, there tends to be a specific power to operate and use the relevant railway. For example, Art 34(1) of the Network Rail (Norton Bridge Area Improvements) Order 2014 provides that 'Network Rail may operate and use the railways and any other elements of the authorised development as a system, or part of a system, of transport for the carriage of passengers and goods'. Similar words are found in, for example, Art 27(1) of the Network Rail (Redditch Branch Enhancement) Order 2013. This is in addition to express provisions granting development consent and conferring power to maintain the authorised development.

Highways

Highway DCOs contain the grant of development consent and the power to maintain the development, but not express provisions empowering the use or operation of the relevant highway (see eg Arts 5–6 of the A14 Cambridge to Huntingdon Improvement Scheme Development Consent Order 2016 and Arts 3–4 of the Lancashire County Council (Torrisholme to the M6 Link (A683 Completion of Heysham to M6 Link Road)) Order 2013). As the highways will be owned and operated by highway authorities with pre-existing statutory powers, no additional power to use the new highway is it seems required.

Gas pipelines

In gas pipeline DCOs, there are provisions authorising the operation and use of the pipe: 'the undertaker may at any time operate and use the authorised development except to the extent that this Order or an agreement made under this Order provides otherwise' (see Art 4 of the Thorpe Marsh Gas Pipeline Order 2016 and Art 6 of the Willington C Gas Pipeline Order 2014).

Power generation facilities

The Brechfa Forest West Wind Farm Order 2013 contains the grant of development consent in Art 3 and the right to maintain in Art 5. Article 7 then provides: 'the undertaker is authorised to operate the generating station comprised in the authorised development'. The explanatory note to the DCO says that the 'Order grants development consent for, and authorises RWE Npower Renewables Limited to construct, operate and maintain a wind electricity generating station'.

Similar wording is used in a range of other orders including the Ferrybridge Multifuel 2 Power Station Order 2015 (Art 6), the Swansea Bay Tidal Generating Station Order 2015 (Art 5), the North Killingholme (Generating Station) Order 2014 (Art 5), the North Blyth Biomass Power Station Order 2013 (Art 6), the Triton Knoll Offshore Wind Farm Order 2013 (Art 5), and the Rookery South (Resource Recovery Facility) Order 2013 (Art 6).

The Hinkley Point C (Nuclear Generating Station) Order 2013 contains the grant of development consent in Art 3 and the power to maintain the authorised project in Art 5. Article 6, headed 'authorisation of use', then provides: 'subject to the provisions of this Order and to the requirements the undertaker may operate and use the authorised project'. The same approach is taken in the Thames Water Utilities Limited (Thames Tideway Tunnel) Order 2014 (see Art 4).

Other power generation DCOs employ similar but slightly different wording:

- Article 7 of the Clocaenog Forest Wind Farm Order 2014 says 'the undertaker is authorised to operate and use the authorised development for generating electricity'.
- Article 6 of the Palm Paper Mill Generating Station Order 2016 provides that 'the undertaker may operate the generating station for which development consent is granted by this Order'.
- Article 5 of the Port Talbot Steelworks Generating Station Order 2015 provides that 'the undertaker is authorised to operate the generating station for which development consent is granted by this Order'.
- Article 5 of the Progress Power (Gas Fired Power Station) Order 2015 and of the Hirwaun Generating Station Order 2015 both provide that 'the undertaker is hereby authorised to operate the generating station comprised in the authorised development'.
- Article 5 of the Knottingley Power Plant Order 2015 provides that 'the undertaker is hereby authorised to operate the generating station and associated plant comprised in the authorised development'.

Overhead lines

In relation to overhead lines, Art 4(2) of the National Grid (North London Reinforcement Project) Order 2014 provides that 'the undertaker may install, and keep installed, above ground the electric lines included in the authorised development'. Article 4(2) of the National Grid (King's Lynn B Power Station Connection) Order 2013 similarly provides that 'the undertaker may install, and keep installed, above ground the electric line included in the authorised development'. In the National Grid (Hinkley Point C Connection Project) Order 2016 similar wording was removed by the Secretary of State from Art 3 of the draft Order as 'unnecessary given the terms of section 16 of the Planning Act 2016' (Secretary of State's decision letter para 143), although it is clear from schedule 5 para 6 of the PA 2008 that a DCO may include such a provision.

Landfill

Not all DCOs contain such express provisions relating to the use or operation of the project. The White Moss Landfill Order 2015 includes in the definition of the project in paragraph 1 of Schedule 1 not only the 'construction of a new hazardous waste landfill facility' but also: 'the operation of a landfill gas collection and flare system, the operation of a leachate collection, treatment and lagoon system, the extraction, stockpiling and exportation of clay, mudstones, coal and other suitable materials including general fill materials and all other associated engineering works to construct the landfill phases'. Paragraph 2 then adds 'continuation of the filling with hazardous waste as shown on the works plan' and 'operation of the interceptor waste treatment facility for the treatment of waste'. This is an alternative means to seek to ensure that the use and operation of the project is expressly authorised by the DCO.

Defence to Proceedings in Respect of Nuisance

Written by: James Pereira QC, ftb
Edited by: Michael Humphries QC, ftb

Introduction

This chapter considers PA 2008, s 158. This section provides statutory authority for certain activities authorised by an order granting development consent, for the purpose of conferring a defence in civil or criminal proceedings in nuisance. Note that s 158 confers statutory authority rather than blanket immunity from actions in nuisance. It must therefore be read alongside relevant case law on the scope of the defence of statutory authority. It should also be read alongside PA 2008, s 152, which provides an entitlement to claim compensation where land has been injuriously affected by the carrying out of works. These and other matters are discussed in more detail below.

Statutory basis

PA 2008, s 158 provides as follows:

> "**Nuisance: statutory authority**
>
> (1) This subsection confers statutory authority for—
>
> (a) carrying out development for which consent is granted by an order granting development consent;
>
> (b) doing anything else authorised by an order granting development consent.
>
> (2) Statutory authority under subsection (1) is conferred only for the purpose of providing a defence in civil or criminal proceedings for nuisance.
>
> (3) Subsections (1) and (2) are subject to any contrary provision made in any particular case by an order granting development consent."

The scope of PA 2008, s 158

The proceedings that fall within PA 2008, s 158(2)

The statutory authority is only conferred for the purpose of providing a defence in civil or criminal proceedings for nuisance: see PA 2008, s 158(2). Such proceedings would include private nuisance and public nuisance at common law.

The position in relation to statutory nuisance proceedings under the Environmental Protection Act 1990 is less clear. The Divisional Court in *Camden LBC v LUL* [2000]

Env LR 369 (DC) at [25] has expressed the preliminary, non-binding, view on a similarly worded provision in the Railways Act 1993, s 122(3) that it would apply to proceedings by way of an appeal against a statutory nuisance abatement notice served under the Environmental Protection Act 1990, s 80 where that notice alleged a statutory nuisance amounting to a common law nuisance, but it would not apply where the notice alleged a statutory nuisance amounting to prejudice to health.

In the same case, the Divisional Court expressed the view that criminal proceedings for a nuisance order under the Environmental Protection Act 1990, s 82 would be criminal proceedings for nuisance. Proceedings under section 82 are started by laying an information in the magistrates' court and are therefore criminal in nature: see *Botross v London Borough of Hammersmith and Fulham* [1995] Env LR 217. Consistent with this view, General Model Provision 7 ('GMP7') in the Infrastructure Planning (Model Provisions) (England and Wales) Order 2009 makes express provision for a defence to proceedings under the Environmental Protection Act 1990, s 82 to be conferred upon a defendant in certain circumstances. This is addressed further below.

Activities that fall within PA 2008, s 158

The statutory authority extends to the carrying out of development for which consent is granted under the DCO (PA 2008, s 158(1)(a)), and to other activities (which need not amount to development) which are authorised by an order granting development consent (PA 2008, s 158(1)(b)). The defence therefore covers not only the construction of an NSIP, but also its operation. It could also extend to other activities that may be authorised by the NSIP, such as those associated with the lopping of trees or the carrying out of survey work.

The scope of a defence of statutory authority

It is important to note that the scope of the defence of statutory authority generally has been the subject of a number of court decisions which are therefore relevant to the scope of PA 2008, s 158.

A defence of statutory authority is only available where the nuisance created could not have been prevented by reasonable measures or due diligence by the perpetrator: see *Allen v Gulf Oil* [1981] AC 1001. It must be the inevitable result of carrying out the development or undertaking the activities in question: see *Managers of the Metropolitan Asylum District v Frederick Hill and Others* (1881) 6 App Cas 193 at 213. Hence where the nuisance has come about because of the negligence of the operator, the defence will not succeed.

Model provisions

As stated above, GMP7 makes express provision for a defence to proceedings for a nuisance order brought by an individual under the Environmental Protection Act 1990, s 82 in certain circumstances. The relevant circumstances are as follows.

For proceedings in relation to a nuisance caused by the carrying out of development, the defendant must show that the nuisance:

- relates to premises used by the undertaker for the purposes of or in connection with the construction or maintenance of the authorised project and that the nuisance is attributable to the carrying out of the authorised project in accordance with a notice served under the Control of Pollution Act 1974 s 60 (control of noise on construction site), or a consent given under s 61 (prior consent for work on construction site) or 65 (noise exceeding registered level); or
- is a consequence of the construction or maintenance of the authorised project and that it cannot reasonably be avoided.

For proceedings relating to nuisance caused by the operation of the project the defendant must show that the nuisance:

- relates to premises used by the undertaker for the purposes of or in connection with the use of the authorised project and that the nuisance is attributable to the use of the authorised project which is being used in accordance with a scheme of monitoring and attenuation of noise agreed with the Commission as described in requirement 25; or
- is a consequence of the use of the authorised project and that it cannot reasonably be avoided.

As a consequence of the above, GMP7 also disapplies certain statutory provisions where the consent relates to the use of premises by the undertaker for the purposes of or in connection with the construction or maintenance of the authorised project. These provisions are the Control of Pollution Act 1974, s 61(9) (consent for work on construction site to include statement that it does not of itself constitute a defence to proceedings under section 82 of the Environmental Protection Act 1990, s 82) and s 65(8) of that Act (corresponding provision in relation to consent for registered noise level to be exceeded).

Guidance

Paragraph 38 of the DCLG Application Form Guidance (2013), referring to Box 19 of the application form, advises that the applicant should refer to the Environmental Protection Act 1990, s 79(1) in order to consider whether the development proposal would engage one or more of that section's issues relating to nuisance. If it does, the applicant's statement should set out its proposals for mitigating or limiting them.

Compensation

It is not the purpose of this work to give a detailed account of the law of compensation. Users of this Service who have a specific issue in relation to compensation should refer to a specialist text on this subject. This article does, however, give an overview of the entitlement to compensation arising under PA 2008, s 152.

Landowners whose ability to bring an action in nuisance has been curtailed by PA 2008, s 158 are provided with a right to claim compensation under PA 2008, s 152 subject to meeting the requirements of that provision. In simple terms, PA 2008, s 152 provides a right to compensation to any person whose land is injuriously affected by the carrying out of authorised works (see s 152(3)) or depreciated in value by physical factors caused by the use of the NSIP (see s 152(7)). Importantly, the right to compensation does not depend upon any land having been acquired by the use of compulsory purchase powers.

Section 152(3) provides that if, by virtue of section 158 or an order granting development consent, there is a defence of statutory authority in civil or criminal proceedings for nuisance in respect of any authorised works than

> '(3) A person by whom or on whose behalf any authorised works are carried out must pay compensation to any person whose land is injuriously affected by the carrying out of the works.'

It is made clear that the Compulsory Purchase Act 1965, s 10(2) (limitation on compensation) applies to sub-s (3) of this section as it applies to that section: see PA 2008, s 152(5). It is also made clear that the Land Compensation Act 1973, Part 1 (compensation for depreciation of land value by physical factors caused by use of public works) applies in relation to authorised works as if: (a) references in that Part to any public works were to any authorised works; (b) references in that Part to the responsible authority were to the person for whose benefit the order granting development consent has effect for the time being; and (c) ss 1(6) and 17 were omitted: see PA 2008, s 152(7).

An order granting development consent may not include provision the effect of which is to remove or modify the application of any of s 152(1)-(7).

Compensation for injurious affection caused by the carrying out of authorised works

It seems likely from the wording of PA 2008, s 152(3) and (4) that the provision is to be applied in a similar manner to section 10 of the Compulsory Purchase Act 1965. However, by analogy with section 10, compensation would be payable where the following criteria are met:

- the loss has resulted from an act made lawful by the order granting development consent;
- the loss is such that in the absence of PA 2008, s 158 it would have given the landowner an entitlement to recover damages;
- the loss must arise from the physical interference with the land or with a right enjoyed with it, and must result in a depreciation of the value of the claimant's land; and
- the loss must arise from the execution of the authorised works and not from their use.

Note that under PA 2008, s 152(4) a dispute as to the principle or the amount of compensation may be referred to the Upper Tribunal (Lands Chamber).

Compensation for depreciation of land value caused by the use of public works

PA 2008, s 152(7) applies the Land Compensation Act 1973, Part 1 with the modifications set out under s 152(7)(a)–(c) (above). The result is that a right to compensation exists where the following conditions are met:

- the value of the claimant's interest in land has been depreciated (Land Compensation Act 1973, s 1(1));
- the depreciation is caused by 'physical factors'. These are defined as noise, vibration, smell, fumes, smoke, artificial lighting and the discharge on to the land in respect of which the claim is made of any solid or liquid substance (Land Compensation Act 1973, s.1(1) and (2));
- the physical factors are caused directly by the use of the authorised works;
- the claimant has a qualifying interest (Land Compensation Act 1973, s 1(1)). [Reference should be made to the Land Compensation Act 1973, s 2 for the specific statutory wording and requirements in relation to qualifying interests. Only an overview is given here.] This means that the claimant must have purchased his interest before the date on which the authorised works were first used, that in the case of a dwelling the claimant has a freehold interest or a tenancy with not less than three years unexpired term remaining at the date of the claim (and where the claimant is entitled to occupy the land he must do so as his residence), and that in the case of property that is not a dwelling, the claimant must be an owner occupier and the land must either be an agricultural unit or have an annual value which is less than the prescribed amount (Land Compensation Act 1973, s 2(1)–(6));
- the claimant has made his claim at the correct time and in the correct manner (see Land Compensation Act 1973, ss 3, 8, 10 and 19 in relation to the manner and timing of making a claim); and
- the compensation claimed exceeds £50 (Land Compensation Act 1973, s 7).

By PA 2008, s 152(7)(b) the compensation is payable by the person for whose benefit the order granting development consent has effect for the time being. Section 152(7)(b), therefore, modifies the effect of the Land Compensation Act 1973, s 1(1) and (4).

Removal of other Consent Requirements

Written by: Michael Humphries QC, ftb

Introduction

In the 2007 White Paper 'Planning for a Sustainable Future', the Government identified one of the problems of the Town and Country Planning Act 1990 regime as being that:[1]

> 'There are too many different and overlapping development consent regimes. A single project can require multiple permissions under several different regimes, particularly projects involving linked developments – for instance, there a port expansion needs road and rail links. Most of these different statutory consent processes have their own procedural rules and, while there are similarities, there are also some important differences. This can significantly increase the costs of applications and can act as a real barrier to bringing forward proposals and to participating in the debate about them.'

In response to this problem, the Government proposed to:[2]

> 'Streamline the procedures for infrastructure projects of national significance by rationalising the different development consent regimes and improving the inquiry procedures for all of them. This will harmonise requirements on developers *and, as far as possible, create a single application process for all of the development authorisations needed for nationally significant infrastructure projects.*' (emphasis added)

The PA 2008 regime clearly aims to meet that objective by removing the requirement to obtain various permissions, consents and authorisations for development where development consent is required. PA 2008, s 33 sets out the effect of the requirement for development consent on various other consent regimes.

As the 2007 White Paper made clear, however, a single application process was only to be created 'as far as possible' and the reality is that the new regime is some way from being a complete 'one stop shop'. PA 2008, s 150, however, does provide a mechanism for including certain additional consents and authorisations within a DCO.

PA 2008, s 150

PA 2008, s 150 provides as follows:

> '(1) An order granting development consent may include provision the effect of which is to remove a requirement for a prescribed consent or

1 Planning for a Sustainable Future (2007) para 2.8(c)
2 Planning for a Sustainable Future (2007) para 2.13(d)

authorisation granted, only if the relevant body had consented to the inclusion of the provision.

(2) 'The relevant body' is the person of body which would otherwise be required to grant the prescribed consent or authorisation.'

The 'prescribed consents or authorisations' for the purposes of PA 2008, s 150 are set out at reg 2 of, and the Schedule to, the Infrastructure Planning (Miscellaneous Prescribed Provisions) Regulations 2010 ('the 2010 Regulations'). The Schedule to the 2010 Regulations identified some 78 'other' consents and authorisations that may be brought within the 2008 Act regime. This Schedule was, however, amended by the Infrastructure Planning (Miscellaneous Prescribed Provisions) (Amendment) Regulations 2013, SI 2013/520 ('the 2013 Regulations') with effect from 6 April 2013.

It is important to note, however, that the effect of the provisions is to enable a DCO to contain provisions for removal of a prescribed consent or authorisation, only where the 'relevant body' that would otherwise be required to grant the prescribed consent or authorisation has consented to the inclusion of the provision.

The 'relevant bodies' under the Schedule

The Schedule (as amended) lists the consents and authorisations by reference to the sections of the relevant legislation. The Schedule does not list the current relevant consenting bodies. Part 1 of the Schedule lists those consents that are relevant to both England and Wales. Part 2 of the Schedule lists those consents that only relate to Wales.

The intention in drafting the list for Wales was to ensure that no devolved consent should be included in a draft DCO without the agreement of the relevant consulting body in Wales.

The following table lists all the consents and authorisations listed in the 2010 Regulations, as amended by the 2013 Regulations. The effect of those amendments was that 16 consents and authorisations that originally appeared in Part 1 of the Schedule (England and Wales) were moved to Part 2 (Wales only). In the table below those consents and authorisations appear in italics. The relevant bodies are also shows for each consent or authorisation:

Act	Section/ Regulation	Consent/ Authorisation	Relevant Consenting Body
PART 1 of SCHEDULE 1 (England and Wales)			
Electricity Act 1989	6	Licences authorising supply	Gas and Electricity Markets Authority
Gas Act 1986	7,7ZA, 7A	Licensing of public gas transporters, gas interconnectors, gas suppliers and gas shippers	Gas and Electricity Markets Authority

Act	Section/ Regulation	Consent/ Authorisation	Relevant Consenting Body
PART 1 of SCHEDULE 1 (England and Wales)			
Petroleum Act 1998	3	Licence to search, bore for and get petroleum	Secretary of State
Petroleum Act 1998	14	Authorisation for construction and use of a pipeline in controlled waters	Secretary of State
Energy Act 2008	4	Licences in relation to combustible gas importation and storage	Secretary of State; Welsh Ministers; Scottish Ministers; Department of Enterprise, Trade and Investment in Northern Ireland
Energy Act 2008	18	Licences in relation to the storage of carbon dioxide	Secretary of State; Welsh Ministers; Scottish Ministers; Department of Enterprise, Trade and Investment in Northern Ireland
Nuclear Industries Security Regulations 2003	5, 6, 8	Approval of security plans	Secretary of State
Justification of Practices Involving Ionising Radiation Regulations 2004	9, 10	Justifying determinations in relation to new and existing practices relating to ionising radiation	Secretary of State; Scottish Ministers; a Northern Ireland department; the National Assembly for Wales
Energy Act 2008	46	Approval of a funded decommissioning programme	Secretary of State
Conservation (Natural Habitat, &c) Regulations 1994	44	Revoked in England and Wales[3]. In Scotland, licence for taking, possession or control of certain specimens	Marine Management Organisation, Countryside Council for Wales, Welsh Ministers

Act	Section/ Regulation	Consent/ Authorisation	Relevant Consenting Body
PART 1 of SCHEDULE 1 (England and Wales)			
Offshore Marine Conservation (Natural Habitats &c) Regulations 2007	49	Licence in relation to the use, capture or keeping of wild birds	Marine Management Organisation
Protection of Badgers Act 1992	10	Licences to kill, take or interfere with badgers	Natural England, Countryside Council for Wales, Welsh Ministers
Wildlife and Countryside Act 1981	16	Licences in relation to wild birds	Natural England, Countryside Council for Wales, Welsh Ministers
Environmental Permitting (England and Wales) Regulations 2010	Permit	Environmental Permit or exemption from the requirement for a Permit	Environment Agency
Water Resources Act 1991	24, 25	Abstraction and impounding licences	Environment Agency
Water Resources Act 1991	32, 109, 164 and byelaws under 5, 6, 6A of Sch 25	Consent for abstraction; consent for structures in over or under a main river; consent for discharges; byelaws for flood defences; byelaws for fisheries purposes and fisheries byelaws for marine or aquatic environmental purposes	Environment Agency
Water Resources Act 1991	73	Ordinary and emergency drought orders	Environment Agency
Water Resources Act 1991	79A	Drought permits	Environment Agency

Act	Section/ Regulation	Consent/ Authorisation	Relevant Consenting Body
PART 1 of SCHEDULE 1 (England and Wales)			
Water Industry Act 1991	166	Consent for certain discharges under s165	Environment Agency
Land Drainage Act 1991	17, 23	S17 repealed. S23 consent for erecting an obstruction in a watercourse	Environment Agency
Greenhouse Gas Emissions Trading Scheme Regulations 2005	Permit	Repealed[4]. Listed as a permit in the 2010 Regulations	Environment Agency
Persistent Organic Pollutants Regulations 2007	8	Authorisation to be dealt with under Part 2 of Annex V of Regulation (EC) No. 850/2004	Environment Agency
Water Industry Act 1991	Part 4, Ch 3	A notice of determination of a reference in relation to discharge of trade effluent into a public sewer	Sewerage undertaker
PART 2 of SCHEDULE 1 (Wales only)			
Planning (Listed Buildings and Conservation Areas) Act 1990	8	Authorisation of works, Listed building consent	Local Planning Authority/ Secretary of State
Planning (Listed Buildings and Conservation Areas) Act 1990	74	Conservation area consent for demolition	Local Planning Authority/ Secretary of State
Ancient Monuments and Archaeological Areas Act 1979	2, 3	Scheduled monument consent	Secretary of State
Protection of Wrecks Act 1973	1	Restricted area licence	Secretary of State

Act	Section/ Regulation	Consent/ Authorisation	Relevant Consenting Body
PART 2 of SCHEDULE 1 (Wales only)			
Town and Country Planning Act 1990	198	Consent under a tree preservation order	National Assembly for Wales
Town and Country Planning Act 1990	211	Consent in relation to trees in a conservation area	Local Planning Authority
Planning (Hazardous Substances) Act 1990	13, 17, 18	Hazardous substance consent	Hazardous Substance Authority, usually the district council
Salmon and Freshwater Fisheries Act 1975	26	Confirmation or variation of an order in relation to limitation of fishing licences	Water authority, confirmed by Welsh Ministers. The Environment Agency may also make orders
Hedgerows Regulations 1997	5	Removal of hedgerows consent	Local Planning Authority
Public Health Act 1936	263	Approval to culvert or cover a watercourse in an urban district	Local Authority
Coast Protection Act 1949	16	Coastal protection work consent	Coast Protection Authority (district council)
Coast Protection Act 1949	18	Excavation of materials on or under the seashore licence	Coast Protection Authority (district council)
Food and Environment Protection Act 1985	8	Licence in relation to deposits into the sea (Scotland only)	Licensing Authority
Water Industry Act 1991	110A	Order of the Authority in relation to new connections to public sewers	Water Services Regulation Authority
Water Industry Act 1991	118	Consent for discharge of trade effluent into a public sewer	Sewerage undertaker

Act	Section/ Regulation	Consent/ Authorisation	Relevant Consenting Body
PART 2 of SCHEDULE 1 (Wales only)			
Clean Air Act 1993	4	Approval of installation notice in relation to a new furnace	Local Authority
Clean Air Act 1993	6, 8, 15	Approval of plant for arresting grit and dust; approval for height of chimney	Local Authority
Clean Air Act 1993	7	Exemption from s6(1) of the Act	Local Authority
Clean Air Act 1993	14	Exemption from height of chimney regulations	Local Authority of Secretary of State
Clean Air Act 1993	16(2)	Height of other chimneys prevention of the smoke, grit, dust or gases from becoming prejudicial to health or a nuisance	Local Authority
Clean Air Act 1993	20	Exemption of fireplaces in relation to smoke in a smoke control area	Local Authority
Environmental Permitting (England and Wales) Regulations	Permit	Environmental Permit where the local authority is the regulator	Local Authority
Pipe-lines Act 1962	15	Consent to place a pipeline in a street	Street Authority
Road Traffic Regulation Act 1984	1, 9, 14, 15, 22B	Traffic regulation order; experimental traffic order; temporary restriction or prohibition on roads; 22B repealed	Local Traffic Authority

Act	Section/ Regulation	Consent/ Authorisation	Relevant Consenting Body
PART 2 of SCHEDULE 1 (Wales only)			
Town and Country Planning Act 1990	247	Stopping up or diversion of a highway order	Secretary of State
Town and Country Planning Act 1990	257	Stopping up or diversion of a footpath, bridleway or restricted byway	Local Authority
Inclosure Act 1845	147	Repealed by Commons Act 2006	
Inclosure Act 1847	4	Repealed by Commons Act 2006	
Inclosure Act 1852	14	Order distinguishing allotments, town and village greens by metes and bounds (but not fenced)	Commissioners
Inclosure Act 1854	5, 9, 11	Order of exchange, partition or division; fencing and making roads dispensed with; order apportioning rent and fixed payments and determining extent, identify and boundaries of land charged	Commissioners
Inclosure Act 1857	1, 5	Disposal of fences; Repealed by Commons Act 2006	Commissioners
Commons Act 1876	15	Consent or authorisation required under byelaws made by owners in relation to pasture land	Lord of the Manor

Act	Section/ Regulation	Consent/ Authorisation	Relevant Consenting Body
PART 2 of SCHEDULE 1 (Wales only)			
Commons Act 1899	1, 10	Consent or authorisations required under byelaws or made under a scheme for regulation and management of a common	District Council
Law of Property Act 1925	193	Impositions of limitations on rights of access	Welsh Ministers
Coity Wallia Commons Act 1976	6, 10	Private Act. Consents in relation to Coity Wallia Common	Conservators
Health and Safety at Work Act 1974	16	Approval of codes of practice	Health and Safety Executive
Ionising Radiations Regulations 1999	5	Authorisation of specified practices in relation to x-ray and accelerator equipment	Health and Safety Executive
Radiation (Emergency Preparedness and Public Information) Regulations 2001	4, 5	Any assessment required in relation to hazard identification and risk evaluation	Health and Safety Executive
Conservation of Seals Act 1970	10	Licence to kill or take seals	Marine Management Organisation
National Parks and Access to the Countryside Act 1949	20	Authorisation pursuant to byelaws for the protection of nature reserves	Natural England
Deer Act 1991	8	Licences in relation to moving deer or taking deer alive	Natural England, Countryside Council for Wales, Welsh Ministers

Act	Section/ Regulation	Consent/ Authorisation	Relevant Consenting Body
PART 2 of SCHEDULE 1 (Wales only)			
Wildlife and Countryside Act 1981	28E	Consent for operations within a SSSI	Natural England
Wildlife and Countryside Act 1981	53	An order in relation to the duty to keep the definitive map and statement under continuous review	Natural England
Countryside and Rights of Way Act 2000	17	A consent or authorisation required under byelaws in relation to rights of access	Natural England
Countryside and Rights of Way Act 2000	24, 25, 26	Direction in relation to the exclusion or restriction of access in relation to land management, fire risks, salt flats and nature conservation	Coastal Margin – Natural England; Land in a National Park – National Parks Authority; any other land – appropriate countryside body
Salmon and Freshwater Fisheries Act 1975	30	Consent for introduction of fish into inland waters	Environment Agency
Import of Live Fish (England and Wales) Act 1980	1	Consent in relation to import, keeping or release of non-native live fish	Environment Agency, Secretary of State and Natural England/ Countryside Council for Wales
Water Resources (Environmental Impact Assessment) Regulations 2003	9	Consent in relation to abstracting or impounding water	Environment Agency

Act	Section/ Regulation	Consent/ Authorisation	Relevant Consenting Body
PART 2 of SCHEDULE 1 (Wales only)			
Environmental Protection (Disposal of Polychlorinated Biphenyls and other Dangerous Substances) (England and Wales) Regulations 2000	9	A registration with regards to inventories of contaminated equipment	Environment Agency
Control of Pesticides Regulations 1986	Consent	Consent in relation to advertising, control, storage, supply and sale of pesticides	Ministers
Hazardous Waste (England and Wales) Regulations 2005	21	A registration in relation to notification of premises	Environment Agency

Obtaining the consent of the relevant body

Experience is tending to demonstrate that the 'relevant bodies' are often reluctant to give up their consenting or authorising powers and that it is, in fact, proving difficult to promoters to include Schedule 1 consents and authorisations in a DCO.[34]

Indeed, the Planning Inspectorate's own guidance in relation to the Countryside Council for Wales as a consenting authority notes that in relation to the consents listed in Part 2 of Schedule 1 to the Regulations:

> 'These are consents that would normally be granted by CCW. CCW would generally not agree to these consents being included within a development consent order but will consider this on a case by case basis.'

PINS Advice Note 11: 'Working with public bodies in the infrastructure planning process' provides the following guidance to promoters:

> 'Certain prescribed consents etc can be consented separately or included in a DCO. s150 of the 2008 Act provides that these consents can only be included in a DCO if the relevant consenting body agrees to their inclusion. *Developers*

3 Currently, Part 1 of Schedule 1 (England and Wales) does not refer to regulations 53, 54, and 55 of the Conservation of Habitats and Species Regulations 2010, which contains the updated provisions.

4 Part 1 of Schedule 1 has not yet been updated to take account of the Greenhouse Gas Emissions Trading Scheme Regulations 2012.

> *will need to engage early in the pre-application stage with consultees that have such consenting powers, so that it is clear by the time an application is submitted whether such consents are to be included in a draft DCO.*' (emphasis added)

Paragraph 27 of the DCLG 'Guidance on the pre-application process' (March 2015) provides the following advice to relevant consenting bodies and promoters:

> 'Where an applicant proposes to include non-planning consents within their Development Consent Order, the bodies that would normally be responsible for granting those consents should make every effort to facilitate this. They should only object to the inclusion of such non-planning consents with good reason, and after careful consideration of reasonable alternatives. It is therefore important that such bodies are consulted at an early stage.'

Expanding and improving the 'one stop shop' approach to consents

On 22 November 2012 DCLG published a consultation seeking views on proposals to expand and improve the 'one stop shop' approach for consents under the 2008 Act. In its response, published in March 2013, the Government announced its proposals to establish a 'Consents Service Unit' (CSU) within PINS and to make changes to streamline the Infrastructure Planning (Miscellaneous Prescribed Provisions) Regulations 2010 and the Infrastructure Planning (Applications: Prescribed Forms and Procedure) Regulations 2009.

In April 2013 the Government established a new 'Consents Service Unit' within PINS and, in its response to consultation document (Major infrastructure planning: expanding and improving the 'one stop shop' approach for consents – summary of responses and government response') is stated (paragraph 14) that:

> 'The Consents Service Unit, to be based in the Planning Inspectorate, will be operational from April 2013 and will offer a bespoke service to those developers that want to use it. It will provide a lead contact to work with the developer and relevant consenting bodies (with a strong emphasis on the pre-application stage), to coordinate a logical and systematic approach to the handling of 12 different consents which may be required in addition to development consent under the 2008 Act. These consents could be required during the construction phase and/or the operational phase. The aim is to ensure that, where possible, these are dealt with in parallel. The Unit's key role will be to facilitate effective and efficient decision-making, including identifying any process blockages and resource needs, and escalate such issues where necessary.'

In May 2013 PINS published the 'Consents Service Unit for Nationally Significant Infrastructure Projects – Prospectus for Developers' and a 'Frequently Asked Questions' document that both explain the workings of the CSU. The Prospectus for Developers was republished in July 2015.

The Discharge of DCO Requirements

Written by: Michael Humphries QC, ftb

Introduction

PA 2008, s 120(1) provides that an order granting development consent may impose 'requirements' in connection with the development for which development consent is granted.

PA 2008, s 120 further provides that:

'(2) The requirements may in particular include –

(a) requirements corresponding to conditions which could have been imposed on the grant of any permission, consent or authorisation, or the giving of any notice, which (but for section 33(1)) would have been required for the development;

(b) requirements to obtain the approval of the Secretary of State or any other person, so far as not within paragraph (a).'

This article considers the following matters in relation to the discharge of DCO requirements:

- Drafting requirements to be discharged;
- The appropriate discharge body;
- Appealing the discharging authority's decision; and
- Fees.

Drafting requirements to be discharged

Requirements are frequently drafted so as to require the submission of written details of an aspect of the development to a 'discharging authority' that then has the power to 'approve' or otherwise such details prior to development, or a stage of the development, commencing. Such pre-commencement requirements are commonplace as planning conditions and considerable judicial authority exists on their interpretation.

The DCO procedure does give the opportunity, however, to create bespoke requirements and definitions to suite the particular circumstances of a project. Three concepts will be considered:

- The definition of the term 'commence';
- The expression 'unless otherwise approved'; and
- Non-material changes.

The definition of the term 'commence'

Model requirement 2 in Schedule 4 to the Infrastructure Planning (Model Provisions) (England and Wales) Order 2010 ('the Model Provisions Order') states that 'The authorised development must be *begun* within [insert number] years of the date of this order.' (emphasis added). PA 2008, s 155 defines when development is taken to have 'begun' for the purposes of s 154 and such a definition is also relevant to a requirement (such as model requirement 2) in a DCO.

The Model Provisions Order, however, also make extensive use of the term 'commence', such as in model requirement 3 ('No authorised development shall commence until …'). However this term is not defined in the Model Provisions Order, either in the General Model Provisions (Schedule 1) definitions or in the 'model requirements' (Schedule 4) definitions. Nor is the term defined in the 2008 Act itself. Thus if the term 'commence' is not to be given its 'ordinary meaning', it may be appropriate to define it in the DCO itself.

> In the Hinkley Point C nuclear generating station DCO (Schedule 2 paragraph 1 – interpretation) the term 'commencement' (and the words 'commence' and 'commenced') as being *'the carrying out of a material operation, as defined in section 155 of the Planning Act 2008 (which explains when development begins), comprised in or carried out for the purposes of the authorised project'*.

In the Hinckley Point C (Connection Project) draft DCO (Schedule 3 paragraph 1 – interpretation) the term 'commence' was defined negatively so as to exclude certain activities that might otherwise have been captured by the ordinary meaning of the word.

The definition adopted was designed to allow the promoter to undertake certain identified preparatory and investigatory works before discharging the terms of any pre-commencement requirement.

The expression 'unless otherwise approved'

Expressions such as 'unless otherwise approved' or 'save to the extent that revised plans [etc] have been submitted to and approved' have been relatively common in planning conditions and are similarly being proposed in DCO requirements.

In the Hinkley Point C nuclear power station DCO requirement PW4 provides that:

> '(1) Buildings and structures comprising Works Nos … shall be carried out in accordance with the plans as set out in … of this Order, *save to the extent that revised plans* relating to the siting, scale or appearance *have been submitted to and approved by the local planning authority*.' (emphasis added)

In relation to planning conditions, the Courts have generally been reluctant to endorse expressions such as 'unless otherwise approved', as they may have the effect of allowing a form of development that was not assessed or permitted: see, for example, *Henry Boot Home Limited v Bassetlaw DC* [2002] EWCA Civ 983 at paras 51-54. Having said that, the Courts have accepted there may be some scope for non-material amendments to a permitted development.

> In *R (Midcounties Co-operative Limited) v Wyre Forest DC* [2009] EWHC 964 the Court considered a planning condition (condition 6) that set a retail floorspace limit but then stated *'unless otherwise agreed in writing with the Local Planning Authority'* and a further condition (condition 4) that required 'strict compliance' with various plans and drawings *'unless other minor variations are agreed in writing after the date of this permission and before implementation with the Local Planning Authority.'*

In relation to the condition 6 'tailpiece' the court held (para 70) that:

> 'As I shall come to in connection with another condition, I accept the existence of a very limited power to make immaterial variations informally. But while the tailpiece in the condition in question could be applied in that way, it contains no words purporting to limits its application.'

In relation to condition 4, however, the Court held (para 79) that:

> 'I do not regard this tailpiece as unlawful. Its clear scope is to enable 'minor variations' to an obligation otherwise to develop 'in strict accordance' with plans and drawings. Both parts of the condition operate to limit the flexibility which the tailpiece provides.'

The court added (para 81) that:

> 'In my judgement this scope covers at least those circumstances in which the change is immaterial in the sense that no reasonable local planning authority could refuse it, or take enforcement proceedings lawfully in respect of its implementation. I do not exclude other jurisprudential bases.'

There does appear to be, therefore, some limited flexibility for a planning condition to vary a permitted development. See also the approach of the Court in *R (Halebank PC) v Halton BC* 2012 EWHC 1889 (Admin) applying the approach in Mid-Counties and rejecting the approach taken by the deputy judge in *R (Warley) v Wealden DC* [2011] EWHC 2083 (Admin) (see paras 100/101).

In the Hinkley Point C nuclear generating station DCO, the applicant included a provision in the following terms (see Schedule 11 para 1(5) (interpretation)):

> 'Where any requirement specifies 'unless otherwise approved' by the discharging authority or requires the applicant to demonstrate the existence of exceptional circumstances such approval shall not be given or exceptional circumstances agreed except in relation to minor or immaterial changes where it has been demonstrated to the satisfaction of the discharging authority that the subject-matter of the approval sought or the undertaker's proposed response to exceptional circumstances is unlikely to give rise to any materially new or materially different environmental effects from those assessed in the Environmental Statement.' (emphasis added)

This form of wording appears to be acceptable to the Secretary of State and may form a precedent for other DCOs.

PINS Advice Note 15: Drafting Development Consent Orders (October 2014) states (para 19.4 and 'Good practice point') that a 'tailpiece' requirement should not allow the local planning authority to approve details which stray outside the parameters set for the development and that applicants should provide 'justification' in relation to each tailpiece proposed.

Non-material changes

PA 2008, s 153, Sch 6, para 2 enables the Secretary of State to make certain changes to a DCO if the Secretary of State is satisfied that the change is not material. In deciding whether a change is material, the Secretary of State must have regard to the effect of the change, together with any previous changes made under paragraph 2, on the DCO as originally made. The power allows the Secretary of State to impose new requirements in connection with the development, as well as removing or altering existing requirements. The power in paragraph 2 may only be exercised on an application made to the Secretary of State made by, or on behalf of, the applicant or a successor in title of the applicant; a person with an interest in land; or, any other person for whose benefit the DCO has effect.

This approach broadly reflects that set out at section 96A of the Town and Country Planning Act 1990. That section allows a local planning authority to make 'non-material changes' to a planning permission. In principle, it would appear that this provision could be applied and adapted to permit a local planning authority to make non-material changes to the requirements under a DCO. PA 2008, s 120(5) allows a DCO to apply, modify or exclude a statutory provision which relates to a matter for which provision may be made in the order, although it would be a matter for the Secretary of State whether such a provision was necessary or appropriate.

The appropriate discharge authority

In the 'model requirements' at Schedule 4 to the Model Provisions Order it is clearly contemplated that DCO requirements will be discharged by the (then) Infrastructure Planning Commission ('the IPC'), now the Planning Inspectorate ('PINS'). Model requirement 3, for example, states that: 'No [stage of the] authorised development shall commence until [for that stage] written details of the following have, after consultation with the relevant planning authority, been *submitted to and approved by the Commission.'* (emphasis added).

Since the 'model requirements' were published in 2009, however, the IPC has made it clear that it is not resourced to act as the 'discharge authority' for DCO requirements and PINS appears to be adopting the same position. In its 'Guidance for local authorities' (March 2010), DCLG stated that:

> 'as is the case under the previous regime, scheme promoters should normally be able to appeal local authority decisions on a subsequent approval – though not by appealing under the TCPA. Instead *the IPC can include provision in each Development Consent Order that allows it to determine any subsequent approval in default of agreement or approval by the LPA*. We will be amending the Infrastructure Planning (Model Provisions) Order 2009 to reflect this is due

course.' (emphasis added). Although no such amendment was made to the Model Provisions Order, the change of emphasis from the Commission as the primary discharge authority to the commission as default or appeal discharge authority is clear.

In 18 January 2012 the IPC stated in a response in its website 'Register of Advice' that 'Generally discharges of requirements are dealt with by the relevant local authority or statutory undertaker rather than the IPC.' In its April 2012 Advice Note 13 PINS stated (page 4) that 'The developer should seek to agree wording for proposed requirements with the body to whom details are to be submitted for subsequent approval, and in any event seek the local planning authority's views on proposed requirements as they will enforce any breach of terms of any order granted.' This last advice appears to contemplate that the 'discharge authority' could be a body other than the local planning authority, although the local planning authority's role as consultee 'in any event' is emphasised as is its role in enforcing any requirements.

This last point seems important. The PA 2008 makes a breach of the terms of a DCO a criminal offence (see s 161), but makes the relevant local planning authority responsible for the service of a notice of unauthorised development under s 169. It is likely, therefore, that in most cases the most appropriate discharge authority for a DCO requirement will be the relevant local planning authority. That is not to suggest that other bodies may not be the discharge authority in particular circumstances, but PINS is likely to need some convincing that a requirement should be discharge by one body, but enforced by another. Certainly the Secretary of State has shown no enthusiasm for take on the role of discharge authority, although the Secretary of State could be asked to take on that role if particular circumstances indicated that it was appropriate.

Certainly the experience so far is that it is the relevant local planning authority which has been given responsibility for the discharge of DCO requirements.

Appealing the discharging authority's decision

Where conditional planning permission is granted under s 72 of the Town and Country Planning Act 1990 an applicant may appeal to the Secretary of State against a local planning authority's decision to 'refuse an application for any consent, agreement or approval of that authority required by a condition imposed on the grant of planning permission or grant it subject to conditions': see s 78(1)(b) of the 1990 Act. Similarly, an applicant may appeal to the Secretary of State where the local planning authority has failed to determine such an application: see s 78(2) of the 1990 Act. Section 79 deals with the determination of appeals under s 78. Regulations and guidance set out the procedures to be followed in relation to such appeals.

No such equivalent procedure is prescribed under the Planning Act 2008 and neither is there a model provision in the Infrastructure Planning (Model Provisions)(England and Wales) Order 2009, SI 2009/2265 ('the Model Provisions Order') that sets out a preferred appeal mechanism following refusal or conditional grant of an application under a DCO requirement.

In broad terms, emerging practice has identified two solutions to this issue, being:

- The application and adaptation of Part III of the Town and Country Planning Act 1990; and
- The creation of a bespoke system for the discharge of requirements.

The application and adaptation of Part III of the Town and Country Planning Act 1990.

This solution simply seeks to incorporate, with any necessary modifications, the system for appealing planning conditions contained within Part III of the Town and Country Planning Act 1990. Typically, a DCO provision will simply allow an appeal against refusal, grant subject to conditions or non-determination of an application to discharge a DCO requirement to be made under Part III of the 1990 Act as if the requirement were a condition under s 78 of that Act. An example of this approach may be found in the Preesall underground gas storage project DCO. In principle, this approach could allow some adaptation of the 1990 Act system by, for example, modifying timescales or other procedural steps. Any wholesale amendment of the 1990 system, however, is likely (in effect) to fall within the second of the above approaches.

The creation of a bespoke system for the discharge of requirements

An alternative approach seeks to create a bespoke system for the discharge of DCO requirements. This approach may be less straight forward, but does give the opportunity to tailor a system for the discharge of DCO requirements to the particular circumstances of the project. For example, it may be possible to create a 'fast track' written representations system with tight timescales for the exchange of representations and other procedural steps.

Such an approach was adopted in the Hinkley Point C nuclear generating station DCO: see Schedule 14 to that Order.

Fees

As stated above, PA 2008 does not create a mechanism for the discharge of DCO requirements and so does not, therefore, specify any fee structure for local planning authorities acting as the discharge authority under any such requirements.

Three potential mechanism exist under which a fee structure may be identified, being:

- Planning Performance Agreements;
- PA 2008, s 106 obligations; and
- DCO provisions/schedules.

Planning Performance Agreements

Planning Performance Agreements (PPAs) between local planning authorities (LPAs) and applicants for major development projects have been around since 2007, following a Planning Advisory Service and ATLAS pilot project in 2006. The Communities and local Government (CLG) and ATLAS Guidance Note, 'Implementing Planning Performance Agreements', advises that 'Planning Performance Agreements are essentially a collaborative project management process primarily aimed at complex development proposals.'. PPAs can be drafted to set *inter alia* target timetables for the performance of identified steps in the consideration of applications for major development projects.

The CLG/ATLAS Guidance Note observes, at paragraph 2.3, that 'The PPA process could be used at any stage in a development project, from Area Action Plan formation through to reserved matters.' It seems clear, therefore, that there is no objection in principle to PPAs being used in the context of the discharge of planning conditions, and, by extension therefore, DCO requirements. A number of bodies have produced 'good practice' guidance on PPAs.

In a circular letter to local authorities from the Department for Communities and Local Government and the Department of Energy and Climate Change dated 16 July 2009, it was made clear that PPAs are a mechanism available to LPAs within the context of PA 2008.

If performance under a PPA would involve an LPA in additional costs beyond those reflected in any application fee, then this can be recovered through the PPA. This may be particularly attractive to local planning authorities discharging 'requirements' under a DCO where there is no formal application fee mechanism. It does need to be stressed, however, that PPAs are collaborative agreements and cannot be imposed on a hostile local planning authority or, for that matter, an unwilling developer.

PA 2008, s 106 obligations

An appropriately drafted planning obligation may present a further or alternative opportunity to set out a mechanism for the payment of fees to local planning authorities discharging DCO requirements. Indeed, the opportunity to submit a unilateral planning obligation may be particularly attractive where a local planning authority is unable or unwilling to enter into a PPA. Such a mechanism may also be drafted so as to incentivise early decision making by the discharge authority.

A unilateral PA 2008, s 106 obligation cannot, however, impose any positive obligation on a non-party. In other words, a unilateral section 106 obligation cannot require a local planning authority to meet particular positive performance targets, although it may provide for payments based on a local planning authority meeting particular timescales for the determination of discharge applications.

In relation to the Preesall underground gas storage project, the applicant recognised that the relevant local planning authority could have resourcing issues in discharging DCO requirements and set up a 'Discharge Contribution' mechanism in Pt 4 of Sch 1 to its s 106 obligation. The Preesall s 106 obligation set up a mechanism for the discharge of DCO requirements that included 'discharge contributions' to cover the local planning authority's costs; 'timescales' for the determination of discharge applications; and 'penalties' in the event of timescales being exceeded.

DCO provisions/schedules

PA 2008, s 120(5)(d) provides that a DCO may include 'This power would appear to be wide enough to allow the DCO to make provision for payments to be made to local planning authorities discharging DCO requirements. Such a provision would appear to be 'incidental' or 'consequential' upon any DCO provision or requirement making a local planning authority the 'discharge authority' for a DCO requirement.

The Relationship between Development Consent and Marine Licensing

Written by: Michael Humphries QC, ftb

Introduction

A number of Nationally Significant Infrastructure Projects (NSIPs) and associated development are proposed partly on land and partly within the UK marine licensing area, where development would normally require a marine licence granted by the Marine Management Organisation (MMO) or the Welsh Government Marine Consents Unit under Part 4 of the Marine and Coastal Access Act 2009. PA 2008 allows a DCO to include a *deemed* marine licence, thereby removing the requirement to seek separate consent under the 2009 Act. This micro-article examines the relationship between development consent and marine licensing.

A general discussion of the role of the MMO within the Planning Act 2008 regime is set out at Annex B of PINS Advice Note 11: working with public bodies in the infrastructure planning process.

Development within the UK marine licencing area

Part 4 of the Marine and Coastal Access Act 2009 sets up a regime for the licensing of 'licensable marine activities' within 'the UK marine licensing area': see ss 65 and 66 of the 2009 Act. There is a long list of 'licensable marine activities' within s 66 of the 2009 Act which would encompass most forms of 'development' likely to be the subject-matter of an application for development consent. 'Section 66(4) of the 2009 Act defines 'the UK marine licensing area' as consisting of 'the UK marine area' other than the Scottish inshore region. The term 'UK marine area' is itself defined in s 42 of the 2009 Act to include the area of sea within the seaward limits of the territorial sea adjacent to the United Kingdom, any area of sea within the limits of the 'exclusive economic zone', and the area of sea within the limits of the UK sector of the continental shelf. The term 'sea' is defined in s 42 to include any area submerged at mean high water spring tide.

PA 2008, s 31 makes it clear that development consent is required for development to the extent that the development is, or forms part of, an NSIP. The classes of NSIP for which development consent is required are defined by ss 14–30 and, in many cases, include: (a) development in waters adjacent to England and Wales up to the limits of the territorial sea; and (b) development in a Renewable Energy Zone (except where the Scottish Ministers have functions). Furthermore, by PA 2008, s 115(1), development consent may also be granted for 'associated development' if it is to be carried out in England, waters adjacent to England up to the limits of the territorial sea, or in a Renewable Energy Zone (except where the Scottish Ministers have functions). Note that a DCO may not include 'associated development' in waters adjacent to Wales.

It is clear from the above, however, that development consent may be required for development that would also be a 'licensable marine activity' under the 2009 Act.

Development consent

By PA 2008, s 103, it is the Secretary of State that has the function of deciding an application for an order granting development consent and, as stated above, development consent may be granted for both the development for which development consent if required (ie the NSIP) and for 'associated development'.

PA 2008, s 149A provides that:

> "(1) An order granting development consent may include provision deeming a marine licence to have been issued under Part 4 of the Marine and Coastal Access Act 2009 (marine licensing) for any activity only if the activity is to be carried out wholly in one or more of the areas specified in subsection (2).
>
> (2) The areas are –
>
> (a) England,
>
> (b) waters adjacent to England up to the seaward limits of the territorial sea,
>
> (c) an exclusive economic zone, except any part of an exclusive economic zone in relation to which the Scottish Ministers have functions,
>
> (d) a Renewable Energy Zone, except any part of a Renewable Energy Zone in relation to which the Scottish Ministers have functions,
>
> (e) an area designated under section 1(7) of the Continental Shelf Act 1964, except any part of that area which is within a part of an exclusive economic zone or Renewable Energy Zone in relation to which the Scottish Ministers have functions."

A deemed marine licence under s 149A is, therefore, part of the DCO granted by the Secretary of State and is not actually a marine licence granted by the MMO under the 2009 Act. Furthermore, to the extent that a DCO includes a deemed marine licence, then it is axiomatic that the 'activities' covered by that deemed licence will not require a separate marine licence granted by the MMO under the 2009 Act.

The role of the MMO in relation to applications for development consent

The MMO has an important role in relation to applications for development consent. This role is set out in s 23 of the 2009 Act, which makes various amendments to PA 2008.

PA 2008, s 42 is amended to inset a new subsection (1)(aa) so that there is a duty to consult the MMO 'in any case where the proposed development would affect, or would be likely to affect, any of the areas specified in subsection (2)'. A new subsection (2) is then inserted, as follows:

'(2) The areas are –

(a) waters adjacent to England up to the seaward limits of the territorial sea,

(b) an exclusive economic zone, except any part of an exclusive economic zone in relation to which the Scottish Ministers have functions,

(c) a Renewable Energy Zone, except any part of a Renewable Energy Zone in relation to which the Scottish Ministers have functions,

(d an area designated under section 1(7) of the Continental Shelf Act 1964, except any part of that area which is within a part of an exclusive economic zone or Renewable Energy Zone in relation to which the Scottish Ministers have functions.'

For shorthand, these are simply referred to below as 'the s 43(2) areas'.

Thus the MMO's role as consultee extends beyond the circumstances where development is actually proposed within any of the s 42(2) areas and includes circumstances where the proposed development would affect, *or would be likely to affect*, any such area.

Interestingly, section 23(7) of the 2009 Act provides that the Secretary of State must give guidance to the MMO as to 'the kind of representations which may be made by the MMO' under (a) Chapter 2 of Part 5 of PA 2008 (pre-application procedure), or (b) Part 6 of that Act (deciding applications for orders granting development consent). This guidance was issued by Defra as 'Government guidance to the Marine Management Organisation (MMO) on its role in relation to applications, and proposed applications, to the Infrastructure Planning Commission (IPC) for development consent under the Planning Act 2008' (September 2008).

Paragraph 29 of the Defra guidance states that;

> "The MMO is the UK Government's expert body on marine management and it is in this capacity that the MMO should contribute to proposed applications. Therefore, when the MMO is consulted it should limit its representations and comments on the proposed application to those matters that directly relate to its marine management role. A matter is directly related to the MMO's functions only insofar as the proposed development involves an activity or operation which the developer intends to carry out in an area, or likely to affect an area, mentioned above [that is, one of the section 42(2) areas]. It would, for example, be appropriate for the MMO to comment on any piers or jetties associated with an onshore power station development, as these may affect the areas specified in the MCA Act."

Section 23 of the 2009 Act also amends s 56 (duty to notify persons of accepted applications) and s 102 (definition of 'interested party') to include reference to the MMO "where the development for which the application seeks development consent would involve the carrying on of any activity" in one or more of the s 42(2) areas.

Thus for the purposes of ss 56 and 102, the MMO's role is confined to circumstances where the 'activity' would actually be carried on within any of the s 42(2) areas.

By making the MMO an 'interested party' it is clearly contemplated that the MMO will be given the opportunity to play a role during the examination of any application for development consent. Paragraph 42 of the Defra guidance states that: 'The MMO will be invited to any specific issue hearings (see section 91 of the Planning Act) or open floor hearings (see section 93 of the Planning Act) where it can submit representations orally.'

Paragraph 43, however, puts this in context by making clear that: 'When the MMO attends a preliminary meeting or subsequent hearings or makes written representations to the IPC, the MMO should limit its representations on the application to those that directly relate to its marine management role, for example, as a licensing authority or marine planning authority.'

DCO 'requirements' and deemed marine licence 'conditions'

PA 2008, s 120 states that:

> '(1) An order granting development consent may impose requirements in connection with the development for which consent is granted.
>
> (2) The requirements may in particular include –
>
> (a) requirements corresponding to conditions which could have been imposed on the grant of any permission, consent or authorisation, or giving of any notice, which (but for section 33(1)) would have been required for the development;
>
> (b) requirements to obtain the approval of the Secretary of State or any other person, so far as not within paragraph (a).
>
> (3) An order granting development consent may make provision relating to, or matters ancillary to, the development for which consent is granted.
>
> (4) The provision that may be made under subsection (3) includes in particular provision for or relating to any of the matters listed in Part 1 of Schedule 5.'

The list of matters in Part 1 of Schedule 5 includes the following:

> '30A Deeming a marine licence under Part 4 of the Marine and Coastal Access Act 2009 to have been given by the Secretary of State for activities specified in the order and subject to such conditions as may be specified in the order.
>
> 30B Deeming any such conditions to have been attached to the marine licence by the Secretary of State under that Part.'

It is important to note, however, that both the 'requirements' under the DCO and the 'conditions' under the deemed marine licence are all part of the DCO granted by the Secretary of State. In other words, the conditions attached to the deemed marine licence are simply DCO provisions that happen to be in a schedule to the

DCO entitled 'Deemed Marine Licence'. A deemed marine licence will typically be included in a schedule to the DCO in a form that mimics an actual marine licence, but that should not obscure its status as part of the development consent granted by the Secretary of State.

This may be relevant in circumstances where a single DCO 'work' is partly on land and partly within the UK marine licensing area. It may be inappropriate, in relation to a single 'work', to have one body (possibly the local planning authority) responsible to the discharge and enforcement of 'requirements' for that part of the work on land and another body (the MMO) responsible for the discharge and enforcement of 'conditions' for that part of the work within the UK marine licensing area.

Exactly this situation occurred in relation to the Preesall Underground Gas Storage DCO, where part of an underground gas storage cavern was several hundred metres below land and part of it was several hundred metres below an estuary that was within the UK marine licencing area. Clearly it made no sense to have the local planning authority responsible for the discharge and enforcement of requirements relating to part of a cavern and the MMO responsible for the discharge and enforcement of identical conditions relating to the other part of a cavern. In that case the promoter and the two discharging /enforcing authorities agreed that the caverns should be granted a deemed marine licence in respect of such parts that fell within the UK marine licencing area, but that they should be exempted from the conditions imposed under the deemed marine licence and, instead, made the subject of requirements under the DCO.

This reallocation of functions between the local planning authority and the MMO does not cause any jurisdictional conflict, however, in circumstances where the deemed marine licence is simply part of the DCO granted by the Secretary of State.

Enforcement of conditions in a deemed marine licence

DCO requirements are enforced under Part 8 of PA 2008. Deemed marine licence conditions, by contrast, are enforced under Part 4 of the 2009 Act.

PA 2008, s 160 makes it an offence to carry out, or cause to be carried out, development for which development consent is required at a time when no development consent is in force in respect of the development. PA 2008, s 161 creates a further offence where, without reasonable excuse, a person: (a) carries out, or causes to be carried out, development in breach of the terms of an order granting development consent; or (b) otherwise fails to comply with the terms of an order granting development consent.

PA 2008, s 161, therefore, makes it an offence not to comply with a DCO 'requirement' and, it might be thought, a deemed marine licence 'condition'. The 2009 Act, however, inserted a new s 149A(4) into PA 2008, which provides as follows in relation to deemed marine licence conditions:

> '(4) A person who fails to comply with such a condition does not commit an offence under section 161 of this Act.'

This provision does not prevent s 161 being used to enforce any DCO requirement, as opposed to deemed marine licence condition, that happens to apply to the UK marine licensing area.

The enforcement provisions for marine licences are set out at Part 4, Chapter 3 of the 2009 Act. Sections 85-89 set out provisions relating to offences where there has been failure to comply with a condition of a marine licence and ss 90–92 set out provisions relating to enforcement notices where there has been failure to comply with a marine licence condition.

Paragraph 45 of the Defra Guidance (above) states that:

> 'The MMO should prosecute any alleged offences in the marine area under the MCA Act, though it is open to bring legal proceedings for offences in the marine area under sections 160 or 161 of the Planning Act 2008 should this be deemed appropriate (for instance, where particular terms of a DCO do not flow into a deemed marine consent).'

Protective Provisions

Written by Richard Honey
Edited by Michael Humphries QC

The nature of protective provisions

Protective provisions are common in DCOs. They impose limitations on the exercise of the powers under the DCO, or give rights to people affected by the DCO, in order to reduce the potential adverse effect of the project. They are normally used to strike a balance in the overall public interest between the competing needs of public authorities and similar organisations that have an interest in the same land or infrastructure.

Protective provisions are usually put in place for those who operate other infrastructure of one sort or another which may be affected by a development, such as highways and rail authorities, electricity and water utilities, communications equipment operators and the like. Protective provisions may occasionally also extend to private parties who may be specially affected by a project.

The nature of protective provisions is such that they tend not only to place restrictions on the promoter's exercise of its powers but also include provisions requiring the protected party to perform functions. Examples of typical or notable protective provisions are given below.

The need for protective provisions

Those authorities at risk of being adversely affected by a project will normally object to the development, due to its effects on their interests, but express a willingness to withdraw the objection if sufficient safeguards can be put in place. It is normally possible to have such safeguards put in place through agreements between the parties, but often objectors will want them included in the DCO in order to provide greater assurance that they will be observed. Often considerable time is spent trying to resolve objections by way of the agreement of protective provisions.

The former Infrastructure Planning (Model Provisions) (England and Wales) Order 2009 included Schedule L into which protective provisions were to be inserted. Protective provisions need not, however, be included in every case. The Brechfa Forest West Wind Farm Order 2013 and the Palm Paper Mill Generating Station Order 2016, for example, do not contain any protective provisions.

Protective provisions at the pre-application stage

It is advisable if at all possible to negotiate and agree protective provisions with those affected by a project during the pre-application stage. This is not always possible, however. In such circumstances, PINS Advice Note 15 (October 2014) recommends (para 3.1) that 'applicants should as a minimum submit on application the standard protective provision of the relevant party with the amendments that the applicant is seeking to it', commenting also that 'submitting blank schedules is not acceptable'. This point has also been made by the Inspectorate in relation to particular applications: 'where protective provisions are to be included in a DCO the Planning Inspectorate would prefer to see them included in the draft DCO that is submitted for acceptance' (register of advice, 5 July 2012, Willington C Gas Pipeline).

Even if protective provisions are included in a draft DCO by agreement, the promoter will still need to satisfy the Examining Authority that they are necessary and appropriate.

Standard protective provisions

Some promoters, such as Network Rail, have their own standard protective provisions, which they include in DCOs that they promote. These contain protections for statutory undertakers and communications network operators. Additional or bespoke provisions are likely to be necessary in the particular circumstances of any case.

Network Rail also has standard protective provisions that it requires to be included in any DCO promoted by another party, which is likely to affect its railway undertaking. An example is the protective provisions included in the A160/A180 (Port of Immingham Improvement) Development Consent Order 2015. The provisions cover matters such as making the exercise of compulsory purchase powers subject to the consent of Network Rail, the approval of designs, carrying out protective works, and remedying harm done by the execution of the works.

PINS Advice Note 15 also recommends that where protective provisions are drafted by others, the drafting is reviewed by the applicant to ensure the provisions 'fit in with the terminology and style of the rest of the DCO and are suitably drafted for use in an SI' (para 3.2).

Negotiating protective provisions post-examination

Negotiations on protective provisions may only be concluded during the course of the examination of a project. The final, agreed provisions will then have to be substituted for whatever had been included in the draft DCO, or inserted if nothing had been included.

In the case of the A14 Cambridge to Huntingdon Improvement DCO, it appears that negotiations broke down shortly before the Secretary of State's decision in relation to land drainage matters, so that both the land drainage consent dis-application and the related protective provisions were removed from the draft shortly before the DCO was made (decision letter, 11 May 2016). Ultimately, the A14 Cambridge to Huntingdon Improvement Scheme Development Consent Order 2016 contained protective provisions in Schedule 9 for the usual statutory undertakers, the Environment Agency, National Grid, Network Rail, Anglian Water, a pipeline operator, and the County Council in relation to watercourses.

For the Port Talbot Steelworks Generating Station Order 2015, proposed protective provisions included in the draft DCO, in favour of Associated British Ports ('ABP'), were omitted by the Secretary of State after the examination, as the promoter and ABP reached a separate agreement following the close of the examination (decision letter, 8 December 2015, para 4.11). There was therefore no longer any need for the provisions to be included in the order. There were, however, protective provisions in Schedule 4 in favour of Network Rail, Western Power Distribution, National Grid and Welsh Water.

Example protective provisions

An example of fairly extensive protective provisions is the Able Marine Energy Park Development Consent Order 2014, which contained protective provisions in Schedule 9. There were protective provisions in favour of the Humber Conservancy, the Environment Agency, the Highways Agency, Network Rail, National Grid, harbour authorities, a number of statutory undertakers, and some private companies. Examples include provisions that substitute rights had to be provided before existing rights were extinguished, and that junction improvements had to be made before any part of the development was implemented. As the Examining authority noted in its report, in this case 'it was evident from an early stage that the negotiation of protective provisions would be a complex and contested process' (report, 24 February 2013, para 19.15). Six versions of the protective provisions were provided during the examination.

Another example of protective provisions on a similar scale are those in the National Grid (Hinkley Point C Connection Project) Order 2016, which contained provisions in Schedule 15 to protect: electricity, gas, water and sewerage undertakers; operators of electronic communications code networks; highway authorities; Network Rail; First Corporate Shipping Limited in relation to its operation of the Bristol Port; the Environment Agency in relation to flood defence and drainage structures; RWE Generation UK plc in relation to its wharf and other facilities for the Aberthaw power station; and CLH Pipeline Systems Ltd in relation to its pipeline.

In the East Midlands Gateway Rail Freight Interchange and Highway Order 2016, Art 38 gave effect to protective provisions in Schedules 15 to 21. They include the provisions broadly summarised below:

- National Grid: rights in relation to apparatus in stopped-up streets, no acquisition of interests other than by agreement, no removal of apparatus until alternative apparatus has been constructed, alternative apparatus to be constructed as agreed with NG, rights for alternative apparatus to be no less favourable, protection of retained apparatus, payment of expenses, an indemnity, ground subsidence monitoring, co-ordination of works, alternative access, and arbitration.
- East Midlands Airport: compliance with the safeguarding strategy for the airport, production of a bird management plan to minimise any bird hazard impact, approval of any radio or solar equipment in the development, access, and arbitration.
- Severn Trent Water: compliance with the Construction Management Strategy for Safeguarding the Derwent Valley Aqueduct.
- Network Rail: limitation on use of certain powers except with the consent of NR, no acquisition of new rights except with the consent of NR, provision

of plans for approval by NR, construction of protective works, making good damage, provision of access and information by both parties, alterations and additions to the works by NR, payment of costs and expenses, dealing with electromagnetic interference, and control over illumination.

- Highways England: approval of detailed design and works programme, approval of contractors, provision of security for the carrying out of the highway works, agreement of traffic management provisions, carrying out works to the satisfaction of HE, payment of costs and expenses, making good defects, insurance, indemnity, and warranties.
- Leicestershire County Council (as highways authority): approval of detailed design and works programme, maintenance, payment, indemnity, bond or alternative security, arbitration, protection of apparatus, satisfactory workmanship, traffic control, approval of contractors, inspection of works, and insurance.
- Tarmac: supply of detailed design information and works programme, not obstruct access to quarry / landfill / bagging plant, alteration of haul roads, payment of expenses, requirement to construct access for Tarmac before existing access is closed, reinstatement, and arbitration.

In the Thorpe Marsh Gas Pipeline Order 2016, Schedule 9 contains protective provisions for Network Rail and National Grid and then generic provisions for the protection of electricity, gas, water and sewerage statutory undertakers (Part 3) and for the protection of operators of electronic communications code networks (Part 4). The provisions of Part 3 include that no apparatus can be acquired other than by agreement, no apparatus can be removed without alternative apparatus being constructed and brought into operation, the imposition of requirements on carrying out of works, the payment of expenses, and making good and paying compensation for any damage done. The provisions of Part 4 include making good and paying compensation for any damage done.

Similar generic provisions are included in other DCOs, including for example Preesall Underground Gas Storage Facility Order 2015 and the A19/A1058 Coast Road (Junction Improvement) Development Consent Order 2016.

Examples of notable protective provisions include:

- Part 3 of Schedule 8 to the Preesall Underground Gas Storage Facility Order 2015, which protects Blackpool BC in relation to trams, including to protect access to tramway property, approval of plans, carrying out protective works, making good damage, paying expenses, an indemnity, and includes an arbitration provision.
- Part 3 of Schedule 13 to the Norfolk County Council (Norwich Northern Distributor Road (A1067 to A47(T))) Order 2015, which protects Anglian Water Services, including prevention of working within standard protection strips around pipes without agreement from AWS, no work to apparatus without all necessary consents being obtained, no acquisition of apparatus other than by agreement, alternative means of access, notification by the undertaker to AWS of the location of previously unmapped assets, and making good damage and paying reasonable compensation.

- Part 1 of Schedule 8 to Swansea Bay Tidal Generating Station Order 2015, which protects Associated British Ports, including preventing acquisition other than with consent of ABP, restriction on the exercise of some powers in respect of ABP's land, approval of plans and arrangements for the development, imposition of requirements by ABP to protect the harbour, remedy of any erosion or accumulation due to the construction of a tidal work, and an indemnity. There are also similar provisions in Part 2 for the benefit of the Neath Port Authority, and provisions in Part 8 for Swansea Council in relation to accumulation in the River Tawe.
- Part 3 of Schedule 10 to the Network Rail (Redditch Branch Enhancement) Order 2013, which protects the Canal and River Trust, including no interference with access to the Worcester and Birmingham Canal or the supply of water to or from the canal without the consent of the CRT, control over the discharge of water to the canal, pre-construction surveying of the canal, approval of plans, imposition of protective works, prevention of pollution, and an indemnity.
- Part 4 of Schedule 7 to the Network Rail (Ipswich Chord) Order 2012, which protects the Felixstowe Dock operators in relation to taking possession of or imposing speed restrictions on the railway, and Part 5 which protects the National Health Service in relation to making parking spaces available to the National Health Service Blood and Transplant authority.

What Ancillary Matters may be included in a DCO

Written by Ned Westaway, ftb
Edited by Michael Humphries QC, ftb

Introduction

Whilst other parts of this work examine the scope of what may be included in a 'nationally significant infrastructure project' and 'associated development', this article considers the dividing line in PA 2008, Part 7 and Sch 5 between what other matters can and cannot be included in a DCO.

Express inclusions

A significant aim of the PA 2008 was to create a 'one-stop shop' for certain major infrastructure project consents. The regime created falls short of that. Nevertheless, a very considerable number of matters may be expressly included in a DCO.

PA 2008, s 120 states that:

> '(3) An order granting development consent may make provision relating to, or to matters ancillary to, the development for which consent is granted.
>
> (4) The provision that may be made under subsection (3) includes in particular provision for or relating to any of the matters listed in Part 1 of Schedule 5.'

The use of the word 'includes' in PA 2008, s 120(4) makes it clear that the items listed in Part 1 of Sch 5 are not intended to be an exhaustive list of the matters for which provision may be made in a DCO. The scope of PA 2008, s 120(3) is sufficiently wide to allow a DCO to make provision for any matter, that is not otherwise excluded, so long as it relates to, or to matters ancillary to, the development for which development consent in granted. Thus, for example, Sch 5 says nothing about the temporary possession of land for construction or maintenance purposes and yet nearly every DCO so far made includes such provision by virtue of the wording of PA 2008, s 120(3). Nevertheless, Sch 5 does helpfully identify a very wide range of matters that may be included in a DCO.

One of the most significant matters that is expressly identified in Sch 5 is the acquisition of land, or rights over land, including Green Belt land (PA 2008, ss 122–134 and 147, Sch 5 paras 1, 2 and 8).

Also of note are:

- The carrying out of specified excavation, mining, quarrying or boring operations (PA 2008, Sch 5 para 4)

- The operation of a generating station (PA 2008, s 140, Sch 5, para 5)
- Keeping electric lines installed above ground (PA 2008, s 141, Sch 5, para 6)
- The use of underground gas storage facilities (PA 2008, s 142, Sch 5, para 7)
- The carrying out of surveys or taking of soil samples (PA 2008, Sch 5, para 12)
- The cutting down, uprooting, topping or lopping trees or shrubs or cutting back their roots (although in Wales this requires the consent of the local planning authority) (PA 2008, Sch 5, para 13)
- The extinguishment or removal of statutory undertakers' rights and the removal, disposal or resiting of apparatus (s PA 2008, s 138, Sch 5, para 14)
- The carrying out of civil engineering or other works (PA 2008, Sch 5, para 15)
- The diversion of watercourses (PA 2008, s 143, Sch 5, para 16)
- The extinguishment of diversion of highways or rights of way (PA 2008, s 136, Sch 5 para 17)
- The charging of tolls, fares, penalty fares and other charges (PA 2008, s 144, Sch 5, para 18)
- The designation, specification of traffic upon, appropriation or transfer of highways (PA 2008, Sch 5, paras 19–23)
- The operation and maintenance of a transport system (PA 2008, Sch 5, para 24)
- The entering into an agreement for the provision of police services (PA 2008, Sch 5, para 25)
- The authorisation of discharges of water into inland waters or underground strata (PA 2008, s 146, Sch 5, para 26)
- The deemed licensing of marine activities (PA 2008, s 149A, Sch 5, paras 30A and 30B)
- The creation, or amendment of the powers and duties, of a harbour authority (PA 2008, s 145, Sch 5, paras 31 and 32, subject to the restriction in s 145(6)(b))
- The transfer of property, rights, liabilities, or functions (PA 2008, Sch 5, para 33)
- The transfer, leasing, suspension, discontinuance and revival of undertakings (PA 2008, Sch 5, para 34)
- The payment of contributions or compensation (PA 2008, Sch 5, paras 35 and 36)
- The submission of disputes to arbitration (PA 2008, Sch 5, para 37)
- The alteration of borrowing limits (PA 2008, Sch 5, para 38)

There is now a body of authorised DCOs where examples of the above provisions may be found. Many of them are also referred to in the (now lapsed) Infrastructure Planning (Model Provisions) (England and Wales) Order 2009.

There are some obvious restrictions on the inclusion of certain provisions. For example, a DCO may only include provisions relating to a harbour authority if the DCO application includes the construction or alteration of harbour facilities. As stated above, s 120(3) requires that any matter for which provision is to be made in a DCO must relate to, or be a matter ancillary to, the development for which consent is granted.

By PA 2008, s 150 (read together with the Infrastructure Planning (Interested Parties and Miscellaneous Prescribed Provisions) Regulations 2015) a DCO may include provisions removing the requirement for a range of further consents and authorisations, but only if the relevant consenting body agrees. There is also a restriction on a DCO permitting works (etc) on common land except in accordance with the compulsory acquisition provisions (which may involve special parliamentary procedure) in PA 2008, ss132 and 133 (s 139).

Relating or ancillary

As stated above, the matters listed in Sch 5 are not exhaustive of what may be included in a DCO under PA 2008, s 120(3). It is therefore possible for a DCO to include other matters of a similar nature. This will comprise matters relating to, or matters ancillary to, the NSIP itself, such as operation and maintenance (see above), but also matters relating or ancillary to any associated development.

There is no guidance on what constitutes an 'ancillary' matter. However, 'ancillary' in the planning context is usually differentiated from 'primary'. In practice, this relies upon a subjective judgment as to type and scale, it is a test of functional relationship rather than extent (see *Main v Secretary of State for the Environment* (1998) 77 P & CR 300).

A good example of the extent of matters that may be regarded as relating to, or ancillary, is the inclusion in the draft DCO for the Silvertown Tunnel of control and charging provisions for the *existing* Blackwall Tunnel. The Explanatory Memorandum explains that '[t]he implementation of user charging is critical to achieving the objectives of the Scheme, by acting as a demand management tool for traffic using the crossings' (para 3.3). The traffic flows on surrounding highway network will be changed by the construction and operation of the Silvertown Tunnel and, in that context, the ability to manage that network is seen as essential to the successful implementation of the Silvertown Tunnel itself. In that case, there is a clear functional link with the proposed development. Charging provisions may, however, not always be acceptable. The inclusion of provisions for the charging of tolls on highways is expressly provided for in the PA 2008 (s 144 and Schedule 5 para 18).

Necessary or expedient to give full effect to DCO

An alternative justification for provisions in a DCO is PA 2008, s 120 (5)(c) under which an order may include 'any provision that appears to the Secretary of State to be necessary or expedient for giving full effect to any other provision of the order'. This provides a useful reserve basis for a DCO to contain consequential provisions, for example a requirement for further consents or the making of TCPA, s 106 agreements to secure the delivery of off-site benefits.

Protective provisions

DCOs routinely include provisions protecting the property or interests of any person affected, or potentially affected, by a scheme (Schedule 5 para 10). They also may impose or exclude liability in respect of acts or omissions (Schedule 5 para 11). Protective provisions are generally reserved for the protection of the property or other assets of statutory undertakers, such as National Grid, the Canal and River Trust or Communication Code operators.

Application, disapplication or modification of statutory provisions

A DCO may also make provision applying, modifying or excluding a statutory provision that relates to any matter in the order (PA 2008, s 120(5)(a)) or making such amendments, repeals or revocations of 'statutory provisions of local application' as appear to the Secretary of State to be necessary or expedient (PA 2008, s120(5)(b)).

These provisions are based upon similar earlier powers for orders under the Transport and Works Act 1992 (s 5) and the Harbours Act 1964 (s 14). They apply to public or private Acts of Parliament, but will be of particular use in respect of private local Acts relating to infrastructure such as railways, that may preclude upgrades or other changes.

Incorporated into the PA 2008, however, the power in a DCO to apply, modify or exclude a statutory provision is of more general application and is not restricted to transport or harbour projects. That was the subject of some concerns during debate in the House of Lords. Responding to those concerns, the then Secretary of State, Lord Adonis, referred to 'a number of safeguards … to ensure that these essential powers are not used inappropriately or without proper scrutiny'. These were: (i) that the promoter of a DCO must include the legislation it is sought to alter in the application; (ii) the form of the draft order will be based on model provisions; (iii) there are limits on the creation of byelaws or criminal offences (but see below), (iv) a DCO may only be approved if it is in accordance the relevant NPS; and (iv) the Secretary of State may change the terms of a DCO if it would contravene EU law or Convention rights.

The (now lapsed) Infrastructure Planning (Model Provisions) (England and Wales) Order 2009 provided generic text in the general model provisions (Schedule 1) and the model provisions for railways (Schedule 2) for the application and modification of existing legislation. Also, model provision 54 of the model provisions for harbours (Schedule 3) provided as follows:

> '(1) Regulation 60 of the Conservation (Natural Habitats, &c.) Regulations 1994 (general development orders) ('the Habitats Regulations') shall not apply to any planning permission which relates to the works authorised by article 7 (subsidiary works) and which is granted by article 3(1) of the Town and Country Planning (General Permitted Development) Order 1995 for the class of development described as permitted development in Part 11 of Schedule 2 to that Order.
>
> (2) Paragraph (1) does not apply if and to the extent that those works—
>
> (a) do not form part of the plan and project which was subject to an appropriate assessment in accordance with regulation 48 of the

Habitats Regulations (assessment of implications for European Site) in connection with the making of this Order; and

(b) are not the subject of a further consent, permission or authorisation by a competent authority as defined in the Habitats Regulations.'

This gives a helpful example of the extent to which PA 2008, s 120(5)(a) may be used to disapply primary legislation. However, attempts to disapply statutory provisions in DCOs may well be controversial. Prospective applicants should identify any statutory modifications or exclusions sought early, and provide a clear and reasoned justification for them.

Certain statutory provisions may not be modified or excluded (PA 2008, s 151), these are:

- Any provision of the Nuclear Installations Act 1965
- Liability for damage and injury due to escape of water from a reservoir constructed after 1930 under the Reservoirs Act 1975
- Civil liability of water undertakers for escapes of water from pipes under the Water Industry Act 1991
- Civil remedies for loss or damage due to water abstraction under the Water Resources Act 1991

Byelaws and the creation of offences

By Sch 5, para 32A a DCO may include provision for the making of byelaws and their enforcement. A DCO may also create offences in connection with any of the following:

'(a) non-payment of tolls, fares or other charges,

(b) a person's failure to give the person's name or address in accordance with provision relating to penalty fares,

(c) enforcement of byelaws, or

(d) construction, improvement, maintenance or management of a harbour' (Schedule 5 para 32B(1)).

Save for these limited examples, a DCO may not create, provide for the creation or alter powers in relation to the creation of offences (PA 2008, s 120(8)).

There are also controls on the severity of any offence thereby created, such that that offence may only be triable only summarily (ie in the magistrates' court) and the sentence is limited to a level 3 fine on the standard scale (currently £1,000) (para 32B(2)).

PA 2008, s 120(9)

Written by: Hereward Phillpot QC, ftb
Edited by: Michael Humphries QC, ftb

PA 2008, s 120(9)

PA 2008, s 120 identifies what may be included in an order granting development consent. PA 2008, s 120(9) provides as follows:

> 'To the extent that provision for or relating to a matter may be included in an order granting development consent, none of the following may include any such provision –
>
> (a) an order under section 14 or 16 of the Harbours Act 1964 (c 40) (orders in relation to harbours, docks and wharves);
>
> (b) an order under section 4(1) of the Gas Act 1965 (c 36) (order authorising storage of gas in underground strata);
>
> (c) an order under section 1 or 3 of the Transport and Works Act 1992 (c 42) (orders as to railways, tramways, inland waterways etc.)'.

The effect of this provision

PA 2008, s 120(9) is not particularly clearly drafted, and (at least initially) this led to different suggested interpretations being advanced as to its meaning and effect.

In approaching its interpretation, it is important to bear in mind that PA 2008, s 120 is not itself concerned with the consenting of development, rather it is concerned only with the nature of the matters ancillary to development (see s 120(3)) which may or may not be authorised via orders under three separate statutory regimes that confer order-making powers.

Restrictions on the consenting of development are to be found elsewhere in the PA 2008. It is clear that once development consent has been granted under the PA 2008 authorising a particular associated development, that development cannot subsequently be authorised under any of these separate order-making powers. This is because PA 2008, s 115(5) applies s 33(2) to 'associated development' for which development consent exists. The effect is to remove jurisdiction for that development under those other statutory regimes.

This statutory restriction operates in one direction only. It prevents the granting of, say, a Harbour Empowerment Order (HEO) for an associated development *after* the grant of a Development Consent Order (DCO) authorising that development, but not before.

Although the matter has not been tested in the courts, it is suggested that the effect of PA 2008, s 120(9) is twofold:

1 Once a DCO has been granted, it operates to prevent the granting of an order under the other statutory regimes which varies the ancillary matters authorised in that DCO. Any such variations would therefore need to be obtained via the procedure in the Infrastructure Planning (Changes to, and Revocation of, Development Consent Orders) Regulations 2011, SI 2011/2055.

2 It prevents promoters from obtaining consent for associated development in a DCO, but at the same time seeking authorisation for the necessary ancillary powers under a separate statutory regime. This supplementing of DCO powers via other statutory regimes is only permissible under PA 2008, s 120(9) where the provisions in question could not have been included in the DCO itself. Now that the former restriction on the creation of offences in a DCO has been revoked, there are likely to be few such provisions in practice.

Parallel applications

Subject to the important issue of relative timing, there is therefore nothing in PA 2008, s 120(9) which would prevent a promoter seeking an order under one of the other statutory regimes whilst at the same time seeking a DCO containing the same or similar provisions.

Neither PA 2008, s 115(5) nor s 120(9) prevents the relevant decision-maker from granting such an order in advance of the same development and ancillary matters being approved in a DCO. This remains the case even where an application has been made for the DCO in question.

This approach was used by EDF Energy in relation to the development of the Hinkley Point C new nuclear power station. EDF's proposal included the construction and operation of a large aggregates jetty (as associated development), to allow the import by sea of the majority of the aggregates needed to construct the power station. The early construction and availability of this jetty facility was considered likely to accelerate the construction of the power station itself, and to reduce its adverse effects, if and when that was authorised under the Planning Act 2008. EDF therefore sought and obtained powers to construct and operate the jetty through an application for a HEO under the Harbours Act 1964 and a Transport and Works Act Order (TWAO) under the Transport and Works Act 1992. Essentially identical powers were sought and subsequently obtained in the DCO.

In advance of the public inquiry into the application for a HEO and TWAO, the Department for Energy and Climate Change wrote to EDF asking for its views on whether PA 2008, s 120(9) caused any difficulties in reconciling the making of a HEO/TWAO with the existence of an application for a DCO which contains the same provisions. EDF responded to say that no such difficulties arose, for reasons which reflect the analysis set out above, and in due course the HEO and TWAO were both made and not challenged.

It should also be noted that shortly after that public exchange of correspondence, the IPC published Annex B to its then Advice Note 11 (Working with Public Bodies), which confirmed that such an approach was legitimate. The same advice is now to be found in Annex B to PINS Advice Note 11.

Part 9

Compulsory Purchase

Compulsory Purchase Powers in a DCO

Written by: Richard Honey, ftb
Edited by: Michael Humphries QC, ftb

Introduction

A development consent order (DCO) under the PA 2008 can authorise the compulsory acquisition of land or of an interest in or right over land. DCOs are unusual in that they are a means by which even purely private developers may secure compulsory purchase powers. Before the PA 2008 this was not possible; save in the case of the privatised utility companies and under the Pipelines Act 1962.

Even so, the Government's policy position appears still to be that promoters should seek to acquire land by negotiation wherever practicable and that powers of compulsory acquisition should only be sought where attempts to acquire land or rights by agreement have failed.

In this article, as in DCOs themselves, references to acquiring a right over land include acquiring it by the creation of a new right as well as by the acquisition of an existing one (PA 2008, s 159(3)). Particular provision is made for the acquisition of rights in relation to underground gas storage facilities, which is dealt with in PA 2008, s 133. That section covers rights to store gas in underground gas storage facilities, to stop up a well, borehole or shaft, or prevent its use by another person, and rights of way over land.

Conditions for the exercise of compulsory purchase powers

There are important conditions attaching to the use of compulsory purchase powers through DCOs. First, a DCO can include provision authorising the compulsory acquisition of land only if the Secretary of State is satisfied that the land (PA 2008, s 122):

- is required for the development to which the development consent relates (s 122(2)(a));
- is required to facilitate that development (s 122(2)(b);
- is incidental to that development (s 122(2)(b)); or
- is replacement land which is to be given in exchange for the order land (s 122(2)(c)).

The Inspectorate has said that the 'facilitate' and 'incidental' provisions in PA 2008, s 122(2)(b) could encompass the acquisition of land for the construction of development (eg a gas pipeline) which was not authorised by the DCO but which would be authorised by a later consent (register of advice, 17 November 2011, North Killinghome Power Project). In this regard, see also footnote 3 at paragraph 5 of the DCLG Guidance on associated development.

These are wide powers of compulsory purchase that are likely to be sufficient for promoters in most, if not all, cases. The further removed the land is from actually being required for the development, however, the more difficult it is likely to be in practice to justify the acquisition of the land in question.

Secondly, a further important condition must be satisfied under PA 2008, s 122(3), namely that there is a 'compelling case in the public interest' for the land to be acquired compulsorily. Whilst this wording reflects a long-standing policy test and had appeared in various court decisions (see, for example, *De Rothschild v Secretary of State For Transport* (1989) 57 P&CR 330), it was not previously a statutory requirement; indeed, s 122 remains the only place where it does appear as a statutory requirement.

Thirdly, a DCO can only authorise compulsory acquisition of land if one of three further conditions is met (PA 2008, s 123). They are that:

- the application for the order included a request for compulsory acquisition of the land to be authorised (s 123(2));
- all persons with an interest in the land consent to the inclusion of the provision (s 123(3)); or
- the prescribed procedure has been followed in relation to the land (s 123(4)).

The third condition above is based on an equivalent provision in the Acquisition of Land Act 1981. It deals with 'additional land', that is land which it is proposed shall be subject to compulsory acquisition and which was not identified in the book of reference submitted with the application. The procedure for the purposes of PA 2008, s (4) is prescribed in the Infrastructure Planning (Compulsory Acquisition) Regulations 2010, SI 2010/104.

Justification for the exercise of compulsory purchase powers

As well as satisfying the fundamental conditions set out above, it is necessary to show that the compulsory purchase proposed is properly justified.

The DCLG 'Guidance related to procedures for the compulsory acquisition of land' (September 2013) explains what justification will be sought for a DCO authorising the compulsory acquisition of land, including factors to which the decision-maker must have regard (paragraphs 8–19). This includes that:

- all reasonable alternatives to compulsory acquisition (including modifications to the scheme) have been explored (paragraph 8);
- the proposed interference with the rights of those with an interest in the land is for a legitimate purpose and is necessary and proportionate (paragraph 8);
- the applicant must have a clear idea of how it intends to use the land to be acquired (paragraph 9);
- there is a reasonable prospect of the requisite funds becoming available (paragraph 9);
- the purposes for which an order authorises the compulsory acquisition of land are legitimate and sufficiently justify interfering with the human rights of those with an interest in the land affected (paragraph 10);

- the land to be acquired is no more than is reasonably required for the purposes of the development (paragraph 11(i));
- there is compelling evidence that the public benefits that would be derived from the compulsory acquisition will outweigh the private loss that would be suffered by those whose land is to be acquired (paragraph 12).

In determining where the balance of public interest lies, the DCLG Guidance makes it clear (paragraph 14) that 'the Secretary of State will weigh up the public benefits that a scheme will bring against any private loss to those affected by compulsory acquisition.'

An applicant will also be required to provide a funding statement providing as much information as possible about the resource implications of both: (a) acquiring the land; and (b) implementing the project for which the land is required (paragraph 17).

Interestingly, the guidance does not say that the compulsory purchase of land is intended as a last resort in the event that attempts to acquire by agreement fail, as is stated for compulsory purchase orders generally in DCLG's 'Guidance on Compulsory Purchase Process and the Crichel Down Rules' (2015).

Nonetheless, applicants should not underestimate how hard it can be to demonstrate that these policy tests are satisfied in practice. In some cases, such as the expansion of an airport or a harbour, it may not be too difficult to show that the particular land is required. Similarly, in the case of linear schemes such as road and rail routes, it may be easier to show that there are no alternatives but to acquire compulsorily the interests in land which have not been acquired by agreement in advance. In other cases, however, such as offsite ecological compensation works or landscape planting, it may be very hard to show that the particular land is required. The DCLG Guidance states (paragraph 11(ii)) that the Secretary of State needs 'to be satisfied that the development *could only* be landscaped to a satisfactory standard if *the land in question* were to be compulsorily acquired' (emphasis added). This could be very hard to demonstrate in practice.

Types of land

There are various protective provisions in the Act for certain types of land, which are explained in turn below. It should be noted that the Growth and Infrastructure Act 2013 reduced the circumstances in which the special parliamentary procedure was to be engaged.

Statutory undertakers

PA 2008, s 127 provides protective provisions for the land of statutory undertakers which apply where land has been acquired, and is used, by a statutory undertaker for the purpose of its undertaking, and the undertaker makes a representation on the application. In those circumstances s 127(2) provides that the DCO can only include provision authorising the compulsory acquisition of the undertaker's land where the Secretary of State is satisfied that the nature and situation of the land are such that either:

- it can be purchased and not replaced without serious detriment to the carrying on of the undertaking, or

- if purchased it can be replaced by other land belonging to, or available for acquisition by, the undertakers without serious detriment to the carrying on of the undertaking.

PA 2008, s 127(5) makes a similar provision in relation to the acquisition of a right over the undertaker's land.

PA 2008, s 138 relates to DCOs which authorise the acquisition of land in which there subsists a right vested in a statutory undertaker for carrying on their operations or where there is on, under or over the land apparatus of the undertaker. This encompasses statutory undertakers as defined in Part 11 of the Town and Country Planning Act 1990 and electronic communications code network operators. The DCO can include provision for the extinguishment of the relevant right, or the removal of the relevant apparatus, only if the Secretary of State is satisfied that this would be necessary for the purpose of carrying out the development to which the DCO relates.

The Growth and Infrastructure Act 2013 had the effect of removing the special parliamentary procedure in cases where a statutory undertaker or local authority holds land.

National Trust

PA 2008, s 130 applies to land belonging to the National Trust which is held by the Trust inalienably. It provides that to the extent that the DCO authorises the compulsory acquisition of such land it must be subject to special parliamentary procedure if a representation has been made by the Trust about the application objecting to the compulsory acquisition of land.

Commons, open spaces etc

Commons and open spaces are covered in PA 2008, ss 131–132, along with land forming part of a fuel or field garden allotment. Section 131 relates to the acquisition of land and s 132 relates to the acquisition of rights over land. Under s 131 a DCO would be subject to special parliamentary procedure save in particular circumstances. Those circumstances are:

- replacement land has been or will be given in exchange for the order land and the replacement land has been or will be vested in the prospective seller and subject to the same rights, trusts and incidents as attach to the order land (s 131(4));
- for open space only, either there is no suitable land available to be given in exchange for the order land or any suitable land available to be given in exchange is available only at prohibitive cost, and it is strongly in the public interest for the development for which the order grants consent to be capable of being begun sooner than is likely to be possible if the order were to be subject (to any extent) to special parliamentary procedure (s 131(4A));
- for open space only, where the order land is being acquired for a temporary (although possibly long-lived) purpose (s 131(4B));

- where the order land does not exceed 200 sq m or is required for the widening or drainage of an existing highway, and the giving in exchange of other land is unnecessary, whether in the interests of the persons, if any, entitled to rights of common or other rights or in the interests of the public (s 131(5)).

PA 2008, s 132 sets out similar provisions in relation to the compulsory purchase of rights over land, although there are differences between the two provisions.

Green Belt

PA 2008, s 147 applies where the DCO includes the compulsory acquisition (or exchange or appropriation) of Green Belt land. It requires that the Secretary of State must notify the relevant local authorities of the proposed acquisition.

Notification requirements

For pre-application consultation, PA 2008, ss 42 and 44 apply to people who are owners, tenants or occupiers of affected land and people the promoter thinks would or might be entitled to make a claim for compensation under s 10 of the Compulsory Purchase Act 1965 or Part I of the Land Compensation Act 1973. The same categories of persons must also be notified under s 56 and s 59.

Where a DCO is made which includes provision authorising the compulsory acquisition of land, PA 2008, s 134 requires that the promoter (known as a prospective purchaser) serve a 'compulsory acquisition notice' on owners, lessees and occupiers of the land that is to be acquired or to subject to rights being acquired. The persons who have to be served are those who would be qualifying persons for the purposes of s 12(1) of the Acquisition of Land Act 1981. The promoter also has to erect a compulsory acquisition notice on a conspicuous object or objects on or near the order land and, so far as practicable, keep it in place for six weeks, and publish a notice in one or more local newspapers.

PA 2008, s 134(7) explains that a compulsory acquisition notice is a notice in the prescribed form describing the order land (or the right if appropriate), stating that the DCO includes provision authorising the compulsory acquisition of land or a right over the land, where and when a copy of the order is available for inspection, and that a person aggrieved by the DCO may challenge it only in accordance with s 118. The form of notice is found in Schedule 1 to the Infrastructure Planning (Compulsory Acquisition) Regulations 2010.

Procedural requirements

There are various procedural provisions which apply to applications for a DCO where compulsory acquisition powers are sought. For example, the Infrastructure Planning (Applications: Prescribed Forms and Procedure) Regulations 2009, SI 2009/2264 require the provision with such applications of:

- a statement of reasons;

- a statement to indicate how the DCO is proposed to be funded;
- a land plan identifying land over which it is proposed to exercise powers of compulsory acquisition or any right to use land; and
- a book of reference.

There are also particular certification requirements in relation to s 56 (notification of an accepted application).

The DCLG Guidance related to procedures for compulsory acquisition provides advice on what is required for the land plans, funding statement and the statement of reasons. The Inspectorate has said that it would be prepared to provide advice on the content of draft funding statements (register of advice, 25 October 2012, Thames Tideway Tunnel). Funding is likely to be more of an issue with DCOs than traditional compulsory purchase orders because the compulsory acquisition powers in a DCO are often given to purely private bodies and carry with them the liability to pay proper compensation for land and rights acquired.

The guidance also encourages the use of alternative dispute resolution techniques to resolve concerns about the compulsory acquisition of land, including both mediation and early neutral evaluation.

The September 2013 version of the DCLG Guidance omitted what was said in the February 2010 version to the effect that a promoter should be negotiating in parallel with the compulsory purchase process to acquire land by agreement. It is unlikely, however, that this omission was intended to signal a significant change of position on the part of the Government. It remains advisable for promoters to seek to acquire land by agreement where possible and where appropriate within the financial constraints of the project.

PA 2008, s 106 provides that in deciding an application for an order granting development consent, representations may be disregarded if they relate to compensation for compulsory acquisition of land or of an interest in or right over land.

The duration of a DCO authorising the compulsory acquisition of land is covered in s 154, which provides that steps in relation to the acquisition must be taken within a particular time limit. That time limit is to be set out in the DCO and is commonly five years.

PA 2008, s 175 extends the blight regime in the Town and Country Planning Act 1990 to include land identified in a DCO to be subject to compulsory acquisition.

Illustrations from practice

An example of a DCO that included compulsory acquisition powers is the Hinkley Point C (Nuclear Generating Station) Order 2013, SI 2013/648, which grants powers for both the compulsory acquisition of land (art 24) and rights over land (art 27). It also includes powers for the temporary possession of land (art 33). It is notable that during the examination of that application the promoter offered a parent company guarantee of £10 million for the funding of compulsory acquisition compensation in order to satisfy the panel that adequate funding was in place. There was also a debate during the application about the permanent acquisition of land in circumstances where it was in fact only required temporarily, albeit for a period of years. The panel considered that if an owner offered to lease the land there would be no justification for compulsory acquisition but, in the absence of such an offer, a compelling case for the acquisition of the freehold would have been made out. The time limit for the exercise of compulsory acquisition powers was set as five years (art 26).

Incorporation of the Compulsory Purchase Code

Written by: Richard Honey, ftb
Edited by: Michael Humphries QC, ftb

Introduction

Where compulsory acquisition powers are incorporated into a development consent order, it is necessary for them to rely on the mechanisms and processes set out in other legislation for their efficacy. The 'compulsory purchase code' is the name that is commonly given to the disparate group statutory provisions that relate to compulsory purchase, supplemented by case law.

Parts of the compulsory purchase code

In essence, there are four parts to the compulsory purchase code being:

- the statutory power authorising compulsory purchase;
- the procedure for seeking an 'order' by which a statutory power authorising compulsory purchase is applied to a particular parcel of land;
- the implementation of the 'order' (particularly in relation to entry on the land and the transfer of title); and
- compulsory purchase compensation.

The statutory power authorising compulsory purchase

In relation to the PA 2008, s 122 grants the statutory power to include provision authorising the compulsory acquisition of land in a DCO. Subject to the requirements of s 122, that power is, therefore, available to any person who may properly apply for a development consent order.

This makes the powers of compulsory purchase potentially available to a whole range of developers who would not otherwise have had direct access to such powers. This can be contrasted to the compulsory purchase powers available under other regimes where the power is normally only available to a clearly defined class of person; for example, the relevant local authority under s 226 of the Town and County Planning Act 1990 or the relevant highway authority under s 239 of the Highways Act 1980. No such limitations exist under the Planning Act 2008.

The procedure for seeking an 'order' by which a statutory power authorising compulsory purchase is applied to a particular parcel of land

The procedure for seeking a development consent order is dealt with elsewhere in this work.

It is worth reminding the reader, however, that the Infrastructure Planning (Compulsory Acquisition) Regulations 2010, SI 2010/104 set out various procedural requirements that relate particularly to the compulsory acquisition of 'additional land' that was not included in the Book of Reference.

The implementation of the 'order' (particularly in relation to entry on the land and the transfer of title)

PA 2008, s 125 relates to the application of certain other parts of the compulsory purchase code in a development consent order and, in particular, relating to the implementation of the compulsory purchase powers within a DCO. The section applies if a DCO includes provision authorising the compulsory acquisition of land. It provides that Part 1 of the Compulsory Purchase Act 1965 ('CPA 1965') (procedure for compulsory purchase) applies to the compulsory acquisition of land under the DCO as it applies to a compulsory purchase to which Part 2 of the Acquisition of Land Act 1981 applies, as if the DCO were a compulsory purchase order under the 1981 Act. The provisions of the CPA 1965 govern the procedures to be followed once the compulsory acquisition of land has been authorised in the DCO.

PA 2008, s 125 provides however that, subject to any contrary provisions made by the DCO, Part 1 of the CPA 1965 will have effect with the omission of s 4 (time limit for exercise of compulsory purchase powers), s 10 (compensation for injurious affection) and paragraph 3(3) of Schedule 3 (provision as to giving of bonds).

The Planning Inspectorate has made clear that 'broadly, the same legislation applies in respect of procedural matters and how compensation is assessed and paid under the 2008 Act regime as for compulsory purchase under other regimes' (register of advice, 16 December 2010, Rampion Offshore Wind Farm).

The effect of PA 2008, s 125 would also apply Part 1 of the CPA 1965 to any acquisition of land following the service of a blight notice on the grounds that the land is blighted because its compulsory purchase is proposed in an application for a DCO. Section 175 amends the Town and Country Planning Act 1990 to apply the blight provisions to land in an application for a DCO or a DCO which is for compulsory acquisition and also land identified in national policy statements as suitable or potentially suitable for a development.

The procedures for implementing compulsory acquisition powers under a DCO are, therefore, the same as those for a compulsory purchase order, namely through Part 1 of the CPA 1965 and notices to treat and of entry. In addition, however, as is explained below, many DCOs also apply the Compulsory Purchase (Vesting Declarations) Act 1981. This creates an alternative means of implementing the compulsory purchase powers contained in a DCO and would allow the use of general vesting declarations.

Compulsory purchase compensation

Section 1 of the Land Compensation Act 1961 provides as follows:

> 'Where by or under any statute (whether passed before or after the passing of this Act) land is authorised to be acquired compulsorily, any question of disputed compensation and, where any part of the land to be acquired is subject to a lease which comprises land not acquired, any question as to the apportionment of the rent payable under the lease, shall be referred to the [Upper Tribunal] 2 and shall be determined by the Tribunal in accordance with the following provisions of this Act.'

Thus, where there is a dispute as to compensation, the compulsory purchase compensation provisions in the LCA 1961 are automatically applied to any compulsory purchase of land by the terms of s 1, unless specifically disapplied. The 'following provisions' of the 1961 Act referred to in s 1 include the six rules for assessing compensation set out in s 5, as follows:

> 'Compensation in respect of any compulsory acquisition shall be assessed in accordance with the following rules:
>
> (1) No allowance shall be made on account of the acquisition being compulsory:
>
> (2) The value of land shall, subject as hereinafter provided, be taken to be the amount which the land if sold in the open market by a willing seller might be expected to realise:
>
> (3) The special suitability or adaptability of the land for any purpose shall not be taken into account if that purpose is a purpose to which it could be applied only in pursuance of statutory powers, or for which there is no market apart from [...] 1 the requirements of any authority possessing compulsory purchase powers:
>
> (4) Where the value of the land is increased by reason of the use thereof or of any premises thereon in a manner which could be restrained by any court, or is contrary to law, or is detrimental to the health of the occupants of the premises or to the public health, the amount of that increase shall not be taken into account:
>
> (5) Where land is, and but for the compulsory acquisition would continue to be, devoted to a purpose of such a nature that there is no general demand or market for land for that purpose, the compensation may, if the [Upper Tribunal] 2 is satisfied that reinstatement in some other place is bona fide intended, be assessed on the basis of the reasonable cost of equivalent reinstatement:
>
> (6) The provisions of rule (2) shall not affect the assessment of compensation for disturbance or any other matter not directly based on the value of land:
>
> and the following provisions of this Part of this Act shall have effect with respect to the assessment.'

These rules form the starting point in most assessments of compulsory purchase compensation, although it needs to be recognised that the 1961 Act contains a number of other important provisions relating to the assessment of compulsory purchase compensation.

Part 1 of the Land Compensation Act 1973 (compensation for depreciation of land value by physical factors caused by use of public works) applies in relation to works authorised under a DCO, by means of s 152(7) of the 2008 Act, as if references in the LCA 1973 to 'public works' were references to 'authorised works' in the DCO. Part 1 of the LCA 1973 is however applied with the omission of s 1(6) and s 17, which relate to statutory immunity from nuisance.

Compensation is payable pursuant to s 165(4), for damage caused to land or chattels in the exercise of a relevant right of entry, by the local authority that authorised the entry to any person suffering damage. In circumstances where a dispute about such compensation is referred to the Upper Tribunal (Lands Chamber) for determination, s 165(6) provides that the provisions of s.4 of the LCA 1961 apply (with any necessary modifications). Section 4 of the LCA 1961 deals with the costs of Tribunal proceedings.

One important aspect of the compulsory purchase code that is amended by the PA 2008 is the disapplication of s 10 of the CPA 1965 (compensation for injurious affection) and its replacement by a bespoke provision. PA 2008, s 152 applies where a person affected by a DCO has no right to claim in nuisance (eg because of the provision in s 158 which gives a defence of statutory authority in civil or criminal proceedings for nuisance). PA 2008, s 152 gives a right to compensation for injurious affection in cases where a person would not be able to succeed in a claim for nuisance in respect of works authorised by the DCO.

By PA 2008, s 152(1), the section applies if by virtue of s 158 of the DCO there is a defence of statutory authority in civil or criminal proceedings for nuisance in respect of any authorised works. It defines 'authorised works' as including both development for which consent is granted by the DCO and anything else authorised by the DCO. The substantive obligation is in s 152(3), which provides that the person by or on whose behalf any authorised works are carried out must pay compensation to any person whose land is injuriously affected by the carrying out of the works. Section 152(8) provides that a DCO may not include provision the effect of which is to remove or modify the application of any of s 152(1)–(7), so that the provision is 'locked-in' to the DCO system.

The provision for compensation in PA 2008, s 152 effectively applies in lieu of s 10 of the CPA 1965. PA 2008, s 152(5) goes as far as to apply the limitation on compensation in s 10(2) of the CPA 1965 to compensation under s 152(3). Furthermore, s 152(6) applies to the construction of s 152(3) 'any rule or principle applied to the construction of section 10'. Section 152(3) provides compensation where 'land is injuriously affected by the carrying out of the works'. Section 10 of the CPA 1965, by contrast, provides compensation where a person's interest in land is injuriously affected by the execution of the works. It appears, therefore, that there is little difference between the ambit of the two provisions and that the intention is that the approach under s 10 of the CPA 1965 would apply to compensation for injurious affection under PA 2008, s 152.

Ability to modify or exclude a 'compensation provision'

It is important to note that the ability to 'modify' the application of a 'compensation provision', that is a provision in or made under an Act which relates to compulsory purchase compensation, is very limited by the terms of PA 2008, s 126 and can only be included to the extent necessary to apply the provision to the compulsory acquisition of land authorised by the order. Furthermore, a DCO may not include a provision the effect of which is to 'exclude' the application of a 'compensation provision'.

That said, there does appear to be some scope to introduce new provisions into a DCO relating to compulsory purchase compensation where the effect does not modify or exclude the application of an existing 'compensation provision'.

Compulsory purchase provisions in DCOs

As the number of projects passing through the Planning Act 2008 regime increases examples are beginning to emerge of additional or alternative compulsory purchase provisions in DCOs made by the Secretary of State. Some of these derive from the (now lapsed) Infrastructure Planning (Model Provisions)(England and Wales) Order 2009 and others are new.

Taking as an example the Hinkley Point C (Nuclear Generating Station) Order 2013, SI 2013/648, the DCO makes various additional provision for the application of the compulsory purchase code. SI 2013/648, art 27(3), Sch 11 provides for the modification of compensation and compulsory purchase statutes to deal with the creation of new rights.

Article 29 provides for the application of the Compulsory Purchase (Vesting Declarations) Act 1981 to the DCO as if it were a compulsory purchase order, with certain modifications. This enables the use of a general vesting declaration with DCOs, as opposed to notices to treat and of entry as would otherwise be the case.

Article 30 empowers the promoter to acquire only so much of, or such rights in, the subsoil of land as may be required, instead of acquiring the whole of the land. In such cases, Art 31 (considered below), applies where the promoter acquires a cellar, vault, arch or other construction forming part of a house, building or manufactory. The word 'manufactory' has been interpreted to mean a building whose main use is for manufacturing purposes, including ancillary or associated structures (see Roots, Humphries et al *The Law of Compulsory Purchase* (2nd edn, Bloomsbury Professional) at para D385).

By contrast, in the Network Rail (North Doncaster Chord) Order 2012, SI 2012/2635, art 27 applies not only to subsoil but also to 'the airspace over the land' (see also eg the Lancashire County Council (Torrisholme to the M6 Link (A683 Completion of Heysham to M6 Link Road)) Order 2013, SI 2013/675, art 25).

Article 31 of the Hinkley Point C (Nuclear Generating Station) Order 2013 deals with the acquisition of part of certain properties. It applies in place of s 8(1) of the CPA 1965 (which would otherwise apply by virtue of PA 2008, s 125) where a notice to treat is served on the owner of land forming only part of a house, building or manufactory or of land consisting of a house with a park or garden, to enable the owner to serve a counter-notice within 21 days objecting to the acquisition but stating that the owner is willing and able to sell the whole of the land. Unless the promoter agrees to acquire the whole then the issue of whether the owner should be required to sell only the land subject to the notice to treat must be referred to the Lands Chamber of the Upper Tribunal for determination. On such a reference the test is whether the land subject to the notice to treat can be acquired without material detriment to the remainder of the land subject to the counter-notice, or, where the land subject to the notice to treat consists of a house with a park or garden, without material detriment to the remainder of the land subject to the counter-notice and without seriously affecting the amenity and convenience of the house. If so, then the owner is required to sell the land subject to the notice to treat. Where under this process a notice to treat is deemed to cover less land or more land than originally specified in the notice, the promoter has 6 weeks in which it can withdraw the notice. If it does, then it must pay the owner compensation for any loss or expense caused by the giving and withdrawing of the notice to treat. Art 31(10) provides that where the owner is required to sell only part of the land or property, compensation is payable by the promoter for severance.

In arts 33 and 34 relating to the temporary use of land for carrying out and maintaining the project, it is provided that s 13 of the CPA 1965 relating to refusal to give possession to the authority applies to the temporary use as it would to the compulsory acquisition of land under the DCO.

There are various provisions in the Hinkley Point C (Nuclear Generating Station) Order 2013 which confer on persons affected by the exercise of powers under the DCO an entitlement to compensation, to be determined under Part 1 of the LCA 1961 where it is disputed. These provisions cover for example:

- any person who suffers loss by the suspension or extinguishment of any private right of way under art 15 (permanent stopping up of streets);
- any person who suffers loss by the suspension of any private right of way under art 17 (temporary stopping up of streets);
- owners and occupiers of any building or land in relation to which rights under art 22 (protective work to buildings) have been exercised for any loss or damage arising to them by reason of the exercise of those rights;
- owners and occupiers of the relevant land for any loss or damage arising by reason of the exercise of the authority conferred by art 23 to survey and investigate land;
- any person who suffers loss by the extinguishment or suspension of any private right of way under art 28 (private rights of way);
- any person who is an owner or occupier of land appropriated under art 32(1) (rights under or over streets), without the promoter acquiring any part of that person's interest in the land, and who suffers loss as a result;
- owners and occupiers of land of which temporary possession is taken under art 33 (temporary use of land for carrying out authorised project) for any loss or damage arising from the exercise in relation to the land of any power conferred by art 33;
- owners and occupiers of land of which temporary possession is taken under art 34 (temporary use of land for maintaining authorised project) for any loss or damage arising from the exercise in relation to the land of the provisions of art 34;

- any person who suffers any loss or damage arising from unnecessary damage to any tree or shrub when carrying out felling or lopping trees under art 41;
- any person who suffers any loss or damage arising from unnecessary damage to any tree or shrub subject to a tree preservation order under art 42.

Moreover, the Lancashire County Council (Torrisholme to the M6 Link (A683 Completion of Heysham to M6 Link Road)) Order 2013, SI 2013/675 contains in art 18 powers temporarily to close, interfere with and undertake works in the Lancaster Canal. art 18(7) provides that any person who suffers loss or damage as the result of either the suspension of any private right of navigation or any effect of the exercise of the art 18 powers on the functioning of any intake or discharge along the canal is entitled to compensation for such loss or damage.

Returning to the Network Rail (North Doncaster Chord) Order 2012, SI 2012/2635, art 41 of that DCO deals with the application of the Land Compensation Act 1973. It provides that regulations on the sound proofing of buildings affected by public works (eg the Noise Insulation (Railways and Other Guided Transport Systems) Regulations 1996, SI 1996/428 and the Noise Insulation Regulations 1975, SI 1975/1763) apply to the railway comprised in the authorised development under the DCO as if that railway was provided or used in the exercise of statutory powers.

Extinguishment of Public Rights of Way

Written by: Alex Booth, ftb
Edited by: Michael Humphries QC, ftb

Introduction

This article is concerned with the extinguishment of public rights of way and, in particular, PA 2008, ss 136 and 137.

Section 136 provides that a DCO may extinguish public rights of way, subject to one of two criteria contained in s 136(1) being met to the satisfaction of the Secretary of State. Section 136 is otherwise concerned with the procedure of extinguishment in circumstances where the land over which the right exists is authorised for acquisition by the DCO.

Section 137 is a discrete provision, relating to the extinguishment of rights over land that accommodates either apparatus belonging to statutory undertakers, or apparatus operated in connection with an electronic communications code network.

To date, the extent to which the relevant provisions have been considered during the examination process is limited. Furthermore, no guidance has yet been issued which might indicate how the provisions are intended to operate.

General provision as to extinguishment

PA 2008, s 136(1) stipulates that a DCO may only extinguish a public right of way if the Secretary of States is satisfied either:

> '(a) an alternative right of way has been or will be provided, or
>
> (b) the provision of an alternative right of way is not required.'

The inclusion of a discretion for the Secretary of State to authorise the extinguishment of a public right of way without replacement, in the event of his/her concluding that such replacement is not required, would appear to provide potential for dispute. The exercise of such discretion would presumably be subject to regulation by the courts by means of judicial review, the period for challenge being limited to six weeks from the date of publication of the order granting development consent by virtue of the Highways Act 1980, s 118(7).

In terms of the tests likely to be applied by the Secretary of State in this context, some limited assistance may be gained from decisions of the Courts in connection with the Highways Act 1980, s 118. Sections 118(1) and (2) require respectively:

(i) that a highways authority, when considering whether to extinguish a public right of way, should determine whether 'it is expedient that the ... way should be stopped upon on the ground that it is not needed for public use'; and

(ii) that the Secretary of State, when considering whether to confirm an order for extinguishment, should only do so having determined that 'it is expedient so to do having regard to the extent … that the path or way would … be likely to be used by the public, and having regard to the effect which the extinguishment or the right of way would have …'

The decisions of Phillips J in *R v Secretary of State ex parte Stewart* (1980) 39 P&CR 534 and Auld J in *R v Secretary of State ex parte Cheshire County Council* [1991] JPL 537 both offer some insight in this regard, though necessarily they are concerned with the statutory wording of s 118 as opposed to PA 2008, s 136. In the former, and as regards the second of the two tests, Phillips J effectively concluded in *ex p Stewart* (p 541) that where there was material demand for the route in question, it would not be 'expedient' to extinguish it.

However, the test in PA 2008, s 136(1)(b) is more broadly worded so as to suggest that a wide range of matters might be taken into consideration by the Secretary of State in the exercise of his discretion; such discretion to be exercised 'in the round'. At present, the extent to which the benefits of delivering the NSIP giving rise to the need for the extinguishment might fall to be considered in this context is unclear. However, it should be noted that, as regards development consented pursuant to the Town and Country Planning Act 1990, s 247 of that Act confers on the Secretary of State a broad discretion to stop up/extinguish any right of way if it is considered 'necessary' to enable development to be carried out. Paragraph 7.15 of the Rights of Way Circular 1/09 speaks in terms of the decision-maker weighing up 'the advantages' of making an order to extinguish a right of way; such 'advantage' must necessarily include the benefit that the consented development would deliver.

As regards provision of alternative routes pursuant to s 136(1)(a), potentially problematic is the absence of any temporal requirement as to when a replacement right of way must take be provided. The reference to an alternative right that 'has been … provided' must of course relate to a right which has come into existence prior to the date of the Secretary of State's decision in respect of the application. However the reference to the Secretary of State being 'satisfied' that an alternative right 'will be provided', without any requirement as to the date by which such replacement provision must available, might be thought to leave some scope for dispute regarding the sufficiency of the replacement right of way.

The provision in practice

The Rookery South development consent order application provides a useful illustration of how the provision may be expected to work in practice.

In that instance the DCO sought (and ultimately published) provided for the extinguishment of two short sections of footpath: see article 11 of and Schedule 3 to the DCO. By way of mitigation, the promoters were also proposing to upgrade various existing routes, as well as to provide limited new stretches of footpath/cycleway; the improvements to be provided by, s 106 obligation. Notwithstanding that the proposed new provision did not in any sense 'replicate' the routes lost (which routes the Examining Panel observed were 'effectively short stubs and [did] not lead anywhere'), the Panel felt able to conclude (para 5.144) that: 'We are satisfied therefore that alternatives would be provided to enable these public rights of way to be extinguished'.

Accordingly, at least in this instance, the decision-maker did not consider that an 'alternative right of way' being provided pursuant to PA 2008, s 136(1)(a) need reflect or even approximate the route which it replaced. Rather, it was enough that an additional route was being provided. This is significant, in that in the ordinary course of events one might have expected a 'replacement' route to serve the same function as the route to be extinguished, on a 'like for like' basis.

Procedural requirements

Extinguishment where land acquired

PA 2008, s 136(2) and (3) are concerned with circumstances where the order granting development consent makes provision for the acquisition of land, compulsorily or by agreement, and the order extinguishes a right of way that is not a right enjoyed be vehicular traffic. Section 136(3) proves in these circumstances that the order granting development consent may not provide for the right of way to be extinguished from a date which is earlier than that on which the order is 'published'.

It is worth pausing to consider the use of the word 'published' in this context. The term is used in a number of provisions within the PA 2008, but is not defined in s 235 or elsewhere. Its precise meaning in the context of PA 2008 is significant, if only because the six week period within which judicial review proceedings must be brought in respect of legal challenge to the grant of a DCO pursuant to the Highways Act 1980, s 118(1), runs from the date on which the DCO or the statement of reasons in respect of it are 'published' (s 118(1)(b)).

As yet there is no judicial interpretation as to the statutory meaning of the term, either in the context of, PA 2008, s 136(3) or anywhere else in the PA 2008. However, read so as to give practical meaning to the provision, it appears that the intention of the draftsman was to preclude the extinguishment of a public right of way by a DCO until such time as the DCO has been formally 'published' by the HMSO (as the Queen's Printer of Acts of Parliament).

Revival of right of way where acquisition of land abandoned

The remaining provisions of PA 2008, s 136 (s 136(4), (5) and (7)) relate to the circumstances where a public right of way has been extinguished by a DCO, but the anticipated acquisition of land over which the right formerly existed has not been completed. In these circumstances, where 'it appears to the Secretary of State that the proposal to acquire the land has been abandoned' (s 136(4)(b)), then the Secretary of State must make an order 'reviving' the extinguished right.

The provision is clearly intended to avoid the permanent loss to the public, of rights of way the extinguishment of which was not ultimately necessary – either because the NSIP was not constructed, or because it was constructed in such a way as did not require acquisition of the land over which the public rights historically ran.

It should be noted that PA 2008, s 136(7) expressly provides that the 'revival' of a right of way pursuant to s 136(5) is no bar to 'the making of a further order extinguishing the right of way'. The use of the term 'further order' suggests that this provision is not intended for some further extinguishment under the existing DCO, but rather either a fresh DCO or else another, wholly separate, order such as one sought pursuant to the Highways Act 1980, s 118ZA.

The 'apparatus' exception

PA 2008, s 137 is engaged where an order granting development consent makes provision for the acquisition of land, compulsorily or by agreement, and a public right of way (not being a right enjoyed by vehicular traffic) exists over the land in circumstances where either 'on, over or under' that land there is:

(a) apparatus belonging to a statutory undertaker (the term statutory undertaker as defined in Part 11 of the 1990 Act); or

(b) electronic communications apparatus kept installed in connection with an electronic communications code network.

In such circumstances, s 137(3) provides that the right of way in question may only be extinguished with the consent of the undertaker or operator of the network in question.

Unsurprisingly, the legislation provides that consent must not be unreasonably withheld: see PA 2008, s 137(4)(b). In this context it should be noted s 137(5) provides that any dispute as to whether or not any party is acting unreasonably in withholding consent, falls to be determined not by the courts, but by the Secretary of State. This jurisdiction on the part of the Secretary of State would however be subject to regulation by the courts by means of judicial review (s 118(7)).

As to when the requirement to secure 'consent' pursuant to PA 2008, s 137 is engaged, it appears at first that that a distinction of sorts is being drawn between statutory undertakers and the operators of an electronic communications code network.

For statutory undertakers generally the protection in PA 2008, s 137 is afforded where there island on, over or under which there is 'apparatus belonging to statutory undertakers'. The test, therefore, is simply one ownership. For electronic communications apparatus, however, that apparatus must be 'kept installed for the purpose of an electronic communications code network' (emphasis added). This appears to imply something other than ownership, but in reality simply reflects the terms of the electronic communications code that provides that apparatus may be installed or 'kept installed' in land.

As regards what comprises 'apparatus' in this context, for the purposes of PA 2008, s 137(2(b) the terminology relating to electronic communications is defined as per the Communications Act 2003, Sch 17, para 1(1). In contrast, there is no definition of the term 'apparatus' as applicable to a statutory undertaker for the purposes of s 137(2)(a). However in, s 138 (a related provision concerned with private, as opposed to public rights), the term 'relevant apparatus' is defined with reference to statutory undertakers as: 'apparatus vested in or belonging to statutory undertakers for the purpose of carrying out their undertaking'.

Notwithstanding the slight difference in terminology in the two provisions (ie 'apparatus' as opposed to 'relevant apparatus'), it would be surprising indeed if the term 'apparatus' were not accorded the same or very similar meaning in both PA 2008, ss 137 and 138. This is perhaps particularly the case given that, for the purposes of an electronic communications code network, s 138 defines 'relevant apparatus' in precisely the same terms as for s 137. As such, whatever else may be in dispute, there seems little doubt that in order for s 137 to engage the apparatus belonging to a the statutory undertaker must be held by that undertaker for 'for the purpose of carrying out [its] undertaking'.

Temporary Possession

Written by: Richard Honey, ftb
Edited by: Michael Humphries QC, ftb

Introduction

It is possible in practice for DCOs to provide for the temporary possession of land for the purposes of the carrying out of the project or maintaining the project once completed. This is the case even though the PA 2008 contains no express power to take temporary possession. Where temporary possession is taken, it would allow the undertaker to occupy and control the land to the exclusion of everyone else, including the landowner and any lessee. It would authorise what would otherwise be a trespass. If the land were subject to a tenancy, taking temporary possession would have no direct legal effect on the operation of the tenancy, which would continue to apply to the land including obligations to pay rent; although such a tenant might seek to argue as against its landlord that the tenancy had become frustrated as the landlord was not providing vacant possession and, in any event, would have a claim in compensation for loss or damage against the person taking temporary possession.

Temporary possession can be both controversial as far as affected landowners and occupiers are concerned, and problematic to operate in practice as far as the compensation provisions are concerned. Periods of temporary possession can last for many years and can also be of uncertain duration as at the date that possession is taken. This can give rise to problems for the assessment of compensation and for the operation of the six year limitation period for compensation claims. Moreover, during this period landowners cannot deal with the land in the way that they normally could and occupiers must remove themselves from the land and seek other land to carry on their operations. Furthermore, the promoter cannot be forced to acquire the land permanently even where the landowner or occupier would prefer that.

Temporary possession powers were included in Model Provisions 28 and 29 of the general model provisions in the Infrastructure Planning (Model Provisions) (England and Wales) Order 2009, SI 2009/2265. Such powers have been included in many DCOs, for example in Articles 31 and 32 of the National Grid (North London Reinforcement Project) Order 2014, SI 2014/1052 and in Articles 28 to 30 of the Network Rail (Norton Bridge Area Improvements) Order 2014, SI 2014/909.

It is important to note that a power of temporary possession is *not* a power of compulsory acquisition, but simply a power to enter on and take temporary possession of land for a specified purpose; the undertaker acquires no interest or right in the land itself.

Temporary use of land for carrying out the authorised project

Model Provision 28 and a number of DCOs grant an undertaker power, in connection with the 'carrying out' of the authorised project, to enter on and take possession of land specified in a schedule to the order for purposes also specified in the schedule related to a specific part of the project. In practice, land subject to temporary possession for the carrying out of the project is included in the definition of 'Order Land' along with the land to be acquired or used within the limits of deviation.

The Planning Inspectorate has advised that where temporary possession of land is required, The Infrastructure Planning (Applications: Prescribed Forms and Procedure) Regulations 2009, SI 2009/2264, reg 7 applies, so that the land plan must identify the plot with a number and state the area in square metres (Register of Advice, 28 February 2011, Willington Gas Pipeline).

It is also possible for a DCO to include a provision to the effect that temporary possession may be taken of not only that land listed in the schedule to the order for temporary possession but also any land subject to compulsory purchase under the order where the compulsory acquisition process has not been commenced. This is intended to allow temporary possession, rather than permanent acquisition, where the promoter decides to switch to temporary possession. The rationale is that if, during the design development process, it appears that permanent acquisition is not necessary for the purposes of the project, and that temporary possession would suffice, the change can be made. This obviously assists the promoter and may in some cases assist the landowner or occupier; sometimes however the landowner or occupier may want the land taken permanently rather than subject to temporary occupation for a period of in some cases many years.

Otherwise, Model Provision 28 provides that the undertaker may not compulsorily acquire land scheduled for only temporary possession (save in relation to acquiring compulsorily rights or subsoil only) and that where the undertaker takes temporary possession of land, it should not be required to acquire the land or any interest in it.

Model Provision 28 also confers powers to remove any buildings and vegetation from the land and to construct temporary works (including the provision of means of access) and buildings on the land. These powers have been widened in some DCOs as made. For example, Article 31 of the North London Reinforcement DCO (SI 2014/1052) also includes powers to construct other works and mitigation works. It is not unusual now for DCO applications to include powers for temporary possession which go beyond the Model Provisions, in allowing works for mitigation, ground strengthening and the like to be constructed and left on land where only temporary possession has been taken so that the works are left there permanently. An example of where the DCO allows the construction of permanent works on land of which only temporary possession is taken is Article 28 of the Norton Bridge Area Improvements Order 2014, SI 2014/909.

The Model Provisions include a requirement on the undertaker, before giving up the temporary possession, to remove all temporary works and restore the land to the reasonable satisfaction of the landowner, subject to a proviso that the undertaker shall not be required to replace a building removed under the temporary possession power. This provision is extended in practice sometimes so that, where permanent works are to be constructed on land temporary possession of which has been taken, the DCO also provides that the undertaker is not required to remove permanent works constructed on the land, eg mitigation or ground strengthening works. This was done, for example, in Article 28 of the Norton Bridge Area Improvements Order 2014, SI 2014/909; see also the Redditch Branch Enhancement Order 2013, SI 2013/2809, the North Doncaster Chord Order 2012, SI 2012/2635 and the Ipswich Chord Order 2012, SI 2012/2284.

The need for clarity over what works are temporary and what works are permanent is important for a variety of reasons, not least the assessment of compensation. The report of the Examining Authority dated 12 June 2012 into the Ipswich Chord Order 2012, SI 2012/2284 records that the draft DCO in that case was altered to clarify which of the proposed works were permanent and which were temporary so that the land had to be restored.

The reinstatement provision can be important in certain cases. In paragraph 97 of the Examining Authority's report on the North Doncaster Chord Order 2012, SI 2012/2635 dated 31 July 2012, the ExA records that the draft DCO contained a provision that the undertaker should not be required to reinstate any ground used during construction and that it questioned whether this was reasonable as the affected land could include farmland. As a result, the undertaker deleted the provision from the draft DCO.

Model Provision 28 provides that the authority for the temporary possession of land for the purposes of carrying out the project ceases five years after the date on which the relevant DCO is made. This is subject to a proviso that the time limit does not prevent the undertaker from remaining in possession of land, if the land was entered and possession was taken before the end of that period. In Network Rail's Norton Bridge DCO (SI 2014/909), the Secretary of State for Transport inserted a provision to make clear that the authority for temporary possession of land granted under that DCO to National Grid (separate from that granted to Network Rail) also expired five years after the DCO comes into force (decision letter dated 31 March 2014, para 38).

Model Provision 28 provides that not less than 14 days' notice has to be given to owners and occupiers before the undertaker enters on and takes temporary possession of land. Some DCOs as made – for example the Redditch Branch Enhancement Order 2012, SI 2013/2189 and the Norton Bridge Area Improvements Order 2014, SI 2014/909 – have voluntarily included 28 days instead of 14 days' notice.

The Crossrail and HS2 Hybrid Bills both included 28 days' notice provisions. The 'Post Legislative Assessment of the Crossrail Act 2008' published by the Department for Transport (Cmd 8676, July 2013) stated that 'the provision for 28 days' notice to be given for temporary possessions has proven to be sufficient'.

The question of 14 or 28 days' notice was the subject of debate in the case of the National Grid (North London Reinforcement Project) Order 2014, SI 2014/1052. The Examining Authority's report dated 23 January 2014 at paragraph 6.137 contained the conclusion that a period of 14 days was 'so short as to be unreasonable' and recommended a change to 28 days. But the Secretary of State disagreed in his decision letter dated 16 April 2014, stating:

> '4.16 The Secretary of State notes the ExA's view [ER 6.137] that a notice period of 14 days for entering on and taking possession of land was unreasonably short. However, taking into account the strong need for the timely delivery of the project to avoid works in the winter months to mitigate harm to European Sites and species, and the need to avoid any delays in the planned outage timetables which have been calculated to be carried out when forecast network demand can accommodate them, the Secretary of State does not agree that the period is unreasonable. A 14 day notice period is consistent with precedents, including the Infrastructure Planning (Model Provisions) (England and Wales) Order 2009 (now repealed), and section 11

> of the Compulsory Purchase Act 1965. The Secretary of State also considers that any unnecessary delays in the ability for NGET to enter on and take temporary possession of land could constrain the delivery of the Project. The Secretary of State considers that a notice period of 14 days is sufficient.'

A time limit is also set on the duration of the occupation. The Model Provisions provide that the undertaker may not, without the agreement of the landowner, remain in possession of any land for longer than one year after the completion of the part of the project specified in the schedule for the relevant land. In the Secretary of State for Transport's decision letter dated 19 March 2013 on the Heysham to M6 Link Road DCO (SI 2013/675) the Secretary of State included references to work numbers in the schedule to the DCO 'so as to provide greater precision about the deadline for LCC to give up possession of land used temporarily for the purposes of the scheme'.

In the Model Provisions, Article 22(3) provides that all private rights of way over land of which temporary possession is taken shall be suspended and unenforceable for as long as the undertaker remains in lawful possession of the land. This has been extended in some DCOs made. For example, in the North London Reinforcement DCO (SI 2014/1052), Article 26(4) covers all private rights and restrictive covenants, rather than just private rights of way.

All temporary possession provisions include an obligation to pay compensation to the owners and occupiers of land for any loss or damage arising from the exercise of any power contained in the relevant article of the DCO. Disputes as to compensation are dealt with by the Upper Tribunal (Lands Chamber) under Part I of the Land Compensation Act 1961. The provisions also contain a saving that the liability to pay compensation does not affect a person's entitlement to compensation under the Planning Act 2008, s 152 (or the Compulsory Purchase Act 1965, s 10, if applicable).

If the land is being used as a business, the compensatable loss will be the genuine net profit which the business would have earned from its legitimate activities on the affected land, over the relevant period of time (see by analogy eg *Pennine Raceway Ltd v Kirklees MBC* [1984] RVR 85 and *Hobbs (Quarries) Ltd v Somerset CC* (1975) 30 P&CR 286). Where land is occupied by someone other than the owner, the relevant period will run from when temporary possession was taken until the earliest possible date on which the owner could have obtained possession of the land. Any entitlement to compensation is subject to the usual requirements of causation, remoteness and mitigation. The burden of proof to establish the loss or damage, and its quantum, will lie on the claimant.

As noted above, the compensation regime is problematic in relation to limitation periods and uncertain durations of possession. The regime also lacks many of the features of compensation for acquisition, such as entitlements to advance payment, loss payments and statutory interest. This adds to the complexity of dealing with compensation for temporary possession and potentially operates to the detriment of landowners and occupiers in certain cases.

Temporary use of land for maintaining authorised project

Model Provision 29 and many DCOs also contain powers for temporary use of land for the purposes of 'maintaining' the authorised project after its completion. The power shares many of the same features with the construction temporary possession power described above. The main features of the maintenance power are:

- the power applies at any time within a specified maintenance period, usually defined as five years from the date on which the relevant part of the project was first opened for use;
- the power does not apply to any house, or garden belonging to a house, or any other building which is occupied at the time;
- the power is to enter on and take temporary possession of any land within the Order limits, provided it is reasonably required for the purpose of maintaining the project
- buildings on the land, provided they are reasonably necessary for the purpose of maintaining the project
- the power is subject to giving 28 days' notice to the owner and occupier of the land;
- the power is limited to allow temporary possession only for so long as may be reasonably necessary to carry out the maintenance of the part of the project for which possession of the land was taken
- before giving up possession, the undertaker must remove all temporary works and restore the land to the reasonable satisfaction of the owners of the land;
- the power is subject to an obligation to pay compensation to the owners and occupiers of the land for any loss or damage arising from the exercise of the power in relation to the land.

Compulsory Purchase Compensation

Written by: Richard Honey, ftb
Edited by: Michael Humphries QC, ftb

Introduction

The Inspectorate has stated in terms that 'the assessment of compensation is complex and governed by other legislation and extensive case law' (register of advice, 21 February 2012, Dyfnant Forest Wind Farm). That is a fair summary of the position. The Inspectorate has also made it clear repeatedly in its register of advice that it will have nothing to do with claims for compensation (see also eg PA 2008, s 102(4)(e)(i)).

That said, the examining authority may, in some cases, need to give some consideration to the overall amount of compensation payable in connection with consideration of whether there are sufficient funds available to pay compensation. In the Hinkley Point case, the promoter had taken expert advice on the likely cost of implementing the proposed development, including the cost of the necessary land acquisition (panel report, 19 December 2012, para 7.35).

A similar position existed in relation to the Rookery South application (panel decision, 13 October 2011, paras 7.25, 7.100). Although the Examining Authority was hesitant to go too far into considering the quantum of compensation (paras 7.81, 7.83), it did accept that 'a misunderstanding of the likely quantum of compensation could lead the Applicant to underestimate the likely compensation payable, which in turn could impact on viability and thus affect the argument for a compelling case' (para 7.98). Ultimately a provision was included in the DCO (Art 8) to the effect that the development could not be commenced unless either a guarantee in respect of the promoter's liabilities to pay compensation or an alternative form of security for that purpose was in place.

Similarly, the Examining Authority may need to consider the availability of compensation in particular circumstances as part of its consideration of the proportionality of the proposed compulsory acquisition of land. In the case of the Ipswich Rail Chord, the authority had to consider the entitlement to compensation of tenants with an interest of less than six months. The Examining Authority concluded that the resultant interference with the tenants' human rights was proportionate and in the public interest (panel report, 12 June 2012, para 5.91; see also the Rookery South decision at paras 7.102-7.103).

An overview of compulsory purchase compensation under the PA 2008

Save in the case of s 10 of the CPA 1965, which is considered further below, the compensation provisions arising from a DCO are substantially the same as other similar orders. The text below gives a very brief overview of the compensation entitlements that arise and the main rules which apply to them.

Value of the land acquired

The principle underlying compensation for compulsory acquisition of land is that fair compensation should be given to the owner whose land has been taken. The aim is to provide a fair financial equivalent for the land taken. The owner is entitled to be compensated fairly and fully for his loss, but he is not entitled to receive more than fair compensation: see *Transport for London v Spirerose* [2009] 1 WLR 1797 at 1822C–D and *Waters v Welsh Development Agency* [2004] 1 WLR 1304 at 1306E, 1309B–D. Compensation cannot, and must not, exceed the owner's total loss, for, if it did, it would put an unfair burden on the public purse and it would transgress the principle of 'equivalence', which is at the root of statutory compensation, namely that the owner shall be paid neither less nor more than his loss (*Horn v Sunderland Corporation* [1941] 2 KB 26 at 49). A claimant is not entitled to receive more than fair compensation: a person is entitled to compensation for losses fairly attributable to the taking of his land, but not to any greater amount (*Director of Buildings and Lands v Shun Fung* [1995] 2 AC 111 at 125D).

The primary statutory rules for assessing compensation are found in s 5 of the LCA 1961. Under s 5(2) of the LCA 1961 the value of land is taken to be the amount which the land if sold in the open market by a willing seller might be expected to realise. As to what the land might be expected to realise, this refers to the expectations of properly qualified persons who have taken pains to inform themselves of all the particulars ascertainable about the property, and its capabilities, and the demand for it (*Inland Revenue Commissioners v Clay* [1914] 3 KB 466 at 475). It must be assumed that the hypothetical vendor and purchaser did whatever reasonable people buying and selling such property would be likely to have done in real life; the hypothetical buyer is assumed to have behaved reasonably and made proper enquiries about the property and not to have appeared too eager to buy (*Ryde v London Regional Transport* [2004] RVR 60 at paras 18–19). So far as possible the assessment of compensation should reflect what would be likely to happen if the property were actually sold at the valuation date (*Waters* at p 1313C).

The principles applying to an open market valuation of land were summarised by Hoffmann LJ in *IRC v Gray* [1994] RVR 129 at 136:

> 'one assumes that the hypothetical vendor and purchaser did whatever reasonable people buying and selling such property would be likely to have done in real life. The hypothetical vendor is an anonymous but reasonable vendor, who goes about the sale as a prudent man of business, negotiating seriously without giving the impression of being either over-anxious or unduly reluctant. The hypothetical buyer is slightly less anonymous. He too is assumed to have behaved reasonably, making proper inquiries about the property and not appearing too eager to buy. But he also reflects reality in that he embodies whatever was actually the demand for that property at the relevant time. It cannot be too strongly emphasised that although the sale is hypothetical, there is nothing hypothetical about the open market in which it is supposed to have taken place. The concept of the open market involves assuming that the whole world was free to bid, and then forming a view about what in those circumstances would in real life have been the best price reasonably obtainable.'

The willing seller is a hypothetical character and the personal characteristics of the actual seller are not to be taken into account.

The starting point is that a search for the value of land at a particular date must take account of the attributes of the land at that date (*Spirerose* at p 1801G). As a generality, land is to be valued in the state in which it was in and in the circumstances prevailing at the valuation date. Where property is to be valued on an open market basis as at a certain date, no counter-factual assumptions should be made other than those which are inherent in the valuation exercise or those which are directed by statute (*Spirerose* at p 1814C). An interest in land is assumed to be sold in the state in which it existed as at the valuation date, taking into account any tenancies or restrictions to which it was subject. There are particular statutory rules and provisions arising from case-law (including *Pointe Gourde v Sub-Intendant of Crown Lands* [1947] AC 565) which require the effect on value of the scheme underlying the compulsory acquisition to be ignored in certain circumstances.

Where a DCO grants the power to create new rights in land it may need to apply parts of the statutory compensation code with necessary modifications: see, for example, Schedule 10 to the Lancashire County Council (Torrisholme to the M6 Link (A683 Completion of Heysham to M6 Link Road)) Order 2013.

Where temporary possession of land is taken, the promoter must pay compensation to the owners and occupiers of the land for any loss or damage arising from the exercise of the power. If the land is being used for the purposes of a business then the compensatable loss may properly reflect net profit which the business would have earned from its legitimate activities on the affected land, over the relevant period of temporary possession: see by analogy *Pennine Raceway Ltd v Kirklees MBC* [1984] RVR 85 and *Hobbs (Quarries) Ltd v Somerset CC* (1975) 30 P&CR 286. Where land is occupied by someone other than the owner, the relevant period would be from when temporary possession was taken until the earliest possible date on which the owner could have obtained possession of the land. The entitlement to compensation would be subject to the usual requirements of causation, remoteness and mitigation. The burden of proof to establish the loss or damage, and its quantum, would lie on the claimant.

Section 37 of the LCA 1973 provides an avenue for compensation where a claimant has no compensatable interest in the land acquired. This would apply to persons in occupation under a licence, a tenancy at will, or holding over after a lease. Section 37 applies where a person is displaced from land in consequence of the acquisition of the land by an authority possessing compulsory purchase powers and he had no compensatable interest in the land but was in lawful possession of it. The displaced person is entitled to a disturbance payment.

Disturbance

Section 5(6) of the LCA 1961 provides compensation for disturbance, known as Rule 6 compensation. This covers both the cost of being disturbed, or 'displaced', from the land, under the first limb, but also, under the second limb, any other matter not directly based on the value of the land. The second limb of Rule 6 was described as being potentially wide in *Ryde* (para 24). Consequential or economic losses other than those directly related to the value of the land itself are in principle recoverable as compensation under the second limb of Rule 6, including on the part of investment owners. A claim under Rule 6 may be made for consequential loss even it does not stem from a loss of occupation.

Any loss recoverable under Rule 6 must be a loss properly and actually incurred by a claimant. Moreover, such claims are subject in law to three particular tests. To be recoverable:

- there must be a causal connection between the compulsory acquisition and the loss (see *Shun Fung* a p 126A);
- the loss must be reasonably foreseeable and not too remote (see *Shun Fung* at p 126D-F); and,
- the claimant must behave reasonably in taking steps to eliminate or reduce any loss (see *Shun Fung* at pp 126F-G, 127C-E, 138A, 138F).

It is the first of these, causation, which seems to give rise to most problems in practice. In *Wrexham Maelor BC v MacDougall* [1993] 2 EGLR 23 at 32J what was recoverable was described by the Court of Appeal as 'significant damage consequent upon the taking of his interest, other than costs and expenses, which is the natural and reasonable consequence of the taking of his interest and not too remote'. In *Shun Fung* it was said that 'there must be a causal connection between the resumption or acquisition and the loss in question' (at 126A).

Pre-possession losses may be claimed if they are due to the compulsory acquisition. They are only recoverable, however, where they are incurred in anticipation of the compulsory acquisition and because of the threat of compulsory acquisition (*Shun Fung* at 137H–138A). Save for the need to avoid double counting in relation to overlap with the value of the land, judged as at the valuation date, there is no difference in principle as to the recoverability of pre and post-possession losses.

A range of losses may be claimed under Rule 6. Lost profits arising from temporary or permanent loss of business as a result of a compulsory acquisition are generally recoverable. The expenses of removal to new premises are generally recoverable, including the costs of searching for and finding alternative premises, removal costs and the costs of setting-up the new premises. Consequential or economic losses, including taxation liabilities, are generally recoverable, subject to compliance with the three fundamental requirements for Rule 6 claims. The Court of Appeal in *Wrexham Maelor BC* recognised that claims for compensation for losses such as lost earnings or lost profits are not excluded in principle. Rule 6 also encompasses compensation for reasonable surveyor's, legal and other professional fees incurred as a direct consequence of the compulsory acquisition, and compensation for the personal time actually and reasonably spent by a claimant dealing with matters caused by the acquisition, and charged at a fair and reasonable hourly rate.

Severance and injurious affection

Where land is taken, a landowner may suffer loss by the detrimental effect of such acquisition on other land that he retains. Section 7 of the CPA 1965 provides compensation for severance and injurious affection. Section 7 provides that in assessing compensation for land taken, regard must be had to the damage to be sustained by the landowner through any injurious effect on that landowner's other land by reason of the exercise of the relevant statutory powers. This has been described as loss caused to the retained land by the works or use of the land acquired for the statutory purpose. Section 7 requires, in effect, that where a person's land is compulsorily acquired, if certain retained land suffers a diminution in value because of the project, then that diminution in value should be included in the compensation paid for the acquisition. Any loss of amenity which affects the value of the retained land could also give rise to a claim for compensation.

The main requirements in a claim for s 7 compensation for injurious affection are:

- land must have been acquired compulsorily from the claimant;
- the harm must be caused by the exercise of the statutory powers;
- injurious affection can arise from both the execution and the use of the works or the land taken, and would include temporary loss during the execution of the works;
- there is no need for there to be an underlying right to claim in tort;
- injurious affection extends beyond matters that would normally be compensatable in tort, such as loss of privacy and general amenity;
- the injurious effect may arise from the works as a whole and not just from that part of the works on the land taken from the owner;
- compensation may (and ought to) be prospective, to include what is reasonably anticipated to happen as it must be claimed once and for all; and
- damage to purely personal rights unconnected with the land is not compensatable.

The 'other land' (the retained land) must be held with the land taken, but it need not be contiguous with or indeed part of the same title, or used in the same way or occupied by the same person, as the land taken. The two parcels of land must merely be owned by the same person and 'so near to each other, and so situated that the possession and control of each gives an enhanced value to all of them' (*Cowper Essex v Acton Local Board* (1889) 14 App Cas 153 at 167).

For there to be a claim for injurious affection under s 7 of the CPA 1965, the value of the owner's retained land must have been depreciated by injurious affection as a result of the construction or use of the scheme or the acquisition of land. Section 7 provides that compensation is payable for injury done 'by the exercise of the powers conferred by… the special Act'. The injury must be caused by the exercise of the relevant statutory powers. The measure of compensation is the diminution in value of the owner's retained land, and compensation is not to be measured by the costs the owner incurs to overcome the consequences of the construction or use of the scheme (*Cowper Essex* at pp 166, 178).

The provisions of PA 2008, s 152 are explained elsewhere in this work. The effect of s 152(3) is that the promoter must pay compensation to any person whose land is injuriously affected by the carrying out of the authorised works. The provision in s 10(2) of the CPA 1965 is to be applied and, furthermore, any rule or principle applied to the construction of s 10 must also be applied to the construction of s 152(3). It appears that the effect of s 152 is intended to be equivalent to that of s 10 of the CPA 1965.

For PA 2008, s 152 to apply it is not necessary for a person to have had any land taken for the scheme. However, the land must be affected in a way that reduces its value and the injury can only arise from the carrying out of the works, not from the subsequent use of the works. Entitlement to compensation would be limited to cases where a person would have had a claim in tort but for the statutory authority conferred by the DCO. Entitlement only arises where a remedy would have been available in damages but for the defence of statutory authority.

The operation of s 10 of the CPA 1965 has become subject to a series of rules or conditions, known as the McCarthy rules after *Metropolitan Board of Works v McCarthy* (1874) LR 7 HL 243. The same rules would apply to a claim under s 152, pursuant to s 152(6). They are:

- the injurious affection must be the consequence of the lawful exercise of statutory powers;
- the injurious affection must be such that, if not done under statutory authority, would have given rise to a cause of action;
- compensation is payable only for damage to the claimant's land or interest in land; and
- compensation is payable in respect of only the execution of works and not their use.

These rules were summarised in *Clift v Welsh Office* [1999] 1 WLR 796 at 801B-C, with another point added: the compensation must be ascertainable in accordance with the general rules applicable to damages in tort. This includes the tortious requirements of foreseeability and directness of harm. The measure of damages is usually the diminution in the value of the interest in land affected, assessed at the date of the injury, for all the anticipated injury. The value of a claimant's interest in land must be affected by physical interference with some legal right, public or private, of which the claimant is entitled to make use in connection with his property (*McCarthy* at 253 and 256), irrespective of whether the damage was caused by permanent or temporary interference.

Damage arising from business lost by reason of an obstruction or interference making land less accessible or attractive to customers is recoverable, where such loss of business reduces the value of land (see *Wildtree Hotels v Harrow LBC* [2001] 2 AC 1). However, compensation is not available for personal losses, including lost business profits.

Another form of injurious affection compensation is provided under Part 1 of the LCA 1973, which is applied to works authorised under a DCO by s 152(7). Part 1 compensation is in essence compensation for depreciation of land value by physical factors caused by use of public works. Section 1 of the LCA 1973 provides that where the value of an interest in land is depreciated by 'physical factors' caused by the use of public works then, subject to certain conditions, compensation is payable for that depreciation. In addition to compensation, reasonable valuation and legal expenses are also payable (s 3(5)). The 'physical factors' are defined in s 1(2) as noise, vibration, smell, fumes, smoke, artificial lighting and the discharge of any solid or liquid substance (eg dust). Noise is the most common physical factor in relation to which claims are made. The source of the physical factors must be situated on or in the public works the use of which is alleged to be their cause.

Part 1 claims may be made one year after the opening of the relevant public work. Compensation is assessed by reference to prices one year after opening, applying s 5(2)–(4) of the LCA 1961, less deduction for betterment. Reasonably expected intensification of the use of the works is taken into account. Section 9 of the LCA 1973 makes similar provision to s 1 but in circumstances where there are alterations to pre-existing public works (eg road widening).

Some additional points

In terms of procedure, the DCLG 'Guidance related to procedures for compulsory acquisition' (February 2010) says that promoters should seek to acquire land by negotiation wherever practicable (para 39). The guidance urges promoters to use alternative dispute resolution including in relation to agreeing the compensation payable for property acquired (para 42). Mediation and early neutral evaluation are mentioned.

It is also notable that the guidance suggests that in order 'to alleviate concerns about future compensation entitlement' a promoter could enter into agreements with those whose land is to be acquired which guarantee a minimum compensation payment, if the project proceeds (para 44). This would be without prejudice to a claimant's ability to seek a higher level of compensation in the future. Such an approach may assist both in allowing those whose land is being acquired to plan for relocating or dealing with the acquisition, as well as reducing the objections which are made to DCOs on a protective basis.

Disputes about compensation which cannot be resolved must be referred to the Lands Chamber of the Upper Tribunal under the Tribunal Procedure (Upper Tribunal) (Lands Chamber) Rules 2010, SI 2010/2600.

The DCLG guidance also refers readers to ODPM circular 06/2004 entitled 'Compulsory Purchase and the Crichel Down Rules' (since superseded by the DCLG 'Guidance on Compulsory Purchase Process and the Crichel Down Rules' (2015)). DCLG also published in October 2004 a series of guidance documents on the compulsory purchase system. These cover compensation to agricultural owners and occupiers, compensation to business owners and occupiers, and compensation to residential owners and occupiers.

More information on compensation for compulsory purchase can be found in Roots et al *The Law of Compulsory Purchase* (2nd edn, Bloomsbury Professional).

Part 10

Environmental Impact Assessment and Habitats Regulations Assessment

Requirement for Environmental Impact Assessment

Written by: Gregory Jones QC, ftb
Edited by: Michael Humphries QC, ftb

What is EIA?

Environmental Impact Assessment (EIA) is a means of drawing together, in a systematic way, an assessment of the likely significant environmental effects arising from a proposed development.

What type of NSIP Projects are Covered by EIA?

The EIA Directive (Directive 85/337/EEC as amended by Directives 97/11/EC and 2003/35/EC now consolidated as European Directive 2011/92/EU) requires that projects of a description contained within Annexes I and II of the Directive likely to have significant effects on the environment by virtue *inter alia* of their nature, size or location are made subject to an assessment of their environmental effects (Article 2(1)).

These projects are defined in Article 4 and listed in Annex I and Annex II of the EIA Directive. An EIA is always required for projects included in Annex I. Projects of the categories listed in Annex II shall be made subject to an assessment when Member States determine that they are likely to have significant effects on the environment.

Those categories of development within Annex I are all assumed to have likely significant environmental effects and thus an EIA is always mandatory for a development of the type included within Annex 1. Those in Annex II will require an EIA, if in the view of the Examining Authority they are likely to have significant effects on the environment. It is important to note that the requirement is triggered by *any* likely significant environmental effects not merely any *adverse* significant environmental effects (*British Telecommunications plc v Gloucester City Council* [2001] EWHC 1001 (Admin); (2002) 2 P&CR 512; *R (Stephen Prophet) v York City Council* [2002] EWHC 588 (Admin). Hence, promoters of NSIPs should assume that it is most likely that all NSIP applications will be subject to EIA. This is because whilst it may be theoretically possible to devise a nationally infrastructure project that does not require an EIA, in practice it is difficult to imagine a nationally significant infrastructure project will not have a likely significant environmental effect, even if its overall effect is beneficial. Indeed, the 'primary position' of the Institute of Environment Management Assessment is that EIA should be made a mandatory requirement for all NSIPs. Its 'secondary position' is that all non-Annex I developments should undergo formal, case by case, screening opinion produced by the EA, developed through consultation with environmental stakeholders.

The Infrastructure Planning (Environmental Impact Assessment) Regulations 2009

The Infrastructure Planning (Environmental Impact Assessment) Regulations 2009, SI 2009/2263 (as amended) ('the IP EIA Regulations') came into force on 1 October 2009 and are intended to set out the procedures that must be followed so that the consideration of applications for NSIPs fully reflect the requirements of the EIA Directive.

The EIA screening and scoping process for NSIPs under the IP EIA Regulations and the PA 2008 is summarised below. See also PINS Advice Note 7: Environmental Impact Assessment: Preliminary Environmental Information, Screening and Scoping.

Summary of EIA Process for NSIP

Screening

- Screening Opinion within 21 days of request

Scoping

- Desk top baseline review and Gap Assessment
- Preliminary stakeholder engagement
- Scoping Report
- Scoping Opinion within 42 days of receiving request

Preliminary Environmental Information

- 28 days consultation as part of PA 2008, ss 42 and 47 consultation

Environmental Impact Assessment

- Baseline
- Project Definition (iterative process)
- Assessing Effects
- Reporting – Environmental Statement (ES)

How to Approach EIA

In seeking to ensure that the NSIP application is made and assessed in accordance with the EIA Directive and Regulations, it is critical to have a basic understanding of the way in which EU law obligations are to be interpreted, particularly those directed towards environmental protection. Such obligations – as Lord Hoffmann made clear in *R v North Yorkshire , ex parte Brown* [2000] 1 AC 397 at 401D – must be interpreted in accordance with the principles of European law. This means, for example, not only examining the English language version of the EIA Directive – and where appropriate a comparison with other language versions – but also possessing an understanding of the purpose of the EIA Directive.

The EIA Directive will also be interpreted in the light of the EU Treaty obligations imposed upon the United Kingdom. In *Berkeley v Secretary of State for the Environment* [2001] 2 AC 603, Lord Hoffmann expressly relied upon what is now article 4(3) of the Treaty on the European Union ('the TEU') in support of his view that national authorities including the courts must ensure the full effectiveness of the EIA Directive by interpreting very narrowly their discretion not to quash a decision taken in breach of the EIA Directive. Article 4(3) of the TEU states that:

> 'The Member States shall take any appropriate measure, general or particular, to ensure fulfilment of the obligations arising out of the Treaties or resulting from the acts of the institutions of the Union (this includes the EIA Directive). The Member States shall facilitate the achievement of the Union's task.'

The European Court of Justice (ECJ) has also relied upon the obligation contained in this Treaty article in order to create the principles of direct and indirect effect (see further below).

Article 191 of the Treaty on the Functioning of the European Union ('the TFEU') is another important Treaty obligation for the purposes of the EIA Directive. It provides amongst other things that:

> 'Union policy on the environment shall aim at a high level of protection taking into account the diversity of situations in the various regions of the Union. It shall be based on the precautionary principle and on the principles that preventive action should be taken, that environmental damage should as a priority be rectified at source and that the polluter should pay.'

See also the Communication from the Commission on the precautionary principle – Brussels, 02.02.2000 COM (2000). The 'precautionary principle' is, for example, relevant to many practical issues in respect of the EIA of an NSIP, such as the quality of scientific evidence required in EIA.

Relationship between the EIA Directive and the NSIP EIA Regulations

If the IP EIA regulations implement the EIA Directive, why can't we forget about the EIA Directive? It is generally accepted that the EIA Directive is capable of 'direct effect' (*Kraaijveld v Gedeputeerde Staten Van Zuid-Holland* (Case C-72/ 95)). This means if the IP EIA Regulations have not correctly implemented the EIA Directive into the English domestic law, an individual may nonetheless rely directly upon rights conferred by the EIA Directive to enforce those rights against emanations of the state such as the Secretary of State. This is so, even if it means quashing development consent granted to a private company or individual (see eg *R v Durham County Council and Sherburn Stone Company Ltd, ex p Huddleston* [2000] 1 WLR 1484).

Where direct effect cannot be relied upon, the IP EIA Regulations must nonetheless be interpreted to give full effect to the requirements of the EIA Directive, even if that means stretching their ordinary meaning in the English language (see, eg Case C-106 *Marleasing SA v La Comercial International de Alimnetacion SA* [1990] ECR I-4135). This practice is sometimes inaccurately referred to as 'indirect effect' or more precisely, as the 'duty of loyalty' or 'cooperation': see also *R v Durham County Council and Sherburn Stone Company Ltd, ex p Huddleston* [2000] 1 WLR 1484.

The Purpose of the EIA Directive

Given that the ECJ takes a so-called purposive approach to the interpretation of EU law, it is important therefore for those applying for development consent to understand two key aspects about the purpose of the EIA Directive. The first is, as Advocate General Elmer stated in *Commission of the European Communities v Federal Republic of Germany* (Case C-431/92) [1995] ECR I-2189, 2208-2209 that:

> 'the provisions of the Directive are essentially of a procedural nature. By the inclusion of information on the environment in the consent procedure it is ensured that the environmental impact of the project shall be included in the public debate and that the decision as to whether consent is to be given shall be adopted on an appropriate basis.' (approved in *Berkeley*).

Accordingly, since its substance is procedure, flaws in procedures adopted in an EIA may be regarded as substantive flaws and are thus less likely to be excused by the courts or the Examining Authority.

The second point is that the purpose of the EIA Directive is not only that the Secretary of State has all the environmental information before him when he makes a decision on whether to make a development consent order, though that is, of course, a key requirement. Lord Bingham in *Berkeley* held that the directly enforceable right of the citizen which is accorded by the EIA Directive is not merely a right to a fully informed decision on the substantive issue. It must have been adopted on an appropriate basis and that requires the inclusive and democratic procedure prescribed by the Directive in which:

> 'the public, however misguided or wrongheaded its views may be, is given an opportunity to express its opinion on the environmental issues.'

As Advocate General Elmer also made clear in *Aannemersbedrijf P K Kraaijeveld BV v Gedeputeerde Staten van Zuid-Holland* (Case C-72/95) [1996] ECR I-5403, 5427, para 70):

> 'Where a member state's implementation of the Directive is such that projects which are likely to have significant effects on the environment are not made the subject of an environmental impact assessment, the citizen is prevented from exercising his right to be heard.'

The importance attached to the right of public participation the EIA decision making process in respect an NSIP has been further emphasised by the Aarhus Convention on Access to Environmental Justice.

Front-loaded EIA

The courts have also stressed the need to ensure that the environmental effects of a development including cumulative effects are assessed at the earliest possible opportunity in the development consent process (see eg *R (Brown) v Carlisle City Council* [2010] EWCA Civ 523 [2011] Env LR 5 and *R (on the application of Barker) v Bromley LBC* [2006] UKHL 52; [2007] Env LR 20 per Lord Hope at [22]). This requirement fits in with the general front loaded philosophy of the NSIP regime.

What is EIA Development?

The NSIP EIA Regulations impose procedural requirements for carrying out EIA for NSIPs which fall to be considered as 'EIA development' under the EIA Regulations.

The schedules to the EIA Regulations contain the following two broad categories of projects:

- Schedule 1 projects replicate those contained in Annex I to the EIA Directive – these are always EIA development and include, for example, nuclear power stations. By definition it is presumed that such projects are always likely to have significant effects upon the environment.
- Schedule 2 projects replicate those contained in Annex I to the EIA Directive and are only EIA development if the individual project is likely to have significant effects on the environment. Schedule 2 includes, for example, wind farms and overhead cables. Schedule 2 to the EIA Regulations applying to NSIPS does not include applicable thresholds and criteria (unlike the Town and Country Planning (Environmental Impact Assessment) Regulations 2011). But it must be recalled that the European Court of Justice has held that the projects identified in Schedule 2 should be given a *'wide scope and broad purpose'* (*Dutch Dykes – Kraaijveld v Gedeputeerde Staten van Zuid-Holland* (*Case C-72/ 95*) [1997]. Env LR 3, 265).

EIA Scoping

Written by: Hereward Phillpot QC, ftb
Edited by: Michael Humphries QC, ftb

The Infrastructure Planning (Environmental Impact Assessment) Regulations 2009, SI 2009/2263

The Infrastructure Planning (Environmental Impact Assessment) Regulations 2009, SI 2009/2263 (the 'EIA Regulations'), reg 8 sets out the procedure for obtaining a written opinion as to the information to be provided in an environmental statement (ie a 'scoping opinion'). The procedure is only available to a person who proposes to make an application for a development consent order ('DCO') (reg 8(1)), or an application to discharge a requirement (reg 8(2)).

The procedure is not compulsory. Whilst it is, therefore, a matter of choice for applicants whether or not they apply for a scoping opinion, in practice almost all do. It is an important part of the Environmental Impact Assessment ('EIA') process and is regarded as good practice. The advantages are obvious, in that obtaining a scoping opinion helps to focus the process of environmental impact assessment and ensure that the concerns of key stakeholders are identified and addressed at an early stage. It also allows issues to be 'scoped out' of the EIA process at an early stage, which can save time and money.

An effective scoping process makes it less likely that the environmental statement ('ES') submitted with the application will be rejected as inadequate, or that requests will need to be made for additional information. There is no obligation to follow the advice given in the scoping opinion, but again, for obvious enough reasons, most applicants will choose to do so to reduce the prospect of their application being rejected.

Procedural steps

The main procedural steps are the same whether the applicant is seeking a scoping opinion from the Secretary of State pursuant to reg 8(1), or from the authority responsible for the discharge of the requirement (the 'relevant authority') pursuant to reg 8(2).

Once a request has been made, the Secretary of State/relevant authority must consult the person who made the request and the 'consultation bodies' (reg 8(6)). Regulation 2(1) defines 'the consultation bodies' as meaning:

> '(a) a body prescribed under section 42(a) (duty to consult) and listed in column 1 of the table set out at Schedule 1 to the Infrastructure Planning (Applications: Prescribed Forms and Procedure) Regulations 2009 where the circumstances set out in column 2 are satisfied in respect of that body;
>
> - each authority that is within section 43 (local authorities for the purposes of section 42(b)); and

- if the land to which the application, or proposed application, relates or any part of that land is in Greater London, the Greater London Authority.'

If a consultation body fails to reply within 28 days of being consulted, the Secretary of State/relevant authority is entitled to assume it has no comments to make.

Before adopting a scoping opinion, the Secretary of State/relevant authority must take into account: (a) the specific characteristics of the particular development; (b) the specific characteristics of development of the type concerned; (c) the environmental features likely to be affected by the development; and (d) in the case of an application to discharge a requirement, the ES submitted with the original application (reg 8(9)).

The Secretary of State/relevant authority must provide a scoping opinion within 42 days from receipt of the request. There are only two exceptions to this timescale. First, where additional information has been requested, the 42-day period runs from receipt of that additional information (reg 8(6)). Secondly, where the request for a scoping opinion has been accompanied by a request for a screening opinion, the 42-day period runs from the date that the screening opinion was adopted (reg 8(7) and (8)).

In practice, most applicants will undertake at least some form of informal consultation with the main consultation bodies before submitting a request to the Secretary of State. This allows their views to be considered and, where appropriate, reflected in the information accompanying the request and reduces the likelihood of significant dispute as to the appropriate scope of the EIA. As explained below, it is also important in enabling the applicant to satisfy the Secretary of State's expectations as to the information that ought to accompany a request for a scoping opinion, and to comply with the guidance issued by the Planning Inspectorate on his behalf.

Documents accompanying request

The formal requirements for making a valid request for a scoping opinion are very limited.

Where the request is to the Secretary of State in relation to a proposed application for a development consent order, the only obligatory requirements are:

- a plan sufficient to identify the land;
- a brief description of the nature and purpose of the development and its possible effects on the environment; and
- such other information or representations as the person making the request may wish to provide or make (reg 8(3)).

Where the request is to a relevant authority in relation to the discharge of a requirement, in addition to the reference number of the DCO, the applicant must provide:

- an explanation of the likely effects on the environment which were not identified at the time the DCO was made; and
- such other information or representations as the person making the request may wish to provide or make (reg 8(4)).

In practice there is generally a need to provide a fairly substantial amount of information with the request in order to make it possible for the decision-maker to give an informed (and thus useful) scoping opinion. The precise level of information that ought to be provided will be a matter of judgment in each individual case, depending on the nature of the development and the area(s) where its effects might occur.

A common approach (and one recommended by the Planning Inspectorate – see below) is to submit a scoping report, which is structured in a similar way to an ES, explaining the nature and purpose of the proposed development, describing the receiving environment, setting out the proposed approach to the process of environmental impact assessment, and then identifying the scope of the proposed assessment on a topic-by-topic basis.

Form of scoping opinion

A number of scoping opinions provided by the IPC and subsequently the Planning Inspectorate (on behalf of the Secretary of State) in relation to on-going projects are available to download from the Planning Inspectorate's website, and provide a useful guide as to what to expect.

The structure adopted by the Planning Inspectorate for its scoping opinions is to provide:

- an executive summary;
- an introductory section which identifies what the Secretary of State has done in order to satisfy the requirements of reg 8 and to inform his opinion;
- a description of the proposed development and the site and surroundings based on the information provided by the applicant, together with the Secretary of State's comments on that information to inform the process of environmental impact assessment;
- specific comments on the applicant's approach to EIA and the relevant topic areas set out in the applicant's scoping report; and
- a final section which does not formally comprise part of the scoping opinion, but responds to other issues the Secretary of State has identified which may help to inform the preparation of the application for the DCO. This might include information on additional procedural steps made necessary (or desirable) by the presence of protected habitats or species in the receiving environment, the need for information on other regulatory regimes etc.

Appended to the scoping opinion should be a list of consultees, copies of the responses received to consultation and general advice on the presentation of information in the ES.

Secretary of State not precluded from asking for further information

Obtaining a scoping opinion, and then undertaking the process of EIA in a way that reflects that opinion, does not guarantee that the resulting ES will be judged to be adequate. Regulation 8(10) makes explicit that neither the Secretary of State nor a relevant authority shall be precluded from asking for further information, notwithstanding what may have been said in the scoping opinion.

Guidance

The Planning Inspectorate's advice on the screening and scoping process is set out in PINS Advice Note 7: Environmental Impact Assessment: Preliminary Environmental Information, Screening and Scoping (March 2015). No further advice has been provided by the Department for Communities and Local Government, although applicants may also wish to have regard to the guidance issued by the European Commission on Scoping in 2001: see 'Guidance on EIA: Scoping' (June 2001).

Information requirements

PINS Advice Note 7 provides the following guidance on information to be included in a scoping request:

> 'The minimum information that the applicant must provide with a scoping request is the same minimum information that must be provided with a screening request. Applicants should consider carefully the best time to request a scoping opinion. In order to gain the most from a scoping opinion, applicants should consider requesting the opinion once there is sufficient certainty about the description of the proposed development and the main elements of the proposed development likely to have a significant environmental effect. Where multiple and varied design and layout options remain under consideration (for example a number of route corridors associated with a proposed linear development), applicants should be aware that the Secretary of State and the consultees would only be able to provide high level comments. In addition, there may be insufficient detail in the scoping request to enable the Secretary of State to agree to scope out certain elements at this time.'

PINS Advice Note 7 makes clear, therefore, that the scoping request must include the same minimum information that must be provided with a screening request. In relation to a screening request the PINS Advice Note suggests that:

> 'The minimum information that applicants must provide with a screening request is set out in the EIA Regulations. This includes a plan, a description of the proposed development, including both the NSIP and any associated development ("the proposed development"), and a description of its possible effects on the environment.
>
> The Planning Inspectorate requests that the following information is shown on the plan:
>
> - the proposed draft DCO site boundary (identified by a red line) including any associated development;
> - any permanent land take required for the proposed development;

- any temporary land take required for construction, including construction compounds;
- any existing infrastructure which would be retained or upgraded for use as part of the proposed development and any existing infrastructure which would be removed; and
- features including planning constraints and designated areas on and around the site, such as national parks or historic landscapes.'

The PINS Advice Note further suggests that, where practical, the information should be set out on a single plan; but that, where more one plan is used, the plans should be a the same scale and a key plan should be used where appropriate.

Furthermore, in dealing with the description of the development and its possible effects on the environment, applicants should:

- set out the information using the headings in Schedule 3 to the EIA Regulations, being:
  - characteristics of the development;
  - location of the development; and
  - characteristics of the potential impacts;
- ensure that all aspects of the environment likely to be significantly affected by the development are addressed.

Developers are advised to consider the timing of any request carefully so as to obtain the most benefit from the process, waiting until there is sufficient certainty about the description of the scheme likely to have a significant environmental effect.

The PINS Advice Note recommends that, as well as the information required for a screening request, a scoping report should contain the following additional information:

- an outline of the main alternatives considered and the reasons for selecting a preferred option;
- results of desktop and baseline studies where available;
- referenced plans presented at an appropriate scale to convey clearly the information and all known aspects associated with the proposal;
- guidance and best practice to be relied upon, and whether this has been agreed with the relevant bodies (for example the statutory nature conservation bodies or local authorities) together with copies of correspondence to support these agreements;
- methods used or proposed to be used to predict impacts and the significance criteria framework used;
- any mitigation proposed and predicted residual impacts;
- where impacts from consequential or cumulative development have been identified, how applicants intend to assess these impacts in the ES (for example, a

high level assessment of the grid connection where this does not form part of the proposed development for a power station);

- an indication of any European designated nature conservation sites that are likely to be significantly affected by the proposed development and the nature of the likely significant impacts on these sites;
- key topics covered as part of applicants' scoping exercise; and
- an outline of the structure of the proposed ES.

It is also suggested that the scoping report should identify the 'elements' of the proposed development likely to have significant environmental effects. Where there is uncertainty, as much detail as possible should be provided in the form of parameters, or a worst case should be assumed.

A completed trans-boundary screening matrix should also be provided to facilitate the Secretary of State's consideration under reg 24 of the EIA Regulations: see also PINS Advice Note 12: Transboundary Impacts.

Procedural advice

Developers are advised to undertake their own informal consultation with the prescribed consultation bodies prior to submitting their request to the Secretary of State, so as to inform the request that they make.

They are also advised to give the Planning Inspectorate a minimum of ten working days' notice in advance of seeking a scoping opinion, accompanied by a GIS shapefile to identify the land in question. This will enable the Planning Inspectorate to allocate resources and identify the prescribed consultation bodies.

PINS Advice Note 7 also contains more detailed advice on referencing and administrative matters, which applicants should follow when preparing their requests.

Consulting on Preliminary Environmental Information

Written by Cain Ormodroyd
Edited by Michael Humphries QC

Where consent is sought for EIA development,[1] the interaction between the Infrastructure Planning (Environmental Impact Assessment) Regulations 2009 ('the Regulations') and the PA 2008 means that there is a legal requirement to consult on 'preliminary environmental information' ('PEI'). The provisions are inelegantly drafted. In order to understand the scope of this obligation and the level of information in practice required it is necessary to have reference to PINS and DCLG guidance.

Consulting on PEI

The Regulations provide by reg 10 that the statement of community consultation ('SoCC') required to be prepared by PA 2008, s 47 must state whether the development is EIA development. The implication of this is that the status of the development as EIA development must be resolved *before* formal pre-application consultation can begin.[2]

If the development is EIA development, the SOCC must also state 'how the applicant intends to publicise and consult on the preliminary environmental information'. Before the SoCC is finalised, relevant local authorities must be consulted. Once it has been finalised the applicant must consult the local community in accordance with it.[3]

PINS (now withdrawn) Advice Note 16 (April 2012) explained that 'when a developer consults a local authority on the SoCC the local authority will need to have the preliminary environmental information so that its response can be an informed one'.[4] Current guidance therefore suggests that PEI must be provided to local authorities when the SoCC is consulted on. It has been suggested in the past that the PEI need not be provided to the local authority[5]. The better view would appear to be that PEI should indeed be provided to the local authority; certainly if it is not then it is hard to see how the local authority can make any meaningful comment on how that information should be consulted on.

Even assuming that PEI is provided to the local authorities under s 47, however, this consultation process is purely on the contents of the SoCC; it does not involve the local authority or any other body commenting directly on the PEI.

1 See article on Requirement For Environmental Impact Assessment.
2 As noted in PINS Advice Note 7.
3 See article on Legal Requirements for a Statement of Community Consultation.
4 PINS (now withdrawn) Advice Note 16 (April 2012), p4.
5 See somewhat ambiguous entries in PINS Register of Advice: Response to Marcus Bate of Pinsent Masons dated 12 December 2011 and Response to Ben Wallace of ESBI Investments dated 26 January 2012.The conflict appears to have been resolved by clarifying that the position as set out in the guidance is the 'ideal' approach: Response to Keith Morrison on 29 July 2013.

The requirement to consult local authorities and other expert bodies arises from PA 2008, s 42. This section, unlike s 47, does not carry even any implied requirement to supply PEI as part of the consultation process. There is accordingly no legal requirement to consult local authorities or other bodies on the PEI itself.

It is nevertheless good practice to ensure that PEI is provided to expert consultees for their comment. PINS (now withdrawn) Advice Note 16 (April 2012) made clear the dangers in general of providing insufficiently detailed information to these consultees as part of the s 42 consultation exercise: 'unless there is a clear iterative consultation process followed and further documentation provided to consultees during the process the developer will risk being unable to demonstrate that the scheme was carefully considered in the light of consultation responses received.'

There is no objection to carrying out the ss 42 and 47 consultation process with local authorities (and others) in tandem, which avoids these problems.

The other option is to provide the information in a phased manner. This is perhaps more suitable for larger, more complex applications where it is not possible to collate all the necessary information at first. In these cases the draft Environmental Statement ('ES') can be provided to consultees later on in the pre-application process.[6]

What information must be included

PEI is defined in somewhat elliptical terms in reg 2(1) of the Regulations as:

> 'information referred to in Part 1 of Schedule 4 which—
>
> (a) has been compiled by the applicant; and
>
> (b) is reasonably required to assess the environmental effects of the development
>
> (and of any associated development)'

Part 1 of Schedule 4 sets out matters which may be required to be included in the ES provided that they are reasonably required to assess the environmental effects of the development and can reasonably be required to be compiled by the applicant. The ES must also include at least the matters set out in Part 2 of Schedule 4.[7]

The difference in the legislation between PEI and ES is therefore slight. PEI amounts to the reasonably required information falling within Part 1 of Schedule 4 which 'has been' compiled, whereas the ES amounts to that information which can reasonably be required to be compiled. In other words, it appears that it is for the applicant to decide what the contents of the PEI should be. When making this decision, a key factor to take into account is the expectation of DCLG that 'as much information as possible' will be provided to consultees[8]. The decision will ultimately be one for applicants to make, however.

6 See PINS Advice Note 7, p11.

7 See article on Preparation of an environmental statement.

8 DCLG Guidance on the pre-application process, paragraph 72.

In practical terms this decision will be shaped by the stage in the pre-application process at which the PEI is compiled. In this respect the applicant faces the familiar balancing exercise in consultation generally between consulting early enough so that the consultation exercise can be shown to be meaningful and late enough so that consultees can be sufficiently informed of the nature of the proposals to make useful comments.

One option is to use the ES itself, or a developed draft of it, as the PEI. The guidance states that this is unlikely to be 'the most appropriate way' to share environmental information with consultees. However, if it is considered 'appropriate' then it is open to applicants to do so: DCLG Guidance on the pre-application process, at paragraphs 72–3. Rather unhelpfully, the guidance does not explain why use of the ES as the PEI will or will not be considered 'appropriate'. It is clearly not about the level of technical information included, because the guidance cautions that applicants 'should be careful not to assume that non-specialist consultees would not be interested in any technical environmental information' and that such information should be included in all consultations.

Another option is to prepare a separate PEI report. This will be necessary if the ES is not in a sufficiently advanced stage to be provided inline with the pre-application procedure. It will be desirable if, notwithstanding the importance of providing as much information as possible, the ES is so long and detailed as to obscure the crucial issues which must be considered by respondents at the consultation stage.

Preparation of an Environmental Statement

Written by: Hereward Phillpot QC, ftb
Edited by: Michael Humphries QC, ftb

Infrastructure Planning (Environmental Impact Assessment) Regulations 2009, SI 1009/2263

The Infrastructure Planning (Environmental Impact Assessment) Regulations 2009, SI 2009/2263 (the 'EIA Regulations'), reg 9 sets out a procedure intended to facilitate the preparation of an environmental statement (ES).

Pursuant to reg 9(1) and (2), the procedure may be triggered by one of four possible events:

- the applicant notifying the Secretary of State under regulation 6(1)(b) of the EIA Regulations that it intends to provide an ES in respect of a proposed application for a development consent order (DCO);
- the applicant notifying the authority responsible for the discharge of a requirement on an existing DCO (the relevant authority) under regulation 6(2)(b) of the EIA Regulations that it intends to provide an updated ES in respect of a proposed application to discharge the requirement;
- the Secretary of State giving a screening opinion in respect of a proposed application for a DCO to the effect that the proposed development is EIA development; or
- the relevant authority giving a subsequent screening opinion to the effect that supplementary information is needed to enable it to determine an application to discharge a requirement.

The procedure itself is prescribed by reg 9(1), and involves a number of steps that the Secretary of State or the relevant authority, as the case may be, must follow.

The consultation bodies (defined in reg 2(1) of the EIA Regulations) must be notified in writing of the name and address of the applicant, and of the duty imposed on those bodies by reg 9(3) to make information available to that person. The duty is subject to the exceptions from the duty to disclose environmental information under the Environmental Information Regulations 2004 or the equivalent Scottish legislation (see reg 9(4)).

The applicant must be notified in writing of the names and addresses of the bodies so notified.

The applicant must also be notified in writing of any person whom it considers: (a) to be, or to be likely to be, affected by or to have an interest in the proposed development; and (b) to be unlikely to become aware of the proposed development by means of the pre-application and application procedure in Part 5 of the Planning Act 2008 (ie pre-application consultation etc).

Preparation of ES

The law, guidance and good practice on the preparation of ES is extensive, and it would be unrealistic to seek to provide a comprehensive guide to those matters in this article. Instead, the article to provide a brief overview of the key points, including those which have now been set down in the guidance issued by the Planning Inspectorate on behalf of the Secretary of State.

General case law

As the courts have become increasingly familiar with the process of EIA, so the potential pitfalls have become better mapped and understood, and the degree of risk associated with the process has reduced and become more readily manageable. A realistic and pragmatic approach to the process of EIA and the contents of ES has developed, recognising that there will often be room for legitimate disagreement as to the appropriate scope and content of an ES, without any issue of law arising.

The following key principles can be discerned:

- The ES does not have to contain every scrap of environmental information, and need only cover the main effects or likely significant effects. Excessive information can be a hindrance to good decision-making (see eg *R v Rochdale Metropolitan Borough Council, ex parte Milne* (2000) 81 P&CR 27; *R (Bedford) v London Borough of Islington* [2002] EWHC 2044 (Admin); *Derbyshire Waste Ltd v Blewett and Secretary of State for the Environment* [2004] EWCA Civ 1508).
- Where a project is to be approved in stages, with details of some matters reserved for approval at a later stage, the ES accompanying the application for the 'in principle' approval must allow the decision-maker to understand the likely significant effects of the project as a whole (see eg *R v London Borough of Bromley, ex parte Barker* [2006] UKHL 52).
- To enable this to be done, clear parameters will need to be established for the purpose of EIA, and secured in the approval so that the effects of the development as approved do not exceed those assessed (see *R v. Rochdale Metropolitan Borough Council, ex parte Milne* (above)). This will often be an important issue with NSIPs, where much of the detail is likely to remain at large at the DCO stage. In this regard, further guidance has been issued by the Planning Inspectorate on how to deal with the resulting uncertainties (see below).
- Where a development is linked to a larger project, the ES for that development must consider the cumulative effects that are likely to arise as a result (see eg *R (Brown) v Carlisle City Council* [2010] EWCA Civ 523).
- It is important that members of the public do not have to engage in a 'paper chase' to piece together the ES, which must therefore be a properly integrated and accessible document accompanied by a non-technical summary (see *Berkeley v Secretary of State for the Environment* [2001] 2 AC 603).
- An ES will not be adequate if it lacks a key piece of information necessary to ascertain whether significant effects are likely. It is not acceptable to leave the gathering of that additional information until after consent has been granted

(*R v Cornwall County Council, ex parte Hardy* [2001] Env LR 25). That is to be distinguished from situations where it is possible to reach a conclusion on likely significant effects without certain information, but provision is made for that information to be gathered after permission is granted so as to inform mitigation measures etc (see eg *R (PPG 11 Ltd) v Dorset County Council* [2003] All ER (D) 68 (Jun)).

- Mitigation measures can be taken into account in determining likely significant effects, although these must be secured in any consent that is granted, and their likely effectiveness must be taken into account (see eg *R (PPG 11 Ltd) v Dorset County Council* (above)).

Guidance

The Planning Inspectorate's guidance relating to environmental impact assessment and the preparation of an ES is contained in a series of Advice Notes. Those of most direct relevance here are Advice Note 3: EIA Consultation and Notification; Advice Note 7: Environmental Impact Assessment: Preliminary Environmental Information, Screening and Scoping; Advice Note 9: Using the 'Rochdale Envelope'; Advice Note 12: Transboundary Impacts; and also Advice Note 17: Cumulative effects assessment.

Advice Note 3: EIA Consultation and Notification

Advice Note 3 sets out the approach to be taken by the Secretary of State when identifying consultation bodies to be notified under reg 9 of the EIA Regulations and, where relevant, consulted on the scope of the ES under reg 8.

It explains that in addition to providing the applicant with the list of the notified consultation bodies, the Secretary of State will also provide details of any 'non-prescribed consultation bodies', where appropriate. These 'non-prescribed' bodies are those with relevant functions and responsibilities but which are not prescribed under s 42(a) of the PA 2008. The applicant is therefore not obliged to consult with them in order to satisfy the pre-application consultation obligations.

The Secretary of State's list of notified consultation bodies will be used in due course as part of the process of determining whether the applicant has complied with the pre-application procedure. If the applicant identifies and consults fewer bodies than appear on the list, a clear explanation will be needed.

The Advice Note sets out in detail the approach that the Secretary of State will adopt when consulting and notifying in relation to the following activities:

- identifying local authorities;
- applying the 'relevance test' of the APFP Regulations;
- applying the 'circumstances test' of the APFP Regulations;
- identifying statutory undertakers as prescribed in the APFP Regulations;
- identifying parish/community councils;
- notifying and consulting in Wales;

- notifying and consulting the devolved administrations and the British Crown dependencies;
- notifying and consulting where a proposed NSIP includes an offshore element; and
- notifying other European Economic Area states.

Advice Note 7: Environmental Impact Assessment: Preliminary Environmental Information, Screening and Scoping

Advice Note 7 explains when a nationally significant infrastructure project should be considered as Environmental Impact Assessment (EIA) development under the Infrastructure Planning (Environmental Impact Assessment) Regulations 2009 (the EIA Regulations). It details the procedural requirements that apply to NSIPs that are EIA development. This includes the role of preliminary environmental information; pre-application consultation requirements on applicants; notification and consultation requirements on the Secretary of State; and the procedures for screening and scoping developments.

Before submitting an application for development consent, an applicant has an opportunity to ask the Secretary of State for a formal written opinion on the information to be included in an ES; this is known as a 'scoping opinion'. Before adopting a scoping opinion the Secretary of State must consult the prescribed bodies, who have 28 days to respond. A separate article in this work details the various legal requirements and guidance relating to scoping.

Advice Note 9: Using the 'Rochdale Envelope'

The principles behind the use of the 'Rochdale Envelope' are considered in Advice Note 9, but the points summarised below are of particular relevance to the preparation of the ES.

- The developer should seek to identify those aspects of the development that are likely to give rise to significant adverse impacts, such that the maximum potential adverse impacts have been properly assessed and can be taken into account.
- The ES must consider the inter-relationship between aspects of the proposed development, and explain how these have been assessed to address the environmental impacts as a whole.
- Where certain details remain unresolved, the ES will need to clearly identify those elements; provide reasons why these cannot be finalised at this stage; and assess variations of the proposals so as to capture the likely worst case within the parameters set (this should be done as simply as possible, and in a manner that aids the making of recommendations and decision-making).
- In identifying potential cumulative impacts with other major developments, applicants should seek to identify relevant developments through consultation with local planning authorities and other relevant authorities on the basis of those that are:
    - under construction;

  - permitted application(s) not yet determined;
  - projects on the Planning Inspectorate's Programme of Projects;
  - identified in the relevant Development Plan (and emerging Development Plans – with appropriate weight being given as they move closer to adoption); and
  - identified in other plans and programmes which set the framework for future development consents/approvals, where such development is likely to come forward.

- The applicant will need to judge whether the undecided parameters are such as to preclude a robust assessment in the ES, and should ensure that the parameters are not so wide ranging as to represent effectively different schemes. The parameters need to be clearly defined in the draft DCO and in the ES.

Advice Note 12: Transboundary Impacts

Regulation 24 of the EIA Regulations sets out the basis for statutory notification and consultation with other European Economic Area Member States ('EEA States'). This applies where the Secretary of State is of the view that an NSIP is likely to have significant effects on the environment in another EEA State; or another EEA State is of the view that its environment is likely to be significantly affected by an NSIP. This duty applies until the decision on the Development Consent Order (DCO) application is made.

In addition, there may be occasions for an applicant to consult directly with bodies in another State. There are also opportunities for other EEA States to become involved in the examination of a DCO application.

Advice Note 12 sets out the procedures for transboundary notification and consultation in association with an application for a DCO under the PA 2008, where such development, in the view of the Secretary of State, has likely significant effects on the environment in other EEA States. It sets out how the obligations under reg 24 of the EIA Regulations will be met, particularly in the light of the statutory timeframes as prescribed by the PA 2008. The applicant has no formal role under the reg 24 process, as the duties prescribed by reg 24 in notifying and consulting with other EEA States on potential transboundary impacts, are the responsibility of the Secretary of State. However, when fulfilling these duties on behalf of the Secretary of State, the Planning Inspectorate uses the information provided by the applicant to assist in determining the potential for likely significant effects on the environment in other EEA States. To this end, The Advice Note provides that the applicant is requested to provide information to the Planning Inspectorate to enable a view to be reached as to whether the development is likely to have significant transboundary effects on other EEA States. The Advice Note makes clear that information about the potential for transboundary effects should be provided by the applicant:

- With the scoping request, if a scoping opinion is requested by the applicant from the Secretary of State under reg 8 of the EIA Regulations, and
- With the DCO application, when submitted to the Secretary of State for acceptance.

Advice Note 17: Cumulative effects assessment

The requirement for cumulative effects assessment (CEA) is set out in Article 4(3) and Article 5(1) of the EIA Directive. With respect to applications for development consent under the PA2008, the requirements of the Directive are implemented through reg 2 of and Sch 4 para 20 to the EIA Regulations.

Advice Note 17 seeks to provide:

- a brief description of the legal context and obligations placed on an applicant, with respect to cumulative effects under national planning policy and the EIA Regulations;
- an overview of the CEA process that applicants may wish to adopt for NSIPs; and
- advice regarding a staged approach and the use of consistent template formats for documenting the CEA within an applicant's ES.

Environmental Impact Assessment: Trans-Boundary Consultation

Written by: Hereward Phillpot QC, ftb
Edited by: Michael Humphries QC, ftb

The issue

When should the Secretary of State initiate the process of trans-boundary consultation on the environmental effects of a proposed nationally significant infrastructure project (NSIP), how is the decision made, and what steps should be taken by promoters to address this question?

The law

The relevant law is to be found in the Infrastructure Planning (Environmental Impact Assessment) Regulations 2009, SI 2009/2263 (the '2009 Regulations'), reg 24 which transpose the requirements of Article 7 of EU Directive 2011/92/EU (the EIA Directive) into domestic law. Article 7 and Regulation 24 apply to European Economic Area ('EEA') States by virtue of section 2(2) of the European Communities Act 1972 as modified by section 2(5) of the European Economic Area Act 1993.

Regulation 24 provides:

'(1) This regulation applies where–

(a) one of the events mentioned in regulation 4(2) occurs; or

(b) it otherwise comes to the attention of the Secretary of State that development proposed to be carried out in England, Wales or Scotland is the subject of an EIA application, and the Secretary of State is of the view that the development is likely to have significant effects on the environment in another EEA State; or

(c) another EEA State likely to be significantly affected by such development so requests.

(2) Where this regulation applies, the Secretary of State must -

(a) send to the EEA State as soon as possible and no later than their date of publication in The London Gazette referred to in sub-paragraph (b), the particulars required by paragraph (3) and, if it thinks fit, the information referred to in paragraph (4);

(b) publish the information in sub-paragraph (a) in a notice placed in–

(i) the London Gazette, in relation to all proposed development; and

(ii) the Edinburgh Gazette, in relation to development proposed to be carried out in Scotland, indicating the address where additional information is available; and

(c) give the EEA State a reasonable time in which to indicate whether it wishes to participate in the procedure for which these Regulations provide.

(3) The particulars mentioned in paragraph (2)(a) are–

(a) a description of the development, together with any available information on its possible significant effect on the environment in another EEA State; and

(b) information on the nature of the decision which may be taken.

(4) Where an EEA State indicates, in accordance with paragraph (2)(c), that it wishes to participate in the procedure for which these Regulations provide, the Secretary of State must as soon as possible send to that EEA State the following information–

(a) a copy of the application concerned;

(b) a copy of any environmental statement in respect of the development to which that application relates; and

(c) relevant information regarding the procedure under these Regulations,

but only to the extent that such information has not been provided to the EEA State earlier in accordance with paragraph 2(a).

(5) The Commission must also ensure that the EEA State concerned is given an opportunity, before development consent for the development is granted, to forward to the Secretary of State, within a reasonable time, the opinions of its public and the authorities referred to in Article 6(1) of the Directive on the information supplied.

(6) The Commission must in accordance with Article 7(4) of the Directive–

(a) enter into consultations with the EEA State concerned regarding, inter alia, the potential significant effects of the development on the environment of that EEA State and the measures envisaged to reduce or eliminate such effects; and

(b) determine in agreement with the other EEA State a reasonable period of time for the duration of the consultation period.

(7) Where an EEA State has been consulted in accordance with paragraph (6), on the determination of the application concerned the Secretary of State must inform the EEA State of the decision and must forward to it a statement of–

(a) the content of the decision and any requirements attached to it;

(b) the main reasons and considerations on which the decision is based including relevant information about the participation of the public; and

(c) a description, where necessary, of the main measures to avoid, reduce and, if possible, offset the major adverse effects of the development.'

Thus the trans-boundary consultation process can be triggered either by the Secretary of State reaching the view that the proposed development is likely to have significant effects on the environment in another EEA State, or as a result of a request from another EEA State. An example of the latter scenario occurred during the process of determining the application for the proposed new nuclear power station at Hinkley Point in Somerset, where the Austrian Government made a request following the close of the examination. The Austrian Government consulted its own people on the proposed application, and the views expressed in response were taken into account by the Secretary of State in reaching his decision.

All NSIPs that are EIA development will be screened by the Planning Inspectorate on the Secretary of State's behalf on a case by case basis for likely significant effects on another EEA State.

In reaching a view on whether to initiate the process, the Secretary of State must decide whether significant environmental effects on other EEA States are 'likely'.

The Court of Appeal has held that for these purposes 'likely' should be interpreted in the same way as it has been where it appears elsewhere in the 2009 Regulations and the EIA Directive (*R (on the application of An Taisce) v (1) The Secretary of State for Energy and Climate Change (2) NNB Generation Company Limited* [2014] EWCA Civ 1111). An Taisce (The National Trust for Ireland) had argued that a significant adverse effect should be considered 'likely' if it cannot be excluded on the basis of objective evidence. This approach, mirroring that taken by the ECJ to the Habitats Directive in the *Waddenzee* case, was rejected by the Court of Appeal, which held that:

1 The words 'likely to have significant effects on the environment' must have the same meaning throughout the EIA Directive.

2 'Likely' for these purposes does not mean more probable than not.

3 There is a clear distinction between the Habitats Directive and the EIA Directive for these purposes.

4 The 'real risk' approach to likelihood that the domestic authorities have so far adopted when considering the EIA Directive embodies a precautionary approach.

5 Adopting An Taisce's suggested approach would be contrary to the objectives of the EIA Directive as the public and decision-makers would be likely to 'lose the wood for the trees', thereby causing the EIA process to become less effective as an aid to good environmental decision-making.

In deciding whether a project is 'likely' to have a significant adverse effect on the environment of another EEA State, the Secretary of State should therefore approach the question on the basis of whether this is a 'real risk' or a 'serious possibility'. This involves considering both the magnitude and complexity of the potential impact, and the probability of it occurring. The greater the potential impact, the lower will be the level of probability at which the competent authority will decide that it should be subject to the environmental impact assessment process (see *Miller v North Yorkshire CC* [2009] EWHC 2172 (Admin) per Hickinbottom J at paragraphs 31 and 32). The competent authority must therefore make a judgment, balancing the severity of any potential environmental harm against the probability of it occurring.

Once triggered, the process takes place in two stages. First, the paragraph (2) stage involves notification of the EEA State concerned, and providing it with an opportunity to consider whether it wishes to participate. For these purposes the EEA State need only be given relatively limited information about the project (paragraph (3)), although in practice it is likely that it would be provided with a copy of the environmental statement.

If the EEA State in question decides that it does not wish to participate, that is the end of the process. However, if it decides to participate it is then sent a copy of the application, the environmental statement and procedural information and given an opportunity to consult its public and provide their views to the Secretary of State (paragraphs (4) and (5)).

It is the EEA State concerned that must consult its public, and not the Secretary of State. The Secretary of State's role is confined to facilitating the process of consultation through notification and the provision of information, and then taking the results of that consultation into account in making his decision on the application. If the consultation process undertaken by the relevant EEA State is materially defective, however, there may be grounds on which the Secretary of State's ultimate decision could be challenged in the Courts.

Guidance

The Planning Inspectorate's guidance on the trans-boundary consultation process is contained in Advice Note 12: Development with significant trans-boundary impacts consultation (2015).

In addition to providing an explanation of the legal background and the approach adopted by the Planning Inspectorate and the Government, Advice Note 12 also guides promoters on their role in making sure that the relevant information is available at the appropriate times.

Whilst it is important to read the guidance as a whole, the following specific guidance is give to applicants:

> 'The Role of the Applicant
>
> The applicant may wish to consider whether to undertake their own consultation with governmental divisions and interest groups within EEA States. This could be informed by an applicant's own research into environmental issues and may also be informed by the transboundary screenings issued by the Secretary of State for the NSIP.
>
> Whilst not a statutory requirement, the applicant is advised to have regard to any transboundary screenings issued by the Secretary of State. The Annex to this Advice Note sets out the criteria and relevant considerations that will be taken into account by the Secretary of State. Where the Secretary of State is of the view that the proposed NSIP is likely to have a significant effect on the environment in another EEA State, the applicant may wish to

> engage with certain appropriate bodies within those States. Such consultation may form part of the applicant's formal or informal consultation under the pre-application stage of the DCO process, and should be evidenced in the consultation report submitted with the DCO application.
>
> The applicant is advised to undertake such consultation to ensure that the potential issues and concerns are addressed, where possible, before the DCO application is submitted, to seek to resolve transboundary effects, which otherwise may become an issue during the examination.'

The Advice Note states that Planning Inspectorate will identify the EEA States to be notified under reg 24 primarily on the basis of the type of NSIP, its location, and the nature of the receiving environment: criteria are given in the Annex to the Advice Note. However, it makes clear that the Planning Inspectorate will exercise reasonable discretion to determine likely significant effects in another EEA State, based in part upon the information supplied by the applicant. In exercising this discretion and identifying that an NSIP is 'likely to have significant effects' on other EEA States, this should be taken as meaning that in the view of the Secretary of State there is a possibility or real risk, embodying a precautionary approach, that the development will have an effect, and not that a development will definitely have an effect. Specific guidance is given on the approach to nuclear power stations.

So far, only one new nuclear power station has been screened by the Planning Inspectorate (using the 2011 version of Advice Note 12), and in that case it was considered that there was compelling evidence that significant trans-boundary effects were not likely. The reason for reaching this view was that reliance could be placed on the strict system of licensing and regulation to ensure that accidental release of radioactive materials was not likely to occur. On the basis that the same system applies to all new nuclear power stations in the United Kingdom, it seems unlikely that any other such proposals would be regarded as likely to give rise to significant trans-boundary effects by reason of accidental release of radioactive materials.

Advice Note 12 also gives guidance on the approach to be taken to the timing of the different stages of the trans-boundary process.

Discussion

The profile of the issue of trans-boundary consultation has been raised as a result of the *An Taisce* litigation. It is also important to note that the Committee set up to monitor compliance with the obligations created by the original legal source of the trans-boundary consultation requirement - the UNECE Convention on Environmental Impact Assessment in a Trans-boundary Conext (the Espoo Convention) – has become increasingly active and interventionist.

Failure to undertake trans-boundary consultation where it ought to have taken place can therefore present a significant litigation risk.

Whilst the Court of Appeal in the *An Taisce* case rejected the argument that a significant trans-boundary effect was 'likely' for these purposes if it cannot be excluded on the basis of objective evidence, it did not entirely close the door on future litigation to determine what is in fact the correct approach to likelihood for the purposes of EIA. On the facts of that particular case it was successfully argued by the Secretary of State and the promoter that no matter how low the threshold might be set by the Court of Justice of the European Union (CJEU), the Secretary of State's decision would still be lawful. Once the Claimant's 'zero risk' approach had been rejected, it was therefore unnecessary to decide whether the 'real risk' approach might be overturned by the CJEU in order to dispose of the case.

However, at paragraph 33 Sullivan LJ said that if the Court of Appeal were a court of final appeal, and it was therefore necessary to apply the '*CILFIT* test':

> '… I could not say that I was convinced that the other Member States and the CJEU would necessarily conclude that the 'real risk' approach is the correct approach to the likelihood of significant effects on the environment for the purposes of the EIA Directive'.

The '*CILFIT* test' is a reference to the case of *CILFIT (Srl) v Ministry of Health* (Case 283/81) [1982] ECR 3415, concerning the approach to be taken by a court of final appeal to the issue of whether or not a reference should be made to the European Court of Justice (CJEU). In the *CILFIT* case the CJEU said that the national court could only refrain from submitting a question of EU law to the CJEU if it is convinced that the correct application of EU law is so obvious as to leave no scope for any reasonable doubt as to the manner in which the question raised is to be resolved, and convinced that the matter would be equally obvious to the courts of the other Member States and the CJEU.

Sullivan LJ's comment seems to create room for future argument as to what the correct approach should be, albeit in another case with stronger facts. Importantly, it creates room for an argument that a reference ought to be made to the CJEU, an outcome which any promoter should regard with great concern because of the considerable delay and uncertainty that a reference necessarily brings with it.

The cautious approach espoused by the guidance would therefore seem prudent. In most cases promoters ought not to have much to fear from the trans-boundary consultation process. If there is a real risk of significant adverse trans-boundary effects, the process of assessment and pre-application consultation itself may be complicated by the need to deal with another State, but if done properly it is likely to be less risky than the alternative.

Habitats Regulations Assessment

Written by: Gregory Jones QC, ftb
Edited by: Michael Humphries QC, ftb

Introduction

This article considers the circumstances in which an NSIP will require an appropriate assessment under the Conservation of Habitats and Species Regulations 2010, SI 2010/490 (as amended) ('the Habitats Regulations'), the information that should inform such an assessment and the consequences arising out of such an assessment.

This article should be read in conjunction with those considering the EIA process, which will often overlap with assessment under the Habitats Regulations. Although the EIA process is designed to *inform* the final decision, whereas assessment under the Habitats Regulations may, in certain circumstances, actually *determine* the final decision, (see eg Lord Carnwath Foreword to Jones: 'Habitats Directive: A Developer's Obstacle Course?).

The legislative background

The UK is bound by the terms of Council Directive 92/43/EEC of 21 May 1992 on the conservation of natural habitats and of wild fauna and flora ('the Habitats Directive') which has been transposed into domestic law through the Habitats Regulations. Although we are here mainly concerned with Articles 2 and 3 of the Habitats Directive, as the case law has emphasised the need for it to be considered as a whole, the whole of Article 6 is set out below:

1 For special areas of conservation, Member States shall establish the necessary conservation measures involving, if need be, appropriate management plans specifically designed for the sites or integrated into other development plans, and appropriate statutory, administrative or contractual measures which correspond to the ecological requirements of the natural habitat types in Annex I and the species in Annex II present on the sites.

2 Member States shall take appropriate steps to avoid, in the special areas of conservation, the deterioration of natural habitats and the habitats of species as well as disturbance of the species for which the areas have been designated, in so far as such disturbance could be significant in relation to the objectives of this Directive.

3 Any plan or project not directly connected with or necessary to the management of the site but likely to have a significant effect thereon, either individually or in combination with other plans or projects, shall be subject to appropriate assessment of its implications for the site in view of the site's conservation objectives. In the light of the conclusions of the assessment of the implications for the site and subject

to the provisions of paragraph 4, the competent national authorities shall agree to the plan or project only after having ascertained that it will not adversely affect the integrity of the site concerned and, if appropriate, after having obtained the opinion of the general public.

4 If, in spite of a negative assessment of the implications for the site and in the absence of alternative solutions, a plan or project must nevertheless be carried out for imperative reasons of overriding public interest, including those of a social or economic nature, the Member State shall take all compensatory measures necessary to ensure that the overall coherence of Natura 2000 is protected. It shall inform the Commission of the compensatory measures adopted.

5 Where the site concerned hosts a priority natural habitat type and/or a priority species, the only considerations which may be raised are those relating to human health or public safety, to beneficial consequences of primary importance for the environment or, further to an opinion from the Commission, to other imperative reasons of overriding public interest.

The effect of these provisions in the UK is that any plan or project which may affect a Special Area of Conservation ('SAC'), a candidate SAC or a Special Protection Area ('SPA') is subject to Regulations. In addition, the UK Government has a policy of applying their provisions to both Ramsar sites and potential SPAs. In the text that follows, these are referred to simply as 'sites'.

The process of assessment under the Habitats Regulations

PINS Advice Note 10 on *Habitats Regulation Assessment* (January 2013) follows the European Commission's *Methodological Guidance on the Provisions of Articles 6(3) and (4) of the Habitats Directive* in breaking down the process down into four stages (screening, appropriate assessment, alternative solutions and imperative reasons of overriding public interest, or 'IROPI'), and that approach is adopted here for consistency.

In relation to stages 3 and 4, it is noted that the Department for the Environment, Food and Rural Affairs has recently consulted upon draft guidance on *Alternative solutions, imperative reasons of overriding public interest (IROPI) and compensatory measures.* It is to be expected that final guidance on these matters will be forthcoming in due course.

Stage 1: Screening

Article 6(3) of the Directive requires an Appropriate Assessment to be carried out where there is a plan or project, that is not connected to the management of the site, but is 'likely to have a significant effect' upon the site either individually or in combination.

In Case C-258/11 *Sweetman v An Bord Pleanála*, in her opinion, the Advocate-General ('the AG') succinctly summed up in plain language the purpose behind this stage as requiring developers to ask the question 'should we bother to check' whether the plan or project adversely affects the integrity of the site? Stage 1 is therefore a preliminary stage.

When is an effect 'likely'? It does not have the same meaning as the English civil law test of 'more likely than not' (ie more than 50%). Applying the so-called 'precautionary approach' (see micro article 100) the courts have given the word 'likely' a much wider definition that an ordinary reading of the word might suggest. While to most it suggests an event that might well occur, cases such as Case C-127/02 *Landelijke Vereniging tot Behoud van de Waddenzee* [2004] ECR I-7405, *R (Loader) v Secretary of State for Communities and Local Government* [2012] EWCA Civ 869 and *R (Bateman) v South Cambridgeshire DC* [2011] EWCA Civ 157 put it beyond doubt that the correct approach is to look for effects that 'such a risk exists if it cannot be excluded on the basis of objective information that the plan or project will have significant effects on the site concerned' and 'in the case of doubt about the absence of significant effects … an assessment must be carried out' (see *Waddenzee*, para 44). An effect is therefore likely where there is only a risk, or a mere possibility, of it occurring.

What is a 'significant effect'? To all intents and purposes, the definition of significant effects appeared settled after *Waddenzee*, which held that where 'a plan or project has an effect on that site but is not likely to undermine its conservation objectives, it cannot be considered likely to have a significant effect on the site concerned' (see para 47). *Waddenzee* continued at para 48 to say that where those objectives were undermined, it necessarily followed that there were significant effects. The focus therefore was clearly on the 'characteristics and specific environmental conditions of the site concerned by that plan or project' that went to the sites conservation objectives (also at para 48).

However, the recent *Sweetman* case, on one reading, modifies this approach. There, the AG's opinion's was that 'significant' set a 'very low' de minimis threshold excluding only those sites that have 'no appreciable effect on the site'. That threshold 'operates as a trigger, in order to determine whether an appropriate assessment must be undertaken'. However, the AG also considered that the threshold was not so low as to not exclude plans or projects 'having any effect whatsoever on the site' (emphasis added) so as not to prevent all activities on or near the site becoming 'impossible by reason of legislative overkill' (see paras 48 to 49).

Although the AG did not refer to *Waddenzee* in this part of her opinion, the Court did in its decision, albeit only to set out what was said in *Waddenzee*: 'Where a plan or project not directly connected with or necessary to the management of a site is likely to undermine the site's conservation objectives, it must be considered likely to have a significant effect on that site. The assessment of that risk must be made in the light of, in particular, the characteristics and specific environmental conditions of the site concerned by such a plan or project' (see para 30). It therefore seems that the better view is that the focus remains on the site's conservation objectives.

In assessing both significance and likelihood, it is permissible and indeed desirable, to have regard to mitigation measures. If the appropriate authority considers that those measures will be effective, it can base its conclusion that significant effects are unlikely upon then, and dispense with the need for an appropriate assessment. In *Feeney v Secretary of State for Transport* [2013] EWHC 1238 (Admin), Ouseley J held that if the appropriate authority 'lawfully concludes that the [mitigation] would exclude [the risk of a significant effect] on the basis of objective information, it is difficult to see on what basis an appropriate assessment could still be required' (see para 53). However, as the

A5 Alliance [2013] NIQB 30 case demonstrates, doubts about the efficacy of proposed mitigation measures will prevent a conclusion that significant effects are unlikely, and an appropriate assessment will be required.

Although the recent decision in *Champion v North Norfolk DC* [2013] EWHC 1065 (Admin) appears to cast doubt on this approach when it comes to mitigation in the form of planning conditions, it is respectfully suggested that the approach is not likely to be followed by the ECJ. There it was held that a decision maker could not determine that no appropriate assessment was required (ie that significant effects were not likely) while at the same time requiring a condition to mitigate effects (as that condition would not be necessary if those effects were not likely). This appears to be taking two limbs of what is a sequential in reverse order. The first question ought to be whether the plan or project has a condition attached to it, and the second question is whether, given that condition, the project is likely to have significant effects. If it is not, then an appropriate assessment will not be required.

The evidence base at Stage 1 screening

Regulation 61(2) of the Habitats Regulations places a mandatory requirement on a person applying for development consent to provide the appropriate authority with such information as may be required: (a) for the purposes of the appropriate assessment; or (b) to enable them to determine whether an appropriate assessment is required. If insufficient information is submitted for those purposes, the competent authority may, and most likely will, refuse to accept the application for a DCO.

It is therefore necessary to engage in a robust process of pre-application consultation with the relevant statutory nature conservation bodies to ensure that the potential impacts of the development have been identified and addressed in sufficient detail before submission. It is likely that this process will overlap with the consultation required for EIA purposes. It is also good practice to consult more widely.

It is noted here that practice in the UK in relation to the information to be provided at the screening stage goes beyond what would otherwise be thought to be required in light of the AG in *Sweetman* characterising the first stage as the 'should we bother to check?' stage. Instead, as PINS Guidance Note 10 makes clear, the level of detail expected to accompany application is high, such that it 'should result in information which will show beyond reasonable doubt whether any European sites are likely to be affected… describe the likely impacts on the conservation objectives of the European sites … and describe whether the impacts are likely to be significantly adverse'. It is therefore the case that a substantial amount of work may have to be undertaken prior to submission in order to clear this hurdle, notwithstanding that the European approach seems to contemplate a less exacting standard at this stage of the process.

PINS Guidance Note 10 lists the following as issues that developers 'may' (read 'should') wish to include in their stage one screening assessment or report:

- a detailed description of the development, processes, timings, and method of work;
- proposed details of the methodology used to determine which European sites to include within the assessment;

- a plan and description of the European site(s) and all of the associated interest features potentially affected;
- an appraisal of the project's likely impacts on the European site(s);
- an outline and interpretation of baseline data;
- an appraisal of any other plans or projects likely to have a significant effect in combination with the proposed development;
- an evaluation of the potential for the scheme to require two or more appropriate assessments by different competent authorities, and;
- a statement which specifies where the site boundaries of the scheme overlap into devolved assemblies or other European member states.

That screening report will have to come to one of two conclusions: (a) there is no potential likely significant effect on a site; or (b) an anticipated potential significant effect on a site exists.

Where screening concludes that there will be no potential likely significant effect on a site, it will be necessary to produce a 'no significant effects screening report'. There is no template for this report, but it must make it clear what the developer's view is and contain sufficient information to enable the competent authority to reach its own (hopefully concurring) view.

Where screening concludes that there is an anticipated potential likely significant effect on a European site, alone of in combination with other projects, the applicant's HRA needs to move to Stage 2 (Appropriate Assessment) of the HRA process.

The report on the outcome of screening assessment should clearly identify which European sites are being taken forward to Stage 2 (Appropriate Assessment) and which have been screened out.

Stage 2: Appropriate Assessment

Having established that a plan or project is likely to have significant effects on the site, the next stage is to subject the plan or project to an 'appropriate assessment of its implications for the site in view of the site's conservation objectives'.

The question the appropriate assessment addresses is whether the plan or project will 'adversely affect the integrity of the site concerned'. It is not immediately clear from the English language version what that phrase means, and its interpretation was precisely the question the court considered in *Sweetman*.

The AG's opinion was that 'integrity' was directed at the 'essential unity' of the site (see paras 53 to 56). Adopting a purposive approach to interpretation, in making the determination as to whether integrity was affected, it was again necessary to focus on why the site was designated and what its conservation objectives were. If attributes of the site going to its designation and conservation objectives were adversely affected by the proposed plan or project, then so would be its integrity. Further, it was necessary to make the assessment on the basis of the precautionary principle – only if the appropriate authority were 'convinced' that the plan or project would not affect the integrity of the site could that finding properly be made (see para 51). On that basis, a temporary loss of part of the site, perhaps during construction works, is less likely to result in an adverse effect on integrity than a permanent loss.

The CJEU expressly adopted the AG's opinion in holding that the integrity of a site will not be adversely affected where the plan or project permits the 'lasting preservation of the constitutive characteristics of the site concerned that are connected to the presence of a natural habitat type whose preservation was the objective justifying the designation of that site…' (see para 39).

The CJEU emphasised (at para 40) that having made that assessment, the precautionary principle required that authorisation could only be granted 'on condition that the competent authorities – once all aspects of the plan or project have been identified which can, by themselves or in combination with other plans or projects, affect the conservation objectives of the site concerned, and in the light of the best scientific knowledge in the field – are certain that the plan or project will not have lasting adverse effects on the integrity of that site. That is so where no reasonable scientific doubt remains as to the absence of such effects.'

The PINS Guidance suggests that as a minimum, the applicant's HRA report should contain:

- evidence about the project's impacts on the integrity of protected sites
- a description of any mitigation measures proposed which avoid or reduce each impact, and any residual effect
- a schedule indicating the timing of mitigation measures in relation to the progress of the development
- cross references to the relevant DCO requirements and development consent obligations that secure these mitigation measures, and identification of any factors that might affect the certainty of their implementation
- a statement as to whether any residual effects constitute an adverse impact on the integrity of European sites
- evidence to demonstrate that the applicant has fully consulted and had regard to comments received by the relevant SNCBs during pre-application consultation.

Stage 3: Assessment of alternative solutions

Where, having carried out an appropriate assessment and come to the view that the integrity of the site will be adversely affected, authorisation can only be granted where a further assessment has been carried out and concluded that there are no alternative *solutions* to the proposed development, not just alternative developments. This is an onerous hurdle to clear and will require a detailed and thorough examination of alternative solutions to deliver the objectives of the project. That assessment will include considering, at a minimum, not going ahead with the project, as well as locating the project in other regions or even countries. It must be objectively demonstrated that there are no other feasible alternatives that will not affect the integrity of the site, and that the proposal is the least damaging of all the solutions as regards the integrity of the site and the habitats and species therein. The assessment of whether there are alternative sites must be based solely on ecological criteria; matters of economics and social policy are only considered at stage 4.

Stage 4: Imperative Reasons of Overriding Public Interest ('IROPI')

If it is concluded that there are no alternative solutions, then development consent can only be granted if there are IROPI for granting consent. In such a case, compensatory measures must be taken.

Where the site hosts a protected species or habitat, IROPI must relate to human health, public safety or beneficial consequences of the development of primary importance to the environment or other reasons of IROPI where the advice of the European Commission has been sought and had regard to. In all other cases, this is unnecessary.

IROPI may be social or economic, but the use of the words 'imperative' and 'overriding' indicate that this too is a high threshold: the development must in essence be indispensable, and the *public* interest in it going ahead must clearly outweigh protecting the conservation objectives of the site.

Compensatory measures

Although not given as a separate stage 5 in the guidance, compensatory measures follow on from a finding that IROPI has been made out. Such measures will need to be agreed with the appropriate statutory nature conservation body and may well be both expensive and a cause of delay. Compensatory measures must protect the overall coherence of the network of European sites and may include extending sites or recreating sites elsewhere. It will usually be necessary, except where this is not possible, for compensatory measures to be delivered before the site is adversely affected. In framing compensatory measures it should be borne in mind that these measures are to 'compensate'; they do not require more than is necessary to replace what is lost.

Part 11

Other Application Documents

Book of Reference

Written by: Richard Honey, ftb
Edited by: Michael Humphries QC, ftb

Introduction

A DCO 'book of reference' is a schedule of parcels of land affected by an order, identifying persons with some connection to the land. A book of reference is not physically part of the DCO (ie it is not a schedule to the order itself), but is a separate document referred to in a DCO and thereby, in effect, incorporated within the terms of the DCO.

The book of reference to a DCO is important because the order will authorise the undertaker to acquire compulsorily the land and rights described in the book of reference and shown on the plans. Similarly, the undertaker may be authorised to remove or reposition apparatus belonging to statutory undertakers, which is described in the book of reference. For the order to work properly in practice, the book of reference needs to be accurate and complete. The book of reference also identifies particular categories of land, such as land forming part of a common, open space, or fuel or field garden allotment.

Where relevant, an application for a DCO should be accompanied by a book of reference (the Infrastructure Planning (Applications: Prescribed Forms and Procedure) Regulations 2009, SI 2009/2264, reg 5(2)(d)).

Requirements

The requirements for a book of reference are specified in reg 7. It has to be in five parts, as follows:

(1) names and addresses for service of each person within Category 1 (owner, lessee, tenant or occupier) and Category 2 (person interested in the land or having power to sell, convey or release the land), as defined in the Planning Act 2008 (PA 2008), s 57, for any land to be subject to:

   (i) powers of compulsory acquisition;

   (ii) rights to use land; or

   (iii) rights to carry out protective works to buildings (eg underpinning or strengthening);

(2) names and addresses for service of each person within Category 3 in s.57 (persons who after diligent enquiry might be entitled to make a relevant claim if the development consent order were to be made and fully implemented);

(3) names of all those entitled to enjoy easements or other private rights over land (including private rights of navigation over water) to be extinguished, suspended or interfered with;

(4) the owner of any Crown interest in the land which is proposed to be used for the purposes of the order;

(5) land:

  (i) the acquisition of which is subject to special parliamentary procedure;

  (ii) which is special category land; and

  (iii) which is replacement land for land being compulsorily acquired.

For each part of the book of reference, the area of the land in m^2 should be stated for each plot of land within which it is intended that all or part of the proposed development and works shall be carried out.

It is important not to omit land that is to be compulsorily acquired from the book of reference, otherwise it may have to be dealt with as 'additional land' under the Infrastructure Planning (Compulsory Acquisition) Regulations 2010, SI 2010/104. Where land is being acquired by agreement it would not need to be included in the book of reference unless for example there are restrictions on the title that need to be overcome. Having said that, undertakers often include land that is to be acquired by agreement to give protection against unknown third party rights or a landowner's failure or inability to complete a sale by agreement.

Guidance

The *Planning Act 2008: Guidance related to procedures for the compulsory acquisition of land* (September 2013) makes some additional practical points, including:

- each part in the book of reference serves a different purpose and persons may need to be identified in one or more parts;
- applicants should not add any further (non-prescribed) parts to a book of reference;
- ambiguous descriptions should be avoided;
- where it is proposed to create and acquire new rights compulsorily they should be clearly identified;
- the book of reference should cross-refer to the relevant articles of the order.

The point that a person can be in more than one PA 2008, s 57 category, and listed in more than one part of the book of reference, is an important one to remember. Persons identified in Part 3 of the book of reference should generally also be recorded in Part 1, as persons within PA 2008, s 57 categories 1 or 2. If there is doubt whether a private right or easement qualifies for Part 1 it should be included in both Parts 1 and 3 so as to err on the side of caution. If a person is not identified in Part 1 of the book of reference then they would not be an affected person under PA 2008, s 92, and would not be notified under PA 2008, s 59, and so would be deprived of the opportunity to seek a compulsory acquisition hearing.

A book of reference may need to be updated during the course of an application, because information changes or new persons are identified. Amended versions could sensibly be provided to the Inspectorate with the PA 2008, s 58 certificate of compliance and also before the end of the examination.

An issue has arisen in practice where applicants have included in books of reference schedules listing 'statutory undertakers and other like bodies having or possibly having a right to keep equipment on, in or over the land within the Order Limits'. The September 2013 DCLG guidance specifically advises that this should not be done (Annex D, para 9). The Inspectorate has advised that this is not something which it expects to see and that, if such a schedule is included, then the reason for it should be explained in the application documentation (register of advice, 19 September 2012, Daventry International Rail Freight Terminal). The Inspectorate has also advised applicants to prepare a justification as to the purpose of such a schedule and the reasons why it has been included in case the inclusion of such a schedule is questioned by the Examining Authority (register of advice, 27 June 2014, Progress Power Station).

Funding Statement

Written by: James Pereira QC, ftb
Edited by: Michael Humphries QC, ftb

The need for a funding statement

Where an applicant for development consent intends to apply for authorisation to compulsorily acquire land, interests in land or a right over land, he is required to provide with the application 'a statement to indicate how an order that contains the authorisation of compulsory acquisition is proposed to be funded': see The Infrastructure Planning (Applications: Prescribed Forms and Procedures) Regulations 2009, SI 2009/2264, reg 5(1)(h) and DCLG Application Form Guidance (2013), paragraph 26. This statement is commonly referred to as a 'funding statement'.

A funding statement must also be produced where it is proposed to include a provision in the DCO to authorise the acquisition of land that was not shown in the book of reference submitted with the application and a person having an interest in the land does not consent to the inclusion of that provision: see the Infrastructure Planning (Compulsory Acquisition) Regulations 2010, SI 2010/104, reg 5. The funding statement in such a case must relate to the funding of the acquisition proposed by the additional provision.

The contents of a funding statement

As to the contends of a funding statement, the DCLG Application Form Guidance (paragraph 26) explains that it should contain

> '... sufficient information to enable the Secretary of State to be satisfied that, if he was to grant the compulsory acquisition request, the proposed development is likely to be undertaken and not be prevented due to difficulties in sourcing and securing the necessary funding.'

A more detailed consideration of what a funding statement should contain is found later in this article.

The purpose of a funding statement

The 2009 version of the DCLG Application Form Guidance (paragraph 24) stated as follows about the need for a funding statement:

> 'This is necessary because it is not appropriate for people's ownership of land, interest in land or rights over land to be compulsorily taken from them, if there is doubt as to whether the development will proceed after those rights, etc, have been taken away.'

This text does not exist in the equivalent paragraph 26 of the 2013 version on the Guidance.

The funding statement in the examination process

More detail on the approach that will be taken is given in the DCLG Guidance on procedures for compulsory acquisition (2013). This advises (paragraph 9) that:

> 'The applicant must have a clear idea of how they intend to use the land which they are proposing to acquire. They should also be able to demonstrate that there is a reasonable prospect of the requisite funds for acquisition becoming available. Otherwise, it will be difficult to show conclusively that the compulsory purchase of land meets the two conditions in section 122 … .'

In summary the two conditions in s 122 referred to above are that the land is required for the development and that there is a compelling case in the public interest for the acquisition.

The resource implications of the proposed scheme are elaborated in the DCGL Guidance on compulsory acquisition procedures (paragraphs 17–18) in the following terms:

> 'Any application for a consent order authorising compulsory acquisition must be accompanied by a statement explaining how it will be funded. This statement should provide as much information as possible about the resource implications of both acquiring the land and implementing the project for which the land is required. It may be that the project is not intended to be independently financially viable, or that the details cannot be finalised until there is certainty about the assembly of the necessary land. In such instances, the applicant should provide an indication of how any potential shortfalls are intended to be met. This should include the degree to which other bodies (public or private sector) have agreed to make financial contributions or to underwrite the scheme, and on what basis such contributions or underwriting is to be made.
>
> The timing of the availability of the funding is also likely to be a relevant factor. Regulation 3(2) of [the Infrastructure Planning (Miscellaneous Prescribed Provisions) Regulations 2010] allows for five years within which any notice to treat must be served beginning on the date on which the order granting development consent is made, though the Secretary of State does have the discretion to make a different provision in an order granting development consent. Applicants should be able to demonstrate that adequate funding is likely to be available to enable the promoter to carry out the compulsory acquisition within the statutory period following the order being made, and that the resource implications of a possible acquisition resulting from a blight notice have been taken account of.'

The guidance on funding in this context is very similar to that given under the general DCLG guidance on compulsory purchase – 'Guidance on Compulsory Purchase Process and the Crichel Down Rules' (2015) in relation to compulsory acquisition under the Acquisition of Land Act 1981: DCLG Guidance, paragraph 14.

Practical issues and experience to date

The decisions and advice to date have highlighted a number of matters for consideration in this context. These are considered under the headings below.

Expect a high level of scrutiny, but note that the process is quite flexible

Applicants can expect that their funding statements and s 106 obligations will be scrutinised very closely by the Inspectorate. It is common for funding issues to be subject to extensive written questions and answers during the examination process, and also to be subject to oral examination at any oral hearing dealing with compulsory purchase. They are also fairly soft targets for objectors. So applicants need to be prepared.

Experience shows that the inquisitorial nature of the examination works well in this context. It should therefore be possible to ensure that all the Inspectors' concerns have been addressed whether by providing greater security or by explaining why such security is not appropriate in the particular case.

The inquisitorial nature of the process can sometimes be daunting for applicants who are used to an adversarial system, because of the more interventionist approach of the decision-maker during the examination. In particular, it is tempting to view questions from the Inspectors as indicating disapproval or criticism. This temptation should be resisted. While each matter must be judged on its merits, questions from Inspectors are just as likely to be motivated by their need to understand the applicant's position and to have matters explained and justified to them more clearly, as they are to be motivated by some underlying criticism of the applicant's case. As with all aspects of the examination process, it is therefore necessary to critically evaluate the questions being put and decide whether they require a change in the applicant's position or simply a better explanation of what that position is.

Contrary to the fears held by some before the new system got underway, Inspectors are generally content to receive updated funding statements and to accommodate travelling drafts of any planning obligation that is being offered to provide the legal safeguards necessary. In this way the relevant documents can be drafted to reflect the issues raised during the examination. There should be no need to be in the dark about the issues by the end of the examination process. See, for example, the extent to which the funding position evolved during the Rookery South examination.

Note too that the advice given by the Secretary of State in the Galloper wind farm application, which contemplated that further information, might be requested from the applicant after the close of the examination if funding became a particular issue or concern. That is obviously a proportionate approach to take where the alternative would be to refuse the application.

Matters to be covered in a funding statement

The DCLG Guidance on compulsory purchase procedures (paragraphs 33–34) indicates that the following should be addressed in the funding statement:

- The resource implications of the project, including:
    - acquiring the land;
    - implementing the project;
- The sources of funding;
- How potential shortfalls in funding are expected to be met;
- The basis upon which funding is being provided;
- The timing of available funding, in particular by reference to:
    - the time period for the exercise of powers of compulsory acquisition;
    - the possibility of a blight notice being served;
- Any uncertainties (e.g. around securing funding, or around the viability of the project), their implications, and how they are to be addressed.

In addition, the following points may be important:

- Contextual points about the standing of the Applicant, its parents, the importance of the project etc.
- Any points thought necessary to address particular funding concerns that have been raised during the application process, particularly where changes have not been made in response to issues raised by the Inspectorate.
- An explanation of how the funding is to be secured. Usually this will be an explanation of how the section 106 obligation which contains the necessary legal requirements for funding security will work.

The relevance of compensation

The extent to which the level of expected compensation is relevant to these issues is a moot point. Traditionally, it is said that matters of compensation are for the Upper Tribunal and not for the authority being asked to approve powers of compulsory acquisition. On the other hand, the level of expected compensation must be relevant to understanding whether the level of any funding is adequate to fund acquisitions.

The Inspectorate has shown itself willing to accept the proposition that a misunderstanding about the likely level of compensation required could undermine an applicant's arguments on whether there is a compelling case: see the Rookery South report at paragraph 7.98. Applicants are naturally – and quite properly – cautious about providing details of the amount of expected compensation. However, one way of dealing with this may for applicants to refer to the fact that expert advice has been taken on quantum, and that the level of funding for compensation that is available is considerably above the level so advised. In this way applicants are able to address this point without being over-exposed to examination of their precise compensation assessment, and while also giving comfort that any potential underestimate of liability is not a cause of concern: see, for example, the Galloper Wind farm Funding Statement at paragraph 4.15.

Single purpose corporate vehicles (SPVs) and parent companies

It is common for the funding statement submitted with the application to be quite light on detail. In particular, where an applicant is an SPV or subsidiary company with limited assets itself, the funding statement can be expected to refer to the financial standing of the parent(s). Usually such statements are superficially very impressive, because the parent company will often be a major corporate body of substance with a huge turnover. Nevertheless, the concern of the Planning Inspectorate is to ensure that the 'particular' applicant has or will have the necessary funds. Accordingly the examination of a funding statement of this sort will inevitably move on from these general statements to the particular issues surrounding the application and applicant in question, and indeed to the detailed mechanisms by which funding security will be secured. Therefore, while there is often good sense in starting out in a fairly high level way, such an approach may not stand up during the course of the examination process.

It is probably the case that publicly funded projects promoted by a public authority will get an easier ride. The notion of compulsory acquisition by a statutory body funded by the public purse is a more comfortable one than such acquisition by a private commercial body. Moreover, there is probably - rightly or wrongly - an implicit acceptance that that standing of a public authority and the public law principles which govern its conduct make it more accountable, and that when a public body says that it will commit funds to a project it will do just that.

Mechanism for securing the funding

The general guidance on the need for funding and the reasons for it has been referred to already. But what of the particular form or mechanism for securing funding in circumstances where there is doubt as to the particular applicants financial standing or the enforceability of any commitments to funding? The short answer is that each case will be judged on its own merits and the Secretary of State does not as yet have any best practice guidance to provide.

Experience of the examination process to date would suggest, however, that a section 106 obligation will usually be required to ensure that the necessary funding will be in place before the project commences.

Applicants that are commercial enterprises, and in particular SPVs, can be expected to have to give consideration to the following being given by way of a planning obligation:

- Security for a particular, or minimum, sum of money for land acquisitions (which applicants usually see as preferable to an open-ended guarantee). It would be appropriate to time limit the duration of any security, provided the time limit is sufficiently lengthy to allow for disputes as to the amount of compensation payable. The type of security that will be provided (bond, bank guarantee, etc) should be specified.
- A power to approve the security, to be held by the local planning authority.
- A covenant not to exercise any powers of compulsory acquisition until the security in question has been approved.

- A covenant that the applicant will not place itself into voluntary liquidation.
- A covenant not to transfer the benefit of the DCO without first procuring equivalent obligations from the transferee. It may also be appropriate for the provisions of the DCO relating to the transfer of powers to third parties to make it clear that the transferee is under the same obligations as the (original) undertaker.

The need to demonstrate funding to meet compensation claims for severance, injurious affection and/or disturbance caused by the construction or operation of the project may well be challenging, as such compensation may be very difficult to quantify before a project has been implemented. Nevertheless, a funding statement should make it clear that such compensation has, at least, been considered where it might be relevant.

Although the DCLG Guidance on compulsory purchase procedures (paragraph 33) also refers to the need to identify the resource implications of 'implementing' the project, it is in the nature of large infrastructure projects that securing the necessary funding for their development in advance of the grant of development consent is often a wholly unrealistic expectation. Nevertheless, the funding statement should address the funding for the implementation of the scheme, even if it is necessary to do so at a relatively high level at the application stage. In some cases more detail will be required.

Development Consent Obligations

Written by Ned Westaway, ftb
Edited by Michael Humphries QC, ftb

Introduction

Agreements entered into pursuant to the Town and Country Planning Act 1990 (TCPA 1990), s 106 ('s 106 obligations'), are an established and valuable mechanism for securing off-site mitigation and/or benefits in connection with planning permissions.

PA 2008, s 174 made a number of amendments to TCPA 1990, ss 106, 106A and 106B, and introduced a new s 106C, enabling similar obligations to be made, modified and discharged in relation to DCOs. Such obligations are referred to in the PA 2008 as 'development consent obligations'. Their use is encouraged by a number of National Policy Statements and they have been widely used.

This article discusses how TCPA 1990, s 106 agreements have been accommodated within the PA 2008 regime and sets out some key considerations relevant to their use and enforcement.

Incorporation of s 106 obligations within DCO regime

By TCPA 1990, s 106(1A) 'the reference to development in subsection (1)(a) includes anything that constitutes development for the purposes of the Planning Act 2008'. This has the effect that s 106 obligations may restrict the ability of a scheme promoter to carry out development consent on his land in any specified way. The other obligations in TCPA 1990, s 106(1), such as requiring land to be used in a specified way or to pay a sum of money to a local planning authority, needed no amendment.

In all cases where a TCPA 1990, s 106 obligation is entered into in connection with an application for a DCO it is known as a 'development consent obligation' (TCPA 1990, s 106(14)). It is a requirement that a development consent obligation is entered into by deed and must contain a statement to the effect that it is a development consent obligation (TCPA 1990, s 106(9)(aa)).

There is nothing to prevent an applicant entering into an ordinary TCPA 1990, s 106 obligation with a local planning authority separately and / or ahead of a development consent application. For example, the Hinkley Point C (Nuclear Generating Station) Order was confirmed in the context of an existing site preparation TCPA 1990, s 106 agreement.

It will clearly be for the Secretary of State, in determining an application for development consent, to consider the adequacy or otherwise of any development consent obligation.

Modification and discharge

Applications to modify or discharge development consent obligations are made directly to the Secretary of State (TCPA 1990, s 106A(3) and (11)(aa)). By TCPA 1990, s 106A(4) a person against whom an obligation is enforceable may, following the 'relevant period' – that is, such period as may be 'prescribed' or the period of five years beginning with the date on which the obligation was entered into – apply to have the obligation modified or discharged.

In respect of TCPA 1990, s 106 obligations entered into on or before 6 April 2010, the Town and Country Planning (Modification and Discharge of Planning Obligations) Regulations 1992, reg 2A 'prescribes' a 'relevant period' in England only of one month beginning with 28 February 2013. While the matter is not free from doubt, given that development consent obligations are a species of TCPA 1990, s 106 obligation, this 'prescribed' 'relevant period' would seem to apply also to the modification or discharge of English development consent obligations entered into on or before 6 April 2010.

There is no 'merits' appeal against the Secretary of State's decision, however by s 106C a challenge by way of judicial review may be brought against any determination that is otherwise than in accordance with the modification or discharge sought, or any non-determination. The claim for judicial review must be filed before six weeks after the date of notification, or in the case of non-determination, a prescribed period (which has yet to be prescribed).

No secondary legislation has yet been brought forward that might help clarify the procedural expectations and set out requirements for applications to modify or discharge development consent obligations. It is likely that the spirit of the Town and Country Planning (Modification and Discharge of Planning Obligations) Regulations 1992 will apply.

Law and guidance on the use of development consent obligations

A number of National Policy Statements make express reference to the use of planning obligations. For example, the Overarching National Policy Statement for Energy (EN-1) encourages the use of planning obligations where appropriate to provide nature conservation enhancement, mitigation and/or compensation around a development site (see eg paras 5.3.15 and 5.3.17).

The National Planning Policy Framework ('NPPF') and Planning Practice Guidance ('PPG') on s 106 obligations will also be relevant. Para 204 of the NPPF provides that s 106 obligations should only be sought where they meet the following tests:

- necessary to make the development acceptable in planning terms;
- directly related to the development; and
- fairly and reasonably related in scale and kind to the development.

In the context of planning permissions, these tests are put on a statutory footing by reg 122(2) of the Community Infrastructure Levy Regulations 2010. That provision does not apply to development consent obligations although, in practice, the Secretary of State is highly unlikely to have regard to a development consent obligation as a reason for granting development unless it meets the tests. It is therefore important that development consent obligations are carefully considered and framed.

An issue can also arise as to the enforceability of obligations. Unless the party entering into the obligation has control of the land to which the obligation relates it will not be enforceable and is likely to be rejected (see *PNH (Properties) Ltd v SSCLG* [2012] EWHC 1998 (Admin)). A DCO example is the National Grid (North London Reinforcement Project) Order 2014, where although the DCO was made, no weight was given to given to a fund proposed by a s 106 obligation to provide enhancements to land outside of the applicant's control.

The issue may be avoided by including a requirement in DCOs that land outside the applicant's control be bound by appropriate obligations before development (or the relevant part of development) can commence. For planning permissions, such an approach has been established, in particular by the Arsenal Stadium development, which has lent its name to the technique (i.e. 'Arsenal' conditions). It is particularly useful for NSIPs where a degree of land assembly is often necessary. Art 60 of the Thames Water Utilities Limited (Thames Tideway Tunnel) Order 2014 is an example of the application of the 'Arsenal' approach for DCOs.

Enforcement of development consent obligations

Development consent obligations are registered as local land charges (TCPA 1990, s 106(11)) and bind successors in title (TCPA 1990, s 106(3)(b)).

A development consent obligation is enforceable by the local planning authority to which it applies. It will become binding upon the making of a DCO and its enforceability will not depend upon its general reasonableness, connection with the development or whether it meets any of the policy tests set out above (see eg *R (Millgate Developments Ltd) v Wokingham BC* [2011] EWCA Civ 1062; [2012] JPL 258).

TCPA 1990, s 106 provides three ways by which a requirement in an obligation may be enforced:

- by injunction (TCPA 1990, s 106(5)),
- by entry onto land to carry out operations and recovery of expenses (TCPA 1990, s 106(6)) or
- by charging the land (TCPA 1990, s 106(11)).

Part 12

Pre-examination, Examination and Post-examination

Timescales for Pre-examination, Examination and Post-examination Procedures

Written by: Isabella Tafur, ftb
Edited by: Michael Humphries QC, ftb

Introduction

One of the guiding principles behind the development consent regime was a need to improve the efficiency of the planning process for dealing with major infrastructure projects, which was too slow and complicated: see Planning for a Sustainable Future, White Paper 2007, paragraph 1.20. The Government considered that prolonged procedures increased costs, resulted in years of blight for individuals and communities and put the country's economic and environmental well-being at risk. As a consequence, the PA 2008 regime contains a prescribed timetable to facilitate faster decision-making.

This article examines the individual elements within the overall prescribed timetable and considers how the timetable is performing in practice.

Acceptance of an application

The timing of any application for development consent under the PA 2008 is, obviously, within the control of the applicant. However, it is from the date of application that the prescribed timetable applies.

The Secretary of State must decide whether or not to accept the application (PA 2008, s 55) within 28 days from the day after the receipt of an application purporting to be an application for development consent under PA 2008, s 37.

The Secretary of State must notify the applicant of its decision of whether it has accepted the application (s 55(6) and (7)). Although there is no prescribed time period for such notification, experience suggests that PINS will notify the applicant promptly.

Notification of acceptance

If the application has been accepted, the applicant must then notify certain persons – as set out in PA 2008, s 56(2) and Sch 1 to the Infrastructure Planning (Applications: Prescribed Forms and Procedure) Regulations 2009 ('the 2009 Regulations') – in accordance with reg 8 of the 2009 Regulations. The notice of acceptance under s 56(2) must also notify such persons of the deadline for making representations to the Secretary of State of their interest in, or objection, to the application (s 56(4)).

The deadline for making representations under section 56(4) must not be earlier than the period of 28 days that begins with the day after the day on which the person receives the notice (s 56(5)). The applicant must also publicise the application in the manner prescribed by reg 9 the 2009 Regulations.

Pursuant to PA 2008, 56, the applicant must certify to the Secretary of State that it has complied with the notification and publication requirements in s 56. This certificate must be in the form prescribed by the 2009 Regulations (set out in Sch 3 to those Regulations), and must be sent to the Secretary of State within 10 *working* days from the deadline set for the making of representations (reg 10 of the 2009 Regulations). Note this is the only reference to 'working days'; all other statutory deadlines under the PA 2008 and the 2009 Regulations are calendar days. At the same time, if the application includes a request to authorise compulsory purchase powers, the applicant must send the Secretary of State a notice of the affected persons (PA 2008, s 59 and reg 10 of the 2009 Regulations): see, for example, the North London Reinforcement Project application for an example of PINS's approach of where all persons under s 56(2) had not been correctly notified.

Initial assessment and preliminary meeting

The Examining Authority must make an initial assessment of the principal issues arising on the application within 21 days from the day after the applicant notified the relevant persons of the acceptance of the application under s 56.

Having made the initial assessment, the Examining Authority must hold a preliminary meeting (PA 2008, s 88), to which it must invite the applicant, interested parties (s 102), statutory parties (s 88(3A)) and each local authority (s 88A). It may also invite other persons.

There is no prescribed timeframe during which the preliminary meeting must be held. This is significant and gives PINS the opportunity to set the date of the preliminary meeting with a view to allowing adequate preparation time for the examination of a complex or controversial application.

At the preliminary meeting, or as soon as practicable thereafter, the Examining Authority must set a timetable for the examination of the application (Infrastructure Planning (Examination Procedure) Rules 2010, SI 2010/103, reg 8). The timetable must set out, *inter alia,* the date by which representations must be received by the Examining Authority; the period within which the Examining Authority will ask questions in writing and seek further written information; the period within which the applicant will have the opportunity to comment in writing on the relevant representations and any responses to written questions; the period within which the applicant and any interested party must agree a statement of common ground and the date of any issue specific hearing.

Examination

The day after the preliminary meeting (or the last day of the preliminary meeting, if it runs over more than one day) is the start date for the examination of the application. The Examining Authority must complete the examination of the application within six months of the start date (PA 2008, s 98).

The Examining Authority must report to the Secretary of State within three months of the deadline for completion of the examination (or, if it completed the examination earlier than that, within three months of completing the examination) (PA 2008, s 98(3)).

There is a power for the Secretary of State to extend this time limit in s 98(4), provided he notifies all interested parties of the new deadline, and publicised the new deadline in the manner he considers appropriate. The Secretary of State must also make a statement to the Houses of Parliament, announcing the new deadline: see the Able Marine Energy Park application for an example of the Secretary of State extending the three month period for making a decision.

Decision

The Secretary of State must then decide an application within three months from the date on which he received the Examining Authority's report (PA 2008, s 107).

The Secretary of State has a power to extend that time limit, pursuant to s 107(3), provided he notifies interested parties of his decision, publicises the new deadline and announces the new deadline to the Houses of Parliament.

Experience so far

Set out at Table 1 below is a summary of the times within which the various procedural steps have been taken for the first 25 projects that have reached the section 55 decision stage (whether to accept the application).

A number of themes emerge:

- the range of periods from acceptance of the application to preliminary meeting is quite wide at 98 days (Redditch Branch Enhancement Scheme and Stafford Area Improvements Norton Bridge Railway) to 215 (North London Electricity Line Reinforcement where there has been a procedural error in the s 56(2) notices – although the typical range is about 100 days to 130 days.
- there appears to be some correlation, although not a particularly strong one, between the length of period from acceptance of the application to preliminary meeting and whether the Examining Authority is a Panel or a single appointed person;
- the range of period from application to decision is relatively constant at between 14 and 18 months (excluding projects that have gone to Special Parliamentary Procedure) and that even for the largest projects, including the Thanes Tideway Tunnel (18 months).

Table 1

PROJECT	APPLICATION	SECTION 55 DECISION	PRELIMINARY MEETING [days after s 55 decision]	REPORT [days after s 55 decision]	DECISION	TOTAL (MONTHS) [days after s 55 decision]	COMMENTS
Overhead electricity line to connect Maesgwyn Wind Farm	3.8.10	31.8.10	N/A				Application not accepted
Rookery South Energy from Waste Generating Station	5.8.10	26.8.10	17.1.11 [144 days]	N/A IPC made the decision	13.10.11	14 [413 days]	DCO only published on 26.3.13 following SPP
Brig y Cwm Energy from Waste Generating Station	31.12.10	26.1.11	7.6.11 [132 days]	N/A			Application withdrawn following refusal to allow amendment
North Doncaster Rail Chord	22.6.11	19.7.11	16.11.11 [120 days]	31.7.12 [378 days]	16.10.12	16 [455 days]	
Ipswich Rail Chord	29.6.11	21.7.11	9.11.11 [111 days]	12.6.12 [327 days]	5.9.12	15 [412 days]	
Kentish Flats Extension	14.10.11	10.11.11	22.2.12 [104 days]	29.11.12 [385 days]	19.2.13	16 [467 days]	
Hinkley Power Station	31.10.11	24.11.11	21.3.12 [118 days]	19.12.12 [391 days]	19.3.13	17 [481 days]	

PROJECT	APPLICATION	SECTION 55 DECISION	PRELIMINARY MEETING [days after s 55 decision]	REPORT [days after s 55 decision]	DECISION	TOTAL (MONTHS) [days after s 55 decision]	COMMENTS
Brechfa Forest West Wind Farm	4.11.11	30.11.11	13.3.12 [104 days]	12.12.12 [378 days]	12.3.13	16 [468 days]	
Galloper Offshore Wind Farm	21.11.11	19.12.11	29.5.12 [162 days]	27.2.13 [436 days]	24.5.2013	18 [522 days]	
Preesall Saltfield Underground Gas Storage	1.12.11	23.12.11	24.4.12 [123 days]	22.1.13 [396 days]	9.4.2013	16 [473 days]	
Heysham to M6 Link Road	6.12.11	23.12.11	3.4.12 [102 days]	19.12.12 [362 days]	19.3.13	15 [452 days]	
Able Marine Energy Park	19.12.11	12.1.12	24.5.12 [133 days]	25.2.13 [410 days]	18.12.13	23 [707 days]	DCO delayed due to SPP
Triton Knoll Offshore Wind Farm	31.1.12	23.2.12	23.7.12 [151 days]	17.4.13 [419 days]	11.7.13	16 [505 days]	
East Northants Resource Management Facility	14.3.12	11.4.12	26.7.12 [106 days]	22.4.13 [376 days]	11.7.13	13 [457 days]	
Port Blyth New Biomass Plant	15.3.12	11.4.12	2.8.12 [113 days]	2.5.13 [386 days]	24.7.13	15 [470 days]	

PROJECT	APPLICATION	SECTION 55 DECISION	PRELIMINARY MEETING [days after s 55 decision]	REPORT [days after s 55 decision]	DECISION	TOTAL (MONTHS) [days after s 55 decision]	COMMENTS
M1 Junction 10a Grade Separation - Luton	29.6.12	27.7.12	15.11.12 [111 days]	13.8.13 [382 days]	30.10.13	15 [461 days]	
Roosecote Biomass Power Station	3.7.12	31.7.12	N/A				Application withdrawn
Kings Lynn B Connection Project	27.7.12	21.8.12	11.1.13 [143 days]	10.10.13 [415 days]	18.12.13	16 [485 days]	
Fieldes Lock - Rail linked power station	14.8.12	7.9.12					Application withdrawn
North London (Electricity Line) Reinforcement	30.8.12	27.9.12	30.4.13 [215 days]	23.1.14 [483 days]	16.4.14	18 567 days]	Preliminary meeting postponed after it became apparent that the applicant had not fully complied with its obligation under s 56(2) to notify certain persons of the application.
Redditch Branch Enhancement Scheme	4.9.12	1.10.12	7.1.13 [98 days]	2.8.13 [305 days]	31.10.13	13 [369 days]	

PROJECT	APPLICATION	SECTION 55 DECISION	PRELIMINARY MEETING [days after s 55 decision]	REPORT [days after s 55 decision]	DECISION	TOTAL (MONTHS) [days after s 55 decision]	COMMENTS
East Anglia ONE Offshore Windfarm	21.11.12	14.12.12	25.6.13 [193 days]	18.3.14 [459 days]	17.6.14	18 [551 days]	
Stafford Area Improvements Norton Bridge Railway	19.12.12	10.1.13	18.4.13 [98 days]	3.1.14 [358 days]	31.3.14	15 [446 days]	
Daventry International Rail Freight Terminal	22.2.13	20.3.13	8.7.2013 [110 days]	7.4.14 [383 days]	3.10.14	18 [563 days]	Re-submitted application following non-acceptance of application on 29.11.12
Thames Tideway Tunnel	28.2.13	27.3.13	12.9.13 [170 days]	12.6.14 [442 days]	12.9.14	17 [535 days]	

From experience, it is also possible to give some broad indications of the likely timetable for an examination. Table 2 below sets out a typical timetable. This can be helpful in identifying potential peak periods of activity.

Table 2

EVENT	APPROX PERIOD AFTER PRELIMINARY MEETING
PRELIMINARY MEETING	0
Notice of procedural decisions following Preliminary Meeting (incl Timetable for examination; ExA's first written questions; Note of Preliminary Meeting)	1-2 weeks
Deadline for receipt of Responses to ExA's first written questions; Written representations; Local Impact Reports	5-6 weeks
Deadline for receipt of Comments on relevant / written reps Comments on LIRs Comments on responses to ExA's first written questions	9-10 weeks
ExA's second written questions	11-12 weeks
Deadline for receipt of Responses to ExA's second written questions	15-16 weeks
Deadline for receipt of Comments on responses to ExA's second written questions	17-18 weeks
Issue specific hearings Compulsory acquisition hearings Open floor hearings	A few days within range (say) 12-20 weeks
CLOSE OF EXAMINATION	24 weeks

Acceptance of an Application

Written by Isabella Tafur, ftb
Edited by Michael Humphries QC, ftb

Following the lengthy pre-submission stage, the submission of a DCO application is something of a milestone for every applicant. After the inevitable flurry of activity in submitting the application documents, the next stage requires the applicant to wait for up to 28 days to learn whether Secretary of State will accept the application.

PA 2008, s 55 – decisions on whether to accept an application

Pursuant to PA 2008, s 55 the Secretary of State must make a decision on whether to accept the application within 28 days, beginning with the day after the application is received.

The Secretary of State may only accept the application if he is satisfied of four things, being;

(a) that the application is for an order granting development consent (PA 2008, s 55(3)(a));

(b) that development consent is required for any of the development to which the application relates (PA 2008, s 55(3)(c));

(c) that the applicant has complied with the pre-application procedure in Chapter 2 of Part 5 of the Act (PA 2008, s 55(3)(e)) and

(d) that the application (including its accompanying documentation) is of a standard that the Secretary of State considers 'satisfactory' (PA 2008, s 55(3)(f)).

This last requirement – that the Secretary of State be satisfied that the application is satisfactory – was introduced by an amendment to the PA 2008 made by the Localism Act 2011.

In deciding whether the applicant has complied with the pre-application procedure under PA 2008, s 55(3)(c), the Secretary of State must have regard to the applicant's consultation report (PA 2008, s 55(4)(a)); the 'adequacy of consultation' representation from local authority consultees who have been consulted pursuant to PA 2008, s 42(1)(b) (PA 2008, s 55(4)(b)) and the extent to which the applicant has had regard to guidance on pre-application procedure issued by the Secretary of State (PA 2008, s 55(4)(c)).

In deciding whether the application is 'satisfactory' under PA 2008, s 55(3)(f), the Secretary of State must have regard to the extent to which the application complies with the requirements in s 37(3) (form and contents of the application) and any standards set under PA 2008, s 37(5) (PA 2008, s 55(5A)). Prior to the amendments made by the Localism Act 2011, an application could only be accepted if it complied with the requirements in PA 2008, s 37(3) and the standards set under PA 2008, s 37(5). The Localism Act has relaxed that requirement, such that the Secretary of State can now accept an application even if those requirements have not been met, provided that he has regard to those requirements in reaching his decision about whether the application is 'satisfactory'.

The Secretary of State must notify the applicant whether he accepts the application or not (PA 2008, s 55(6) and (7)). If he does not consider that the application can be accepted, then he must also provide his reasons for that view. PA 2008, s 55 contemplates that the applicant may modify the application in response to a negative decision from the Secretary of State, and provides that, in such event, the decision as to whether to accept the modified application should be determined in the same way as the original application (PA 2008, s 55(8)). Any challenge to a refusal to accept an application has to be made by judicial review pursuant to PA 2008, s 118(3).

Notification of an accepted application

On the acceptance of an application, the applicant must notify prescribed persons of that acceptance pursuant to PA 2008, s 56. Regulation 8 of and Schedule 1 to the Infrastructure Planning (Applications: Prescribed Forms and Procedure) Regulations 2009 ('APFP Regulations 2009') set out the persons to be notified, and the information to be included in the notification.

At the same time as it notifies prescribed persons under PA 2008, s 56, the applicant must send a copy of the s 56 notice to those persons who were notified to the applicant as persons whom the Secretary of State considered would be, or would be likely to be, affected by or have an interest in the proposed development and who would be unlikely to have become aware of the proposed development through the pre-submission consultation and publicity (reg 13(2)(a) of the Infrastructure Planning (EIA) Regulations 2009) ('the EIA Regulations 2009'). The Secretary of State must also send to the 'consultation bodies' (as defined in paragraph 2 of the EIA Regulations 2009) a copy of the accepted application, a map showing the location of the proposed development and a copy of the Environmental Statement (reg 13(2(b) of the EIA Regulations).

The applicant must also publish a notice of the acceptance in accordance with reg 9 of the APFP Regulations 2009.

Acceptance checklist

The Planning Inspectorate (Major Applications and Plans Directorate) uses a non-statutory checklist to assist in and inform its decision as to whether to accept an application. The checklist is included as Appendix 3 to PINS Advice Note 6: How to Submit Your Application. The checklist is in tabular form, with the requirements for acceptance and relevant statutory references in the left-hand column and notes in the right-hand column directing the approach the Planning Inspectorate should take in considering each requirement. For example, at section 2.3 the application checklist asks '*Did the applicant consult the following about the proposed application: [...] s 42(1)(d) each person in one or more of s.44 categories?*' and in the right-hand column it explains that in considering this question, the Examining authority should '*Compare the applicant's list of s42 consultees with book of reference*'.

Whilst applicants are advised in PINS Advice Note 6 that they may find it helpful to refer to the checklist in preparing their applications, they are also warned that completion of the checklist by the applicant itself should not be seen as a guarantee that the application will be accepted. Even so, many applicants do complete the form in order to assist the Examining Authority and direct it to the relevant sections of the application documentation.

Even though Applicants make every effort to ensure that their applications comply with all relevant formalities and requirements, inevitably things will sometimes go wrong. In such cases, the question will be whether the Secretary of State considers that the application is, nonetheless, 'satisfactory'. There is little in the way of guidance as to how the Secretary of State will determine that question and it is, therefore, useful to consider other application checklists in order to gauge the Secretary of State's likely approach to irregularities in the application documents.

In the Glyn Rhonwy Pumped Storage DCO application, the Examining Authority noted in the application checklist that the Works Plans did not indicate any limits of deviation, but considered that the limits of deviation would be unlikely to have a bearing on the pre-application consultations and concluded that they were sufficient for acceptance.

In respect of the North London Heat and Power Project DCO, the Examining authority noted in the acceptance checklist some inconsistencies regarding consultation, in that a number of consultees listed in the Consultation Report had been excluded from the Book of Reference without justification. It also expressed concern over the lack of precision in the upper limit of generating capacity in the application documents including the draft DCO, which referred to an upper capacity of 'around 70 megawatts'. Notwithstanding these concerns, the Secretary of State found that the application was satisfactory and simply issued advice pursuant to PA 2008, s 51 to the applicant on how to rectify the concerns it during the examination process.

In the Hirwaun Power Station application checklist, the Examining authority noted that two required consultees did not appear to have been consulted, and that 'a small number of precautionary ones' were also missing without explanation. There were also three inconsistencies between the Book of Reference, the Explanatory Memorandum and the Consultation Report, but the Secretary of State considered that the application was 'satisfactory' nonetheless, and that all of the matters identified in the checklist were capable of being addressed during the examination of the application.

It would appear, therefore, that the Secretary of State will consider an application 'satisfactory' where any error is capable of being corrected in the post acceptance period and where there is no substantial prejudice to another party.

PA 2008, s 56 Notice and Relevant Representations

Written by: Hereward Phillpot QC, ftb
Edited by: Michael Humphries QC, ftb

PA 2008, s 56(2) notice

The PA 2008, s 56(2) places a duty on the applicant to give notice of the application to certain individuals and organisations.

The form and content of the notice

The notice must include the information prescribed by the Infrastructure Planning (Applications: Prescribed Forms and Procedure) Regulations 2009, SI 2009/2264, reg 8(2): see PA 2008, s 56(3).

The applicant must make available to each person required to be notified a copy of the application and certain prescribed documents: see PA 2008, ss 56(6)(b), 37(3)(d) and SI 2009/2264, reg 6.

Who must be notified?

Notification must be given to 'such persons as may be prescribed' (PA 2008, s 56(2)(a)), the identity of 'such persons' to be determined by reference to SI 2009/2264, reg 8(1), Sch 1. Column 1 of SI 2009/2264, Sch 1 provides a list of statutory bodies, and Column 3 identifies the circumstances in which each of those bodies must be notified. For example, Natural England must be notified in the case of all applications likely to affect land in England

Notification must also be given to the Marine Management Organisation ('MMO') where the proposed development involves activity within its jurisdiction (PA 2008, s 56(2)(aa), (2A)), each local authority that is within PA 2008, s 56A (PA 2008, s 56(2)(b)), the Greater London Authority ('GLA') where the application site (or part of it) is within Greater London (PA 2008, s 56(2)(c)), and each person who is within one or more of the categories set out in PA 2008, s 57 (PA 2008, s 56(2)(d)).

PA 2008, s 57 identifies three categories of person. Those who the applicant knows, after making diligent inquiry, have a legal interest in, and/or are occupiers of, land forming all or part of the application site, fall within 'Category 1': see PA 2008, s 57(1). Those known to have an interest in, or the power to sell and convey or release, such land, fall within 'Category 2': see PA 2008, s 57(2). Category 3 is less straightforward, and comprises those that the applicant thinks would or might be entitled to 'make a relevant claim' if the order were to be made and fully implemented: see PA 2008, s 57(4)–(6). A 'relevant claim' for these purposes is defined by subsection (6) as one under section 10 of the Compulsory Purchase Act 1965 (compensation where satisfaction not made for the taking, or injurious affection, of land subject to compulsory purchase), Part 1 of the Land Compensation Act 1973 (compensation for depreciation of land value by physical works caused by use of public works), or PA 2008, s 152(3) (a claim by a person whose land is injuriously affected by the carrying out of works authorised by the DCO).

Publicity

In addition to the requirement to notify certain persons, the applicant must also publicise the application in the prescribed manner: see PA 2008, s 56(7). SI 2009/2264, reg 9 stipulates that this is to be done by way of a notice containing specified details, published in the same way as a proposed application and also displayed at or near to the site.

PA 2008, s 56(4) deadline for receipt of relevant representations

The applicant's notice must also identify the deadline for receipt by the Secretary of State of representations giving notice of the person's interest in, or objection to, the application: see section 56(4). The minimum period that must be allowed is 28 days beginning with the day after that on which the person receives the notice: see PA 2008, s 56(5). The same minimum period has been prescribed for the purposes of the publicity notice under PA 2008, s 56(7): see PA 2008, s 56(8) and SI 2009/2264, reg 9(3).

PA 2008, s 102(2), (4) definition of 'representation' and 'relevant representation'

PA 2008, s 102(1) defines who will qualify as an 'interested party' for the purposes of the examination into the application and, in addition to the applicant, comprises those falling into one of the three categories identified in PA 2008, s 57 (above), the MMO (where relevant), the local authorities and the GLA (where relevant), and anyone who has 'made a relevant representation'.

This is important as, once a person has acquired the status of an 'interested party', such a person also acquires certain rights before, during and after the examination process. These include the right to be invited to a preliminary meeting; the right to require, and be heard at, an open-floor hearing; the right to be heard at an issue-specific hearing, if one is held; the right to be notified of when the Examining Authority has completed its examination; and the right to be notified of the decision: see paragraph 16 of the CLG Guidance on the examination of applications (March 2015).

A 'representation' for these purposes is defined inclusively, so as to include evidence: see PA 2008, s 102(2). A 'relevant representation' is one that satisfies all of the following requirements (PA 2008, s 102(4)):

- it is about the application;
- it is made in the prescribed form and manner, and within the prescribed time limit;

- it contains material 'of a prescribed description'; and
- it is not concerned with compensation for compulsory acquisition, the merits of policy in the NPS, and is not vexatious or frivolous (for example, where the points raised are considered to be so trivial in the context of the application that they are not worthy of serious consideration).

The CLG Guidance on the examination process cautions that deciding to treat a representation as 'vexatious or frivolous' is not a step to be undertaken lightly, as a person aggrieved by such a decision may challenge it by way of judicial review. In borderline cases, the guidance recommends giving the benefit of the doubt to the person making the representation: see CLG Guidance on the examination of applications, paragraph 27. That would appear to be sensible.

The Infrastructure Planning (Interested Parties) Regulations 2010, SI 2010/102 prescribe the form and manner in which relevant representations must be made. SI 2010/102, reg 4 requires relevant representations to be in the form of a registration form, and to include certain basic information about the person registering (for example, name, address of the person/agent, interest in land affected by the application (if any) etc), as well as 'an outline of the principal submissions which the person registering intends to make in respect of the application' (SI 2010/102, reg 4(e)). It must also state whether the person registering intends to make oral representations at any hearings that may be held (SI 2010/102, reg 4(f)).

Guidance on what is meant by an 'outline of the principal submissions' is to be found in the CLG Guidance on the examination process at paragraphs 23-24. A person's relevant representation does not need to set out in full the arguments which the person intends to make during the examination, but it should contain sufficient information to enable the Examining Authority to understand which aspects of the application the person supports or objects to, and the reasons why. This will help the Examining Authority identify the main issues likely to feature in the examination, guide its structure and programme, and suggest where interested parties with similar cases might consider collaborating to present a joint case.

The guidance also suggests that this process of considering the relevant representations will help the Examining Authority to see whether there are any relevant issues at risk of not being properly covered, and how to remedy this. In practice this is unlikely to arise very often, as the prolonged and detailed pre-application process should ensure that all of the potentially important issues are flushed out in advance of the application being made.

Infrastructure Planning (Examination Procedure) Rules 2010, SI 2010/103

Rule 3 – relevant representations

Further provision in relation to relevant representations is made in the Infrastructure Planning (Examination Procedure) Rules 2010, SI 2010/103, r 3.

Those making relevant representations must ensure that they are received by the Examining Authority by the later of the dates specified in the notices required by PA 2008, s 56(4), (8). Any written comment on relevant representations that are made must be received either by the date on which the preliminary meeting is held, or, if later, the date specified in the timetable set by the Examining Authority pursuant to SI 2010/103, r 8.

The Examining Authority can ask for further information about matters contained in a relevant representation, or a comment made in respect of such a representation, and set a date by which such information must be provided.

All relevant representations and comments must be made available by the Examining Authority as soon as practicable after receipt, in accordance with SI 2010/103, r 21. This involves publishing the material on the PINS website http://infrastructure.planningportal.gov.uk/ and making hard copies available for inspection and copying – see SI 2010/103, r 21(2).

Time periods

Later representations

The examination process involves a series of stages at which further representations will be sought by the Examining Authority from interested parties. At the preliminary meeting, or as soon as practicable thereafter, the Examining Authority will publish a timetable in accordance with SI 2010/103, r 8. That timetable will set a date for the making of written representations, for the Examining Authority to ask questions in writing about any matter contained in the application, in relevant representations, written representations, or anything else it considers relevant, and for the applicant and interested parties to comment in writing on any relevant or written representations or responses provided to written questions.

The timetable will tend to evolve during the course of the examination, with further deadlines being set for additional rounds of questions and comments, hearings and written representations. In order to keep the examination to time, these deadlines are generally fairly tight, and a great deal of effort is required in order adequately to deal with the multiple (and often complex) matters of law and evidence arising in the limited time available.

SI 2010/103, r 23 – allowing extra time

The Examining Authority does have the power to allow extra time for the taking of any step which may or must be taken under the 2010 Rules: see SI 2010/103, r 23.

Whilst this is a power exercised from time to time (see, for example, the extension of time allowed for the making of comments on written representations in the Able marine energy park examination), the Examining Authority is likely to be reluctant to allow more time unless there are very good reasons for doing so and it would not put at risk the prospects of finishing the examination on time. Generalised pleas for more time because of the very significant administrative and cost burdens involved in sticking to the tight timetables needed to complete the examination on time are likely to be refused (see, for example, the Examining Authority's rejection of a request made for an extension of time by the joint local authorities at the examination into the proposals for a new nuclear power station at Hinkley Point C in Somerset).

Interested Parties

Written by: Hereward Phillpot QC, ftb
Edited by: Michael Humphries QC, ftb

PA 2008, ss 102, 102A, 102B

The main participants in an examination held under the PA 2008 are those who have, or acquire, the status of 'interested parties'. Designation as an interested party carries with it important consequences in terms of notification, the right to make and receive representations, and the right to require and to participate in hearings.

PA 2008, s 102

PA 2008, s 102(1) defines who is or may become an 'interested party' for the purposes of the examination of any individual application.

The applicant and the local authority in whose area the land is located are automatically accorded the status of Interested Parties (s 102(1)(a),(c) and (8)). In addition, the Marine Management Organisation and the Greater London Authority are automatically given the status of interested parties where the development proposed falls within their respective areas of jurisdiction (s 102(1)(ba) and (d)).

Other persons can become interested parties in the following ways:

- By reason of being notified of the application in accordance with s 56(2)(a) (s 102(1)(aa)) (see Micro-article 124 above).
- By reason of a decision by the Examining Authority under s.102A that the person is within one of the categories set out in s 102B (s 102(1)(ab) (see below).
- In the case of 'statutory parties' (see s 88(3)(c) and below) and local authorities within s 88A, by notifying the Examining Authority of a desire to become an interested party following the preliminary meeting (s 102(1)(ca)).
- By making a relevant representation (s 102(1)(e)) (see Micro-article 124 above for the definition of a 'relevant representation').

Once a person has become an interested party, he may choose to relinquish that status by notifying the Examining Authority to that effect (s 102(1ZA). For example, various Interested Parties wrote to the Examining Authority to relinquish their status during the examination into the East Northants Research Management Facility.

PA 2008, ss 102A and 102B

The purpose of PA 2008, ss 102A and 102B is to enable the Examining Authority to accord interested party status to those who should have been, but were not, notified of the acceptance of the application under section 56 (and thus acquired interested party status via that route).

PA 2008, s 102A allows for those who consider themselves to be in this position to ask the Examining Authority to become interested parties. On receipt of a request which meets the requirements set out in section 102A(1), the Examining Authority must decide whether the person is within one or more of the categories set out in section 102B. If it is satisfied to that effect, it must then notify that person and the applicant that the person has become an interested party (s 102A(3)).

There are four requirements which PA 2008, s 102A(1) sets before the obligation under subsection (2) arises:

- The person must have made a request to the Examining Authority to become an Interested Person;
- The request must state that the person claims to be within one or more of the categories in section 102B;
- The person must not have been notified of the acceptance of the application in accordance with section 56(2)(d); and
- The applicant must have issued a section 58 certificate in relation to the application (certifying compliance with the section 56 requirement to notify persons of the accepted application).

PA 2008, s 102B identifies three categories of person, corresponding to the categories of person who should have been notified under section 56(2)(d) (see Article 124 above).

The Infrastructure Planning (Interested Parties) Regulations 2010, SI 2010/102

As explained above, PA 2008, s 102(1) provides that a 'statutory party' may become an interested party. Section 88(3A) provides that a 'statutory party' means a person specified in, or of a description specified in, regulations made by the Secretary of State.

The Infrastructure Planning (Interested Parties) Regulations 2010, SI 2010/102 contain the relevant specifications. Regulation 3 provides that the persons specified for these purposes are:

- Those listed in Column 1 of the Schedule to the Regulations in the circumstances specified in Column 2 to that Schedule; and
- Any affected person.

Column 1 lists various persons, and Column 2 lists the circumstances in which those persons are deemed to be statutory parties. So, for example, the Welsh Ministers are a statutory party for all applications likely to affect land in Wales, and the Health and Safety Executive is a statutory party for all applications.

Affected persons are defined in regulation 2(1) as meaning a person whose name has been given to the Examining Authority in a notice under PA 2008, s 59 (notice of persons interested in land to which a compulsory acquisition request relates). All 'affected persons' are therefore also interested parties, and have all the entitlements associated with that status. In addition, they may also request that a compulsory acquisition hearing be held to consider the issues arising in connection with the proposed compulsory acquisition of land.

Status of 'Interested Parties' in the examination process

The Act provides Interested Parties with a particular status in the examination process. In particular:

- Interested Parties must be invited to the preliminary meeting (PA 2008, s 88(3)(b)) and have a right to participate in that meeting (s 88(4)(a)).
- Procedural decisions made by the Examining Authority must be notified to all Interested Parties (s 89(2A) and (4)).
- In determining whether a hearing should be held, the Examining Authority is required to ensure that 'an interested party has a fair chance to put the party's case' (s 91(1)(b)), and hence Interested Parties have a special status when considering the fairness of the examination procedure.
- Interested Parties are entitled to make oral representations at hearings (s 91(3)).
- Interested Parties are entitled to require to be heard at an open floor hearing (s 93(1)) and to make oral representations about the application at that hearing (s 93(3)).
- Notification of, and participation in, site visits is limited to Interested Parties Infrastructure Planning (Examination Procedure) Rules 2010, rule 16 (see eg the invitation to Interested Parties to make submissions on locations for the site visit at the Galloper Offshore Windfarm examination).
- The Secretary of State must notify Interested Parties of the deadline for the decision on the application, and of any changes to that deadline (s 98).

Participation by those who are not Interested Parties

The Examining Authority retains a discretion to allow participation in the examination by those who are not interested Parties. It is a discretion that has already been exercised in a number of examinations, including those into the Triton Knoll Offshore Wind Farm and Preesall Saltfield Underground Gas Storage proposals.

The CLG Guidance has this to say about the exercise of that discretion:

> 'It is for the Examining Authority to decide whether to allow persons other than those categorised as interested parties to participate in the examination of the application, including expert witnesses. But where a request is received from an interested party to allow an expert witness to take part in the examination of the application, the Secretary of State considers that this should be given serious consideration, in the interests of informed decision making' (paragraph 43).

This needs to be read and understood together with paragraph 29 of the CLG Guidance, which states that where an interested party wishes to take part in an oral hearing, they may appoint a representative, including a legal representative, to speak on their behalf at the hearing.

In practice the nature and format of issue specific hearings often makes it necessary for the panel's questions to be answered by more than one person. For example, a question might require both the explanation of a point of law, or DCO drafting, and the giving of expert evidence on the practicalities lying behind that point. Participants at issue specific hearings sometimes therefore adopt an approach whereby questions are dealt with by a rotating cast of individuals from within the team. Lawyers cannot give evidence, and whilst they can relay instructions to the panel in response to questions, it will often be much more sensible and efficient simply to ask the relevant member of the team to deal with a point. That should not require an application for the Examining Authority's consent on each occasion, and a pragmatic approach seems to have been adopted in hearings so far.

Local Impact Reports

Written by: Hereward Phillpot QC, ftb
Edited by: Michael Humphries QC, ftb

PA 2008, s 60

PA 2008, s 60 provides that certain local authorities are to be invited to produce a 'Local Impact Report' (LIR) in order to inform the examination of the likely impact of the proposed development on that authority's area. In some cases the invitation to produce such a report will be made to a number of different authorities who may choose to co-operate to produce a combined LIR (for example, at the examination into the Galloper Offshore Windfarm proposal Suffolk CC and Suffolk Coastal DC provided at joint LIR: see preliminary meeting notes at paragraphs 4.18-4.19). There is no obligation on an authority that receives such an invitation to produce a LIR, but it is strongly encouraged to do so: see PINS Advice Note 1: Local Impact Reports.

The Act defines a LIR as follows: 'a report in writing giving details of the likely impact of the proposed development on the authority's area (or any part of that area)' (PA 2008, s 60(3)).

PA 2008, s 104(2)(b) imposes an obligation upon the Secretary of State to have regard to any LIR submitted to him within the relevant time limit.

Procedural requirements and timescales

The invitation to produce a LIR is triggered by a notice given by the Secretary of State (section 60(2)), which must also specify the deadline for receipt of the LIR (PA 2008, s 60(5)). The Secretary of State must give the requisite notice once the application has been accepted and he has received a PA 2008, s 58 certificate (certifying compliance with the requirements of section 56) and (where it applies) notification under section 59.

PINS Advice Note 1: Local Impact Reports explains that the Examining Authority will take account of the complexity of the application and other relevant matters, and also the overall timescale set by the Act for examining the application. In practice, this last factor means that the deadline set by the notice is likely to be quite short.

The deadline for receipt of the LIR will be one of the items included amongst the procedural decisions made following the preliminary meeting, together with the period within which Interested Parties (including the applicant) will have the opportunity to make written comments on any LIRs that are submitted.

Authorities are advised in PINS Advice Note 1 not to wait until the deadline has been set before commencing the preparation of their LIR, because of the scale of the task and the limited time likely to be available between notification and expiry of the deadline. The consultation and pre-application periods are likely to be the most appropriate time to commence the evaluation of impacts and gathering of material. The LIR can then be compiled once the application has been accepted and the invitation to submit a LIR has been received. The Examining Authority may agree to an extension of time for an authority to complete its LIR, but this is likely to be a discretion exercised only rarely, and then only to allow a limited additional period of time (see, for example, the approach taken in the examination into the Brechfa Forest West Wind Farm application).

Authorities should also take account of the other deadlines that are likely to be looming for them at this stage of the examination, such as those for production of Statements of Common Ground and written representations (see, for example, the notes of the Hinkley Point C preliminary meeting at paragraphs 5.2, 5.11-5.16).

PA 2008, s 56A identifies which adjoining authorities (unitary authorities, lower-tier district councils and upper-tier county councils), in addition to the authority (or authorities) within whose area the development is to be located, are to be invited to submit a LIR. In respect of offshore proposals, it may be the case that there are no local authorities who would be invited to produce a LIR, although in those circumstances the nearest local authority has sometimes voluntarily produced a LIR in any event (see, for example, the discussion reported in the notes of the Triton Knoll Offshore Windfarm preliminary meeting at paragraphs 3.24 to 3.26).

Contents and style of a LIR

Provided that the LIR satisfies the statutory definition, the precise style and content of the document is a matter of choice for each individual authority.

Contents

Section 10 of the CLG's Guidance for local authorities contains some guidance on the contents of LIR, but it is somewhat limited. It explains two important points:

1 There is no need for the LIR to replicate the Environmental Impact Assessment produced by the applicant. This is of great practical significance because of the highly complex and technical nature of such assessments, and the length of the Environmental Statements to which the assessment process leads.

2 The LIR should be distinguished from any representation a local authority may choose to make in respect of the merits of an application. Again, this is a significant point because maintaining that distinction should make the task of producing the LIR more manageable, and help the authority to focus on the proper role of that document.

More detailed guidance is available in PINS Advice Note 1: Local Impact Reports, which contains the following very helpful list of topics that may be of assistance in compiling the LIR:

1 Site description and surroundings/location

2 Details of the proposal

3 Relevant planning history and any issues arising

4 Relevant development plan policies, supplementary planning guidance or documents, development briefs or approved master-plans and an appraisal of their relationship and relevance to the proposals

5 Relevant development proposals under consideration or granted permission but not commenced or completed

6 Local area characteristics such as urban and landscape qualities and nature conservation sites

7 Local transport patterns and issues

8 Site and area constraints

9 Designated sites

10 Socio-economic and community matters

11 Consideration of the impact of the proposed articles and requirements within the draft Order (such as the scheme) in respect of all of the above

12 DCO obligations and their impact on the local authority's area.

Both the CLG Guidance and the PINS Advice Note stress the importance of using the LIR to provide local knowledge and experience, and evidence of local concerns and issues to the Examining Authority. Examples given in the PINS Advice Note include local evidence of flooding, local social or economic issues or local knowledge of travel patterns to community facilities. This should ensure that local issues which might not otherwise come to the attention of the examination are properly taken into account.

PINS Advice Note 1 indicates that LIRs are also expected to contain the local authority's appraisal of the proposed development's compliance with local policy and guidance. This may well be a material consideration, but it must also be remembered that the development plan has no particular status in decision-making under the PA 2008.

PINS Advice Note 1 encourages local authorities to give their views on the relative importance of different social, environmental or economic issues and the impact of the scheme on them, on the basis that they are well placed to appreciate the impacts of proposals, for example in terms of employment, local services, associated development, or DCO obligations under s174 of the PA 2008.

National Policy Statements (NPSs) may also be helpful to local authorities in preparing their LIRs as a guide to matters of local impact that are likely to be relevant to the determination of an application. However, local authorities are advised by in PINS Advice Note 1 that there is no need for them to undertake an assessment of compliance with an NPS as this would duplicate the Examining Authority's role.

PINS Advice Note 1 also suggests that where an NPS is locationally specific, the local authority should consider those local impacts of a development proposal which would not have been considered at the national policy development stage. In such instances there may be local impacts on sensitive receptors not apparent at the NPS stage, stemming from, for example, the particular layout, design, scale, appearance, or access arrangements of the scheme.

An important task for local authorities in compiling the LIR is to consider in detail the impact of the proposed DCO articles, requirements and DCO obligations, and any changes or additions which the local authority consider to be needed. These matters are likely to be the focus of much of the Examining Authority's attention during the course of the examination, and it is essential that local authorities get to grips with the detail of these matters at the earliest opportunity. By doing so, they will also help to ensure that their LIR and written representations are properly focussed, and maximise the prospects of influencing the Secretary of State's decision.

Style

PINS Advice Note 1 suggests that the LIR should consist of a statement of positive, neutral and negative local impacts, but it does not need to contain a balancing exercise between positives and negatives, as that is a matter for the Examining Authority; nor does it need to take the form of a formal committee report.

Emerging good practice

It is inevitable that the approach taken to the production of the LIR will differ from authority to authority and from project to project. Much may depend on the scale and complexity of the individual proposal, and the extent to which it has been possible to agree statements of common ground with the applicant.

For example, in the Hinkley Point C examination, the two District Councils and the County Council produced a joint LIR. The LIR was a very substantial document, supported by detailed appendices, but its nature and scale were not dictated simply by the complex nature and scale of the development to be assessed and the fact that it involved multiple sites in a number of quite different locations. In that case there had been a failure to agree much in the way of common ground in advance of the production of the LIR, and the impacts were in dispute between the authorities and the applicant.

The overall structure of the LIR in that case was as follows:

1 An Executive Summary, identifying the structure and role of the LIR, its contents and the key impacts identified.

2 A main LIR, divided into three parts:

   a Site related matters.

   b opic-based matters.

   c Community/area based matters.

3 A set of Appendices, comprising:

   a Figures

   b Topic papers (the evidence and supporting data said to justify the impacts articulated in the main LIR).

   c A list of documents used in compiling the LIR.

   d Preliminary comments on draft requirements.

Whilst the contents and focus of the LIR were the subject of lengthy and detailed criticism by the applicant during the examination process, the broad structure adopted may nevertheless offer some assistance for other authorities dealing with large and complicated applications.

By contrast, the LIR submitted in the Preesall Saltfield Underground Gas Storage examination was a relatively simple, single volume document of just under 50 pages in length. That relatively modest document was supplemented by a series of Statements of Common Ground, to which it made cross-reference as appropriate, and might be seen as representing a more manageable approach in less complex cases.

Initial Assessment of Issues

Written by: Isabella Tafur, ftb
Edited by: Michael Humphries QC, ftb

Introduction

While it is for the Examining Authority to decide how to examine an application, in making any decision about how the application will be examined, it must comply with the provisions in the PA 2008, Chapter 6. Pursuant to PA 2008, s 88, the examining authority must make an initial assessment of the principal issues arising on the application prior to the Preliminary Meeting.

Initial assessment of the principal issues

In making its initial assessment of the principal issues, the Examining Authority will have regard to the application documents and is also likely to take into account the relevant representations received from interested parties: see para 37 of the DCLG Guidance 'Planning Act 2008: Guidance for the examination of applications for development consent' and PINS Advice note 8.3 (under the heading 'What is a relevant representation?).

Rule 5 of the Infrastructure Planning (Examination Procedure) Rules 2010, SI 2010/103 requires the Examining Authority to make the initial assessment of issues within 21 days from the day after the deadline for the receipt of representations by the Secretary of State (as specified by the applicant in its PA 2008, s 56 notification letter).

Notification of the initial assessment

Having made the initial assessment of principal issues, the Examining Authority will hold a Preliminary Meeting. Rule 6 of the Infrastructure Planning (Examination Procedure) Rules 2010 requires the Examining Authority to give notice of that Meeting, and to notify all those invited of the matters to be discussed at the Preliminary Meeting. This is done by a 'Rule 6 letter'.

The Examining Authority's initial assessment of principal issues will usually be listed as Appendix C to the Rule 6 letter. The Examining Authority makes it clear that it is not a comprehensive or exclusive list of all relevant matters, as it will have regard to all the important and relevant matters raised during the examination. This last point is important, as the list of principal issues will not preclude parties from raising other issues, nor the Examining Authority from considering them during the examination.

The initial assessment of principal issues will also usually then form an agenda item at the Preliminary Meeting allowing parties the opportunity to comment on the initial assessment list and raise potential additional issues. PINS Advice Note 8.1 states that 'The meeting may include questions and answers about the key issues that will need to be examined, the timetable for the examination and other important organisational details.'

At, or more usually following, the Preliminary Meeting the Examining Authority will set out the timetable for the examination: see Rule 8 of the Infrastructure Planning (Examination Procedure) Rules 2010. This is usually done by issuing a 'Rule 8 letter' a few days after the close of the Preliminary Meeting. The Rule 8 letter will also contain the Examining Authority's list of principal issues or refer back to the initial assessment of principal issues if the list has not changed.

Conclusion

Given the relatively short time-scales for responding to written questions during the examination period, the initial assessment of principal matters can provide applicants and interested parties with a useful steer in identifying areas in which further work could usefully be focused.

Examples of initial assessments

Typically the list of principal issues will include numbered headings, with short explanatory notes below. Below are a number of examples of the lists of principal issues generated by the applications for development consent for three very different types of NSIP.

Rampion offshore wind farm

1 *Biodiversity, biological environment and ecology*

Including effects on marine and terrestrial life, onshore and offshore ornithology and on protected areas and species including in combination effects.

2 *Compulsory powers*

Including whether there is a compelling case in the public interest.

3 *Development Consent Order and Deemed Marine Licence*

Including consideration of the appropriateness of the powers that would be conferred and whether the Order and the Licence would secure the mitigation relied on by the applicant in the Environmental Statement or which is otherwise considered necessary (Note: This topic will necessarily have to be considered on a ' without prejudice' basis.)

4 *Effects during construction and operation*

Including the cable route corridor, substation site and effect of electro-magnetic fields on receptors.

5 *Landscape/seascape, visual and heritage*

Including effects on the South Downs National Park, the Sussex Heritage Coast and on heritage assets including buried archaeological remains onshore and offshore.

6 *Marine and coastal physical processes*

Including waste and debris with dredging and disposal, chemical pollutants, scouring and scour protection, effects on the coast (erosion and flooding), effects on sea defences and physical effects on port approaches (eg deep water channels).

7 *Navigation and risk*

Including safety during construction and operation, effects of maintenance of shipping lanes and anchorages, effects on commercial and recreational vessels, local ports and search and rescue operations.

8 *Socio-economic*

Including effects on tourism and recreation (land and water based), effects on local businesses (land and water based) and effects on nearby ports and commercial fishing.

9 *Transport and traffic*

Including effects that traffic generated by the proposal could have on the highway network during construction and operation, environmental effects, in combination effects with other proposals and effects on other road users.

Daventry International rail freight terminal

1 *Combination with other development proposals*

- The relationship between the proposed development and the adjacent major sustainable urban extension (SUE) of Rugby, both forming part of the former Rugby Radio Station site.
- The policy and development plan context for examining the application.
- The details of the application particularly concerning a new junction with the A5, rail connections, and the main warehouse buildings within the context of the parameters included in the main site and rail framework plans and schedule.

2 *Transport*

- The calculation of additional traffic generated by the proposed development, the impact on the trunk road network, the adequacy of proposals for junction improvements and mitigating transport impacts on local roads and communities adjacent to the development.
- The capacity of the rail network to accommodate the predicted additional rail flows from the development.

3 *Heritage impacts*

- The consequences of the development for the scale of mediaeval and later ridge and furrow cultivation which has survived as a feature of the former Rugby Radio Station site.
- The extent to which the proposed Lilbourne Meadows provide for a satisfactory retention of the existing ridge and furrow.

4 *Landscape and visual impacts*

- The impact of lighting from the proposed development on surrounding areas.
- The extent to which the proposed warehousing buildings will be visible from surrounding areas, including the degree to which these would result in adverse visual impacts and the likely success of proposed mitigation.
- The nature and adequacy of Lilbourne Meadows to provide a visual buffer between Lilbourne and the main development, and the mechanisms for implementation.

5 *Ecology impacts*

- The nature and adequacy of Lilbourne Meadows to provide habitat mitigation for protected species

6 *Drainage and flooding*

- Given the large area of hard standing proposed, the suitability of land drainage proposals, including the diversion of Clifton Brook and its tributary.

7 *Traffic management*

- How the impact of heavy goods vehicles on the local environment can be mitigated, for example restricting/preventing the use of laybys for overnight lorry parking to reduce the consequent general degradation and appearance of the area caused by litter, low standard of maintenance and misuse of land.

8 *Construction impacts*

- The impact from vibration during the construction phase.
- The effects of earthwork operations during construction on dust emissions and reduction in air quality.

9 *Noise*

- The impact of noise generated by the railway proposals (including on the proposed SUE development) and from HGV traffic to and from the site once the development is operational.
- Given that the site is proposed to be operated 24-hours a day, noise impacts generated from the main site on Lilbourne village.

Thames Tideway tunnel

1 *Air quality and emissions*

Matters include but are not limited to:

- The effects on air quality from dust and particulates from construction and transportation.
- Odour, particularly during operation.
- Adequacies of the baseline assessment, the assessments of likely significant effects and any proposed monitoring regime and mitigation. Any measures to avoid, reduce and compensate for adverse impacts.

2 *Biodiversity, biological environment and ecology*

Matters include but are not limited to:

- Implications for European sites and protected species.
- Loss of or change to habitats, both estuarine and terrestrial, including timing of works and activities and resultant seasonal effects.
- Potential impacts of waste disposal transportation and method and location of disposal.
- Adequacies of the baseline assessment, the assessments of likely significant effects and any proposed monitoring regime and mitigation. Any measures to avoid, reduce and compensate for adverse impacts.

3 *Coastal/river change*

Matters include but are not limited to:

- The effects of the application proposals on channel, bank and foreshore erosion and deposition (affecting flood defence structures, transport infrastructure, ecology, recreation and heritage assets).
- Restoration of and works to foreshore.
- Any proposed monitoring and measures to avoid, reduce and compensate for adverse impacts.

4 *Compulsory acquisition and related matters*

Matters include but are not limited to:

- Justification for compulsory acquisition of the land, rights and powers that are sought by the draft development consent order.
- Alternatives both in relation to individual plots and specific sites.
- Statutory undertaker land and apparatus and potential detriment to the carrying on of an undertaking and any need for replacement land in that context.
- Open space land and rights over that land, loss of open space and any need for replacement land in that context.

- Resource implications in particular the availability and certainty of funding for the project, blight and hardship matters and compensation.
- Considerations in relation to mooring rights and displacement both permanent and temporary.
- Protective provisions and indemnities.
- Limitations on rights of way, access and works to property likely to have a direct effect beyond the property interests and Book of Reference defined limits of compulsory acquisition sought.

5 *Design, landscape and visual impact*

Matters include but are not limited to:

- The extent to which the design would be attractive, durable, resilient and adaptable and whether the project would demonstrate good design in terms of siting in relation to existing and proposed townscape, landscape, local context and setting.
- The main alternatives to the designs considered.
- Visual impact and public perceptions of the landscape, riverscape and townscape of the area.
- Loss of and change to existing tree and vegetation cover, the duration of impact and the delivery mechanisms and timescales for mitigation.
- The extent to which the design would meet the functional objectives of the project and operational, safety and security requirements.

6 *Flood risk and climate change*

Matters include but are not limited to:

- Appropriate adaptation and consequential impacts and mitigation.
- Potential impact of settlement on flood defence assets.
- The extent to which design and landscape measures maximise permeability and the potential for preventing rainwater from entering the sewerage system.
- Lifetime and capacity of new infrastructure.
- Any update required against UK Climate Projections.

7 *Historic environment*

Matters include but are not limited to:

- The effects on the significance of buildings and structures identified as heritage assets.
- The effects of settlement on heritage assets.
- The effects on the settings of heritage assets and the wider historic environment.
- The measures to protect heritage assets which are as yet undiscovered.

8 *Land use including regeneration and open space*

Matters include but are not limited to:

- The effects on current and planned regeneration schemes and housing delivery.
- The effects on open space including Metropolitan Open Land.

9 *Noise and disturbance*

Matters include but are not limited to:

- The effects of noise and vibration on residential amenity (including shift workers) and other sensitive receptors such as recording studios and schools.
- Noise and vibration from transportation particularly during construction.
- Use of assessment methodologies and mitigation and thresholds proposed for construction and operational noise levels and the 'Thames Tideway Tunnel noise insulation and temporary re-housing policy' and 'compensation programmes'.

10 *Rationale for the selection of worksites and drive strategies*

Matters include but are not limited to:

- Detail of specific sites, routes, designs, layout, construction programmes and operational processes.
- Sites and alternatives including Carnwath Road Riverside, Chambers Wharf and the matters relating to the drive to versus the drive from these locations, Deptford Church Street, King Edward Memorial Park Foreshore and the considerations raised by the potential for use of land at Heckford Street.

11 *Socio-economic effects*

Matters include but are not limited to:

- Health and wellbeing including any measures to avoid, reduce or compensate for adverse impacts.
- The effects of the proposed development on the community including amenity, use and enjoyment of open space and equalities impacts.
- The effects on river access, occupiers (residential, leisure and business) and users.
- The effects on schools, businesses and tourism.
- Baseline assessment methodologies and mitigation.

12 *Traffic, travel and transportation*

Matters include but are not limited to:

- The effects in relation to waste management and disposal strategy.
- The effects of settlement on transportation bridges and tunnels (road, rail and pedestrian/cycle etc).

- The effects on existing transport networks (highway, waterway, rail and pedestrian/cycle etc) and parking and the capacity for and impacts on existing users.

13 *Water quality and resources*

Matters include but are not limited to:

- The effects of proposed project on water quality – discharges during construction, maintenance periods and operation.
- The effects of the proposed design for reduction of discharges from each combined sewer overflow connection site.
- Relationship with the River Basin Management Plans, estuary management plan and water resources management plans and the requirements of the Water Framework Directive.
- Mitigation and management during construction, operational and decommissioning phases.

Statements of Common Ground

Written by: James Pereira QC, ftb
Edited by: Michael Humphries QC, ftb

Introduction

Paragraph 58 of the DCLG Guidance for the examination of applications for development consent (March 2015) describes a statement of common ground in the following way:

> 'A statement of common ground is a written statement prepared jointly by the applicant and another party or parties, setting out any matters on which they agree. As well as identifying matters which are not in real dispute, it may also be useful for a statement to identify areas where agreement has not been reached. The statement should include references to show where those matters are dealt with in the written representations or other documentary evidence.'

Statements of common ground are given legislative recognition in rule 8 of the Infrastructure Planning (Examination Procedure) Rules 2010, SI 2010/103 (as amended), which provides that among the matters to be included in the timetable which is set at, or shortly after, the Preliminary Meeting on the DCO application, is the period within which the application and any interested party must agree a statement of common ground.

The purpose of a statement of common ground

Statements of common ground are useful documents to assist the parties and the Examining Authority in identifying and understanding what are the issues of dispute and what are the issues that are agreed between the parties to the statement. This is useful to ensure that the evidence and the examination focuses on the material differences between the parties. The effective use of such statements is expected to lead to a more efficient examination process.

The form and content of statements of common ground

A statement of common ground is a written statement prepared jointly by the parties to the statement. It will usually be signed by a representative from each party. It is possible for the parties to an examination to enter into more than one statement of common ground, and for there to be different statements of common ground between different parties.

The content of a statement of common ground will depend upon the subject-matter of the statement, which in turn will depend upon the issues raised by the particular application. Paragraphs 61/62 of the DCLG Guidance for the examination of applications for development consent (March 2015) advises as follows:

> 'The statement should be clear about the basic information on which the parties have agreed, such as the precise nature of the proposed infrastructure, a description of the site and its planning history. Effective cross-referencing of other application documents should be used in order to avoid duplication between documents and keep the volume of examination material to the necessary minimum.
>
> In addition to basic information agreement can often be reached on technical matters and topics that rely on basic statistical data. For example, the evidence to be submitted on traffic flows. Ideally, agreement should also be sought before the examination commences about any requirements (i.e. conditions) that should be attached to a Development Consent Order if granted.'

The following points should be noted:

- It would be usual for there to be statements of common ground between the applicant for the DCO and the main statutory parties who are relevant to the application. This might include, for example, bodies such as the local planning authority, the local highway authority, the Environment Agency, Natural England, English Heritage and, where appropriate, the Marine Management Organisation.
- Cross referencing to other documents that are before the Examining Authority, or annexing documents that support propositions in the statement of common ground, can be a useful means of increasing the weight that such documents carry. It also helps the reader of the statement to understand the basis of the agreement (or disagreement), which in turn will help to shape the examination process.
- Statements of common ground are often made on a topic or issue basis. For example, in any one application there may be a statement of common ground setting out a general description of the project, another statement of common ground on pre-application procedures, another on noise impacts, another on nature conservation matters, and so on.
- In cases where the statement of common ground concerns matters of expert evidence and opinion, it is good practice for it to be signed by the parties' relevant experts, and for it to carry an appropriate experts' declaration. This will assist the examining authority in assessing the weight to be given to the statement, and will help it decide who to question about the statement, should questioning be necessary.

The timing of statements of common ground

It is usual for the Examining Authority to set a deadline for the submission of statements of common ground in the formal letter which is sent out after the Preliminary Meeting has been held following acceptance of the DCO application. However, the early submission of statements of common ground is encouraged, and applicants are advised that they need not wait until the examination period to prepare or submit statements of common ground. The DCLG Guidance gives particular encouragement to reaching agreement about any requirements (ie conditions) that should be attached to a development consent order if granted before the examination commences. The

Planning Officer's Society has endorsed the DCLG's encouragement of making statements of common ground at the pre-application stage (see paragraph 3.28 of 'Responding to Nationally Significant Infrastructure Projects' Advice Note, August 2010 (Planning Officer's Society)).

Preparing statements of common ground

There is no set way of preparing a statement of common ground. Paragraph 63 of the DCLG Guidance for the examination of applications for development consent (March 2015) advises as follows:

> 'How such agreement is reached will vary depending on the nature and complexity of the application and the matters at issue. Where there are only two or three major parties involved and the issues are fairly straightforward, the Examining Authority is likely to expect the parties to have considered producing a statement of common ground containing agreed facts or setting out those areas where agreement will not be reached. For more complex applications it is likely that the Examining Authority will expect the applicant to agree a number of statements of common ground with different parties, each focused on separate aspects of the application.'

It is to be remembered that the parties are expected to co-operate with the examination process, and hence in the preparation of statements of common ground. Where the statements involve matters of expert opinion, any experts involved in preparing the statement of common ground should do so in accordance with their overriding duty to the Examining Authority.

The effect of a statement of common ground

It is important to recognise that the Examining Authority is not bound to accept the contents of a statement of common ground, nor are participants in the examination process who are not parties to the statement. Parties to statements of common ground therefore need to be prepared to answer questions on the contents of the statement and to justify the agreement reached.

As paragraph 64 of the DCLG Guidance for the examination of applications for development consent (March 2015) makes clear:

> '... the duty of the Examining Authority is not simply to accept the statement of common ground or to react to the evidence presented. The role of the Examining Authority is to ensure that all aspects of any given matter are explored thoroughly, especially with regard to the matters fundamental to the decision, rather than simply accepting the statement of common ground without question.
>
> Consequently, the Examining Authority should probe the evidence thoroughly if their judgement or professional expertise indicates that either:
>
> - all of the evidence necessary for a soundly reasoned decision has not been put before them, or

- that a material part of the evidence in front of them has not been adequately tested.'

However, it is important that any questioning or challenge to the statement of common ground from the Examining Authority is conducted fairly. It is good practice to ensure that fair, advanced, warning is given by the Examining Authority of any questioning or examination of matters that are agreed in the statement of common ground. In extreme cases, where the parties have proceeded on the basis that an issue is agreed but the decision-maker goes back on that agreement in its decision without giving fair warning to the parties, and without allowing them to comment, the courts may be prepared to quash the decision as being procedurally unfair: see *Edward Ware New Homes v Secretary of State* [2003] EWCA Civ 566, where an Inspector's decision letter following a planning appeal was quashed because he had reached a contrary view on an issue which was agreed in the statement of common ground between the parties at the inquiry, and which had not been treated as controversial at the inquiry, without giving the parties the opportunity to comment first.

Compulsory Acquisition Hearings

Written by: Richard Honey, ftb
Edited by: Michael Humphries QC, ftb

Introduction

This article examines the various provisions relating to a compulsory purchase hearing. Unlike an issue specific hearing, a compulsory acquisition hearing may be required as of right in defined circumstances.

Requiring a compulsory acquisition hearing

Where an application for a development consent order (DCO) includes a request for authorisation of compulsory acquisition of land or an interest in or right over land, the Examining Authority must fix, and cause each 'affected person' to be informed of, the deadline by which an affected person must notify the Secretary of State that the person wishes a compulsory acquisition hearing to be held (PA 2008, s 92(2)).

PA 2008, s 92(5) defines an 'affected person' by reference to section 59(4) of the Planning Act 2008 which states that 'A person is an affected person … if the applicant, after making diligent inquiry, knows that the person is interested in the land to which the compulsory acquisition request relates or any part of that land.'

At or as soon as practical after the end of the Preliminary Meeting for an examination held pursuant to PA 2008, s 88, rule 8 of the Infrastructure Planning (Examination Procedure) Rules 2010, SI 2010/103 ('the 2010 Rules') require the Examining Authority to set the timetable for the examination of the application including '(g) the date by which any affected person must notify the Examining authority or their wish to be heard at a compulsory acquisition hearing'. This timetable is set out in what is generally known as the Examining Authority's Rule 8 letter. Rule 13 of the 2010 Rules provides that at least 21 days notice must be given of a deadline for an affected person to give notice requesting a compulsory acquisition hearing.

If any such a request is duly made, then PA 2008, s 92(3) makes clear that a compulsory acquisition hearing must be held. The 2010 Rules also provide that at least 21 days notice must be given to an affected person of the date, time and place of the compulsory acquisition hearing itself (rule 13(3)). In practice considerably more notice is likely to be given.

Arrangements for compulsory acquisition hearings

The Preliminary Meeting held under rule 7 will usually consider, where necessary, how compulsory acquisition hearings are to be arranged and timetabled, prior to the timetable actually being issued. Even before then, it is normal for persons to have indicated in their relevant representations whether they qualify as an affected person and whether they would like a compulsory acquisition hearing to be held.

It is possible for the Examining Authority to consider all compulsory acquisition requests relating to the same application at the same compulsory acquisition hearing, although it can also convene separate compulsory acquisition hearings (rule 15(2)).

The conduct of compulsory acquisition hearings

It is for the Examining Authority to decide how a compulsory acquisition hearing is to be conducted (PA 2008, s 94(3)). Within that context, however, both the applicant and each affected person are 'entitled' to make oral representations about the compulsory acquisition of land at a compulsory acquisition hearing (s 92(4)).

The DCLG 'Guidance for the examination of applications for development consent' (March 2015) states that a compulsory acquisition hearing is intended to consider the issues arising in connection with the authorisation of the compulsory acquisition of land (para 31). It also says that affected persons 'may make oral representations about the compulsory acquisition requests' (para 87) and that 'a key matter to be considered will be whether there is a compelling case in the public interest for the compulsory acquisition of land' (para 91).

The general provisions in relation to hearings at a DCO examination are found in PA 2008, ss 94, 95 and 95A. A hearing must be in public (s 94(2). The Examining Authority has the power to decide how the hearing is to be conducted. PA 2008, s 94(4) states that it is for the authority to decide whether a person making oral representations may be questioned, and the matters on which they may be questioned, as well as the amount of time for making representations and asking questions. PA 2008, s 94(7) goes on to provide that the Examining Authority must apply the principle that any oral questioning should be undertaken by the Examining Authority itself, except where the it thinks that oral questioning by another person is necessary in order to ensure 'adequate testing of any representations' or 'that a person has a fair chance to put the person's case'. The Examining Authority can refuse to allow representations to be made at a hearing for a number of reasons, including that they relate to compensation for compulsory acquisition of land or of an interest in or right over land (s 94(8)).

The 2010 Rules set more detailed rules for the conduct of hearings. Rule 14(2) obliges the Examining Authority to identify at the start of any hearing the matters to be considered at the hearing and any matters on which they require further explanation. Rule 14(3) provides that oral representations must be based on representations submitted in writing earlier in the process, but rule 14(4) allows other issues to be referred to. Rule 14(9) entitles an affected person to be represented by any other person at a hearing.

The DCLG 'Guidance for the examination of applications for development consent' (March 2015) provides that hearings should be 'carried out as efficiently as possible, whilst remaining fair to all parties and thorough in their examination of evidence' (para 90). In relation to compulsory acquisition, it is likely that the Examining Authority will allow more latitude to objectors than in other types of hearings, as they are subject to appropriation of land or rights against their will.

The DCLG guidance provides that the examining authority 'will probe, test and assess the evidence through direct questioning of persons making oral representations' (para 96). The Examining Authority is able to appoint a barrister or solicitor itself to test evidence through oral questioning. The DCLG guidance also says that the Examining authority may allow cross-examination 'where it considers that this is necessary to ensure the adequate testing of any representations, or where it considers that it is necessary to allow an interested party a fair chance to put their case' (para 98) and goes on to say that the authority 'will ensure that parties are not denied the opportunity to ask questions where the answers are required in order to complete their cases' (para 99).

It is possible for the Examining Authority to allow witnesses to be called at compulsory acquisition hearings. The DCLG guidance explains that although there is no automatic right to call witnesses, the authority has the discretion to allow this to be done either by the authority of its own volition or upon the request of a party (para 101).

Whilst PA 2008, s 92 entitles certain parties to make 'oral representations' and s 94 places limits on the questioning of a person making oral representations other, that is, than by the Examining Authority itself, experience so far suggests that Examining Authorities do on occasion conduct compulsory acquisition hearings in a reasonably formal way.

For example, at the first compulsory acquisition hearing in June 2011, which was in relation to an application for an energy recovery facility at Rookery South, the Examining Authority allowed the calling and cross-examination of witnesses by counsel and the making of opening and closing submissions, over four days. The main issues covered at that hearing were the justification for the development proposed (scale and need), alternative sites and the policy context. The Examining Authority's decision dated 13 October 2011 records that at the hearing 'some issues relevant to the consideration of the grant of development consent were examined further in the context of compulsory acquisition' (para 7.87).

In this context it is perhaps interesting to note that, in relation to compulsory purchase orders, the Compulsory Purchase (Inquiries Procedure) Rules 2007, SI 2007/3617 set out an entitlement to cross-examine witnesses (rule 16(3)).

Other compulsory acquisition hearings have been structured more like other hearings, that is, with an agenda of issues to be addressed in turn and very much led by the Inspector(s) (see, for example, the Ipswich Rail Chord agenda for hearing in February 2012 and the King's Lynn B Power Station Connection agenda for hearing in April 2013). In other cases witnesses have prepared statements of evidence in support of the acquisition (see, for example, the Redditch Branch Enhancement hearing in April 2013).

Perhaps the underlying message here is that practice is still emerging, but the procedural rules are sufficiently flexible to allow a range of responses appropriate to the particular circumstances.

Open Floor Hearings

Written by: Hereward Phillpot QC, ftb
Edited by: Michael Humphries QC, ftb

PA 2008, s 93

PA 2008, s 93 establishes a duty on the Examining Authority to cause an open floor hearing (OFH) to be held where one is duly requested by an interested party (IP). The purpose of an OFH is to hear, first hand, from IPs about their thoughts on the proposed development.

The Examining Authority must first fix and inform IPs of a deadline by which they must notify the Secretary of State of their wish to be heard at an OFH (PA 2008, s 93(1)). Where at least one notification has been received in time, the Examining Authority is obliged to cause an OFH to be held (s 93(2)), at which each IP is entitled to make oral representations about the application.

The deadline for the purposes of PA 2008, s 93(1) must be at least 21 days after the date on which notice of the deadline is given (Infrastructure Planning (Examination Procedure) Rules 2010, SI 2010/103 (the 2010 Rules), r 13(1)). The Examining Authority must notify all IPs of the date of any OFH as soon as practicable after the expiry of the deadline (r 13(3)).

Procedural rules

The 2010 Rules do not make very detailed provision for the procedure to be adopted at hearings, leaving the precise procedure to the discretion of the Examining Authority. They do, however, set some important ground ruless, which apply to both OFHs and issue specific hearings (ISH).

The Examining Authority shall determine the procedure at the hearing (r 14(1)), identifying at the start of the hearing the matters to be considered, and any matters where it requires further explanation from IPs (r 14(2)). That does not prevent additional matters being referred to during the hearing, subject to the Examining Authority's discretion as to how the hearing is to be conducted (r 14(4)).

Any oral representations must be based on either the relevant or written representations made by or on behalf of the IP (r 14(3)).

The Examining Authority may proceed with the OFH even if the IP who requested it does not attend (r 14(7)).

DCLG/PINS Guidance

The main guidance on hearings (including OFHs) is provided in the DCLG Guidance document *Planning Act 2008: Guidance for the examination of applications for development consent.* A summary of some of the points made in the CLG Guidance is to be found in PINS *Advice Note 8.5: Participating in the examination*, but the latter document adds nothing of substance.

The DCLG Guidance explains that, subject to the Examining Authority's powers of control over the conduct of the hearing, all IPs will have an opportunity to make oral representations about the application (paragraph 85). However, it also underlines the point that it is for the Examining Authority to determine how the hearing is conducted, including the amount of time to be allowed for the making of a person's representations. The Examining Authority is expected to use this power to ensure that hearings are carried out 'as efficiently as possible, whilst remaining fair to all parties and thorough in their examination of evidence' (paragraph 86). In practice the emphasis has tended to be on efficiency and expedition, not only to keep the examination timetable on track, but also to try to make time for all IPs to have their say. IPs will generally be reminded that the process is primarily a written one, and that there is no need to repeat points that have already been made in writing.

Those with similar interests, who are likely to submit similar evidence, are encouraged to work to agree upon a spokesperson to put forward a joint case. Repetition of points is strongly discouraged (paragraph 91).

Any questioning of IPs will generally be undertaken by the Examining Authority itself, or an advocate appointed to assist it, and should not be aggressively adversarial (paragraph 92). In certain circumstances cross-examination may be allowed (paragraphs 93 and 95), but in practice this would be highly unusual (see below) and there will generally be little if anything to be gained on the part of the applicant from the cross-examination of IPs at an OFH.

There is no automatic right to call witnesses at hearings, but the Examining Authority has a discretion to permit any person other than the IP to make oral representations. Where an IP asks for an expert witness to be allowed to take part in the examination, the request should not be denied unreasonably (paragraph 97). In practice evidence from expert witnesses will tend to be confined to ISHs.

The recording and filming of proceedings is allowed, subject to it not disrupting the hearing (paragraph 98).

Practice at OFHs

The following points can be made about the emerging practice at OFHs:

- PINS makes audio recordings of the hearings, and these recordings (together with written summaries) are made available on the PINS website. Listening to these recordings provides an invaluable insight into how an OFH is likely to be conducted.
- The Examining Authority does not generally allow IPs to use the OFH as an opportunity to question the applicant.
- Responses by the applicant to points made by IPs at OFHs will generally be expected to be provided in writing in due course (sometimes alongside responses made to written representations).

- Therefore, whilst a representative of the applicant will usually be in attendance, this may well not be the applicant's advocate.
- If large numbers of IPs register a wish to speak at an OFH, then the time available for each IP will be correspondingly limited (for example, in some of the OFHs held in relation to EDF's application for its new nuclear power station at Hinkley Point in Somerset, a limit of 3 minutes per person was adopted). Objectors should therefore be aware that mass participation in an OFH may ultimately be counter-productive.
- Although there can be a temptation on the part of applicants to view OFHs as little more than an opportunity for objectors to let off steam (akin to hearing from members of the public in a planning inquiry under the Town and Country Planning Act 1990, s 78), this would be a mistake. The Examining Authority appears to be very conscious of the additional burden placed upon its shoulders by the inquisitorial nature of the examination system, and will tend to pick up and pursue any apparently well-founded concerns raised by IPs. Applicants should therefore take care to note what is said at OFHs, particularly by members of the Examining Authority in response to concerns that are aired before them.
    - Do the members of the Examining Authority appear to be interested in and/or sympathetic to particular points raised by IPs?
    - What questions do the members of the Examining Authority ask IPs, and what (if any) further details emerge in answer to those questions?
    - Are any reassurances given to IPs that particular issues that are raised will be a focus of later hearings (eg on requirements)?

Meritorious concerns raised by IPs at an OFH will generally be revisited by the Examining Authority at the relevant moment in issue specific hearings later in the examination, and/or in written questions. A well-advised applicant will therefore pay heed to these advanced indications, and prepare its responses accordingly.

Site Inspections

Written by: Gregory Jones QC, ftb
Edited by: Michael Humphries QC, ftb

Introduction

Site inspections are invariably carried out in respect of all planning appeals to the Planning Inspectorate whether the appeals are by way of written representations, hearings or public inquiry conducted under the Town and Country Planning Act 1990 (as amended) (TCPA 1990). Accordingly, whilst there is no direct case authority upon the conduct of site inspections carried out by the Examining Authority under the PA 2008 or of the Infrastructure Planning (Examination Procedure) Rules 2010, SI 2010/103 ('the Examination Procedure Rules') in respect of NSIPs, there is an established body of case law on the conduct of site inspections by planning inspectors, see for example, the Planning Inspectorate Good Practice Note 13 at http://www.planningportal.gov.uk/uploads/pins/gpa_13.pdf which gives general guidance on the conduct of site inspections carried out under the Town and Country Planning Act 1990.

Although strictly speaking, the PINS Guidance Note 13 on site inspections applies only to inspections conducted under the TCPA 1990 its guidance on site inspections for hearings does appear to represent a statement of good practice for the conduct of hearings for DCO applications under the Planning Act 2008. This is helpful because only brief guidance on the conduct of site inspections in respect of NSIPs is given in the DCLG 'Guidance on the examination of applications for development consent' ('the DCLG Examination Guidance').

Unaccompanied site inspections

It is common practice for the persons appointed to examine applications for development consent to make a site visit to familiarise themselves with the proposed development area: see paragraph 99 of the DCLG Examination Guidance.

Rule 16(1) of the Examination Procedure Rules provides that the Examining Authority may make an unaccompanied inspection of an application site before, or during the examination, without giving notice to the persons entitled to take part in the examination.

Such inspections are commonly known as an 'unaccompanied site inspection.' They frequently take place in ordinary planning appeals whether they are conducted by written representations, hearing or public inquiry.

The Examining Authority must ensure that it acts fairly and lawfully in the conduct of any site visits. Accordingly, it is submitted that the Examining Authority should, as matter of good practice, let the parties know what the Examining Authority has seen on the unaccompanied site visit. The best way to do this is to make a written record of the unaccompanied site visit available to the parties –it can be put on the hearing website- describing anything which it saw on the site visit which it considers might be of potential relevance to determination of the application. This allows the parties an opportunity to make representation about anything which the Examining Authority has seen.

In *R (London Borough of Haringey) v The Secretary of State for Communities and Local Government, O.A Kwateng (Ebenezer Community Learning Centre)* [2008] EWHC 1201 (Admin) a planning inspector on a site inspection had observed that neighbouring buildings were being used for educational purposes and relied upon that fact in arriving at his decision to grant planning permission. The High Court quashed his decision, holding not only that it was unfair not to raise this new matter with the parties and allow them a fair opportunity to make representations upon it but also because it subsequently proved that he had made an error of fact in assuming that the educational use was lawful or had been tolerated by the local planning authority. The same principles would appear to apply to a site inspection under the Planning Act 2008.

An unaccompanied site visit might require the Examining Authority to gain access to the site from the owner of the site. The Examining Authority should be wary of engaging in any conversation other than normal pleasantries and certainly not discuss matters relating to the application with, or in the presence of, the owner or his representatives (see *Wilkson Properties Ltd v Royal Borough of Kensington and Chelsea* [2010] EWHC 3274; [2011] JPL 1083).

Accompanied site inspections

Rule 16(2) of the Examination Procedure Rules allows the Examining Authority 'before the completion of its examination of the application or specified matters, inspect any site to which the application or specified matters relate in the company of any interested party or their representative.' This power is more widely drafted than the power to carry out an unaccompanied site visit under rule 16(1). The former is restricted to an inspection of the application site, the latter permits the Examining Authority to conduct an accompanied site inspection to 'any site' to which 'the application or specified matters relate.' This may, for example, allow the Examining Authority, where such issues are relevant, to inspect sites which are said to be comparable sites, or alternatives sites, or sites which are said to be impacted by the proposed development.

It is important to note that rule 16(2) of the Examination Procedure Rules grants a power; it does not impose an obligation. Having said that, where a decision maker has a power, it has a corresponding duty to consider whether to exercise it (see eg *Stovin v Wise* [1996] 3 WLR 388). Thus, an Examining Authority is obliged, at least, to consider any request by an interested party to conduct an accompanied inspection at any such site coming within rule 16(2) of the Examination Procedure Rules. It is for the Examining Authority to determine whether such an inspection is required.

Sometimes landowners are reluctant to allow opposing parties to accompany inspectors on site visits. There are, indeed, instances where planning inspectors considering applications under the TCPA 1990 have gone on site inspections where third parties have been excluded from attending by the land owner. Such approach is said not to be unfair where the local planning authority that has refused to grant planning permission is also present on the site visit to represent the 'opposition side'. This view is open to considerable doubt.

In applications under the PA 2008, however, the role of the local planning authority is quite different and an Examining Authority should be extremely wary of conducting an accompanied site inspection where a particular party has been refused access by the landowner. An Examining Authority could refuse a request for an accompanied site inspection under rule 16(2) of the Examination Procedure Rules. This may not be a significant problem where the site in question is the application site because the Examining Authority has the power to go on an unaccompanied site inspection under rule 16(1) of the Examination Procedure Rules. However, the Examining Authority has no power to go on an unaccompanied site inspection of any site that is not part of the application site. In practice, a landowner who is a party to the proceedings would be well advised not to refuse access to the representatives of an opposing party, since the absence of an accompanied site inspection on their land is likely to tell against the landowner's case whether it be as a promoter or as objector to the NSIP application.

Not surprisingly rule 16 (3) of the Examination Procedure Rules provides that where the Examining Authority intends to make an accompanied site inspection 'it must notify all interested parties of the date, time and place at which it proposes to make the inspection.' However, rule 16(4) of the Examination Procedure Rules provides the Examining authority 'shall not be bound to defer an [accompanied site] inspection *... where an interested party is neither present nor represented at the time appointed.'* (emphasis added). However, this does not mean that the Examining authority can fix the time of the accompanied site visit without regard for the availability of the interested parties. Like any decision it must be exercised fairly and in a way which would not unfairly cause prejudice to any particular party.

Paragraph 101 of the DCLG Examination Guidance makes clear that 'The Examining Authority will refuse to hear evidence or other submissions during any accompanied visit. It is acceptable, however, for people to draw their attention to particular features of the site and its surroundings.' If something arises at the site inspection which is relevant and which has not been addressed at the hearing, the Examining authority should, depending on the circumstances, either reopen the hearing or invite the matter to be addressed by the parties in writing, rather than discussing the matter with the representatives of the parties who happened to be at the site inspection (see *R (London Borough of Haringey) v The Secretary of State for Communities and Local Government, O.A Kwateng (Ebenezer Community Learning Centre)* (above).

In *Fox v Secretary of State for the Environment* [1993] JPL 448 an inspector who travelled to a site inspection in a car with one of the parties was criticised by the High Court, as was the inspector who went for a drink with both parties and then stayed behind to finish his drink with the local planning authority witness when the applicant had finished up and left (*Cotterell v Secretary of State for the Environment* [1991] JPL 1155). In both cases the decisions were not quashed because the other party had known what had happened and agreed or waived his right to object. Nonetheless, it is not conduct to be encouraged. It is submitted that the distinguished editors of *De Smith's Judicial Review* (6th Edition, Sweet & Maxwell) are correct when they state at 10:058: 'There is little doubt that an inspector who accepts hospitality or a lift on the site visit from one party in the absence of the other would be disqualified for bias, but this would not be the case where the inspector had asked sought and obtained the consent of the parties.'

By contrast, it is respectfully submitted that the courts in England and Wales are unlikely to follow the approach recently adopted by the High Court of Northern Ireland in *Alternative A5 Alliance's Application for Judicial Review* [2013] NIQB 30 which found that there was no apparent bias where inspectors, on more than one occasion, rode in cars with officers employed in the promotion of a road scheme without notifying objectors, still less, getting their consent.

Procedures Following Completion of Examination

Written by: Isabella Tafur, ftb
Edited by: Michael Humphries QC, ftb

Introduction

The timetables for the examination of applications under the PA 2008 are considered in an article entitled 'Timescales for applications'. The examination must be completed within six months, from the day after the preliminary meeting. When the Examining authority has completed its examination, it must inform each of the interested parties of that fact (PA 2008, s 99). The focus of this article is the procedure following completion of the examination.

Reporting to the Secretary of State

Within three months from the deadline for completion of the examination, or, if the examination closed earlier, within three months from the date of its closure, the Examining authority must make a report to the Secretary of State, setting outs its findings and conclusions in respect of the application, and its recommendation as to the decision to be made (PA 2008, s 98(3) and the Infrastructure Planning (Examination Procedure) Rules 2010, SI 2010/103, r 19).

There is no statutory provision governing the form of the Examining Authority's report. However, reports generally provide a file reference at the outset (summarising the dates on which the application was made, received and accepted; the dates on which the examination commenced and closed and a brief summary of the development), followed by a summary of the Examining Authority's recommendation and the main body of the report. With certain minor variations, the main body of the reports often follow a format such as this: introduction, main features of the proposal, legal and policy context, findings and conclusions on main issues, overall conclusion and recommendation on the case for development consent, compulsory acquisition, the development consent order, overall conclusions and recommendation.

Extending the deadline for the report

The period for making the report can be extended by the Secretary of State, who is empowered pursuant to PA 2008, s 98(4) to set a later date for any of the deadlines set out in PA 2008, s 98. The same deadline may be extended more than once, and can be extended even after the deadline has already passed (PA 2008, s 98(5)).

Where the power of extension is exercised, the Secretary of State must notify each interested party of the new deadline, must publicise a new deadline in such a manner as he thinks appropriate and must make a statement (either written or oral) to the House of Parliament of which he is a member, announcing the new deadline.

The Secretary of State's decision

Having received the report from the Examining Authority, the Secretary of State must make a decision on the application within three months of its receipt – or within three months of the deadline under PA 2008, s 98(3) – whichever is the earlier date (PA 2008, s 107(1)).

If the Secretary of State differs from the Examining Authority on any matter of fact mentioned in, or appearing to the Secretary of State to be material to, a conclusion reached by the Examining Authority, or if he takes into account new evidence or new matters of fact, and is for that reason disposed to disagree with a recommendation made by the Examining Authority, he must not come to a decision at variance with the recommendation without first notifying all interested parties of his disagreement with the Examining Authority and the reasons for it, and giving them an opportunity to make representations in writing in respect of any new evidence or new matter of fact (SI 2010/103, r 19(3)). SI 2010/103, r 10 (which makes provisions in respect of written representations, such as empowering the Examining Authority to accept representations by persons who are not interested parties, and ensuring that interested parties are given the opportunity to comment on representations) will apply to any such representation in writing, save that paragraphs (2) and (4) will not apply (which require a minimum period of 21 days to be allowed for the submission of representations and require the representation to identify those parts of the application with which it agrees and disagrees).

Extending the deadline for the decision

Similar to the power of extension under PA 2008, s 98(4), the Secretary of State is also empowered to extend the deadline for making his decision, pursuant to PA 2008, s 107(3). Again, he can extend a deadline more than once, and may extend it even after the date for the deadline has passed. If the deadline is extended, the Secretary of State must make a statement (either written or oral) to the House of Parliament of which he is a member, and must publish that statement in such a form and manner as he considers appropriate.

Experience so far

So far, the power to extend the deadline for the Examining authority to provide a report to the Secretary of State (PA 2008, s 98(4)) has not been exercised in any of the DCO applications submitted to the Planning Inspectorate. In relation to the Thanes Tideway Tunnel DCO application, the applicant made an application to extend the length of the examination but this was refused by the Secretary of State.

The power to extend the deadline for making a decision has been exercised once (pursuant to PA 2008, s 107(3)), in respect of the Able Marine Energy Park application. The Secretary of State for Transport issued a statement on 21 May 2013, explaining that he had decided to set a new deadline for the decision to 24 July 2013 (an extension of two months) in order to allow the applicant to negotiate with the

Crown Estate the terms of a lease of land that was required for the project and in order to ensure compliance with PA 2008, s 135 and the Crown Estate's statutory duties (https://www.gov.uk/government/speeches/planning-act-2008-application-for-the-proposed-able-marine-energy-park-development-consent-order).

Decision-Making where there is no National Policy Statement

Written by Hereward Phillpot QC
Edited by Michael Humphries QC

The legislation

Part 6 of the PA 2008 makes separate provision for the approach to decision-making in relation to an application for an order granting development consent depending on whether or not a National Policy Statement ('NPS') has effect in relation to development of the description to which the application relates.

Where an NPS *'has effect'* in relation to development of the description to which the application relates (PA 2008, s 104(1)), the decision must be reached in accordance with *'any relevant national policy statement'* (PA 2008, s 104(3)). Where PA 2008, s 104 does not apply in relation to an application, the decision must be reached in accordance with the provisions of section 105. The clear implication here appears to be that a 'relevant' NPS is one which 'has effect' in relation to that description of development.

The expression 'has effect' is worthy of some consideration, however, as an NPS may not 'have effect' in relation to all forms of development to which it seemingly relates. Thus NPS EN-1 states (para 1.4.5) that 'Insofar as this NPS has effect in relation to applications for the development of new nuclear power stations, it only has effect in relation to applications for development of new nuclear power stations on sites listed in EN-6.' Thus an application for a new nuclear power station on a site not listed in NPS EN-6 would, apparently, fall within section 105.

PA 2008, s 105(2) provides that, in deciding an application to which section 104 does not apply, the Secretary of State must have regard to:

(a) any local impact report submitted within the specified deadline;

(b) any matters prescribed in relation to development of the description to which the application relates; and

(c) any other matters which the Secretary of State thinks are both important and relevant to the Secretary of State's decision.

This is a materially different and less prescriptive approach than that provided for by PA 2008, s 104. The most obvious difference, clearly, is that there is no equivalent in section 105 to the PA 2008, s 104(3) duty to decide the application in a particular way (ie in accordance with the NPS unless ...). Nevertheless, an application determined under section 105 may still have regard to an NPS where the Secretary of State considers it both important and relevant to the decision. This might be the case, for example, where a nuclear power station was proposed on a site not identified in NPS EN-6 (see above).

The Infrastructure Planning (Decisions) Regulations 2010 set out the prescribed matters for the purposes of PA 2008, s 105(2)(b). The prescribed matters are as follows:

- *Listed buildings, conservation areas and scheduled monuments* – Regulation 3 imposes duties similar to those which apply to determinations under the Town and Country Planning Acts.
- *Deemed consents under the Marine and Coastal Access Act 2009* – Regulation 3A applies where a deemed marine licence has been applied for, and requires the Secretary of State to have regard to:
  - the need to protect the environment;
  - the need to protect human health; and
  - the need to prevent interference with legitimate uses of the sea.
- *Hazardous substances* – Regulation 6 provides that where the development would involve the presence of certain hazardous substances, the Secretary of State must have regard to:
  - any current or contemplated use of the land to which the application relates;
  - the way in which other land in the vicinity is being used or is likely to be used; and
  - any planning permission or development consent that has been granted for development of that other land in the vicinity.
- *Biological diversity* – Regulation 7 requires the Secretary of State to have regard to the UN Environmental Programme Convention on Biological Diversity of 1992 (and, in Scotland, to any strategy designated under s 2(1) of the Nature Conservation (Scotland) Act 2004).

In the usual way, the requirements which govern applications for EIA development – such as the prohibition on granting consent without consideration of environmental information (Regulation 3 of the Infrastructure Planning (Environmental Impact Assessment) Regulations 2009) – will apply to decisions made under PA 2008, s 105. The difference is that there will be no NPS to provide guidance on how the environmental impacts should be treated for the purposes of decision-making.

The same would be true for any application which engages the provisions of the Conservation of Habitats and Species Regulations 2010, or other similar statutory regimes of relevance to applications for development consent.

Likewise, the statutory tests for authorising compulsory acquisition (PA 2008, s 122) and the relevant guidance (DCLG, Planning Act 2008: Guidance related to procedures for the compulsory acquisition of land, September 2013) are the same whether or not there is a relevant NPS in place, and are dealt with elsewhere in this book. However, in practical terms it is likely to be somewhat harder to satisfy those tests, because of the requirement to establish need and to deal with potential alternatives in the absence of an NPS which makes provision for these matters.

Case law

So far there has only been one case in the Administrative Court dealing with the approach to decision-making under PA 2008, s 105. In *R (David Gate) v The Secretary of State for Transport* [2013] EWHC 2937 (Admin), Turner J dismissed an application for judicial review of the decision by the Secretary of State to make The Lancashire County Council (Torrisholme to the M6 Link (A683 Completion of Heysham to M6 Link Road)) Order 2013.

This was a decision made before the National Networks NPS, and hence under section 105. One of the grounds of challenge was that the Secretary of State had erred in basing his decision, at least in part, in reliance upon various NPS which were said not to be material to the type of development under consideration.

Dismissing this ground of challenge, Turner J referred to PA 2008, s 105(2)(c) and said (paragraphs 56–58) that:

> 'It must follow, and common sense would in any event dictate, that the decision maker is not precluded from taking into account matters incorporated within national policy statements which are not directly applicable to the development so long as he considers that they are both important and relevant to his decision.
>
> The Examining Authority in this case specifically and accurately noted both the absence of a directly applicable national policy statement and the requirement to have regard to important and relevant matters under section 105. He went on to refer to the national policy statements in respect of ports and of nuclear power generation in this specific context. Heysham is a port and the site of two nuclear power stations. There is a possibility that a third may be constructed here.
>
> Against this background, it is clear that the Examining Authority was fully aware of the fact that the national policy statements had no direct application to this project. No objection could reasonably have been taken if the defendant had simply articulated matters relevant to Heysham's status as a port and site of nuclear power generation without reference to national policy statements and the fact that national policy statements were referred to does not vitiate the relevance of the matters which they contain. Once the matters are correctly categorised as relevant then it is a matter for the defendant to determine what weight to give them subject to the very limited constraints of judicial review. …'

There are perhaps three main points to take from this:

- taken into account by the Secretary of State under section 105(2)(c) was 'relevant to the Secretary of State's decision';
- if something is relevant, the weight to attach to it (and hence whether it is 'important' under section 105(2)(c)) is a matter of planning judgment for the Secretary of State; and
- an NPS dealing with a different type of development can be relevant and important in appropriate circumstances.

Practical points

It is likely that there will be relatively few NSIPs promoted in the absence of a relevant NPS; save in relation to business and commercial NSIPs. There have not been many so far, and most of the planned NPSs are now in place. The outcome of an application for development consent and compulsory acquisition powers in the absence of a NPS establishing need, and setting clear criteria to determine the acceptability of the proposed development, is necessarily less predictable.

That has not prevented some applications from coming forward in the absence of a directly applicable NPS. In addition to the Heysham Link Road (above), an application for a Tidal Lagoon at Swansea Bay was approved by the Secretary of State for Energy and Climate Change in June 2015, even though this was not a technology covered by the Energy NPSs. However, the Energy NPSs were treated as being important and relevant to the decision because they established a national need for the development of new nationally significant electricity generating and network infrastructure (see the Secretary of State's decision letter at paragraphs 11–12). It was not therefore necessary for the applicant to establish the need for the proposed development from first principles in a policy vacuum.

As this was Welsh case, the Welsh Government's guidance in 'Planning Policy Wales' was also taken into account, alongside local development plan policy.

Within England, the National Planning Policy Framework (NPPF) would also be likely to be regarded as important and relevant; something which paragraph 3 of the NPPF specifically contemplates. The NPPF states that it does not contain specific policies for NSIPs (paragraph 3), and therefore the approach to decision-making in paragraph 14 of the NPPF would not be directly applicable. In practice, however, it may well be that a fairly similar balancing approach would be applied in determining an application for development consent to that set by paragraph 14 where development plan policies are absent, silent or out of date. In those circumstances the NPPF provides that planning permission should be granted unless:

> '– any adverse impacts of doing so would significantly and demonstrably outweigh the benefits, when assessed against the policies in this Framework taken as a whole; or
>
> – specific policies in this Framework indicate development should be restricted'

In the Swansea Tidal Lagoon decision, the Secretary of State described the case for authorising the proposed development (paragraph 95) by reference to:

> '… the national need for the proposed Development and that the potential adverse local impacts of the Development do not outweigh the benefits of the scheme' (emphasis added).

This mirrors the language used in PA 2008, s 104(7), and the approach to determining whether development is or is not sustainable pursuant to paragraph 14 of the NPPF; see per Jay J in *Cheshire East BC v SSCLG* [2016] EWHC 571 (Admin). If the adverse impacts do not outweigh the benefits, and need has been established, it may well be that only something akin to the possible obstacles identified in PA 2008, s 104(4)–(6) would lead to the refusal of development consent.

Part 13

Correction of Errors, Changes and Revocation

Correction of Errors in Development Consent Decisions

Written by: Isabella Tafur, ftb
Edited by: Michael Humphries QC, ftb

Introduction

Pursuant to the PA 2008, s 119, Sch 4, the Secretary of State may correct certain errors in development consent decisions. The documents that can be corrected are:

(a) where development consent has been granted, errors in development consent order; and

(b) where development consent has been refused, errors in the refusal letter.

The Act, however, only allows corrections to 'correctable errors'. These are defined as errors or omissions that are part of the document recording the decision, but are *not* part of the statement of reasons for the decision (PA 2008, Sch 4, para 1(3)). Any error in the statement of reasons for the decision cannot, therefore, be corrected. Furthermore, there is no power of correction in relation to DCO provisions included pursuant to PA 2008, Sch 5, paras 30A and 30B which relate to deemed marine licences (see PA 2008, Sch 4, para 1(11)).

Where the development consent order was required to be contained in a statutory instrument, the correction of any error/omission must also be made by an order contained in a statutory instrument (PA 2008, Sch 4, para 1(8)). As soon as possible after the instrument containing the order is made, the Secretary of State must deposit a copy of it in the office of the Clerk of the Parliaments (PA 2008, Sch 4, para 1(10)).

Conditions

The Secretary of State may only correct an error or omission if the following conditions are satisfied:

(a) the Secretary of State has received a written request to correct the error/omission from any person before the end of the relevant period (PA 2008, Sch 4, para 5(a)); or

(b) the Secretary of State has sent a statement in writing to the applicant, explaining the error/omission and stating that the Secretary of State is considering making the correction before the end of the relevant period (PA 2008, Sch 4, para 5(b)).

The 'relevant periods are:

(a) if development consent has been granted, the Secretary of State will only have the power to correct an error if the request is received/statement is sent before the expiry of 6 weeks, beginning with the day on which the order was published, or, if later, the day on which the statement of reasons for making the order was published (PA 2008, Sch 4, para 1(6)(a) and s 118(1)(b)); or

(b) if development consent is refused, the Secretary of State will only have the power to correct an error if the request is received/statement is sent before the expiry of 6 weeks, beginning with the day on which the statement of reasons for refusal is published (PA 2008, Sch 4, para 1(6)(b) and s 118(1)(b)).

Furthermore, the Secretary of State must inform each relevant local planning authority that the request has been made/statement has been sent (PA 2008, Sch 4, para 1(7)).

Correction notices

If a written request has been received or a statement sent, the Secretary of State must issue a correction notice (PA 2008, Sch 4, para 2(1)). The correction notice must be served as soon as practicable after making the correction or deciding not to make the correction (PA 2008, Sch 4, para 2(2)). The notice must specify the correction of the error/omission or give notice of the decision not to correct the error/omission, and it must be given to the applicant, each local planning authority for all (or any part) of the area in which the development is situated, and to the person who requested the correction (PA 2008, Sch 4, para 2(3)). The Secretary of State may also give to the notice to other persons, but is not obliged to do so (PA 2008, Sch 4, para 2(4)).

Effect of a correction

If a correction is made to a decision, the original decision (whether the development consent order or the refusal of development consent) remains in force, but is treated as corrected by the terms specified in the correction notice (PA 2008, Sch 4, para 3(1)). The correction takes effect from the date the correction notice is issued or, if the correction is required to be made by statutory instrument, the date specified in the order.

Where a correction is not made, the original decision continues to have full force and effect (PA 2008, Sch 4, para 3(2)).

Examples of correction notices

An example of a correction notice can be seen in relation to the Galloper Wind Farm Order 2013, SI 2013/1203 (the Order). The Secretary of State's notice and correction order can be downloaded from the following website:

http://infrastructure.planningportal.gov.uk/projects/eastern/galloper-offshore-wind-farm/?document=&ipcsection=search&from=01-07-2013&to=15-09-2013&btnSearch=Search

The notice explains that the Secretary of State has received a request from the applicant to correct certain errors in the Order. It goes on to set out the corrections that the Secretary of State has made as a result of that request. In summary, these are as follows:

(a) corrections to plan references (which had failed to take account of the updated versions which had been submitted before the Order was made);

(b) a correction to the definition, in the interpretation section of the Order, of 'the percentage reduction' as it did not reflect the Secretary of State's conclusions in his decision letter in respect of the maximum number of predicted lesser black-backed gull mortalities which should be attributed to the development;

(c) a correction to the section of the Order dealing with the approval of detailed wind turbine design parameters to correct the fact that it erroneously prevented works commencing onshore until the wind turbine approval process had been completed;

(d) a correction to the section of the Order dealing with aids to navigation to correct the fact that it erroneously prevented works commencing onshore until 14 days after the required notification to Defence Infrastructure Safeguarding.

The notice also sets out those corrections requested by the applicant, which the Secretary of State decided not to make. He declined to amend Article 4 of the Order (which dealt with the maintenance of the authorised project), which the applicant had requested be amended to make clear that maintenance works within the scope of the environmental statement needed no further approval. The Secretary of State considered that the wording of Article 4 properly reflected his intention and that it would not be appropriate to treat the requested change as a 'correctable error'.

The applicant also requested that the words in Article 13 (dealing with street works) be amended by the deletion of the certain words to reflect an agreement the applicant had given to EDF Energy to protect the latter's interests. The Secretary of State considered that as EDF's interests were secured by way of a separate private legal agreement, such a change to the Order was not essential. The notice explained that the wording in the Order had been used in other DCOs and that it would not be appropriate to treat the requested change as a 'correctable error'.

The Galloper Wind Farm (Correction) Order 2013, SI 2013/2086 came into effect on 21 August 2013. The Schedule to SI 2013/2086 contains a table that sets out the relevant provision of the original Development Consent Order which is to be modified (in the first column), the erroneous text (in the second column) and the replacement text (in the third column).

Relationship with other provisions

It is worth noting the relationship between the power to correct errors (in PA 2008, Sch 4) and the power to make changes to, and revocation of, development consent orders (in PA Sch 6, para 3) provides that the Secretary of State may by order make a change to, or revoke, a development consent order without an application being made if he is satisfied that –

(a) the development consent order contains a significant error; and

(b) it would *not* be appropriate for the error to be corrected by means of the power conferred by PA 2008, Sch 4, para 1 (see above) or by PA 2008, Sch 6, para 2 (non-material changes).

It is not entirely clear in what circumstances it would not be 'appropriate' for an error to be corrected under PA 2008, Sch 4, para 1 or Sch 6, para 2, but might still be appropriate to correct such error under PA 2008, Sch 6.

Note also the relationship between PA 2008, Sch 4 and PA 2008, s 161 (breach of terms of order granting development consent). PA 2008, s 161(3) provides that it is a defence for a person charged with an offence under s 161(1) to prove that:

(a) the breach or failure to comply occurred only because of an error or omission in the order; and

(b) a correction notice specifying the correction of the error or omission has been issued under PA 2008, Sch 4, para 2.

Conclusion

Errors and omissions in development consent orders, and in notices refusing development consent can, in certain circumstances, be corrected. Any person may request such a correction, or the Secretary of State may unilaterally decide to make a correction, within the statutory period during which a legal challenge can be made to a decision to grant or refuse an application for development consent. To date this is a power that has only rarely been invoked.

Changes to and Revocation of Development Consent Orders

Written by Isabella Tafur
Edited by Michael Humphries QC

Introduction

Once a development consent order has been made, the Secretary of State may make changes to, or indeed revoke the DCO pursuant to s 153 of and Sch 6 to the PA 2008. This is distinct from the Secretary of State's power to correct any errors in a DCO under s 119 of and Sch 4 to the PA 2008 (see article 141).

Paragraph 2 of Sch 6 authorises the Secretary of State to make non-material changes to a DCO, and para 3 of Sch 6 authorises the making of material changes to, and the revocation of, DCOs. The power to make material changes under para 3 includes a power to require the removal or alteration of buildings or works; require the discontinuance of a use of land; impose specified requirements in connection with the continuance of a use of land; impose new requirements in connection with the relevant development and to remove or alter existing requirements (PA 2008, Sch 6, para 5). Material changes to a DCO can only be made within four years of the date on which the development was substantially complete (PA 2008, Sch 6, para 5), but this time limit does not prevent the Secretary of State from revoking a DCO or making changes to the requirements on a DCO at any time.

The procedure for applying for changes to be made to DCOs and the consultation requirements in respect of such applications are set out in the Infrastructure Planning (Changes to, and Revocation of, Development Consent Orders) Regulations 2011 (as amended) ('2011 Regulations'). The Department for Communities and Local Government has issued 'Guidance on changes to development consent orders' (December 2015).

Non-material changes to a DCO

Under para 2 of Sch 6 to PA 2008, the Secretary of State may make non-material changes to a DCO. This includes a power to impose new requirements or to remove or alter existing requirements on a DCO but it does not authorise the making of any changes to a deemed marine licence under the Marine and Coastal Access Act 2009. It will be for the Secretary of State to decide whether the proposed change is material, having regard to the effect of the change, together with any previous non-material changes, on the DCO as originally made.

The Guidance on changes to DCOs provides advice on the types of change that are likely to be material. It explains that changes should be treated as material if they would require an updated ES to take account of new, or materially different, likely significant effects on the environment or if they are likely to invoke the need for a Habitats Regulations Assessment or the need for a new or additional licence in respect of a European Protected Species. Equally, a change should be treated as material if it would authorise the compulsory acquisition of any land or interest in land and the potential impact of the proposed changes on local people will be a consideration in determining whether a change is material.

An application for the making of a non-material change to a DCO can be made by the person who applied for the DCO or a successor in title; any person with an interest in the land to which the DCO relates or any other person for whose benefit the DCO has effect. The application must be made in accordance with the requirements of reg 4 of the 2011 Regulations and must be accompanied by a consultation and publicity statement. The fee for making such an application is currently £6,891 (reg 5 of the 2011 Regulations).

Pursuant to reg 6 of the 2011 Regulations, the applicant must publish a notice of the application explaining its main elements, in a local newspaper for at least two successive weeks and in any other publication necessary to ensure that notice of the application is given in the vicinity of the land. The publication must include details of how to respond to the publicity and must allow at least 28 days for responses to be made.

The applicant must send a copy of the notice to each person for whose benefit the DCO has effect, each person who was notified of the original application under section 56 of PA 2008, and any other person who may be directly affected by the proposed change (reg 7 of the 2011 Regulations), unless the Secretary of State has given written consent that the applicant need not consult any such persons. If the Secretary of State authorises the applicant not to consult any such person, he must publish his reasons for doing so on its website.

There is no statutory timetable for making the decision in respect of a non-material change. However, the Guidance explains (at para 37) that where the applicant has complied with all necessary procedural requirements and has provided all the information and documents necessary for a decision to be made, a decision should normally be expected within 6 weeks of the closing date for responses to publicity and consultation.

If the change is made to the DCO, the Secretary of State must notify its decision to the applicant, any person consulted about the application and any person who made a relevant representation in response to the publicity or consultation exercises (reg 8 of the 2011 Regulations).

Material changes to, and revocation of, a DCO

Pursuant to para 3 of Sch 6 to PA 2008, the Secretary of State may make changes to, or revoke a DCO, either on receipt of an application or, in certain circumstances, without any application being made. An application may be made by the original applicant or a successor in title; a person with an interest in the land; or any other person for whose benefit the DCO has effect. A local planning authority ('LPA') can also make such an application provided the Secretary of State is satisfied that the DCO authorised development wholly or partly in the area of that LPA, the development has been begun but been abandoned and the amenity of other land in the LPA's area or an adjoining area is adversely affected by the condition of the land. The power can only be exercised without any application if the Secretary of State is satisfied that the DCO contains a significant error and that it would not be appropriate for the error to be corrected under Sch 4 (correction of errors) or para 2 of Sch 6 (non-material changes) or if the Secretary of State is satisfied that, if the development were carried out in accordance with the DCO, there would be a contravention of EU law or a Convention right, or there are other exceptional circumstances that make it appropriate to exercise the power.

The applicant must consult those persons prescribed by reg 10 of the 2011 Regulations in respect of a proposed application under this provision and must allow a period of at least 28 days for representations to be made. Prior to carrying out that consultation exercise, the applicant must notify the Secretary of State of the proposed application (reg 12 of the 2011 Regulations). Unless the applicant has the written consent of the Secretary of State to dispense with any of these requirements, a notice of the proposed application must also be published in one or more local newspapers for at least two successive weeks, as well as once in the London Gazette and, if land in Scotland is affected, the Edinburgh Gazette. If the proposed application relates to offshore development, a notice must be published once in Lloyd's List and once in an appropriate fishing trade journal (reg 14 of the 2011 Regulations). A notice must also be displaced on the land, or as close to it as is reasonably practicable. Once the application has been made, notice must be given to persons prescribed by reg 19 of the 2011 Regulations and a notice must be published again in the relevant newspapers etc., in accordance with reg 14.

The application must contain the information prescribed by reg 16 of the 2011 Regulations and must be accompanied, among other things, by a statement as to whether the application involves EIA development and by a consultation report. Unless the application is made by the LPA, a fee of £4,500 is payable on the making of the application, with further fees payable at pre-examination and examination stages (reg 18 of and Sch 2 to the 2011 Regulations).

The Secretary of State may refuse to determine an application for a change to a DCO. In particular, the Secretary of State may exercise this power if it is considered that the development that would be authorised as a result of the change should properly be the subject of a new application for a DCO.

In some cases, the Secretary of State may decide that it is not necessary for an Examining body to examine the application, in which case he must notify the applicant and all those who had made relevant representations of this decision and publish the reasons for the decision on the website, allowing a period of at least 28 days for representations to be made (regs 21A and 21B of the 2011 Regulations).

An application under this section will be treated as a 'subsequent application' for the purposes of regs 3 (prohibition on granting consent without consideration of environmental information), 6 (procedure for establishing whether environmental impact assessment is required), 8 (application for a scoping opinion), 18 (subsequent application for EIA development) and 19 (subsequent application not complying with EIA requirements) of the Infrastructure Planning (EIA) Regulations 2009 (reg 17 of the 2011 Regulations).

Regulations 22–41 of the 2011 Regulations set down the procedures for the appointment of the Examining body and the conduct of the examination, which are akin to the procedures for the examination of a DCO. Where an Examining body has been appointed to examine the application, it must complete its examination within 4 months of the start day (i.e. the day of the preliminary meeting) (reg 42 of the 2011 Regulations) and report to the Secretary of State within two months of the completion of the examination (reg 43 of the 2011 Regulations). The Secretary of State must decide the application within two months of receiving the report from the Examining body, or within two months of the deadline for receiving that report, whichever is the earliest (reg 49 of the 2011 Regulations). If the Secretary of State has determined the application without examination by an Examining body, then it must determine the application within two months of issuing the notification under reg 21A that such examination was not necessary.

Where a material change is made to a DCO, the DCO will continue in force and the change will take effect from the date on which the Secretary of State gives notice of his decision or, if the change to the DCO is required to be made by a statutory instrument, the date specified in the order making the change. If a DCO is revoked, the revocation takes effect on the date specified in the order making the revocation or, where there is no date specified, the date on which the order making the revocation is made (reg 53 of the 2011 Regulations).

Where the change or revocation to a DCO is made by the Secretary of State without any application, the procedure set out in Part 3 of the 2011 Regulations applies. This requires the Secretary of State to give notice to prescribed persons of his intention to consider making such an order and to publish a notice in relevant newspapers etc. in accordance with the requirements in reg 14 of the 2011 Regulations. Once the decision has been made, the Secretary of State must notify the persons prescribed by reg 58 of the 2011 Regulations.

Compensation

Where a material change is made to a DCO, or a DCO is revoked, any person who has incurred expenditure in carrying out work (i.e. in the preparation of plans or other similar matters of preparatory work) which is rendered abortive by the change or revocation can claim compensation from the Secretary of State, as can any person who has otherwise sustained any loss or damage which is directly attributable to the change or revocation (para 6 of Sch 6 to PA 2008). However, no compensation is payable in respect of any works done before the DCO was made or in respect of any other loss or damage arising out of anything done or omitted to be done before the DCO was made (other than loss or damage consisting of the depreciation of the value of an interest in land).

Any claim for compensation must be made in accordance with reg 61 of the 2011 Regulations and must be made within 12 months of the notification of the Secretary of State's decision to make the change or revoke the DCO under regs 50 or 57. Any dispute as to the compensation payable will be referred to the Upper Tribunal for determination.

Changes made to DCOs to date

To date (May 2015), no material changes have been made to a DCO and there have been no revocations, but non-material changes have been made in respect of four

DCOs: Heysham link road, Galloper wind farm, Hinkley Point C nuclear power station and East Anglia ONE wind farm.

In respect of the Heysham link road, the non-material change authorised in March 2015 permitted the realignment of the slip road at junction 34 of the M6 by a maximum of 11.7 metres form the alignment authorised by the original DCO. The change would not require the exercise of any new compulsory acquisition powers and would avoid the need to divert a National Grid high pressure gas pipeline.

In July 2015 a non-material change was made to the Galloper wind farm DCO authorising an increase in the permitted monopole diameter from a maximum of 7.0 metres to a maximum of 7.5 metres.

A non-material change to the Hinkley Point C DCO was authorised in September 2015 to allow changes to a number of service buildings. The change authorised nine new or relocated structures for the safe operation of plant and the movement of 15 structures from their consented locations. No changes were proposed to the tallest buildings or to the overall site footprint.

In respect of East Anglia ONE, the Secretary of State made a non-material change to the DCO in March 2016, allowing the applicant the option to construct either a 750MW wind farm with a High Voltage Alternating Current ('HVAC') transmission system or the 1200MW wind farm with a High Voltage Direct Current transmission system for which development consent had been granted. The change to the HVAC system would generate a need for an increase in the height of the electrical equipment at the onshore sub-station.

Part 14

Legal Challenges

Legal Challenge to Grant of Development Consent

Written by: Richard Honey, ftb
Edited by: Michael Humphries QC, ftb

Introduction

A legal challenge to the grant of development consent is by way of judicial review. The normal principles and procedures of judicial review generally apply, subject to the provisions of PA 2008, s 118. In particular, there is a six-week time limit for bringing judicial review proceedings.

PA 2008, s 118(1)

PA 2008, s 118 governs legal challenges relating to applications for orders granting development consent. Section 118(1) (as amended) provides that:

> 'A court may entertain proceedings for questioning an order granting development consent only if
>
> (a) the proceedings are brought by a claim for judicial review, and
>
> (b) the claim form is filed before the end of the period of 6 weeks beginning with the day after -
>
> (i) the day on which the order is published, or,
>
> (ii) if later, the day on which the statement of reasons for making the order is published.'

This six-week time limit was unusual when the Act was introduced, but it is now the standard time limit for judicial review of planning decisions given the change made in July 2013 by the Civil Procedure (Amendment No 4) Rules 2013, SI 2013/1412.

The requirement to 'publish' the order is contained in PA 2008, s 117. The order must be published 'in such manner as the Secretary of State thinks appropriate' (s 117(3)), unless the order:

- makes by-laws,
- introduces offences,
- applies, modifies or excludes a statutory provision, or
- amends, repeals or revokes a statutory provision of local application,

in which case it must be contained in a statutory instrument (s 117(4)). Statutory instruments are officially published by Her Majesty's Stationery Office (HMSO) on the website of The National Archives (www.legislation.gov.uk), where new statutory instruments are listed by publication date.

The requirement to 'publish' a statement of reasons for a decision to grant development consent is contained in PA 2008, s 116. The statement must again be published 'in such manner as the Secretary of State thinks appropriate' (s 116(3)).

Typically an Order granting development consent and the Secretary of State's statement of reasons for making the Order will be published simultaneously on the Planning Inspectorate's website (infrastructure.planningportal.gov.uk).

In *R (oao Williams) v Secretary of State for Climate Change* [2015] EWHC 1202 (Admin) Lindblom J (as he then was) said (para 45) that:

> 'The way in which an order and the Secretary of State's statement of reasons for making it are to be 'published' is not prescribed by section 118. But in my view the placing of the order on the Planning Inspectorate's infrastructure planning website ..., together with the Secretary of State's decision letter and the Examining Authority's report, and, on the same day, the notification of the interested parties, both by email and post, that this had been done, was enough to constitute publication of the order, and the reasons why it was made, within the meaning of section 118.'

In the case of Rookery South, where there was the special parliamentary procedure to be followed subsequent to the panel's decision, the Inspectorate advised that 'in cases where special parliamentary procedure applies, the publication of the order, for the purposes of PA 2008, s 118, will follow the special parliamentary procedure' (register of advice, 18 November 2011, Rookery South Energy from Waste Generating Station).

Date from which time runs

Readers are referred to s 118 (as amended by the Criminal Justice and Courts Act 2015) for details of the date from which the six week time limit runs in each given circumstances (see PA 2008, s 118(1)–(7) inclusive).

It should be noted that in the section as originally enacted, time ran from the day beginning with the event specified in s 118(1)–(7) and, in the case of s 118(1) from the day on which the order was published or, if later the day of which the statement of reasons for making the order was published. The words 'beginning with' in PA 2008, s 118 contrasted with the word 'from' which is used in r 54.5 of the Civil Procedure Rules (CPR) for judicial reviews generally. This led to two challenges to the Thames Tideway Tunnel DCO being held to be out of time when the applicants calculated the six weeks from the day after the publication of the DCO and their applications for judicial review were dismissed: see *R (oao Blue Green London Plan and LB Southwark) v Secretary of State for Environment Food and Rural Affairs* [2015] EWHC 495 (Admin).

Following the decision in these challenges the wording of s 118(1) was amended so as to provide that a challenge by way of judicial review must be made within the period of six weeks 'beginning with *the day after*' (emphasis added) the publication of the DCO and Statement of Reasons.

For example: if an Order and statement of reasons were published on 5 January, the first day of the six weeks would be 6 January, and the time for challenge would expire on 17 February.

Accuracy is vital bearing in mind the inability of the court to extend time where there is a statutory time limit (see below).

The time limit of six weeks is set by statute

The time limit of six weeks for challenges to is one set by statute (ie by the terms of s 118 and not by the Civil Procedure Rules) and thus it is important to note that the court has no power or discretion to extend it: see *Mucelli v Government of Albania* [2009] 1 WLR 276.

Procedural issues

Promptness

Apart from the six-week time limit, the requirement for promptness in the CPR r 54.5(1)(a) appears not to apply to judicial reviews within the scope of PA 2008, s 118, because r 54.5(3) states that the rule does not apply when any other enactment specifies a shorter time limit for making a claim for judicial review; s 118 would be such an enactment.

Although the requirement for promptness in the CPR would appear not to apply to judicial reviews brought under PA 2008, s 118, the 'undue delay' provision in s 31(6) of the Senior Courts Act 1981 would still apply. Section 31(6) provides that where the High Court considers that there has been undue delay in making an application for judicial review, the court may refuse to grant permission or relief, if it considers that the granting of the relief sought would be likely to cause substantial hardship to, or substantially prejudice the rights of, any person, or would be detrimental to good administration. Section 31(7) says that this provision is 'without prejudice to any enactment or rule of court which has the effect of limiting the time within which an application for judicial review may be made'. Accordingly, 'undue delay' together with one of the harms identified in s 31(6) (substantial hardship, substantial prejudice of rights, or detriment to good administration) would allow a court to refuse permission or relief, even where a claim was brought within six weeks. It is, however, unlikely that, save in exceptional circumstances, a court would regard six weeks for bringing a claim as representing 'undue delay'. Nonetheless, potential claimants would need to bear this in mind and could not simply wait until the end of the six-week period to bring a claim.

Pre-action protocol for judicial review

The courts will normally expect the Pre-Action Protocol for Judicial Review produced under the CPR to be followed before proceedings are commenced. Given the abridged time limit under PA 2008, s 118 (six weeks instead of three months) there is likely to be a question as to whether full compliance with the pre-action protocol is practical. In a letter dated 11 November 2011, solicitors for an objector to the Rookery South Energy from Waste Generating Station application said that the pre-action protocol did not apply in light of the timetable (copy published on the register of advice). In a response of the same date, Helen Adlard, the IPC's Director of Legal Services, stated that the pre-action protocol did apply and suggested that in circumstances where the DCO had not yet been made it would be 'highly appropriate' to warn the decision-maker of the grounds of challenge envisaged.

When the new six-week time limit for judicial review of planning decisions was introduced in July 2013 the pre-action protocol was amended to advise that the 'protocol may not be appropriate in cases where one of the shorter time limits … applies. In those cases, the parties should still attempt to comply with this protocol but the court will not apply normal cost sanctions where the court is satisfied that it has not been possible to comply because of the shorter time limits'. In practice claimants and respondents ought to try to comply with the pre-action protocol, although the normal periods for compliance may have to be abridged.

There are two main stages under the pre-action protocol. First, the claimant sends a letter before claim which should identify the issues in dispute and establish whether litigation can be avoided. A standard form letter before claim is included in Annex A to the protocol. The letter should contain the date and details of the decision being challenged and a clear summary of the facts on which the claim is based. It should also contain the details of any relevant information that the claimant is seeking and an explanation of why this is considered relevant. The second stage is the letter of response, sent by the proposed defendant and any interested parties, following the standard form set out in Annex B to the protocol. The letter should be sent within 14 days, or, if this is not possible, then the defendant should send an interim response and propose a reasonable extension of time. If the claim is being conceded in full, in part or not at all, the reply should say so in clear and unambiguous terms. Where appropriate the letter should contain a fuller explanation of the decision being challenged, deal with any points of dispute, and enclose any relevant documents.

Alternative dispute resolution

In applications for judicial review there is generally an encouragement by the courts to consider alternative dispute resolution: see eg *R (Cowl) v Plymouth City Council (Practice Note)* [2002] 1 WLR 803 and the pre-action protocol. However, given the nature of the grant of development consent by means of a DCO the ability to use ADR in this context is almost non-existent.

Standing

To be able to bring a claim for judicial review a claimant must have a sufficient interest in the matter to which the claim relates. Standing is a ground on which both permission and substantive relief may be refused, but the test at the permission stage is lower, essentially to exclude troublemakers. The importance and merits of the claim can alter the degree of standing required. A 'sufficient interest' has been given a wide and flexible interpretation by the courts. In planning and environmental cases, a reasonably low threshold is usually applied, including those with a general interest in the issue to be determined. Representative and campaign groups would usually be regarded as having sufficient standing.

Claim Form

A judicial review claim is commenced using the Part 8 claim procedure. The claim form should be accompanied by a detailed statement of the claimant's grounds, a statement of the facts relied on, and any applications eg for directions. The claim form must be served within seven days from issue, and an acknowledgement of service filed by the defendant and interested parties within 21 days of service, including a statement of grounds for contesting the claim.

Permission to bring an application for judicial review

There is a permission stage in all applications for judicial reviews that will apply also to challenges to the making of a DCOs under PA 2008, s 118(1). It is necessary for a claimant to secure permission from the court to bring an application for judicial review. This is usually considered first by a judge on the papers. At the 'permission stage' the court will consider the merits of the claim against the relevant test: whether the claim discloses an arguable case. Permission should not be granted for judicial review claims that are misguided complaints of administrative error. The purpose of the permission stage is to protect public authorities against weak and vexatious claims. The court will make an order giving or refusing permission, and giving any directions. Permission may be granted with conditions or only on certain of the grounds sought.

If permission is refused it is possible then to renew the application for permission at an oral hearing before a single judge, usually listed for 30 minutes. If permission is refused after an oral hearing then a right of appeal lies to the Court of Appeal. Sometimes, in urgent or complex cases, a judge will order a permission hearing without a paper decision being reached, or that there be a rolled-up hearing, where permission and the substantive case are considered at the same hearing. In July 2013 the CPR were changed to remove the right to reconsideration at a hearing of the refusal of permission in cases where the application was certified as totally without merit by the judge considering the application on the papers.

As far as the costs of the permission stage are concerned, a successful defendant should be entitled to recover the cost for its acknowledgement of service, including the preparation of summary grounds of resistance, but not of any pre-action correspondence (see *R (Mount Cook) v Westminster CC* [2004] 2 P&CR 22 at para 76(1) *and R (Ewing) v Office of the Deputy Prime Minister* [2006] 1 WLR 1260 at 1267A-B). Defendants are not generally entitled to their costs of attending any oral permission hearing, but may be awarded them in certain circumstances as an exception.

Grounds for judicial review

If permission is granted, the defendant and any interested parties must within 35 days serve detailed grounds for contesting the claim and any written evidence. Skeleton arguments must be filed and served before the hearing. The court's permission is required if a claimant seeks to rely on grounds other than those for which he has been given permission to proceed. Where justified by urgency, for example where a development needs to commence, it is possible to seek to have the hearing expedited.

If a claim is commenced in, or transferred to, an Administrative Court location outside London it is likely that the claim will be heard more quickly.

The grounds of challenge to the grant of consent are likely often to feature issues of European law, for example arising in connection with the EIA Directive, the Birds Directive or the Habitats Directive. It is also inevitable that some challenges will seek to rely on human rights issues, such as Articles 6 (fair hearing) and 8 (home and family life) and Article 1 of the First Protocol (property). There may also be arguments in relation to statutory duties such as the public sector equality duty in s 149 of the Equality Act 2010, breach of which would give rise to grounds for judicial review.

Otherwise, grounds of judicial review of the grant of development consent will be the same as for any judicial review. These will include: error of law; excess of power, ie going beyond the powers conferred by statute; jurisdictional error; unauthorised delegation; acting as if discretion is fettered; over-rigid adherence to policy or rules; irrelevant considerations taken in to account, or a refusal to take in to account relevant considerations; irrationality; acting in bad faith; failure to observe procedural rules; procedural unfairness; breach of right to a fair hearing; actual or apparent bias; failure to give adequate reasons; misinterpretation of policy; fundamental error of fact; lack of evidence for a conclusion; proportionality; failure properly to consult; and, breach of a substantive or procedural legitimate expectation.

The ambit of judicial review is quite limited and so gives defendants a fair degree of protection from challenges. The merits of the decision cannot be considered. Matters of judgment are the exclusive province of the decision-maker. The assessment of facts and weighing of considerations is in the hands of the decision-maker alone and the court has no power to intervene. A decision-maker is entitled to attach what weight it pleases to relevant considerations, and the courts will not entertain a submission that undue weight was given to one consideration or too little weight was given to another. If a matter would not have caused the decision-maker to reach a different conclusion then it is irrelevant whether it was taken in to account; and, if a judge is uncertain whether a matter would have made a difference to a decision then he cannot conclude that the decision was invalid. Where there is a factual error which is insignificant or insubstantial then the relevant decision will not be quashed. Where it can be shown that notwithstanding any error the decision-maker would have reached the same decision on the other factors stated, the court will not interfere.

Other issues during conduct of proceedings

Orders for disclosure against a respondent can be made, but disclosure is not required. Such orders are fairly rare, since questions of fact play much less part in judicial review proceedings than in other cases and since the decision and the basis for it is usually clearly evidenced (eg by a panel report). However, there has been a trend towards increasing disclosure in judicial review cases. The Secretary of State will normally hold the relevant documents that are not already in the public domain, such as those relating to Ministerial consideration of whether or not to grant a DCO. Traditionally there has been a duty of candour on public authorities voluntarily to provide full and frank disclosure of relevant material to a challenger. Lord Donaldson MR said in *R v Lancashire CC ex p Huddleston* [1986] 2 All ER 941 that judicial review was 'a process which falls to be conducted with all the cards face upwards on the table and the vast majority of the cards will start in the authority's hands'. The courts have made it clear that the duty of candour is a very high and important duty to assist the court with full and accurate explanations of all the facts relevant to the issues the court must decide. An authority should explain fully what it has done and why it has done it, so far as is necessary fairly to meet the challenge made. The duty of candour had perhaps not been working so well in recent years. But following the decisions in *Tweed v Parades Commission* [2007] 1 AC 650, *R (Al-Sweady) v Secretary of State for Defence* [2009] EWHC 2387 (Admin) and *R (Shoesmith) v Ofsted* [2010] EWHC 852 (Admin), it is increasingly common for a defendant to provide something like disclosure.

Cross-examination is unusual in judicial review proceedings (see eg *R (Bancoult) v Foreign Secretary* [2012] EWHC 2115 (Admin)). Cross-examination is exceptional because the primary facts are often not in dispute, or at least those asserted by the defendant are undisputed, and the authority may normally be relied upon to disclose relevant documents pursuant to its duty of candour. But the court retains a discretion to permit cross-examination and should do so if it is necessary for the claim to be, and be seen to be, determined fairly and justly.

Remedies

The remedy sought in judicial review is likely to be the quashing of the DCO. It may also be that a declaration is sought as to what the correct legal position is on some issue. In judicial review all remedies are discretionary, so even where a decision has been held by the court to be unlawful it may be that it is not quashed. However, discretion must be exercised judicially and in most cases in which a decision has been found to be flawed it would not be a proper exercise of discretion to refuse to quash it *(R (Edwards) v Environment Agency* [2008] UKHL 22 at para 63).

Costs

In relation to costs of judicial reviews generally, Part 45 of the CPR now provides a regime of fixed costs in claims to which the Aarhus Convention applies. This is likely to cover most if not all challenges to DCOs, depending on the actual grounds of challenge, as the Aarhus Convention applies to environmental matters generally. CPR rr 45.41 to 45.44 enable a claimant to tick a box on the claim form to seek costs protection, which will apply unless it is successfully challenged by a defendant. The only ground for challenging the application of this fixed costs regime is that the claim is not one within the ambit of the Aarhus Convention. Where the rules apply, the total costs recoverable from a claimant are limited to £5,000 (individual) or £10,000 (others) and the costs recoverable by a claimant are limited to £35,000.

Otherwise there remains an ability for a claimant to apply for a protective costs order in accordance with the principles set out in *R (Corner House Research) v Secretary of State for Trade and Industry* [2005] EWCA Civ 192. The basic guidelines for the award of a PCO are:

- the issues raised are of general public importance;
- the public interest requires that those issues be resolved;

- the claimant has no private interest in the outcome;
- having regard to the financial resources and the costs, it is fair and just to make the order; and
- if the order is not made, the claimant will probably discontinue the proceedings and will be acting reasonably in so doing.

It was also said that if the claimant's lawyers were acting *pro bono* then it would be likely to enhance the merits of the application. These conditions have been applied flexibly in subsequent cases.

Where the grant of development consent is challenged, the promoter will be an interested party. A promoter is entitled to, and in practice is likely to, participate in the judicial review in order to seek to uphold the DCO. The Secretary of State, represented usually by the Treasury Solicitor, will be the defendant. As such, the role of a promoter is somewhat limited. It is unlikely that a third party in such a judicial review would be awarded their costs if the challenge is dismissed (see *Bolton MDC v SSE* [1995] 1 WLR 1176), although two sets of costs are awarded in some cases.

Generally

Given the scale and significance of projects authorised by DCOs, and the limited ability of objectors to probe applications through the PA 2008 process, it is likely that a substantial proportion of DCOs granted will be challenged by judicial review.

Judicial reviews were launched, for example, upon the making of the Rookery South, Hinkley Point and the Heysham to M6 link road DCOs. In relation to Rookery South, the challenge was brought by a waste company who objected to the DCO and petitioned in relation to the special parliamentary procedure. The grounds of challenge include the basis for the decision to include compulsory purchase powers and that the special parliamentary procedure does not provide for an environmental impact assessment process. In relation to Hinkley Point, judicial review proceedings were brought by Greenpeace and An Taisce, the former in relation to the policy effect of the lack of a long-term waste disposal facility and the latter in relation to trans-boundary effects and the failure to consult the Irish government. The Heysham to M6 link road challenge was brought by a campaign group. The grounds included challenges relating to whether the project was properly within the Planning Act 2008 regime, on pre-application consultation, the use of the National Policy Statement, alternatives and ecology.

Judicial reviews will be dealt with by the Planning Court, which forms part of the Administrative Court of the Queen's Bench Division of the High Court.

Legal Challenge to Refusal of Development Consent

Written by: Richard Honey, ftb
Edited by: Michael Humphries QC, ftb

Introduction

A legal challenge to the refusal of development consent is by way of judicial review. The normal principles and procedures of judicial review generally apply, subject to the provisions of PA 2008, s 118. In particular, there is a six-week time limit for bringing judicial review proceedings.

The main principles and procedural provisions relating to judicial review are considered in another article in this work entitled 'Legal challenge to grant of development consent'. Those principles and procedural provisions, however, also apply to the challenge of a refusal of an application for development consent; subject to some key differences that are considered below.

PA 2008, s 118(2)

PA 2008, s 118 governs legal challenges relating to the refusal of development consent. Section 118(2) (as amended) provides that:

> 'A court may entertain proceedings for questioning a refusal of development consent only if
>
> (a) the proceedings are brought by a claim for judicial review, and
>
> (b) the claim form is filed before the end of the period of 6 weeks beginning with the day after the day on which the statement of reasons for the refusal is published.'

This six-week time limit was unusual when the Act was introduced, but it is now the standard time limit for judicial review of planning decisions given the change made in July 2013 by the Civil Procedure (Amendment No 4) Rules 2013, SI 2013/1412.

The requirement to 'publish' a statement of reasons for a decision to refuse development consent is contained in PA 2008, s 116. The statement must be published 'in such manner as the Secretary of State thinks appropriate' (s 116(3)).

Procedural issues

Standing

A promoter bringing such a judicial review would have no problem establishing standing. The decision would be defended by the Secretary of State. It is unlikely that an objector to the DCO would actively participate in the judicial review, although that would in practice depend on the circumstances of each case and the grounds of challenge.

Grounds for judicial review

As to grounds of judicial review, a promoter might be arguing that there has been an error of law in the sense that a legal test has been misconstrued and applied more rigorously than it ought to have been. It is, however, more likely that a promoter would be challenging on the grounds for example of: over-rigid adherence to policy or rules; irrelevant considerations taken in to account, or a refusal to take in to account relevant considerations; irrationality; failure to observe procedural rules; procedural unfairness; failure to give adequate reasons; misinterpretation of policy; fundamental error of fact; and, lack of evidence for a conclusion. Other grounds may of course be applicable in particular cases.

Other issues during conduct of proceedings

Where a DCO has been refused contrary to the recommendation of a panel's report, the promoter is likely to wish to secure, by way of disclosure, all documents evidencing the consideration of the application by the Minister and his advisers. This could be secured under the duty of candour or by way of an application for specific disclosure, if necessary.

Remedy

The remedy sought in judicial review is likely to be the quashing of the Secretary of State's decision to refuse consent. If the challenge is successful, the Secretary of State will then have to re-decide the application. Where the error of law lies with the Examining Authority, it may be advisable to seek an order that the report should be quashed as well, but that is unlikely to be necessary. It has been held in relation to comparable decisions that where a decision is quashed then 'the Secretary of State had to start again de novo with a clean sheet' (*Kingswood v SSE* (1989) 57 P&CR 153 at 162). The Judge in *Kingswood* went on to conclude that 'there can be no doubt that the Secretary of State must consider the matter de novo in circumstances where a decision is quashed' (p163). It may also be that a declaration is sought as to what the legal position is.

Costs

In relation to costs it is possible that a promoter would be able to take advantage of the fixed costs regime in Part 45 of the CPR. Although it will depend on the precise grounds of challenge, it is entirely possible that such a challenge would be a claim to which the Aarhus Convention would apply. It is, however, to be doubted that it would be worthwhile to engage this fixed costs regime. First, the costs of the Secretary of State using the Treasury Solicitor and counsel from the Attorney General's panel are not likely to be great, although they will be higher if the defendant goes off-panel and instructs a QC. Secondly, the reciprocal cap of £35,000 is likely to cover only a very small proportion of a claimant promoter's costs.

The availability of the £10,000 cap means however that a promoter would be able to launch a judicial review with limited prospects of success, knowing that costs exposure would be limited if the case were lost. Given how much would have been invested by a promoter in taking a DCO application through examination, some promoters might see the limited further expense of a judicial review as being a worthwhile investment, even if there were only very limited prospects of success.

Generally

The first judicial review by a promoter of a refusal of development consent was in relation to the Preesall Underground Gas Storage DCO: see *R (oao Halite Enery Group Ltd) v Secretary of State for Climate Change and Energy* [2014] EWHC 17 (Admin). The challenge was successful and led to the redetermination and, ultimately, to the grant of development consent for the project. The High Court decision raised important issues relating to the inquisitorial role of the Examining Authority, fairness in the examination process and the proper interpretation of policy in NPSs.

Legal Challenge to Decision Not to Accept Application

Written by: Richard Honey, ftb
Edited by: Michael Humphries QC, ftb

Introduction

A legal challenge to a decision not to accept an application would be by way of judicial review. The normal principles and procedures of judicial review generally apply, subject to the provisions of PA 2008, s 118. In particular, there is a six-week time limit for bringing judicial review proceedings.

The main principles and procedural provisions relating to judicial review are considered in another article in this work entitled 'Legal challenge to grant of development consent'. Those principles and procedural provisions, however, also apply to a challenge to a decision not to accept an application for development consent; subject to some key differences that are considered below.

PA 2008, s 118(3)

PA 2008, s 118 governs legal challenges relating to a decision not to accept an application. Section 118(3) (as amended) provides that:

> 'A court may entertain proceedings for questioning a decision of the Secretary of State under section 55 not to accept an application for an order granting development consent only if
>
> (a) the proceedings are brought by a claim for judicial review, and
>
> (b) the claim form is filed before the end of the period of 6 weeks beginning with the day after the day on which the Secretary of State notifies the applicant as required by subsection (7) of that section.'

This six-week time limit was unusual when the Act was introduced, but it is now the standard time limit for judicial review of planning decisions given the change made in July 2013 by the Civil Procedure (Amendment No 4) Rules 2013, SI 2013/1412.

PA 2008, s 55 provides that the Secretary of State has 28 days after receipt of what purports to be an application for a development consent order to decide whether or not to accept the application. Section 55(7) provides that if the Secretary of State is of the view that the application cannot be accepted, he must notify the applicant of that and the reasons for it. This is the start date for the six-week period.

Procedural issues

Standing

A promoter bringing such a judicial review would have no problem establishing standing and the Planning Inspectorate's decision not to accept an application would be defended by the relevant Secretary of State. It is unlikely that an objector to the DCO would actively participate in the judicial review, although that would in practice depend on the circumstances of each case and the grounds of challenge. If, for example, the applicant was not accepted on grounds relating to adequacy of consultation, it is not inconceivable that a local authority that had given an adverse 'adequacy of consultation representation' (see s 55(4)(b) and (5)) might wish to participate in the judicial review.

Grounds for judicial review

PA 2008, s 55(3) provides that the Secretary of State may accept an application only if he concludes:

(a) that it is an application for an order granting development consent,

(c) that development consent is required for any of the development to which the application relates,

(e) that the applicant has, in relation to a proposed application that has become the application, complied with Chapter 2 of Part 5 (pre-application procedure), and

(f) that the application (including accompaniments) is of a standard that the Secretary of State considers satisfactory.

[NB some earlier parts of s 55(3) were repealed by the Localism Act 2011.]

In relation to PA 2008, s 55(3)(e) above, that is, pre-application procedure, s 55(4) identifies a number of matters to which the Secretary of State must 'have regard' when reaching his conclusion, being:

(a) the consultation report received under PA 2008, s 37(3)(c),

(b) any adequacy of consultation representation received by the Secretary of State from a local authority consultee, and

(c) the extent to which the applicant has had regard to any guidance issued under section 50.

In relation to PA 2008, s 55(3)(f) above, that is, whether the application is of a 'satisfactory' standard, s 55(5A) identifies a number of further matters to which the Secretary of State must 'have regard' when reaching his conclusion, being the extent to which:

(a) the application complies with the requirements in section 37(3) (form and contents of application) and any standards set under section 37(5), and

(b) any applicable guidance given under section 37(4) has been followed in relation to the application.

It can be readily seen, therefore, that inherent in any decision not to accept an application under PA 2008, s 55 are a number of judgments by the Secretary of State that are susceptible to scrutiny in any application judicial review. The Inspectorate could, for example, misunderstand or misinterpret one of the matters in s 55(3), including, for example, whether the pre-application procedures have been properly complied with.

PA 2008, s 55(3)(f) (application of a 'satisfactory' standard) was a matter added to s 55(3) on 1 April 2012 by the Localism Act 2011. This appears to be an additional matter to those in ss 55(3)(a), (c) and (e), rather than a standard against which those other matters should be tested. Thus it would appear that even if an application is of a standard that the Secretary of State considers 'satisfactory' (s 55(3)(f)), he must still be satisfied that it has also 'complied' with Chapter 2 of Part 5 of the Act (s 55(3)(e)). This understanding of how s 55(3) operates has not, however, been tested in the courts.

The reasons given pursuant to PA 2008, s 55(7) could also be inadequate, although reasons challenges often simply result in the reasons being 'corrected'.

Beyond such grounds focused on the requirements of s 55 itself, all the other usual grounds for judicial review would apply. Having said that, however, a challenge alleging that a decision not to accept an application on the basis of 'irrationality' would be likely to struggle to succeed. For a conclusion to be irrational or perverse it must be one that that no reasonable person in the position of the Secretary of State, properly directing himself on the relevant material, could have reached *(Seddon v Secretary of State for the Environment* (1981) 42 P&CR 26). The courts have made it clear that they will require 'something overwhelming' from a claimant before allowing a challenge of this sort (*Associated Provincial Picture Houses v Wednesbury Corporation* [1948] 1 KB 223 at 230; see also 233-234). A claimant alleging that the Inspectorate has reached a *Wednesbury* unreasonable conclusion on a matter of judgment faces a particularly daunting task: see, for example, *R (Newsmith Stainless Ltd) v Secretary of State for the Environment, Transport and the Regions* [2001] EWHC Admin 74 at para 8.

PA 2008, s 55(4)(c) required the Secretary of State to have regard, in reaching the conclusion in s 55(3)(e) (pre-application procedures), to the extent to which the applicant has had regard to any guidance issued by the Secretary of State under s 50. Clearly if an applicant had correctly followed DCLG Guidance on an issue on which its application was later not accepted under s 55, that could raise issues of legitimate expectation: see eg *R v North and East Devon Health Authority, ex parte Coughlan* [2001] QB 213 and *Nadarajah & Abdi v Home Secretary* [2005] EWCA Civ 1363.

Other issues during conduct of proceedings

Where a decision has been made not to accept an application, the promoter is likely to wish to secure by way of disclosure all documents evidencing the consideration of the application by the Inspectorate, including the PA 2008, s 55 application checklist. This is likely to contain more detailed reasons than those set out pursuant to s 55(7). This could be secured under the duty of candour or by way of an application for specific disclosure, if necessary.

Generally

Although PA 2008, s 118(3) applies to a decision not to accept an application it does not apply to a decision to accept an application. Such a challenge would be caught by s 118(7) which applies to 'proceedings for questioning anything else done, or omitted to be done, by the Secretary of State in relation to an application for an order granting development consent'.

As a decision under PA 2008, s 55 is a procedural decision, rather than a substantive decision, and some at least of the impediments to acceptance could be cured by an applicant supplying further or different information, it is a decision which might lead to a different outcome if taken a second time in different circumstances. It is not therefore a final decision in one sense in that the Inspectorate could change its mind in the light of further information. This seems also to be the intention of s 55(8) that provides that 'If in response the applicant modifies (or further modifies) the application, subsections (2) to (7) then apply to the application as modified.'

This is, therefore, one area of judicial review in connection with the PA 2008 where both the pre-action protocol and alternative dispute resolution might have an important role in removing to reducing the need for judicial review. If errors are point out to, and accepted by, the Planning Inspectorate and/or the applicant, then there may be scope to re-submit or modify the application so that the re-submitted or modified application could be accepted.

The position with the Daventry International Rail Freight Terminal application, which was not accepted by the Inspectorate due to non-compliance with PA 2008, s 55(3)(e) and s 55(3)(f), is illustrated by the meeting note published on the register of advice (5 December 2012) and subsequent correspondence (19 December 2012). Following the Planning Inspectorate's decision not to accept, a meeting was held between the Planning Inspectorate and the promoter to agree the way forward; this led to an acceptable re-submission of the application. In the letter dated 28 November 2012 containing the notification of the decision not to accept the application the Inspectorate had stated:

> 'We would also encourage you to meet with us so we can advise how best to address the issues to help facilitate a new application at the earliest opportunity.'

Legal Challenge to Other Action of Secretary of State

Written by: Alex Booth, ftb
Edited by: Michael Humphries QC, ftb

Introduction

PA 2008, s 118 deals with legal challenges to applications for orders granting development consent. Its purpose is, in effect, to regulate the timescales within which a challenge by way of judicial review may be brought against a decision of the Secretary of State in relation to an application for an order granting development consent. PA 2008, s 118 identifies six specific 'decisions' to which its provisions relate and then provides a general provision covering anything else done, or omitted to be done, by the Secretary of State. This general provision does not cover challenges to national policy statements, which are specifically dealt with under PA 2008, s 13.

The specific 'decisions' covered by PA 2008, s 118 comprise:

- an order granting development consent (s 118(1));
- a refusal of development consent (s 118(2));
- a decision under s 55 *not* to accept an application for an order granting development (s 118(3));
- a decision under Sch 4 para 1 in relation to an error or omission in a decision document (s 118(4));
- a decision under Sch 6 para 2(1) to make a change to an order granting development consent (s 118(5)); and
- a decision under Sch 6 para 3(1) to make a change to, or revoke, an order granting development consent.

In the case of each of these specific decisions a challenge may *only* be brought by way of judicial review where the claim form is filed before the end of the period of six weeks 'beginning with the day after' the date of an event identified in the individual provision.

The 2008 Act recognises, however, that there could be other decisions of the Secretary of State, or the Examining Authority on behalf of the Secretary of State, which do not fall within the above six cases and where a legal challenge could otherwise be brought under the normal judicial review timescales. As stated above, to deal with this eventuality the Act provides a general provision covering 'anything else done, or omitted to be done, by the Secretary of State' (s 118(7)). This article examines this general provision.

As yet, of the various applications for judicial review that have lodged in respect of the development consent process, none have been brought pursuant to the general provision under s 118(7).

PA 2008, s 118(7)

PA 2008, s 118(7) (as amended) provides as follows:

> 'A court may entertain proceedings for questioning anything else done, or omitted to be done, by the Secretary of State in relation to an application for an order granting development consent only if –
>
> (a) the proceedings are brought by a claim for judicial review, and
>
> (b) the claim form is filed before the end of the period of 6 weeks beginning with the day after the relevant day.'

It is important to note that a court may entertain proceedings for questions anything else done, or omitted to be done, 'only' if brought by judicial review before the end of six weeks beginning with the day after the 'relevant day'. The effect of s 118(7) is, therefore, to 'oust' any other avenue of legal challenge and impose a strict six-week time limit.

It is also important to note that PA 2008, s 118(7) is directed to anything done, or omitted to be done, 'in relation to an application' for development consent. It is not absolutely clear, therefore, whether it covers an act or omission of the Secretary of State during the pre-application procedures under the 2008 Act. Certainly the point did not appear to have been raised be the defendant in the *Innovia Cellophane Ltd* challenge to the (former) Infrastructure Planning Commission's grant of s 53 authorisation in respect of the then proposed Hinkley Point C application for development consent: see *R (Innovia Cellophane Ltd) v Infrastructure Planning Commission* [2011] EWHC 2883.

Within six weeks 'beginning with' the 'relevant day'

The period within which a claim may be brought is identified as 'beginning with the day after the relevant day' (s 118(7)(b)). The 'relevant day' is itself defined (s 118(8)) as meaning the day on which:

- the application for development consent is withdrawn;
- the order granting development consent or the statement of reasons in respect of that order is 'published', whichever is the later;
- the statement of reasons for refusing to grant development consent is 'published'.

The first of these potential starting dates envisages a scenario in which an applicant for development consent has withdrawn its application, but a person still wishes to challenge a decision of the Secretary of State. Whilst it is not immediately obvious why a person might still wish to challenge a decision of the Secretary of State after an application for a development consent order has been withdrawn, it might be relevant, for example, where the Secretary of State had authorised entry on land by the promoter of a project under PA 2008, s 53 before the application for development consent had been withdrawn. Such a claim would allow a landowner to challenge a 'redundant' s 53 authorisation.

It is worth noting that this 'withdrawn' application scenario provides the only opportunity for a challenge to be brought in respect of a decision of the Secretary of

State prior to either the publication of the order or, alternatively, the publication of the statement of reasons for its refusal.

Thus the effect of PA 2008, s 118 in general, and s 118(7) in particular, is to mean that a legal challenge may not be brought in respect of a decision of the Secretary of State from the making of the application until the grant or refusal of consent (subject to the 'withdrawn' application point). Thus a challenge may not be brought to any procedural decision taken during the examination of an application for development consent. The absence of any means of challenge during an examination may, however, mean storing up trouble for later in the process. Indeed, an applicant may even recognise that a particular act or omission by the Examining Authority, on behalf of the Secretary of State, at an early stage in the examination process could afford potential claimants with a fertile ground of challenge, but then be left waiting until the order is granted to see whether a challenge is indeed brought. Thus there is a risk that considerable resources may be expended during the remainder of the examination and ultimately be wasted.

A further point to consider within the context of timing, concerns the second of the start dates identified above, and the fact that the claim form may only be filed during the period of six weeks 'beginning with the day after' the 'publication' of a development consent order.

The requirement to 'publish' the order is contained in PA 2008, s 117. The order must be published 'in such manner as the Secretary of State thinks appropriate' (s 117(3)), unless the order:

- makes by-laws,
- introduces offences,
- applies, modifies or excludes a statutory provision, or
- amends, repeals or revokes a statutory provision of local application,

in which case it must be contained in a statutory instrument (s 117(4). Statutory instruments are officially published by Her Majesty's Stationery Office (HMSO) on the website of The National Archives (www.legislation.gov.uk), where new statutory instruments they are listed by publication date.

The requirement to 'publish' a statement of reasons for a decision to grant development consent is contained in PA 2008, s 116. The statement must again be published 'in such manner as the Secretary of State thinks appropriate' (s 116(3)).

Typically an Order granting development consent and the Secretary of State's statement of reasons for making the Order will be published simultaneously on the Planning Inspectorate's website (infrastructure.planningportal.gov.uk).

In *R (oao Williams) v Secretary of State for Climate Change* [2015] EWHC 1202 (Admin) Lindblom J (as he then was) said (para 45) that:

> 'The way in which an order and the Secretary of State's statement of reasons for making it are to be 'published' is not prescribed by section 118. But in my view the placing of the order on the Planning Inspectorate's infrastructure planning website …, together with the Secretary of State's decision letter and the Examining Authority's report, and, on the same day, the notification of

> the interested parties, both by email and post, that this has been done, was enough to constitute publication of the order, and the reasons why it was made, within the meaning of section 118.'

The requirement to 'publish' a statement of reasons for a decision to refuse development consent is contained in PA 2008, s 116. The statement must be published 'in such manner as the Secretary of State thinks appropriate' (s 116(3)).

The effect of PA 2008, s 118 delaying legal challenge until the 'publication' of a development consent order can be seen in relation to FCC Environmental Ltd (formerly Waste Recycling Group Ltd) in respect of its s 118(1) claim for judicial review of the development consent order granted to Covanta Rookery South Ltd for a resource recovery facility in Bedfordshire. In that instance, the Infrastructure Planning Commission issued its statement of reasons for the grant of development consent on 13 October 2011 and made a draft DCO on 22 November 2011. The draft was placed before Parliament on 29 November that year, but thereafter underwent special parliamentary procedure. The DCO was then 'published' on 26 March 2013, and it was only at that stage that judicial review proceedings were, or indeed could be, lodged.

Matters for challenge

There are a limited number of matters which might conceivably form the basis of a challenge pursuant to PA 2008, s 118(7), since in most cases proceedings are likely to be brought either pursuant to s 118(1) (challenge to order granting development consent) or s 118(2) (challenge to refusal of development consent). Although as yet there is no legal authority upon the point, such would appear to be the case even if the substance of a complaint related to a procedural decision of the Secretary of State during the examination period. Thus a decision in respect of an application made by an objector that an examination should be suspended pursuant to regulation 17 of the Infrastructure Planning (Environmental Impact Assessment) Regulations 2009, SI 2009/2263, on the basis of the inadequacy of an environmental statement, might well still be made under s 118(1) if development consent were granted; notwithstanding it was a procedural decision on which the claim was founded.

As such, it is only certain discrete actions of the Secretary of State that would fall to be challenged pursuant to PA 2008, s 118(7) such as, by way of example, the decision to issue a certificate pursuant to s 127(2) approving the compulsory acquisition of land held by a statutory undertaker.

In such an instance, the subject-matter of the challenge would not comprise part of the decision reached in respect of the DCO application itself, but would instead comprise an associated but distinct determination. In this example PA 2008, s 118(7) would be relevant as a challenge to the decision to issue/refuse certification for compulsory purchase pursuant to s 127 would not comprise 'proceedings for questioning an order granting development consent' under s 118(1).

It may be that the full scope of PA 2008, s 118(7) will only become apparent as the provision is tested in the courts. For the present, however, it would appear that it will have only limited application.

Part 15

Enforcement

Enforcement Under the Planning Act 2008

Written by: Michael Humphries QC, ftb

Introduction

PA 2008, Part 8 sets up the system of 'enforcement' under the Act for: (a) development without development consent; and (b) breach of the terms of an order granting development consent. It is worth noting at the outset that the PA 2008 enforcement system is radically different from that under the Town and Country Planning Act 1990.

In broad terms, PA 2008 creates two criminal offences:

(a) the carrying out of development for which development consent is required without first obtaining without development consent (s 160); and

(b) the carrying out of development in breach of the terms of a DCO or otherwise failing to comply with the terms of a DCO (s 161).

Only where a person has been found guilty of an offence under either of these provisions may a local planning authority serve a 'notice of unauthorised development' requiring 'steps' to be carried out to rectify the position. This is in sharp contrast to the 1990 Act regime where breaches of planning control are first made subject to civil enforcement and on then, in certain circumstances, made the subject-matter of an offence. A local planning authority may, however, apply to the High Court for an injunction to restrain any actual or apprehended activity that would be an offence under PA 2008, s 160 or 161.

This article will consider:

- Offences;
- Notices of unauthorised development; and
- Injunctions.

Offences

PA 2008, ss 160 and 161

PA 2008, Part 8 creates two primary offences, those being under ss 160 and 161.

PA 2008, s 160

PA 2008, s 160 provides that:

> '(1) A person commits an offence if the person carries out, or causes to be carried out, development for which development consent is required at a time when no development consent is in force in respect of the development.'

A person guilty of an offence under this section is liable to a fine not exceeding £50,000 on summary conviction, or an unlimited fine for conviction on indictment: see s 160(2).

The reference in PA 2008, s 160(1) to development for which development consent is 'required' relates directly to s 31 and the requirement for development consent for development to the extent that 'the development is or forms part of a nationally significant infrastructure project.' This again relates back to s 14, which defines the term 'nationally significant infrastructure project', and the various thresholds in ss 15–30.

It seems unlikely that an infrastructure developer would deliberately carry out development requiring development consent without first having obtained a DCO and so offences are likely to fall within two broad categories, being:

- Development thought to be within PA 2008 regime that extends physically or functionally beyond that actually granted by a DCO; or
- Development thought to be outside PA 2008 regime that has breached some NSIP threshold.

In relation to the first of these categories, it is clearly within the power of the promoter to ensure that any DCO is drafted so as to grant the necessary consent to carry out the development. It is for this reason that 'parameters' and the concept of the 'Rochdale envelope' are so important.

In relation to the second category above, it will be particularly important for any developer proposing an infrastructure project to ascertain with some certainty whether such project falls within the scope of PA 2008 as any error of understanding could result in a criminal conviction. Such an error may be made, for example, where what is being proposed is an 'alteration' to an existing infrastructure development, that alteration itself falling above a relevant threshold. An offence will be committed under this section notwithstanding that planning permission, or other consent, may have been granted for the development by a local planning authority or other decision-maker acting under the same error of understanding.

Clearly the criminal law standard of proof (ie beyond reasonable doubt) will apply to any proceedings under PA 2008, s 160.

PA 2008, s 161

PA 2008, s 161 provides that:

> '(1) A person commits an offence if without reasonable excuse the person –
>
> (a) carries out, or causes to be carried out, development in breach of the terms of an order granting development consent, or
>
> (b) otherwise fails to comply with the terms of an order granting development consent.'

Again, a person guilty of an offence under this section is liable to a fine not exceeding £50,000 on summary conviction, or an unlimited fine for conviction on indictment: see PA 2008, s 160(2).

It is important to note that by virtue of s PA 2008, ss 161(2) and 149A(4), a person who fails to comply with a 'condition' under a deemed 'marine licence' does not commit an offence under s 161, although breach of requirement for, or conditions of, a marine licence would be an offence under s 85 of the Marine and Coastal Access Act 2009.

The offence under PA 2008, s 161 may be committed where a person either: (a) carries out development in 'breach' of the terms of an order (s 161(1)(a)); or (b) 'fails to comply with the terms' of an order (s 161(1)(b)). In this context, the expression 'the terms of an order' would appear to comprise the articles in the body of the DCO, the contents of its schedules (including any plans) and, in particular, its 'requirements'.

PA 2008, s 161(1)(a) appears to contemplate the person committing the offence undertaking some positive action in 'carrying out development' in breach of the terms of a DCO which does exist for the project. This offence can be distinguished, therefore, from that under s 160 where the carrying out of development is at a time where there is no DCO for that project. An offence under this provision might comprise, for example, the carrying out of development in breach of a requirement first to submit details for approval by the local planning authority.

By contrast, PA 2008, s 161(1)(b) does not require the person committing the offence to be 'carrying out development' and so would be particularly relevant during the operational stages of any project. An offence under this provision might comprise, for example, operating the project in breach of any requirement relating to hours of operation.

The offence created under PA 2008, s 161 does introduce the potential defence of 'reasonable excuse', which was absent from s 160. The term 'reasonable excuse', which also appears in ss 53(6) and 168, is not defined in PA 2008, although it is a concept that occurs in other legislation. In such circumstances, it would appear that the words should be given their ordinary meaning and that an 'excuse' (in other words, an explanation for not complying with the terms of a DCO) will have to be advanced by a defendant, which will have to be judged 'reasonable' in considering whether an offence has been committed under s 161.

PA 2008, s 161(3) also makes it a defence under s 161 to prove that: (a) the breach or failure to comply occurred only because of 'an error or omission in the order'; and (b) a 'correction notice' specifying the correction of the error or omission has been issued under para 2 of Sch 4 to PA 2008.

Clearly, as with an offence under PA 2008, s 160, the criminal law standard of proof (ie beyond reasonable doubt) will apply to any proceedings under s 161.

Time limits

PA 2008, s 162 sets certain time limits for charging a person with an offence under ss 160 and 161. Section 162(1) provides that a person may not be charged with an offence under s 160 or 161 after the end of:

- the 'relevant four-year period'; or
- in certain circumstances, the 'extended period'.

The four-year period

PA 2008, s 162(2) provides that:

> 'The 'relevant 4-year period means –
>
> (a) in the case of an offence under section 160, the period of 4 years beginning with the date on which the development was substantially completed;
>
> (b) in the case of an offence under section 161, the period of 4 years beginning with the later of –
>
> (i) the date on which the development was substantially completed, and
>
> (ii) the date on which the breach or failure to comply occurred.'

The term 'substantially completed' in s 162(2) reflects the same language s section 171B of the Town and Country Planning Act 1990 and the case law that has developed under that section is likely to be highly material in relation to s 162(2).

The extended period

The 'extended period' applies where an information notice has been served under PA 2008, s 167 (see below) or an injunction applied for under s 171 (see below): see s 162(3). In such circumstances, s 162(4) provides that the four-year period runs from:

- the date of service of any information notice;
- the date of any application for an injunction;
- the later of those dates, if both apply.

The relevant local planning authority

For the purposes of PA 2008, Part 8, the term 'the relevant local planning authority' in relation to any land is defined by s 173 as the local planning authority for the area in which the land is situated.

Where, however, there is both a district planning authority and a county planning authority for an area then:

- if the 'relevant development' (see s 173(6)) is the construction or alteration of a hazardous waste facility within s 14(1)(p), the relevant local planning authority is the county planning authority (s 173(4)); and
- in any other case, the relevant local planning authority is the district planning authority (s 173(5)).

Rights of entry

PA 2008, s 163 provides a right to enter land 'without warrant' if the 'relevant local planning authority' 'has reasonable grounds for suspecting' that an offence under s 160 or 161 'is being, or has been, committed' on or in respect of the land.

The person authorised to enter the land under PA 2008, s 163 may 'at any reasonable hour' enter the land for the purpose of *'ascertaining whether'* an offence under s 160 or 161 has been, or is being, committed on the land: see s 163(2); although the person may only enter a building occupied as a dwelling on the giving of 24 hours' notice to the occupier of the building: see s 163(3).

This power clearly relates to any offence under PA 2008, s 160 or 161 that 'is being, or has been' committed; but not to 'apprehended' future offences. To the extent, therefore, that s 171 allows a local planning authority to apply for an injunction to restrain an 'apprehended' 'prohibited activity' (i.e. an anticipated future offence under s 160 or 161), s 163 would not give the relevant local planning authority power to enter the land.

PA 2008, s 164 gives the relevant local planning authority power to enter land 'under warrant' where: (a) admission to the land has been refused, or a refusal is reasonably apprehended; or (b) the case is one of urgency.

PA 2008, s 165 set out various supplementary provisions relating to the rights of entry under ss 163 and 164, including in relation to matters such as the wilful obstruction of a person exercising a right of entry as above, and compensation for damage caused to the land and chattels in the exercise of any such right of entry.

Information notices

An 'information notice' may be served under PA 2008, s 167 where it appears to 'the relevant local planning authority' that an offence under s 160 or 161 'may have been committed on or in respect of the land'.

This power clearly relates to offences that 'may have' been committed (ie 'past' offences), rather than anticipated future offences under PA 2008, s 160 or 161. As with the right to enter under s 163, therefore, to the extent that s 171 allows a local planning authority to apply for an injunction to restrain an 'apprehended' 'prohibited activity' (ie an anticipated future offence), section 167 would not allow the relevant local planning authority to require the giving of information to that 'apprehended' activity.

By virtue of PA 2008, s 167(2), such a notice may only be served by 'the relevant local planning authority' and, by s 167(3), may only be served on any person who: (a) is the owner or occupier of the land or has any other interest in it; or (b) is carrying out operations on the land or is using it for any purpose. Thus the power is wide enough to require information from contractors or others carrying out development.

An information notice may require (s 167(4)) the person served to give:

- information about any operations being carried out in, on, over or under the land, any use of the land and any other activities being carried out in, on, over or under the land; and

- information about the provisions of any order granting development consent for development of the land.

Notices of unauthorised development

PA 2008, s 169 provides for the relevant local planning authority to serve a 'notice of unauthorised development' where a person is found guilty of an offence under s 160 or 161.

The first thing to note is that such a notice can only *follow* successful criminal proceedings under PA 2008, s 160 or 161; a notice under s 169 cannot be served in advance of, or in parallel with, such proceedings. This is in sharp contrast with the approach under the Town and Country Planning Act 1990 where civil enforcement precedes any criminal proceedings.

Where the offence in respect of which a person has been found guilty is under PA 2008, s 160, then the relevant local planning authority may serve a notice of unauthorised development on the person by under s 169(2), requiring such 'steps' as may be specified in the notice to be taken:

- to remove the development; and
- to restore the land on which the development has been carried out to its condition before the development was carried out.

The notice of unauthorised development must specify the period within which any 'steps' are required to be taken and may specify different periods for different steps: see s 169(5).

Where the offence in respect of which a person has been found guilty is under PA 2008, s 161, then the relevant local planning authority may serve a notice of unauthorised development on the person by under s 169(4), requiring the person to remedy the breach or failure to comply.

Although PA 2008, s 169(4) does not refer to 'steps' required to be taken to remedy the breach or failure to comply, and therefore it is not clear whether s 169(5) applies, it would appear prudent to set out in the notice any period, or periods, within which the person is to remedy the breach or failure to comply.

PA 2008, s 170 sets out various matters relating to the execution of works required by notice of unauthorised development, including in relation to liability for expenses incurred in complying with any such notice (s 170(2)).

Injunctions

A 'local planning authority' may apply to the High Court for an injunction pursuant to PA 2008, s 171 if it considers it 'necessary or expedient' for any 'actual or apprehended prohibited activity' to be restrained by injunction.

For these purposes a 'prohibited activity' means an activity that constitutes an offence under PA 2008, s 160 or 161 in relation to land in the area of the local planning authority: see s 171(2).

PA 2008, s 171 makes it clear that an application for an injunction may be brought by 'a local planning authority' for the land in respect of which the 'prohibited activity' has taken place; thus the exercise of the power is not restricted to the 'relevant local planning authority' under s 173. Consequently, for land where there is both a district planning authority and a county planning authority, it would appear that either may make an application for an injunction under s 171.

It is important to note that a local planning authority may apply for an injunction under PA 2008, s 171 for any 'actual' or 'apprehended' prohibited activity. An 'actual' prohibited activity is clearly one that has occurred or is occurring. The term 'apprehended' is not one that is defined in PA 2008 but, given its ordinary meaning, an 'apprehended' prohibited activity is clearly one that is reasonably anticipated. Indeed, as injunctions are not granted lightly by the High Court, one might expect a local planning authority to have to demonstrate fairly clear grounds for 'apprehending' that an offence is likely to be committed under s 160 or 161.

On an application under PA 2008, s 171 the court may grant such an injunction as it 'thinks fit' for the purpose of restraining the prohibited activity: see s 171(3).

Part 16

Miscellaneous Issues

Amendments to a DCO Application

Written by: Isabella Tafur, ftb
Edited by: Michael Humphries QC, ftb

Introduction

Circumstances may arise in which an application for a development consent order requires amendment after it has been accepted by the Secretary of State. There has been some dispute as to the extent to which amendments can be made to the application post-acceptance.

This article examines the extent to which is it possible to amend a DCO application post-acceptance.

PA 2008, s 114

PA 2008, s 114(1) provides that when the Secretary of State has decided an application for an order granting development consent, he or she must either

- make the order granting development consent; or
- refuse development consent.

PA 2008, s 114(1) is not explicit on the point as to whether the Secretary of State can make the order 'with or without modifications', but there is nothing in s 114(1) to limit the Secretary of State's power to make such order he thinks fit.

PA 2008, s 114(2) empowers the Secretary of State to make provision regulating the procedure to be followed if he proposes to make an order granting development consent in terms which are materially different from those proposed in the application. No such 'provision' has so far been made by regulation or otherwise, save in relation to compulsory acquisition by the Infrastructure Planning (Compulsory Acquisition) Regulations 2010, SI 2010/104. However, there is nothing in s 114(2) that 'requires' the Secretary of State to make provision for any particular procedure if he proposed to make an order granting development consent on terms materially different from those proposed in the application.

Thus the better view is PA 2008, s 114 does allow the Secretary of State to make an order granting development consent on terms materially different from those applied for. This view appears to be entirely consistent with the, so-called, Bob Neill letter.

On 28 November 2011 the then Secretary of State, Bob Neill MP, wrote to Sir Michael Pitt on the scope of s 114 in the context of the Brig y Cwm application. He set out the Government's position as follows:

> 'My Department has received representation questioning whether section 114(1) empowers the decision-maker to make a development consent order in different terms from that applied for. This was the subject of an amendment laid at the Lord Report stage of the Localism Bill, and in response, Earl

Attlee confirmed the Government's view, that section 114(1) clearly places the responsibility for making a development consent order on the decision-maker, and does not limit the terms in which it can be made. If follows from this that the decision-maker has them power under section 114(1) to make a development consent order which is different from that originally applied for, and that no regulations are needed under section 114(2) in order to do so.

The power to make regulations in section 114(2) is unconnected, and has no bearing on the extent of the s 114(1) power. Section 114(2) merely provides the Secretary of State with a power to make regulations about how material changes should be dealt with, if he thinks it appropriate to do so.'

The Examination Procedure Rules

The Infrastructure Planning (Examination Procedure) Rules 2010, SI 2010/103, r 2 provides that amendments can be made to an application post-acceptance, by defining 'application' in the following way:

'an application for development consent under section 37 (application for orders granting development consent) and includes –

(a) part of an application;

(b) any accompanying documents and further representations made by the applicant; and

(c) any amendments made to the application.' [emphasis added].

Guidance on making a change to a DCO application

In the Bob Neill letter, the Secretary of State also commented that:

'This power provided by section 114(1) is, of course, limited in a number of ways. If the Examining Authority decides to consider material changes to an application as part of the examination, the Examining Authority will need to act reasonably, and in accordance with the principles of natural justice. In particular the principles arising from the *Wheatcroft* case must be fully addressed, which essentially require that anyone affected by amended proposals must have a fair opportunity to have their views heard and properly taken into account regarding them.

... Depending on the circumstances, in accordance with the principles set out in *Wheatcroft*, the Examining Authority may need to:

- extend the examination using the power in section 98(4) of the Act to consult interested parties on the effect of the proposed amendments, and allow time to consider any amendments accepted for examination
- take into account what publicity (if any) the promoter has carried out to ensure people who are not interested parties have an opportunity to make representations

- use the general power to control the examination of an application in section 87(1) of the 2008 Act to make changes to the timetable to allow for representations to be made regarding any such amendments
- exercise its discretion under rules 10(3) and 14(10) of the Infrastructure Planning (Examination Procedure) Rules 2010 to permit representations to be made by people who are not interested parties in cases where it is appropriate to do so.'

DCLG Guidance for the examination of applications for development consent (March 2015) (paragraph 109–115) gives the following guidance on changing a draft development consent order post-acceptance:

> 'It is expected that applications will be as well prepared as possible prior to submission and an application will not be accepted if it is not of a satisfactory standard. However, the Government recognises that there are occasions when applicants may need to make material changes to a proposal after an application has been accepted for examination. Reasons for this could include, for example, regulatory changes, technical developments or the discovery of previously unknown factors arising from representations received after acceptance or examination submissions.
>
> However, if it is determined that a proposed change is of such a degree that it constitutes a materially different project then the applicant will need to determine how best to proceed. The applicant may decide to withdraw their existing application and restart the pre-application process or continue with their application in its original form or they may decide to submit an alternative proposal for change. It should be noted that the Examining Authority will not be able to indicate what degree of change would be acceptable in advance of the applicant submitting a proposed change.
>
> It is important for all parties to remember that it is for the applicant to decide whether or not to propose a change to a proposal during the examination. Other parties can highlight those areas where they think a proposal should be changed during their discussion with the applicant in the pre-application period and also in their written representations.
>
> Before proposing a change, applicants should carefully consider the impact that it will have on any non-planning permits which they are seeking alongside their Development Consent Order. A change in the Development Consent Order may mean that it is not possible to issue these non-planning permits to the same timescale as the Development Consent Order.
>
> In considering a proposed material change to an application and before making a procedural decision about whether and how to examine the changed application, the Examining Authority will need to ensure it is able to act reasonably and fairly, in accordance with the principles of natural justice and in doing so, there will be a number of factors to consider such as:
>
> - whether the application (as changed) is still of a sufficient standard for examination;

- whether sufficient consultation on the changed application can be undertaken to allow for the examination to be completed within the statutory timetable of 6 months; and
- whether any other procedural requirements can still be met.

It is expected that applicants will discuss the implications of any changes they wish to make with relevant statutory consultees and notify the Examining Authority at the earliest opportunity. This should allow the Examining Authority to accommodate any appropriate consultation on the change within the six month examination period.

If an applicant seeks to introduce a material change during the final stages of the examination period, it is unlikely to be accepted on the basis that the application cannot be examined within the statutory timetable without breaching the principles of fairness and reasonableness.'

The DCLG Guidance has now been supplemented by PINS Advice Note 16: How to request a change which may be material (July 2015). The Advice Note states that:

> 'This advice note is intended to build on the Examination Guidance and sets out a structured approach in order to establish greater certainty about how applicants may make a request for a material change, as well as the implications of doing so. This note is relevant to the pre examination and examination stages as the only time during which a request to make a material change to an application may be capable of being considered by the appointed ExA.' (preamble)

And later:

> 'The justification for making a material change after an application has been accepted for examination must be robust and there should be good reasons as to why the matters driving the change were not identified and dealt with proactively at the pre-application stage. Before an applicant makes a material change request it should carefully consider how it will impact upon the other interested parties and the examination timetable.' (para 1.3)

Within that context, the Advice Note covers the following issues:

- What constitutes a material change;
- Key steps in requesting a potential material change to an application;
- Information required with a material change request;
- The role of the Examining Authority; and
- Timing implications.

Before making any application to make a material change to an application after it has been accepted for examination, it will be important to consider carefully the information that PINS will require in support of any such application. The PINS Advice Note states (Figure 2) that the following information will be required:

> 'a. A clear description of the proposed change, including any new/altered works and any new/altered ancillary matters.

b. A statement setting out the rationale and pressing need for making the change with reference to Examination Guidance on examinations of applications for development consent, National Policy Statement as appropriate and any other important and relevant matters.

c. A full schedule of all application documents and plans listing consequential revisions to each document and plan or a "no change" annotation. The schedule should include an update of any consents/ licences required and whether (given the proposed change to the application) there will be any impediment to securing the consents/ licences before the examination is concluded.

d. A track changed version of the draft DCO showing each proposed change, and a track changed revised explanatory memorandum. If drafting changes have been made to the draft DCO during the course of the examination, applicants should check with the ExA which version of the draft DCO and explanatory memorandum should be used for this purpose.

e. If the proposed change involves changes to the Order land, confirmation that the Infrastructure Planning (Compulsory Acquisition) Regulations 2010 (the CA Regulations) are not engaged including if appropriate a copy of the consent obtained from persons with an interest in the additional land. If the CA Regulations are engaged applicants must provide the information prescribed by Regulation 5 of the CA Regulations and should clarify how it is considered that the procedural requirements of the CA Regulations can be met within the statutory examination period.

f. If the proposed change results in any new likely significant environmental effects, provision of other environmental information and confirmation that:

    i. the effects have been adequately assessed and that the environmental information has been subject to publicity. Whilst not statutorily required, the publicity should reflect the requirements of Regulations 17(3) (a) to (e) of the Infrastructure Planning (Environmental Impact Assessment) Regulations 2009 (the EIA Regulations) and applicants should also submit copies of any representations received in response to this publicity with the change request.

    ii. any consultation bodies who might have an interest in the proposed changes have been consulted (reflecting the requirements of Regulation 17 (3) (g) and (h) of the EIA regulations). It is recommended that applicants submit copies of any responses received from consultation bodies with the change request. NB. applicants should identify those consultation bodies who were consulted on the proposed changes but NOT on the original application.

g. Where (proportionate) additional non-statutory consultation has been carried out (either voluntarily or at the direction of the ExA) a consultation statement confirming who has been consulted in relation to the proposed change should be submitted. Copies of any consultation responses received by the applicant should also be included with any request, as an Annex.'

Costs in DCO Examinations

Written by: Douglas Edwards QC, ftb
Edited by: Michael Humphries QC, ftb

Introduction

At the conclusion of the examination process it may be that one or more of the interested parties, affected persons or indeed any other person who takes part in an examination wishes to claim the costs, or some of the costs, they incurred in that process from another person. This chapter considers the power to make costs, the procedure for applying for costs, the approach that will be taken to such applications, and also gives some examples of situations were costs awards may be appropriate.

The Department for Communities and Local Government published its guidance on *Award of costs: examination of applications for development consent orders* in July 2013, which replaces the Infrastructure Planning Commission's earlier *Policy on the Award of Costs in Relation to Examinations of Nationally Significant Infrastructure Project Applications.*

It is important to note that the costs guidance in relation to appeals under the Planning Acts, namely Circular 03/2009 on *Costs awards in appeals and other planning proceedings*, expressly does not apply to the development consent process under the PA 2008.

The power to award costs

PA 2008, s 95(4) applies section 250(5) of the Local Government Act 1972 to examinations by the Examining Authority of applications for development consent orders. It consequently gives the Examining Authority the power to award costs in the same way that an Inspector may award costs at a planning inquiry.

Procedure for claiming costs

Who can apply?

Standing to apply for costs is broad; any party who took part in the Examination can apply. That includes interested parties under PA 2008, s 102, affected persons under PA 2008, s 59, additional affected persons and additional interested parties under regulation 2 of the Infrastructure Planning (Compulsory Acquisition) Regulations 2010, and any other person who took part in the examination. The use of the term 'party' in this chapter refers to all such categories of person.

Time limits

An application for costs must be made within 28 days of the Examining Authority giving notice that it has completed its examination. Failure to apply within 28 days will usually result in the Examining Authority refusing to consider the application, unless good reason can be shown for applying late. It is therefore always best practice to apply within the 28 days.

In the event that the examination comes to an early end, perhaps because the application for development consent is withdrawn or because the examination is cancelled, the 28 day period begins to run from the date on which the Examining Authority gives notification of that withdrawal or the cancellation.

Procedure

In either case, the application for costs should be made in writing to the Planning Inspectorate at Temple Quay House, 2 The Square, Temple Quay, Bristol, BS1 6PN. There is no particular format for the application, but it should set out the broad nature of the costs claimed, the basis on which costs are sought (ie the conduct complained of) and should explain how costs have been incurred as a result of that conduct.

The costs application will be assessed by the same Examining Authority which considered the main application for development consent, but as the costs decision is made after the conclusion of the examination it is obviously made separately and a party who, for instance, unsuccessfully opposes development consent, may still be awarded their costs.

Upon receipt of an application for costs, the Examining Authority will first contact the parties against whom costs are sought and require them to respond within a set period of time. It will then invite final comments from the party who applied for costs, again within a set period of time. The Examining Authority will then take all of these submissions into account in reaching a decision.

Assessment of costs

Beyond determining whether an award of costs will be full or partial (see below), the Examining Authority's decision will not settle the amount of costs that should be paid. Therefore, when a party receives a full or partial costs award, the next step will be for that party to contact the paying party and attempt to agree the costs payable.

If the parties cannot agree, then the matter will require detailed assessment by a Costs Officer of the Senior Court Costs Office at Cliffords Inn, Fetter Lane, London, EC4A 1DQ and on 020 7947 7124. Part 47 of the Civil Procedure Rules and its accompanying Practice Direction will apply to any detailed assessment.

Given the various stages in the process it will therefore be appreciated that the final costs decision may come some time after the completion of the examination, and indeed after the initial costs application.

Enforcement

It is to be hoped that matters do not reach this stage, but if after having received a costs award and having the amount of those costs determined by agreement or on detailed assessment, those costs are not then paid, the costs award can be enforced through the courts. Part 70 of the Civil Procedure Rules and its accompanying Practice Direction will apply.

Approach taken to applications for costs

Principles applied

The starting point of any assessment of costs is that, unlike in most litigation, in the ordinary course of events all parties should bear their own costs. An award of costs must therefore be seen as being out of the ordinary, and should be made against this background.

The Examining Authority is most likely to award costs where the following three conditions are satisfied:

- first, the application for costs has been made in a timely manner within 28 days of the completion of the examination;
- secondly, the party from whom costs are sought has acted unreasonably; and
- thirdly, that unreasonable behaviour has caused, in whole or in part, the party seeking their costs to incur wasted or otherwise unnecessary expenditure.

As is therefore apparent, the key issue will be whether the other party acted unreasonably. The courts have been clear that in the context of cost awards, 'unreasonable' is to be given its ordinary English meaning.

Although the costs awarded can only relate to those incurred in the examination itself, the conduct complained of can relate to the pre-examination period or indeed even to the period before the application for development consent was submitted. The key is that the conduct caused costs to be incurred in the examination.

Examples of 'unreasonable' conduct

The list of unreasonable conduct is never closed, but common examples of procedure related behaviour that may be found an award of costs include:

- submitting documents late;
- failing to cooperate or to respond to reasonable requests in a timely fashion;
- submitting new or substantial evidence late, especially where this then requires other parties to submit further evidence in response;
- failing to agree on a statement of common ground or factual matters where this increases the amount of work other parties have to complete on other documents;
- withdrawing evidence at a late stage, especially where other parties have prepared on the basis of the withdrawn documents;
- failing to appear at a hearing or a site visit; and

- withdrawing the development consent application itself where no material change in circumstance can be identified to justify such a course of action, unless other exceptional circumstances can be shown.

Examples of substantive unreasonable behaviour could include:

- submitting a development consent application that is plainly contrary to policy (ie the content of a National Policy Statement);
- making submissions, or acting, contrary to established case law;
- pursuing objections that fail to accord proper weight to policy statements and which fail to provide objective evidence in support of the objection; and
- a local authority requiring the development consent applicant to enter into a obligation which fails to comply with para 204 of the National Planning Policy Framework, or an applicant failing to enter into such an obligation where the Examining Authority consider it necessary.

Compulsory acquisition

An exception to the need to show unreasonable behaviour occurs in development consent applications where the applicant seeks authorisation to compulsorily acquire land. Here an objector will be entitled to costs if they:

(a) maintain their objection throughout the process prior to the Secretary of State's decision (or withdrawal of the application for development consent and/or compulsory acquisition powers);

(b) participate in the examination by way of representations; and

(c) have their objection upheld by the Secretary of State, either through the wholesale refusal of development consent or by way of a development consent order that does not include compulsory acquisition powers (or if the applicant withdraws their request as in (a) above).

If an objector is unsuccessful under (c), they may still be entitled to costs if they can show unreasonable behaviour in the normal way. Partial success in an objection to compulsory acquisition (i.e. through the exclusion of only some land from the Order) will usually be met with a partial award of costs.

Different time limits also apply in this case. The application for costs should be made within 28 days of notification of the Secretary of State's decision, or withdrawal of the application.

Basis of assessment

Where the Examining Authority decides to make an award of costs it has two options available: a full award, or a partial award.

- A full award will provide for the payment of all of a party's necessary and reasonable costs incurred in its taking part in the examination, including preparation for and involvement in the examination, and the costs of applying for costs.

- A partial award by contrast will award a party its necessary and reasonable costs insofar as they relate to the unreasonable conduct of another, or to a specific part of the examination.

What is included within recoverable costs?

A party may have to incur costs for a number of reasons, including: obtaining professional advice or representation; drafting; document preparation; travel; and accommodation. So long as the unreasonable behaviour can be shown to have caused those costs to be incurred, those costs are in principle, and subject to their being necessary and reasonable, recoverable.

NSIPs and Town or Village Greens

Written by: Gregory Jones QC, ftb
Edited by: Michael Humphries QC, ftb

Introduction

A NSIP just like any other development might be thwarted by the land, or part of the land, being successfully registered as a Town or Village Green (TGV).

Town and village greens developed under customary law as areas of land where local people indulged in lawful sports and pastimes. These might include organised or ad-hoc games, picnics, fetes and similar activities. The court has taken a fairly wide approach and held such activities might include dog walking.

Most greens were registered in the late 1960s under the Commons Registration Act 1965. Provided the right to apply has not been excluded, anyone can apply under section 15(1) of the Commons Act 2006 to register land as a green if it has been used by local people for lawful sports and pastimes 'as of right' – that is without permission, force or secrecy- for at least 20 years (see DEFRA further fact sheet https://www.gov.uk/town-and-village-greens-how-to-register).

Pilot implementation areas

Those promoting NSIPs should check to see whether the site in question is included within any of the pilot implementation areas. In relation to the pilot implementation areas for Part 1 of the Commons Act 2006 (Devon, Kent (but not including unitary authorities in these first two counties), Cornwall, Hertfordshire, Herefordshire, Lancashire (but not Blackpool), and Blackburn with Darwen), the procedures, forms and guidance for applications under section 15 have been revised, and are now contained in the Guidance to Applicants in the pilot implementation areas.

Growth and Infrastructure Act 2013

The new Growth and Infrastructure Act 2013 (GIA 2013) introduces wide ranging implications for landowners and developers, including the introduction of significant changes to the procedure for registering land as a town or village green. The provisions are as yet untested in the courts. They are of great importance to any NSIP promoter who fears that its land may be subject a TVG application.

GIA 2013, s 16 inserted a new s 15C and Sch 1A into the Commons Act 2006. The new Sch 1A prescribes a series of nine occurrences (defined as 'trigger events') which, once triggered, will prevent the commons registration authority from registering the affected land as a town or village green.

Each trigger event is linked to procedures contained in existing planning or infrastructure legislation. Each may be "terminated' following specified further events.

The remainder of this article summarises the nine trigger events and terminating events in the Commons Act 2006, Sch 1A

Trigger Events

Planning applications

This trigger event relates to 'an application for planning permission in relation to the land which would be determined under the Town and Country Planning Act 1990 (TCPA 1990), s 70 is first publicised in accordance with requirements imposed by a development order by virtue of section 65(1) of that Act.' It occurs following receipt of a valid application by the local planning authority - the date of publication of notice of the application in accordance with Article 13 of the Town and Country Planning (Development Management Procedure) (England) Order 2010 (as amended) – namely: publication on the local authority's website site display/serving the notice on any adjoining owner or occupier placing notice in a locally circulating newspaper.

It is lost if the application is withdrawn the local planning authority refuse to determine the application on the basis that it is a 'repeat application' the application is refused and all legal avenues for appeal are exhausted permission is granted but the development is not begun within the period permitted by the permission.

Urgent Crown development

This trigger event arises where there is an application for planning permission made in relation to 'the land under s 293A of the 1990 Act is first publicised in accordance with subsection (8) of that section'. It relates to applications to the Secretary of State by the Crown for urgent developments of national importance. It occurs on the date of publication of notice of the application in accordance with art 13 of the Town and Country Planning (Development Management Procedure) (England) Order 2010, SI 2010/2184 (as amended) – namely:

(a) publication on the local authority's website site;

(b) display/serving the notice on any adjoining owner or occupier

(c) placing notice in a locally circulating newspaper

It is lost if the application is withdrawn or the application is refused and all legal avenues to appeal exhausted or permission is granted but the development is not begun within the period permitted by the permission.

Publication of a draft development plan document (identifying the land for potential development)

This trigger event arises where 'a draft of a development plan document which identifies the land for potential development is published for consultation in accordance with regulations under section 17(7) of the 2004 Act.' It relates to the publication by a local authority of a draft development plan document containing a statement which: encourages the development of use of the land over a specified period allocates the land for a particular type of development or use guides the determination of planning applications in respect of the land. It occurs when the draft development plan document is published by being made available for inspection at the local authority's offices and website notification is sent to relevant consultation bodies.

It is terminated when the draft development plan document is withdrawn the draft development plan document is adopted but this latter event is itself a new trigger (see further below).

Adoption of a development plan document (identifying the land for potential development)

This trigger event arises where 'a development plan document which identifies the land for potential development is adopted under section 23(2) or (3) of the 2004 Act.' It relates to the adoption of a development plan document (identifying the land for potential development – as above) following independent examination.

It occurs on the date of adoption following a resolution by the local planning authority and is terminated if: the development plan document is revoked or the policy relating to the land in question is superseded

Publication of a draft neighbourhood development plan (identifying the land for potential development)

This trigger is 'a proposal for a neighbourhood development plan which identifies the land for potential development is published by a local planning authority for consultation in accordance with regulations under paragraph 4(1) of Schedule 4B of the 1990 Act as it applies by virtue of section 38A(3) of the 2004 Act'.

It occurs upon the publication by a local authority of a draft neighbourhood development plan following submission by a parish council or designated neighbourhood forum when the draft neighbourhood development plan is published by: notice on the local authority's website and in such other manner as the local authority considers is likely to bring the proposal to the attention of people who live, work or carry on business in the neighbourhood area notification is sent to those bodies initially consulted by the parish council or designated neighbourhood forum.

It is terminated if the draft neighbourhood development plan is withdrawn the draft neighbourhood development plan is adopted but this leads to another trigger event, see below.

Making of a neighbourhood development plan (identifying the land for potential development)

This trigger event is where 'a neighbourhood development plan which identifies the land for potential development is made under section 38A of the 2004 Act'. It relates to the making by a local authority of a neighbourhood development plan (identifying the land for potential development – as above) following: independent examination and a local referendum. It occurs upon the publication by the local authority of its 'decision statement' following the making of the neighbourhood development plan.

It terminates where the plan ceases to have effect, is revokes, or where a policy relating to the development on land is superseded by another policy.

Saved structure plans and local plans identifying the land for potential development extant on 25 April 2013

This trigger arises where 'a development plan for the purposes of TCPA 1990, s 27 or 54, or anything treated as contained in such a plan by virtue of Schedule 8 to the Planning and Compulsory Purchase Act 2004, continues to have effect (by virtue of that Schedule) on the commencement of section 16 of the Growth and Infrastructure Act 2013 and identifies the land for potential development.' It relates to extant structure plans, unitary development plans or local plans identifying the land for potential development and which predate the Planning and Compulsory Purchase Act 2004 which have been saved by the Secretary of State.

It came into force on 25 April 2013 (if the plan was extant on that date) and is terminated when a new policy replacing the saved policy is first published or adopted.

Publication of a proposed application for a nationally significant infrastructure project

This trigger is where 'a proposed planning application for an order granting development consent under section 114 of the 2008 Act in relation to the land is first publicised in accordance with section 48 of that Act ' It relates to proposed applications for nationally significant infrastructure project consent. It occurs upon the publication by the applicant of notice of the proposed application in local and national newspaper.

It is lost on the earlier of: the period of two years following the final newspaper publication the publication by the Secretary of State of an accepted application.

Publication of an accepted application for a nationally significant infrastructure project

This trigger event relates to where 'a proposed planning application for an order granting development consent under section 114 of the 2008 Act in relation to the land is first publicised in accordance with section 48 of that Act.' It is in respect of accepted applications for nationally significant infrastructure project consents. It occurs upon the publication by the applicant of notice of the application in local and national newspapers.

It is lost if the application is withdrawn or the application is refused and all legal avenues to appeal exhausted or consent is granted but the development is not begun within the period permitted by the consent.

The Changes Introduced by the Infrastructure Act 2015

Written by Hereward Phillpot QC
Edited by Michael Humphries QC

Introduction

Part 5 of the Infrastructure Act 2015 ('IA 2015') makes a number of amendments to the PA 2008, seeking to improve certain aspects of the process for approving nationally significant infrastructure projects (NSIPs') based on experience so far.

There are three main changes introduced by the IA 2015:

(a) earlier appointment of the Examining Authority ('ExA') (IA 2015, s 26);

(b) the introduction of two-person panels (IA 2015, s 27); and

(c) streamlining of the process for making changes to development consent orders ('DCOs') (IA 2015, s 28).

Section 26 came into force on 12 April 2015, and applies to applications made under s 37 of the PA 2008 from that date onwards. Section 27 has not been brought into force at the date of writing (May 2016). Section 28 came into force on 14 July 2015, and applies to applications made for a change to a DCO under para 3(1) of Sch 6 to the PA 2008 from that date onwards.

Earlier appointment of the ExA

Under s 61 of the PA 2008 as originally enacted, the ExA could only be appointed by the Secretary of State after he had received confirmation from the applicant that the post-acceptance publicity stage had been completed (either in the form of a certificate under s 58(2) or a notice under s 59). The effect of this was to introduce a period of 'dead time' between the point of acceptance and the point at which the ExA was able to engage with the application and the applicant. This hiatus would tend to last between one and two months.

The effect of s 26 of the IA 2015 is to amend s 61 of the PA 2008 to allow the ExA to be appointed by the Secretary of State immediately after the application has been accepted.

This change should remove the current problem with the handling of the application, and allow for earlier engagement between the applicant and the ExA. In an inquisitorial process where the particular views and preferences of the individuals making up the ExA are so important, early engagement can be beneficial for all parties. For example, if it becomes apparent following the ExA's initial review that some issue requires further work (perhaps involving the need for additional consultation), there ought to be more time available in which to achieve that. Furthermore, any 'dead time' is unwelcome in a process which is intended to speed up the approval of important strategic projects, and in which time is a precious commodity.

Two-person panels

Section 65 of the PA 2008 provides that where the ExA comprises a panel, it must be made up of a minimum of three and a maximum of five persons. Where a panel of three has been appointed, and one ceases to act, another panel member must therefore be appointed (PA 2008, s 68(3)).

Section 27 of the IA 2015 allows for a panel of two persons to be appointed, and accordingly removes the obligation to appoint an additional panel member if one person in a panel of three has to cease to act.

As a consequential change, s 27(4) extends the principle of majority voting (with the lead member having the casting vote) to two person panels.

This is a practical and sensible change, introducing a welcome additional element of flexibility. It should also save money for applicants in appropriate cases by removing the need to fund additional panel members where two persons can adequately deal with the issues.

Streamlining the process for changing DCOs

The need to make changes

It will not infrequently be the case that, following a decision by the Secretary of State to make a DCO, it becomes apparent that it is necessary, or at least desirable, to make changes to it.

NSIPs tend to be at an early stage of the design process when a DCO is granted. That is particularly so for the larger and more complex projects, and for those using relatively innovative technology.

Certain types of NSIP are also subject to separate statutory regimes to regulate the safety of their operation, and the requirements subsequently imposed pursuant to those regimes can lead to the need for different or additional development, outside the parameters set by the DCO. An example of this can be seen in the case of the Hinkley Point C DCO, where the requirements set by the nuclear safety process (informed by lessons learned from the experience at Fukushima) meant that additional buildings and (in some cases) larger buildings had to be provided within the 'nuclear island', going beyond what had been anticipated and approved in the DCO. There was therefore no option but to seek approval from the Secretary of State for the necessary changes to be made to the DCO.

In addition, the contractors who will be responsible for implementing the development are generally only appointed after a DCO has been granted. Their involvement in the process can often generate different ideas as to how the project ought to be constructed so as to save time and cost, and/or further limit adverse environmental effects from the construction process. However, if putting their suggestions into action would require the project to go beyond the parameters set by the DCO, it will only be possible to realise those benefits if the DCO is changed.

Whilst some flexibility can be (and generally is) built into DCOs to cater for these possibilities, there are important limits:

(a) it will only be possible to build in flexibility based on what is known and anticipated at the time;

(b) all flexibility needs to be justified, particularly in cases where a consequential effect is the need to seek powers of compulsory acquisition over additional land; and

(c) too much flexibility can make the process of environmental impact assessment very difficult.

The difficulty with the Schedule 6 process

Schedule 6 to the PA 2008 establishes a distinction between 'non-material' and 'material' changes to DCOs. It is with the 'material change' process that the difficulty lies.

The main difficulty with the process for making 'material' changes to a DCO is that it is lengthy, and little different in practice from what would be required for an application for an entirely new DCO.

The details of the process are to be found in Part 2 of the Infrastructure Planning (Changes to, and Revocation of, Development Consent Orders) Regulations 2011 ('the 2011 Regulations').

In circumstances where the funding for NSIPs is often time-constrained, and delay can be extremely expensive, it is perhaps unsurprising that prior to the IA 2015 reforms no applications had been made for changes described by the applicant as 'material'. The process for approving non-material changes set out in Part 1 of the 2011 Regulations is relatively short and simple, and applications have been made for non-material changes (see eg Hinkley Point C and the Heysham to M6 Link Road project).

The changes introduced by the IA 2015

Section 28 of the IA 2015 has made a significant change to the process for approving material changes to DCOs by giving the Secretary of State a discretion whether or not to hold an examination before determining the application.

The change will benefit those applicants who need to make changes that are at the lower end of materiality, but are sufficiently substantial that treating them as 'non-material' is either not an option at all or would make any approval potentially vulnerable to legal challenge. In those cases it may now be possible to dispense with the need for an examination, and instead determine the application through a much shorter written procedure. This allows for a more proportionate and tailored approach to be adopted.

The process has also been streamlined to some extent through the detailed revisions introduced using secondary legislation: the Infrastructure Planning (Changes to, and Revocation of, Development Consent Orders) (Amendment) Regulations 2015 ('the 2015 Regulations'). The key changes that have been made are as follows:

(a) It is now only necessary to consult those who are directly affected by the proposed changes, rather than all of those who were consulted on the original application (reg 5(1) of the 2015 Regulations; reg 10 of the 2011 Regulations).

(b) There is no longer any general duty of community consultation (reg 5(2) of the 2015 Regulations; reg 13 of the 2011 Regulations).

(c) Where no examination is judged to be required, a short process for the submission of further written representations has been introduced (reg 5(7) of the 2015 Regulations; new regs 21A and 21B of the 2011 Regulations).

(d) Where an examination is required, the time limits for the key stages have been reduced as follows:

  (i) the examination will now last a maximum of four months instead of six (reg 5(10) of the 2015 Regulations; reg 42(2) of the 2011 Regulations);

  (ii) the time limit for the examining body to report to the Secretary of State is now two months following the end of the examination, instead of three (reg 5(11) of the 2015 Regulations; reg 43 of the 2011 Regulations); and

  (iii) the Secretary of State is to make his decision by the end of 2 months following receipt of the report, instead of 3 (reg 5(12) of the 2015 Regulations; reg 49 of the 2011 Regulations).

Even though the savings in time and effort that will flow from those changes are meaningful, the overall time needed for applications to go through the examination process may still prove off-putting for many projects. That may be unavoidable given the need to ensure that applications for major projects are properly scrutinised before they are determined, and that those likely to be most affected are given a fair and effective opportunity to have their say as part of that process. Applicants should therefore continue to do all they can to seek to anticipate and justify the need for suitable flexibility when preparing their DCOs.

Part 17

Case summaries

Case Summary

Written by Michael Humphries QC, ftb

R (oao INNOVIA CELLOPHANE LTD) v THE INFRASTRUCTURE PLANNING COMMISSION and NNB GENERATION COMPANY LTD

[2011] EWHC 2883 (Admin)

High Court

Cranston J

Judgment: 4 November 2011

BACKGROUND

NNB Generation Company Ltd ('NNB') is a subsidiary of EDF Energy (UK) Ltd ('EDF') and in November 2009 had notified The Infrastructure Planning Commission ('the IPC') of a proposed application to build a new nuclear power station at Hinkley Point, Somerset. The proposed nuclear power station was known as Hinkley Point C ('HPC'). NNB submitted its application for development consent for HPC in October 2011 under section 37 of the Planning Act 2008.

During 2009, 2010 and 2011 NNB undertook pre-application consultation in relation to its proposed application for HPC. During pre-application consultation, NNB identified land owned by Innovia Cellophane Ltd ('Innovia') at Bridgewater as suitable for accommodation for construction workers. The consultation documentation referred to the building of short term, temporary accommodation for workers that could not find accommodation locally. The proposed campus would be able to accommodate up to about 1,075 workers (later reduced to about 850) in individual en suite rooms. There would be restaurants, bars and other facilities. Whilst the buildings proposed would not be suitable for conversion into housing, the infrastructure was to be designed to allow for the later building of houses.

From late 2009 NNB and Innovia undertook negotiations on the acquisition of the land. These included requests by NNB for access to the land in order to undertake surveys necessary for the making of an application for development consent. During November 2010 NNB sent Innovia correspondence identifying a list of proposed surveys. NNB did not receive a satisfactory response from Innovia and in January 2011 submitted an application to the IPC for authorisation to access the land under section 53 of the Planning Act 2008. Innovia objected to the section 53 application. There followed a period of negotiations for voluntary access between NNB and Innovia, but these were ultimately unsuccessful.

On 19 April 2011 the IPC issues authorisation to access the land under section 53 of the 2008 Act ('the authorisation'). The authorisation was subject to 'conditions' set out in the schedule.

Innovia challenged the IPC's authorisation by judicial review brought under section 118 of the Planning Act 2008.

By the time of the hearing of the judicial review NNB had entered onto the land several times under the section 53 authorisation.

DECISION

The judicial review was brought under three grounds being:

- Dwellings are excluded from the definition of 'Associated Development' under the Planning Act 2008;
- Section 53 authorisation should be a 'last resort'; and
- The conditions attached to the authorisation were unenforceable.

Dwellings excluded from Associated Development

Innovia argued that the section 53 authorisation was unlawful because it purported to authorise access for development that did not fall within the section 115 definition of 'associated development'.

The definition of 'associated development' is set out in section 115 of the Planning Act 2008 means development that is 'associated' with development for which development consent is required (ie a Nationally Significant Infrastructure Project ('NSIP')) or any part of it, and is not 'the construction or extension of one or more dwellings'. The issue, therefore, turned on whether the campus accommodation proposed comprised 'dwellings'.

At the time of the judicial review (2011) the IPC was also 'required' by section 115(6) (since repealed) to have regard to any guidance issued by the Secretary of State. DCLG had issued 'Guidance on associated development' in September 2009 (since superseded by DCLG Guidance on associated development applications for major infrastructure projects' (April 2013)).

In the key passages in his judgement on the definition of 'dwelling' Cranston J held as follows:

> '27. One aspect of that is that the 2008 Act is part of the package of planning legislation on the statute book. It draws on the pre-existing planning legislation with various cross-references to the Town and Country Planning Act 1990 and the incorporation of concepts from it. Where definitions are different from those in the 1990 Act this is made clear in the 2008 Act: for example, ss.32(2)-(3). Construing statutes in pari materia is probably no more than a recognition of the reality that the drafter of a later statute, obviously related to an earlier one, will have employed a word or concept in the sense that has become accepted in the interpretation of the earlier. Dwelling house is well understood in the context of the Town and Country Planning Act 1990 and secondary legislation made under it. In *Gravesham Borough Council v Secretary of State for the Environment* (1982) 47 P&CR 142 the issue was whether a weekend and holiday chalet was a dwelling house for the purposes of the General Development Order 1977, which

conferred various permitted development rights. McCullough J said that a dwelling-house was a building of a particular kind. He then examined various circumstances where a building was a dwelling house and said:

'What have these examples in common? All are buildings that ordinarily afford the facilities required for day-to-day private domestic existence.

This characteristic is lacking in hotels, holiday camps, hostels, residential schools, naval and military barracks and similar places where people may eat, sleep and perhaps spend 24 hours a day. Quite clearly, none of these is a dwelling house'(at 146).

28. That analysis was endorsed by the Court of Appeal in *Moore v Secretary of State for the Environment* (1998) 77 P&CR 114. Particularly striking is that the statutory context there was quite different than in the Gravesham case but the same meaning was given to the term. So dwelling house has a well established meaning in the planning legislation and is distinct from hostels and other forms of non-permanent accommodation which is not self-contained. The obvious application here is that the proposed campus type accommodation on the Bridgwater land is akin to the hostel mentioned by McCullough J, with its single rooms, supported by catering and other facilities elsewhere on the site.

29. In my opinion, the statutory object and Parliamentary intention confirm that this is the correct interpretation of the term dwelling in section 115 of the 2008 Act. As already explained the 2008 Act aimed to create a streamlined, efficient and predictable planning system for nationally significant infrastructure projects. One way it did this was by rationalising the development consent regimes to create, as far as possible, a single consent regime with a harmonised set of requirements and procedures. That key purpose is given effect to in section 115(1) by permitting applications for development consent to cover not just the nationally significant infrastructure project itself but also associated development such as, as in this case, the specially built, temporary campus type accommodation for the large number of workers needed for its construction. To allow the local planning authority to determine the issue of this accommodation would lead to the piecemeal consent system which the 2008 Act was intended to overcome.'

On the basis of this analysis it was concluded that the temporary campus style accommodation proposed did not fall within the definition of 'dwelling' for the purposes of section 115 and so the proposed workers accommodation was 'associated development'.

Section 53 authorisation should be a 'last resort'

In IPC Advice Note 5 'Section 53: Rights of Entry' (May 2010) (since superseded by PINS Advice Note 5 'Section 53: Rights of Entry' (April 2012)) the IPC advised that 'Requests for authorisation should only be made as a last resort.'

Innovia claimed that the IPC had failed to 'grapple' with this issue in granting NNB authorisation as Innovia were prepared to grant access and negotiations were continuing.

In the key passages in his judgement on the meaning of 'last resort' Cranston J held as follows:

> '34 In my judgment, it cannot be said that the Commission's decision to issue the section 53 authorisation as a last resort was in any way disproportionate or flawed. In making that judgment all the circumstances were relevant, including the fact that after a prolonged period the parties had not been able to reach agreement. …
>
> 35 There was no need for the Commission, in reaching its conclusion, to determine whose fault it was that agreement between the parties had not been reached. I reject the claimants' contention that so long as they as the landowners were prepared to negotiate in good faith the presumption should be that reasonable efforts have not been exhausted. In practice that would give a landowner a ransom over a project, because negotiations in good faith could continue almost indefinitely. Such an approach would not accord with the Commission's statutory remit. Ultimately at what point negotiations can be judged to have failed, and the last resort reached, is a matter of judgement for the Commission, in the light of all the circumstances. From the history of the negotiations I have outlined above, the fact is that over a prolonged period, and for whatever reason, the claimants and NNB had not reached any sensible agreement to give NNB access to the land. Given that history, and the Commission's statutory remit to decide applications for nationally significant infrastructure projects expeditiously, there was nothing flawed about the Commission's conclusion that the section 53 authorisation was required as a last resort.
>
> 36 The last resort policy accords with article 1 protocol 1 of the Convention. The context here is not a taking of land but an application for an authorisation to carry out surveys on the land under a set of conditions which ensures that any damage caused is remedied. There is no permanent taking of any rights over the land and the claimants are left in possession of it. The grant of the authorisation was in accord with the statutory requirements in section 53 and was considered necessary, as a last resort, to allow an application for a nationally significant infrastructure project to be progressed. There was no disproportionate or unlawful interference with Convention rights.'

Key is the passage in the judgement that makes clear that even if landowners are still willing to negotiate in good faith there is no presumption that reasonable efforts have not been exhausted.

The conditions attached to the authorisation were unenforceable

Section 53(4)(c) of the 2008 Act states that an authorised party must comply with any conditions subject to which the authorisation is granted but is silent as to the means of enforcement for any breach of the duty.

The section 53 authorisation granted to NNB was subject to conditions, one of which stated that those entering on the land should not cause or permit and pollution or contamination. Innovia argued that the IPC acted unlawfully in granting the authorisation because, although it stated that the attached conditions were necessary to protect the Innovia's interests, the conditions were unenforceable.

Innovia argued that the contamination of the land, as a result of the manufacturing processes in the factory over many years, provided a high level of potential risk from any person carrying out surveys. Innovia raised concerns about their position under the Health and Safety at Work Act 1974 and potential occupier's liability.

In the key passages in his judgement on the conditions imposed Cranston J held as follows:

> '39 ... The Commission was entitled to conclude that the conditions of access in the section 53 authorisation appropriately responded to the claimants' concerns. It was not required to impose conditions which dealt with every possible situation. In the event of the conditions not being complied with, the right of entry ceases. There is nothing of substance in the concerns about potential occupier's liability or under the health and safety at work legislation. Such liability is limited if persons take reasonable precautions. The claimants can hardly argue that they will not do that.'

Cranston J also held that it was reasonable to take into account the fact that NNB had highly experienced staff with extensive knowledge of health and safety law, working with highly reputable consultants.

The claim for judicial review was dismissed

Case Summary

Written by Michael Humphries QC, ftb

R (oao DAVID GATE on behalf of TRANSPORT SOLUTIONS FOR LANCASTER AND MORECAMBE) and the secretary of state for transport and LANCASHIRE COUNTY COUNCIL

[2013] EWHC 2937 (Admin)

High Court

Turner J

Judgment: 4 October 2013

BACKGROUND

Lancashire County Council ('LCC') had long standing proposals to provide a link road between the M6 Motorway and the port of Heysham on Morcambe Bay. Part of the link road had already been built when LCC was granted development consent by the Lancashire County Council (Torrisholme to the M6 Link (A683 Completion of Hersham to M6 Link Road)) Order 2013 ('the Order') for the final stretch of road linking Heysham with the M6.

The development comprises a 4.8km long dual carriageway connecting a previously built length of the A683 Heysham to M6 Link, at a junction near Torrisholme, to junction 34 of the M6 near Halton ('the M6 Link Road'). Whilst the M6 junction was to be a highway for which the Secretary of State would be the highway authority, the dual carriageway was a highway in respect of which it was intended that LCC would be the highway authority.

The decision to make the order was challenged by way of claim for judicial review under section 118 of the Planning Act 2008 by a Mr Gate on behalf of a campaigning group called 'Transport Solutions for Lancaster and Morecambe' ('TSLM') who were opposed to the Order for the M6 Link Road along its proposed alignment.

DECISION

TSLM brought its challenge on five grounds, as follows:

- Ground 1 – The defendant had no power to make the order.
- Ground 2 – The consultation process was flawed.
- Ground 3 – The defendant wrongly took into account inapplicable National Policy Statements.
- Ground 4 – The defendant wrongly dismissed alternative alignments of the proposed route.
- Ground 5 – Inadequate consideration was given to otter welfare.

Ground 1 – The defendant had no power to make the order

This ground focused on the issue of whether the Order could grant development consent for a highway in respect of which LCC would become highway authority.

Section 115(1) of the Planning Act 2008 provides that:

> 'Development for which development consent may be granted
>
> (1) Development consent may be granted for development which is—
>
> (a) development for which development consent is required, or
>
> (b) associated development.'

Section 115(2) of the 2008 Act provides insofar as is relevant that:

> '(2) "Associated development" means development which—
>
> (a) is associated with the development within subsection (1)(a) (or any part of it)…'

Finally, section 31 of the 2008 Act provides that:

> 'Consent under this Act ("development consent") is required for development to the extent that the development is or forms part of a nationally significant infrastructure project.'

Thus the issue came down to whether:

- The dual carriageway was an NSIP or part of an NSIP; or
- The dual carriageway was 'Associated Development'.

Section 14 provides that *'In this Act 'nationally significant infrastructure project' means a project which consists of any of the following: … (h) highway related development'* (emphasis added). The definition of a highway-related development in section 22 of the Planning Act 2008 provides that:

> '(1) Highway-related development is within section 14(1)(h) only if the development is—
>
> (a) construction of a highway in a case within subsection (2),
>
> … .
>
> (2) Construction of a highway is within this subsection only if the highway will (when constructed) be wholly in England and—
>
> (a) the Secretary of State will be the highway authority for the highway, or
>
> (b) the highway is to be constructed for a purpose connected with a highway for which the Secretary of State is (or will be) the highway authority.' (emphasis added)

Turner J rejected first an argument that the consented project was 'one complete scheme', on the basis that the ordinary meaning of the words 'consists of' in section 14 require that the project must fall entirely within the relevant definition of an NSIP;

otherwise the word 'includes' or an equivalent would have been used. As it was clear that the dual carriageway was not a highway for which the Secretary of State would be the highway authority the project could not all fall within section 22(2)(a).

Next, however, Turner J examined whether the dual carriageway was a highway 'constructed for a purpose connected with a highway for which the Secretary of State is [or will be] the highway authority' within section 22(2)(b).

On this issue he concluded as follows:

> '23. In the circumstances of this case I am entirely satisfied that the dual carriageway which is intended to fall within the auspices of Lancashire as highway authority ("the Lancashire highway") was indeed constructed for a purpose connected with the highway in respect of which the defendant is intended to be the highway authority (the defendant's highway").
>
> 24. These are my reasons:
>
> i. Part of the purpose of the 2008 Act was to streamline the process of obtaining consent for national projects. By the operation of section 33 of the Act, where a proposed project falls within the parameters of "development consent" then it is not necessary to obtain any of that wide range of other consents, permissions and authorisations which would otherwise burden the developer. If section 22(2)(b) were given too narrow an interpretation then the danger would arise that many projects would be doubly encumbered by the need to obtain development consent in respect of one part of it and the requirement to comply with the residual panoply of consents which would otherwise be covered by section 33 in respect of the rest. Far from being streamlined, the process would become unattractively more elaborate than under the old regime. This is precisely the result which would ensue if the claimant were to succeed on this point in the circumstances of this case.
>
> ii. The purpose of a motorway is not fulfilled merely by the provision of junctions. The roads which lead from those junctions are all likely to be connected to the purpose of the junctions which they serve to a greater or lesser extent and over a distance which will vary from case to case. The point at which any given road leading from a motorway junction could be said to be sufficiently remote so as no longer to be connected with the purpose of the junction is a matter of judgment which the decision maker with the requisite combination of expertise and familiarity with the detail of the proposed development and its context will usually be best placed to judge. I would expect those circumstances in which such a decision would fall within the legitimate purview of judicial review to be rare.
>
> iii. The facts of this case fully justify the inclusion of the Lancashire highway within the parameters of the application for development consent. The works to the motorway junction and the relatively

> short length of dual carriageway leading towards Heysham are to a significant degree mutually dependent for the fulfilment of their respective and overlapping purposes. To attempt to separate them would be wholly artificial.'

Whilst this effectively dealt with Ground 1, Turner J went on to deal with some other arguments that had been raised under this ground.

First he dealt with an argument suggesting that the effect of section 33 (Effect of requirement for development consent on other consent regimes) was such that a highway granted development consent under the Planning Act 2008 could not later become a highway for which the county council became highway authority. At paragraph 26 of his judgment he made clear that:

> '... it was contended that the effect of section 33(4) of the 2008 Act, which precludes the making of an order under section 10 of the Highways Act 1980 that the Highway should become a trunk road, would in this case have the effect of preventing the defendant in perpetuity from becoming the highway authority in respect of the Lancashire highway. This, it is argued would produce absurd results. In my judgment, however, the role of section 33 is limited in operation to the statutory regime which may be deployed to obtain orders to permit the project to proceed and does not create a bar to the subsequent re-allocation of responsibilities between highway authorities thereafter in accordance with the established statutory regime. The risk of an absurd result does not therefore arise.' (emphasis added)

He also made clear (paragraph 29) that, had he not found that the dual carriageway was to be constructed for s purpose 'connected with' the Secretary of State's highway, he would not have gone on to decide that the dual carriageway was 'associated with' the development of the motorway junction for the purposes of section 115. He came to this conclusion on the basis that, in the context of the DCLG 'Guidance on associated development', the dual carriageway could not be said to be subordinate or of secondary significance to the motorway junction.

The application failed on Ground 1.

Ground 2 – The consultation process was flawed

This ground was based on the contention that the decision making process was undermined by flawed consultation.

After reviewing the requirements for community consultation in section 47 and the duty to take consultation responses into account in section 49, Turner J proceeds to identify what he called the 'central complaint' which the claimants made, being that the consultation was launched on the assumption that the project would proceed along a particular geographical route and that representations about alternative routes would not be entertained.

Having reviewed the history of the consultation process, Turner J came to the following conclusions:

'49. … a decision following a consultation process is not unlawful simply because it is possible in hindsight to conceive of a process that would have been an improvement on that which was actually carried out. In the circumstances of this case, I decline to conclude that the matters complained of by the claimant are of sufficient practical substance to render the decision unlawful. I note, in particular:

i. Notwithstanding the wording of the section 47 statement and supporting information, the local community (or, at least, the interested part of it) was undeterred in its determination to exhume the issue of preferred route which Lancashire thought had been put to rest in 2007. The section 37(3)(c) Consultation Report records that the most frequently raised issues included location of the route.

ii. The Examining Authority, who was in a better position than this court to form a judgment on the issue, found at paragraphs 215 and 216 of his recommendation: "Some IPs raised concerns over the adequacy of the pre-application process. This was a matter considered at the acceptance stage. I am satisfied that even if some representatives of the consultants may have given unhelpful comments at public exhibitions and meetings, it was clear that the consultation process and the ability to make representations on the DCO did allow objections in principle and fundamental alternatives to be canvassed and not just minor alterations, notwithstanding the long history that had led to the DCO scheme… Moreover, I am satisfied that no persons have been precluded or hindered from making their cases against the proposal on whatever basis they consider relevant."

iii. The consultation process in respect of the proposed development was generally very thorough and robust including, as it did, five public exhibitions each lasting about six hours, meetings with affected parties and community groups, news letters and a website page.

iv. There was no evidence before the Examining Authority (or before me) to suggest that there had been any significant change in circumstances between 2007 and 2013 which would have been likely to justify a reversal of the arguments in favour of the western route.

v. There were clear arguments of proportionality which would justify the concentration of consultative minds on the proposed changes to the earlier project rather than radically different proposals which had very limited prospects indeed of displacing the favoured northern route.

50. In the circumstances, I am satisfied that, although in one limited respect the consultation process fell short of ideal, it is not the function of this court retrospectively to micromanage for perfection. Taken as a whole, the consultation process was a fair one and not susceptible to review.'

The application failed on Ground 2.

Ground 3 – The defendant wrongly took into account inapplicable National Policy Statements

At the time of the examination into the M6 Link Road project there was no designated National Policy Statement (NPS) for national networks (including highways). Despite that the Examining Authority had clearly had regard to the NPSs in respect of ports and nuclear power stations, although it had clearly recognised that they had no direct application to the project.

Whilst section 104 (2)(a) provides that *'(2) In deciding the application the Panel or Council must have regard to — (a) any national policy statement which has effect in relation to development of the description to which the application relates (a "relevant national policy statement")'* the application for the M6 Link Road had to be determined under section 105(2), which provides that:

> '(2) In deciding the application the Secretary of State must have regard to—
>
> ...
>
> (c) any other matters which the Secretary of State thinks are both important and relevant to the Secretary of State's decision.'

On this ground turner J had no difficulty in concluding that:

> '56. It must follow, and common sense would in any event dictate, that the decision maker is not precluded from taking into account matters incorporated within national policy statements which are not directly applicable to the development so long as he considers that they are both important and relevant to his decision.'

The application failed on Ground 3.

Ground 4 – The defendant wrongly dismissed alternative alignments of the proposed route

This ground was based on the contention that the Secretary of State wrongly rejected alternative routes on the basis that they would have adverse effects on European Protected Sites (EPSi) and Species (EPSp) and that the proposed development ran through green belt land.

Having reviewed that consideration that was given to these issues by the Secretary of State, Turner J concluded that:

> '65. Ultimately, it is neither necessary nor desirable that the consideration of possible alternative routes in the context of the determination of an application for development consent should be entered into with the same level of expert scrutiny and assessment as the development itself. Such an approach would be likely to be disproportionate in time, effort and expense. The Examining Authority set out his reasons for rejecting alternatives in coherent and compelling detail. His conclusions were neither unlawful nor irrational.'

Ground 5 – Inadequate consideration was given to otter welfare

The final ground upon which Transport Solutions criticises the Secretary of State's decision is based on the contention that the consent failed properly to deal with the potential impact of the development on the welfare of otters.

Turner J drew attention to regulation 41 of the Conservation of Habitats and Species Regulations 2010 ('the 2010 Regulations') that makes it an offence to deliberately disturb a European protected species or to damage or destroy a breeding site to resting place of such an animal.

It seemed to be accepted that Otters lived in the vicinity of a new bridge across the River Lune required for the M6 Link Road. In essence, the concern seems to have been that as otters are a mobile species there was uncertainty about where they would be then construction started. LCC undertook to carry out further detailed surveys before construction was to begin and to apply to Natural England for a licence under section 53 of the 2010 Regulations at that stage, if necessary. The Secretary of State concluded, on the evidence, that it was not likely that the proosed development would harm otters in those ways prohibited by the Regulations and that, even if it did, Natural England would be likely to issue a licence.

Turner J quoted the judgment of Lord Brown in *R (Morge) v Hampshire CC* [2011] 1 WLR 268 where the Supreme Court considered the proper scope of the European Directive that was subsequently implemented domestically in the 2010 Regulation, as follows:

> '29 … the planning committee['s] only obligation under regulation 3(4) is, I repeat, to "have regard to the requirements of the Habitats Directive so far as [those requirements] may be affected by" their decision whether or not to grant a planning permission. Obviously, in the days when the implementation of such a permission provided a defence to the regulation 39 offence of acting contrary to article 12(1), the planning committee, before granting a permission, would have needed to be satisfied either that the development in question would not offend article 12(1) or that a derogation from that article would be permitted and a licence granted. Now, however, I cannot see why a planning permission (and, indeed, a full planning permission save only as to conditions necessary to secure any required mitigating measures) should not ordinarily be granted save only in cases where the planning committee conclude that the proposed development would both (a) be likely to offend article 12(1) and (b) be unlikely to be licensed pursuant to the derogation powers. After all, even if development permission is given, the criminal sanction against any offending (and unlicensed) activity remains available and it seems to me wrong in principle, when Natural England have the primary responsibility for ensuring compliance with the Directive, also to place a substantial burden on the planning authority in effect to police the fulfilment of Natural England's own duty.
>
> 30 Where, as here, Natural England express themselves satisfied that a proposed development will be compliant with article 12, the planning authority are to my mind entitled to presume that that is so. The

> planning committee here plainly had regard to the requirements of the Directive: they knew from the officers' decision report and addendum report (see para 8 above and the first paragraph of the addendum report as set out in para 72 of Lord Kerr of Tonaghmore JSC's judgment) not only that Natural England had withdrawn their objection to the scheme but also that necessary measures had been planned to compensate for the loss of foraging…'

In this context he considered that the approach of the Examining Authority and the Secretary of State was 'both pragmatic and in accordance with the Regulations' (paragraph 72).

The challenge failed on Ground 5.

The application for judicial review was dismissed.

Case Summary

Written by Michael Humphries QC, ftb

HALITE ENERGY GROUP LIMITED v THE SECRETARY OF STATE FOR ENERGY AND CLIMATE CHANGE

[2014] EWHC 17 (Admin)

High Court

Patterson J

Judgment: 17 January 2014

BACKGROUND

Halite Energy Group ('Halite') made an application for development consent dated 30 November 2011 for the purpose of creating an underground gas storage facility at Preesall, Lancashire. The purpose of the application was to inject gas into, store gas in, and extract gas from underground caverns with a total storage capacity of up to 900 million cubic metres (mcm) and a working gas capacity of up to 600 mcm. A parallel application for deemed hazardous substance consent was made at the same time. The facility was to comprise up to 19 operational storage caverns created by solution mining in the Preesall halite (ie rock salt) deep underground. The creation of the underground gas storage caverns was a Nationally Significant Infrastructure Project ('NSIP') by virtue of section 17 of the Planning Act 2008.

There had been two applications for planning permission for the development of an underground gas storage facility at Preesall in 2004 and 2009; both had been refused. These applications had been refused, inter alia, due to the application containing insufficient geological information.

The 'examination' of the application for development consent took place between 24 April 2012 and 24 October 2012.

The Examining Authority reported to the Secretary of State on 21 January 2014 recommending that consent be granted subject to various requirements. One of those requirements (Requirement 6) required the undertaker to provide further geological information to the local mineral planning authority (Lancashire CC) to demonstrate, before development commenced, that the minimum working gas capacity of the proposed facility would exceed 300 mcm.

In his decision dated 9 April 2013, the Secretary of State decided under section 114 of the Planning Act 2008 to refuse the application for development consent. He also refused the parallel application for hazardous substances consent.

Halite challenged the Secretary of State's refusal of development consent under section 118(2) of the Planning Act 2008.

DECISION

Patterson J identified three essential grounds of appeal, as follows:

- Was there a breach of natural justice in that Halite was dealt with unfairly?
- What is the proper interpretation of paragraph 2.8.9 of NPS EN-4?
- Was the Secretary of State's decision irrational?

Ground 1 – Was there a breach of natural justice in that Halite was dealt with unfairly?

Patterson J identified that a central issue in the determination of the application for development consent was whether the benefit of the gas storage outweighed the visual impacts of the surface infrastructure. The issue for the court, however, was whether the process by which the Secretary of State had reached his decision on that issue had been conducted fairly.

Patterson J drew attention to one of the leading authorities on breaches of natural justice in planning cases, as follows:

> "38. The case of *Castleford Homes Limited v Secretary of State for the Environment, Transport and the Regions* [2001] EWHC 77 dealt with the issue of breach of natural justice in the context of three alternative developments for residential development. Mr Justice Ouseley dealt with the legal position at [52] and [53] where he said,
>
> "52. The relevant law, though not cited to me, is to be found in cases such as Fairmount Investment Ltd. -v- The Secretary of State for the Environment [1976] 1 WLR 1255at p.1266; and H. Sabey & Co. Ltd. -v- The Secretary of State for the Environment [1978] 1 All E.R. 586. Did the Claimant have a "fair crack of the whip?" Was the Claimant deprived of an opportunity to present material by an approach on the part of the Inspector which he did not and could not reasonably have anticipated? Or is he trying to improve his case subsequently, having been substantially aware of, or alerted to, the key issues at the Inquiry? Did he simply fail to realise that he might lose on an aspect which was fairly and squarely at issue and hence fail to put forward his fall-back case? Those are the sort of questions which can be used to guide a conclusion as to whether the manner in which a particular issue was dealt with at an Inquiry involved a breach of natural justice and was unfair.
>
> 53. It is always difficult for parties to an Inquiry to know how far it is necessary to go in order to deal with the contingent ramifications of the process yet to be undertaken by an Inspector of analysing the arguments, accepting some in whole or in part and rejecting others. It is obviously helpful if an Inspector does flag up issues which the parties do not appear to have fully appreciated or explored. The point at which a failure to do so, amounts to a breach of the rules of natural justice and becomes

unfair, is a question of degree, there being no general requirement for an inspector to reveal any provisional thinking. It involves a judgment being made as to what is fair or unfair in a particular case."

39. The claimant submits that here the ExA was conducting an inquisitorial process. The applicant, therefore, had to be in a position where he could fairly meet their concerns. He was entitled to a "fair crack of the whip" which he did not get."

The judgement then examines the factual matrix in some detail before turning to a 'discussion' of the issues.

At paragraphs 79-80 of the judgement Patterson J reviews the nature and objectives of the new 'examination' process and observes, as follows, at paragraphs 81/82:

"81. … As a rule there is no cross-examination at the hearings or on the written documents submitted in response to the Panel's questions. The onus is, therefore, on the ExA to ensure that material matters of concern, which may or may not, have been raised by others who have made representations on the planning application are raised with all parties in a fair and transparent way. In particular, where matters raised or of concern relate to the principal controversial issues, there is a duty upon the ExA to provide all parties with the opportunity to comment upon them before reaching their final conclusions.

82. The questions which Ouseley J set out in Castleford Homes on the sort of issues which could be used to guide a conclusion as to whether the manner in which a particular issue was dealt with at an inquiry involved a breach of natural justice and was unfair, are just as apposite to a process of examination by an ExA as they are to parties at an inquiry. The fundamental issue here is whether there was a fair process in the particular circumstances of this examination? If there was not, the supplemental question is, what are the consequences?"

In this context Patterson J identified three further questions as follows:

- Should the claimant have recognised that deficiencies in the geological data and its interplay with the COMAH regime had become an issue?
- Did the ExA mislead themselves on the geological issues by requiring the claimant to demonstrate its position to too high a standard – beyond reasonable doubt – and act in a way that was unfair?
- To what extent, if at all, did any deficiencies in the examination affect the defendant's ultimate decision?

Should the claimant have recognised that deficiencies in the geological data and its interplay with the COMAH regime had become an issue?

Importantly, there was a Statement of Common Ground (SoCG) between Halite and Lancashire CC as to the adequacy of the geological data supplied with the application. In relation to the SoCG Patterson J stated as follows:

"86. A SOCG has been described by PINS as a crucial component of the inquiry process. As part of the highly focussed modern inquiry

> regime parties are entitled to rely upon the content of the SOCG as determinative, as between themselves, of the issues contained within it. Although an examination is not an inquiry I can see no basis for any lesser weight to attach to a SOCG in an examination process. Of course, an ExA is not bound by the SOCG. In this case with their own expert advisor on geological issues it was entirely foreseeable that they would examine its contents critically. However, if there was to be a fundamental disagreement with the contents of the SOCG it was reasonable to expect that would be raised with the parties in a transparent manner. If an ISH was not considered necessary by the ExA then, at the very least, further questions should have been raised which made clear the areas of concern to the ExA and which gave the claimant the opportunity to rebut the various scenarios and "extreme circumstances" which were postulated in the Panel Report. In the absence of either of those events as the examination progressed it was not unreasonable for the claimant to expect that geological issues were no longer a main controversial issue."

This is an important indication of the importance to be attached to SoCGs in the 'examination' process under the Planing Act 2008.

There was no Issue Specific Hearing (ISH) on geology issues during the examination; although one was held on the relationship between the Planning Act 2008 regime and that under the Control of Major Accident Hazards (COMAH) regime.

In that context, and after reviewing the conduct of the examination, Patterson J concluded on this further question that:

> "95. There was nothing, therefore, to indicate to the claimant that the agreed joint expert view set out in the SOCG was being challenged or upturned in the way that it eventually transpired in the Panel Report. The ExA clearly had concerns about the boundaries of the planning system and its overlap with the COMAH process which was understandable. It did not, however, explore its concerns about the prospect of reduced working gas storage or the likelihood or consequences thereof save in the sole question by Ms Gawith. In those circumstances it is putting it too high to say that the claimant should have recognised the full extent or significance of the issue that was finally taken against it."

<u>Did the ExA mislead themselves on the geological issues by requiring the claimant to demonstrate its position to too high a standard – beyond reasonable doubt – and act in a way that was unfair?</u>

In a number of places in the Examining Authority's report they express themselves as not being satisfied that the suitability of the geology had been proved "beyond reasonable doubt". The Secretary of State even quoted one of those passages in his dicision letter, without disavowal.

The test of 'beyond reasonable doubt' was clearly not the standard of proof normally applied in planning law cases – that being the text of 'on a balance of probabilities' – and Halite challenged the Examining Authority's reasoning and the Secretary of State's decision on this basis.

Patterson J concluded as follows:

> "96. The failure on the part of the ExA to explore with the claimant, or any of the parties, the three scenarios referred to in their report and/or the calculations contained in paragraphs 5.76 to 5.78 in conjunction with examining the geological issues so that they were "certain" or that the geology was proved beyond "reasonable doubt", in my judgment, demonstrates a lack of transparent and fair process. Those were matters which bore directly upon the conclusions reached not only by the claimant's consultants, Mott McDonald, but also by Atkins and LCC, generally, and in the SOCG.
>
> 97. Those matters went to the heart of the likelihood of being able to construct the development as proposed in the application. They provided a vital step in the ExA's reasoning. … The claimant needed to have the opportunity to deal with those matters to have a fair hearing.
>
> 98. I accept entirely that there is no obligation on the ExA to share its provisional conclusions, as Mr Hudson says in his witness statement. In my judgment, however, there is an obligation on the ExA to share the route to such conclusions where they relate to a main issue at the examination and the route and thinking is based on options that have not been in the public domain.
>
> 99. As to the standard of proof, the defendant submits that the ExA were using "beyond reasonable doubt" as a synonym for 'demonstrate'. If the phrase was used on only one occasion, and bearing in mind that one must read the decision letter as a whole, I would be more sympathetic to that submission. Unfortunately, the several references to "beyond reasonable doubt" [5.62], [5.65], [7.11], the expression of the need for "certainty" [5.47] and for "full demonstration" [5.58], have led me somewhat reluctantly to the conclusion that the panel applied or are likely to have applied the wrong standard of proof to this material issue. Not only is that an error of law, it is unfair to the claimant."

Three particular points emerge:

- there is no obligation on the Examining Authority to share its provisional conclusions;
- there is, however, an obligation on the Examining Authority to share the route to such conclusions where they relate to a main issue at the examination and the route and thinking is based on options that have not been in the public domain; and
- 'beyond reasonable doubt' is the wrong standard of proof in decision-making under the Planning Act 2008.

<u>To what extent, if at all, did any deficiencies in the examination affect the defendant's ultimate decision?</u>

Patterson J concluded at paragraphs 100-103 of her judgement that the Secretary of State had clearly relied on the Examining Authority's findings and conclusions on the central issue of the sufficiency of the geological information before him and, as that approach was flawed because of "a lack of fair and transparent process" (paragraph 103) in parts of the examination on the part of the Examining Authority, that lack of fair process had infected the Secretary of State's decision.

Patterson J held that the judicial review challenge succeeded on Ground 1 (paragraph 103).

Ground 2 – What is the proper interpretation of paragraph 2.8.9 of NPS EN-4?

Paragraph 2.8.9 of NPS EN-4 reads:

> "Applicants should undertake and supply to the IPC, a detailed geological assessment to demonstrate the suitability of the geology at the site for the type of underground gas storage proposed. When considering storage in porous rock, in a depleted or partially depleted oil or gas field or aquifer applicants should undertake a detailed geological assessment to determine suitability of the rocks for underground gas storage. When considering storage in a salt cavity, the geological assessment should include depth below surface, salt thickness, salt purity and presence of shale bands which could affect cavern design. In addition, a study of the geological integrity of the overlying strata and potential for collapse, taking account of the proposed minimum and maximum working pressures will need to be undertaken. The assessment should include construction, operational and decommissioning phases and should cover the long term integrity of the affected strata after decommissioning or closure of the storage facility. The IPC will consider the geological assessment alongside the environmental assessment if the former does not form part of the ES."

The Examining Authority had interpreted the words "to demonstrate the suitability of the geology at the site for the type of underground gas storage proposed" to mean that Halite had to prove the 'minimum capacity' that the facility would achieve. Furthermore, as this was not considered to have been demonstrated 'beyond reasonable doubt', the application was not in accordance with the NPS and the section 104(3) presumption in favour of granting development consent did not apply.

Halite argued, however, that this was a fundamental misinterpretation of paragraph 2.8.9 of NPS EN-4.

Patterson J held on this issue that:

> "122. The natural meaning of the words in paragraph 2.8.9 is, in my judgement, clear. They are seeking a detailed geological appraisal to demonstrate the suitability of the site for the development proposed. It is no more than that. The ordinary meaning of "suitability" would not necessarily include capacity. The geological assessment is to show that the type of medium is appropriate or fit for the purpose for which it is proposed. The fact that the paragraph appears under the section entitled "factors influencing site selection" endorses that view. The paragraph is advising applicants to establish whether the site is geologically fit for the intended purpose. That is why the subsequent paragraph refers to safety

as an additional factor to be considered when considering where to site gas storage facilities. If capacity was a necessary part of the geological assessment then I would have expected it to be mentioned expressly. It is not. Other aspects which have to be taken into account as part of the detailed geological study are. Doubtless on many occasions capacity will be taken into account as part of the geological assessment but, in my judgement, the wording of paragraph 2.8.9 does not make it an absolute requirement that it has to be.

...

131 It follows that, whilst detailed geological data for the site of the proposals is required under NPS EN-4 that does not necessarily have to include capacity. To so hold would be to place too absolute a requirement on the contents of the geological assessment that is not supported by language or meaning of paragraph 2.8.9 of EN-4. ..."

Patterson J held that the judicial review challenge also succeeded on Ground 2.

Was the Secretary of State's decision irrational?

In the light of her previous conclusions Patterson J dealt with this ground briefly, as follows:

"133. It is clear that there were real deficiencies in the reasoning of the Secretary of State in his decision letter. He was rejecting the recommendation of the ExA but, because he adopted their approach to the geological assessment, including the standard to which they had to be satisfied, was flawed in his approach. He failed to express any reasons for so doing. Further, he failed to consider that whereas the approach of the Panel was to recommend approval of the project subject to an amended R6 because he took a different view whether that involved different considerations. Those deficiencies are such, as in my judgment, as to make his decision irrational."

The judicial review, therefore, also succeeded on Ground 3.

The claim for judicial review, therefore, succeeded on all grounds and the decision of the Secretary of State to refuse development consent was quashed.

Case Summary

Written by Michael Humphries QC, ftb

FCC ENVIRONMENT (UK) LTD v THE SECRETARY OF STATE FOR ENERGY AND CLIMATE CHANGE and COVANTA ROOKERY SOUTH LTD

[2014] EWHC 947 (Admin)

High Court

Mitting J

Judgment: 6 February 2014

[2015] EWCA Civ 55

Court of Appeal

Aikins LJ, Sullivan LJ and Black LJ

Judgment: 5 February 2015

BACKGROUND

On 4 August 2010 Covanta Rookery South Ltd ('Covanta') applied for development consent under section 37 of the Planning Act 2008 to build a combined waste treatment and electricity generating plant on a site mostly owned by them at Rookery South, Bedfordshire. The proposed waste treatment and electricity plant was a Nationally Significant Infrastructure Project by virtue of section 15 of the 2008 Act.

Bedford Borough Council and Central Bedfordshire Council ('the local authorities') owned part of the land required to construct the plant, comprising the subsoil of an access road, and FCC Environment (UK) Ltd ('FCC'), a rival operator, enjoyed the benefit of a restrictive covenant over the land that prohibited the construction and operation of the proposed waste processing plant.

The draft development consent order ('DCO') submitted by Covanta included powers for the compulsory purchase of land, including the local authorities land and the extinguishment of certain rights over land.

Section 128 of the 2008 Act affords protection to certain landowners, including local authorities, whose land is subject to compulsory acquisition, such that an order granting development consent is subject to special parliamentary procedure ('SPP') if a local authority has made, and not withdrawn, a representation about the making of the order. In relation to the proposed facility at Rookery South the local authorities had made, and not withdrawn, such representations.

The procedural requirements for SPP are set out in the Statutory Orders (Special Procedure) Act 1945. The effect was to require an order granting development consent, which included provision authorising the compulsory acquisition of land owned by a local authority to be laid before Parliament (section 1(2) of the 1945 Act). Those opposed had 21 days in which to petition Parliament. A Joint Committee of both Houses would then consider the matter and report to Parliament. If it reported the order without amendment, it would come into effect on the date on which its report was laid before Parliament (section 6(1). If it reported with amendments, or if it was not approved, legislation would be required (section 6(2) and (3)). The Secretary of State's only responsibility was to publish Parliament's approval. The Secretary of State had a residual power to change or revoke an order once made in the circumstances set out in Schedule 6 (section 153) to the Planning Act 2008.

After examining the application a Panel of the Infrastructure Planning Commission ('IPC') decided to make the order, and submitted it to the Secretary of State on 13 October 2011. The order was made on 11 November 2011. SPP was then activated by petitions from the local authorities, FCC and others.

A Joint Committee then heard the petitions and reported the order, without amendments, on 13 February 2013. It came into effect automatically and immediately under section 6(1) of the 1945 Act. FCC then applied to the Secretary of State to exercise his power to revoke the order under Schedule 6 of the 2008 Act; he refused to do so.

FCC then brought proceedings by way of judicial review under section 118 of the 2008 Act to challenge the Secretary of State's decision not to revoke the order.

DECISION

FCC's challenge raised two issues being:

- The adequacy of the Panel's reasons for including provision for compulsory acquisition of the benefit of the restrictive covenant enjoyed by FCC; and
- A contention that the environmental impact assessment ('EIA') relied on by the IPC was out of date when Parliament approved the order.

In the Court of Appeal, the Appellant (FCC) challenged the High Court's decision on three grounds.

Ground 1

In the High Court, Mitting J considers the first issue (above) at paragraphs 11 to 20 of his judgement.

The issue turned, to a considerable degree, on the interesting relationship between (a) section 104(3) (development consent should be granted for development in accordance with the NPS) and (b) the requirements of section 122 where land is being compulsorily acquired, and in particular the section 122(3) requirement that the decision-maker must be satisfied that there is a compelling case in the public interest for the land to be compulsorily acquired. The argument focussed particularly on the advice on alternatives in NPS EN-1 (paragraph 4.4.3) and that at paragraphs 20, 29 and 31 of the DCLG 'Guidance related to procedures for compulsory acquisition' (February 2010) (since superseded by DCLG 'Guidance related to procedures for compulsory acquisition' (September 2013)).

In this context Mitting J made the following observations:

> "17. That guidance [ie the DCLG guidance] and reasoning reflects a tension between the mandatory requirement to apply National Policy Statements and the need to examine alternatives to compulsory purchase of the land in question. [Counsel] for the Secretary of State, and [Counsel] for Covanta, submit that the Commission must apply relevant National Policy Statements to issues arising under section 122(3). I agree. Section 104(3) requires the Commission to decide the application for an order granting development consent. When, as here, the order includes provision for compulsory acquisition, the requirement in section 104(3) must apply to deciding that part of the application as well. They submit, however, that the Commission retains the power in principle to refuse to include provision for compulsory acquisition, if not satisfied of the compelling case in the public interest for the land to be acquired compulsorily.
>
> 18. For my part I find it difficult to conceive of circumstances in which the Panel in applying statutory guidance, as it must, which established an urgent need for development, could legitimately conclude that there was not a compelling case as a necessary element of the scheme, justifying compulsory acquisition of rights in land. To that extent, the established distinction between tests for the grant of planning consent and the grant of a power of compulsory acquisition (see *Trusthouse Forte Hotels Ltd v Secretary of State for the Environment* (1986) 53 P&CR 293 at page 299, paragraph 2 and page 300, paragraph 6) has been modified by statute.'

Mitting J then went on to consider the Panel's reasoning in relation to the issue of 'alternatives' and concluded that it was adequate.

At first instance, therefore, FCC failed on the first issue (above). Mitting J's reasoning in his paragraph 18 (above) was, however, challenged in the Court of Appeal.

Ground 1 in the Court of Appeal related to the reasoning in Mitting J's paragraph 18 and it was common ground between the parties that his approach was erroneous.

In respect of the relationship between sections 104 and 122, the Court endorsed (para 10) the approach set out in the Skeleton Argument of counsel for the Secretary of State that:

> '35 (1) Section 104(3) of the 2008 Act requires "the application" to be decided in accordance with any relevant NPS;
>
> (2) The tests for whether to grant powers of compulsory acquisition are set by section 122(2) and (3) of the 2008 Act and include, in section 122(3), that there must be "a compelling case in the public interest";
>
> (3) Where "the application" includes proposed powers of compulsory acquisition of land, in assessing whether there is a "compelling case in the public interest" pursuant to section 122(3), the decision-maker will have to make that assessment in accordance with the contents of any relevant NPS by virtue of section 104(3);

(4) However, where, as in the present case, the NPS establishes an urgent need for development, this does not mean that the "compelling case in the public interest" test is automatically and necessarily met – section 104(3) means that, in assessing whether there is a "compelling case in the public interest", the need for the development must be treated as established and cannot be questioned, but it may be possible to meet the need without the use of the requested powers of compulsory acquisition;

(5) This is a reflection of the fact that section 104(3) is a broad provision, dealing with the determination of the application as a whole and leading to an order granting development consent which may include compulsory acquisition provisions, whereas section 122(3) is a narrower test dealing specifically with compulsory acquisition powers;

(6) The full and proper application of the section 122(3) test is guaranteed by section 104(6) which disapplies the requirement in section 104(3) where it would lead to unlawfulness under any enactment (ie including under a different provision of the 2008 Act) – thus, if there was any potential conflict between sections 104(3) and 122(3), the "compelling public interest" test in section 122(3) would not be overridden by section 104(3).

36. In this way, there is no conflict between section 104(3) and section 122(3). They each operate distinctly in the determination of the application overall (in the case of section 104(3)) and a request for compulsory acquisition powers (in the case of section 122(3)). To the extent that any conflict might otherwise arise because of the terms of particular provisions in an NPS, the conflict is avoided by virtue of section 104(6).'

This approach must be correct and is helpful clarification of the relationship between the need for nationally significant infrastructure projects as set out in an NPS and the quite separate duty to establish a 'compelling case in the public interest' when seeking to compulsorily acquire land.

Ground 2

Ground 2 in the Court of Appeal was a reasons challenge relating to whether potential alternatives to the proposed development had been properly considered in the Examining Authority's report and Secretary of State's decision. This part of the Court of Appeal's judgment is very much confined to the facts of the particular case.

Ground 3

Ground 3 in the Court of appeal related to the second of the two issues identified above; namely, whether the Environmental Statement was out of date by the time Parliament approved the Order.

In relation to this ground, FCC accepted that the requirements of the EIA Directive were fulfilled during the determination by the Panel, and at the time of the making of its order, 22 November 2011, but not during the special procedure, or at the time the order came into effect on its approval by Parliament on 13 February 2013. By then, FCC submitted, it was out of date.

The foundation of FCC's argument was that determination of the application for development consent was a composite procedure, and that until it concluded Covanta were not entitled to proceed with its project. Therefore, within the autonomous meaning of 'development consent' in European law, the requirement for an up-to-date assessment of environmental effects was not fulfilled.

Mitting J identified a preliminary obstacle to this argument (paragraph 23) in that, in so far as the efficacy of Parliament's enquiry into environmental effects was being criticized, the Speakers of both Houses of Parliament had not been served with the claim form and invited to make representation. Nor had the inadequacy of environmental impact assessment been raised before the joint Committee.

Mitting J also concluded (paragraphs 24-26), however, that the IPC was the 'competent authority' for the purposes of the EIA Directive, as it was (before the Localism Act 2011) the IPC that made the decision to make the DCO and not the Secretary or State or Parliament. Thus the decision to make the order had been made in 2011, before the environmental information was said to be out of date, and not when it took effect in 2013.

The EIA challenge, therefore, also failed in the High Court.

The Court of Appeal agreed with Mitting J's reasoning on this issue and endorsed the conclusion that it was the IPC, and not Parliament, that was the competent authority for the purposes of the PA 2008. Thus the 'decision' on the development consent had been taken in 2011 when the environmental information was fresh and not in 2013 when it took effect following 'special parliamentary procedure'. The reasoning leading to this conclusion may, however, no longer be safe following the passing of the Localism Act 2011, which made the Secretary of State the decision-maker in relation to the grant of development consent.

The Court of Appeal also drew attention to the decisions in *R (Wells) v Secretary of State for Transport* [2004] 1 CMLR 31 and *R (Barker) v Bromley LBC* [2006] QB 764, but distinguished the circumstances of a 'two stage' outline planning permission requiring the submission and approval of details from the circumstances under the PA 2008 where the environmental effects of a proposed development were fully considered on the grant of development consent.

The appeal was, therefore, dismissed.

Case Summary

Written by Michael Humphries QC, ftb

R (oao AN TAISCE (THE NATIONAL TRUST FOR IRELAND)) and THE SECRETARY OF STATE FOR ENERGY AND CLIMATE CHANGE and NNB GENERATION COMPANY LTD

[2013] EWHC 4161 (Admin)

High Court

Patterson J

Judgment: 20 December 2013

[2014] EWCA Civ 1111

Court of Appeal

Sullivan LJ; Gloster LJ and Longmore LJ

Judgment: 1 August 2014

BACKGROUND

On 31 October 2011 NNB Generation Company Limited ('NNB'), a subsidiary of EDF Energy (UK) Ltd ('EDF'), made an application to the Infrastructure Planning Commission ('IPC') for development consent to build and operate a new nuclear power station at Hinkley Point, Somerset; the power station was to be known as Hinkley Point C (HPC).

The consenting procedure for a new nuclear power station is complex and involved various consents and permissions. At first instance, Patterson J set out the background to the claim, including the regulatory context, at paragraphs 5-62 of her judgment. This was not challenged and was gratefully adopted by Sullivan LJ (paragraph 3) in the Court of Appeal.

A number of points may be made briefly:

- In its 2008 White Paper entitled 'Meeting the Energy Challenge' the government set out its proposals for a new consenting regime for future nuclear power stations.
- The new regime comprises:
    - The grant of development consent under the Planning Act 2008;
    - The identification of suitable sites for new nuclear power stations in National Policy Statements ('NPSs'), through a process of 'strategic siting assessment' ('SSA') and 'strategic environmental assessment' ('SEA');
    - The 'justification' of the use of ionising radiation by new nuclear reactor designs pursuant to the Justification of Practices Involving Ionising Radiation Regulations 2004; and

  - ○ The approval of nuclear reactor designs through a process of 'generic design assessment' ('GDA') undertaken by the Office of Nuclear Regulation ('ONR') and the Environment Agency ('EA').

- In addition, it is necessary for a nuclear power station operator to obtain a nuclear site licence ('NSL') issued by the ONR under the Nuclear Installations Act 1965 and environmental permits granted by the EA under the Environmental Permitting Regulations.
- In October 2010 the Secretary of State made the Justification Decision (Generation of Electricity by the EPR Nuclear Reactor) Regulations 2010.
- The ONR was formed on 1 April 2011 as an executive agency of the Health and Safety Executive ('HSE') and, together with the EA, developed a process of GDA for new reactor designs.
- In June 2011 the IPC published its Advice Note 12 on development with significant transboundary effects (later superseded by PINS Advice Note 12: Transboundary Impacts Consultation (April 2012)).
- On 19 July 2011 the Secretary of State designated the six energy NPSs, including NPS EN-6 on nuclear generation. EN-6 identified eight sites for new nuclear power stations, including that for HPC.
- On 29 July 2011 NNB applied for a NSL. A license was subsequently granted which came into force on 3 December 2012.

On 31 October 2011 NNB made its application for development consent for HPC under section 37 of the Planning Act 2008. The examination into the application ran between 21 March 2012 and 21 September 2012. On 19 March 2013 the Secretary of State granted development consent for HPC. In making his decision the Secretary of State reiterated that the nuclear safety aspects of the project were regulated by the ONR and EA, that a nuclear site license had been granted (26 November 2012) and that the GDA process concluded (13 December 2012). He also took account of his Justification Decision of October 2010.

The issue raised by An Taisce was whether, in granting development consent, the Secretary of State had failed to comply with Regulation 24 of the Infrastructure Planning (Environmental Impact Assessment) Regulations 2009 and Article 7 of Directive 2011/92/EU ('the EIA Directive') in that he had failed to consult the public in the Republic of Ireland about likely significant effects of HPC on the environment in the Republic of Ireland (ie transboundary effects).

The Secretary of State had not conducted transboundary consultation in accordance with Regulation 24 and Article 7 because he did not consider that the HPC project was "likely to have significant effects on the environment of another Member State". A transboundry screening assessment carried out by PINS had concluded on the basis of licensing and monitoring conditions impacts would not be significant.

An Taisce brought an application for judicial review, under section 118 of the Planning Act 2008, challenging the Secretary of State's decision to grant development consent for HPC. This came before the High Court as a 'rolled up' hearing (ie of permission to bring judicial review and the substantive issues) with the agreement of all parties.

The legal framework for the challenge was set out at paragraphs 63-79 of the judgment of Patterson J; it was not in dispute in either the High Court or the Court of Appeal.

DECISION

Patterson J identified three grounds of challenge, as follows:

- the defendant misdirected himself as to the meaning of Regulation 24 and Article 7 in considering only impacts arising from the ordinary regulated operation of the nuclear power station and not "unlikely", but nevertheless possible, impacts from other scenarios;
- the defendant failed to comply with Regulation 24 and Article 7 by omitting to take into account the possible impacts arising from unplanned or accidental effects of the development; and/or
- because the meaning of Article 7 is unclear the court should make a reference to the CJEU.

In a detailed and closely reasoned judgment, Patterson J rejected the claimant's arguments on all three grounds and refused to quash the Secretary of State's decision to grant development consent for HPC.

In the Court of Appeal, Sullivan LJ gave the only reasoned judgment, with which Gloster LJ and Longmore LJ agreed.

In the Court of Appeal the argument focussed on Article 7, rather than Regulation 24, and Sullivan LJ characterised the grounds as follows:

> '8. The Claimant contends that there was a failure to comply with Article 7 of the Directive. The Defendant failed to consult the public in the Republic of Ireland in accordance with Article 7 because:
>
> 1) He misdirected himself as to the meaning of "likely" within Article 7 by "scoping out" severe nuclear accidents on the basis that they were very unlikely (Ground 1 "likelihood"); and
>
> 2) Even if he was correct as to the meaning of "likely", the Defendant erred in relying on the existence of the UK nuclear regulatory regime to fill gaps in current knowledge when reaching his conclusion as to the likelihood of nuclear accidents (Ground 2 "regulatory regime").'

Ground 1 - Likelihood

Article 7 of the EIA Directive provides as follows:

> '1. Where a Member State is aware that a project is likely to have significant effects on the environment in another Member State or where a Member State likely to be significantly affected so requests, the Member State in whose territory the project is intended to be carried out shall send to the affected Member State as soon as possible and no later than when informing its own public, inter alia:

(a) a description of the project, together with any available information on its possible transboundary impact;

(b) information on the nature of the decision which may be taken.

The Member State in whose territory the project is intended to be carried out shall give the other Member State a reasonable time in which to indicate whether it wishes to participate in the environmental decision-making procedures referred to in Article 2(2), and may include the information referred to in paragraph 2 of this Article.

2. If a Member State which receives information pursuant to paragraph 1 indicates that it intends to participate in the environmental decision-making procedures referred to in Article 2(2), the Member State in whose territory the project is intended to be carried out shall, if it has not already done so, send to the affected Member State the information required to be given pursuant to Article 6(2) and made available pursuant to points (a) and (b) of Article 6(3).

3. The Member States concerned, each insofar as it is concerned, shall also:

(a) Arrange for the information referred to in paragraphs 1 and 2 to be made available, within a reasonable time, to the authorities referred to in Article 6(1) and the public concerned in the territory of the Member State likely to be significantly affected; and

(b) ensure that the authorities referred to in Article 6(1) and the public concerned are given an opportunity, before development consent for the project is granted, to forward their opinion within a reasonable time on the information supplied to the competent authority in the Member State in whose territory the project is intended to be carried out."

Sullivan LJ pointed out (paragraph 9) that the words 'likely to have significant effects on the environment' occur in a number of places in the EIA Directive: in recitals (7) and (9), in Articles 1(1), 2(1) and 7(1), and in a slightly different formulation 'likely significant effects of the proposed project on the environment' in Annex IV. In similar vein, an Environmental Statement must include 'the data required to identify and assess the main effects which the project is likely to have on the environment': see Article 5(3).

In that context he made two points at the outset (paragraph 11) being that:

- The words 'likely to have significant effects on the environment' must have the same meaning throughout the EIA Directive (not least because the environmental information to be supplied to the authorities and the public in the other Member State under Article 7 is the information that must be provided under Article 6 to the public in the Member State in which the project is located); and
- Whatever that meaning might be, in the context of the EIA Directive the word 'likely' does not mean, as an English lawyer might suppose, more probable than not.

The Court of Justice of the European Union ('CJEU') has not ruled on the meaning of 'likely to have significant effects on the environment' in the EIA Directive. The Domestic authorities were considered by Patterson J in paragraphs 123-126 of her judgment. None of those authorities, however, was binding on the Court of Appeal. In *R (Morge) v Hampshire County Council* [2010] EWCA Civ 608 [2010] PTSR 1882, Ward LJ recorded the parties' agreement that 'likely' connotes real risk and not probability (paragraph 80). In *R (Bateman) v South Cambridgeshire District Council* [2011] EWCA Civ 157 Moore-Bick LJ expressed the view in paragraph 17 that something more than a bare possibility is probably required, though any serious possibility 'would suffice', but he did not find it necessary to reach a final decision on the question (paragraph 19).

An Taisce's submission was that a project is "likely to have significant effects on the environment" if such effects "cannot be excluded on the basis of objective evidence". This submission was founded on the decision of the Grand Chamber of the CJEU in Case C-127/02 *Landelijke Vereniging tot Behoud van de Waddenzee and Nederlandse Vereniging tot Bescherming van Bogels v Staatssecretaris van Landbouw, Natuurbeheer en Visserij* ("Waddenzee"). Waddenzee was concerned with the Habitats Directive, not the EIA Directive, Article 6(3) of which materially provides that:

> "Any plan or project not directly connected with or necessary to the management of the site but likely to have a significant effect thereon, either individually or in combination with other plans or projects, shall be subject to appropriate assessment of its implications for the site in view of the site's conservation objectives. ..." (emphasis added)

In paragraphs 42-44 of its judgment the Grand Chamber in Waddenzee said:

> "42. As regards Article 2(1) of Directive 85/337 [now Article 2(1) of the EIA Directive], the text of which, essentially similar to Article 6(3) of the Habitats Directive, provides that "Member States shall adopt all measures necessary to ensure that, before consent is given, projects likely to have significant effects on the environment ... are made subject to an assessment with regard to their effects', the Court has held that these are projects which are likely to have significant effects on the environment (see to that effect Case C-117/02 Commission v Portugal [2004] ECR I-5517, paragraph 85).
>
> ...
>
> 44. In the light, in particular, of the precautionary principle, which is one of the foundations of the high level of protection pursued by Community policy on the environment, in accordance with the first subparagraph of Article 174(2) EC, and by reference to which the Habitats Directive must be interpreted, such a risk exists if it cannot be excluded on the basis of objective information that the plan or project will have significant effects on the site concerned (see, by analogy, inter alia Case C-180/96 United Kingdom v Commission [1998] ECR I-2265, paragraphs 50, 105 and 107). ...
>
> 45. In the light of the foregoing, ... the first sentence of Article 6(3) of the Habitats Directive must be interpreted as meaning that any plan or project not directly connected with or necessary to the management of

the site is to be subject to an appropriate assessment of its implications for the site in view of the site's conservation objectives if it cannot be excluded, on the basis of objective information, that it will have a significant effect on that site, either individually or in combination with other plans or projects." (emphasis added)

Sullivan LJ dealt with the central issue in the An Taisce argument as follows:

"37. The Claimant's challenge to the Defendant's decision in this case does not simply depend upon the proposition that the Grand Chamber's approach in Waddenzee to the meaning of "likely to have a significant effect" in the Habitats Directive should be carried over into the EIA Directive, it also depends upon a very literal meaning being given to the Grand Chamber's words "cannot be excluded on the basis of objective information" in its judgment in Waddenzee. If a remote risk can properly be excluded, the Claimant does not challenge the Defendant's assessment that the remoteness of the risk in this case was such that it could be excluded. In order to succeed in this claim the Claimant has to establish that any risk, no matter how remote, cannot be excluded unless it has been demonstrated that there is no possibility of its occurring. It is, in effect a "zero risk" approach to the likelihood of significant environmental effects.

38. It would be surprising if the Grand Chamber had intended to impose such a high and inflexible threshold for "appropriate assessment", even in the context of the Habitats Directive. However purposive the interpretation of the Habitats Directive, its text cannot be ignored. The word "likely", and the concept of likelihood, implies at least some degree of flexibility. There comes a point when the probability (to use the word in Annex III to the EIA Directive) of a significant effect is so remote that it ceases to be "likely", however broad the concept of likelihood. In Waddenzee the Grand Chamber said that, following an appropriate assessment, a project could be authorised only if the competent authority "have made certain that it will not adversely affect the integrity of that site. That is the case where no reasonable scientific doubt remains as to the absence of such effects...." ... . Thus, certainty was equated with the absence of reasonable scientific doubt.

39. Even if the Waddenzee approach to likelihood is carried over into the EIA Directive, it must be open to a competent authority to conclude that the risk of a significant adverse effect on the environment is so remote (e.g. if it is more remote than the risk of a meteorite of over a kilometre hitting the earth) that there is "no reasonable scientific doubt" as to the absence of that adverse effect for the purpose of the EIA Directive. The competent authority does not have to be satisfied that there is no risk, however remote, that a severe nuclear accident will occur in order to be satisfied that there is "no reasonable scientific doubt" that such an accident will not occur. This approach is consistent with the guidance that is contained in the Planning Inspectorate's Advice note 12: Development with significant transboundary impacts consultation.

...

42. In the present case, it is common ground that the probability of a severe nuclear accident is very low indeed. There may be an issue as to just how low that probability is … but there is no doubt that the Defendant was entitled to describe it in his decision as a "very low probability". The issue, therefore, is whether the risk of a significant effect on the environment can properly be excluded on the basis of a very low probability, or only upon the basis of a zero probability. In this case we are concerned with a proposal for a nuclear power station, and the environmental consequences of a severe nuclear accident. In that context, for obvious reasons, "very low probability" means very low probability indeed, far below the levels of probability (or "risk") that might be regarded as acceptable in the context of other developments. … .

43. Annex III requires the Member States to consider both the magnitude and complexity of an environmental impact and the probability of such an impact when deciding whether an Annex II project is likely to have significant effect on the environment (see paragraph 22 above). As a matter of common sense, the greater the potential impact, the lower will be the level of probability at which the competent authority will decide that it should be subjected to the environmental impact assessment process: see *Miller v North Yorkshire County Council*, [2009] EWHC 2172 (Admin) per Hickinbottom J at paragraphs 31 and 32. This leaves an area of judgment for the competent authority balancing the severity of any potential environmental harm against the probability of it occurring. It recognises the fact that some significant effects on the environment, e.g. a significant radiological impact, are much more significant than others. Given the wide range of projects covered by the EIA Directive and the express requirement to consider the probability of any impact, I am satisfied that, even if it is appropriate to apply the "cannot be excluded on the basis of objective evidence" approach to the likelihood of significant effects on the environment in the EIA Directive, there is no realistic prospect of the Claimant's "zero risk" approach being adopted by the CJEU. I would add that our attention was not drawn to any decision of a Court in which the Claimant's approach to exclusion has been adopted. However purposive the interpretation of the EIA Directive, a "zero risk" approach to likelihood would be an interpretative step too far and would frustrate, rather than further the purpose of the Directive."

On that basis Ground 1 failed.

Ground 2 – the existence on the UK nuclear regulatory regime to fill gaps in current knowledge

Sullivan LJ drew attention to the fact that this issue had been dealt with at paragraphs 177-193 of Patterson J's judgment at first instances. He quoted her conclusion at paragraph 193 as follows:

"In my judgment there is no reason that precludes the Secretary of State from being able to have regard to, and rely upon, the existence of a stringently

> operated regulatory regime for future control. Because of its existence, he was satisfied, on a reasonable basis, that he had sufficient information to enable him to come to a final decision on the development consent application. In short, the Secretary of State had sufficient information at the time of making his decision to amount to a comprehensive assessment for the purposes of the Directive. The fact that there were some matters still to be determined by other regulatory bodies does not affect that finding. Those matters outstanding were within the expertise and jurisdiction of the relevant regulatory bodies which the defendant was entitled to rely upon."

Sullivan LJ agreed with the judge's conclusions on this issue (paragraph 46) and made it clear that had this ground of challenge stood alone he would not have granted permission to apply for judicial review.

He went on, however, to make the following helpful comments:

> "48. Many major developments, particularly the kind of projects that are listed in Annex I to the EIA Directive, are not designed to the last detail at the environmental impact assessment stage. There will, almost inevitably in any major project, be gaps and uncertainties as to the detail, and the competent authority will have to form a judgment as to whether those gaps and uncertainties mean that there is a likelihood of significant environmental effects, or whether there is no such likelihood because it can be confident that the remaining details will be addressed in the relevant regulatory regime. In paragraph 38 of his judgment in R (Jones) v Mansfield District Council [2004] 2 P & CR 14, Dyson LJ (as he then was) adopted paragraphs 51 and 52 of the judgment of Richards J (as he then was) which included the following passage:
>
> "It is for the authority to judge whether a development would be likely to have significant effects. The authority must make an informed judgment, on the basis of the information available to it and having regard to any gaps in that information and to any uncertainties that may exist, as to the likelihood of significant environmental effects. Everything depends on the circumstances of the individual case.""

In this context Sullivan LJ stated, having commented on the "elaborate regulatory regime for nuclear power stations" in the UK, that "it might be thought that this case was the paradigm of a case in which a planning decision-taker could reasonably conclude that there was no likelihood of significant environmental effects because any remaining gaps in the details of the project would be addressed by the relevant regulatory regime" (paragraph 50).

In this basis Ground 2 failed.

Sullivan LJ also decided that a reference to the CJEU was not necessary.

The Court of Appeal dismissed the application for judicial review.

Case Summary

Written by Michael Humphries QC, ftb

R (oao MICHAEL WILLIAMS) v SECRETARY OF STATE FOR CLIMATE CHANGE and RWE INNOGY UK LTD

[2015] EWHC 1202 (Admin)

High Court

Lindblom J

Judgment: 30 April 2015

BACKGROUND

In March 2013 RWE Npower Renewables Limited made an application for development consent under section 37 of the PA 2008 in respect of the construction of up to 32 wind turbine generators, each with a height to blade tip of 145 metres, together with related infrastructure and various other works ('Clocaenog Forest Wind Farm'). The installed capacity was to be between 64 and 96 megawatts. The application site, about 1,580 hectares of forest, lay within an area identified by the Welsh Government as one of seven capable of accommodating large wind farms. There were ten dwellings near the application site. Mr Williams and his wife own one of them. They and other local residents objected.

The application did not include a proposal for the connection to the national grid. When it was made, alternative alignments for the grid connection were being considered – one running to the north, the other to the south. The choice between those two routes would depend on the route ultimately favoured by the distribution network operator, and the connection to the grid was to be the subject of a separate application, made later.

The Secretary of State made the DCO for the Clocaenog Forest Wind Farm on 12 September 2014 and the Claimant, Mr Williams, made his application for judicial review on 24 October 2014.

Three main issues were raised during the 'rolled up' permission hearing on this application, being:

- first, whether the Secretary of State ought to have regarded the 'project' as including the connection to the grid;
- secondly, whether, under regulation 6(3) of the Habitats Regulations, he was required to undertake an 'appropriate assessment' either of a larger project embracing the connection to the grid or of the project as submitted to him in combination with the grid connection; and
- thirdly, whether, if the court finds that he was required to undertake an appropriate assessment, it should nevertheless withhold relief in the exercise of its discretion.

However, following the hearing and before Lindblom J (as he then was) was able to deliver his reserved judgment, the solicitors acting for the Interested Party, who were intending to develop and operate the wind farm, wrote to the Administrative Court Office raising a jurisdictional issue; namely, that the application for judicial review had been made out of time under s 118 of the PA 2008. This jurisdictional issue arose following the decisions of Ouseley J in two applications for judicial review in relation to the Thames Tideway Tunnel DCO where the same point had arisen on almost precisely the same facts: R (oao Blue Green London Plan and oao LB Southwark) v Secretary of State for Communities and local Government and Thames Water [2015] EWHC 495 (Admin). Lindblom J invited written submissions from the parties on the jurisdictional issue before giving judgment.

DECISION

The decision of Lindblom J in this challenge deals solely with the jurisdictional issue and, having dismissed the claim on that basis, he declined to give judgment on the three issues argued at the hearing.

The jurisdictional issue related to the running of time under s 118 of the PA 2008, but in order to understand the s 118 issue it is also necessary to consider s 117.

It is important to note at the outset that the wording of s 118 has been amended since judgment was given in Blue Green London Plan, LB Southwark and Williams and those decisions would now be decided differently on their particular facts.

Section 117 of the 2008 Act, under the heading 'Orders granting development consent: formalities', provides that:

> '(1) This section applies in relation to an order granting development consent.
>
> ...
>
> (3) Except in a case within subsection (4), the Secretary of State must publish the order in such manner as the Secretary of State thinks appropriate.
>
> (4) If the order includes provision –
>
> > (a) made under section 120(3) for or relating to any of the matters listed in paragraphs 32A and 32B of Schedule 5, or
> >
> > (b) made in the exercise of any of the powers conferred by section 120(5)(a) or (b), the order must be contained in a statutory instrument.
>
> ...
>
> (6) As soon as practicable after the instrument containing the order is made, the Secretary of State must deposit in the office of the Clerk of the Parliaments a copy of –
>
> > (a) the instrument,
> >
> > (b) the latest version of any plan supplied by the applicant in connection with the application for the order contained in the instrument, and

(c) the statement of reasons prepared under section 116(1).

…'. (emphasis added)

Prior to its amendment, s 118 of the 2008 Act provided, under the heading 'Legal challenges relating to applications for orders granting development consent', that:

'(1) A court may entertain proceedings for questioning an order granting development consent only if –

(a) the proceedings are brought by a claim for judicial review, and

(b) the claim form is filed during the period of 6 weeks beginning with –

(i) the day on which the order is published, or

(ii) if later, the day on which the statement of reasons for making the order is published.

(2) A court may entertain proceedings for questioning a refusal of development consent only if –

(a) the proceedings are brought by a claim for judicial review, and

(b) the claim form is filed during the period of 6 weeks beginning with the day on which the statement of reasons for the refusal is published.

….' (emphasis added).

Thus for Mr Williams the issue was that his claim form had to be 'filed during the period of 6 weeks beginning with … the day on which the order is published' and, if the Order was published on 12 September 2014, the six weeks ran out on 23 October 2014, the day before he actually filed it.

As mentioned above, s 118 has subsequently been amended, with effect from 13 April 2015, by section 92(4) of the Criminal Justice and Courts Act 2015. The words 'before the end of' have now been substituted for the word 'during', and the words 'the day after' have been inserted after the words 'beginning with'. Corresponding amendments were also made to other parts of s 118 and, indeed, to s 13 (Legal challenges relating to NPSs).

Thus the decision in the *Williams* challenge is, to some extent, now academic. The decision is helpful, however, in identifying what is meant by the term 'published' and this remains relevant for the amended s 118. This latter point was not taken in the *London Blue Green Plan* and *LB Southwark* challenges.

As set out above, s 118(1)(b)(i) makes clear that time runs from 'the day on which the order is published' and s 117(3) provides that 'the Secretary of State must publish the order in such manner as the Secretary of State thinks appropriate'. A complicating factor, however, is that where a DCO is also a statutory instrument (as is usually the case) s 117(6) prescribes certain further formalities. Lindblom J dealt with these issues head on in his judgment, as follows:

'43. The critical question therefore is whether the Clocaenog Forest Wind Farm Order was published, within the meaning of section 118(1), on 12 September 2014.

44. In my view it was. I base that conclusion on a straightforward interpretation of the statutory formula in section 118(1)(b) of the 2008 Act – "the day on which the order is published" or, if later, "the day on which the statement of reasons for making the order is published". The words mean what they say. What they mean, in their ordinary sense, is the day on which the order, or the statement of the Secretary of State's reasons for making it, is put into the public domain. The concept of publication in this context, I think, reflects the normal meaning of the verb to "publish" – to "[make] generally known, declare or report openly; announce ..." (Shorter Oxford English Dictionary, sixth edition). The same may be said of the concept of the Secretary of State's reasons for a refusal of development consent being "published", as the parallel provision for that eventuality is framed in section 118(2)(b). Here again the focus is on the reasons for the Secretary of State's decision being made known to the general public, as well as to those members of the public particularly affected by it. The critical step, which starts the period for challenge, is the publication of the Secretary of State's reasons for his decision.

45. The way in which an order and the Secretary of State's statement of reasons for making it are to be "published" is not prescribed by section 118. But in my view the placing of the order on the Planning Inspectorate's infrastructure planning website on 12 September 2014, together with the Secretary of State's decision letter and the Examining Authority's report, and, on the same day, the notification of interested parties, both by e-mail and by post, that this had been done, was enough to constitute publication of the order, and the reasons why it was made, within the meaning of section 118. It enabled any interested party, including Mr Williams, to consider, with the benefit of legal advice, whether there were grounds for a claim for judicial review, and, if there were, to launch a challenge within the statutory period of six weeks. The fact that the Secretary of State chose to publish the order in that way but then went on to publish it in other ways as well does not mean that he failed to publish it, and his reasons for making it, on 12 September 2014. Putting both the order and the reasons on the Government's legislation.gov.uk website, producing it and sending it out in printed form, and placing notices in the London Gazette and in the local press to announce the decision were all separate and additional acts of publication. But the order and reasons had been published on 12 September 2014. This was all that was necessary to start the period within which a legal challenge to the order could be made.

46. I do not accept that the provisions of section 117 point to some other understanding of section 118. There is clearly a difference between the concept of publishing a development consent order by making it known to the public that the order has been made, and the concept of the formalities involved in the making of a statutory instrument. Section 117(3) allows the Secretary of State to publish an order granting development consent "in such manner as [he] thinks appropriate" unless the order falls within the ambit of section 117(4), in which case it "must be contained in a statutory instrument". The status

of a development consent order as a statutory instrument, if it has to be in that form, requires a particular statutory process to be followed. That process has to be followed, no matter how the Secretary of State has initially published the order and his reasons for making it. The relevant provisions of the 1946 Act and 1947 regulations lay down the procedure by which statutory instruments are to be promulgated, and provide differently for local instruments and general instruments in the formal steps required. In this case it was necessary for the development consent order to be contained in a statutory instrument. As a local instrument it was exempt from the requirements of section 2(1) of the 1946 Act. Mr Hunter does not suggest that any of the necessary formalities under the 1946 Act and 1947 regulations were neglected. But in any event the order and the Secretary of State's reasons for making it were in the public domain on 12 September 2014, and interested parties had been told on the same day that this was so. That is the crucial point.

47. If Parliament had intended to include in section 118 different concepts of a development consent order being "published" depending on whether or not it was required to be contained in a statutory instrument, I think it would have done so. Had the intention been to provide that the period for challenge would start only when a particular requirement of the 1946 Act or the 1947 regulations had been discharged, this could have been done. But it was not. I doubt that such provisions would have been conducive to clarity, certainty and consistency in the statutory regime for challenging decisions on applications for development consent orders. The fact is, however, that section 118 was not drafted in that way. And I do not think the court should imply into it provisions that Parliament did not see fit to insert.

48. The same may be said of the requirements of the 2009 regulations. If Parliament had intended the time limit in section 118 to begin on the day on which a particular requirement of regulation 23 of the 2009 regulations was satisfied – presumably the requirement in paragraph (2)(c) that the public be informed of the decision "by publication of a notice of the decision in the manner prescribed in paragraph (3)" – it could and would have done so. Again, however, it did not. And again, I see no reason to read such a provision into section 118.

49. So one is left with the simple concept of a development consent order being published on the day when the order itself and the Secretary of State's reasons for making it are made known to the public. That is how section 118(1)(b) of the 2008 Act should be understood.'

Thus to 'publish' a DCO for the purposes of s 118, it is sufficient for the Secretary of State to place the Order on the Planning Inspectorate's website.

Mr William's claim was, therefore, dismissed for want of jurisdiction.

Case Summary

Written by Michael Humphries QC, ftb

R (oao BLUE GREEN LONDON PLAN and oao LB SOUTHWARK) v SECRETARY OF STATE FOR COMMUNITIES AND LOCAL GOVERNMENT and SECRETARY OF STATE FOR ENVIRONMENT, FOOD AND RURAL AFFAIRS

[2015] EWHC 495 (Admin)

High Court

Ouseley J

Judgment: 15 January 2015

On appeal by Blue Green London Plan only:

[2015] EWCA Civ 876

Court of Appeal

Sales LJ

Judgment: 24 June 2015

[NB The High Court made an order releasing its judgment in this application from the general prohibition on citing permission judgments: Practice Direction (Citation of Authorities) [2001] 1WLR 1001.]

[NB In the Court of Appeal this appeal was considered at the same hearing as that brought by Thames Blue Green Economy Limited as they were challenges to the same DCO. They were, however, separate challenges, despite similarities in the Applicants' names.]

BACKGROUND

On 12 September 2014 the Secretaries of State for Communities and Local Government and for Environment, Food And Rural Affairs made and published the Thames Water Utilities Limited (Thames Tideway Tunnel) Order 2014. A number of challenges were brought, including those by a Mr Stevens, in person on behalf of Blue Green London Plan, and by the London Borough of Southwark ('the Applicants'). Thames Water Utilities Limited was an interested party in both claims and appeared at the hearing.

The Applicants filed their claims on 24 October 2014. The Secretaries of State and the interested party said that the last day for filing was 23 October 2014. The question then arose at the permission hearing as to whether the Court had jurisdiction to hear the claims. This had to be determined before the Court could, if it had jurisdiction, consider the substantive merits of the claims.

[NB The effect of this decision has now been reversed by amendments to s 118 of the PA 2008 made by the Criminal Justice and Courts Act 2015.]

DECISION

The relevant statutory provision of the PA 2008 for bringing a claim against the making of a DCO is s 118, which (at the time of these applications) provided that:

> '(1) A court may entertain proceedings for questioning an order granting development consent only if
>
> (a) the proceedings are brought by a claim for judicial review, and
>
> (b) the claim form is filed during the period of six weeks beginning with:
>
> (i) the day on which the order is published …' (emphasis added)

The High Court (Ouseley J) observed that there are three parts to this formulation. First, that the court is able to 'entertain' proceedings only if those proceedings are brought as required and that that language was only apt to create a jurisdictional bar to a claim that does not meet the requirements. Second, that the proceedings are to be brought by a claim for judicial review. Third, that there is a statutory time limit of six weeks.

The first issue was the starting point of that six weeks time limit. On this point, Ouseley J held that:

> '15 [Counsel for LB Southwark] submits that the claim form was filed during the period of six weeks beginning with the day on which the order was published, because the wording, "six weeks beginning with", is the same as, "six weeks beginning after" that day.
>
> 16 In my judgment, it is perfectly clear that, as a matter of ordinary statutory construction, a period of six weeks beginning with the day on which an event occurred includes the day on which the event occurred.
>
> 17 I reach that conclusion by reference to clear authority, although, as [Counsel for LB Southwark] says, none of them directly deal with Section 118 itself, but with statutory wording in cognate fields.
>
> 18 I start with the decision of the Court of Appeal in Okolo v Secretary of State for the Environment and another [1997] 4 AER 242 . The court had to construe Section 23(4) of the Acquisition of Land Act 1981, which provided that:
>
> "An application to the High Court under this section shall be made within six weeks … from the date on which notice of the confirmation or making of the order is first published in accordance with this Act."
>
> 19 The Court of Appeal, see page 246 letters C to D per Lord Justice Schiemann, regarded it as manifest that the counting of the period of six weeks, or 42 days, started on the day after the order was published. That is what was meant by six weeks "from the date" on which the notice was published. That is, of course, different from the statutory language with which I am concerned.

20 The distinction is borne out by two other decisions. The first is the decision in Hinde v Rugby Borough Council [2011] EWHC 3684 Admin, in which Mr David Elvin QC, sitting as a Deputy High Court Judge, had to construe the provisions of Section 113 of the Planning and Compulsory Purchase Act 2004. This provided, in relation to a development plan document, that an application to the High Court:

> "Must be made not later than the end of the period of six weeks starting with the relevant date."

> 21 The Deputy Judge drew attention to the distinction between the language of "starting with" in Section 113 of the 2004 Act and the language of Section 23(4) of the 1981 Act, "from the date".
>
> 22 He rejected a number of other arguments which found echoes in those of [Counsel for LB Southwark] here. He said in paragraph 10 that if he were to approach that section without authority, he would have had no hesitation in accepting the submissions by counsel on behalf of the interested party that Section 111 clearly required the calculation of six weeks to start with, that is include, the date of adoption. He also took the view it was clear that time could not be extended. He elaborated his reasoning.
>
> 23 I draw particular attention to that, because in the next case to which I refer, *Barker v Hambleton District Council [2012] EWCA Civ 610, the Court of Appeal* specifically found itself in "complete agreement with the judgment of the Deputy Judge in Hinde". In that case, the Court of Appeal again had to consider Section 113 of the 2004 Act.
>
> 24 Having commented on the clarity and incisiveness of Mr Elvin's judgment, the Court of Appeal considered arguments advanced by [Counsel] on behalf of the claimant in that case, which again were echoed by some of [Counsel for LB Southwark's] submissions.
>
> 25 I note at the end of paragraph 12 that the Court of Appeal, through Lord Justice Maurice Kay, specifically drew attention to the contrast between the language of some Acts in the planning sphere, which use the words "from the relevant date" and those at Section 113 which use the words "starting with". He said, after referring to Okolo:

> "However, Section 113 of the Planning and Compulsory Purchase Act 2004 expressly departed from that model. 'Starting with' is not the same as the word 'from' and I can see no basis for any kind of presumption that, in using different language, Parliament was intending it to mean precisely the same as the discarded language."

. . .

31 It is accordingly clear that there is a distinction to be drawn — a vital distinction — between how one interprets and applies a period starting with the date of the event and how one applies a period which commences from or after the date on which an event occurs.

32 [Counsel for LB Southwark] submitted, however, that the effect of Section 118(1)(a) was to bring about a different result from that which applied in cases where there was a statutory appeal. That was because it was required that challenges be brought by judicial review. It was Section 31 of the Senior Courts Act 1981 which thus had to be examined. This provides:

> "1) An application to the High Court for one or more of the following forms of relief, namely (a) a mandatory, prohibiting or quashing order … shall be made in accordance with the rules of the court by a procedure to be known as an application for judicial review."

33 It was contended from that that the language of Section 31(4) imported the requirement that the application be made in accordance with the rules of court. That meant that one was entitled to look and see what the language of the rules of court were and how they had been interpreted.

34 CPR 54.5 deals with the time limit for filing claim forms. 54.5.1 provides that the claim form must be filed (a) promptly and (b) in any event not later than three months after the grounds to make the claim first arose. I emphasise that, in the enactment of the CPR, the language chosen was "after the grounds".

35 [Counsel for LB Southwark] rightly points out that that has been interpreted by the *Court of Appeal in R (Berky) v Newport City Council [2012] EWCA Civ 378 [2012] 2 CMLR 44* as excluding the day on which grounds first arose. This is made clear in the judgment of Lord Justice Carnwath at page 32 and of Lord Justice Moore-Bick at 40, paragraph 48, who said that the natural meaning of the expression "not later than three months after the grounds to make the claim first arose" is that the three months begins to run on the day after the grounds first arose.

36 It is to be noted that the Court of Appeal was construing a rule the language of which is akin to the language of Okolo, and not a rule the language of which was akin to that in Hinde and Barker.

37 There is no surprise that it should have reached the conclusion it did about what that rule meant. But that does not mean that the different words of Section 118(1) should be construed as if they were the words of Section 23(4) of the Acquisition of Land Act. Nothing in the decision in Berky could sensibly be seen as diminishing the effect of the decision in Barker as to what the words "beginning with" by contrast to the language of CPR 54.5actually meant.

38 I am not clear, I have to accept, that the decision in Berky was cited in Barker, coming as it did, it appears, but a few days before. At all events, there is no conflict at all between those two lines of authority, construing, as they are, different statutory provisions which have a clearly different natural meaning.

39 It therefore avails [Counsel for LB Southwark] nothing to refer to this claim having to be brought by way of judicial review, incorporating Section 31(1), in accordance with the rules, to say that the natural meaning should be given a completely different meaning and that by using the words "beginning with" Parliament must be taken to have meant "after".

40 I should just add as well that it seems to me that her argument must fall foul of the provisions of Part 54.5.3, which says that Rule 54.5 does not apply when any other enactment specifies a shorter time limit for making the claim for judicial review. It is perfectly clear that Section 118 does indeed provide for a shorter time limit. Not merely does it do so by providing six weeks rather than three months, but by shortening the period from when the six weeks runs.

41 For the sake of completeness I should just note that this is not a claim that falls under CPR 54.5.5, because the 2008 Act is not one of the Planning Acts as defined by Section 336 of the Town and Country Planning Act 1990, which is what the Planning Act means in 54.5.5.'

This on the first issue – the starting point of the six weeks time limit – it is clear that the works "beginning with (i) the day on which the order is published" includes that day. On that basis, time ran out on 23 October 2014 and the Applicants' claims were out of time. As noted above, the effect of this decision has now been reversed by the Criminal Justice and Courts Act 2015, which has amended s 118 to read:

'(1) A court may entertain proceedings for questioning an order granting development consent only if—

(a) the proceedings are brought by a claim for judicial review, and

(b) the claim form is filed [before the end of] the period of 6 weeks beginning with [the day after] —

(i) the day on which the order is published ...'

On this formulation of s 118 time would have ended on 24 October 2014 and the Applicants' claims would have just been in time.

The second issue that arose was whether the Court had power to extend time.

On this issue Ouseley J held that:

'43 In my judgment, there is no power to extend time. Plainly, Section 118 contains no such power. Indeed, the jurisdictional language of its opening phrases shows that such a power is rather unlikely to be found. There are no provisions that assist [Counsel for LB Southwark] in this argument. She referred to Section 31(1) of the Senior Courts Act but that does not itself contain a power to extend time.

44 It would have to be argued that the reference in Section 31(1) to an application being made in accordance with the rules of court by a procedure to be known as an application for judicial review, incorporated more general powers within the rules of court for the extension of time. But it clearly does not do so. CPR 54.5.3 clearly precludes the operation of the longer time limits. CPR 3.1 cannot help, because that provides that, except where these rules provide otherwise, the court may extend or shorten the time for compliance with any rule, practice direction or court order. It gives it no power to extend, or indeed, for that matter, to shorten a time limit set out by statute.

45 It is perfectly clear from the decision of the House of Lords in Mucelli, and the Supreme Court in Pomiechowski, that the language of giving

notice of appeal in accordance with the rules of court did not suffice to bring into that Act, the Extradition Act 2003, the power to extend time. If ever an Act were to do so it would have been the Extradition Act 2003, with its engagement of human rights considerations and extremely short time available for the giving of notices of appeal, often by unrepresented people in custody. But it was held on two occasions in those two cases that, in reality, there was no such power to be given to the language of in accordance with the rules of court.

46 That must apply to the position here. As I say, in principle, the language of Section 118 is inconsistent with giving Section 31 any such effect in this area.

47 Accordingly, I conclude that these two applications were out of time and that there is no power to extend time. …'

Thus the Court held clearly that there is no power to extend the statutory six weeks time limit in s 118. This point remains important, even in the context of the amended s 118.

Mr Stevens, on behalf of Blue Green London Plan, sought permission to appeal this decision in the Court of Appeal. In that Court, Sales LJ held that:

'27 So far as the judge's interpretation of section 118 is concerned (by which the judge determined that the 6-week period had to, as the statute says, be treated as commencing on the day on which the order was published, namely 12 September 2014), I do not consider that Mr Stevens has any real prospects of success on appeal. In my view, as a matter of interpretation of the statute, the judge was plainly right in the interpretation that he gave to the Act.'

Permission to appeal was, therefore, refused.

Case Summary

Written by Michael Humphries QC, ftb

R (oao THAMES BLUE GREEN ECONOMY LIMITED) v SECRETARY OF STATE FOR COMMUNITIES AND LOCAL GOVERNMENT and SECRETARY OF STATE FOR ENVIRONMENT, FOOD AND RURAL AFFAIRS

[2015] EWHC 727 (Admin)

High Court

Ouseley J

Judgment: 16 January 2015

On appeal by Thames Blue Green Economy Limited:

[2015] EWCA Civ 876

Court of Appeal

Sales LJ

Judgment: 24 June 2015

[NB The transcript of the High Court decision in this application is not widely available, despite the Court making an order releasing the judgement from the general prohibition on citing permission judgements: *Practice Direction (Citation of Authorities)* [2001] 1WLR 1001.]

[NB In the Court of Appeal this appeal was considered at the same hearing as that brought by Blue Green London Plan as they were challenges to the same DCO. They were, however, separate challenges, despite similarities in the Applicants' names.]

BACKGROUND

On 12 September 2014 the Secretaries of State for Communities and Local Government and for Environment, Food and Rural Affairs made and published the Thames Water Utilities Limited (Thames Tideway Tunnel) Order 2014. A number of challenges were brought, including that by Thames Blue Green Economy Ltd. Thames Water Utilities Limited was an interested party in the claim and appeared at the hearing.

At the examination into the Thames Tideway Tunnel DCO a group known as Thamesbank and, later, Thames Blue Green Economy (which became incorporated as Thames Blue Green Economy Limited during the High Court proceedings) objected to the Thames Tideway Tunnel project on the grounds, amongst others, that a tunnel was the wrong solution to the problem of waste water pollution in the River Thames and that 'blue-green' solutions, such as sustainable urban drainage ('SUDs'), should be preferred instead.

The process leading to the designation of the National Policy Statement for Waste Water ('the NPS') had considered various strategic alternative solutions for dealing with problems of waste water pollution in the River Thames. The NPS set out its conclusions on the need for waste water infrastructure to resolve these problems and then considered, in some detail, the various alternative solutions considered.

At paragraph 2.6.34 it stated that:

> 'The examining authority and the decision maker should undertake any assessment of an application for the development of the Thames Tunnel on the basis that the national need for this infrastructure has been demonstrated. The appropriate strategic alternatives to a tunnel have been considered and it has been concluded that it is the only option to address the problem of discharging unacceptable levels of untreated sewage into the River Thames within a reasonable time at a reasonable cost.'

And at paragraph 3.4.1 it also concluded that:

> 'Part 2 of this NPS provides an overview of the strategic alternatives both to the general nationally significant need for waste water infrastructure and to the project-specific need for the Thames Tunnel … These strategic alternatives do not need to be assessed by the examining authority or the decision maker.'

This policy position in the NPS has to be seen in the context of the provisions of s 104, which provide that:

> '(2) In deciding the application the Secretary of State must have regard to
>
> - (a) any national policy statement …
> - (b) any local impact report …
> - … and
> - (d) any other matters which the Secretary of State thinks are both important and relevant to the Secretary of State's decision.
>
> (3) <u>The Secretary of State must decide the application [for an order granting development consent] in accordance with any relevant national policy statement, except to the extent that one or more of sub-sections (4) to (8) applies.</u>
>
> …
>
> (7) This sub-section applies if the Secretary of State is satisfied that <u>the adverse impact of the proposed development would outweigh its benefits</u>.' (emphasis added)

In this context, the Examining Authority took the decision that it would not entertain representations that challenged the 'tunnel' solution that had been identified in the NPS. In granting development consent, the Secretaries of State did not demure from the Examining Authority's position on this point and made it clear that they had relied on the NPS.

In relation to the disregarding of material, s 87 of the PA 2008 provides that:

> '(1) It is for the Examining authority to decide how to examine the application.

(2) [that] in making any decision about [that it must] — comply with —

(i) the following provisions of this Chapter …..

…

(3) The Examining authority may in examining the application disregard representations if the Examining authority considers that the representations

(a) are vexatious or frivolous,

(b) relate to the merits of policy set out in a national policy statement, or

(c) relate to compensation for compulsory acquisition of land or of an interest in or right over land.'

(emphasis added)

Section 106 sets out a similar provision in respect the disregard of material for the Secretary of State's decision making.

Thames Blue Green Economy Limited's application for permission to bring judicial review proceedings was first refused on the papers and the hearing before Ouseley J was, therefore, a renewed oral application.

Before the High Court the Applicant advanced two principal arguments being:

1 that the Examining Authority had a discretion to exclude material under s 87, but had failed to exercise that discretion because it had wrongly concluded that it was bound to exclude the representations that Thames Blue Green Economy Limited had put forward and, furthermore, that s 104 required such material to be considered; and

2 that the Examining Authority's approach was not consistent with the Environmental Impact Assessment Directive and, in particular, Articles 6.4 and 7.

Ground 1 – the discretion to exclude material

In the High Court, Ouseley J focused first on the s 87 argument:

'31. I turn to the submission which initially focussed on Section 87(3) but needs, in reality, to focus on Section 104(7) as well. It was not disputed but that Section 87 (3) created a discretion through the use of the word "may" in contrast with the use of the word "must" in Section 87(2) for the examining authority to have regard to representations falling within either (a) or (b) or (c), that is to say vexatious ones, ones relating to the merits of policy and those relating to the compensation for compulsory acquisition. The gravamen of [Counsel for Thames Blue Green Economy Limited]'s submissions was that the procedural decision and the elaboration in the examining authority's report, its reasoning not being dissented from by the Secretary of State and stated to be his reasoning as well, showed that in reality no discretion had been exercised at all. The panel had considered itself obliged to ignore the representations which Thamesbank wished to put forward. That, submitted [Counsel for Thames Blue Green Economy Limited], is the only conclusion which should be drawn or at least was a conclusion which arguably could be drawn in the last sentence of paragraph 16.25 of their report.

32. In my judgment it is perfectly obvious that the panel considered what Thamesbank asked them to consider and reached a decision that they would disregard it under Section 87(3)(b) as it was judged by them to relate to the merits of policy set out in a NPS. Indeed, that conclusion is inevitable. That is exactly what the purpose of the representations was. It was to persuade the examining authority to recommend and the Secretary of State then to accept a recommendation that the tunnel scheme should be refused in favour of an unspecified but preferable project for an alternative strategy for dealing with the problems.

33. The gravamen, as the case was analysed, was whether this was a lawful approach having regard to Section 104(7). It is clear to my mind that that is where the focus of the argument has to lie. It was not disputed by [Counsel for Thames Blue Green Economy Limited] that because the Secretaries of State were obliged by Section 104(3) to decide the development consent application in accordance with any relevant national policy statement, unless an exception applied, the material which Thamesbank had disregarded could only be relevant to the decision and hence to the examining authority's consideration if it fell within one of the exceptions to Section 104(3), in this case if it fell within Section 104(7). There was absolutely no point - and this is really what the panel are saying – in exercising their discretion to admit material which is irrelevant. And there can be no complaint about a discretion being exercised to refuse to admit irrelevant material, and it is material that would be irrelevant because it would fall outside the scope of any decision which the Secretary of State would make.

34. That of course does not remove all scope from Section 87(3) for a discretion which might be exercised. As [Counsel], for Thames Water Utilities Ltd, points out, the words "relate to the merits of policy" are wider than those which might lawfully require a decision under Section 104(3) which was not in accordance with the relevant NPS. I am satisfied that it is clear beyond argument that there is no breach of Section 87(3) unless the evidence could be admitted lawfully to reach a decision not in accordance with the NPS by virtue of Section 104(7).'

Thus Ouseley J accepted that it was right for the Examining Authority to disregard material under s 87(3) where they considered that it challenged the merits of Government policy, subject to the all important question as to whether they were obliged to have regard to that same material because of the terms of s 104 and, in particular, the combination of s 104(3) and s 104(7).

Ouseley J dealt with this issue in the following passage:

37. … Section 104 deals with the decision on a particular project for which a Development Consent Order has been applied for. Section

104(3) requires the decision to be made in accordance with the NPS. No decision for a non-tunnel scheme, no decision rejecting a tunnel scheme on the grounds that a non-tunnel scheme might be better could possibly come within the scope of Section 104(3). It is a forbidden decision. It is a forbidden decision unless it comes within an exception, and Section 104(7) is the only provision. However it needs to be clear that the ability to reach a decision that is not in accordance with any relevant NPS only applies once the Secretary of State "is satisfied that the adverse impact of the proposed development would outweigh its benefits". It is not a provision which enables the Secretary of State to consider alternatives in order to reach a decision that the adverse impact of the proposed development would outweigh its benefits.

38. The natural meaning of the language of Section 104(7) is that the adverse impact of the development proposed in the Development Consent Order must first be shown to outweigh the benefits of the project applied for in the development consent. It neither adds to the adverse impact nor detracts from it, nor does it add to or detract from its benefits that some different scheme might be thought to have greater benefits or lesser impact. It is clear that that does not mean that there is an obligation to grant a development consent regardless of the overall balance because one might outweigh the other and, indeed, particular features might be too objectionable to enable development consent to be granted or would require variation. But it is important that that conclusion be set in the context of this Act.

39. The question of strategic alternatives that are not in accordance with the NPS is decided first through the process of developing and then designating a NPS. That process involves strategic environmental assessment of the project, of its nature, Parliamentary consideration and public participation through those processes. It involves the conclusion through that that the tunnel is the correct solution and that no strategic alternative is better. That issue is not to be revisited.

40. It is perfectly clear that this is a conscious, deliberate two-stage way of dealing with the problem of public participation both in the policy and in the detail of development consent and avoiding the problem of deciding both detail and what government policy should be and what strategic alternatives need to be considered at the same time. It was well known by the time the 1998 Act was passed, particularly from the Heathrow Terminal 5 Inquiry, that leaving government policy and strategic alternatives and detail to be resolved all at the same time meant that infrastructure planning took a wholly inordinate length of time in the views of those who passed this Act. It was to come to a different way of dealing with, first, strategic policy considerations, what was government policy to be and then, with development consent process, adjusting the normal planning process that was required.

41. [Counsel for Thames Blue Green Economy Limited]'s submissions prayed in aid a conventional planning argument that where a proposal does harm it will be relevant to the consideration of its merits to

consider whether or not there is an alternative way of achieving the same ends with a lesser impact somewhere else. That is a conventional planning approach which has become familiar over the years, never mind for the moment precisely what level of harm has to be shown before consideration of alternatives becomes permissible.

42. That is not the process which Parliament has set out in the 2008 Act for dealing with nationally significant infrastructure projects. The process is perfectly clear. First of all, the strategic nature of what is required to meet the needs is considered. It is considered with the benefit of the strategic environmental assessment, sustainability appraisal, public participation and Parliamentary designation. It is part of the procedure that those decisions are not then revisited. Section 87(3), Section 106 and, more particularly, Section 107(3) and (7) [sic – should be s 104(3) and (7)] are designed to make a two-stage process effective. It is designed to avoid it being said by those who participate at the development consent stage that the examining authority and Secretaries of State are obliged to go back and consider what ought to have been the position in the NPS when it has already been through all the procedures through which it has been.

43. Accordingly, I am entirely satisfied that the Secretary of State could not, conformably with his duties, have taken account of the Thamesbank strategic tunnel development to reach a decision not in accordance with a NPS. It would have been irrelevant for the panel to have considered that material and it was entitled to refuse to do so, in my judgment, exercising its discretion in the only way it was possible for it rationally to be exercised.'

This passage is important in a number of respect, including the reminder at paragraphs 41 / 42 that 'conventional' planning arguments relating to alternatives where a 'need' case is advanced do not fit within the process which Parliament set out in the PA 2008 for dealing with nationally significant infrastructure projects. As paragraph 38 makes clear, s 104(3) requires a decision to be taken in accordance with a relevant NPS unless the adverse impacts of <u>that</u> development outweighs its benefits; and it neither adds to or detracts from the benefits / impacts of that project that some other project may have greater or lesser benefits or impacts. This is of considerable importance in understanding the proper approach to alternatives under s 104.

Ouseley J refused permission on Ground 1.

In the Court of Appeal Sales LJ said (para 12) that he "agreed with the reasoning of the judge" and with the reasoning on Sullivan LJ, who had refused permission on the paper application to the Court of Appeal, and made it clear that the argument on section 104(7) and section 87(3) of the Act did not have any real prospect of success. He refused permission.

Sales LJ also made clear (para 14) that if some new circumstances did arise after the designation of an NPS, then the 2008 Act had a mechanism (PA 2008, s 6) for the review of that NPS and it would be open to someone to approach the Secretary of State to request such a review. That, he considered, would be the proper way in which such matters should be taken into account.

Ground 2 – Environmental Impact Assessment Directive
This ground argued that, amongst other things, that as Article 6.4 of the EAI Directive said that "The public concerned shall be given early and effective opportunities to particulate in environmental decision making" and that for that purpose they shall "be entitled to express comments and opinions when all options are open to the competent authority" before the decision is taken, then that meant that Thames Blue Green Economy Limited was entitled under the Directive to have made representations to the Examining Authority on the Thames Tideway Tunnel DCO about non-tunnel solutions to the problem of waste water pollution in the River Thames.

Ouseley J deal with this ground, as follows:

> '45. … Article 5 of Directive 2011/92 EU on the assessment of the effects on certain public and private projects on the environment reads:
>
> "1 In the case of projects which … are to be made subject to an environmental impact assessment in accordance with this Article and Articles 6 to 10, Member States shall adopt the necessary measures to ensure that the … [appropriate information is supplied in the appropriate form]."
>
> Article 6 deals with the content, including the way content of information is supplied and how it is made available to the public concerned. It says, amongst other matters:
>
> "6.4 The public concerned shall be given early and effective opportunities to participate in the environmental decision-making procedures referred to in Article 2 (2) and shall, for that purpose, be entitled to express comments and opinions when all options are open to the competent authority or authorities before the decision on the request for development consent is taken."
>
> Article 8 provides:
>
> "The results of consultations and the information gathered pursuant to Articles ….. 6 ….. shall be taken into consideration in the development consent procedure."
>
> 46. It is contended that Article 6.4 and in particular the reference to expressing opinions "when all options are open" means that the Secretaries of State were obliged to keep open non-strategic alternatives because they would be options within the meaning of Article 6.4. And if the interpretation which I have regarded as obviously correct is right, then that contravenes the Directive's provisions in Article 6.4. In my judgment that is completely misconceived. Article 6.4 with reference to options is not dealing with the entitlement to raise strategic alternatives in relation to project consent. The Directive usually deals expressly with those alternatives which they require to be considered. "Options" does not mean alternatives.
>
> 47. What it is seeking to emphasise, particularly in the context of Article 6 read as a whole, is the stage in the decision-making process at which the environmental information has to be available for comment, that is to say it has to be made available when the decision to grant or refuse,

and the conditions and terms of the grant or refusal, remain open, and are not closed.

48. The second point I make is that the Directive has to be understood in the context of the sort of decision with which it is concerned. It is concerned with Development Consent Orders amongst others. It is not requisite for the applicant to set out alternatives of a different nature to show that they had been considered. There is no such obligation in relation to project development consent. There is an obligation however to do that in relation to strategic environmental assessment. It cannot be the case that through the use of the word "options" the EIA was intending to impose a requirement to consider - by that side wind - that which expressly is not required in the content of the information for the benefit of the public or the decision-maker, but yet is expressly required in the consideration of a plan or programme.

49. The European Union must be taken to have understood that it had made a strategic environmental assessment directive to deal with plans or programmes which set the framework for decisions or would influence them as a matter of law in just the way that the NPS does. It cannot have envisaged that all that process would be undertaken again through the use of the word "options" in an environmental impact assessment directive.

50. It must be remembered that the Strategic Environmental Assessment Directive was introduced to deal with this mischief: by the time projects - which is what the EIA is concerned with - came to be considered, the pass would often have been sold by a prior plan or programme which could not be considered in the EIA. It was in recognition of that limitation that Strategic Environmental Assessment was introduced. It was not to take over the domestic decision-making process so long as that decision-making process has enabled both the plan and programme to be considered for SEA purposes and has enabled the project to be considered for EIA. Both those requirements are satisfied.

51. I have no doubt that that submission is wrong.

52. I would finally say in relation to Article 8 that it is clear that the environmental information to be taken into account is only that which is material to the decision to be made, and the possible existence of strategic alternatives which the environmental assessment itself has not covered, are entirely outwith its scope for these purposes.'

Thus two points are made. First, that when Article 6.4 refers to being able to participate when 'options' are open, it is not referring to 'alternatives' to the project, but the options to grant or refuse an application and, indeed, options relating to the conditions and terms of the grant or refusal. Secondly, that in using the term 'options', the EIA Directive cannot have intended that decisions on strategic alternatives that were the subject matter of Strategic Environmental Assessment ('SEA') can be revisited at the development consent stage.

In the Court of Appeal, Sales LJ relied on the refusal by Sullivan LJ of the paper application to the Court of Appeal. Sullivan LJ had said that:

> 'The second ground of appeal ignores the role of the Strategic Environmental Impact Assessment Directive. The 'options' that are still open at the EIA stage may well have been narrowed by the consideration and rejection of alternatives to the project under an SEA. Ground 2 effectively argues that alternatives which have been rejected at the SEA stage must be reconsidered at the EIA stage because 'all options' must be left open. Construing those words in the EIA Directive in isolation and in a literal manner is not a sensible interpretation of the EIA Directive in a context which includes the SEA Directive. The two Directives are intended to compliment, not duplicate, each other.'

Sales LJ considered that permission should be refused on this ground also for essentially the same reason.

Again, this reinforces the importance for the consideration of alternatives of the two-stage process that is inherent in SEA followed by EIA.

Case Summary

Written by Michael Humphries QC, ftb

R (oao SCARISBRICK) v SECRETARY OF STATE FOR COMMUNITIES AND LOCAL GOVERNMENT and WHITEMOSS LANDFILL LTD

[2016] EWHC 715 (Admin)

High Court

Cranston J

Judgment: 16 February 2016

BACKGROUND

This was an application for permission to bring a claim for judicial review under s 118 in relation to the White Moss Landfill Order 2015. The DCO had granted development consent for development and the compulsory acquisition of land at White Moss Landfill Ltd's (the interested party) existing site at Whitemoss for hazardous waste landfill.

The ground pursued at the oral permission hearing centred on the issue of 'need' and how this had been treated by the Examining Authority and the Secretary of State. The need for hazardous waste facilities is covered by the National Policy Statement for Hazardous Waste, published in 2013.

DECISION

Counsel for the Applicant (Scarisbrick) contended that it was arguable that in approving this site, the Examining Authority and the Secretary of State had misdirected themselves as to the meaning and requirements of the NPS and that they unlawfully failed to assess whether there was a need for the capacity that this landfill site will provide. He submitted that it was arguable that the 'accepted' or 'demonstrated' need in the NPS was the need for this type of facility; as he put it, a need at the strategic level, not whether there was a need for any particular hazardous waste facility, and certainly not for this proposed hazardous waste facility, for which the Interested Party had sought permission. In other words, he argued that whilst the NPS forecloses consideration of the principle of hazardous waste landfills, it should not be interpreted as prescribing the need for any particular hazardous waste facility, however large. In this context, Counsel for the Applicant argued that the 'need' established in the NPS could not be relied on in considering site specific issues such as green belt and compulsory purchase, and that it was inconsistent with the Habitats Directive.

Cranston J dealt with this issue as follows:

> '29 In my view, the wording of the NPS is clear, in particular the final sentence of the summary section 3.1: in other words, an application is to be assessed on the basis that need has been demonstrated. Thus

an assessment of need is not required in the context of any particular application which exceeds the threshold. In my view, there is no question but that this reading is supported by other passages in the NPS, such as paragraph 3.4.14, namely that the Examining Authority should examine applications for infrastructure covered by the NPS on the basis that need has been demonstrated. There is no support for reading these passages as meaning that the NPS is recognising a general strategic need for relevant infrastructure but requiring an assessment of need in an individual case. If the NPS had intended this it would have said so. As to the policy arguments, other parts of the NPS set out the rationale as to why need is to be assumed. The overall amount of hazardous waste will continue to be significant, it says, despite economic downturns and other factors, and landfill facilities, although they should be a last resort, will continue to have a place. There is also the reference to the time limits on existing planning consents for landfill sites and thus the need for new capacity.

30 In my view, the other arguments which Mr Wolfe advanced do not lead to a contrary conclusion. He invoked the 2010 Strategy but, as the NPS suggests, events to some extent have moved on from the position stated there. Moreover, the NPS states explicitly that it prevails over the documents. There is no basis for suggesting an incompatibility with the Habitats Directive, Green Belt policy, the statutory provisions for compulsory acquisitions or the ECHR. For example, in the case where a particular proposal for infrastructure has an impact on a European site so as to require imperative reasons of overriding public interest (the Habitats Directive point), need might be relevant to the existence of such imperative reasons, but it would not of itself establish such reasons without further assessment nor create any presumption that the IROPI test is met. Similarly with Green Belt, need is taken into account, as the Examining Authority did but, as [Counsel for the Secretary of State] in my view correctly put it, does not act as a trump card. So, in this case, the NPS establishes need, that is a material planning consideration and the Examining Authority took it into account, along with other factors, giving it considerable weight.'

On this basis permission for bring a claim for judicial review was refused.

This decision is a helpful re-affirmation of the important role played by NPSs in the establishment of need in the PA 2008 regime.

Appendix

Planning Act 2008

Planning Act 2008 c. 29

An Act to establish the Infrastructure Planning Commission and make provision about its functions; to make provision about, and about matters ancillary to, the authorisation of projects for the development of nationally significant infrastructure; to make provision about town and country planning; to make provision about the imposition of a Community Infrastructure Levy; and for connected purposes.

[26th November 2008]

BE IT ENACTED by the Queen's most Excellent Majesty, by and with the advice and consent of the Lords Spiritual and Temporal, and Commons, in this present Parliament assembled, and by the authority of the same, as follows:—

Part 1 [Infrastructure planning: fees][1]

1–3 …

Repealed by Localism Act 2011, ss 128(2), 237, Sch 13, paras 1, 2, Sch 25, Pt 20 as from 1 April 2012.

1 Words substituted by Localism Act 2011, s 128(2), Sch 13, paras 1, 3(1), (5) (15 January 2012 for the purpose of conferring power on the Secretary of State to make regulations or rules; 1 April 2012 otherwise).

4 Fees

(1) The Secretary of State may make regulations providing for the [charging of fees by the Secretary of State in connection with the performance of any of the Secretary of State's major-infrastructure functions][1].

(2) Regulations under subsection (1) may in particular make provision—

(a) about when a fee (including a supplementary fee) may, and may not, be charged;

(b) about the amount which may be charged;

(c) about what may, and may not, be taken into account in calculating the amount charged;

(d) about who is liable to pay a fee charged;

(e) about when a fee charged is payable;

(f) about the recovery of fees charged;

(g) about waiver, reduction or repayment of fees;

(h) about the effect of paying or failing to pay fees charged;

(i) for the supply of information for any purpose of the regulations.

(3) The regulations may provide for the amounts of fees to be calculated by reference to costs [incurred by the Secretary of State][2]—

(a) in the performance of any of [the Secretary of State's major-infrastructure functions][3], and

(b) in doing anything which is calculated to facilitate, or is conducive or incidental to, the performance of any of [the Secretary of State's major-infrastructure functions][3].

[(4) In this section 'the Secretary of State's major-infrastructure functions' means—

(a) the Secretary of State's functions under Parts 2 to 8 and under Part 12 so far as applying for the purposes of those Parts,

(b) the giving of advice to which section 51 applies, and

(c) the Secretary of State's functions, in relation to proposed applications for orders granting development consent, under statutory provisions implementing—

(i) Council Directive 85/337/EC on the assessment of the effects of certain public and private projects on the environment, as amended from time to time, or

(ii) provisions of an EU instrument which from time to time replace provisions of that Directive.

(5) In subsection (4)(c) 'statutory provision' means a provision of an Act or of an instrument made under an Act.][4]

1 Words substituted by Localism Act 2011, s 128(2), Sch 13, paras 1, 3(1), (2) (15 January 2012 for the purpose of conferring power on the Secretary of State to make regulations or rules; 1 April 2012 otherwise).
2 Words substituted by Localism Act 2011, s 128(2), Sch 13, paras 1, 3(1), (3)(a) (15 January 2012 for the purpose of conferring power on the Secretary of State to make regulations or rules; 1 April 2012 otherwise).
3 Words substituted by Localism Act 2011, s 128(2), Sch 13, paras 1, 3(1), (3)(b) (15 January 2012 for the purpose of conferring power on the Secretary of State to make regulations or rules; 1 April 2012 otherwise).
4 Added by Localism Act 2011, s 128(2), Sch 13, paras 1, 3(1), (4) (15 January 2012 for the purpose of conferring power on the Secretary of State to make regulations or rules; 1 April 2012 otherwise).

Part 2 National policy statements

5 National policy statements

(1) The Secretary of State may designate a statement as a national policy statement for the purposes of this Act if the statement—

(a) is issued by the Secretary of State, and

(b) sets out national policy in relation to one or more specified descriptions of development.

(2) In this Act 'national policy statement' means a statement designated under subsection (1) as a national policy statement for the purposes of this Act.

(3) Before designating a statement as a national policy statement for the purposes of this Act the Secretary of State must carry out an appraisal of the sustainability of the policy set out in the statement.

(4) A statement may be designated as a national policy statement for the purposes of this Act only if the consultation and publicity requirements set out in section 7, and the parliamentary requirements set out in section 9, have been complied with in relation to it [and—][1]

[(a) the consideration period for the statement has expired without the House of Commons resolving during that period that the statement should not be proceeded with, or

(b) the statement has been approved by resolution of the House of Commons—

(i) after being laid before Parliament under section 9(8), and

(ii) before the end of the consideration period.][1]

[(4A) In subsection (4) 'the consideration period', in relation to a statement, means the period of 21 sitting days beginning with the first sitting day after the day on which the statement is laid before Parliament under section 9(8), and here 'sitting day' means a day on which the House of Commons sits.][2]

(5) The policy set out in a national policy statement may in particular—

(a) set out, in relation to a specified description of development, the amount, type or size of development of that description which is appropriate nationally or for a specified area;

(b) set out criteria to be applied in deciding whether a location is suitable (or potentially suitable) for a specified description of development;

(c) set out the relative weight to be given to specified criteria;

(d) identify one or more locations as suitable (or potentially suitable) or unsuitable for a specified description of development;

(e) identify one or more statutory undertakers as appropriate persons to carry out a specified description of development;

(f) set out circumstances in which it is appropriate for a specified type of action to be taken to mitigate the impact of a specified description of development.

(6) If a national policy statement sets out policy in relation to a particular description of development, the statement must set out criteria to be taken into account in the design of that description of development.

(7) A national policy statement must give reasons for the policy set out in the statement.

(8) The reasons must (in particular) include an explanation of how the policy set out in the statement takes account of Government policy relating to the mitigation of, and adaptation to, climate change.

(9) The Secretary of State must—

(a) arrange for the publication of a national policy statement[.]

[...][3]

(10) In this section 'statutory undertakers' means persons who are, or are deemed to be, statutory undertakers for the purposes of any provision of Part 11 of TCPA 1990.

1 Added by Localism Act 2011, s 130(1), (2) (1 April 2012).
2 Added by Localism Act 2011, s 130(1), (3) (1 April 2012).
3 Repealed by Localism Act 2011, s 237, Sch 25, Pt 20 (1 April 2012).

6 Review

(1) The Secretary of State must review each national policy statement whenever the Secretary of State thinks it appropriate to do so.

(2) A review may relate to all or part of a national policy statement.

(3) In deciding when to review a national policy statement the Secretary of State must consider whether—

(a) since the time when the statement was first published or (if later) last reviewed, there has been a significant change in any circumstances on the basis of which any of the policy set out in the statement was decided,

(b) the change was not anticipated at that time, and

(c) if the change had been anticipated at that time, any of the policy set out in the statement would have been materially different.

(4) In deciding when to review part of a national policy statement ('the relevant part') the Secretary of State must consider whether—

(a) since the time when the relevant part was first published or (if later) last reviewed, there has been a significant change in any circumstances on the basis of which any of the policy set out in the relevant part was decided,

(b) the change was not anticipated at that time, and

(c) if the change had been anticipated at that time, any of the policy set out in the relevant part would have been materially different.

(5) After completing a review of all or part of a national policy statement the Secretary of State must do one of the following—

(a) amend the statement;

(b) withdraw the statement's designation as a national policy statement;

(c) leave the statement as it is.

(6) Before amending a national policy statement the Secretary of State must carry out an appraisal of the sustainability of the policy set out in the proposed amendment.

(7) The Secretary of State may amend a national policy statement only if the consultation and publicity requirements set out in section 7, and the parliamentary requirements set out in section 9, have been complied with in relation to the proposed amendment [and—][1]

[(a) the consideration period for the amendment has expired without the House of Commons resolving during that period that the amendment should not be proceeded with, or

(b) the amendment has been approved by resolution of the House of Commons—

(i) after being laid before Parliament under section 9(8), and

(ii) before the end of the consideration period.][1]

[(7A) In subsection (7) 'the consideration period', in relation to an amendment, means the period of 21 sitting days beginning with the first sitting day after the day on which the amendment is laid before Parliament under section 9(8), and here 'sitting day' means a day on which the House of Commons sits.][2]

(8) Subsections (6) [to (7A)][3] do not apply if the Secretary of State thinks that the proposed amendment (taken with any other proposed amendments) does not materially affect the policy as set out in the national policy statement.

(9) If the Secretary of State amends a national policy statement, the Secretary of State must—

(a) arrange for the amendment, or the statement as amended, to be published, and

(b) lay the amendment, or the statement as amended, before Parliament.

1 Added by Localism Act 2011, s 130(1), (5) (1 April 2012).
2 Added by Localism Act 2011, s 130(1), (6) (1 April 2012).
3 Words substituted by Localism Act 2011, s 130(1), (7) (1 April 2012).

[6A Interpretation of sections 5(4) and 6(7)

(1) This section applies for the purposes of section 5(4) and 6(7).

(2) The consultation and publicity requirements set out in section 7 are to be treated as having been complied with in relation to a statement or proposed amendment ('the final proposal') if—

(a) they have been complied with in relation to a different statement or proposed amendment ('the earlier proposal'),

(b) the final proposal is a modified version of the earlier proposal, and

(c) the Secretary of State thinks that the modifications do not materially affect the policy as set out in the earlier proposal.

(3) The consultation and publicity requirements set out in section 7 are also to be treated as having been complied with in relation to a statement or proposed amendment ('the final proposal') if—

(a) they have been complied with—

(i) in relation to a different statement or proposed amendment ('the earlier proposal'), and

(ii) in relation to modifications of the earlier proposal ('the main modifications'),

(b) the final proposal is a modified version of the earlier proposal, and

(c) there are no modifications other than the main modifications or, where the modifications include modifications other than the main modifications, the Secretary of State thinks that those other modifications do not materially affect the policy as set out in the earlier proposal modified by the main modifications.

(4) If section 9(8) has been complied with in relation to a statement or proposed amendment ('the final proposal'), the parliamentary requirements set out in section 9(2) to (7) are to be treated as having been complied with in relation to the final proposal where—

(a) the final proposal is not the same as what was laid under section 9(2), but

(b) those requirements have been complied with in relation to what was laid under section 9(2).

(5) Ignore any corrections of clerical or typographical errors in what was laid under section 9(8).][1]

1 Added by Localism Act 2011, s 130(1), (8) (1 April 2012).

[6B Extension of consideration period under section 5(4A) or 6(7A)

(1) The Secretary of State may—

(a) in relation to a proposed national policy statement, extend the period mentioned in section 5(4A), or

(b) in relation to a proposed amendment of a national policy statement, extend the period mentioned in section 6(7A),

by 21 sitting days or less.

(2) The Secretary of State does that by laying before the House of Commons a statement—

(a) indicating that the period is to be extended, and

(b) setting out the length of the extension.

(3) The statement under subsection (2) must be laid before the period would have expired without the extension.

(4) The Secretary of State must publish the statement under subsection (2) in a way the Secretary of State thinks appropriate.

(5) The period may be extended more than once.][1]

1 Added by Localism Act 2011, s 130(1), (8) (1 April 2012).

7 Consultation and publicity

(1) This section sets out the consultation and publicity requirements referred to in sections 5(4) and 6(7).

(2) The Secretary of State must carry out such consultation, and arrange for such publicity, as the Secretary of State thinks appropriate in relation to the proposal.

This is subject to subsections (4) and (5).

(3) In this section 'the proposal' means—

(a) the statement that the Secretary of State proposes to designate as a national policy statement for the purposes of this Act, or

(b) (as the case may be) the proposed amendment.

(4) The Secretary of State must consult such persons, and such descriptions of persons, as may be prescribed.

(5) If the policy set out in the proposal identifies one or more locations as suitable (or potentially suitable) for a specified description of development, the Secretary of State must ensure that appropriate steps are taken to publicise the proposal.

(6) The Secretary of State must have regard to the responses to the consultation and publicity in deciding whether to proceed with the proposal.

8 Consultation on publicity requirements

(1) In deciding what steps are appropriate for the purposes of section 7(5), the Secretary of State must consult—

(a) each local authority that is within subsection (2)[, (3) or (3A)][1], and

(b) the Greater London Authority, if any of the locations concerned is in Greater London.

(2) A local authority is within this subsection if any of the locations concerned is in the authority's area.

(3) A local authority ('A') is within this subsection if—

(a) any of the locations concerned is in the area of another local authority ('B'), [...][2]

[(aa) B is a unitary council or a lower-tier district council, and][2]

(b) any part of the boundary of A's area is also a part of the boundary of B's area.

[(3A) If any of the locations concerned is in the area of an upper-tier county council ('C'), a local authority ('D') is within this subsection if—

(a) D is not a lower-tier district council, and

(b) any part of the boundary of D's area is also part of the boundary of C's area.][3]

(4) In this section 'local authority' means—

(a) a county council, or district council, in England;

(b) a London borough council;

(c) the Common Council of the City of London;

(d) the Council of the Isles of Scilly;

(e) a county council, or county borough council, in Wales;

(f) a council constituted under section 2 of the Local Government etc. (Scotland) Act 1994 (c. 39);

(g) a National Park authority;

(h) the Broads Authority.

[(5) In this section—

'lower-tier district council' means a district council in England for an area for which there is a county council;

'unitary council' means a local authority that is not an upper-tier county council, a lower-tier district council, a National Park authority or the Broads Authority;

'upper-tier county council' means a county council in England for each part of whose area there is a district council.][4]

1 Words substituted by Localism Act 2011, s 130(1), (9) (1 April 2012).
2 Added by Localism Act 2011, s 130(1), (10) (1 April 2012).
3 Added by Localism Act 2011, s 130(1), (11) (1 April 2012).
4 Added by Localism Act 2011, s 130(1), (12) (1 April 2012).

9 Parliamentary requirements

(1) This section sets out the parliamentary requirements referred to in sections 5(4) and 6(7).

(2) The Secretary of State must lay the proposal before Parliament.

(3) In this section 'the proposal' means—

(a) the statement that the Secretary of State proposes to designate as a national policy statement for the purposes of this Act, or

(b) (as the case may be) the proposed amendment.

(4) Subsection (5) applies if, during the relevant period—

(a) either House of Parliament makes a resolution with regard to the proposal, or

(b) a committee of either House of Parliament makes recommendations with regard to the proposal.

(5) The Secretary of State must lay before Parliament a statement setting out the Secretary of State's response to the resolution or recommendations.

(6) The relevant period is the period specified by the Secretary of State in relation to the proposal.

(7) The Secretary of State must specify the relevant period in relation to the proposal on or before the day on which the proposal is laid before Parliament under subsection (2).

[(8) After the end of the relevant period, but not before the Secretary of State complies with subsection (5) if it applies, the Secretary of State must lay the proposal before Parliament.

(9) If after subsection (8) has been complied with—

(a) something other than what was laid under subsection (8) becomes the proposal, or

(b) what was laid under subsection (8) remains the proposal, or again becomes the proposal, despite the condition in section 5(4)(a) not having been met in relation to it,

subsection (8) must be complied with anew.

(10) For the purposes of subsection (9)(a) and (b) ignore any proposal to correct clerical or typographical errors in what was laid under subsection (8).][1]

1 Added by Localism Act 2011, s 130(1), (13) (1 April 2012).

10 Sustainable development

(1) This section applies to the Secretary of State's functions under sections 5 and 6.

(2) The Secretary of State must, in exercising those functions, do so with the objective of contributing to the achievement of sustainable development.

(3) For the purposes of subsection (2) the Secretary of State must (in particular) have regard to the desirability of—

(a) mitigating, and adapting to, climate change;

(b) achieving good design.

11 Suspension pending review

(1) This section applies if the Secretary of State thinks that the condition in subsection (2) or (3) is met.

(2) The condition is that—

(a) since the time when a national policy statement was first published or (if later) last reviewed, there has been a significant change in any circumstances on the basis of which any of the policy set out in the statement was decided,

(b) the change was not anticipated at that time, and

(c) if the change had been anticipated at that time, any of the policy set out in the statement would have been materially different.

(3) The condition is that—

(a) since the time when part of a national policy statement ('the relevant part') was first published or (if later) last reviewed, there has been a significant change in any circumstances on the basis of which any of the policy set out in the relevant part was decided,

(b) the change was not anticipated at that time, and

(c) if the change had been anticipated at that time, any of the policy set out in the relevant part would have been materially different.

(4) The Secretary of State may suspend the operation of all or any part of the national policy statement until a review of the statement or the relevant part has been completed.

(5) If the Secretary of State does so, the designation as a national policy statement of the statement or (as the case may be) the part of the statement that has been suspended is treated as having been withdrawn until the day on which the Secretary of State complies with section 6(5) in relation to the review.

12 …

Repealed by Localism Act 2011, s 237, Sch 25, Pt 20 as from 1 April 2012.

13 Legal challenges relating to national policy statements

(1) A court may entertain proceedings for questioning a national policy statement or anything done, or omitted to be done, by the Secretary of State in the course of preparing such a statement only if—

(a) the proceedings are brought by a claim for judicial review, and

(b) the claim form is filed [before the end of][1] the period of 6 weeks beginning with [the day after][2]—

(i) the day on which the statement is designated as a national policy statement for the purposes of this Act, or

(ii) (if later) the day on which the statement is published.

(2) A court may entertain proceedings for questioning a decision of the Secretary of State not to carry out a review of all or part of a national policy statement only if—

(a) the proceedings are brought by a claim for judicial review, and

(b) the claim form is filed [before the end of][1] the period of 6 weeks beginning with [the day after][2] the day of the decision not to carry out the review.

(3) A court may entertain proceedings for questioning a decision of the Secretary of State to carry out a review of all or part of a national policy statement only if—

(a) the proceedings are brought by a claim for judicial review, and

(b) the claim form is filed [before the end of][1] the period of 6 weeks beginning with [the day after][2] the day on which the Secretary of State complies with section 6(5) in relation to the review concerned.

(4) A court may entertain proceedings for questioning anything done, or omitted to be done, by the Secretary of State in the course of carrying out a review of all or part of a national policy statement only if—

(a) the proceedings are brought by a claim for judicial review, and

(b) the claim form is filed [before the end of][1] the period of 6 weeks beginning with [the day after][2] the day on which the Secretary of State complies with section 6(5) in relation to the review concerned.

(5) A court may entertain proceedings for questioning anything done by the Secretary of State under section 6(5) after completing a review of all or part of a national policy statement only if—

(a) the proceedings are brought by a claim for judicial review, and

(b) the claim form is filed [before the end of][1] the period of 6 weeks beginning with [the day after][2] the day on which the thing concerned is done.

(6) A court may entertain proceedings for questioning a decision of the Secretary of State as to whether or not to suspend the operation of all or part of a national policy statement under section 11 only if—

(a) the proceedings are brought by a claim for judicial review, and

(b) the claim form is filed [before the end of][1] the period of 6 weeks beginning with [the day after][2] the day of the decision.

1 Words substituted by Criminal Justice and Courts Act 2015, s 92(3)(a) (13 April 2015).
2 Words added by Criminal Justice and Courts Act 2015, s 92(3)(b) (13 April 2015).

Part 3 Nationally significant infrastructure projects

General

14 Nationally significant infrastructure projects: general

(1) In this Act 'nationally significant infrastructure project' means a project which consists of any of the following—

(a) the construction or extension of a generating station;

(b) the installation of an electric line above ground;

(c) development relating to underground gas storage facilities;

(d) the construction or alteration of an LNG facility;

(e) the construction or alteration of a gas reception facility;

(f) the construction of a pipe-line by a gas transporter;

(g) the construction of a pipe-line other than by a gas transporter;

(h) highway-related development;

(i) airport-related development;

(j) the construction or alteration of harbour facilities;

(k) the construction or alteration of a railway;

(l) the construction or alteration of a rail freight interchange;

(m) the construction or alteration of a dam or reservoir;

(n) development relating to the transfer of water resources;

(o) the construction or alteration of a waste water treatment plant [or of infrastructure for the transfer or storage of waste water][1];

(p) the construction or alteration of a hazardous waste facility;

[(q) development relating to a radioactive waste geological disposal facility.][2]

(2) Subsection (1) is subject to sections 15 to [30A][3].

(3) The Secretary of State may by order—

(a) amend subsection (1) to add a new type of project or vary or remove an existing type of project;

(b) make further provision, or amend or repeal existing provision, about the types of project which are, and are not, within subsection (1).

(4) An order under subsection (3)(b) may amend this Act.

(5) The power conferred by subsection (3) may be exercised to add a new type of project to subsection (1) only if—

(a) a project of the new type is a project for the carrying out of works in one or more of the fields specified in subsection (6), and

(b) the works are to be carried out wholly in one or more of the areas specified in subsection (7).

(6) The fields are—

(a) energy;

(b) transport;

(c) water;

(d) waste water;

(e) waste.

(7) The areas are—

(a) England;

(b) waters adjacent to England up to the seaward limits of the territorial sea;

(c) in the case of a project for the carrying out of works in the field of energy, a Renewable Energy Zone, except any part of a Renewable Energy Zone in relation to which the Scottish Ministers have functions.

1 Words added by Infrastructure Planning (Waste Water Transfer and Storage) Order 2012, SI 2012/1645, art 2(1), (2) (23 June 2012: insertion has effect subject to supplementary provision specified in SI 2012/1645, art 3).

2 Added by Infrastructure Planning (Radioactive Waste Geological Disposal Facilities) Order 2015, SI 2015/949, art 2(1), (2)(a) (27 March 2015).

3 Word substituted by Infrastructure Planning (Radioactive Waste Geological Disposal Facilities) Order 2015, SI 2015/949, art 2(1), (2)(b) (27 March 2015).

Energy

15 Generating stations

(1) The construction or extension of a generating station is within section 14(1)(a) only if the generating station is or (when constructed or extended) is expected to be within subsection (2) or (3).

(2) A generating station is within this subsection if—

(a) it is in England or Wales,

[(aa) it does not generate electricity from wind,][1]

(b) it is not an offshore generating station, and

(c) its capacity is more than 50 megawatts.

(3) A generating station is within this subsection if—

(a) it is an offshore generating station, and

(b) its capacity is more than 100 megawatts.

(4) An 'offshore' generating station is a generating station that is—

(a) in waters in or adjacent to England or Wales up to the seaward limits of the territorial sea, or

(b) in a Renewable Energy Zone, except any part of a Renewable Energy Zone in relation to which the Scottish Ministers have functions.

1 Added by Infrastructure Planning (Onshore Wind Generating Stations) Order 2016, SI 2016/306, art 3 (5 March 2016).

16 Electric lines

(1) The installation of an electric line above ground is within section 14(1)(b) only if (when installed) the electric line will be—

(a) wholly in England,

(b) wholly in Wales,

(c) partly in England and partly in Wales, or

(d) partly in England and partly in Scotland, subject to subsection (2).

(2) In the case of an electric line falling within subsection (1)(d), the installation of the line above ground is within section 14(1)(b) only to the extent that (when installed) the line will be in England.

(3) The installation of an electric line above ground is not within section 14(1)(b)—

(a) if the nominal voltage of the line is expected to be less than 132 kilovolts, [...][1]

[(aa) if the length of the line (when installed) will be less than two kilometres,

(ab) if—

(i) the line will replace an existing line,

(ii) the nominal voltage of the line is expected to be greater than the nominal voltage of the existing line (but see subsection (3A)),

(iii) the height above the surface of the ground of any support for the line will not exceed the height of the highest existing support or support which is being replaced by more than 10 per cent, and

(iv) where the line is to be installed in a different position from the existing line, the distance between any new support and the existing line will not exceed 60 metres and the existing line will be removed within twelve months from the date on which the installation of the line which replaces it is complete,][2]

(b) to the extent that (when installed) the line will be within premises in the occupation or control of the person responsible for its installation [, or][3]

[(c) if section 37(1) of the Electricity Act 1989 (consent required for overhead lines) does not apply to it by virtue of the Overhead Lines (Exemption) (England and Wales) Regulations 2009 (S.I. 2009/640), as amended by the Overhead Lines (Exempt Installations) (Consequential Provisions) Order 2010.][3]

[(3A) Paragraph (ab)(ii) of subsection (3) (condition that nominal voltage of line expected to be greater than nominal voltage of existing line) does not apply if any part of the line (when installed) will be within a European site or an SSSI.][2]

[(4) In this section—

'European site' has the same meaning as in the Conservation of Habitats and Species Regulations 2010 (S.I. 2010/490);

'existing line' means an electric line which—

(a) has been installed or is kept installed above ground in accordance with a consent granted under section 37(1) of the Electricity Act 1989 or an order granting development consent; or

(b) has been installed above ground and is an electric line to which section 37(1) of the Electricity Act 1989 does not apply by virtue of—

(i) paragraph 5(4) or (5) of Schedule 17 to that Act, or

(ii) the Overhead Lines (Exemption) (England and Wales) Regulations 2009 (S.I. 2009/640), as amended by the Overhead Lines (Exempt Installations) (Consequential Provisions) Order 2010;

'premises' includes any land, building or structure;

'SSSI' means a site of special scientific interest notified under sections 28 to 28D of the Wildlife and Countryside Act 1981.][4]

1 Word repealed by Overhead Lines (Exempt Installations) Order 2010, SI 2010/277, art 2(a) (1 March 2010).
2 Added by Planning Act 2008 (Nationally Significant Infrastructure Projects) (Electric Lines) Order 2013, SI 2013/1479, art 2(a), (b) (18 June 2013).
3 Added by Overhead Lines (Exempt Installations) Order 2010, SI 2010/277, art 2(b) (1 March 2010).
4 Substituted by Planning Act 2008 (Nationally Significant Infrastructure Projects) (Electric Lines) Order 2013, SI 2013/1479, art 2(c) (18 June 2013).

17 Underground gas storage facilities

(1) Development relating to underground gas storage facilities is within section 14(1)(c) only if the development is within subsection (2), (3) or (5).

(2) Development is within this subsection if—

(a) it is the carrying out of operations for the purpose of creating underground gas storage facilities in England, or

(b) it is starting to use underground gas storage facilities in England,

and the condition in subsection (4) is met in relation to the facilities.

(3) Development is within this subsection if—

(a) it is starting to use underground gas storage facilities in Wales,

(b) the facilities are facilities for the storage of gas underground in natural porous strata,

(c) the proposed developer is a gas transporter, and

(d) the condition in subsection (4) is met in relation to the facilities.

(4) The condition is that—

(a) the working capacity of the facilities is expected to be at least 43 million standard cubic metres, or

(b) the maximum flow rate of the facilities is expected to be at least 4.5 million standard cubic metres per day.

(5) Development is within this subsection if—

(a) it is the carrying out of operations for the purpose of altering underground gas storage facilities in England, and

(b) the effect of the alteration is expected to be—

(i) to increase by at least 43 million standard cubic metres the working capacity of the facilities, or

(ii) to increase by at least 4.5 million standard cubic metres per day the maximum flow rate of the facilities.

(6) 'Underground gas storage facilities' means facilities for the storage of gas underground in cavities or in porous strata.

(7) In this section—

'maximum flow rate', in relation to underground gas storage facilities, means the maximum rate at which gas is able to flow out of the facilities, on the assumption that—

(a) the facilities are filled to maximum capacity, and

(b) the rate is measured after any processing of gas required on its recovery from storage;

'working capacity', in relation to underground gas storage facilities, means the capacity of the facilities for storage of gas underground, ignoring any capacity for storage of cushion gas.

(8) In subsection (7) 'cushion gas' means gas which is kept in underground gas storage facilities for the purpose of enabling other gas stored there to be recovered from storage.

18 LNG facilities

(1) The construction of an LNG facility is within section 14(1)(d) only if (when constructed) the facility will be in England and—

(a) the storage capacity of the facility is expected to be at least 43 million standard cubic metres, or

(b) the maximum flow rate of the facility is expected to be at least 4.5 million standard cubic metres per day.

(2) The alteration of an LNG facility is within section 14(1)(d) only if the facility is in England and the effect of the alteration is expected to be—

(a) to increase by at least 43 million standard cubic metres the storage capacity of the facility, or

(b) to increase by at least 4.5 million standard cubic metres per day the maximum flow rate of the facility.

(3) 'LNG facility' means a facility for—

(a) the reception of liquid natural gas from outside England,

(b) the storage of liquid natural gas, and

(c) the regasification of liquid natural gas.

(4) In this section—

'maximum flow rate', in relation to a facility, means the maximum rate at which gas is able to flow out of the facility, on the assumption that—

(a) the facility is filled to maximum capacity, and

(b) the rate is measured after regasification of the liquid natural gas and any other processing required on the recovery of the gas from storage;

'storage capacity' means the capacity of the facility for storage of liquid natural gas.

(5) The storage capacity of an LNG facility is to be measured as if the gas were stored in regasified form.

19 Gas reception facilities

(1) The construction of a gas reception facility is within section 14(1)(e) only if (when constructed)—

(a) the facility will be in England and will be within subsection (4), and

(b) the maximum flow rate of the facility is expected to be at least 4.5 million standard cubic metres per day.

(2) The alteration of a gas reception facility is within section 14(1)(e) only if—

(a) the facility is in England and is within subsection (4), and

(b) the effect of the alteration is expected to be to increase by at least 4.5 million standard cubic metres per day the maximum flow rate of the facility.

(3) 'Gas reception facility' means a facility for—

(a) the reception of natural gas in gaseous form from outside England, and

(b) the handling of natural gas (other than its storage).

(4) A gas reception facility is within this subsection if—

(a) the gas handled by the facility does not originate in England, Wales or Scotland,

(b) the gas does not arrive at the facility from Scotland or Wales, and

(c) the gas has not already been handled at another facility after its arrival in England.

(5) 'Maximum flow rate' means the maximum rate at which gas is able to flow out of the facility.

20 Gas transporter pipe-lines

(1) The construction of a pipe-line by a gas transporter is within section 14(1)(f) only if (when constructed) each of the conditions in subsections (2) to (5) is expected to be met in relation to the pipe-line.

(2) The pipe-line must be wholly or partly in England.

(3) Either—

(a) the pipe-line must be more than 800 millimetres in diameter and more than 40 kilometres in length, or

(b) the construction of the pipe-line must be likely to have a significant effect on the environment.

(4) The pipe-line must have a design operating pressure of more than 7 bar gauge.

(5) The pipe-line must convey gas for supply (directly or indirectly) to at least 50,000 customers, or potential customers, of one or more gas suppliers.

(6) In the case of a pipe-line that (when constructed) will be only partly in England, the construction of the pipe-line is within section 14(1)(f) only to the extent that the pipe-line will (when constructed) be in England.

(7) 'Gas supplier' has the same meaning as in Part 1 of the Gas Act 1986 (c. 44) (see section 7A(11) of that Act).

21 Other pipe-lines

(1) The construction of a pipe-line other than by a gas transporter is within section 14(1)(g) only if (when constructed) the pipe-line is expected to be—

(a) a cross-country pipe-line,

(b) a pipe-line the construction of which would (but for section 33(1) of this Act) require authorisation under section 1(1) of the Pipe-lines Act 1962 (c. 58) (cross-country pipe-lines not to be constructed without authorisation), and

(c) within subsection (2).

(2) A pipe-line is within this subsection if one end of it is in England or Wales and—

(a) the other end of it is in England or Wales, or

(b) it is an oil or gas pipe-line and the other end of it is in Scotland.

(3) For the purposes of section 14(1)(g) and the previous provisions of this section, the construction of a diversion to a pipe-line is treated as the construction of a separate pipe-line.

(4) But if—

(a) the pipe-line to be diverted is itself a nationally significant pipe-line, and

(b) the length of the pipe-line which is to be diverted has not been constructed,

the construction of the diversion is treated as the construction of a cross-country pipe-line, whatever the length of the diversion.

(5) For the purposes of subsection (4), a pipe-line is a nationally significant pipe-line if—

(a) development consent is required for its construction by virtue of section 14(1)(g), and has been granted, or

(b) its construction has been authorised by a pipe-line construction authorisation under section 1(1) of the Pipe-lines Act 1962 (c. 58).

(6) 'Diversion' means a lateral diversion of a length of a pipe-line (whether or not that pipe-line has been constructed) where the diversion is beyond the permitted limits.

(7) The permitted limits are the limits of lateral diversion permitted by any of the following granted in respect of the construction of the pipe-line—

(a) development consent;

(b) authorisation under the Pipe-lines Act 1962;

(c) planning permission.

Transport

[22 Highways

(1) Highway-related development is within section 14(1)(h) only if the development is—

(a) construction of a highway in a case within subsection (2),

(b) alteration of a highway in a case within subsection (3), or

(c) improvement of a highway in a case within subsection (5).

(2) Construction of a highway is within this subsection only if—

(a) the highway will (when constructed) be wholly in England,

(b) the Secretary of State [or a strategic highways company][1] will be the highway authority for the highway, and

(c) the area of development is greater than the relevant limit set out in subsection (4).

(3) Alteration of a highway is within this subsection only if—

(a) the highway is wholly in England,

(b) the Secretary of State [or a strategic highways company][1] is the highway authority for the highway, and

(c) the area of development is greater than the relevant limit set out in subsection (4).

(4) For the purposes of subsections (2)(c) and (3)(c) the relevant limit —

(a) in relation to the construction or alteration of a motorway, is 15 hectares,

(b) in relation to the construction or alteration of a highway, other than a motorway, where the speed limit for any class of vehicle is expected to be 50 miles per hour or greater, is 12.5 hectares, and

(c) in relation to the construction or alteration of any other highway is 7.5 hectares.

(5) Improvement of a highway is within this subsection only if—

(a) the highway is wholly in England,

(b) the Secretary of State [or a strategic highways company][1] is the highway authority for the highway, and

(c) the improvement is likely to have a significant effect on the environment.

(6) Highway-related development does not fall within section 14(1)(h) if—

(a) an order mentioned in section 33(4) has been made in relation to the development before 1 March 2010,

(b) a further order is needed in relation to the development, and

(c) not more than 7 years have elapsed since the making of the earlier order.

(7) Alteration of a highway is not within section 14(1)(h) if

(a) planning permission has been granted for a development,

(b) the alteration is necessary as a result of the development, and

(c) the developer has asked for the alteration to be made to the highway.

(8) Alteration of a highway is not within section 14(1)(h) if—

(a) an order mentioned in section 33(4) has been made in relation to local highway works,

(b) the alteration is necessary as a result of the local highway works, and

(c) the local highway authority responsible for the local highway works has asked for the alteration to be made to the highway.

(9) In this section—

'area of development'—

(a) in relation to construction of a highway, means the land on which the highway is to be constructed and any adjoining land expected to be used in connection with its construction;

(b) in relation to alteration of a highway, means the land on which the part of the highway to be altered is situated and any adjoining land expected to be used in connection with its alteration;

'local highway authority' has the meaning given by section 329(1) of the Highways Act 1980;

'local highway works' means works carried out by or on behalf of a local highway authority in relation to a highway for which it is the highway authority (and the local highway authority is referred to in this section as 'responsible' for those works);

'motorway' means a highway which is a special road in accordance with section 16 of the Highways Act 1980;

['strategic highways company' means a company for the time being appointed under Part 1 of the Infrastructure Act 2015.][1]][2]

1 Words added by Infrastructure Act 2015, s 1(6), Sch 1, para 153 (12 February 2015).
2 Substituted by Highway and Railway (Nationally Significant Infrastructure Project) Order 2013, SI 2013/1883, art 3 (25 July 2013).

23 Airports

(1) Airport-related development is within section 14(1)(i) only if the development is—

(a) the construction of an airport in a case within subsection (2),

(b) the alteration of an airport in a case within subsection (4), or

(c) an increase in the permitted use of an airport in a case within subsection (7).

(2) Construction of an airport is within this subsection only if (when constructed) the airport—

(a) will be in England or in English waters, and

(b) is expected to be capable of providing services which meet the requirements of subsection (3).

(3) Services meet the requirements of this subsection if they are—

(a) air passenger transport services for at least 10 million passengers per year, or

(b) air cargo transport services for at least 10,000 air transport movements of cargo aircraft per year.

(4) Alteration of an airport is within this subsection only if—

(a) the airport is in England or in English waters, and

(b) the alteration is expected to have the effect specified in subsection (5).

(5) The effect is—

(a) to increase by at least 10 million per year the number of passengers for whom the airport is capable of providing air passenger transport services, or

(b) to increase by at least 10,000 per year the number of air transport movements of cargo aircraft for which the airport is capable of providing air cargo transport services.

(6) 'Alteration', in relation to an airport, includes the construction, extension or alteration of—

(a) a runway at the airport,

(b) a building at the airport, or

(c) a radar or radio mast, antenna or other apparatus at the airport.

(7) An increase in the permitted use of an airport is within this subsection only if—

(a) the airport is in England or in English waters, and

(b) the increase is within subsection (8).

(8) An increase is within this subsection if—

(a) it is an increase of at least 10 million per year in the number of passengers for whom the airport is permitted to provide air passenger transport services, or

(b) it is an increase of at least 10,000 per year in the number of air transport movements of cargo aircraft for which the airport is permitted to provide air cargo transport services.

(9) In this section—

'air cargo transport services' means services for the carriage by air of cargo;

'air passenger transport services' means services for the carriage by air of passengers;

'air transport movement' means a landing or take-off of an aircraft;

'cargo' includes mail;

'cargo aircraft' means an aircraft which is—

(a) designed to transport cargo but not passengers, and

(b) engaged in the transport of cargo on commercial terms;

'English waters' means waters adjacent to England up to the seaward limits of the territorial sea;

'permitted' means permitted by planning permission or development consent.

24 Harbour facilities

(1) The construction of harbour facilities is within section 14(1)(j) only if (when constructed) the harbour facilities—

(a) will be in England or Wales or in waters adjacent to England or Wales up to the seaward limits of the territorial sea, and

(b) are expected to be capable of handling the embarkation or disembarkation of at least the relevant quantity of material per year.

(2) The alteration of harbour facilities is within section 14(1)(j) only if—

(a) the harbour facilities are in England or Wales or in waters adjacent to England or Wales up to the seaward limits of the territorial sea, and

(b) the effect of the alteration is expected to be to increase by at least the relevant quantity per year the quantity of material the embarkation or disembarkation of which the facilities are capable of handling.

(3) 'The relevant quantity' is—

(a) in the case of facilities for container ships, 500,000 TEU;

(b) in the case of facilities for ro-ro ships, 250,000 units;

(c) in the case of facilities for cargo ships of any other description, 5 million tonnes;

(d) in the case of facilities for more than one of the types of ships mentioned in paragraphs (a) to (c), an equivalent quantity of material.

(4) For the purposes of subsection (3)(d), facilities are capable of handling an equivalent quantity of material if the sum of the relevant fractions is one or more.

(5) The relevant fractions are—

(a) to the extent that the facilities are for container ships—

$x / 500{,}000$

where $\times$ is the number of TEU that the facilities are capable of handling;

(b) to the extent that the facilities are for ro-ro ships—

y / 250,000

where y is the number of units that the facilities are capable of handling;

(c) to the extent that the facilities are for cargo ships of any other description—

z / 5,000,000

where z is the number of tonnes of material that the facilities are capable of handling.

(6) In this section—

'cargo ship' means a ship which is used for carrying cargo;

'container ship' means a cargo ship which carries all or most of its cargo in containers;

'ro-ro ship' means a ship which is used for carrying wheeled cargo;

'TEU' means a twenty-foot equivalent unit;

'unit' in relation to a ro-ro ship means any item of wheeled cargo (whether or not self-propelled).

25 Railways

(1) Construction of a railway is within section 14(1)(k) only if—

(a) the railway will (when constructed) be wholly in England,

(b) the railway will (when constructed) be part of a network operated by an approved operator,

[(ba) the railway will (when constructed) include a stretch of track that—

(i) is a continuous length of more than 2 kilometres, and

(ii) is not on land that was operational land of a railway undertaker immediately before the construction work began or is on land that was acquired at an earlier date for the purpose of constructing the railway,][1]

and

(c) the construction of the railway is not permitted development.

(2) Alteration of a railway is within section 14(1)(k) only if—

(a) the part of the railway to be altered is wholly in England,

(b) the railway is part of a network operated by an approved operator,

[(ba) the alteration of the railway will include laying a stretch of track that—

(i) is a continuous length of more than 2 kilometres, and

(ii) is not on land that was operational land of a railway undertaker immediately before the alteration work began or is on land that was acquired at an earlier date for the purpose of the alteration,][1] and

(c) the alteration of the railway is not permitted development.

[(2A) Construction or alteration of a railway is not within section 14(1)(k) to the extent that it takes place on the operational land of a railway undertaker unless that land was acquired for the purpose of the construction or alteration.][1]

(3) Construction or alteration of a railway is not within section 14(1)(k) to the extent that the railway forms part (or will when constructed form part) of a rail freight interchange.

(4) 'Approved operator' means a person who meets the conditions in subsections (5) and (6).

(5) The condition is that the person must be—

(a) a person who is authorised to be the operator of a network by a licence granted under section 8 of the Railways Act 1993 (c. 43) (licences for operation of railway assets), or

(b) a wholly-owned subsidiary of a company which is such a person.

(6) The condition is that the person is designated, or is of a description designated, in an order made by the Secretary of State.

(7) In this section—

'network' has the meaning given by section 83(1) of the Railways Act 1993 (c. 43);

['operational land' has the same meaning as in the TCPA 1990;][1]

'permitted development' means development in relation to which planning permission is granted by article 3 of the Town and Country Planning (General Permitted Development) Order 1995;

['railway undertaker' has the same meaning as in Part 17 of Schedule 2 to the Town and Country Planning (General Permitted Development) Order 1995;][1]

'wholly-owned subsidiary' has the same meaning as in the Companies Act 2006 (c. 46) (see section 1159 of that Act).

(8) [In the definition of 'permitted development' in subsection (7), the reference][2] to the Town and Country Planning (General Permitted Development) Order 1995 is to that Order as it has effect immediately before the day on which this section comes fully into force.

1 Added by Highway and Railway (Nationally Significant Infrastructure Project) Order 2013, SI 2013/1883, art 4(1)-(5).
2 Substituted by Highway and Railway (Nationally Significant Infrastructure Project) Order 2013, SI 2013/1883, art 4(1), (6).

26 Rail freight interchanges

(1) The construction of a rail freight interchange is within section 14(1)(l) only if (when constructed) each of the conditions in subsections (3) to (7) is expected to be met in relation to it.

(2) The alteration of a rail freight interchange is within section 14(1)(l) only if—

(a) following the alteration, each of the conditions in subsections (3)(a) and (4) to (7) is expected to be met in relation to it, and

(b) the alteration is expected to have the effect specified in subsection (8).

(3) The land on which the rail freight interchange is situated must—

(a) be in England, and

(b) be at least 60 hectares in area.

(4) The rail freight interchange must be capable of handling—

(a) consignments of goods from more than one consignor and to more than one consignee, and

(b) at least 4 goods trains per day.

(5) The rail freight interchange must be part of the railway network in England.

(6) The rail freight interchange must include warehouses to which goods can be delivered from the railway network in England either directly or by means of another form of transport.

(7) The rail freight interchange must not be part of a military establishment.

(8) The effect referred to in subsection (2)(b) is to increase by at least 60 hectares the area of the land on which the rail freight interchange is situated.

(9) In this section—

'goods train' means a train that (ignoring any locomotive) consists of items of rolling stock designed to carry goods;

'military establishment' means an establishment intended for use for naval, military or air force purposes or for the purposes of the Department of the Secretary of State responsible for defence.

(10) The following terms have the meanings given by section 83(1) of the Railways Act 1993—

'network';

'rolling stock';

'train'.

Water

27 Dams and reservoirs

(1) The construction of a dam or reservoir is within section 14(1)(m) only if—

(a) the dam or reservoir (when constructed) will be in England,

(b) the construction will be carried out by one or more water undertakers, and

(c) the volume of water to be held back by the dam or stored in the reservoir is expected to exceed 10 million cubic metres.

(2) The alteration of a dam or reservoir is within section 14(1)(m) only if—

(a) the dam or reservoir is in England,

(b) the alteration will be carried out by one or more water undertakers, and

(c) the additional volume of water to be held back by the dam or stored in the reservoir as a result of the alteration is expected to exceed 10 million cubic metres.

(3) 'Water undertaker' means a company appointed as a water undertaker under the Water Industry Act 1991 (c. 56).

28 Transfer of water resources

(1) Development relating to the transfer of water resources is within section 14(1)(n) only if—

(a) the development will be carried out in England by one or more water undertakers,

(b) the volume of water to be transferred as a result of the development is expected to exceed 100 million cubic metres per year,

(c) the development will enable the transfer of water resources—

(i) between river basins in England,

(ii) between water undertakers' areas in England, or

(iii) between a river basin in England and a water undertaker's area in England, and

(d) the development does not relate to the transfer of drinking water.

(2) In this section—

'river basin' means an area of land drained by a river and its tributaries;

'water undertaker' means a company appointed as a water undertaker under the Water Industry Act 1991;

'water undertaker's area' means the area for which a water undertaker is appointed under that Act.

Waste water

29 Waste water treatment plants

(1) The construction of a waste water treatment plant is within section 14(1)(o) only if the treatment plant (when constructed)—

(a) will be in England, and

(b) is expected to have a capacity exceeding a population equivalent of 500,000.

[(1A) The construction of infrastructure for the transfer or storage of waste water is within section 14(1)(o) only if —

(a) the works will be carried out wholly in England and the infrastructure will (when constructed) be wholly in England,

(b) the main purpose of the infrastructure will be—

(i) the transfer of waste water for treatment, or

(ii) the storage of waste water prior to treatment,

or both, and

(c) the infrastructure is expected to have a capacity for the storage of waste water exceeding 350,000 cubic metres.][1]

(2) The alteration of a waste water treatment plant is within section 14(1)(o) only if—

(a) the treatment plant is in England, and

(b) the effect of the alteration is expected to be to increase by more than a population equivalent of 500,000 the capacity of the plant.

[(2A) The alteration of infrastructure for the transfer or storage of waste water is within section 14(1)(o) only if—

(a) the works will be carried out wholly in England and the part of the infrastructure to be altered is wholly in England,

(b) the main purpose of the infrastructure is —

(i) the transfer of waste water for treatment, or

(ii) the storage of waste water prior to treatment,

or both, and

(c) the effect of the alteration is expected to be to increase the capacity of the infrastructure for the storage of waste water by more than 350,000 cubic metres.][1]

(3) 'Waste water' includes domestic waste water, industrial waste water and urban waste water.

(4) The following terms have the meanings given by regulation 2(1) of the Urban Waste Water Treatment (England and Wales) Regulations 1994 (S.I. 1994/2841)—

'domestic waste water';

'industrial waste water';

'population equivalent';

'urban waste water'.

1 Inserted by Infrastructure Planning (Waste Water Transfer and Storage) Order 2012, SI 2012/1645, art 2(1), (3) (23 June 2012: insertions have effect subject to supplementary provision specified in SI 2012/1645, art 3).

Waste

30 Hazardous waste facilities

(1) The construction of a hazardous waste facility is within section 14(1)(p) only if—

(a) the facility (when constructed) will be in England,

(b) the main purpose of the facility is expected to be the final disposal or recovery of hazardous waste, and

(c) the facility is expected to have the capacity specified in subsection (2).

(2) The capacity is—

(a) in the case of the disposal of hazardous waste by landfill or in a deep storage facility, more than 100,000 tonnes per year;

(b) in any other case, more than 30,000 tonnes per year.

(3) The alteration of a hazardous waste facility is within section 14(1)(p) only if—

(a) the facility is in England,

(b) the main purpose of the facility is the final disposal or recovery of hazardous waste, and

(c) the alteration is expected to have the effect specified in subsection (4).

(4) The effect is—

(a) in the case of the disposal of hazardous waste by landfill or in a deep storage facility, to increase by more than 100,000 tonnes per year the capacity of the facility;

(b) in any other case, to increase by more than 30,000 tonnes per year the capacity of the facility.

(5) The following terms have the same meanings as in the Hazardous Waste (England and Wales) Regulations 2005 (S.I. 2005/894) (see regulation 5 of those regulations)—

'disposal';

'hazardous waste';

'recovery'.

(6) 'Deep storage facility' means a facility for the storage of waste underground in a deep geological cavity.

[30A Radioactive waste geological disposal facilities

(1) A radioactive waste geological disposal facility means a facility which meets the conditions in subsection (2).

(2) The conditions are that—

(a) the main purpose of the facility is expected to be the final disposal of radioactive waste,

(b) the part of the facility where radioactive waste is to be disposed of is expected to be constructed at a depth of at least 200 metres beneath the surface of the ground or seabed, and

(c) the natural environment which surrounds the facility is expected to act, in combination with any engineered measures, to inhibit the transit of radionuclides from the part of the facility where radioactive waste is to be disposed of to the surface.

(3) Development is within section 14(1)(q) only if the development is within subsection (4) or (6) of this section.

(4) Development is within this subsection if—

(a) it is the construction of one or more boreholes, and the carrying out of any associated excavation, construction or building work,

(b) the borehole or boreholes will be constructed, and any associated excavation, construction or building work will be carried out, in England or waters adjacent to England up to the seaward limits of the territorial sea, and

(c) the conditions in subsection (5) are met in relation to each borehole.

(5) The conditions are that—

(a) the borehole is expected to be constructed to a depth of at least 150 metres beneath the surface of the ground or seabed, and

(b) the main purpose of constructing the borehole is to obtain information, data or samples to determine the suitability of a site for the construction or use of a radioactive waste geological disposal facility.

(6) Development is within this subsection if—

(a) it is the construction of a radioactive waste geological disposal facility, and

(b) the facility (when constructed) will be in England or waters adjacent to England up to the seaward limits of the territorial sea.

(7) In this section—

'disposal' in relation to radioactive waste means emplacement in an appropriate facility without the intention to retrieve;

'radioactive waste' has the same meaning as in the Environmental Permitting (England and Wales) Regulations 2010 (see paragraph 3(1) of Part 2 of Schedule 23 to those regulations).][1]

1 Added by Infrastructure Planning (Radioactive Waste Geological Disposal Facilities) Order 2015, SI 2015/949, art 2(1), (3) (27 March 2015).

Part 4 Requirement for development consent

31 When development consent is required

Consent under this Act ('development consent') is required for development to the extent that the development is or forms part of a nationally significant infrastructure project.

32 Meaning of 'development'

(1) In this Act (except in Part 11) 'development' has the same meaning as it has in TCPA 1990.

This is subject to subsections (2) and (3).

(2) For the purposes of this Act (except Part 11)—

(a) the conversion of a generating station with a view to its being fuelled by crude liquid petroleum, a petroleum product or natural gas is treated as a material change in the use of the generating station;

(b) starting to use a cavity or strata for the underground storage of gas is treated as a material change in the use of the cavity or strata;

(c) an increase in the permitted use of an airport is treated as a material change in the use of the airport.

(3) For the purposes of this Act (except Part 11) the following works are taken to be development (to the extent that they would not be otherwise)—

(a) works for the demolition of a listed building or its alteration or extension in a manner which would affect its character as a building of special architectural or historic interest;

(b) demolition of a building in a conservation area;

(c) works resulting in the demolition or destruction of or any damage to a scheduled monument;

(d) works for the purpose of removing or repairing a scheduled monument or any part of it;

(e) works for the purpose of making any alterations or additions to a scheduled monument;

(f) flooding or tipping operations on land in, on or under which there is a scheduled monument.

(4) In this section—

'conservation area' has the meaning given by section 91(1) of the Listed Buildings Act;

'flooding operations' has the meaning given by section 61(1) of the Ancient Monuments and Archaeological Areas Act 1979 (c. 46);

'listed building' has the meaning given by section 1(5) of the Listed Buildings Act;

'permitted' means permitted by planning permission or development consent;

'petroleum products' has the meaning given by section 21 of the Energy Act 1976 (c. 76);

'scheduled monument' has the meaning given by section 1(11) of the Ancient Monuments and Archaeological Areas Act 1979 (c. 46);

'tipping operations' has the meaning given by section 61(1) of that Act.

33 Effect of requirement for development consent on other consent regimes

(1) To the extent that development consent is required for development, none of the following is required to be obtained for the development or given in relation to it—

(a) planning permission;

(b) consent under section 10(1), 11(1) or 12(1) of the Green Belt (London and Home Counties) Act 1938 (c. xciii) (erection of buildings and construction of sewer main pipes, watercourses and electric lines etc. on Green Belt land);

(c) a pipe-line construction authorisation under section 1(1) of the Pipe-lines Act 1962 (c. 58) (authorisation for construction of cross-country pipe-lines);

(d) authorisation by an order under section 4(1) of the Gas Act 1965 (c. 36) (storage of gas in underground strata);

[…][1]

(f) to the extent that the development relates to land in England, consent under section 2(3) or 3 of the Ancient Monuments and Archaeological Areas Act 1979;

(g) to the extent that the development relates to land in England, notice under section 35 of the Ancient Monuments and Archaeological Areas Act 1979;

(h) consent under section 36 or 37 of the Electricity Act 1989 (c. 29) (construction etc. of generating stations and installation of overhead lines);

(i) to the extent that the development relates to land in England, consent under section 8(1), (2) or (3) of the Listed Buildings Act;

(j) to the extent that the development relates to land in England, consent under section 74(1) of the Listed Buildings Act.

(2) To the extent that development consent is required for development, the development may not be authorised by any of the following—

(a) an order under section 14 or 16 of the Harbours Act 1964 (c. 40) (orders in relation to harbours, docks and wharves);

(b) an order under section 4(1) of the Gas Act 1965 (order authorising storage of gas in underground strata);

(c) an order under section 1 or 3 of the Transport and Works Act 1992 (c. 42) (orders as to railways, tramways, inland waterways etc.).

(3) Subsection (2) is subject to section 34.

(4) If development consent is required for the construction, improvement or alteration of a highway, none of the following may be made or confirmed in relation to the highway or in connection with the construction, improvement or alteration of the highway—

(a) an order under section 10 of the Highways Act 1980 (c. 66) (general provisions as to trunk roads) directing that the highway should become a trunk road;

(b) an order under section 14 of that Act (supplementary orders relating to trunk roads and classified roads);

(c) a scheme under section 16 of that Act (schemes authorising the provision of special roads);

(d) an order under section 18 of that Act (supplementary orders relating to special roads);

(e) an order or scheme under section 106 of that Act (orders and schemes providing for construction of bridges over or tunnels under navigable waters);

(f) an order under section 108 or 110 of that Act (orders authorising the diversion of navigable and non-navigable watercourses);

(g) an order under section 6 of the New Roads and Street Works Act 1991 (c. 22) (toll orders).

[(5) The Secretary of State may by order—

(a) amend subsection (1) or (2)—

(i) to add or remove a type of consent, or

(ii) to vary the cases in relation to which a type of consent is within that subsection;

(b) make further provision, or amend or repeal provision, about—

(i) the types of consent that are, and are not, within subsection (1) or (2), or

(ii) the cases in relation to which a type of consent is, or is not, within either of those subsections.

(6) In this section 'consent' means—

(a) a consent or authorisation that is required, under legislation, to be obtained for development,

(b) a consent, or authorisation, that—

(i) may authorise development, and

(ii) is given under legislation, or

(c) a notice that is required by legislation to be given in relation to development.

(7) In subsection (6) 'legislation' means an Act or an instrument made under an Act.

(8) An order under subsection (5) may not affect—

(a) a requirement for a devolved consent to be obtained for, or given in relation to, development, or

(b) whether development may be authorised by a devolved consent.

(9) A consent is 'devolved' for the purposes of subsection (8) if—

(a) provision for the consent would be within the legislative competence of the National Assembly for Wales if the provision were contained in an Act of the Assembly,

(b) provision for the consent is, or could be, made by the Welsh Ministers in an instrument made under an Act,

(c) the consent is not within subsection (6)(c) and the Welsh Ministers have a power or duty—

(i) to decide, or give directions as to how to decide, whether the consent is given,

(ii) to decide, or give directions as to how to decide, some or all of the terms on which the consent is given, or

(iii) to revoke or vary the consent, or

(d) the consent is within subsection (6)(c) and the notice has to be given to the Welsh Ministers or otherwise brought to their attention.

(10) An order under subsection (5)(b) may amend this Act.][1]

1 Repealed by Growth and Infrastructure Act 2013, s 18(3)(a) (25 June 2013).
2 Added by Localism Act 2011, s 131(1), (2) (1 April 2012).

34 Welsh offshore generating stations

(1) Section 33(2) does not prevent an order under section 3 of the Transport and Works Act 1992 (c. 42) from authorising the carrying out of works consisting of the construction or extension of a generating station that is or (when constructed or extended) will be a Welsh offshore generating station.

(2) A 'Welsh offshore generating station' is a generating station that is in waters in or adjacent to Wales up to the seaward limits of the territorial sea.

(3) If, by virtue of subsection (1), an order under section 3 of the Transport and Works Act 1992 authorises the carrying out of any works, development consent is treated as not being required for the carrying out of those works.

[35 Directions in relation to projects of national significance

(1) The Secretary of State may give a direction for development to be treated as development for which development consent is required.

This is subject to the following provisions of this section and section 35ZA.

(2) The Secretary of State may give a direction under subsection (1) only if—

(a) the development is or forms part of—

(i) a project (or proposed project) in the field of energy, transport, water, waste water or waste, or

(ii) a business or commercial project (or proposed project) of a prescribed description,

(b) the development will (when completed) be wholly in one or more of the areas specified in subsection (3), and

(c) the Secretary of State thinks the project (or proposed project) is of national significance, either by itself or when considered with—

(i) in a case within paragraph (a)(i), one or more other projects (or proposed projects) in the same field;

(ii) in a case within paragraph (a)(ii), one or more other business or commercial projects (or proposed projects) of a description prescribed under paragraph (a)(ii).

(3) The areas are—

(a) England or waters adjacent to England up to the seaward limits of the territorial sea;

(b) in the case of a project for the carrying out of works in the field of energy, a Renewable Energy Zone, except any part of a Renewable Energy Zone in relation to which the Scottish Ministers have functions.

(4) The Secretary of State may give a direction under subsection (1) only with the consent of the Mayor of London if—

(a) all or part of the development is or will be in Greater London, and

(b) the development is or forms part of a business or commercial project (or proposed project) of a description prescribed under subsection (2)(a)(ii).

(5) Regulations under subsection (2)(a)(ii) may not prescribe a description of project which includes the construction of one or more dwellings.][1]

1 Sections 35 and 35ZA substituted for s 35 by Growth and Infrastructure Act 2013, s 26(1), (2) (25 April 2013).

[35ZA Directions under sections 35: procedural matters

(1) The power in section 35(1) to give a direction in a case within section 35(2)(a)(i) (projects in the field of energy etc) is exercisable only in response to a qualifying request if no application for a consent or authorisation mentioned in section 33(1) or (2) has been made in relation to the development to which the request relates.

(2) The power in section 35(1) to give a direction in a case within section 35(2)(a)(ii) (business or commercial projects of prescribed description) is exercisable only in response to a qualifying request made by one or more of the following—

(a) a person who proposes to carry out any of the development to which the request relates;

(b) a person who has applied, or proposes to apply, for a consent or authorisation mentioned in section 33(1) or (2) in relation to any of that development;

(c) a person who, if a direction under section 35(1) is given in relation to that development, proposes to apply for an order granting development consent for any of that development.

(3) If the Secretary of State gives a direction under section 35(1) in relation to development, the Secretary of State may—

(a) if an application for a consent or authorisation mentioned in section 33(1) or (2) has been made in relation to the development, direct the application to be treated as an application for an order granting development consent;

(b) if a person proposes to make an application for such a consent or authorisation in relation to the development, direct the proposed application to be treated as a proposed application for development consent.

(4) A direction under section 35(1), or subsection (3) of this section, may be given so as to apply for specified purposes or generally.

(5) A direction under subsection (3) may provide for specified provisions of or made under this or any other Act—

(a) to have effect in relation to the application, or proposed application, with any specified modifications, or

(b) to be treated as having been complied with in relation to the application or proposed application.

(6) If the Secretary of State gives a direction under subsection (3), the relevant authority must refer the application, or proposed application, to the Secretary of State instead of dealing with it themselves.

(7) If the Secretary of State is considering whether to give a direction under subsection (3), the Secretary of State may direct the relevant authority to take no further action in relation to the application, or proposed application, until the Secretary of State has decided whether to give the direction.

(8) The Secretary of State may require an authority within subsection (9) to provide any information required by the Secretary of State for the purpose of enabling the Secretary of State to decide—

(a) whether to give a direction under section 35(1), and

(b) the terms in which such a direction should be given.

(9) An authority is within this subsection if an application for a consent or authorisation mentioned in section 33(1) or (2) in relation to the development has been, or may be, made to it.

(10) If the Secretary of State decides to give a direction under section 35(1), the Secretary of State must give reasons for the decision.

(11) In this section—

'qualifying request' means a written request, for a direction under section 35(1) or subsection (3) of this section, that—

(a) specifies the development to which it relates, and

(b) explains why the conditions in section 35(2)(a) and (b) are met in relation to the development;

'relevant authority'—

(a) in relation to an application for a consent or authorisation mentioned in section 33(1) or (2) that has been made, means the authority to which the application was made, and

(b) in relation to such an application that a person proposes to make, means the authority to which the person proposes to make the application.][1]

1 Sections 35 and 35ZA substituted for s 35 by Growth and Infrastructure Act 2013, s 26(1), (2) (25 April 2013).

[35A Timetable for deciding request for direction under section 35

(1) This section applies if the Secretary of State receives a qualifying request from a person ('R').

(2) The Secretary of State must make a decision on the qualifying request before the primary deadline, subject to subsection (3).

(3) Subsection (2) does not apply if, before the primary deadline, the Secretary of State asks R to provide the Secretary of State with information for the purpose of enabling the Secretary of State to decide—

(a) whether to give the direction requested, and

(b) the terms in which it should be given.

(4) If R—

(a) is asked under subsection (3) to provide information, and

(b) provides the information sought within the period of 14 days beginning with the day on which R is asked to do so,

the Secretary of State must make a decision on the qualifying request before the end of the period of 28 days beginning with the day the Secretary of State receives the information.

(5) In this section—

'the primary deadline' means the end of the period of 28 days beginning with the day on which the Secretary of State receives the qualifying request;

'qualifying request' has the meaning given by [section 35ZA(11)][1].][2]

1 Word substituted by Growth and Infrastructure Act 2013, s 26(1), (3) (25 April 2013).
2 Added by Localism Act 2011, s 132(10) (1 April 2012).

36 Amendments consequential on development consent regime

Schedule 2 makes amendments consequential on the development consent regime.

Part 5 Applications for orders granting development consent

Chapter 1 Applications

37 Applications for orders granting development consent

(1) An order granting development consent may be made only if an application is made for it.

(2) An application for an order granting development consent must be made to the [Secretary of State][1].

(3) An application for an order granting development consent must [, so far as necessary to secure that the application (including accompaniments) is of a standard that the Secretary of State considers satisfactory][2] —

(a) specify the development to which it relates,

(b) be made in the prescribed form,

(c) be accompanied by the consultation report, and

(d) be accompanied by documents and information of a prescribed description.

(4) The [Secretary of State][1] may give guidance about how the requirements under subsection (3) are to be complied with.

(5) The [Secretary of State][1] may set standards for—

(a) the preparation of a document required by subsection (3)(d);

(b) the coverage in such a document of a matter falling to be dealt with in it;

(c) all or any of the collection, sources, verification, processing and presentation of information required by subsection (3)(d).

(6) The [Secretary of State][1] must publish, in such manner as [the Secretary of State][3] thinks appropriate, any guidance given under subsection (4) and any standards set under subsection (5).

(7) In subsection (3)(c) 'the consultation report' means a report giving details of—

(a) what has been done in compliance with sections 42, 47 and 48 in relation to a proposed application that has become the application,

(b) any relevant responses, and

(c) the account taken of any relevant responses.

(8) In subsection (7) 'relevant response' has the meaning given by section 49(3).

1 Word substituted by Localism Act 2011, s 128(2), Sch 13, paras 1, 5(1), (2) (1 April 2012).
2 Words inserted by Localism Act 2011, s 137(1), (5) (1 April 2012).
3 Word substituted by Localism Act 2011, s 128(2), Sch 13, paras 1, 5(1), (3) (1 April 2012).

38 ...

Repealed by Localism Act 2011, ss 128(2), 237, Sch 13, paras 1, 6, Sch 25, Pt 20 as from 1 April 2012.

39 Register of applications

(1) The [Secretary of State][1] is to maintain a register of applications received by [the Secretary of State][2] for orders granting development consent ('the register').

(2) Where the [Secretary of State][1] receives an application for an order granting development consent, [the Secretary of State][2] must cause details of the application to be entered in the register.

(3) The [Secretary of State][1] must publish the register or make arrangements for inspection of the register by the public.

(4) The [Secretary of State][1] must make arrangements for inspection by the public of—

(a) applications received by the [Secretary of State][1] for orders granting development consent,

(b) consultation reports received by the [Secretary of State][1] under section 37(3)(c), and

(c) accompanying documents and information received by the [Secretary of State][1] under section 37(3)(d).

1 Word substituted by Localism Act 2011, s 128(2), Sch 13, paras 1, 7(1), (2) (1 April 2012).
2 Word substituted by Localism Act 2011, s 128(2), Sch 13, paras 1, 7(1), (3) (1 April 2012).

40 Applications by the Crown for orders granting development consent

(1) This section applies to an application for an order granting development consent made by or on behalf of the Crown.

(2) The Secretary of State may by regulations modify or exclude any statutory provision relating to—

(a) the procedure to be followed before such an application is made;

(b) the making of such an application;

(c) the decision-making process for such an application.

(3) A statutory provision is a provision contained in or having effect under this Act or any other enactment.

Chapter 2 Pre-application procedure

41 Chapter applies before application is made

(1) This Chapter applies where a person ('the applicant') proposes to make an application for an order granting development consent.

(2) In the following provisions of this Chapter—

'the proposed application' means the proposed application mentioned in subsection (1);

'the land' means the land to which the proposed application relates or any part of that land;

'the proposed development' means the development for which the proposed application (if made) would seek development consent.

[42 Duty to consult

(1) The applicant must consult the following about the proposed application—

(a) such persons as may be prescribed,

(aa) the Marine Management Organisation, in any case where the proposed development would affect, or would be likely to affect, any of the areas specified in subsection (2),

(b) each local authority that is within section 43,

(c) the Greater London Authority if the land is in Greater London, and

(d) each person who is within one or more of the categories set out in section 44.

(2) The areas are—

(a) waters in or adjacent to England up to the seaward limits of the territorial sea;

(b) an exclusive economic zone, except any part of an exclusive economic zone in relation to which the Scottish Ministers have functions;

(c) a Renewable Energy Zone, except any part of a Renewable Energy Zone in relation to which the Scottish Ministers have functions;

(d) an area designated under section 1(7) of the Continental Shelf Act 1964, except any part of that area which is within a part of an exclusive economic zone or Renewable Energy Zone in relation to which the Scottish Ministers have functions.][1]

1 Existing s 42 renumbered as s 42(1) and s 42(1)(aa) and (2) inserted by Marine and Coastal Access Act 2009, s 23(1), (2) (1 April 2010).

43 [Local authorities for purposes of section 42(1)(b)][1]

(1) A local authority is within this section if the land is in the authority's area.

(2) A local authority ('A') is within this section if—

(a) the land is in the area of another local authority ('B'), [...][2]

[(aa) B is a unitary council or a lower-tier district council, and][2]

(b) any part of the boundary of A's area is also a part of the boundary of B's area.

[(2A) If the land is in the area of an upper-tier county council ('C'), a local authority ('D') is within this section if—

(a) D is not a lower-tier district council, and

(b) any part of the boundary of D's area is also part of the boundary of C's area.][3]

[(3) In this section—

'local authority' means—

(a) a county council, or district council, in England;

(b) a London borough council;

(c) the Common Council of the City of London;

(d) the Council of the Isles of Scilly;

(e) a county council, or county borough council, in Wales;

(f) a council constituted under section 2 of the Local Government etc (Scotland) Act 1994;

(g) a National Park authority;

(h) the Broads Authority;

'lower-tier district council' means a district council in England for an area for which there is a county council;

'unitary council' means a local authority that is not an upper-tier county council, a lower-tier district council, a National Park authority or the Broads Authority;

'upper-tier county council' means a county council in England for each part of whose area there is a district council.][4]

1 Heading substituted by Marine and Coastal Access Act 2009, s 23(1), (3)(a) (1 April 2010).
2 Added by Localism Act 2011, s 133(1), (2) (1 April 2012).
3 Added by Localism Act 2011, s 133(1), (3) (1 April 2012).
4 Substituted by Localism Act 2011, s 133(1), (4) (1 April 2012).

44 [Categories for purposes of section 42(1)(d)][1]

(1) A person is within Category 1 if the applicant, after making diligent inquiry, knows that the person is an owner, lessee, tenant (whatever the tenancy period) or occupier of the land.

(2) A person is within Category 2 if the applicant, after making diligent inquiry, knows that the person—

(a) is interested in the land, or

(b) has power—

(i) to sell and convey the land, or

(ii) to release the land.

(3) An expression, other than 'the land', that appears in subsection (2) of this section and also in section 5(1) of the Compulsory Purchase Act 1965 (c. 56) has in subsection (2) the meaning that it has in section 5(1) of that Act.

(4) A person is within Category 3 if the applicant thinks that, if the order sought by the proposed application were to be made and fully implemented, the person would or might be entitled—

(a) as a result of the implementing of the order,

(b) as a result of the order having been implemented, or

(c) as a result of use of the land once the order has been implemented,

to make a relevant claim.

This is subject to subsection (5).

(5) A person is within Category 3 only if the person is known to the applicant after making diligent inquiry.

(6) In subsection (4) 'relevant claim' means—

(a) a claim under section 10 of the Compulsory Purchase Act 1965 (c. 56) (compensation where satisfaction not made for the taking, or injurious affection, of land subject to compulsory purchase);

(b) a claim under Part 1 of the Land Compensation Act 1973 (c. 26) (compensation for depreciation of land value by physical factors caused by use of public works) [;][2]

[(c) a claim under section 152(3).][2]

1 Heading substituted by Marine and Coastal Access Act 2009, s 23(1), (3)(b) (1 April 2010).
2 Added by Localism Act 2011, s 135(1), (8) (1 April 2012).

45 Timetable for consultation under section 42

(1) The applicant must, when consulting a person under section 42, notify the person of the deadline for the receipt by the applicant of the person's response to the consultation.

(2) A deadline notified under subsection (1) must not be earlier than the end of the period of 28 days that begins with the day after the day on which the person receives the consultation documents.

(3) In subsection (2) 'the consultation documents' means the documents supplied to the person by the applicant for the purpose of consulting the person.

46 Duty to notify [Secretary of State][1] of proposed application

(1) The applicant must supply the [Secretary of State][2] with such information in relation to the proposed application as the applicant would supply to the [Secretary of State][2] for the purpose of complying with section 42 if the applicant were required by that section to consult the [Secretary of State][2] about the proposed application.

(2) The applicant must comply with subsection (1) on or before commencing consultation under section 42.

1 Word substituted by Localism Act 2011, s 128(2), Sch 13, paras 1, 8(1), (3) (1 April 2012).
2 Word substituted by Localism Act 2011, s 128(2), Sch 13, paras 1, 8(1), (2) (1 April 2012).

47 Duty to consult local community

(1) The applicant must prepare a statement setting out how the applicant proposes to consult, about the proposed application, people living in the vicinity of the land.

(2) Before preparing the statement, the applicant must consult each local authority that is within section 43(1) about what is to be in the statement.

(3) The deadline for the receipt by the applicant of a local authority's response to consultation under subsection (2) is the end of the period of 28 days that begins with the day after the day on which the local authority receives the consultation documents.

(4) In subsection (3) 'the consultation documents' means the documents supplied to the local authority by the applicant for the purpose of consulting the local authority under subsection (2).

(5) In preparing the statement, the applicant must have regard to any response to consultation under subsection (2) that is received by the applicant before the deadline imposed by subsection (3).

(6) Once the applicant has prepared the statement, the applicant [must—][1]

[(za) make the statement available for inspection by the public in a way that is reasonably convenient for people living in the vicinity of the land,][1]

(a) [publish,][2] in a newspaper circulating in the vicinity of the land[, a notice stating where and when the statement can be inspected][3], and

(b) [publish the statement in such manner][4] as may be prescribed.

(7) The applicant must carry out consultation in accordance with the proposals set out in the statement.

1 Words and para (za) substituted for words by Localism Act 2011, s 134(a) (1 April 2012).
2 Word inserted by Localism Act 2011, s 134(b)(i) (1 April 2012).
3 Words inserted by Localism Act 2011, s 134(b)(ii) (1 April 2012).
4 Words substituted by Localism Act 2011, s 134(c) (1 April 2012).

48 Duty to publicise

(1) The applicant must publicise the proposed application in the prescribed manner.

(2) Regulations made for the purposes of subsection (1) must, in particular, make provision for publicity under subsection (1) to include a deadline for receipt by the applicant of responses to the publicity.

49 Duty to take account of responses to consultation and publicity

(1) Subsection (2) applies where the applicant—

(a) has complied with sections 42, 47 and 48, and

(b) proposes to go ahead with making an application for an order granting development consent (whether or not in the same terms as the proposed application).

(2) The applicant must, when deciding whether the application that the applicant is actually to make should be in the same terms as the proposed application, have regard to any relevant responses.

(3) In subsection (2) 'relevant response' means—

(a) a response from a person consulted under section 42 that is received by the applicant before the deadline imposed by section 45 in that person's case,

(b) a response to consultation under section 47(7) that is received by the applicant before any applicable deadline imposed in accordance with the statement prepared under section 47, or

(c) a response to publicity under section 48 that is received by the applicant before the deadline imposed in accordance with section 48(2) in relation to that publicity.

50 Guidance about pre-application procedure

(1) Guidance may be issued about how to comply with the requirements of this Chapter.

(2) Guidance under this section may be issued by [...][1] the Secretary of State.

(3) The applicant must have regard to any guidance under this section.

1 Words repealed by Localism Act 2011, s 237, Sch 25, Pt 20 (1 April 2012).

Chapter 3 Assistance for applicants and others

51 Advice for potential applicants and others

(1) [This section applies to advice][1] about—

(a) applying for an order granting development consent;

(b) making representations about an application, or a proposed application, for such an order.

[(3) The Secretary of State may by regulations make provision about the giving of advice to which this section applies.

(4) In particular, regulations under subsection (3) may make provision that has the effect that—

(a) a request for advice made by an applicant, potential applicant or other person, or

(b) advice given to an applicant, potential applicant or other person,

must be, or may be, disclosed by the Secretary of State to other persons or to the public generally.][2]

1 Words substituted by Localism Act 2011, s 128(2), Sch 13, paras 1, 10(1), (2) (15 January 2012 for the purpose of conferring power on the Secretary of State to make regulations or rules; 1 April 2012 otherwise).

2 Section 51(3)-(4) substituted for s 51(2)-(4) by Localism Act 2011, s 128(2), Sch 13, paras 1, 10(1), (3) (15 January 2012 for the purpose of conferring power on the Secretary of State to make regulations or rules; 1 April 2012 otherwise).

52 Obtaining information about interests in land

(1) Where a person is applying, or proposes to apply, for an order granting development consent, [subsections (2) and (2A) apply][1] for the purpose of enabling the person ('the applicant') to comply with provisions of, or made under, Chapter 2 of this Part or Chapter 1 of Part 6.

(2) The [Secretary of State][2] may authorise the applicant to serve a notice on a person mentioned in subsection (3) requiring the person ('the recipient') to give to the applicant in writing the name and address of any person the recipient believes is one or more of the following—

(a) an owner, lessee, tenant (whatever the tenancy period) or occupier of the land;

(b) a person interested in the land;

(c) a person having power—

(i) to sell and convey the land, or

(ii) to release the land.

[(2A) The Secretary of State may authorise the applicant to serve a notice on a person mentioned in subsection (3) requiring the person ('the recipient') to give to the applicant in writing the name and address of any person the recipient believes is a person who, if the order sought by the application or proposed application were to be made and fully implemented, would or might be entitled—

(a) as a result of the implementing of the order,

(b) as a result of the order having been implemented, or

(c) as a result of the use of the land once the order has been implemented,

to make a relevant claim.][3]

(3) The persons are—

(a) an occupier of the land;

(b) a person who has an interest in the land as freeholder, mortgagee or lessee;

(c) a person who directly or indirectly receives rent for the land;

(d) a person who, in pursuance of an agreement between that person and a person interested in the land, is authorised to manage the land or to arrange for the letting of it.

(4) A notice under subsection (2) [or (2A)][4] must—

(a) be in writing,

(b) state that the [Secretary of State][2] has authorised the applicant to serve the notice,

(c) specify or describe the land to which the application, or proposed application, relates,

(d) specify the deadline by which the recipient must give the required information to the applicant, and

(e) draw attention to the provisions in subsections (6) to (9).

(5) A deadline specified under subsection (4)(d) in a notice must not be earlier than the end of the 14 days beginning with the day after the day on which the notice is served on the recipient of the notice.

[(5A) A notice under subsection (2A) must explain the circumstances in which a person would or might be entitled as mentioned in that subsection.][5]

(6) A person commits an offence if the person fails without reasonable excuse to comply with a notice under subsection (2) [or (2A)][4] served on the person.

(7) A person commits an offence if, in response to a notice under subsection (2) [or (2A)][4] served on the person—

(a) the person gives information which is false in a material particular, and

(b) when the person does so, the person knows or ought reasonably to know that the information is false.

(8) If an offence under this section committed by a body corporate is proved to have been committed with the consent or connivance of, or to be attributable to any neglect on the part of—

(a) a director, manager, secretary or other similar officer of the body,

(b) a person purporting to act in any such capacity, or

(c) in a case where the affairs of the body are managed by its members, a member of the body,

that person, as well as the body, is guilty of that offence and liable to be proceeded against accordingly.

(9) A person guilty of an offence under this section is liable on summary conviction to a fine not exceeding level 5 on the standard scale.

(10) In subsections [(2) to (3)][6] 'the land' means—

(a) the land to which the application, or proposed application, relates, or

(b) any part of that land.

(11) Any other expression that appears in either of paragraphs (b) and (c) of subsection (2) and also in section 5(1) of the Compulsory Purchase Act 1965 (c. 56) has in those paragraphs the meaning that it has in section 5(1) of that Act.

[(12) In subsection (3) as it applies for the purposes of subsection (2A) 'the land' also includes any relevant affected land (see subsection (13)).

(13) Where the applicant believes that, if the order sought by the application or proposed application were to be made and fully implemented, there would or might be persons entitled—

(a) as a result of the implementing of the order,

(b) as a result of the order having been implemented, or

(c) as a result of the use of the land once the order has been implemented,

to make a relevant claim in respect of any land or in respect of an interest in any land, that land is 'relevant affected land' for the purposes of subsection (12).

(14) In this section 'relevant claim' means—

(a) a claim under section 10 of the Compulsory Purchase Act 1965 (compensation where satisfaction not made for compulsory purchase of land or not made for injurious affection resulting from compulsory purchase);

(b) a claim under Part 1 of the Land Compensation Act 1973 (compensation for depreciation of land value by physical factors caused by use of public works);

(c) a claim under section 152(3).][7]

1 Words substituted by Localism Act 2011, s 135(1), (2) (1 April 2012).
2 Word substituted by Localism Act 2011, s 128(2), Sch 13, paras 1, 11 (1 April 2012).
3 Added by Localism Act 2011, s 135(1), (3) (1 April 2012).
4 Words inserted by Localism Act 2011, s 135(1), (4) (1 April 2012).
5 Added by Localism Act 2011, s 135(1), (5) (1 April 2012).
6 Words substituted by Localism Act 2011, s 135(1), (6) (1 April 2012).
7 Added by Localism Act 2011, s 135(1), (7) (1 April 2012).

53 Rights of entry

(1) Any person duly authorised in writing by the [Secretary of State][1] may at any reasonable time enter any land for the purpose of surveying and taking levels of it[, or in order to facilitate compliance with the provisions mentioned in subsection (1A),][2] in connection with—

(a) an application for an order granting development consent, whether in relation to that or any other land, that has been accepted by the [Secretary of State][1],

(b) a proposed application for an order granting development consent, or

(c) an order granting development consent that includes provision authorising the compulsory acquisition of that land or of an interest in it or right over it.

[(1A) Those provisions are any provision of or made under an Act for the purpose of implementing—

(a) Council Directive 85/337/EEC of 27 June 1985 on the assessment of the effects of certain public and private projects on the environment, as amended from time to time,

(b) Council Directive 92/43/EC of 21 May 1992 on the conservation of natural habitats and of wild fauna and flora, as amended from time to time, or

(c) any EU instrument from time to time replacing all or any part of either of those Directives.][3]

(2) Authorisation may be given by the [Secretary of State][1] under subsection (1)(b) in relation to any land only if it appears to the [Secretary of State][1] that—

(a) the proposed applicant is considering a distinct project of real substance genuinely requiring entry onto the land [.][4]

[...][4]

(3) Subject to subsections (9) and (10), power conferred by subsection (1) to survey land includes power to search and bore for the purpose of ascertaining the nature of the subsoil or the presence of minerals or other matter in it.

[(3A) Power conferred by subsection (1) for the purpose of complying with the provisions mentioned in subsection (1A) includes power to take, and process, samples of or from any of the following found on, in or over the land—

(a) water,

(b) air,

(c) soil or rock,

(d) its flora,

(e) bodily excretions, or dead bodies, of non-human creatures, or

(f) any non-living thing present as a result of human action.][5]

(4) A person authorised under subsection (1) to enter any land—

(a) must, if so required, produce evidence of the person's authority, and state the purpose of the person's entry, before so entering,

(b) may not demand admission as of right to any land which is occupied unless 14 days' notice of the intended entry has been given to the occupier, and

(c) must comply with any other conditions subject to which the [Secretary of State's][6] authorisation is given.

(5) A person commits an offence if the person wilfully obstructs a person acting in the exercise of power under subsection (1).

(6) A person guilty of an offence under subsection (5) is liable on summary conviction to a fine not exceeding level 3 on the standard scale.

(7) Where any damage is caused to land or chattels—

(a) in the exercise of a right of entry conferred under subsection (1), or

(b) in the making of any survey for the purpose of which any such right of entry has been conferred, compensation may be recovered by any person suffering the damage from the person exercising the right of entry.

(8) Any question of disputed compensation under subsection (7) must be referred to and determined by the [Upper Tribunal][7].

(9) No person may carry out under subsection (1) any works authorised by virtue of subsection (3) unless notice of the person's intention to do so was included in the notice required by subsection (4)(b).

(10) The authority of the appropriate Minister is required for the carrying out under subsection (1) of works authorised by virtue of subsection (3) if—

(a) the land in question is held by statutory undertakers, and

(b) they object to the proposed works on the ground that execution of the works would be seriously detrimental to the carrying-on of their undertaking.

(11) In subsection (10)—

'the appropriate Minister' means—

(a) in the case of land in Wales held by water or sewerage undertakers, the Welsh Ministers, and

(b) in any other case, the Secretary of State;

'statutory undertakers' means persons who are, or who are deemed to be, statutory undertakers for the purposes of any provision of Part 11 of TCPA 1990.

1 Word substituted by Localism Act 2011, s 128(2), Sch 13, paras 1, 12(1), (2) (1 April 2012).
2 Words inserted by Localism Act 2011, s 136(1), (2) (1 April 2012).
3 Added by Localism Act 2011, s 136(1), (3) (1 April 2012).
4 Repealed by Localism Act 2011, s 237, Sch 25, Pt 20 (1 April 2012).
5 Added by Localism Act 2011, s 136(1), (5) (1 April 2012).
6 Word substituted by Localism Act 2011, s 128(2), Sch 13, paras 1, 12(1), (3) (1 April 2012).
7 Words substituted by Transfer of Tribunal Functions (Lands Tribunal and Miscellaneous Amendments) Order 2009, SI 2009/1307, art 5(1), (2), Sch 1, paras 291, 292 (1 October 2009: substitution came into force on 1 June 2009 but could not take effect until the commencement of Planning Act 2008, s 53(8) on 1 October 2009).

54 Rights of entry: Crown land

(1) [Subsections (1) to (3A) of section 53][1] apply to Crown land subject to subsections (2) and (3) of this section.

(2) A person must not enter Crown land unless the person ('P') has the permission of—

(a) a person appearing to P to be entitled to give it, or

(b) the appropriate Crown authority.

(3) In section 53(3), the words 'Subject to subsections (9) and (10)' must be ignored.

(4) Subsections (4) to (6) and (9) to (11) of section 53 do not apply to anything done by virtue of subsections (1) to (3) of this section.

1 Words substituted by Localism Act 2011, s 136(1), (6) (1 April 2012).

Part 6 Deciding applications for orders granting development consent

Chapter 1 Handling of application by Commission

55 Acceptance of applications

(1) The following provisions of this section apply where the [Secretary of State][1] receives an application that purports to be an application for an order granting development consent.

(2) The [Secretary of State][1] must, by the end of the period of 28 days beginning with the day after the day on which [the Secretary of State][2] receives the application, decide whether or not to accept the application.

(3) The [Secretary of State][1] may accept the application only if the [Secretary of State][1] concludes—

(a) that it is an application for an order granting development consent,

[…][3]

(c) that development consent is required for any of the development to which the application relates,

[…][3]

(e) that the applicant has, in relation to a proposed application that has become the application, complied with Chapter 2 of Part 5 (pre-application procedure) [, and][4]

[(f) that the application (including accompaniments) is of a standard that the Secretary of State considers satisfactory.][4]

(4) The [Secretary of State][1], when deciding whether [the Secretary of State][2] may reach the conclusion in subsection (3)(e), must have regard to—

(a) the consultation report received under section 37(3)(c),

(b) any adequacy of consultation representation received by [the Secretary of State][2] from a local authority consultee, and

(c) the extent to which the applicant has had regard to any guidance issued under section 50.

(5) In subsection (4)—

'local authority consultee' means—

(a) a local authority consulted under [section 42(1)(b)][5] about a proposed application that has become the application, or

(b) the Greater London Authority if consulted under [section 42(1)(c)][6] about that proposed application;

'adequacy of consultation representation' means a representation about whether the applicant complied, in relation to that proposed application, with the applicant's duties under sections 42, 47 and 48.

[(5A) The Secretary of State, when deciding whether the Secretary of State may reach the conclusion in subsection (3)(f), must have regard to the extent to which—

(a) the application complies with the requirements in section 37(3) (form and contents of application) and any standards set under section 37(5), and

(b) any applicable guidance given under section 37(4) has been followed in relation to the application.][7]

(6) If the [Secretary of State][1] accepts the application, [the Secretary of State][2] must notify the applicant of the acceptance.

(7) If the [Secretary of State][1] is of the view that [the application cannot be accepted, the Secretary of State][8] must—

(a) notify that view to the applicant, and

(b) notify the applicant of [the Secretary of State's][9] reasons for that view.

(8) If in response the applicant modifies (or further modifies) the application, subsections (2) to (7) then apply in relation to the application as modified.

1 Word substituted by Localism Act 2011, s 128(2), Sch 13, paras 1, 13(1), (2) (1 April 2012).
2 Word substituted by Localism Act 2011, s 128(2), Sch 13, paras 1, 13(1), (3) (1 April 2012).
3 Repealed by Localism Act 2011, s 237, Sch 25, Pt 21 (1 April 2012).
4 Added by Localism Act 2011, s 137(1), (3) (1 April 2012).
5 Words substituted by Marine and Coastal Access Act 2009, s 23(1), (4)(a) (1 April 2010).
6 Words substituted by Marine and Coastal Access Act 2009, s 23(1), (4)(b) (1 April 2010).
7 Added by Localism Act 2011, s 137(1), (4) (1 April 2012).
8 Words substituted by Localism Act 2011, s 128(2), Sch 13, paras 1, 13(1), (4)(a) (1 April 2012).
9 Word substituted by Localism Act 2011, s 128(2), Sch 13, paras 1, 13(1), (4)(b) (1 April 2012).

56 Notifying persons of accepted application

(1) Subsections (2), (6) and (7) apply where the [Secretary of State][1] accepts an application for an order granting development consent.

(2) The applicant must give notice of the application to—

(a) such persons as may be prescribed,

[(aa) the Marine Management Organisation, in any case where the development for which the application seeks development consent would involve the carrying on of any activity in one or more of the areas specified in subsection (2A),][2]

[(b) each local authority that is within section 56A,][3]

(c) the Greater London Authority if the land to which the application relates, or any part of it, is in Greater London, and

(d) each person who is within one or more of the categories set out in section 57.

[(2A) The areas are—

(a) waters in or adjacent to England up to the seaward limits of the territorial sea;

(b) an exclusive economic zone, except any part of an exclusive economic zone in relation to which the Scottish Ministers have functions;

(c) a Renewable Energy Zone, except any part of a Renewable Energy Zone in relation to which the Scottish Ministers have functions;

(d) an area designated under section 1(7) of the Continental Shelf Act 1964, except any part of that area which is within a part of an exclusive economic zone or Renewable Energy Zone in relation to which the Scottish Ministers have functions.][4]

(3) Notice under subsection (2) must be in such form and contain such matter, and be given in such manner, as may be prescribed.

(4) The applicant must, when giving notice to a person under subsection (2), notify the person of the deadline for receipt by the [Secretary of State][1] of representations giving notice of the person's interest in, or objection to, the application.

(5) A deadline notified under subsection (4) must not be earlier than the end of the period of 28 days that begins with the day after the day on which the person receives the notice.

(6) The applicant must make available, to each person to whom notice is given under subsection (2), a copy of—

(a) the application, and

(b) the documents and information that were required by section 37(3)(d) to accompany the application.

(7) The applicant must publicise the application in the prescribed manner.

(8) Regulations made for the purposes of subsection (7) must, in particular, make provision for publicity under subsection (7) to include a deadline for receipt by the [Secretary of State][1] of representations giving notice of persons' interests in, or objections to, the application.

(9) A deadline specified in accordance with subsection (8) does not apply to a person to whom notice is given under subsection (2).

1 Word substituted by Localism Act 2011, s 128(2), Sch 13, paras 1, 14 (1 April 2012).
2 Added by Marine and Coastal Access Act 2009, s 23(1), (5)(a) (1 April 2010).
3 Substituted by Localism Act 2011, s 138(1), (2) (1 April 2012).
4 Added by Marine and Coastal Access Act 2009, s 23(1), (5)(b) (1 April 2010).

[56A Local authorities for the purposes of sections 56(2)(b) and 60(2)(a)

(1) A local authority is within this section if the land is in the authority's area.

(2) A local authority ('A') is within this section if—

(a) the land is in the area of another local authority ('B'),

(b) B is a unitary council or a lower-tier district council, and

(c) any part of the boundary of A's area is also a part of the boundary of B's area.

(3) If the land is in the area of an upper-tier county council ('C'), a local authority ('D') is within this section if—

(a) D is not a lower-tier district council, and

(b) any part of the boundary of D's area is also part of the boundary of C's area.

(4) In this section—

'the land' means the land to which the application concerned relates or any part of that land;

'local authority' has the meaning given in section 102(8);

'lower-tier district council' means a district council in England for an area for which there is a county council;

'unitary council' means a local authority that is not an upper-tier county council, a lower-tier district council, a National Park authority or the Broads Authority;

'upper-tier county council' means a county council in England for each part of whose area there is a district council.][1]

1 Added by Localism Act 2011, s 138(1), (3) (1 April 2012).

57 Categories for purposes of section 56(2)(d)

(1) A person is within Category 1 if the applicant, after making diligent inquiry, knows that the person is an owner, lessee, tenant (whatever the tenancy period) or occupier of the land.

(2) A person is within Category 2 if the applicant, after making diligent inquiry, knows that the person—

(a) is interested in the land, or

(b) has power—

(i) to sell and convey the land, or

(ii) to release the land.

(3) An expression, other than 'the land', that appears in subsection (2) of this section and also in section 5(1) of the Compulsory Purchase Act 1965 (c. 56) has in subsection (2) the meaning that it has in section 5(1) of that Act.

(4) A person is within Category 3 if the applicant thinks that, if the order sought by the application were to be made and fully implemented, the person would or might be entitled—

(a) as a result of the implementing of the order,

(b) as a result of the order having been implemented, or

(c) as a result of use of the land once the order has been implemented,

to make a relevant claim.

This is subject to subsection (5).

(5) A person is within Category 3 only if the person is known to the applicant after making diligent inquiry.

(6) In subsection (4) 'relevant claim' means—

(a) a claim under section 10 of the Compulsory Purchase Act 1965 (compensation where satisfaction not made for the taking, or injurious affection, of land subject to compulsory purchase);

(b) a claim under Part 1 of the Land Compensation Act 1973 (c. 26) (compensation for depreciation of land value by physical factors caused by use of public works) [;][1]

[(c) a claim under section 152(3).][1]

(7) In this section 'the land' means the land to which the application relates or any part of that land.

1 Added by Localism Act 2011, s 135(1), (9) (1 April 2012).

58 Certifying compliance with section 56

(1) Subsection (2) applies where—

(a) the [Secretary of State][1] has accepted an application for an order granting development consent, and

(b) the applicant has complied with section 56 in relation to the application.

(2) The applicant must, in such form and manner as may be prescribed, certify to the [Secretary of State][1] that the applicant has complied with section 56 in relation to the application.

(3) A person commits an offence if the person issues a certificate which—

(a) purports to be a certificate under subsection (2), and

(b) contains a statement which the person knows to be false or misleading in a material particular.

(4) A person commits an offence if the person recklessly issues a certificate which—

(a) purports to be a certificate under subsection (2), and

(b) contains a statement which is false or misleading in a material particular.

(5) A person guilty of an offence under this section is liable on summary conviction to a fine not exceeding level 5 on the standard scale.

(6) A magistrates' court may try an information relating to an offence under this section whenever laid.

(7) Section 127 of the Magistrates' Courts Act 1980 (c. 43) has effect subject to subsection (6) of this section.

1 Word substituted by Localism Act 2011, s 128(2), Sch 13, paras 1, 15 (1 April 2012).

59 Notice of persons interested in land to which compulsory acquisition request relates

(1) This section applies where—

(a) the [Secretary of State][1] has accepted an application for an order granting development consent, and

(b) the application includes a request for an order granting development consent to authorise compulsory acquisition of land or of an interest in or right over land (a 'compulsory acquisition request').

(2) The applicant must give to the [Secretary of State][1] a notice specifying the names, and such other information as may be prescribed, of each affected person.

(3) Notice under subsection (2) must be given in such form and manner as may be prescribed.

(4) A person is an 'affected person' for the purposes of this section if the applicant, after making diligent inquiry, knows that the person is interested in the land to which the compulsory acquisition request relates or any part of that land.

1 Word substituted by Localism Act 2011, s 128(2), Sch 13, paras 1, 16 (1 April 2012).

60 Local impact reports

(1) Subsection (2) applies where the [Secretary of State][1] —

(a) has accepted an application for an order granting development consent, and

(b) has received—

(i) a certificate under section 58(2) in relation to the application, and

(ii) where section 59 applies, a notice under that section in relation to the application.

(2) The [Secretary of State][1] must give notice in writing to each of the following, inviting them to submit a local impact report [to the Secretary of State][2] —

[(a) each local authority that is within section 56A, and][3]

(b) the Greater London Authority if the land to which the application relates, or any part of it, is in Greater London.

(3) A 'local impact report' is a report in writing giving details of the likely impact of the proposed development on the authority's area (or any part of that area).

(4) 'The proposed development' is the development for which the application seeks development consent.

(5) A notice under subsection (2) must specify the deadline for receipt by the [Secretary of State][1] of the local impact report.

1 Word substituted by Localism Act 2011, s 128(2), Sch 13, paras 1, 17(1), (2) (1 April 2012).
2 Words substituted by Localism Act 2011, s 128(2), Sch 13, paras 1, 17(1), (3) (1 April 2012).
3 Substituted by Localism Act 2011, s 138(1), (4) (1 April 2012).

61 Initial choice of Panel or single [appointed person][1]

[(1) Subsection (2) applies where the Secretary of State has accepted an application for an order granting development consent.][2]

[(2) The Secretary of State must decide whether the application—

(a) is to be handled by a Panel under Chapter 2, or

(b) is to be handled by a single appointed person under Chapter 3.

(3) The Secretary of State must publish the criteria that are to be applied in making decisions under subsection (2).][3]

1 Word substituted by Localism Act 2011, s 128(2), Sch 13, paras 1, 18(1), (4) (1 April 2012).
2 Substituted by Infrastructure Act 2015, s 26 (12 April 2015).
3 Section 61(2)-(3) substituted for s 61(2)-(5) by Localism Act 2011, s 128(2), Sch 13, paras 1, 18(1), (3) (1 April 2012).

62 Switching from single [appointed person][1] to Panel

(1) Subsection (2) applies where an application for an order granting development consent is being handled by a single [appointed person][1] under Chapter 3.

[(2) The Secretary of State may decide that the application should instead be handled by a Panel under Chapter 2.

(3) The Secretary of State must publish the criteria that are to be applied in making decisions under subsection (2).][2]

1 Word substituted by Localism Act 2011, s 128(2), Sch 13, paras 1, 19(1), (2) (1 April 2012).
2 Section 62(2)-(3) substituted for s 62(2)-(5) by Localism Act 2011, s 128(2), Sch 13, paras 1, 19(1), (3) (1 April 2012).

63 …

Repealed by Localism Act 2011, s 237, Sch 25, Pt 20 (1 April 2012).

Chapter 2 The Panel procedure

Panels

64 Panel for each application to be handled under this Chapter

(1) This Chapter applies where—

(a) the [Secretary of State][1] accepts an application for an order granting development consent, and

(b) under section 61(2) or 62(2), it is decided that the application is to be handled by a Panel under this Chapter.

(2) There is to be a Panel (referred to in this Chapter as 'the Panel') to handle the application.

1 Word substituted by Localism Act 2011, s 128(2), Sch 13, paras 1, 21 (1 April 2012).

65 Appointment of members, and lead member, of Panel

[(1) The Secretary of State must appoint—

(a) three, four or five persons to be members of the Panel, and

(b) one of those persons to chair the Panel.][1]

(2) In this Chapter 'the lead member' means the person who for the time being is appointed to chair the Panel.

[...][2]

1 Substituted by Localism Act 2011, s 128(2), Sch 13, paras 1, 22(1), (2) (1 April 2012).
2 Repealed by Localism Act 2011, ss 128(2), 237, Sch 13, paras 1, 22(1), (3), Sch 25, Pt 20 (1 April 2012).

66 Ceasing to be member, or lead member, of Panel

[...][1]

(2) The person appointed to be the lead member ceases to hold that office if the person ceases to be a member of the Panel.

(3) A person may resign from membership of the Panel by giving notice in writing to the [Secretary of State][2].

(4) The lead member may resign that office, without also resigning from membership of the Panel, by giving notice in writing to the [Secretary of State][2].

(5) The [Secretary of State][3] —

(a) may remove a person ('the Panel member') from membership of the Panel if the [Secretary of State][4] is satisfied that the Panel member is unable, unwilling or unfit to perform the duties of Panel membership;

(b) may remove the lead member from that office, without also removing the lead member from membership of the Panel, if the [Secretary of State][4] is satisfied that the lead member is unable, unwilling or unfit to perform the duties of the office.

1 Repealed by Localism Act 2011, ss 128(2), 237, Sch 13, paras 1, 23(1), (2), Sch 25, Pt 20 (1 April 2012).
2 Word substituted by Localism Act 2011, s 128(2), Sch 13, paras 1, 23(1), (3) (1 April 2012).
3 Words substituted by Localism Act 2011, s 128(2), Sch 13, paras 1, 23(1), (4)(a) (1 April 2012).
4 Word substituted by Localism Act 2011, s 128(2), Sch 13, paras 1, 23(1), (4)(b) (1 April 2012).

67 ...

Repealed by Localism Act 2011, ss 128(2), 237, Sch 13, paras 1, 24, Sch 25, Pt 20 (1 April 2012).

68 Additional appointments to Panel

(1) Subsections (2) and (3) apply at any time after the initial members of the Panel have been appointed under section 65(1)(a).

[(2) The Secretary of State may appoint a person to be a member of the Panel, but this power may not be exercised so as to cause the Panel to have more than five members.][1]

(3) If at any time the Panel has only two members or a single member, it is the duty of the [Secretary of State][2] to ensure that the power under subsection (2) is exercised so as to secure that the Panel again has at least three members.

(4) A person appointed under subsection (2) becomes a member of the Panel in addition to any person who is otherwise a member of the Panel.

[...][3]

1 Substituted by Localism Act 2011, s 128(2), Sch 13, paras 1, 25(1), (2) (1 April 2012).
2 Words substituted by Localism Act 2011, s 128(2), Sch 13, paras 1, 25(1), (3) (1 April 2012).
3 Repealed by Localism Act 2011, ss 128(2), 237, Sch 13, paras 1, 25(1), (4), Sch 25, Pt 20 (1 April 2012).

69 Replacement of lead member of Panel

(1) Subsection (2) applies where a person ceases to hold the office of lead member.

(2) The [Secretary of State][1] must appoint a member of the Panel to chair the Panel.

(3) A person may be appointed under subsection (2) even though that person was not a member of the Panel when the vacancy arose.

[...][2]

1 Words substituted by Localism Act 2011, s 128(2), Sch 13, paras 1, 26(1), (2) (1 April 2012).
2 Repealed by Localism Act 2011, ss 128(2), 237, Sch 13, paras 1, 26(1), (3), Sch 25, Pt 20 (1 April 2012).

70 ...

Repealed by Localism Act 2011, ss 128(2), 237, Sch 13, paras 1, 27, Sch 25, Pt 20 (1 April 2012).

71 Supplementary provision where Panel replaces single [appointed person][1]

(1) Subsections (2) and (3) apply where this Chapter applies as the result of a decision under section 62(2).

(2) [An appointed person][2]—

(a) may be appointed under section 65(1)(a) or 68(2) as a member of the Panel, and

(b) if a member of the Panel, may be appointed under section 65(1)(b) or 69(2) to chair the Panel.

(3) The Panel may, so far as it thinks appropriate, decide to treat things done by or in relation to [an appointed person][3] in proceedings under Chapter 3 on the application as done by or in relation to the Panel.

(4) Where the Panel makes a decision under subsection (3), the lead member is under a duty to ensure that the membership of the Panel has the necessary knowledge of the proceedings under Chapter 3 on the application.

[(5) In this section 'appointed person' means a person appointed to handle the application under Chapter 3.][4]

1 Word substituted by Localism Act 2011, s 128(2), Sch 13, paras 1, 28(1), (5) (1 April 2012).
2 Words substituted by Localism Act 2011, s 128(2), Sch 13, paras 1, 28(1), (2) (1 April 2012).
3 Words substituted by Localism Act 2011, s 128(2), Sch 13, paras 1, 28(1), (3) (1 April 2012).
4 Added by Localism Act 2011, s 128(2), Sch 13, paras 1, 28(1), (4) (1 April 2012).

72 Panel ceasing to have any members

(1) If the Panel ceases to have any members, a new Panel must be constituted under section 65(1).

(2) At times after the new Panel has been constituted (but subject to the further application of this subsection in the event that the new Panel ceases to have any members), references in this Chapter to the Panel are to be read as references to the new Panel.

(3) The new Panel may, so far as it thinks appropriate, decide to treat things—

(a) done by or in relation to a previous Panel appointed to handle the application, or

(b) treated under section 71(3) as done by or in relation to a previous Panel appointed to handle the application,

as done by or in relation to the new Panel.

(4) Where the Panel makes a decision under subsection (3), the lead member is under a duty to ensure that the membership of the Panel has the necessary knowledge of the proceedings on the application up until the reconstitution of the Panel.

(5) The power under section 68(2) is not exercisable at times when the Panel has no members.

73 Consequences of changes in Panel

(1) The Panel's continuing identity is to be taken not to be affected by—

(a) any change in the membership of the Panel;

(b) the Panel's coming to have only two members or a single member;

(c) any change in the lead member;

(d) a vacancy in that office.

(2) When there is a change in the membership of the Panel, the lead member is under a duty to ensure that the membership of the Panel after the change has the necessary knowledge of the proceedings on the application up until the change.

(3) Subsection (2) does not apply where the change occurs as a result of the Panel being reconstituted as required by section 72(1).

Panel's role in relation to application

74 Panel to decide, or make recommendation in respect of, application

[...][1]

(2) [The Panel][2] has the functions of—

(a) examining the application, and

(b) making a report to the Secretary of State on the application setting out—

(i) the Panel's findings and conclusions in respect of the application, and

(ii) the Panel's recommendation as to the decision to be made on the application.

(3) The Panel's functions under this section are to be carried out in accordance with Chapter 4.

[...][1]

1 Repealed by Localism Act 2011, ss 128(2), 237, Sch 13, paras 1, 29(1), (2), (4), Sch 25, Pt 20 (1 April 2012).

2 Words substituted by Localism Act 2011, s 128(2), Sch 13, paras 1, 29(3) (1 April 2012).

75 Decision-making by the Panel

(1) The making of a decision by the Panel requires the agreement of a majority of its members.

(2) The lead member has a second (or casting) vote in the event that the number of members of the Panel agreeing to a proposed decision is the same as the number of members not so agreeing.

76 Allocation within Panel of Panel's functions

(1) This section applies in relation to the Panel's examination of the application.

(2) The Panel, as an alternative to itself undertaking a part of the examination, may allocate the undertaking of that part to any one or more of the members of the Panel.

(3) Where there is an allocation under subsection (2)—

(a) anything that under Chapter 4 is required or authorised to be done by or to the Panel in connection with the allocated part of the examination may be done by or to the member or members concerned (or by or to the Panel), and

(b) findings and conclusions of the member or members concerned in respect of the matters allocated are to be taken to be the Panel's.

(4) Subsection (3)(b) has effect subject to any decision of the Panel, made on the occasion of making the allocation or earlier, as to the status of any such findings or conclusions.

(5) Where there is an allocation under subsection (2) to two or more of the members of the Panel, the making of a decision by the members concerned requires the agreement of all of them.

77 Exercise of Panel's powers for examining application

(1) In this section 'procedural power' means any power conferred on the Panel for the purposes of its examination of the application.

(2) A procedural power, as well as being exercisable by the Panel itself, is also (subject to subsection (3)) exercisable by any one or more of the members of the Panel.

(3) The Panel may decide to restrict or prohibit the exercise of a procedural power otherwise than by the Panel itself.

(4) Subsection (2)—

(a) applies whether or not there is an allocation under section 76(2), and

(b) where there is such an allocation, is in addition to section 76(3)(a).

(5) Subsection (3) does not authorise curtailment of a power conferred by section 76(3)(a).

Chapter 3 The [single appointed person][1] procedure

The single [appointed person][1]

78 Single [appointed person][1] to handle application

(1) This Chapter applies where—

(a) the [Secretary of State][2] accepts an application for an order granting development consent, and

(b) under section 61(2), it is decided that the application is to be handled by a single [appointed person][3] under this Chapter.

(2) In this Chapter ['the single appointed person'][4] means the person who is appointed to handle the application under this Chapter.

1 Word substituted by Localism Act 2011, s 128(2), Sch 13, paras 1, 30(1), (5), (6) (1 April 2012).
2 Word substituted by Localism Act 2011, s 128(2), Sch 13, paras 1, 30(1), (2) (1 April 2012).
3 Word substituted by Localism Act 2011, s 128(2), Sch 13, paras 1, 30(1), (3) (1 April 2012).
4 Word substituted by Localism Act 2011, s 128(2), Sch 13, paras 1, 30(1), (4) (1 April 2012).

[79 Appointment of single appointed person

The Secretary of State must appoint a person to handle the application.][1]

1 Substituted by Localism Act 2011, s 128(2), Sch 13, paras 1, 31 (1 April 2012).

80 Ceasing to be the single [appointed person][1]

[...][2]

(2) A person may resign from being the single [appointed person][3] by giving notice in writing to the [Secretary of State][4].

(3) The [Secretary of State][5] may remove a person ('the appointee') from being the single [appointed person][6] [if the Secretary of State][7] is satisfied that the appointee is unable, unwilling or unfit to perform the duties of the single [appointed person][6].

1 Word substituted by Localism Act 2011, s 128(2), Sch 13, paras 1, 32(1), (5) (1 April 2012).
2 Repealed by Localism Act 2011, ss 128(2), 237, Sch 13, paras 1, 32(1), (2), Sch 25, Pt 20 (1 April 2012).
3 Word substituted by Localism Act 2011, s 128(2), Sch 13, paras 1, 32(1), (3)(a) (1 April 2012).
4 Word substituted by Localism Act 2011, s 128(2), Sch 13, paras 1, 32(1), (3)(b) (1 April 2012).
5 Words substituted by Localism Act 2011, s 128(2), Sch 13, paras 1, 32(1), (4)(a) (1 April 2012).
6 Word substituted by Localism Act 2011, s 128(2), Sch 13, paras 1, 32(1), (4)(b) (1 April 2012).
7 Words substituted by Localism Act 2011, s 128(2), Sch 13, paras 1, 32(1), (4)(c) (1 April 2012).

81 ...

Repealed by Localism Act 2011, ss 128(2), 237, Sch 13, paras 1, 33, Sch 25, Pt 20 (1 April 2012).

82 Appointment of replacement single [appointed person][1]

(1) Where a person ceases to be the single [appointed person][1], a new appointment of a person to handle the application must be made under section 79.

(2) Where that happens, the new single [appointed person][1] may, so far as may be appropriate, decide to treat things done by or in relation to any previous single [appointed person][1] as done by or in relation to the new single [appointed person][1].

(3) Where the single [appointed person][1] makes a decision under subsection (2), the single [appointed person][1] is under a duty to acquire the necessary knowledge of the previous proceedings on the application.

1 Words substituted by Localism Act 2011, s 128(2), Sch 13, paras 1, 34 (1 April 2012).

Single [appointed person][1]'s role in relation to application

83 Single [appointed person][1] to examine and report on application

(1) The single [appointed person][1] has the functions of—

(a) examining the application, and

(b) making a report [to the Secretary of State][2] on the application setting out—

(i) the single [appointed person][1]'s findings and conclusions in respect of the application, and

(ii) the single [appointed person][1]'s recommendation as to the decision to be made on the application.

[...][3]

(3) The single [appointed person][1]'s functions under subsection (1) are to be carried out in accordance with Chapter 4.

[...][3]

1 Words substituted by Localism Act 2011, s 128(2), Sch 13, paras 1, 35(1), (2) (1 April 2012).
2 Words inserted by Localism Act 2011, s 128(2), Sch 13, paras 1, 35(1), (3) (1 April 2012).
3 Repealed by Localism Act 2011, ss 128(2), 237, Sch 13, paras 1, 35(1), (4), (5), Sch 25, Pt 20 (1 April 2012).

Commission's role in respect of application

84–85 ...

Repealed by Localism Act 2011, ss 128(2), 237, Sch 13, paras 1, 36, Sch 25, Pt 20 (1 April 2012).

Chapter 4 Examination of applications under Chapter 2 or 3

86 Chapter applies to examination by Panel or single [appointed person][1]

(1) This Chapter applies—

(a) in relation to the examination of an application by a Panel under Chapter 2, and

(b) in relation to the examination of an application by a single [appointed person][1] under Chapter 3.

(2) In this Chapter as it applies in relation to the examination of an application by a Panel under Chapter 2, 'the Examining authority' means the Panel.

(3) In this Chapter as it applies in relation to the examination of an application by a single [appointed person][1] under Chapter 3, 'the Examining authority' means the single [appointed person][1].

1 Word substituted by Localism Act 2011, s 128(2), Sch 13, paras 1, 37 (1 April 2012).

87 Examining authority to control examination of application

(1) It is for the Examining authority to decide how to examine the application.

(2) The Examining authority, in making any decision about how the application is to be examined, must—

(a) comply with—

(i) the following provisions of this Chapter, and

(ii) any rules made under section 97[.][1]

[...][1]

(3) The Examining authority may in examining the application disregard representations if the Examining authority considers that the representations—

(a) are vexatious or frivolous,

(b) relate to the merits of policy set out in a national policy statement, or

(c) relate to compensation for compulsory acquisition of land or of an interest in or right over land.

1 Repealed by Localism Act 2011, ss 128(2), 237, Sch 13, paras 1, 38, Sch 25, Pt 20 (1 April 2012).

88 Initial assessment of issues, and preliminary meeting

(1) The Examining authority must make such an initial assessment of the principal issues arising on the application as the Examining authority thinks appropriate.

(2) After making that assessment, the Examining authority must hold a meeting.

(3) The Examining authority must invite to the meeting—

(a) the applicant, [...][1]

(b) each other interested party,

[(c) each statutory party, and

(d) each local authority that is within section 88A,][2]

whether or not the Examining authority is required by rules under section 97, or chooses, also to invite other persons.

[(3A) In subsection (3)(c) 'statutory party' means a person specified in, or of a description specified in, regulations made by the Secretary of State.][3]

(4) The purposes of the meeting are—

(a) to enable invitees present at the meeting to make representations to the Examining authority about how the application should be examined,

(b) to discuss any other matter that the Examining authority wishes to discuss, and

(c) any other purpose that may be specified in rules under section 97.

(5) Subsections (2) to (4) do not prevent the Examining authority holding other meetings.

(6) Rules under section 97—

(a) may (in particular) make provision supplementing subsections (1) to (4), and

(b) must make provision as to when the assessment under subsection (1) is to be made and as to when the meeting required by subsection (2) is to be held.

1 Word repealed by Localism Act 2011, s 138(1), (5)(a) (15 January 2012 for the purpose of conferring power on the Secretary of State to make regulations; 1 April 2012 otherwise).
2 Added by Localism Act 2011, s 138(1), (5)(b) (15 January 2012 for the purpose of conferring power on the Secretary of State to make regulations; 1 April 2012 otherwise).
3 Added by Localism Act 2011, s 138(1), (5)(c) (15 January 2012 for the purpose of conferring power on the Secretary of State to make regulations; 1 April 2012 otherwise).

[88A Local authorities for the purposes of section 88(3)(d)

(1) A local authority ('A') is within this section if—

(a) the land is in the area of another local authority ('B'),

(b) B is a unitary council or a lower-tier district council, and

(c) any part of the boundary of A's area is also a part of the boundary of B's area.

(2) If the land is in the area of an upper-tier county council ('C'), a local authority ('D') is within this section if—

(a) D is not a lower-tier district council, and

(b) any part of the boundary of D's area is also part of the boundary of C's area.

(3) In this section—

'the land' means the land to which the application relates or any part of that land;

'local authority' has the meaning given in section 102(8);

'lower-tier district council' means a district council in England for an area for which there is a county council;

'unitary council' means a local authority that is not an upper-tier county council, a lower-tier district council, a National Park authority or the Broads Authority;

'upper-tier county council' means a county council in England for each part of whose area there is a district council.][1]

1 Added by Localism Act 2011, s 138(1), (6) (1 April 2012).

89 Examining authority's decisions about how application is to be examined

(1) The Examining authority must in the light of the discussion at the meeting held under section 88(2) make such procedural decisions as the Examining authority thinks appropriate.

(2) The decisions required by subsection (1) may be made at or after the meeting.

[(2A) Upon making the decisions required by subsection (1), the Examining authority must inform each person mentioned in section 88(3)(c) and (d)—

(a) of those decisions, and

(b) that the person may notify the Examining authority in writing that the person is to become an interested party.][1]

(3) The Examining authority may make procedural decisions otherwise than as required by subsection (1), and may do so at any time before or after the meeting.

(4) The Examining authority must inform each interested party of any procedural decision made by the Examining authority.

(5) In this section 'procedural decision' means a decision about how the application is to be examined.

1 Added by Localism Act 2011, s 138(1), (7) (1 April 2012).

90 Written representations

(1) The Examining authority's examination of the application is to take the form of consideration of written representations about the application.

(2) Subsection (1) has effect subject to—

(a) any requirement under section 91, 92 or 93 to cause a hearing to be held, and

(b) any decision by the Examining authority that any part of the examination is to take a form that is neither—

(i) consideration of written representations, nor

(ii) consideration of oral representations made at a hearing.

(3) Rules under section 97 may (in particular) specify written representations about the application which are to be, or which may be or may not be, considered under subsection (1).

91 Hearings about specific issues

(1) Subsections (2) and (3) apply where the Examining authority decides that it is necessary for the Examining authority's examination of the application to include the consideration of oral representations about a particular issue made at a hearing in order to ensure—

(a) adequate examination of the issue, or

(b) that an interested party has a fair chance to put the party's case.

(2) The Examining authority must cause a hearing to be held for the purpose of receiving oral representations about the issue.

(3) At the hearing, each interested party is entitled (subject to the Examining authority's powers of control over the conduct of the hearing) to make oral representations about the issue.

(4) Where the Examining authority is a Panel acting under Chapter 2, any two or more hearings under subsection (2) may be held concurrently.

92 Compulsory acquisition hearings

(1) This section applies where the application includes a request for an order granting development consent to authorise compulsory acquisition of land or of an interest in or right over land (a 'compulsory acquisition request').

(2) The Examining authority must fix, and cause each affected person to be informed of, the deadline by which an affected person must notify the [Secretary of State][1] that the person wishes a compulsory acquisition hearing to be held.

(3) If the [Secretary of State][1] receives notification from at least one affected person before the deadline, the Examining authority must cause a compulsory acquisition hearing to be held.

(4) At a compulsory acquisition hearing, the following are entitled (subject to the Examining authority's powers of control over the conduct of the hearing) to make oral representations about the compulsory acquisition request—

(a) the applicant;

(b) each affected person.

(5) A person is an 'affected person' for the purposes of this section if the person's name has been given to the [Secretary of State][1] in a notice under section 59.

1 Word substituted by Localism Act 2011, s 128(2), Sch 13, paras 1, 39 (1 April 2012).

93 Open-floor hearings

(1) The Examining authority must fix, and cause the interested parties to be informed of, the deadline by which an interested party must notify the [Secretary of State][1] of the party's wish to be heard at an open-floor hearing.

(2) If the [Secretary of State][1] receives notification from at least one interested party before the deadline, the Examining authority must cause an open-floor hearing to be held.

(3) At an open-floor hearing, each interested party is entitled (subject to the Examining authority's powers of control over the conduct of the hearing) to make oral representations about the application.

1 Word substituted by Localism Act 2011, s 128(2), Sch 13, paras 1, 40 (1 April 2012).

94 Hearings: general provisions

(1) The following provisions of this section apply—

(a) to a hearing under section 91(2),

(b) to a compulsory acquisition hearing (see section 92), and

(c) to an open-floor hearing (see section 93).

(2) The hearing—

(a) must be in public, and

(b) must be presided over by one or more of the members of the Panel or (as the case may be) the single [appointed person][1].

(3) It is for the Examining authority to decide how the hearing is to be conducted.

(4) In particular, it is for the Examining authority to decide—

(a) whether a person making oral representations at the hearing may be questioned at the hearing by another person and, if so, the matters to which the questioning may relate;

(b) the amount of time to be allowed at the hearing—

(i) for the making of a person's representations (including representations made in exercise of an entitlement under section 91(3), 92(4) or 93(3)), or

(ii) for any questioning by another person.

(5) The Examining authority's powers under subsections (3) and (4) are subject to—

(a) subsection (2), and

(b) any rules made under section 97.

(6) Although the Examining authority's powers under subsections (3) and (4) may be exercised for the purpose of controlling exercise of an entitlement under section 91(3), 92(4) or 93(3), those powers may not be exercised so as to deprive the person entitled of all benefit of the entitlement.

(7) In making decisions under subsection (4)(a), the Examining authority must apply the principle that any oral questioning of a person making representations at a hearing (whether the applicant or any other person) should be undertaken by the Examining authority except where the Examining authority thinks that oral questioning by another person is necessary in order to ensure—

(a) adequate testing of any representations, or

(b) that a person has a fair chance to put the person's case.

(8) The Examining authority may refuse to allow representations to be made at the hearing (including representations made in exercise of an entitlement under section 91(3), 92(4) or 93(3)) if the Examining authority considers that the representations—

(a) are irrelevant, vexatious or frivolous,

(b) relate to the merits of policy set out in a national policy statement,

(c) repeat other representations already made (in any form and by any person), or

(d) relate to compensation for compulsory acquisition of land or of an interest in or right over land.

1 Word substituted by Localism Act 2011, s 128(2), Sch 13, paras 1, 41 (1 April 2012).

95 Hearings: disruption, supervision and costs

(1) Where an interested party or any other person behaves in a disruptive manner at a hearing, the Examining authority may decide to do any one or more of the following—

(a) exclude the person from all, or part, of the remainder of the hearing;

(b) allow the person to continue to attend the hearing only if the person complies with conditions specified by the Examining authority;

(c) exclude the person from other hearings;

(d) direct that the person is allowed to attend other hearings only if the person complies with conditions specified by the Examining authority.

(2) In this section 'hearing' means—

(a) a preliminary meeting under section 88,

(b) a hearing under section 91(2),

(c) a compulsory acquisition hearing (see section 92),

(d) an open-floor hearing (see section 93),

(e) any other meeting or hearing that the Examining authority causes to be held for the purposes of the Examining authority's examination of the application, or

(f) a site visit.

[...][1]

(4) Subsection (5) of section 250 of the Local Government Act 1972 (c. 70) (provisions about costs applying where Minister causes a local inquiry to be held) applies in relation to the Examining authority's examination of the application as it applies in relation to an inquiry under that section, but with references to the Minister causing the inquiry to be held being read as references to the Examining authority.

This is subject to subsection (5) of this section.

(5) Subsections (6) to (8) of section 210 of the Local Government (Scotland) Act 1973 (c. 65) (provisions about expenses applying where Minister causes a local inquiry to be held) apply in relation to the Examining authority's examination of the application in so far as relating to a hearing held in Scotland as they apply in relation to an inquiry under that section, but with references to the Minister causing the inquiry to be held being read as references to the Examining authority.

1 Repealed by Public Bodies (Abolition of Administrative Justice and Tribunals Council) Order 2013, SI 2013/2042, art 2(2), Schedule, para 40(a) (19 August 2013).

[95A Hearings: defence and national security

(1) Subsection (2) applies if the Secretary of State is satisfied that if all or part of the Examining Authority's examination of the application takes the form of a meeting or hearing—

(a) the making of particular oral representations at such a meeting or hearing would be likely to result in the disclosure of information as to defence or national security, and

(b) the public disclosure of that information would be contrary to the national interest.

(2) The Secretary of State may direct that representations of a description specified in the direction may be made only to persons of a description so specified (instead of being made in public).

(3) If the Secretary of State gives a direction under subsection (2), the Attorney General or (where the representations are to be made in Scotland) the Advocate General for Scotland may appoint a person (an 'appointed representative') to represent the interests of an interested party who (by virtue of the direction) is prevented from being present when the representations are made.

(4) Rules under section 97 may (in particular) make provision as to the functions of an appointed representative.

(5) The Secretary of State may direct a person (a 'responsible person') to pay the fees and expenses of an appointed representative if the Secretary of State thinks that the responsible person is interested in a meeting or hearing in relation to any representations that are the subject of a direction under subsection (2).

(6) Subsections (7) and (8) apply if the Secretary of State gives a direction under subsection (5).

(7) If the appointed representative and the responsible person are unable to agree the amount of the fees and expenses, the amount must be determined by the Secretary of State.

(8) The Secretary of State must cause the amount agreed between the appointed representative and the responsible person, or determined by the Secretary of State, to be certified.

(9) An amount so certified is recoverable from the responsible person as a civil debt.

(10) In this section 'representations' includes evidence.][1]

1 Added by Localism Act 2011, s 128(2), Sch 13, paras 1, 42 (15 January 2012).

96 Representations not made orally may be made in writing

(1) Subsection (2) applies where—

(a) a person asks the Examining authority to be allowed to make oral representations about the application at a hearing,

(b) the person does not (for whatever reason) make the representations orally at a hearing,

(c) written representations from the person are received by the [Secretary of State][1] before the Examining authority completes the Examining authority's examination of the application, and

(d) the written representations state that they are ones that the person asked to be allowed to, but did not, make orally at a hearing.

(2) The Examining authority must consider the written representations as part of the Examining authority's examination of the application, subject to section 87(3).

1 Word substituted by Localism Act 2011, s 128(2), Sch 13, paras 1, 43 (1 April 2012).

97 Procedure rules

(1) The Lord Chancellor or (if subsection (2) applies) the Secretary of State [...][1] may make rules regulating the procedure to be followed in connection with the Examining authority's examination of the application.

(2) This subsection applies if the development to which the application relates (or part of the development) is the construction (other than by a gas transporter) of an oil or gas cross-country pipe-line—

(a) one end of which is in England or Wales, and

(b) the other end of which is in Scotland.

(3) Rules under subsection (1) may make provision for or in connection with authorising the Examining authority, alone or with others, to enter onto land, including land owned or occupied otherwise than by the applicant, for the purpose of inspecting the land as part of the Examining authority's examination of the application.

(4) Rules under subsection (1) may regulate procedure in connection with matters preparatory to the Examining authority's examination of the application, and in connection with matters subsequent to the examination, as well as in connection with the conduct of the examination.

(5) Power under this section to make rules includes power to make different provision for different purposes.

(6) Power under this section to make rules is exercisable by statutory instrument.

(7) A statutory instrument containing rules under this section is subject to annulment pursuant to a resolution of either House of Parliament.

1 Words repealed by Public Bodies (Abolition of Administrative Justice and Tribunals Council) Order 2013, SI 2013/2042, art 2(2), Schedule, para 40(b) (19 August 2013).

98 Timetable for examining, and reporting on, application

(1) The Examining authority is under a duty to complete the Examining authority's examination of the application by the end of the period of 6 months beginning with the day after the start day.

(2) The start day is the day on which the meeting required by section 88 is held or, if that meeting is held on two or more days, the later or latest of those days.

(3) [[The Examining authority is under a duty to make its report under section 74(2)(b) or 83(1)(b)][2] by the end of the period of 3 months beginning with—

(a) the deadline for completion of its examination of the application, or

(b) (if earlier) the end of the day on which it completes the examination.][1]

(4) The [Secretary of State][3] may set a date for a deadline under this section that is later than the date for the time being set.

(5) The power under subsection (4) may be exercised—

(a) more than once in relation to the same deadline;

(b) after the date for the time being set for the deadline.

[(6) Subsections (7) and (8) apply where the power under subsection (4) is exercised.

(7) The Secretary of State must—

(a) notify each interested party of the new deadline, and

(b) publicise the new deadline in such manner as the Secretary of State thinks appropriate.

(8) The Secretary of State exercising the power must make a statement, to the House of Parliament of which that Secretary of State is a member, announcing the new deadline.

(9) A statement under subsection (8) may be written or oral.][4]

1 Words and (a) and (b) substituted for words by Localism Act 2011, s 139(1), (2) (1 April 2012).

2 Words substituted by Localism Act 2011, s 128(2), Sch 13, paras 1, 44(1), (2) (1 April 2012).
3 Words substituted by Localism Act 2011, s 128(2), Sch 13, paras 1, 44(1), (3) (1 April 2012).
4 Section 98(6)-(9) substituted for s 98(6) by Localism Act 2011, s 128(2), Sch 13, paras 1, 44(1), (4) (1 April 2012).

99 Completion of Examining authority's examination of application

When the Examining authority has completed its examination of the application, it must inform each of the interested parties of that fact.

100 Assessors

(1) The [Secretary of State][1] may, at the request of the Examining authority, appoint a person to act as an assessor to assist the Examining authority in the Examining authority's examination of the application.

(2) A person may be appointed as an assessor only if it appears to the [Secretary of State][2] that the person has expertise that makes the person a suitable person to provide assistance to the Examining authority.

1 Words substituted by Localism Act 2011, s 128(2), Sch 13, paras 1, 45(1), (2) (1 April 2012).
2 Word substituted by Localism Act 2011, s 128(2), Sch 13, paras 1, 45(1), (3) (1 April 2012).

101 Legal advice and assistance

(1) The [Secretary of State][1] may, at the request of the Examining authority, appoint a barrister, solicitor or advocate to provide legal advice and assistance to the Examining authority in connection with its examination of the application.

(2) The assistance that may be given by a person appointed under subsection (1) includes carrying out on behalf of the Examining authority any oral questioning of a person making representations at a hearing.

1 Words substituted by Localism Act 2011, s 128(2), Sch 13, paras 1, 46 (1 April 2012).

102 Interpretation of Chapter 4: 'interested party' and other expressions

(1) For the purposes of this Chapter, a person is an 'interested party' if—

(a) the person is the applicant,

[(aa) the person has been notified of the acceptance of the application in accordance with section 56(2)(d),

(ab) the Examining authority has under section 102A decided that it considers that the person is within one or more of the categories set out in section 102B,][1]

[(ba) the person is the Marine Management Organisation and the development for which the application seeks development consent would involve the carrying on of any activity in one or more of the areas specified in subsection (1A),][2]

[(c) the person is a local authority in whose area the land is located, (ca) the person—

(i) is mentioned in section 88(3)(c) or (d), and

(ii) has notified the Examining authority as mentioned in section 89(2A)(b),][3]

(d) the person is the Greater London Authority and the land is in Greater London, or

(e) the person has made a relevant representation.

[(1ZA) But a person ceases to be an 'interested party' for the purposes of this Chapter upon notifying the Examining authority in writing that the person no longer wishes to be an interested party.][4]

[(1A) The areas are—

(a) waters in or adjacent to England up to the seaward limits of the territorial sea;

(b) an exclusive economic zone, except any part of an exclusive economic zone in relation to which the Scottish Ministers have functions;

(c) a Renewable Energy Zone, except any part of a Renewable Energy Zone in relation to which the Scottish Ministers have functions;

(d) an area designated under section 1(7) of the Continental Shelf Act 1964, except any part of that area which is within a part of an exclusive economic zone or Renewable Energy Zone in relation to which the Scottish Ministers have functions.][5]

(2) In this Chapter 'representation' includes evidence, and references to the making of a representation include the giving of evidence.

[...][6]

(4) A representation is a relevant representation for the purposes of subsection (1) to the extent that—

(a) it is a representation about the application,

(b) it is made to the [Secretary of State][7] in the prescribed form and manner,

(c) it is received by the [Secretary of State][7] no later than the deadline that applies under section 56 to the person making it,

(d) it contains material of a prescribed description, and

(e) it does not contain—

(i) material about compensation for compulsory acquisition of land or of an interest in or right over land,

(ii) material about the merits of policy set out in a national policy statement, or

(iii) material that is vexatious or frivolous.

[...][6]

(8) In [subsection (1)(c)][8] 'local authority' means—

(a) a county council, or district council, in England;

(b) a London borough council;

(c) the Common Council of the City of London;

(d) the Council of the Isles of Scilly;

(e) a county council, or county borough council, in Wales;

(f) a council constituted under section 2 of the Local Government etc. (Scotland) Act 1994 (c. 39);

(g) a National Park authority;

(h) the Broads Authority.

(9) In this section 'the land' means the land to which the application relates or any part of that land.

1 Section 102(1)(aa) and (ab) substituted for s 102(1)(b) by Localism Act 2011, s 138(1), (8)(a) (1 April 2012).
2 Added by Marine and Coastal Access Act 2009, s 23(1), (6)(a) (1 April 2010).
3 Section 102(1)(c) and (ca) substituted for s 102(1)(c) by Localism Act 2011, s 138(1), (8)(b) (1 April 2012).
4 Added by Localism Act 2011, s 138(1), (8)(c) (1 April 2012).
5 Added by Marine and Coastal Access Act 2009, s 23(1), (6)(b) (1 April 2010).
6 Repealed by Localism Act 2011, ss 138(1), (8)(d), (e), 237, Sch 25, Pt 21 (1 April 2012).
7 Word substituted by Localism Act 2011, s 128(2), Sch 13, paras 1, 47 (1 April 2012).
8 Words substituted by Localism Act 2011, s 138(1), (8)(f) (1 April 2012).

[102A Persons in certain categories may ask to become interested parties etc

(1) Subsection (2) applies if—

(a) a person makes a request to the Examining authority to become an interested party,

(b) the request states that the person claims to be within one or more of the categories set out in section 102B,

(c) the person has not been notified of the acceptance of the application in accordance with section 56(2)(d), and

(d) the applicant has issued a certificate under section 58 in relation to the application.

(2) The Examining authority must decide whether it considers that the person is within one or more of the categories set out in section 102B.

(3) If the Examining authority decides that it considers that the person is within one or more of the categories set out in section 102B, the Examining authority must notify the person, and the applicant, that the person has become an interested party under section 102(1)(ab).

(4) If the Examining authority thinks that a person might successfully make a request mentioned in subsection (1)(a), the Examining authority may inform the person about becoming an interested party under section 102(1)(ab).

But the Examining authority is under no obligation to make enquiries in order to discover persons who might make such a request.][1]

1 Added by Localism Act 2011, s 138(1), (9) (1 April 2012).

[102B Categories for the purposes of section 102A

(1) A person is within Category 1 if the person is an owner, lessee, tenant (whatever the tenancy period) or occupier of the land.

(2) A person is within Category 2 if the person—

(a) is interested in the land, or

(b) has power—

(i) to sell and convey the land, or

(ii) to release the land.

(3) An expression, other than 'the land', that appears in subsection (2) of this section and also in section 5(1) of the Compulsory Purchase Act 1965 has in subsection (2) the meaning that it has in section 5(1) of that Act.

(4) A person is within Category 3 if, should the order sought by the application be made and fully implemented, the person would or might be entitled—

(a) as a result of the implementing of the order,

(b) as a result of the order having been implemented, or

(c) as a result of use of the land once the order has been implemented,

to make a relevant claim.

(5) In subsection (4) 'relevant claim' means—

(a) a claim under section 10 of the Compulsory Purchase Act 1965 (compensation where satisfaction not made for the taking, or injurious affection, of land subject to compulsory purchase);

(b) a claim under Part 1 of the Land Compensation Act 1973 (compensation for depreciation of land value by physical factors caused by use of public works);

(c) a claim under section 152(3).

(6) In this section 'the land' means the land to which the application relates or any part of that land.][1]

1 Added by Localism Act 2011, s 138(1), (9) (1 April 2012).

Chapter 5 Decisions on applications

103 [Secretary of State is to decide applications][1]

(1) The Secretary of State has the function of deciding an application for an order granting development consent [.][2]

[...][2]

[...][3]

1 Heading substituted by Localism Act 2011, s 128(2), Sch 13, paras 1, 48(1), (4) (1 April 2012).
2 Word and s 103(1)(a)-(b) repealed by Localism Act 2011, ss 128(2), 237, Sch 13, paras 1, 48(1), (2), Sch 25, Pt 20 (1 April 2012).
3 Repealed by Localism Act 2011, ss 128(2), 237, Sch 13, paras 1, 48(1), (3), Sch 25, Pt 20 (1 April 2012).

104 [Decisions in cases where national policy statement has effect][1]

(1) This section applies in relation to an application for an order granting development consent if [a national policy statement has effect in relation to development of the description to which the application relates][2].

(2) In deciding the application the [Secretary of State][3] must have regard to—

(a) any national policy statement which has effect in relation to development of the description to which the application relates (a 'relevant national policy statement'),

[(aa) the appropriate marine policy documents (if any), determined in accordance with section 59 of the Marine and Coastal Access Act 2009,][4]

(b) any local impact report (within the meaning given by section 60(3)) submitted to the [Secretary of State][5] before the deadline specified in a notice under section 60(2),

(c) any matters prescribed in relation to development of the description to which the application relates, and

(d) any other matters which the [Secretary of State][3] thinks are both important and relevant to [the Secretary of State's][6] decision.

(3) The [Secretary of State][7] must decide the application in accordance with any relevant national policy statement, except to the extent that one or more of subsections (4) to (8) applies.

(4) This subsection applies if the [Secretary of State][7] is satisfied that deciding the application in accordance with any relevant national policy statement would lead to the United Kingdom being in breach of any of its international obligations.

(5) This subsection applies if the [Secretary of State is][8] satisfied that deciding the application in accordance with any relevant national policy statement would lead to the [Secretary of State being in breach of any duty imposed on the Secretary of State][9] by or under any enactment.

(6) This subsection applies if the [Secretary of State][10] is satisfied that deciding the application in accordance with any relevant national policy statement would be unlawful by virtue of any enactment.

(7) This subsection applies if the [Secretary of State][10] is satisfied that the adverse impact of the proposed development would outweigh its benefits.

(8) This subsection applies if the [Secretary of State][10] is satisfied that any condition prescribed for deciding an application otherwise than in accordance with a national policy statement is met.

(9) For the avoidance of doubt, the fact that any relevant national policy statement identifies a location as suitable (or potentially suitable) for a particular description of development does not prevent one or more of subsections (4) to (8) from applying.

1 Heading substituted by Localism Act 2011, s 128(2), Sch 13, paras 1, 49(1), (7) (1 April 2012).
2 Words substituted by Localism Act 2011, s 128(2), Sch 13, paras 1, 49(1), (2) (1 April 2012).
3 Words substituted by Localism Act 2011, s 128(2), Sch 13, paras 1, 49(1), (3)(a) (1 April 2012).
4 Added by Marine and Coastal Access Act 2009, s 58(5) (12 November 2010).
5 Word substituted by Localism Act 2011, s 128(2), Sch 13, paras 1, 49(1), (3)(b) (1 April 2012).
6 Word substituted by Localism Act 2011, s 128(2), Sch 13, paras 1, 49(1), (3)(c) (1 April 2012).
7 Words substituted by Localism Act 2011, s 128(2), Sch 13, paras 1, 49(1), (4) (1 April 2012).
8 Words substituted by Localism Act 2011, s 128(2), Sch 13, paras 1, 49(1), (5)(a) (1 April 2012).
9 Words substituted by Localism Act 2011, s 128(2), Sch 13, paras 1, 49(1), (5)(b) (1 April 2012).
10 Words substituted by Localism Act 2011, s 128(2), Sch 13, paras 1, 49(1), (6) (1 April 2012).

105 [Decisions in cases where no national policy statement has effect][1]

(1) This section applies in relation to an application for an order granting development consent [if section 104 does not apply in relation to the application][2].

(2) In deciding the application the Secretary of State must have regard to—

(a) any local impact report (within the meaning given by section 60(3)) submitted to the [Secretary of State][3] before the deadline specified in a notice under section 60(2),

(b) any matters prescribed in relation to development of the description to which the application relates, and

(c) any other matters which the Secretary of State thinks are both important and relevant to the Secretary of State's decision.

1 Heading substituted by Localism Act 2011, s 128(2), Sch 13, paras 1, 50(1), (4) (1 April 2012).
2 Words substituted by Localism Act 2011, s 128(2), Sch 13, paras 1, 50(1), (2) (1 April 2012).
3 Word substituted by Localism Act 2011, s 128(2), Sch 13, paras 1, 50(1), (3) (1 April 2012).

106 Matters that may be disregarded when deciding application

(1) In deciding an application for an order granting development consent, the [Secretary of State][1] may disregard representations if the [Secretary of State][1] considers that the representations—

(a) are vexatious or frivolous,

(b) relate to the merits of policy set out in a national policy statement, or

(c) relate to compensation for compulsory acquisition of land or of an interest in or right over land.

(2) In this section 'representation' includes evidence.

1 Words substituted by Localism Act 2011, s 128(2), Sch 13, paras 1, 51 (1 April 2012).

107 Timetable for decisions

(1) [The [Secretary of State][2] is under a duty to decide an application for an order granting development consent by the end of the period of 3 months beginning with—

(a) the [deadline under section 98(3)][3], or

(b) (if earlier) the end of the day on which the Secretary of State receives a report on the application under section 74(2)(b) or 83(1)(b).][1]

[...][4]

(3) The [Secretary of State][5] may set a date for the deadline under subsection (1) that is later than the date for the time being set.

[...][4]

(5) The power under subsection (3) may be exercised—

(a) more than once in relation to the same deadline;

(b) after the date for the time being set for the deadline.

[(6) Subsection (7) applies where the power under subsection (3) is exercised.

(7) The Secretary of State exercising the power must make a statement, to the House of Parliament of which that Secretary of State is a member, announcing the new deadline.

(8) A statement under subsection (7) must be published in such form and manner as the Secretary of State considers appropriate.

(8A) A statement under subsection (7) may be written or oral.][6]

1 Words substituted, existing text renumbered as s 107(1)(a), word is inserted and a new s 107(1)(b) inserted by Localism Act 2011, s 139(1), (3) (1 April 2012).
2 Words substituted by Localism Act 2011, s 128(2), Sch 13, paras 1, 52(1), (2)(a) (1 April 2012).
3 Words substituted by Localism Act 2011, s 128(2), Sch 13, paras 1, 52(1), (2)(b) (1 April 2012).
4 Repealed by Localism Act 2011, s 237, Sch 25, Pt 20 (1 April 2012).
5 Words substituted by Localism Act 2011, s 128(2), Sch 13, paras 1, 52(1), (4) (1 April 2012).
6 Section 107(6)-(8A) substituted for s 107(6)-(9) by Localism Act 2011, s 128(2), Sch 13, paras 1, 52(1), (6) (1 April 2012).

Chapter 6 Suspension of decision-making process

108 Suspension during review of national policy statement

(1) This section applies where—

(a) an application is made for an order granting development consent for development of a description in relation to which a national policy statement has effect, and

(b) the Secretary of State thinks that, as a result of a change in circumstances since the national policy statement was first published or (if later) the statement or any part of it was last reviewed, all or part of the statement should be reviewed before the application is decided.

(2) The Secretary of State may direct that, until the review has been completed and the Secretary of State has complied with section 6(5) in relation to the review, [examination of the application by a Panel under Chapter 2, or a single appointed person under Chapter 3, is suspended (if not already completed).][1]

1 Words substituted by Localism Act 2011, s 128(2), Sch 13, paras 1, 53 (1 April 2012).

Chapter 7 Intervention by Secretary of State

109-113 ...

Repealed by Localism Act 2011, ss 128(2), 237, Sch 13, para 54, Sch 25, Pt 20 (1 April 2012).

Chapter 8 Grant or refusal

114 Grant or refusal of development consent

(1) When [the Secretary of State][1] has decided an application for an order granting development consent, the [Secretary of State][2] must either—

(a) make an order granting development consent, or

(b) refuse development consent.

(2) The Secretary of State may by regulations make provision regulating the procedure to be followed if the [Secretary of State][3] proposes to make an order granting development consent on terms which are materially different from those proposed in the application.

1 Word substituted by Localism Act 2011, s 128(2), Sch 13, paras 1, 55(1), (2)(a) (1 April 2012).
2 Words substituted by Localism Act 2011, s 128(2), Sch 13, paras 1, 55(1), (2)(b) (1 April 2012).
3 Words substituted by Localism Act 2011, s 128(2), Sch 13, paras 1, 55(1), (3) (1 April 2012).

115 Development for which development consent may be granted

(1) Development consent may be granted for development which is—

(a) development for which development consent is required, or

(b) associated development[, or

(c) related housing development.][1]

(2) 'Associated development' means development which—

(a) is associated with the development within subsection (1)(a) (or any part of it),

(b) *is not* [does not consist of or include][2] the construction or extension of one or more dwellings, and

(c) is within subsection (3) or (4).

(3) Development is within this subsection if it is to be carried out wholly in one or more of the following areas—

(a) England;

(b) waters adjacent to England up to the seaward limits of the territorial sea;

(c) in the case of development in the field of energy, a Renewable Energy Zone, except any part of a Renewable Energy Zone in relation to which the Scottish Ministers have functions.

(4) Development is within this subsection if—

(a) it is to be carried out wholly in Wales,

(b) it is the carrying out or construction of surface works, boreholes or pipes, and

(c) the development within subsection (1)(a) with which it is associated is development within section 17(3).

[(4B) 'Related housing development' means development which—

(a) consists of or includes the construction or extension of one or more dwellings,

(b) is on the same site as, or is next to or close to, any part of the development within subsection (1)(a), or is otherwise associated with that development (or any part of it),

(c) is to be carried out wholly in England, and

(d) meets the condition in subsection (4C).

(4C) Development meets the condition in this subsection if the development within subsection (1)(a) to which it is related is to be carried out in one or more of the following areas—

(a) England;

(b) waters adjacent to England up to the seaward limits of the territorial sea.][1]

(5) To the extent that development consent is granted for associated development [or related housing development][1], section 33 applies to the development as it applies to development for which development consent is required.

[...][3]

[(7) The Secretary of State, in deciding an application for an order granting development consent for development that includes related housing development, must take into account any matters set out in guidance published by the Secretary of State.][1]

1 Inserted by Housing and Planning Act 2016, s 160(1), (2), (4), (5), (6) (on a date to be appointed)
2 Substituted for preceding words in italics by Housing and Planning Act 2016, s 160(1), (3) (on a date to be appointed)
3 Repealed by Localism Act 2011, ss 128(2), 237, Sch 13, paras 1, 56, Sch 25, Pt 20 (1 April 2012).

116 Reasons for decision to grant or refuse development consent

(1) The [Secretary of State][1] must prepare a statement of [the Secretary of State's][2] reasons for deciding to—

(a) make an order granting development consent, or

(b) refuse development consent.

(2) The [Secretary of State][3] must provide a copy of the statement to each person who is an interested party in relation to the application for the purposes of Chapter 4 (see section 102).

(3) The [Secretary of State][4] must publish the statement in such manner as [the Secretary of State][5] thinks appropriate.

[...][6]

1 Words substituted by Localism Act 2011, s 128(2), Sch 13, paras 1, 57(1), (2)(a) (1 April 2012).
2 Word substituted by Localism Act 2011, s 128(2), Sch 13, paras 1, 57(1), (2)(b) (1 April 2012).
3 Words substituted by Localism Act 2011, s 128(2), Sch 13, paras 1, 57(1), (3) (1 April 2012).
4 Words substituted by Localism Act 2011, s 128(2), Sch 13, paras 1, 57(1), (4)(a) (1 April 2012).
5 Words substituted by Localism Act 2011, s 128(2), Sch 13, paras 1, 57(1), (4)(b) (1 April 2012).
6 Repealed by Localism Act 2011, ss 128(2), 237, Sch 13, paras 1, 57(1), (5), Sch 25, Pt 20 (1 April 2012).

117 Orders granting development consent: formalities

(1) This section applies in relation to an order granting development consent.

[...][1]

(3) Except in a case within subsection (4), the [Secretary of State][2] must publish the order in such manner as [the Secretary of State][3] thinks appropriate.

[(4) If the order includes provision—

(a) made under section 120(3) for or relating to any of the matters listed in paragraphs 32A and 32B of Schedule 5, or

(b) made in the exercise of any of the powers conferred by section 120(5)(a) or (b),

the order must be contained in a statutory instrument.][4]

[...][1]

(6) As soon as practicable after the instrument [containing the order is made, the Secretary of State][5] must deposit in the office of the Clerk of the Parliaments a copy of—

(a) the instrument,

(b) the latest version of any plan supplied by the applicant in connection with the application for the order contained in the instrument, and

(c) the statement of reasons prepared under section 116(1).

[...][1]

1 Repealed by Localism Act 2011, ss 128(2), 237, Sch 13, paras 1, 58(1), (2), Sch 25, Pt 20 (1 April 2012).
2 Words substituted by Localism Act 2011, s 128(2), Sch 13, paras 1, 58(1), (3)(a) (1 April 2012).
3 Words substituted by Localism Act 2011, s 128(2), Sch 13, paras 1, 58(1), (3)(b) (1 April 2012).
4 Substituted by Localism Act 2011, s 128(2), Sch 13, paras 1, 58(1), (4) (1 April 2012).
5 Words substituted by Localism Act 2011, s 128(2), Sch 13, paras 1, 58(1), (5) (1 April 2012).

Chapter 9 Legal challenges

118 Legal challenges relating to applications for orders granting development consent

(1) A court may entertain proceedings for questioning an order granting development consent only if—

(a) the proceedings are brought by a claim for judicial review, and

(b) the claim form is filed [before the end of][1] the period of 6 weeks beginning with [the day after][2]—

(i) the day on which the order is published, or

(ii) if later, the day on which the statement of reasons for making the order is published.

(2) A court may entertain proceedings for questioning a refusal of development consent only if—

(a) the proceedings are brought by a claim for judicial review, and

(b) the claim form is filed [before the end of][1] the period of 6 weeks beginning with [the day after][2] the day on which the statement of reasons for the refusal is published.

(3) A court may entertain proceedings for questioning a decision of the [Secretary of State][3] under section 55 not to accept an application for an order granting development consent only if—

(a) the proceedings are brought by a claim for judicial review, and

(b) the claim form is filed [before the end of][1] the period of 6 weeks beginning with [the day after][2] the day on which the [Secretary of State][3] notifies the applicant as required by subsection (7) of that section.

(4) A court may entertain proceedings for questioning a decision under paragraph 1 of Schedule 4 in relation to an error or omission in a decision document only if—

(a) the proceedings are brought by a claim for judicial review, and

(b) the claim form is filed [before the end of][1] the period of 6 weeks beginning with the day [after the day][2] on which a correction notice in respect of the error or omission is issued under paragraph 2 of that Schedule or, if the correction is required to be made by order contained in a statutory instrument, the day [after the day][2] on which the order is published.

(5) A court may entertain proceedings for questioning a decision under paragraph 2(1) of Schedule 6 to make a change to an order granting development consent only if—

(a) the proceedings are brought by a claim for judicial review, and

(b) the claim form is filed [before the end of][1] the period of 6 weeks beginning with the day [after the day][2] on which notice of the change is given under paragraph 2(12)(b) of that Schedule or, if the change to the order is required to be made by order contained in a statutory instrument, the day [after the day][2] on which the order making the change is published.

(6) A court may entertain proceedings for questioning a decision under paragraph 3(1) of Schedule 6 to make a change to, or revoke, an order granting development consent only if—

(a) the proceedings are brought by a claim for judicial review, and

(b) the claim form is filed [before the end of][1] the period of 6 weeks beginning with the day [after the day][2] on which notice of the change or revocation is given under paragraph 4(6) of that Schedule or, if the change or revocation is required to be made by order contained in a statutory instrument, the day [after the day][2] on which the order making the change or revocation is published.

(7) A court may entertain proceedings for questioning anything else done, or omitted to be done, by the Secretary of State [...][4] in relation to an application for an order granting development consent only if—

(a) the proceedings are brought by a claim for judicial review, and

(b) the claim form is filed [before the end of][1] the period of 6 weeks beginning with [the day after][2] the relevant day.

(8) 'The relevant day', in relation to an application for an order granting development consent, means the day on which—

(a) the application is withdrawn,

(b) the order granting development consent is published or (if later) the statement of reasons for making the order is published, or

(c) the statement of reasons for the refusal of development consent is published.

(9) Subsections (7) and (8) do not apply in relation to—

(a) a failure to decide an application for an order granting development consent, or

(b) anything which delays (or is likely to delay) the decision on such an application.

1 Words substituted by Criminal Justice and Courts Act 2015, s 92(4)(a)(i), (b)(i), (c)(i) (13 April 2015).
2 Words added by Criminal Justice and Courts Act 2015, s 92(4)(a)(ii), (b)(ii), (c)(ii) (13 April 2015).
3 Word substituted by Localism Act 2011, s 128(2), Sch 13, paras 1, 59(1), (2) (1 April 2012).
4 Words repealed by Localism Act 2011, ss 128(2), 237, Sch 13, paras 1, 59(1), (3), Sch 25, Pt 20 (1 April 2012).

Chapter 10 Correction of errors

119 Correction of errors in development consent decisions

Schedule 4 (correction of errors in development consent decisions) has effect.

Part 7 Orders granting development consent

Chapter 1 Content of orders

General

120 What may be included in order granting development consent

(1) An order granting development consent may impose requirements in connection with the development for which consent is granted.

(2) The requirements may in particular include[—][1]

[(a) requirements corresponding to conditions which could have been imposed on the grant of any permission, consent or authorisation, or the giving of any notice, which (but for section 33(1)) would have been required for the development;

(b) requirements to obtain the approval of the Secretary of State or any other person, so far as not within paragraph (a).][1]

(3) An order granting development consent may make provision relating to, or to matters ancillary to, the development for which consent is granted.

(4) The provision that may be made under subsection (3) includes in particular provision for or relating to any of the matters listed in Part 1 of Schedule 5.

(5) An order granting development consent may—

(a) apply, modify or exclude a statutory provision which relates to any matter for which provision may be made in the order;

(b) make such amendments, repeals or revocations of statutory provisions of local application as appear to the [Secretary of State][2] to be necessary or expedient in consequence of a provision of the order or in connection with the order;

(c) include any provision that appears to the [Secretary of State][2] to be necessary or expedient for giving full effect to any other provision of the order;

(d) include incidental, consequential, supplementary, transitional or transitory provisions and savings.

(6) In subsection (5) 'statutory provision' means a provision of an Act or of an instrument made under an Act.

(7) Subsections (3) to (6) are subject to subsection (8) and the following provisions of this Chapter.

[(8) With the exception of provision made under subsection (3) for or relating to any of the matters listed in paragraph 32B of Schedule 5, an order granting development consent may not include—

(a) provision creating offences,

(b) provision conferring power to create offences, or

(c) provision changing an existing power to create offences.][3]

(9) To the extent that provision for or relating to a matter may be included in an order granting development consent, none of the following may include any such provision—

(a) an order under section 14 or 16 of the Harbours Act 1964 (c. 40) (orders in relation to harbours, docks and wharves);

(b) an order under section 4(1) of the Gas Act 1965 (c. 36) (order authorising storage of gas in underground strata);

(c) an order under section 1 or 3 of the Transport and Works Act 1992 (c. 42) (orders as to railways, tramways, inland waterways etc.).

1 Existing text renumbered as s 120(2)(a) and s 120(2)(b) inserted by Localism Act 2011, s 140 (1 April 2012).
2 Words substituted by Localism Act 2011, s 128(2), Sch 13, paras 1, 60(1), (2) (1 April 2012).
3 Substituted by Localism Act 2011, s 128(2), Sch 13, paras 1, 60(1), (3) (1 April 2012).

121 ...

Repealed by Localism Act 2011, ss 128(2), 237, Sch 13, paras 1, 61, Sch 25, Pt 20 (1 April 2012).

Compulsory acquisition

122 Purpose for which compulsory acquisition may be authorised

(1) An order granting development consent may include provision authorising the compulsory acquisition of land only if the [Secretary of State][1] is satisfied that the conditions in subsections (2) and (3) are met.

(2) The condition is that the land—

(a) is required for the development to which the development consent relates,

(b) is required to facilitate or is incidental to that development, or

(c) is replacement land which is to be given in exchange for the order land under section 131 or 132.

(3) The condition is that there is a compelling case in the public interest for the land to be acquired compulsorily.

1 Words substituted by Localism Act 2011, s 128(2), Sch 13, paras 1, 62 (1 April 2012).

123 Land to which authorisation of compulsory acquisition can relate

(1) An order granting development consent may include provision authorising the compulsory acquisition of land only if the [Secretary of State][1] is satisfied that one of the conditions in subsections (2) to (4) is met.

(2) The condition is that the application for the order included a request for compulsory acquisition of the land to be authorised.

(3) The condition is that all persons with an interest in the land consent to the inclusion of the provision.

(4) The condition is that the prescribed procedure has been followed in relation to the land.

1 Words substituted by Localism Act 2011, s 128(2), Sch 13, paras 1, 62 (1 April 2012).

124 ...

Repealed by Localism Act 2011, ss 128(2), 237, Sch 13, paras 1, 63, Sch 25, Pt 20 (1 April 2012).

125 Application of compulsory acquisition provisions

(1) This section applies if an order granting development consent includes provision authorising the compulsory acquisition of land.

(2) Part 1 of the Compulsory Purchase Act 1965 (c. 56) (procedure for compulsory purchase) applies to the compulsory acquisition of land under the order—

(a) as it applies to a compulsory purchase to which Part 2 of the Acquisition of Land Act 1981 (c. 67) applies, and

(b) as if the order were a compulsory purchase order under that Act.

(3) Part 1 of the Compulsory Purchase Act 1965, as applied by subsection (2), has effect with the omission of the following provisions—

(a) section 4 (time limit for exercise of compulsory purchase powers);

(b) section 10 (compensation for injurious affection);

(c) […][1].

(4) In so far as the order includes provision authorising the compulsory acquisition of land in Scotland—

(a) subsections (2) and (3) do not apply, and

(b) the Acquisition of Land (Authorisation Procedure) (Scotland) Act 1947 (c. 42) ('the 1947 Act') applies to the compulsory acquisition of that land under the order as if the order were a compulsory purchase order as defined in section 1(1) of that Act.

(5) The 1947 Act, as applied by subsection (4), has effect with the omission of the following provisions—

(a) Parts 2 and 3 of the First Schedule (compulsory purchase by Ministers and special provisions as to certain descriptions of land);

(b) section 116 of the Lands Clauses Consolidation (Scotland) Act 1845 (c. 19) (time limit for exercise of compulsory purchase powers) (that section being incorporated into the 1947 Act by paragraph 1 of the Second Schedule to the 1947 Act).

(6) Subsections (2) to (5) are subject to any contrary provision made by the order granting development consent.

1 Repealed by Housing and Planning Act 2016, s 190, Sch 16, para 17 (13 July 2016).

126 Compensation for compulsory acquisition

(1) This section applies in relation to an order granting development consent which includes provision authorising the compulsory acquisition of land.

(2) The order may not include provision the effect of which is to modify the application of a compensation provision, except to the extent necessary to apply the provision to the compulsory acquisition of land authorised by the order.

(3) The order may not include provision the effect of which is to exclude the application of a compensation provision.

(4) A compensation provision is a provision of or made under an Act which relates to compensation for the compulsory acquisition of land.

127 Statutory undertakers' land

(1) This section applies in relation to land ('statutory undertakers' land') if—

(a) the land has been acquired by statutory undertakers for the purposes of their undertaking,

(b) a representation has been made about an application for an order granting development consent before the completion of the examination of the application, and the representation has not been withdrawn, and

(c) as a result of the representation the [Secretary of State][1] is satisfied that—

(i) the land is used for the purposes of carrying on the statutory undertakers' undertaking, or

(ii) an interest in the land is held for those purposes.

(2) An order granting development consent may include provision authorising the compulsory acquisition of statutory undertakers' land only to the extent that the [Secretary of State is satisfied of the matters set out in subsection (3).][2]

(3) The matters are that the nature and situation of the land are such that—

(a) it can be purchased and not replaced without serious detriment to the carrying on of the undertaking, or

(b) if purchased it can be replaced by other land belonging to, or available for acquisition by, the undertakers without serious detriment to the carrying on of the undertaking.

(4) Subsections (2) and (3) do not apply in a case within subsection (5).

(5) An order granting development consent may include provision authorising the compulsory acquisition of a right over statutory undertakers' land by the creation of a new right over land only to the extent that the [Secretary of State is satisfied of the matters set out in subsection (6).][2]

(6) The matters are that the nature and situation of the land are such that—

(a) the right can be purchased without serious detriment to the carrying on of the undertaking, or

(b) any detriment to the carrying on of the undertaking, in consequence of the acquisition of the right, can be made good by the undertakers by the use of other land belonging to or available for acquisition by them.

[…][3]

(8) In this section—

'statutory undertakers' has the meaning given by section 8 of the Acquisition of Land Act 1981 (c. 67) and also includes the undertakers—

(a) which are deemed to be statutory undertakers for the purposes of that Act, by virtue of another enactment;

(b) which are statutory undertakers for the purposes of section 16(1) and (2) of that Act (see section 16(3) of that Act).

(9) In the application of this section to a statutory undertaker which is a health service body (as defined in section 60(7) of the National Health Service and Community Care Act 1990 (c. 19)), references to land acquired or available for acquisition by the statutory undertakers are to be construed as references to land acquired or available for acquisition by the Secretary of State for use or occupation by the body.

1 Words substituted by Localism Act 2011, s 128(2), Sch 13, paras 1, 64(1), (2) (1 April 2012).

2 Words substituted by Growth and Infrastructure Act 2013, s 23(1), (2)(a), (b) (25 June 2013).
3 Repealed by Growth and Infrastructure Act 2013, s 23(1), (2)(c) (25 June 2013).

128, 129 ...

Repealed by Growth and Infrastructure Act 2013, s 24(1) (25 June 2013).

130 National Trust land

(1) This section applies to land belonging to the National Trust which is held by the Trust inalienably.

(2) An order granting development consent is subject to special parliamentary procedure, to the extent that the order authorises the compulsory acquisition of land to which this section applies, if the condition in subsection (3) is met.

(3) The condition is that—

(a) a representation has been made by the National Trust about the application for the order granting development consent before the completion of the examination of the application, [...][1]

[(aa) the representation contains an objection to the compulsory acquisition of the land, and][1]

(b) the [objection][2] has not been withdrawn.

[(3A) In a case to which this section applies and to which section 131 or 132 also applies, special parliamentary procedure—

(a) may be required by subsection (2) whether or not also required by section 131(3) or 132(2), and

(b) may be required by section 131(3) or 132(2) whether or not also required by subsection (2).][3]

(4) In this section 'held inalienably', in relation to land belonging to the National Trust, means that the land is inalienable under section 21 of the National Trust Act 1907 (c. cxxxvi) or section 8 of the National Trust Act 1939 (c. lxxxvi).

(5) In this section 'the National Trust' means the National Trust for Places of Historic Interest or Natural Beauty incorporated by the National Trust Act 1907 (c. cxxxvi).

1 Added by Localism Act 2011, s 141(1), (3)(a) (1 April 2012).
2 Word substituted by Localism Act 2011, s 141(1), (3)(b) (1 April 2012).
3 Added by Growth and Infrastructure Act 2013, s 24(5) (25 June 2013).

131 Commons, open spaces etc: compulsory acquisition of land

(1) This section applies to any land forming part of a common, open space or fuel or field garden allotment.

(2) This section does not apply in a case to which section 132 applies.

(3) An order granting development consent is subject to special parliamentary procedure, to the extent that the order authorises the compulsory acquisition of land to which this section applies, [unless—

(a) the Secretary of State is satisfied that one of subsections (4) to (5) applies, and

(b) that fact, and the subsection concerned, are recorded in the order or otherwise in the instrument or other document containing the order.][1]

(4) This subsection applies if—

(a) replacement land has been or will be given in exchange for the order land, and

(b) the replacement land has been or will be vested in the prospective seller and subject to the same rights, trusts and incidents as attach to the order land.

[(4A) This subsection applies if—

(a) the order land is, or forms part of, an open space,

(b) none of the order land is of any of the other descriptions in subsection (1),

(c) either—

(i) there is no suitable land available to be given in exchange for the order land, or

(ii) any suitable land available to be given in exchange is available only at prohibitive cost, and

(d) it is strongly in the public interest for the development for which the order grants consent to be capable of being begun sooner than is likely to be possible if the order were to be subject (to any extent) to special parliamentary procedure.

(4B) This subsection applies if—

(a) the order land is, or forms part of, an open space,

(b) none of the order land is of any of the other descriptions in subsection (1), and

(c) the order land is being acquired for a temporary (although possibly long-lived) purpose.][2]

(5) This subsection applies if—

(a) the order land does not exceed 200 square metres in extent or is required for the widening or drainage of an existing highway or partly for the widening and partly for the drainage of such a highway, and

(b) the giving in exchange of other land is unnecessary, whether in the interests of the persons, if any, entitled to rights of common or other rights or in the interests of the public.

[...][3]

(11) If an order granting development consent authorises the compulsory acquisition of land to which this section applies, it may include provision—

(a) for vesting replacement land given in exchange as mentioned in subsection (4)(a) in the prospective seller and subject to the rights, trusts and incidents mentioned in subsection (4)(b), and

(b) for discharging the order land from all rights, trusts and incidents to which it is subject.

(12) In this section—

'common', 'fuel or field garden allotment' and 'open space' have the same meanings as in section 19 of the Acquisition of Land Act 1981 (c. 67);

'the order land' means the land authorised to be compulsorily acquired;

'the prospective seller' means the person or persons in whom the order land is vested;

'replacement land' means land which is not less in area than the order land and which is no less advantageous to the persons, if any, entitled to rights of common or other rights, and to the public.

1 Words substituted by Growth and Infrastructure Act 2013, s 24(2)(a) (25 June 2013).
2 Added by Growth and Infrastructure Act 2013, s 24(2)(b) (25 June 2013).
3 Repealed by Growth and Infrastructure Act 2013, s 24(2)(c) (25 June 2013).

132 Commons, open spaces etc: compulsory acquisition of rights over land

(1) This section applies to any land forming part of a common, open space or fuel or field garden allotment.

(2) An order granting development consent is subject to special parliamentary procedure, to the extent that the order authorises the compulsory acquisition of a right over land to which this section applies by the creation of a new right over land, [unless—

(a) the Secretary of State is satisfied that one of subsections (3) to (5) applies, and

(b) that fact, and the subsection concerned, are recorded in the order or otherwise in the instrument or other document containing the order.][1]

(3) This subsection applies if the order land, when burdened with the order right, will be no less advantageous than it was before to the following persons—

(a) the persons in whom it is vested,

(b) other persons, if any, entitled to rights of common or other rights, and

(c) the public.

(4) This subsection applies if—

(a) replacement land has been or will be given in exchange for the order right, and

(b) the replacement land has been or will be vested in the persons in whom the order land is vested and subject to the same rights, trusts and incidents as attach to the order land (ignoring the order granting development consent).

[(4A) This subsection applies if—

(a) the order land is, or forms part of, an open space,

(b) none of the order land is of any of the other descriptions in subsection (1),

(c) either—

(i) there is no suitable land available to be given in exchange for the order right, or

(ii) any suitable land available to be given in exchange is available only at prohibitive cost, and

(d) it is strongly in the public interest for the development for which the order grants consent to be capable of being begun sooner than is likely to be possible if the order were to be subject (to any extent) to special parliamentary procedure.

(4B) This subsection applies if—

(a) the order land is, or forms part of, an open space,

(b) none of the order land is of any of the other descriptions in subsection (1), and

(c) the order right is being acquired for a temporary (although possibly long-lived) purpose.][2]

(5) This subsection applies if—

(a) the order land does not exceed 200 square metres in extent or the order right is required in connection with the widening or drainage of an existing highway or in connection partly with the widening and partly with the drainage of such a highway, and

(b) the giving of other land in exchange for the order right is unnecessary, whether in the interests of the persons, if any, entitled to rights of common or other rights or in the interests of the public.

[…][3]

(11) If an order granting development consent authorises the compulsory acquisition of a right over land to which this section applies by the creation of a new right over land, it may include provision—

(a) for vesting replacement land given in exchange as mentioned in subsection (4)(a) in the persons in whom the order land is vested and subject to the rights, trusts and incidents mentioned in subsection (4)(b), and

(b) for discharging the order land from all rights, trusts and incidents to which it has previously been subject so far as their continuance would be inconsistent with the exercise of the order right.

(12) In this section—

'common', 'fuel or field garden allotment' and 'open space' have the same meanings as in section 19 of the Acquisition of Land Act 1981 (c. 67);

'the order land' means the land to which this section applies over which the order right is to be exercisable;

'the order right' means the right authorised to be compulsorily acquired;

'replacement land' means land which will be adequate to compensate the following persons for the disadvantages which result from the compulsory acquisition of the order right—

(a) the persons in whom the order land is vested,

(b) the persons, if any, entitled to rights of common or other rights over the order land, and

(c) the public.

1 Words substituted by Growth and Infrastructure Act 2013, s 24(3)(a) (25 June 2013).
2 Added by Growth and Infrastructure Act 2013, s 24(3)(b) (25 June 2013).
3 Repealed by Growth and Infrastructure Act 2013, s 24(3)(c) (25 June 2013).

133 Rights in connection with underground gas storage facilities

(1) This section applies if—

(a) the development to which an order granting development consent relates is development within section 14(1)(c), and

(b) the order authorises the compulsory acquisition of one or more rights within subsection (2).

(2) The rights are—

(a) a right to store gas in underground gas storage facilities;

(b) a right to stop up a well, borehole or shaft, or prevent its use by another person;

(c) a right of way over land.

(3) If the right within subsection (2) is an existing right to store gas in underground gas storage facilities, this Act has effect in relation to the compulsory acquisition of the right with the omission of section 131.

(4) If the order authorises the compulsory acquisition of the right by the creation of a new right within subsection (2), this Act has effect in relation to the compulsory acquisition of the right with the omission of sections 127 to 132.

134 Notice of authorisation of compulsory acquisition

(1) This section applies if—

(a) an order is made granting development consent, and

(b) the order includes provision authorising the compulsory acquisition of land.

(2) In this section—

'the order land' means—

(a) in a case where the order granting development consent authorises the compulsory acquisition of a right over land by the creation of a new right, the land over which the right is to be exercisable;

(b) in any other case where the order granting development consent authorises the compulsory acquisition of land, the land authorised to be compulsorily acquired;

'the prospective purchaser' means—

(a) in a case where the order granting development consent authorises the compulsory acquisition of a right over land by the creation of a new right, the person for whose benefit the order authorises the creation of the right;

(b) in any other case where the order granting development consent authorises the compulsory acquisition of land, the person authorised by the order to compulsorily acquire the land.

(3) After the order has been made, the prospective purchaser must—

[(za) make a copy of the order available, at a place in the vicinity of the land, for inspection by the public at all reasonable hours,][1]

(a) serve a compulsory acquisition notice [...][2] on each person to whom subsection (4) applies, and

(b) affix a compulsory acquisition notice to a conspicuous object or objects on or near the order land.

(4) This subsection applies to any person who, if the order granting development consent were a compulsory purchase order, would be a qualifying person for the purposes of section 12(1) of the Acquisition of Land Act 1981 (c. 67) (notice to owners, lessees and occupiers).

(5) A compulsory acquisition notice which is affixed under subsection (3)(b) must—

(a) be addressed to persons occupying or having an interest in the order land, and

(b) so far as practicable, be kept in place by the prospective purchaser until the end of the period of 6 weeks beginning with the date on which the order is published.

(6) The prospective purchaser must also publish a compulsory acquisition notice in one or more local newspapers circulating in the locality in which the order land is situated.

(7) A compulsory acquisition notice is a notice in the prescribed form—

(a) describing the order land,

(b) in a case where the order granting development consent authorises the compulsory acquisition of a right over land by the creation of a new right, describing the right,

(c) stating that the order granting development consent includes provision authorising the compulsory acquisition of a right over the land by the creation of a right over it or (as the case may be) the compulsory acquisition of the land, […][3]

[(ca) stating where and when a copy of the order is available for inspection in accordance with subsection (3)(za), and][3]

(d) stating that a person aggrieved by the order may challenge the order only in accordance with section 118.

[…][4]

1 Added by Localism Act 2011, s 142(1), (2)(a) (1 April 2012).
2 Words repealed by Localism Act 2011, ss 142(1), (2)(b), 237, Sch 25, Pt 21 (1 April 2012).
3 Added by Localism Act 2011, s 142(1), (3) (15 January 2012 for the purpose of conferring power on the Secretary of State to make regulations; 1 April 2012 otherwise).
4 Repealed by Localism Act 2011, ss 142(1), (4), 237, Sch 25, Pt 21 (1 April 2012).

Miscellaneous

135 Orders: Crown land

(1) An order granting development consent may include provision authorising the compulsory acquisition of an interest in Crown land only if—

(a) it is an interest which is for the time being held otherwise than by or on behalf of the Crown, and

(b) the appropriate Crown authority consents to the acquisition.

(2) An order granting development consent may include any other provision applying in relation to Crown land, or rights benefiting the Crown, only if the appropriate Crown authority consents to the inclusion of the provision.

(3) The reference in subsection (2) to rights benefiting the Crown does not include rights which benefit the general public.

(4) For the purposes of this section 'the Crown' includes—

(a) the Duchy of Lancaster;

(b) the Duchy of Cornwall;

(c) the Speaker of the House of Lords;

(d) the Speaker of the House of Commons;

(e) the Corporate Officer of the House of Lords;

(f) the Corporate Officer of the House of Commons.

136 Public rights of way

(1) An order granting development consent may extinguish a public right of way over land only if the [Secretary of State][1] is satisfied that—

(a) an alternative right of way has been or will be provided, or

(b) the provision of an alternative right of way is not required.

(2) The following provisions of this section apply if—

(a) an order granting development consent makes provision for the acquisition of land, compulsorily or by agreement,

(b) the order extinguishes a public right of way over the land, and

(c) the right of way is not a right enjoyable by vehicular traffic.

(3) The order granting development consent may not provide for the right of way to be extinguished from a date which is earlier than the date on which the order is published.

(4) Subsection (5) applies if—

(a) the order granting development consent extinguishes the right of way from a date ('the extinguishment date') which is earlier than the date on which the acquisition of the land is completed, and

(b) at any time after the extinguishment date it appears to the [Secretary of State][2] that the proposal to acquire the land has been abandoned.

(5) The [Secretary of State][2] must by order direct that the right is to revive.

[...][3]

(7) Nothing in subsection (5) prevents the making of a further order extinguishing the right of way.

1 Words substituted by Localism Act 2011, s 128(2), Sch 13, paras 1, 66(1), (2) (1 April 2012).
2 Words substituted by Localism Act 2011, s 128(2), Sch 13, paras 1, 66(1), (3) (1 April 2012).
3 Repealed by Localism Act 2011, ss 128(2), 237, Sch 13, paras 1, 66(1), (4), Sch 25, Pt 20 (1 April 2012).

137 ...

Repealed by Growth and Infrastructure Act 2013, s 23(3) (25 June 2013).

138 Extinguishment of rights, and removal of apparatus, of statutory undertakers etc.

(1) This section applies if an order granting development consent authorises the acquisition of land (compulsorily or by agreement) and—

(a) there subsists over the land a relevant right, or

(b) there is on, under or over the land relevant apparatus.

(2) 'Relevant right' means a right of way, or a right of laying down, erecting, continuing or maintaining apparatus on, under or over the land, which—

(a) is vested in or belongs to statutory undertakers for the purpose of the carrying on of their undertaking, or

(b) is conferred by or in accordance with the electronic communications code on the operator of an electronic communications code network.

(3) 'Relevant apparatus' means—

(a) apparatus vested in or belonging to statutory undertakers for the purpose of the carrying on of their undertaking, or

(b) electronic communications apparatus kept installed for the purposes of an electronic communications code network.

(4) The order may include provision for the extinguishment of the relevant right, or the removal of the relevant apparatus, [only if the Secretary of State is satisfied that the extinguishment or removal is necessary for the purpose of carrying out the development to which the order relates.][1]

[(4A) In this section 'statutory undertakers' means persons who are, or are deemed to be, statutory undertakers for the purpose of any provision of Part 11 of TCPA 1990.

(4B) In this section the following terms have the meanings given in paragraph 1(1) of Schedule 17 to the Communications Act 2003— 'electronic communications apparatus'; 'electronic communications code'; 'electronic communications code network'; 'operator'.][2]

[...][3]

1 Words substituted by Growth and Infrastructure Act 2013, s 23(4)(a) (25 June 2013).
2 Added by Growth and Infrastructure Act 2013, s 23(4)(b) (25 June 2013).
3 Repealed by Growth and Infrastructure Act 2013, s 23(4)(c) (25 June 2013).

139 Common land and rights of common

(1) An order granting development consent may not include provision the effect of which is to exclude or modify the application of a provision of or made under the Commons Act 2006, except in accordance with section 131 or 132.

(2) For the purposes of section 38(6)(a) of the Commons Act 2006, works carried out under a power conferred by an order granting development consent are not to be taken to be carried out under a power conferred by or under an enactment, except in a case to which section 131 or 132 applies.

(3) An order granting development consent may not authorise the suspension of, or extinguishment or interference with, registered rights of common, except in accordance with section 131 or 132.

(4) 'Registered rights of common' means rights of common registered under—

(a) the Commons Act 2006, or

(b) the Commons Registration Act 1965.

140 Operation of generating stations

An order granting development consent may include provision authorising the operation of a generating station only if the development to which the order relates is or includes the construction or extension of the generating station.

141 Keeping electric lines installed above ground

An order granting development consent may include provision authorising an electric line to be kept installed above ground only if the development to which the order relates is or includes the installation of the line above ground.

142 Use of underground gas storage facilities

An order granting development consent may include provision authorising the use of underground gas storage facilities only if the development to which the order relates is or includes development within section 17(2), (3) or (5).

143 Diversion of watercourses

(1) An order granting development consent may include provision authorising the diversion of any part of a navigable watercourse only if the condition in subsection (2) is met.

(2) The new length of watercourse must be navigable in a reasonably convenient manner by vessels of a kind that are accustomed to using the part of the watercourse which is to be diverted.

(3) In deciding whether the condition in subsection (2) is met, the effect of any bridge or tunnel must be ignored if the construction of the bridge or tunnel is part of the development for which consent is granted by the order granting development consent.

(4) If an order granting development consent includes provision authorising the diversion of any part of a navigable watercourse, the order is also to be taken to authorise the diversion of any tow path or other way adjacent to that part.

144 Highways

(1) An order granting development consent may include provision authorising the charging of tolls in relation to a highway only if a request to that effect has been included in the application for the order.

(2) If an order granting development consent includes provision authorising the charging of tolls in relation to a highway, the order is treated as a toll order for the purposes of sections 7 to 18 of the New Roads and Street Works Act 1991 (c. 22).

[(2A) Subsection (2) does not apply to an order that includes provision authorising other charges in respect of the use or keeping of motor vehicles on roads.

(2B) In subsection (2A)—

'motor vehicle' has the meaning given in section 185(1) of the Road Traffic Act 1988, except that section 189 of that Act (exceptions: certain pedestrian controlled vehicles and electrically assisted pedal cycles) applies as it applies for the purposes of the Road Traffic Acts;

'road' has the meaning given in section 142(1) of the Road Traffic Regulation Act 1984.][1]

[...][2]

1 Added by Growth and Infrastructure Act 2013, s 27(1), (2) (25 June 2013).
2 Repealed by Growth and Infrastructure Act 2013, s 27(1), (3) (25 June 2013).

145 Harbours

(1) An order granting development consent may include provision for the creation of a harbour authority only if—

(a) the development to which the order relates is or includes the construction or alteration of harbour facilities, and

(b) the creation of a harbour authority is necessary or expedient for the purposes of the development.

(2) An order granting development consent may include provision changing the powers or duties of a harbour authority only if—

(a) the development to which the order relates is or includes the construction or alteration of harbour facilities, and

(b) the authority has requested the inclusion of the provision or has consented in writing to its inclusion.

(3) An order granting development consent may include provision authorising the transfer of property, rights or liabilities from one harbour authority to another only if—

(a) the development to which the order relates is or includes the construction or alteration of harbour facilities, and

(b) the order makes provision for the payment of compensation of an amount—

(i) determined in accordance with the order, or

(ii) agreed between the parties to the transfer.

(4) An order granting development consent which includes provision for the creation of a harbour authority, or changing the powers or duties of a harbour authority, may also make other provision in relation to the authority.

This is subject to subsection (6).

(5) Subject to subsection (6), the provision which may be included in relation to a harbour authority includes in particular—

(a) any provision in relation to a harbour authority which could be included in a harbour revision order under section 14 of the Harbours Act 1964 (c. 40) by virtue of any provision of Schedule 2 to that Act;

(b) provision conferring power on the authority to change provision made in relation to it (by the order or by virtue of this paragraph), where the provision is about—

(i) the procedures (including financial procedures) of the authority;

(ii) the power of the authority to impose charges;

(iii) the power of the authority to delegate any of its functions;

(iv) the welfare of officers and employees of the authority and financial and other provision made for them.

(6) The order may not include provision—

(a) which, by virtue of any other provision of this Act, is not permitted to be included in an order granting development consent;

(b) conferring power on a harbour authority to delegate, or makes changes to its powers so as to permit the delegation of, any of the functions mentioned in paragraphs (a) to (f) of paragraph 9B of Schedule 2 to the Harbours Act 1964.

146 Discharge of water

(1) This section applies if—

(a) an order granting development consent includes provision authorising the discharge of water into inland waters or underground strata, and

(b) but for the order, the person to whom development consent is granted would have had no power to take water, or to require discharges to be made, from the inland waters or other source from which the discharges authorised by the order are intended to be made.

(2) The order does not have the effect of conferring any such power on that person.

147 Development of Green Belt land

(1) This section applies if an order granting development consent includes provision—

(a) authorising the acquisition of Green Belt land, compulsorily or by agreement,

(b) authorising the sale, exchange or appropriation of Green Belt land, or

(c) freeing land from any restriction imposed upon it by or under the Green Belt (London and Home Counties) Act 1938 (c. xciii), or by a covenant or other agreement entered into for the purposes of that Act.

(2) The [Secretary of State][1] must notify the relevant local authorities of the provision made by the order.

[...][2]

(4) The relevant local authorities are—

(a) each local authority in whose area all or part of the land is situated,

(b) any local authority in whom all or part of the land is vested, and

(c) each contributing local authority.

(5) In this section 'local authority' and 'contributing local authority' have the same meanings as in the Green Belt (London and Home Counties) Act 1938 (c. xciii) (see section 2(1) of that Act).

1 Words substituted by Localism Act 2011, s 128(2), Sch 13, paras 1, 68(1), (2) (1 April 2012).
2 Repealed by Localism Act 2011, ss 128(2), 237, Sch 13, paras 1, 68(1), (3), Sch 25, Pt 20 (1 April 2012).

148, 149 ...

Repealed by Marine and Coastal Access Act 2009, s 321, Sch 22, Pt 2 (6 April 2011).

[149A Deemed consent under a marine licence

(1) An order granting development consent may include provision deeming a marine licence to have been issued under Part 4 of the Marine and Coastal Access Act 2009 (marine licensing) for any activity only if the activity is to be carried out wholly in one or more of the areas specified in subsection (2).

(2) The areas are—

(a) England,

(b) waters adjacent to England up to the seaward limits of the territorial sea,

(c) an exclusive economic zone, except any part of an exclusive economic zone in relation to which the Scottish Ministers have functions,

(d) a Renewable Energy Zone, except any part of a Renewable Energy Zone in relation to which the Scottish Ministers have functions,

(e) an area designated under section 1(7) of the Continental Shelf Act 1964, except any part of that area which is within a part of an exclusive economic zone or Renewable Energy Zone in relation to which the Scottish Ministers have functions.

(3) Subsections (4) and (5) apply if an order granting development consent includes provision—

(a) deeming a marine licence to have been granted under Part 4 of the Marine and Coastal Access Act 2009 subject to specified conditions, and

(b) deeming those conditions to have been attached to the marine licence by the Secretary of State under that Part.

(4) A person who fails to comply with such a condition does not commit an offence under section 161 of this Act.

(5) Sections 68 (notice of applications) and 69(3) and (5) (representations) of the Marine and Coastal Access Act 2009 do not apply in relation to the deemed marine licence.][1]

1 Added by Marine and Coastal Access Act 2009, s 112(1), Sch 8, para 4(1), (2) (6 April 2011).

150 Removal of consent requirements

(1) An order granting development consent may include provision the effect of which is to remove a requirement for a prescribed consent or authorisation to be granted, only if the relevant body has consented to the inclusion of the provision.

(2) 'The relevant body' is the person or body which would otherwise be required to grant the prescribed consent or authorisation.

151 Liability under existing regimes

An order granting development consent may not include provision the effect of which is to exclude or modify the application of—

(a) any provision of the Nuclear Installations Act 1965 (c. 57);

(b) section 28 of, and Schedule 2 to, the Reservoirs Act 1975 (c. 23) (liability for damage and injury due to escape of water from a reservoir constructed after 1930);

(c) section 209 of the Water Industry Act 1991 (c. 56) (civil liability of water undertakers for escapes of water from pipes);

(d) section 48A of the Water Resources Act 1991 (c. 57) (civil remedies for loss or damage due to water abstraction).

152 Compensation in case where no right to claim in nuisance

(1) This section applies if, by virtue of section 158 or an order granting development consent, there is a defence of statutory authority in civil or criminal proceedings for nuisance in respect of any authorised works.

(2) 'Authorised works' are—

(a) development for which consent is granted by an order granting development consent;

(b) anything else authorised by an order granting development consent.

(3) A person by whom or on whose behalf any authorised works are carried out must pay compensation to any person whose land is injuriously affected by the carrying out of the works.

(4) A dispute as to whether compensation under subsection (3) is payable, or as to the amount of the compensation, must be referred to the [Upper Tribunal][1].

(5) Subsection (2) of section 10 of the Compulsory Purchase Act 1965 (c. 56) (limitation on compensation) applies to subsection (3) of this section as it applies to that section.

(6) Any rule or principle applied to the construction of section 10 of that Act must be applied to the construction of subsection (3) of this section (with any necessary modifications).

(7) Part 1 of the Land Compensation Act 1973 (c. 26) (compensation for depreciation of land value by physical factors caused by use of public works) applies in relation to authorised works as if—

(a) references in that Part to any public works were to any authorised works;

(b) references in that Part to the responsible authority were to the person for whose benefit the order granting development consent has effect for the time being;

(c) sections 1(6) and 17 were omitted.

(8) An order granting development consent may not include provision the effect of which is to remove or modify the application of any of subsections (1) to (7).

1 Words substituted by Transfer of Tribunal Functions (Lands Tribunal and Miscellaneous Amendments) Order 2009, SI 2009/1307, art 5(1), (2), Sch 1, paras 291, 293 (1 March 2010: substitution came into force on 1 June 2009 but could not take effect until the commencement of Planning Act 2008, s 152(4) on 1 March 2010).

Chapter 2 Changes to, and revocation of, orders

153 Changes to, and revocation of, orders granting development consent

Schedule 6 (changes to, and revocation of, orders granting development consent) has effect.

Chapter 3 General

154 Duration of order granting development consent

(1) Development for which development consent is granted must be begun before the end of—

(a) the prescribed period, or

(b) such other period (whether longer or shorter than that prescribed) as is specified in the order granting the consent.

(2) If the development is not begun before the end of the period applicable under subsection (1), the order granting development consent ceases to have effect at the end of that period.

(3) Where an order granting development consent authorises the compulsory acquisition of land, steps of a prescribed description must be taken in relation to the compulsory acquisition before the end of—

(a) the prescribed period, or

(b) such other period (whether longer or shorter than that prescribed) as is specified in the order.

(4) If steps of the prescribed description are not taken before the end of the period applicable under subsection (3), the authority to compulsorily acquire the land under the order ceases to have effect.

155 When development begins

(1) For the purposes of this Act (except Part 11) development is taken to begin on the earliest date on which any material operation comprised in, or carried out for the purposes of, the development begins to be carried out.

(2) 'Material operation' means any operation except an operation of a prescribed description.

156 Benefit of order granting development consent

(1) If an order granting development consent is made in respect of any land, the order has effect for the benefit of the land and all persons for the time being interested in the land.

(2) Subsection (1) is subject to subsection (3) and any contrary provision made in the order.

(3) To the extent that the development for which development consent is granted is development within section 17(3), the order granting the consent has effect for the benefit of a person for the time being interested in the land only if the person is a gas transporter.

157 Use of buildings in respect of which development consent granted

(1) If development consent is granted for development which includes the erection, extension, alteration or re-erection of a building, the order granting consent may specify the purposes for which the building is authorised to be used.

(2) If no purpose is so specified, the consent is taken to authorise the use of the building for the purpose for which it is designed.

158 Nuisance: statutory authority

(1) This subsection confers statutory authority for—

(a) carrying out development for which consent is granted by an order granting development consent;

(b) doing anything else authorised by an order granting development consent.

(2) Statutory authority under subsection (1) is conferred only for the purpose of providing a defence in civil or criminal proceedings for nuisance.

(3) Subsections (1) and (2) are subject to any contrary provision made in any particular case by an order granting development consent.

159 Interpretation: land and rights over land

(1) This section applies for the purposes of this Part.

(2) 'Land' includes any interest in or right over land.

(3) Acquiring a right over land includes acquiring it by the creation of a new right as well as by the acquisition of an existing one.

Part 8 Enforcement

Offences

160 Development without development consent

(1) A person commits an offence if the person carries out, or causes to be carried out, development for which development consent is required at a time when no development consent is in force in respect of the development.

(2) A person guilty of an offence under this section is liable [on summary conviction, or on conviction on indictment, to a fine][1].

(3) […][2]

1 Words substituted by Legal Aid, Sentencing and Punishment of Offenders Act 2012 (Fines on Summary Conviction) Regulations 2015, SI 2015/664, reg 4(1), Sch 4, para 41(1), (2)(a) (12 March 2015).
2 Repealed by Legal Aid, Sentencing and Punishment of Offenders Act 2012 (Fines on Summary Conviction) Regulations 2015, SI 2015/664, reg 4(1), Sch 4, para 41(1), (2)(b) (12 March 2015).

161 Breach of terms of order granting development consent

(1) A person commits an offence if without reasonable excuse the person—

(a) carries out, or causes to be carried out, development in breach of the terms of an order granting development consent, or

(b) otherwise fails to comply with the terms of an order granting development consent.

(2) Subsection (1) is subject to [section 149A(4)][1].

(3) It is a defence for a person charged with an offence under this section to prove that—

(a) the breach or failure to comply occurred only because of an error or omission in the order, and

(b) a correction notice specifying the correction of the error or omission has been issued under paragraph 2 of Schedule 4.

(4) A person guilty of an offence under this section is liable on summary conviction, or on conviction on indictment, to a fine][2].

(5) [...][3]

1 Words substituted by Marine and Coastal Access Act 2009, s 112(1), Sch 8, para 4(1), (3) (6 April 2011).
2 Words substituted by Legal Aid, Sentencing and Punishment of Offenders Act 2012 (Fines on Summary Conviction) Regulations 2015, SI 2015/664, reg 4(1), Sch 4, para 41(1), (3)(a) (12 March 2015).
3 Repealed by Legal Aid, Sentencing and Punishment of Offenders Act 2012 (Fines on Summary Conviction) Regulations 2015, SI 2015/664, reg 4(1), Sch 4, para 41(1), (3)(b) (12 March 2015).

162 Time limits

(1) A person may not be charged with an offence under section 160 or 161 after the end of—

(a) the relevant 4-year period, or

(b) if subsection (3) applies, the extended period.

(2) The 'relevant 4-year period' means—

(a) in the case of an offence under section 160, the period of 4 years beginning with the date on which the development was substantially completed;

(b) in the case of an offence under section 161, the period of 4 years beginning with the later of—

(i) the date on which the development was substantially completed, and

(ii) the date on which the breach or failure to comply occurred.

(3) This subsection applies if during the relevant 4-year period—

(a) an information notice has been served under section 167, or

(b) an injunction has been applied for under section 171.

(4) The 'extended period' means the period of 4 years beginning with—

(a) the date of service of the information notice, if subsection (3)(a) applies;

(b) the date of the application for the injunction, if subsection (3)(b) applies;

(c) the later (or latest) of those dates, if both paragraphs (a) and (b) of subsection (3) apply.

Rights of entry

163 Right to enter without warrant

(1) This section applies in relation to any land if the relevant local planning authority has reasonable grounds for suspecting that an offence under section 160 or 161 is being, or has been, committed on or in respect of the land.

(2) A person authorised in writing by the relevant local planning authority may at any reasonable hour enter the land for the purpose of ascertaining whether an offence under section 160 or 161 is being, or has been, committed on the land.

(3) A person may enter a building used as a dwelling-house under subsection (2) only if 24 hours' notice of the intended entry has been given to the occupier of the building.

164 Right to enter under warrant

(1) This section applies if it is shown to the satisfaction of a justice of the peace on sworn information in writing—

(a) that there are reasonable grounds for suspecting that an offence under section 160 or 161 is being, or has been, committed on or in respect of any land, and

(b) that the condition in subsection (2) is met.

(2) The condition is that—

(a) admission to the land has been refused, or a refusal is reasonably apprehended, or

(b) the case is one of urgency.

(3) The justice of the peace may issue a warrant authorising any person who is authorised in writing for the purpose by the relevant local planning authority to enter the land.

(4) For the purposes of subsection (2)(a) admission to land is to be regarded as having been refused if no reply is received to a request for admission within a reasonable period.

(5) A warrant authorises entry on one occasion only and that entry must be—

(a) before the end of the period of one month beginning with the date of the issue of the warrant, and

(b) at a reasonable hour, unless the case is one of urgency.

165 Rights of entry: supplementary provisions

(1) A person authorised to enter land in pursuance of a right of entry conferred under or by virtue of section 163 or 164 ('a relevant right of entry')—

(a) must, if so required, produce evidence of the authority and state the purpose of entry before entering the land,

(b) may take on to the land such other persons as may be necessary, and

(c) must, if the person leaves the land at a time when the owner or occupier is not present, leave it as effectively secured against trespassers as it was found.

(2) A person commits an offence if the person wilfully obstructs a person acting in the exercise of a relevant right of entry.

(3) A person guilty of an offence under subsection (2) is liable on summary conviction to a fine not exceeding level 3 on the standard scale.

(4) If any damage is caused to land or chattels in the exercise of a relevant right of entry, compensation may be recovered by any person suffering the damage from the local planning authority that authorised the entry.

(5) Except so far as otherwise provided by regulations, any question of disputed compensation under subsection (4) is to be referred to and determined by the [Upper Tribunal][1].

(6) In relation to the determination of any such question, the provisions of [section 4 of the Land Compensation Act 1961 (c. 33)][2] apply subject to any necessary modifications and to any other prescribed modifications.

1 Words substituted by Transfer of Tribunal Functions (Lands Tribunal and Miscellaneous Amendments) Order 2009, SI 2009/1307, art 5(1), (2), Sch 1, paras 291, 294(a) (1 March 2010: substitution came into force on 1 June 2009 but could not take effect until the commencement of the Planning Act 2008, s 165(5) on 1 March 2010).

2 Words substituted by Transfer of Tribunal Functions (Lands Tribunal and Miscellaneous Amendments) Order 2009, SI 2009/1307, art 5(1), (2), Sch 1, paras 291, 294(b) (1 March 2010: substitution came into force on 1 June 2009 but could not take effect until the commencement of the Planning Act 2008, s 165(5) on 1 March 2010).

166 Rights of entry: Crown land

Sections 163 and 164 do not apply to Crown land.

Information notices

167 Power to require information

(1) This section applies in relation to any land if it appears to the relevant local planning authority that an offence under section 160 or 161 may have been committed on or in respect of the land.

(2) The relevant local planning authority may serve an information notice.

(3) The information notice may be served on any person who—

(a) is the owner or occupier of the land or has any other interest in it, or

(b) is carrying out operations on the land or is using it for any purpose.

(4) The information notice may require the person on whom it is served to give such of the following information as may be specified in the notice—

(a) information about any operations being carried out in, on, over or under the land, any use of the land and any other activities being carried out in, on, over or under the land, and

(b) information about the provisions of any order granting development consent for development of the land.

(5) An information notice must inform the person on whom it is served of the likely consequences of a failure to respond to the notice.

(6) A requirement of an information notice is complied with by giving the required information to the relevant local planning authority in writing.

168 Offences relating to information notices

(1) A person commits an offence if without reasonable excuse the person fails to comply with any requirement of an information notice served under section 167 before the end of the period mentioned in subsection (2)

(2) The period referred to in subsection (1) is the period of 21 days beginning with the day on which the information notice is served.

(3) A person guilty of an offence under subsection (1) is liable on summary conviction to a fine not exceeding level 3 on the standard scale.

(4) A person commits an offence if the person—

(a) makes any statement purporting to comply with a requirement of an information notice which he knows to be false or misleading in a material respect, or

(b) recklessly makes such a statement which is false or misleading in a material respect.

(5) A person guilty of an offence under subsection (4) is liable on summary conviction to a fine not exceeding level 5 on the standard scale.

Notices of unauthorised development

169 Notice of unauthorised development

(1) Subsection (2) applies if a person is found guilty of an offence under section 160 committed on or in respect of any land.

(2) The relevant local planning authority may serve a notice of unauthorised development on the person requiring such steps as may be specified in the notice to be taken—

(a) to remove the development, and

(b) to restore the land on which the development has been carried out to its condition before the development was carried out.

(3) Subsection (4) applies if a person is found guilty of an offence under section 161 committed on or in respect of any land.

(4) The relevant local planning authority may serve a notice of unauthorised development on the person requiring the person to remedy the breach or failure to comply.

(5) A notice of unauthorised development—

(a) must specify the period within which any steps are required to be taken, and

(b) may specify different periods for different steps.

(6) Where different periods apply to different steps, references in this Part to the period for compliance with a notice of unauthorised development, in relation to any step, are to the period within which the step is required to be taken.

(7) A notice of unauthorised development must specify such additional matters as may be prescribed.

170 Execution of works required by notice of unauthorised development

(1) If any of the steps specified in a notice of unauthorised development have not been taken before the end of the period for compliance with the notice, the relevant local planning authority may—

(a) enter the land on which the development has been carried out and take those steps, and

(b) recover from the person who is then the owner of the land any expenses reasonably incurred by it in doing so.

(2) Where a notice of unauthorised development has been served in respect of development—

(a) any expenses incurred by the owner or occupier of the land for the purposes of complying with it, and

(b) any sums paid by the owner of the land under subsection (1) in respect of expenses incurred by the relevant local planning authority in taking steps required by it,

are to be deemed to be incurred or paid for the use and at the request of the person found guilty of the offence under section 160 or 161.

(3) Regulations may provide that all or any of the following sections of the Public Health Act 1936 (c. 49) are to apply, subject to such adaptations and modifications as may be specified in the regulations, in relation to any steps required to be taken by a notice of unauthorised development—

section 276 (power of local authorities to sell materials removed in executing works under that Act subject to accounting for the proceeds of sale);

section 289 (power to require the occupier of any premises to permit works to be executed by the owner of the premises);

section 294 (limit on liability of persons holding premises as agents or trustees in respect of the expenses recoverable under that Act).

(4) Regulations under subsection (3) applying all or any of section 289 of that Act may include adaptations and modifications for the purpose of giving the owner of land to which such a notice relates the right, as against all other persons interested in the land, to comply with the requirements of the notice.

(5) Regulations under subsection (3) may also provide for the charging on the land on which the development is carried out of any expenses recoverable by the relevant local planning authority under subsection (1).

(6) A person commits an offence if the person wilfully obstructs a person acting in the exercise of powers under subsection (1).

(7) A person guilty of an offence under subsection (6) is liable on summary conviction to a fine not exceeding level 3 on the standard scale.

Injunctions

171 Injunctions

(1) A local planning authority may apply to the court for an injunction if it considers it necessary or expedient for any actual or apprehended prohibited activity to be restrained by injunction.

(2) Prohibited activity means activity that constitutes an offence under section 160 or 161 in relation to land in the area of the local planning authority.

(3) On an application under this section the court may grant such an injunction as the court thinks fit for the purpose of restraining the prohibited activity.

(4) In this section 'the court' means the High Court or [the county court][1].

1 Words substituted by Crime and Courts Act 2013, s 17(5), Sch 9, para 52(1)(b), (2) (22 April 2014: subject to transitional provision specified in Crime and Courts Act 2013 (Commencement No. 10 and Transitional Provision) Order 2014, SI 2014/954, art 3).

Isles of Scilly

172 Isles of Scilly

(1) The Secretary of State may by order provide for the exercise by the Council of the Isles of Scilly in relation to land in the Council's area of any functions exercisable by a local planning authority under any provision of this Part.

(2) Before making an order under this section the Secretary of State must consult the Council of the Isles of Scilly.

The relevant local planning authority

173 The relevant local planning authority

(1) This section applies for the purposes of this Part.

(2) The relevant local planning authority in relation to any land is the local planning authority for the area in which the land is situated. This is subject to subsections (3) to (5).

(3) Subsections (4) and (5) apply if the land is in an area for which there is both a district planning authority and a county planning authority.

(4) If any of the relevant development is the construction or alteration of a hazardous waste facility within section 14(1)(p), the relevant local planning authority is the county planning authority.

(5) In any other case, the relevant local planning authority is the district planning authority.

(6) 'The relevant development' is—

(a) if the relevant offence is an offence under section 160 or 161(1)(a), the development referred to in section 160(1) or 161(1)(a);

(b) if the relevant offence is an offence under section 161(1)(b), the development to which the order granting development consent mentioned in section 161(1)(b) relates.

(7) 'The relevant offence' is the offence by reference to which a provision of this Part confers a function on a local planning authority.

Part 9 Changes to existing planning regimes

Chapter 1 Changes related to development consent regime

174–177 ...

Amend Town and Country Planning Act 1990 and Town and Country Planning (Scotland) Act 1997.

Grants

178 Grants for advice and assistance: Scotland

(1) The Secretary of State may make grants for the purpose of assisting any person to provide advice and assistance in connection with any matter which is related to the application of this Act to Scotland.

(2) The Secretary of State may, as respects any such grant, provide that it is to be subject to such terms and conditions as the Secretary of State thinks appropriate.

179 ...

Repealed by Local Democracy, Economic Development and Construction Act 2009, s 146(1), Sch 7, Pt 4 (1 April 2010 as SI 2009/3318).

Chapter 2 Other changes to existing planning regimes

180 ...

Amends Planning and Compulsory Purchase Act 2004.

181 ...

Repealed by Local Democracy, Economic Development and Construction Act 2009, s 146(1), Sch 7, Pt 4 (1 April 2010 as SI 2009/3318).

182-186 ...

Amend Planning and Compulsory Purchase Act 2004.

Determination of applications

187 Power to decline to determine applications: amendments

Schedule 7 (power to decline to determine applications: amendments) has effect.

188-192 ...

Amend Town and Country Planning Act 1990.

Trees

193 Existing tree preservation orders: transitional provision

(1) This section applies to a tree preservation order made before the appointed day.

(2) With effect from the beginning of the appointed day, a tree preservation order to which this section applies shall have effect with the omission of all of its provisions other than any that have effect for the purpose of identifying the order or for the purpose of identifying the trees, groups of trees or woodlands in respect of which the order—

(a) is in force, or

(b) may at any later time be in force.

(3) In this section—

'the appointed day'—

(a) in relation to England means the day on which subsection (1) comes fully into force in relation to England, and

(b) in relation to Wales means the day on which subsection (1) comes fully into force in relation to Wales;

'tree preservation order' means an order made under, or an order having effect as if made under, section 198(1) of TCPA 1990.

Use of land

194 Use of land: power to override easements and other rights

(1) […][1]

(2) The Welsh Ministers may by order amend Schedule 4 to the Welsh Development Agency Act 1975 (c. 70) for the purpose of authorising the use in accordance with planning permission of land acquired under section 21A of that Act, even if the use involves—

(a) interference with an interest or right to which paragraph 6 of that Schedule applies, or

(b) a breach of a restriction as to the user of land arising by virtue of a contract.

(3) The power to make an order under subsection (2) is exercisable by statutory instrument.

(4) The power includes—

(a) power to make different provision for different purposes (including different areas);

(b) power to make incidental, consequential, supplementary, transitional or transitory provision or savings.

(5) No order may be made under subsection (2) unless a draft of the instrument containing the order has been laid before, and approved by resolution of, the National Assembly for Wales.

1 Repealed by Housing and Planning Act 2016, s 206, Sch 19, paras 13, 14 (13 July 2016).

195–196 …

Amend Town and Country Planning Act 1990, Planning (Listed Buildings and Conservation Areas) Act 1990 and Planning (Hazardous Substances) Act 1990.

Appeals

197 Appeals: miscellaneous amendments

Schedule 11 (appeals: miscellaneous amendments) has effect.

198-201 ...

Amend Town and Country Planning Act 1990 and Planning and Compensation Act 1991.

Part 10 Wales

202 ...

Amends Government of Wales Act 2006.

203 Power to make provision in relation to Wales

(1) The Welsh Ministers may by order make provision—

(a) which has an effect in relation to Wales that corresponds to the effect an England-only provision has in relation to England;

(b) conferring power on the Welsh Ministers to do anything in relation to Wales that corresponds to anything the Secretary of State has power to do by virtue of an England-only provision.

(2) The England-only provisions are—

section 184 (correction of errors in decisions);

section 189 (compensation where development order or local development order withdrawn);

section 190 (power to make non-material changes to planning permission);

section 194(1) and Schedule 9 (use of land: power to override easements and other rights);

section 195 (applications and appeals by statutory undertakers);

section 196 and Schedule 10 (determination of procedure for certain proceedings);

paragraphs 2(3) and (4) and 3(3) of Schedule 7.

(3) Before an England-only provision is brought into force—

(a) the reference in subsection (1)(a) to the effect an England-only provision has is to be read as a reference to the effect the provision would have, if it were in force;

(b) the reference in subsection (1)(b) to anything the Secretary of State has power to do by virtue of an England-only provision is to be read as a reference to anything the Secretary of State would have power to do by virtue of the provision, if it were in force.

(4) The Welsh Ministers may by order make provision for the purpose of reversing the effect of any provision made in exercise of the power conferred by subsection (1).

(5) The Secretary of State may make an order in consequence of an order under subsection (1) for the purpose of ensuring that an England-only provision continues to have (or will when brought into force have) the effect in relation to England that it would have had if the order under subsection (1) had not been made.

(6) An order under this section may amend, repeal, revoke or otherwise modify a provision of—

(a) an Act, or

(b) an instrument made under an Act.

(7) The powers of the Welsh Ministers to make orders under this section are exercisable by statutory instrument.

(8) Those powers include—

(a) power to make different provision for different purposes (including different areas);

(b) power to make incidental, consequential, supplementary, transitional or transitory provision or savings.

(9) No order may be made by the Welsh Ministers under this section unless a draft of the instrument containing the order has been laid before, and approved by resolution of, the National Assembly for Wales.

204 Wales: transitional provision in relation to blighted land

(1) During the transitional period the repeal by PCPA 2004 of paragraphs 1 to 4 of Schedule 13 to TCPA 1990 in relation to Wales is subject to subsection (2).

(2) That repeal does not affect anything which is required or permitted to be done for the purposes of Chapter 2 of Part 6 of TCPA 1990 (interests affected by planning proposals: blight) in relation to land falling within any of paragraphs 1, 2, 3 and 4 of Schedule 13 to TCPA 1990.

(3) The transitional period is the period during which—

(a) in the case of land falling within paragraph 1 of Schedule 13 to TCPA 1990, a structure plan continues to be or to be comprised in the development plan for an area in Wales by virtue of Part 3 of Schedule 5 to the Local Government (Wales) Act 1994 (c. 19) and Part 1A of Schedule 2 to TCPA 1990;

(b) in the case of land falling within paragraph 2 of Schedule 13 to TCPA 1990, a local plan continues to be or to be comprised in the development plan for an area in Wales by virtue of Part 3 of Schedule 5 to the Local Government (Wales) Act 1994 and Part 1A of Schedule 2 to TCPA 1990;

(c) in the case of land falling within paragraphs 3 or 4 of Schedule 13 to TCPA 1990, a unitary development plan continues to form part of the development plan for an area in Wales by virtue of article 3(1) and (2) of the PCPA No.6 Order 2005.

(4) In this section 'PCPA No.6 Order 2005' means the Planning and Compulsory Purchase Act 2004 (Commencement No.6, Transitional Provisions and Savings) Order 2005 (S.I. 2005/2847).

(5) This section is deemed to have come into force on the same day as the repeal of paragraphs 1 to 4 of Schedule 13 to TCPA 1990 came into force in relation to Wales (see Article 2(e) and (g) of the PCPA No.6 Order 2005).

Part 11 Community Infrastructure Levy

205 The levy

(1) The Secretary of State may with the consent of the Treasury make regulations providing for the imposition of a charge to be known as Community Infrastructure Levy (CIL).

(2) In making the regulations the Secretary of State shall aim to ensure that the overall purpose of CIL is to ensure that costs incurred in [supporting][1] the development of an area can be funded (wholly or partly) by owners or developers of land [in a way that does not make development of the area economically unviable][2].

(3) The Table describes the provisions of this Part.

Section	**Topic**
Section 206	The charge
Section 207	Joint committees
Sections 208 and 209	Liability
Section 210	Charities
Section 211	Amount
Sections 212 to 214	Charging schedule
Section 215	Appeals
[Sections 216 to 216B][3]	Application
Section 217	Collection
Section 218	Enforcement
Section 219	Compensation
Section 220	Procedure
Section 221	Secretary of State
Section 222	CIL regulations and orders: general
Section 223	Relationship with other powers
Section 224	Amendments
Section 225	Repeals

(4) In those sections regulations under this section are referred to as 'CIL regulations'.

1 Words substituted by Localism Act 2011, s 115(1), (2)(a) (15 January 2012 subject to transitional and savings provisions specified in SI 2012/57, arts 6, 7, 9, 10 and 11).

2 Words inserted by Localism Act 2011, s 115(1), (2)(b) (15 January 2012 subject to transitional and savings provisions specified in SI 2012/57, arts 6, 7, 9, 10 and 11).
3 Words substituted by Localism Act 2011, s 115(1), (3) (15 January 2012 subject to transitional and savings provisions specified in SI 2012/57, arts 6, 7, 9, 10 and 11).

206 The charge

(1) A charging authority may charge CIL in respect of development of land in its area.

(2) A local planning authority is the charging authority for its area.

(3) But—

(a) the Mayor of London is a charging authority for Greater London (in addition to the local planning authorities),

(b) the Broads Authority is the only charging authority for the Broads (within the meaning given by section 2(3) of the Norfolk and Suffolk Broads Act 1988 (c. 4)), and

(c) the Council of the Isles of Scilly is the only charging authority for the Isles of Scilly.

(4) CIL regulations may provide for any of the following to be the charging authority for an area, or in the case of Greater London one of the charging authorities, in place of the charging authority under subsection (2), (3)(b) or (c)—

(a) a county council,

(b) a county borough council,

(c) a district council,

(d) a metropolitan district council, and

(e) a London borough council (within the meaning of TCPA 1990).

(5) In this section, 'local planning authority' has the meaning given by—

(a) section 37 of PCPA 2004 in relation to England, [except that a Mayoral development corporation is a local planning authority for the purposes of this section only if it is the local planning authority for all purposes of Part 2 of PCPA 2004 in respect of the whole of its area and all kinds of development,][1] and

(b) section 78 of PCPA 2004 in relation to Wales.

[(6) CIL regulations may make transitional provision in connection with, or in anticipation of, a Mayoral development corporation—

(a) becoming a charging authority as a result of the operation of subsection (2), or

(b) ceasing to be a charging authority as a result of the operation of that subsection.][2]

1 Words inserted by Localism Act 2011, s 222, Sch 22, paras 59, 61(2) (15 January 2012).
2 Added by Localism Act 2011, s 222, Sch 22, paras 59, 61(3) (15 January 2012).

207 Joint committees

(1) This section applies if a joint committee that includes a charging authority is established under section 29 of PCPA 2004.

(2) CIL regulations may provide that the joint committee is to exercise specified functions, in respect of the area specified in the agreement under section 29(1) of PCPA 2004, on behalf of the charging authority.

(3) The regulations may make provision corresponding to provisions relating to joint committees in Part 6 of the Local Government Act 1972 (c. 70) in respect of the discharge of the specified functions.

208 Liability

(1) Where liability to CIL would arise in respect of proposed development (in accordance with provision made by a charging authority under and by virtue of section 206 and CIL regulations) a person may assume liability to pay the levy.

(2) An assumption of liability—

(a) may be made before development commences, and

(b) must be made in accordance with any provision of CIL regulations about the procedure for assuming liability.

(3) A person who assumes liability for CIL before the commencement of development becomes liable when development is commenced in reliance on planning permission.

(4) CIL regulations must make provision for an owner or developer of land to be liable for CIL where development is commenced in reliance on planning permission if—

(a) nobody has assumed liability in accordance with the regulations, or

(b) other specified circumstances arise (such as the insolvency or withdrawal of a person who has assumed liability).

(5) CIL regulations may make provision about—

(a) joint liability (with or without several liability);

(b) liability of partnerships;

(c) assumption of partial liability (and subsection (4)(a) applies where liability has not been wholly assumed);

(d) apportionment of liability (which may—

(i) include provision for referral to a specified person or body for determination, and

(ii) include provision for appeals);

(e) withdrawal of assumption of liability;

(f) cancellation of assumption of liability by a charging authority (in which case subsection (4)(a) applies);

(g) transfer of liability (whether before or after development commences and whether or not liability has been assumed).

(6) The amount of any liability for CIL is to be calculated by reference to the time when planning permission first permits the development as a result of which the levy becomes payable.

(7) CIL regulations may make provision for liability for CIL to arise where development which requires planning permission is commenced without it (and subsection (6) is subject to this subsection).

(8) CIL regulations may provide for liability to CIL to arise in respect of a development where—

(a) the development was exempt from CIL, or subject to a reduced rate of CIL charge, and

(b) the description or purpose of the development changes.

209 Liability: interpretation of key terms

(1) In section 208'development' means—

(a) anything done by way of or for the purpose of the creation of a new building, or

(b) anything done to or in respect of an existing building.

(2) CIL regulations may provide for—

(a) works or changes in use of a specified kind not to be treated as development;

(b) the creation of, or anything done to or in respect of, a structure of a specified kind to be treated as development.

(3) CIL regulations must include provision for determining when development is treated as commencing.

(4) Regulations under subsection (3) may, in particular, provide for development to be treated as commencing when some specified activity or event is undertaken or occurs, where the activity or event—

(a) is not development within the meaning of subsection (1), but

(b) has a specified kind of connection with a development within the meaning of that subsection.

(5) CIL regulations must define planning permission (which may include planning permission within the meaning of TCPA 1990 and any other kind of permission or consent (however called, and whether general or specific)).

(6) CIL regulations must include provision for determining the time at which planning permission is treated as first permitting development; and the regulations may, in particular, make provision—

(a) about outline planning permission;

(b) for permission to be treated as having been given at a particular time in the case of general consents.

(7) For the purposes of section 208—

(a) 'owner' of land means a person who owns an interest in the land, and

(b) 'developer' means a person who is wholly or partly responsible for carrying out a development.

(8) CIL regulations may make provision for a person to be or not to be treated as an owner or developer of land in specified circumstances.

210 Charities

(1) CIL regulations must provide for an exemption from liability to pay CIL in respect of a development where—

(a) the person who would otherwise be liable to pay CIL in respect of the development is a relevant charity in England and Wales, and

(b) the building or structure in respect of which CIL liability would otherwise arise is to be used wholly or mainly for a charitable purpose of the charity within the meaning of [section 2 of the Charities Act 2011][1].

(2) CIL regulations may—

(a) provide for an exemption from liability to pay CIL where the person who would otherwise be liable to pay CIL in respect of the development is an institution established for a charitable purpose;

(b) require charging authorities to make arrangements for an exemption from, or reduction in, liability to pay CIL where the person who would otherwise be liable to pay CIL in respect of the development is an institution established for a charitable purpose.

(3) Regulations under subsection (1) or (2) may provide that an exemption or reduction does not apply if specified conditions are satisfied.

(4) For the purposes of subsection (1), a relevant charity in England and Wales is an institution which—

(a) is registered in the register of charities kept by the Charity Commission under [section 29 of the Charities Act 2011][2], or

(b) is a charity within the meaning of [section 1(1) of the Charities Act 2011 but is not required to be registered in the register kept under section 29 of that Act][3].

(5) In subsection (2), a charitable purpose is a purpose falling within [section 3(1) of the Charities Act 2011;][4] but CIL regulations may provide for an institution of a specified kind to be, or not to be, treated as an institution established for a charitable purpose.

1 Words substituted by Charities Act 2011, 354(1), Sch 7, para 136(1), (2) (14 March 2012: substitution has effect subject to transitional provisions and savings specified in Charities Act 2011, s 354(1), (2), Sch 7, para 2, Sch 8).
2 Words substituted by Charities Act 2011, 354(1), Sch 7, para 136(1), (3)(a) (14 March 2012: substitution has effect subject to transitional provisions and savings specified in Charities Act 2011, s 354(1), (2), Sch 7, para 2, Sch 8).
3 Words substituted by Charities Act 2011, 354(1), Sch 7, para 136(1), (3)(b) (14 March 2012: substitution has effect subject to transitional provisions and savings specified in Charities Act 2011, s 354(1), (2), Sch 7, para 2, Sch 8).
4 Words substituted by Charities Act 2011, 354(1), Sch 7, para 136(1), (4) (14 March 2012: substitution has effect subject to transitional provisions and savings specified in Charities Act 2011, s 354(1), (2), Sch 7, para 2, Sch 8).

211 Amount

(1) A charging authority which proposes to charge CIL must issue a document (a 'charging schedule') setting rates, or other criteria, by reference to which the amount of CIL chargeable in respect of development in its area is to be determined.

(2) A charging authority, in setting rates or other criteria, must have regard, to the extent and in the manner specified by CIL regulations, to—

(a) actual and expected costs of infrastructure (whether by reference to lists prepared by virtue of section 216(5)(a) or otherwise);

(b) matters specified by CIL regulations relating to the economic viability of development (which may include, in particular, actual or potential economic effects of planning permission or of the imposition of CIL);

(c) other actual and expected sources of funding for infrastructure.

(3) CIL regulations may make other provision about setting rates or other criteria.

(4) The regulations may, in particular, permit or require charging authorities in setting rates or other criteria—

(a) to have regard, to the extent and in the manner specified by the regulations, to actual or expected administrative expenses in connection with CIL;

[(aa) to have regard, to the extent and in the manner specified by the regulations, to actual and expected costs of anything other than infrastructure that is concerned with addressing demands that development places on an area (whether by reference to lists prepared by virtue of section 216(5)(a) or otherwise);

(ab) to have regard, to the extent and in the manner specified by the regulations, to other actual and expected sources of funding for anything other than infrastructure that is concerned with addressing demands that development places on an area;][1]

(b) to have regard, to the extent and in the manner specified by the regulations, to values used or documents produced for other statutory purposes;

(c) to integrate the process, to the extent and in the manner specified by the regulations, with processes undertaken for other statutory purposes;

(d) to produce charging schedules having effect in relation to specified periods (subject to revision).

(5) The regulations may permit or require charging schedules to adopt specified methods of calculation.

(6) In particular, the regulations may—

(a) permit or require charging schedules to operate by reference to descriptions or purposes of development;

(b) permit or require charging schedules to operate by reference to any measurement of the amount or nature of development (whether by reference to measurements of floor space, to numbers or intended uses of buildings, to numbers or intended uses of units within buildings, to allocation of space within buildings or units, to values or expected values or in any other way);

(c) permit or require charging schedules to operate by reference to the nature or existing use of the place where development is undertaken;

(d) permit or require charging schedules to operate by reference to an index used for determining a rate of inflation;

(e) permit or require charging schedules to operate by reference to values used or documents produced for other statutory purposes;

(f) provide, or permit or require provision, for differential rates, which may include provision for supplementary charges, a nil rate, increased rates or reductions.

(7) A charging authority may consult, or take other steps, in connection with the preparation of a charging schedule (subject to CIL regulations).

[(7A) A charging authority must use appropriate available evidence to inform the charging authority's preparation of a charging schedule.

(7B) CIL regulations may make provision about the application of subsection (7A) including, in particular—

(a) provision as to evidence that is to be taken to be appropriate,

(b) provision as to evidence that is to be taken to be not appropriate,

(c) provision as to evidence that is to be taken to be available,

(d) provision as to evidence that is to be taken to be not available,

(e) provision as to how evidence is, and as to how evidence is not, to be used,

(f) provision as to evidence that is, and as to evidence that is not, to be used,

(g) provision as to evidence that may, and as to evidence that need not, be used, and

(h) provision as to how the use of evidence is to inform the preparation of a charging schedule.][2]

(8) The regulations may require a charging authority to provide in specified circumstances an estimate of the amount of CIL chargeable in respect of development of land.

(9) A charging authority may revise a charging schedule.

(10) This section and sections 212, 213 and 214(1) and (2) apply to the revision of a charging schedule as they apply to the preparation of a charging schedule.

1 Added by Localism Act 2011, s 115(1), (4) (15 January 2012 subject to transitional and savings provisions specified in SI 2012/57, arts 6, 7, 9, 10 and 11).
2 Added by Localism Act 2011, s 114(1), (2) (16 November 2011: insertion does not apply in relation to cases where an examiner submits recommendations to a charging authority before the coming into force of Localism Act 2011, s 114, but subject to that the cases in relation to which this amendment applies include a case in which steps in relation to the charging schedule have been taken before then).

212 Charging schedule: examination

(1) Before approving a charging schedule a charging authority must appoint a person ('the examiner') to examine a draft.

(2) The charging authority must appoint someone who, in the opinion of the authority—

(a) is independent of the charging authority, and

(b) has appropriate qualifications and experience.

(3) The charging authority may, with the agreement of the examiner, appoint persons to assist the examiner.

[(4) In this section and sections 212A and 213'the drafting requirements' means the requirements of this Part and CIL regulations (including the requirements to have regard to the matters listed in section 211(2) and (4)), so far as relevant to the drafting of the schedule.

(7) The examiner must consider whether the drafting requirements have been complied with and—

(a) make recommendations in accordance with section 212A, and

(b) give reasons for the recommendations.][1]

(8) The charging authority must publish the recommendations and reasons.

(9) CIL regulations must require a charging authority to allow anyone who makes representations about a draft charging schedule to be heard by the examiner; and the regulations may make provision about timing and procedure.

(10) CIL regulations may make provision for examiners to reconsider their decisions with a view to correcting errors (before or after the approval of a charging schedule).

(11) The charging authority may withdraw a draft.

1 Section 212(4) and (7) substituted for s 212(4)-(7) by Localism Act 2011, s 114(1), (3) (16 November 2011: substitution does not apply in relation to cases where an examiner submits recommendations to a charging authority before the coming into force of Localism Act 2011, s 114, but subject to that the cases in relation to which this amendment applies include a case in which steps in relation to the charging schedule have been taken before then).

[212A Charging schedule: examiner's recommendations

(1) This section applies in relation to the examination, under section 212, of a draft charging schedule.

(2) If the examiner considers—

(a) that there is any respect in which the drafting requirements have not been complied with, and

(b) that the non-compliance with the drafting requirements cannot be remedied by the making of modifications to the draft,

the examiner must recommend that the draft be rejected.

(3) Subsection (4) applies if the examiner considers—

(a) that there is any respect in which the drafting requirements have not been complied with, and

(b) that the non-compliance with the drafting requirements could be remedied by the making of modifications to the draft.

(4) The examiner must—

(a) specify the respects in which the drafting requirements have not been complied with,

(b) recommend modifications that the examiner considers sufficient and necessary to remedy that non-compliance, and

(c) recommend that the draft be approved with—

(i) those modifications, or

(ii) other modifications sufficient and necessary to remedy that non-compliance.

(5) Subject to subsections (2) to (4), the examiner must recommend that the draft be approved.

(6) If the examiner makes recommendations under subsection (4), the examiner may recommend other modifications with which the draft should be approved in the event that it is approved.

(7) If the examiner makes recommendations under subsection (5), the examiner may recommend modifications with which the draft should be approved in the event that it is approved.][1]

1 Added by Localism Act 2011, s 114(1), (4) (16 November 2011: insertion does not apply in relation to cases where an examiner submits recommendations to a charging authority before the coming into force of Localism Act 2011, s 114, but subject to that the cases in relation to which this amendment applies include a case in which steps in relation to the charging schedule have been taken before then).

213 Charging schedule: approval

[(1) A charging authority may approve a charging schedule only if—

(a) the examiner makes recommendations under section 212A(4) or (5), and

(b) the charging authority has had regard to those recommendations and the examiner's reasons for them.

(1A) Accordingly, a charging authority may not approve a charging schedule if, under section 212A(2), the examiner recommends rejection.

(1B) If the examiner makes recommendations under section 212A(4), the charging authority may approve the charging schedule only if it does so with modifications that are sufficient and necessary to remedy the non-compliance specified under section 212A(4)(a) (although those modifications need not be the ones recommended under section 212A(4)(b)).

(1C) If a charging authority approves a charging schedule, it may do so with all or none, or some one or more, of the modifications (if any) recommended under section 212A(6) or (7).

(1D) The modifications with which a charging schedule may be approved include only—

(a) modifications required by subsection (1B), and

(b) modifications allowed by subsection (1C).][1]

(2) A charging authority (other than the Mayor of London) must approve a charging schedule—

(a) at a meeting of the authority, and

(b) by a majority of votes of members present.

(3) The Mayor of London must approve a charging schedule personally.

[(3A) Subsection (3B) applies if—

(a) the examiner makes recommendations under section 212A(4), and

(b) the charging schedule is approved by the charging authority.

(3B) The charging authority must publish a report setting out how the charging schedule as approved remedies the non-compliance specified under section 212A(4)(a).

(3C) CIL regulations may make provision about the form or contents of a report under subsection (3B).][2]

(4) CIL regulations may make provision for the correction of errors in a charging schedule after approval.

[(5) In this section 'examiner' means examiner under section 212.][3]

1 Section 213(1)-(1D) substituted for s 213(1) by Localism Act 2011, s 114(1), (5) (16 November 2011: substtitution does not apply in relation to cases where an examiner submits recommendations to a charging authority before the coming into force of Localism Act 2011, s 114, but subject to that the cases in relation to which this amendment applies include a case in which steps in relation to the charging schedule have been taken before then).

2 Added by Localism Act 2011, s 114(1), (6) (16 November 2011: insertion does not apply in relation to cases where an examiner submits recommendations to a charging authority before the coming into force of Localism Act 2011, s 114, but subject to that the cases in relation to which this amendment applies include a case in which steps in relation to the charging schedule have been taken before then).

3 Added by Localism Act 2011, s 114(1), (7) (16 November 2011: insertion does not apply in relation to cases where an examiner submits recommendations to a charging authority before the coming into force of Localism Act 2011, s 114, but subject to that the cases in relation to which this amendment applies include a case in which steps in relation to the charging schedule have been taken before then).

214 Charging schedule: effect

(1) A charging schedule approved under section 213 may not take effect before it is published by the charging authority.

(2) CIL regulations may make provision about publication of a charging schedule after approval.

(3) A charging authority may determine that a charging schedule is to cease to have effect.

(4) CIL regulations may provide that a charging authority may only make a determination under subsection (3) in circumstances specified by the regulations.

(5) A charging authority (other than the Mayor of London) must make a determination under subsection (3)—

(a) at a meeting of the authority, and

(b) by a majority of votes of members present.

(6) The Mayor of London must make a determination under subsection (3) personally.

215 Appeals

(1) CIL regulations must provide for a right of appeal on a question of fact in relation to the application of methods for calculating CIL to a person appointed by the Commissioners for Her Majesty's Revenue and Customs.

(2) The regulations must require that the person appointed under subsection (1) is—

(a) a valuation officer appointed under section 61 of the Local Government Finance Act 1988 (c. 41), or

(b) a district valuer within the meaning of section 622 of the Housing Act 1985 (c. 68).

(3) Regulations under this section or section 208(5)(d)(ii) may, in particular, make provision about—

(a) the period within which the right of appeal may be exercised,

(b) the procedure on an appeal, and

(c) the payment of fees, and award of costs, in relation to an appeal.

(4) In any proceedings for judicial review of a decision on an appeal, the defendant shall be the Commissioners for Her Majesty's Revenue and Customs and not the person appointed under subsection (1).

216 Application

(1) Subject to [sections 216A(1), 216B(2) and 219(5)][1], CIL regulations must require the authority that charges CIL to apply it, or cause it to be applied, to [supporting development by funding the provision, improvement, replacement, operation or maintenance of infrastructure][2].

(2) In [this section (except subsection (3)) and sections 216A(2) and 216B(2)][3] 'infrastructure' includes—

(a) roads and other transport facilities,

(b) flood defences,

(c) schools and other educational facilities,

(d) medical facilities,

(e) sporting and recreational facilities,[and][4]

(f) open spaces [.][5]

[...][6]

(3) The regulations may amend subsection (2) so as to—

(a) add, remove or vary an entry in the list of matters included within the meaning of 'infrastructure';

(b) list matters excluded from the meaning of 'infrastructure'.

(4) The regulations may specify—

(a) works, installations and other facilities [whose provision, improvement or replacement may or is to be, or may not][7] be, funded by CIL, [(aa) maintenance activities and operational activities (including operational activities of a promotional kind) in connection with infrastructure that may or are to be, or may not be, funded by CIL,

(ab) things within section 216A(2)(b) that may or are to be, or may not be, funded by CIL passed to a person in discharge of a duty under section 216A(1),

(ac) things within section 216B(2)(b) that may or are to be, or may not be, funded by CIL to which provision under section 216B(2) relates,][8]

(b) criteria for determining the areas [that may benefit from funding][9] by CIL in respect of land, and

(c) what is to be, or not to be, treated as funding.

(5) The regulations may—

(a) require charging authorities to prepare and publish a list of [what is][10] to be, or may be, wholly or partly funded by CIL;

(b) include provision about the procedure to be followed in preparing a list (which may include provision for consultation, for the appointment of an independent person or a combination);

(c) include provision about the circumstances in which a charging authority may and may not apply CIL to [anything][11] not included on the list.

(6) In making provision about funding the regulations may, in particular—

(a) permit CIL to be used to reimburse expenditure already incurred;

(b) permit CIL to be reserved for expenditure that may be incurred [in the future][12] ;

(c) permit CIL to be applied (either generally or subject to limits set by or determined in accordance with the regulations) to administrative expenses in connection with infrastructure [or anything within section 216A(2)(b) or 216B(2)(b)][13] or in connection with CIL;

(d) include provision for the giving of loans, guarantees or indemnities;

(e) make provision about the application of CIL where [anything][14] to which it was to be applied no longer [requires][15] funding.

(7) The regulations may—

(a) require a charging authority to account separately, and in accordance with the regulations, for CIL received or due;

(b) require a charging authority to monitor the use made and to be made of CIL in its area;

(c) require a charging authority to report on actual or expected charging, collection and application of CIL;

(d) permit a charging authority to cause money to be applied in respect of things done outside its area;

(e) permit a charging authority or other body to spend money;

(f) permit a charging authority to pass money to another body (and in paragraphs (a) to (e) a reference to a charging authority includes a reference to a body to which a charging authority passes money in reliance on this paragraph).

1 Word substituted by Localism Act 2011, s 115(1), (5)(a)(i) (15 January 2012 subject to transitional and savings provisions specified in SI 2012/57, arts 6, 7, 9, 10 and 11).
2 Words substituted by Localism Act 2011, s 115(1), (5)(a)(ii) (15 January 2012 subject to transitional and savings provisions specified in SI 2012/57, arts 6, 7, 9, 10 and 11).
3 Words substituted by Localism Act 2011, s 115(1), (5)(b) (15 January 2012 subject to transitional and savings provisions specified in SI 2012/57, arts 6, 7, 9, 10 and 11).
4 Word inserted by Community Infrastructure Levy Regulations 2010, SI 2010/948, reg 63(1), (2) (6 April 2010).
5 Word substituted by Community Infrastructure Levy Regulations 2010, SI 2010/948, reg 63(1), (3) (6 April 2010).
6 Repealed by Community Infrastructure Levy Regulations 2010, SI 2010/948, reg 63(1), (4) (6 April 2010).
7 Words substituted by Localism Act 2011, s 115(1), (5)(c) (15 January 2012 subject to transitional and savings provisions specified in SI 2012/57, arts 6, 7, 9, 10 and 11).
8 Added by Localism Act 2011, s 115(1), (5)(d) (15 January 2012 subject to transitional and savings provisions specified in SI 2012/57, arts 6, 7, 9, 10 and 11).
9 Words substituted by Localism Act 2011, s 115(1), (5)(e) (15 January 2012 subject to transitional and savings provisions specified in SI 2012/57, arts 6, 7, 9, 10 and 11).
10 Words substituted by Localism Act 2011, s 115(1), (5)(f) (15 January 2012 subject to transitional and savings provisions specified in SI 2012/57, arts 6, 7, 9, 10 and 11).
11 Word substituted by Localism Act 2011, s 115(1), (5)(g) (15 January 2012 subject to transitional and savings provisions specified in SI 2012/57, arts 6, 7, 9, 10 and 11).
12 Words substituted by Localism Act 2011, s 115(1), (5)(h) (15 January 2012 subject to transitional and savings provisions specified in SI 2012/57, arts 6, 7, 9, 10 and 11).
13 Words inserted by Localism Act 2011, s 115(1), (5)(i) (15 January 2012 subject to transitional and savings provisions specified in SI 2012/57, arts 6, 7, 9, 10 and 11).
14 Words substituted by Localism Act 2011, s 115(1), (5)(j)(i) (15 January 2012 subject to transitional and savings provisions specified in SI 2012/57, arts 6, 7, 9, 10 and 11).
15 Word substituted by Localism Act 2011, s 115(1), (5)(j)(ii) (15 January 2012 subject to transitional and savings provisions specified in SI 2012/57, arts 6, 7, 9, 10 and 11).

[216A Duty to pass receipts to other persons

(1) CIL regulations may require that CIL received in respect of development of land in an area is to be passed by the charging authority that charged the CIL to a person other than that authority.

(2) CIL regulations must contain provision to secure that money passed to a person in discharge of a duty under subsection (1) is used to support the development of the area to which the duty relates, or of any part of that area, by funding—

(a) the provision, improvement, replacement, operation or maintenance of infrastructure, or

(b) anything else that is concerned with addressing demands that development places on an area.

(3) A duty under subsection (1) may relate to—

(a) the whole of a charging authority's area or the whole of the combined area of two or more charging authorities, or

(b) part only of such an area or combined area.

(4) CIL regulations may make provision about the persons to whom CIL may or must, or may not, be passed in discharge of a duty under subsection (1).

(5) A duty under subsection (1) may relate—

(a) to all CIL (if any) received in respect of the area to which the duty relates, or

(b) such part of that CIL as is specified in, or determined under or in accordance with, CIL regulations.

(6) CIL regulations may make provision in connection with the timing of payments in discharge of a duty under subsection (1).

(7) CIL regulations may, in relation to CIL passed to a person in discharge of a duty under subsection (1), make provision about—

(a) accounting for the CIL,

(b) monitoring its use,

(c) reporting on its use,

(d) responsibilities of charging authorities for things done by the person in connection with the CIL,

(e) recovery of the CIL, and any income or profits accruing in respect of it or from its application, in cases where—

(i) anything to be funded by it has not been provided, or

(ii) it has been misapplied,

including recovery of sums or other assets representing it or any such income or profits, and

(f) use of anything recovered in cases where—

(i) anything to be funded by the CIL has not been provided, or

(ii) the CIL has been misapplied.

(8) This section does not limit section 216(7)(f).][1]

1 Added by Localism Act 2011, s 115(1), (6) (15 January 2012 subject to transitional and savings provisions specified in SI 2012/57, arts 6, 7, 9, 10 and 11).

[216B Use of CIL in an area to which section 216A(1) duty does not relate

(1) Subsection (2) applies where—

(a) there is an area to which a particular duty under section 216A(1) relates, and

(b) there is also an area to which that duty does not relate ('the uncovered area').

(2) CIL regulations may provide that the charging authority that charges CIL received in respect of development of land in the uncovered area may apply the CIL, or cause it to be applied, to—

(a) support development by funding the provision, improvement, replacement, operation or maintenance of infrastructure, or

(b) support development of the uncovered area, or of any part of that area, by funding anything else that is concerned with addressing demands that development places on an area.

(3) Provision under subsection (2) may relate to the whole, or part only, of the uncovered area.

(4) Provision under subsection (2) may relate—

(a) to all CIL (if any) received in respect of the area to which the provision relates, or

(b) such part of that CIL as is specified in, or determined under or in accordance with, CIL regulations.][1]

1 Added by Localism Act 2011, s 115(1), (6) (15 January 2012 subject to transitional and savings provisions specified in SI 2012/57, arts 6, 7, 9, 10 and 11).

217 Collection

(1) CIL regulations must include provision about the collection of CIL.

(2) The regulations may make provision for payment—

(a) on account;

(b) by instalments.

(3) The regulations may make provision about repayment (with or without interest) in cases of overpayment.

(4) The regulations may make provision about payment in forms other than money (such as making land available, carrying out works or providing services).

(5) The regulations may permit or require a charging authority or other public authority to collect CIL charged by another authority; and section 216(7)(a) and (c) apply to a collecting authority in respect of collection as to a charging authority.

(6) Regulations under this section may replicate or apply (with or without modifications) any enactment relating to the collection of a tax.

(7) Regulations under this section may make provision about the source of payments in respect of Crown interests.

218 Enforcement

(1) CIL regulations must include provision about enforcement of CIL.

(2) The regulations must make provision about the consequences of late payment and failure to pay.

(3) The regulations may make provision about the consequences of failure to assume liability, to give a notice or to comply with another procedure under CIL regulations in connection with CIL.

(4) The regulations may, in particular, include provision—

(a) for the payment of interest;

(b) for the imposition of a penalty or surcharge;

(c) for the suspension or cancellation of a decision relating to planning permission;

(d) enabling an authority to prohibit development pending assumption of liability for CIL or pending payment of CIL;

(e) conferring a power of entry onto land;

(f) requiring the provision of information;

(g) creating a criminal offence (including, in particular, offences relating to evasion or attempted evasion or to the provision of false or misleading information or failure to provide information, and offences relating to the prevention or investigation of other offences created by the regulations);

(h) conferring power to prosecute an offence;

(i) for enforcement of sums owed (whether by action on a debt, by distraint against goods or in any other way);

(j) conferring jurisdiction on a court to grant injunctive or other relief to enforce a provision of the regulations (including a provision included in reliance on this section);

(k) for enforcement in the case of death or insolvency of a person liable for CIL.

(5) CIL regulations may include provision (whether or not in the context of late payment or failure to pay) about registration or notification of actual or potential liability to CIL; and the regulations may include provision—

(a) for the creation of local land charges;

(b) for the registration of local land charges;

(c) for enforcement of local land charges (including, in particular, for enforcement—

(i) against successive owners, and

(ii) by way of sale or other disposal with consent of a court);

(d) for making entries in statutory registers;

(e) for the cancellation of charges and entries.

(6) Regulations under this section may—

(a) replicate or apply (with or without modifications) any enactment relating to the enforcement of a tax;

(b) provide for appeals.

(7) Regulations under this section may provide that any interest, penalty or surcharge payable by virtue of the regulations is to be treated for the purposes of sections 216 to 220 as if it were CIL.

(8) The regulations providing for a surcharge or penalty must ensure that no surcharge or penalty in respect of an amount of CIL exceeds the higher of—

(a) 30% of that amount, and

(b) £20,000.

(9) But the regulations may provide for more than one surcharge or penalty to be imposed in relation to a CIL charge.

(10) The regulations may not authorise entry to a private dwelling without a warrant issued by a justice of the peace.

(11) Regulations under this section creating a criminal offence may not provide for—

(a) [...][1]

(b) a maximum term of imprisonment exceeding 6 months on summary conviction, or

(c) a maximum term of imprisonment exceeding 2 years on conviction on indictment.

(12) The Secretary of State may by order amend subsection (11) to reflect commencement of section 283 of the Criminal Justice Act 2003 (c. 44).

(13) In this Part a reference to administrative expenses in connection with CIL includes a reference to enforcement expenses.

1 Repealed by Legal Aid, Sentencing and Punishment of Offenders Act 2012 (Fines on Summary Conviction) Regulations 2015, SI 2015/664, reg 4(2), Sch 4, para 92 (12 March 2015).

219 Compensation

(1) CIL regulations may require a charging authority or other public authority to pay compensation in respect of loss or damage suffered as a result of enforcement action.

(2) In this section, 'enforcement action' means action taken under regulations under section 218, including—

(a) the suspension or cancellation of a decision relating to planning permission, and

(b) the prohibition of development pending assumption of liability for CIL or pending payment of CIL.

(3) The regulations shall not require payment of compensation—

(a) to a person who has failed to satisfy a liability to pay CIL, or

(b) in other circumstances specified by the regulations.

(4) Regulations under this section may make provision about—

(a) the time and manner in which a claim for compensation is to be made, and

(b) the sums, or the method of determining the sums, payable by way of compensation.

(5) CIL regulations may permit or require a charging authority to apply CIL (either generally or subject to limits set by or determined in accordance with the regulations) for expenditure incurred under this section.

(6) A dispute about compensation may be referred to and determined by the [Upper Tribunal][1].

(7) In relation to the determination of any such question, the provisions of [section 4 of the Land Compensation Act 1961 (c. 33)][2] apply subject to any necessary modifications and to the provisions of CIL regulations.

1 Words substituted by Transfer of Tribunal Functions (Lands Tribunal and Miscellaneous Amendments) Order 2009, SI 2009/1307, art 5(1), (2), Sch 1, paras 291, 296(a) (1 June 2009).

2 Words substituted by Transfer of Tribunal Functions (Lands Tribunal and Miscellaneous Amendments) Order 2009, SI 2009/1307, art 5(1), (2), Sch 1, paras 291, 296(b) (1 June 2009).

220 Community Infrastructure Levy: procedure

(1) CIL regulations may include provision about procedures to be followed in connection with CIL.

(2) In particular, the regulations may make provision about—

(a) procedures to be followed by a charging authority proposing to begin charging CIL;

(b) procedures to be followed by a charging authority in relation to charging CIL;

(c) procedures to be followed by a charging authority proposing to stop charging CIL;

(d) consultation;

(e) the publication or other treatment of reports;

(f) timing and methods of publication;

(g) making documents available for inspection;

(h) providing copies of documents (with or without charge);

(i) the form and content of documents;

(j) giving notice;

(k) serving notices or other documents;

(l) examinations to be held in public in the course of setting or revising rates or other criteria or of preparing lists;

(m) the terms and conditions of appointment of independent persons;

(n) remuneration and expenses of independent persons (which may be required to be paid by the Secretary of State or by a charging authority);

(o) other costs in connection with examinations;

(p) reimbursement of expenditure incurred by the Secretary of State (including provision for enforcement);

(q) apportionment of costs;

(r) combining procedures in connection with CIL with procedures for another purpose of a charging authority (including a purpose of that authority in another capacity);

(s) procedures to be followed in connection with actual or potential liability for CIL.

(3) CIL regulations may make provision about the procedure to be followed in respect of an exemption from CIL or a reduction of CIL; in particular, the regulations may include provision—

(a) about the procedure for determining whether any conditions are satisfied;

(b) requiring a charging authority or other person to notify specified persons of any exemption or reduction;

(c) requiring a charging authority or other person to keep a record of any exemption or reduction.

(4) A provision of this Part conferring express power to make procedural provision in a specified context includes, in particular, power to make provision about the matters specified in subsection (2).

(5) A power in this Part to make provision about publishing something includes a power to make provision about making it available for inspection.

(6) Sections 229 to 231 do not apply to this Part (but CIL regulations may make similar provision).

221 Secretary of State

The Secretary of State may give guidance to a charging authority or other public authority (including an examiner appointed under section 212) about any matter connected with CIL; and the authority must have regard to the guidance.

222 Regulations and orders: general

(1) CIL regulations—

(a) may make provision that applies generally or only to specified cases, circumstances or areas,

(b) may make different provision for different cases, circumstances or areas,

(c) may provide, or allow a charging schedule to provide, for exceptions,

(d) may confer, or allow a charging schedule to confer, a discretionary power on the Secretary of State, a local authority or another specified person,

(e) may apply an enactment, with or without modifications, and

(f) may include provision of a kind permitted by section 232(3)(b) (and incidental, supplemental or consequential provision may include provision disapplying, modifying the effect of or amending an enactment).

(2) CIL regulations—

(a) shall be made by statutory instrument, and

(b) shall not be made unless a draft has been laid before and approved by resolution of the House of Commons.

(3) An order under section 218(12) or 225(2)—

(a) shall be made by statutory instrument, and

(b) may include provision of a kind permitted by subsection (1)(a), (b) or (f) above, but may not amend an Act of Parliament in reliance on subsection (1)(f).

(4) An order under section 218(12) shall be subject to annulment in pursuance of a resolution of either House of Parliament.

(5) An order under section 225(2) shall be subject to annulment in pursuance of a resolution of the House of Commons.

223 Relationship with other powers

(1) CIL regulations may include provision about how the following powers are to be used, or are not to be used—

(a) section 106 of TCPA 1990 (planning obligations), and

(b) section 278 of the Highways Act 1980 (c. 66) (execution of works).

(2) CIL regulations may include provision about the exercise of any other power relating to planning or development.

(3) The Secretary of State may give guidance to a charging or other authority about how a power relating to planning or development is to be exercised; and authorities must have regard to the guidance.

(4) Provision may be made under subsection (1) or (2), and guidance may be given under subsection (3), only if the Secretary of State thinks it necessary or expedient for—

(a) complementing the main purpose of CIL regulations,

(b) enhancing the effectiveness, or increasing the use, of CIL regulations,

(c) preventing agreements, undertakings or other transactions from being used to undermine or circumvent CIL regulations,

(d) preventing agreements, undertakings or other transactions from being used to achieve a purpose that the Secretary of State thinks would better be achieved through the application of CIL regulations, or

(e) preventing or restricting the imposition of burdens, the making of agreements or the giving of undertakings, in addition to CIL.

(5) CIL regulations may provide that a power to give guidance or directions may not be exercised—

(a) in relation to matters specified in the regulations,

(b) in cases or circumstances specified in the regulations,

(c) for a purpose specified in the regulations, or

(d) to an extent specified in the regulations.

224 …

Amends Local Government Act 1972, Norfolk and Suffolk Broads Act 1988, Deregulation and Contracting Out Act 1994 and Greater London Authority Act 1999.

225 Community Infrastructure Levy: repeals

(1) The following provisions of PCPA 2004 shall cease to have effect—

(a) sections 46 to 48 (planning contribution), and

(b) paragraph 5 of Schedule 6 (repeal of sections 106 to 106B of TCPA 1990 (planning obligations)).

(2) The Treasury may by order repeal the Planning-gain Supplement (Preparations) Act 2007 (c. 2).

Part 12 Final provisions

The Crown and Parliament

226 The Crown

(1) This Act binds the Crown, subject to subsections (2) and (3).

(2) Sections 40, 54, 135, 166, 228 and 231 make special provision in relation to the application of some provisions of this Act to the Crown.

(3) The amendments made by this Act bind the Crown only to the extent that the provisions amended bind the Crown.

227 'Crown land' and 'the appropriate Crown authority'

(1) In this Act, 'Crown land' and 'the appropriate Crown authority' must be read in accordance with this section.

(2) 'Crown land' is land in which there is a Crown interest or a Duchy interest.

(3) For the purposes of this section, a Crown interest is any of the following—

(a) an interest belonging to Her Majesty in right of the Crown or in right of Her private estates;

(b) an interest belonging to a government department or held in trust for Her Majesty for the purposes of a government department;

(c) an interest belonging to an office-holder in the Scottish Administration or held in trust for Her Majesty for the purposes of the Scottish Administration by such an office-holder;

(d) the interest of the Speaker of the House of Lords in those parts of the Palace of Westminster and its precincts occupied on 23 March 1965 by or on behalf of the House of Lords;

(e) the interest of the Speaker of the House of Commons in those parts of the Palace of Westminster and its precincts occupied on 23 March 1965 by or on behalf of the House of Commons;

(f) the interest in any land of—

(i) the Corporate Officer of the House of Lords;

(ii) the Corporate Officer of the House of Commons;

(iii) those two Corporate Officers acting jointly;

(g) such other interest as the Secretary of State specifies by order.

(4) For the purposes of this section, a Duchy interest is—

(a) an interest belonging to Her Majesty in right of the Duchy of Lancaster, or

(b) an interest belonging to the Duchy of Cornwall.

(5) 'The appropriate Crown authority' in relation to any land is—

(a) in the case of land belonging to Her Majesty in right of the Crown and forming part of the Crown Estate, the Crown Estate Commissioners;

(b) in relation to any other land belonging to Her Majesty in right of the Crown, the government department or, as the case may be, office-holder in the Scottish Administration, having the management of the land;

(c) in relation to land belonging to Her Majesty in right of Her private estates, a person appointed by Her Majesty in writing under the Royal Sign Manual or, if no such appointment is made, the Secretary of State;

(d) in relation to land belonging to Her Majesty in right of the Duchy of Lancaster, the Chancellor of the Duchy;

(e) in relation to land belonging to the Duchy of Cornwall, such person as the Duke of Cornwall, or the possessor for the time being of the Duchy, appoints;

(f) in the case of land belonging to a government department or held in trust for Her Majesty for the purposes of a government department, the department;

(g) in the case of land belonging to an office-holder in the Scottish Administration or held in trust for Her Majesty for the purposes of such an office-holder, the office-holder;

(h) in relation to Westminster Hall and the Chapel of St Mary Undercroft, the Lord Great Chamberlain and the Speakers of the House of Lords and the House of Commons acting jointly;

(i) in relation to Her Majesty's Robing Room in the Palace of Westminster, the adjoining staircase and ante-room and the Royal Gallery, the Lord Great Chamberlain.

(j) in relation to land in which there is a Crown interest by virtue of subsection (3)(d) or (f)(i), the Corporate Officer of the House of Lords;

(k) in relation to land in which there is a Crown interest by virtue of subsection (3)(e) or (f)(ii), the Corporate Officer of the House of Commons;

(l) in relation to land in which there is a Crown interest by virtue of subsection (3)(f)(iii), those two Corporate Officers acting jointly.

(6) If any question arises as to what authority is the appropriate Crown authority in relation to any land it must be referred to the Treasury, whose decision is final.

(7) References to Her Majesty's private estates must be construed in accordance with section 1 of the Crown Private Estates Act 1862 (c. 37).

(8) References to an office-holder in the Scottish Administration are to be construed in accordance with section 126(7) of the Scotland Act 1998 (c. 46).

228 Enforcement in relation to the Crown and Parliament

(1) No act or omission done or suffered by or on behalf of the Crown constitutes an offence under this Act.

(2) For the purposes of this section 'the Crown' includes—

(a) the Duchy of Lancaster;

(b) the Duchy of Cornwall;

(c) the Speaker of the House of Lords;

(d) the Speaker of the House of Commons;

(e) the Corporate Officer of the House of Lords;

(f) the Corporate Officer of the House of Commons.

Service of notices and other documents

229 Service of notices: general

(1) A notice or other document required or authorised to be served, given or supplied under this Act may be served, given or supplied in any of these ways—

(a) by delivering it to the person on whom it is to be served or to whom it is to be given or supplied,

(b) by leaving it at the usual or last known place of abode of that person or, in a case where an address for service has been given by that person, at that address,

(c) by sending it by post, addressed to that person at that person's usual or last known place of abode or, in a case where an address for service has been given by that person, at that address,

(d) by sending it in a prepaid registered letter, or by the recorded delivery service, addressed to that person at that person's usual or last known place of abode or, in a case where an address for service has been given by that person, at that address,

(e) in a case where an address for service using electronic communications has been given by that person, by sending it using electronic communications, in accordance with the condition set out in subsection (2), to that person at that address,

(f) in the case of an incorporated company or body—

(i) by delivering it to the secretary or clerk of the company or body at their registered or principal office,

(ii) by sending it by post, addressed to the secretary or clerk of the company or body at that office,

(iii) by sending it in a prepaid registered letter or, or by the recorded delivery service, addressed to the secretary or clerk of the company or body at that office.

(2) The condition mentioned in subsection (1)(e) is that the notice or other document must be—

(a) capable of being accessed by the person mentioned in that provision,

(b) legible in all material respects, and

(c) in a form sufficiently permanent to be used for subsequent reference.

(3) For the purposes of subsection (2), 'legible in all material respects' means that the information contained in the notice or document is available to that person to no lesser extent than it would be if served, given or supplied by means of a notice or document in printed form.

(4) Subsection (1)(c), (e) and (f)(ii) do not apply to the service, giving or supply of any of the following—

(a) notice under section 53(4)(b);

(b) a compulsory acquisition notice under section 134;

(c) notice under section 163(3);

(d) an information notice under section 167;

(e) a notice of unauthorised development under section 169.

(5) This section is without prejudice to section 233 of the Local Government Act 1972 (c. 70) (general provisions as to service of notices by local authorities).

(6) This section is subject to any contrary provision made by or under this Act.

230 Service of documents to persons interested in or occupying premises

(1) Subsection (2) applies if—

(a) a notice or document is required or authorised to be served on or given or supplied to any person as having an interest in premises, and the name of that person cannot be ascertained after reasonable inquiry, or

(b) a notice or document is required or authorised to be served on or given or supplied to any person as an occupier of premises.

(2) The notice or document is to be taken to be duly served, given or supplied if either the condition in subsection (3) or the condition in subsection (4) is met.

(3) The condition is that the notice or document—

(a) is addressed to the person either by name or by the description of 'the owner' or, as the case may be, 'the occupier' of the premises (describing them), and

(b) is delivered or sent—

(i) in the case of a notice mentioned in section 229(4), in the manner specified in section 229(1)(a), (b) or (d), and

(ii) in any other case, in the manner specified in section 229(1)(a), (b), (c) or (d).

(4) The condition is that the notice or document is so addressed and is marked in such a manner as may be prescribed for securing that it is plainly identifiable as an important communication and—

(a) it is sent to the premises in a prepaid registered letter or by the recorded delivery service and is not returned to the authority sending it, or

(b) it is delivered to a person on those premises, or is affixed conspicuously to an object on those premises.

(5) Subsection (6) applies if—

(a) a notice or other document is required to be served on or given or supplied to all persons who have interests in or are occupiers of premises comprised in any land, and

(b) it appears to the authority required or authorised to serve, give or supply the notice or other document that any part of that land is unoccupied.

(6) The notice or other document is to be taken to be duly served on or given or supplied to all persons having interests in, and on any occupiers of, premises comprised in that part of the land (other than a person who has given to that authority an address for the service of the notice or document on him) if—

(a) it is addressed to 'the owners and any occupiers' of that part of the land (describing it), and

(b) it is affixed conspicuously to an object on the land.

(7) This section is subject to any contrary provision made by or under this Act.

231 Service of notices on the Crown and Parliament

(1) Any notice or other document required under this Act to be served on or given or supplied to the Crown must be served on or given or supplied to the appropriate Crown authority.

(2) Sections 229 and 230 do not apply for the purposes of the service, giving or supply of such a notice or document.

(3) For the purposes of this section 'the Crown' includes—

(a) the Duchy of Lancaster;

(b) the Duchy of Cornwall;

(c) the Speaker of the House of Lords;

(d) the Speaker of the House of Commons;

(e) the Corporate Officer of the House of Lords;

(f) the Corporate Officer of the House of Commons.

General

232 Orders and regulations

(1) Subsections (2) and (3) apply to a power to make an order or regulations conferred on the Secretary of State by this Act, except—

(a) power to make an order granting development consent;

(b) a power conferred by paragraph 1(4) of Schedule 4;

(c) a power to make changes to, or revoke, an order granting development consent;

(d) a power conferred by Part 11 or section 237 or 241.

(2) The power is exercisable by statutory instrument.

(3) The power includes—

(a) power to make different provision for different purposes (including different areas);

(b) power to make incidental, consequential, supplementary, transitional or transitory provision or savings.

(4) A statutory instrument containing an order or regulations under this Act is subject to annulment pursuant to a resolution of either House of Parliament.

This is subject to subsection (5) (and section 222(5)).

(5) Subsection (4) does not apply to a statutory instrument containing—

(a) an order granting development consent;

(b) an order made by virtue of paragraph 1(8) of Schedule 4;

(c) an order changing or revoking an order granting development consent;

(d) an order under [section 14(3), 33(5), 111, 160(3), 161(5), 172(1), 203(5) or 227(3)(g)][1];

(e) regulations under [section 35(2)(a)(ii), 104(2)(c) or 105(2)(b)][2].

(6) No order may be made under [section 14(3), 33(5), 111, 160(3), 161(5), 203(5) or 227(3)(g)][3] unless a draft of the instrument containing the order has been laid before, and approved by resolution of, each House of Parliament.

(7) No regulations may be made under [section 35(2)(a)(ii), 104(2)(c) or 105(2)(b)][4] unless a draft of the instrument containing the regulations has been laid before, and approved by resolution of, each House of Parliament.

1 Word inserted by Localism Act 2011, s 131(1), (3)(a) (1 April 2012).
2 Words inserted by Growth and Infrastructure Act 2013, s 26(1), (4)(a) (25 April 2013).
3 Word inserted by Localism Act 2011, s 131(1), (3)(b) (1 April 2012).
4 Words inserted by Growth and Infrastructure Act 2013, s 26(1), (4)(b) (25 April 2013).

233 Directions

(1) A direction given under this Act must be in writing.

(2) A power conferred by this Act to give a direction includes power to vary or revoke the direction.

234 Abbreviated references to Acts

In this Act—

'the Hazardous Substances Act' means the Planning (Hazardous Substances) Act 1990 (c. 10);

'the Listed Buildings Act' means the Planning (Listed Buildings and Conservation Areas) Act 1990 (c. 9);

'PCPA 2004' means the Planning and Compulsory Purchase Act 2004 (c. 5);

'TCPA 1990' means the Town and Country Planning Act 1990 (c. 8).

235 Interpretation

(1) In this Act (except in Part 11)—

'airport' has the meaning given by section 82(1) of the Airports Act 1986 (c. 31);

'alteration', in relation to an airport, must be read in accordance with section 23(6);

'alteration', in relation to a highway, includes stopping up the highway or diverting, improving, raising or lowering it;

'appropriate Crown authority' has the meaning given by section 227;

'building' has the meaning given by section 336(1) of TCPA 1990;

[...][1]

'construction', in relation to so much of a generating station as comprises or is to comprise renewable energy installations, has the same meaning as in Chapter 2 of Part 2 of the Energy Act 2004 (c. 20) (see section 104 of that Act) (and related expressions must be read accordingly);

'construction', in relation to a pipe-line, includes placing (and related expressions must be read accordingly);

[...][1]

'cross-country pipe-line' has the same meaning as in the Pipe-lines Act 1962 (c. 58) (see section 66 of that Act);

'Crown land' has the meaning given by section 227;

[...][1]

'development' has the meaning given by section 32;

'development consent' has the meaning given by section 31;

'electric line' has the same meaning as in Part 1 of the Electricity Act 1989 (c. 29) (see section 64(1) of that Act);

'extension', in relation to a generating station, has the meaning given by section 36(9) of the Electricity Act 1989 (and 'extend' must be read accordingly);

'gas' includes natural gas;

'gas reception facility' must be read in accordance with section 19(3);

'gas transporter' has the same meaning as in Part 1 of the Gas Act 1986 (c. 44) (see section 7(1) of that Act);

'generating station' has the same meaning as in Part 1 of the Electricity Act 1989 (see section 64(1) of that Act);

'goods' has the meaning given by section 83(1) of the Railways Act 1993 (c. 43);

'Green Belt land' has the meaning given by section 2(1) of the Green Belt (London and Home Counties) Act 1938 (c. xciii);

'harbour' and 'harbour authority' have the meanings given by section 57(1) of the Harbours Act 1964 (c. 40);

'highway' has the meaning given by section 328 of the Highways Act 1980 (c. 66);

'highway authority' has the same meaning as in the Highways Act 1980 (c. 66) (see sections 1 to 3 of that Act);

'improvement', in relation to a highway, has the meaning given by section 329(1) of the Highways Act 1980;

'inland waters' has the same meaning as in the Water Resources Act 1991 (c. 57) (see section 221(1) of that Act);

'land' includes buildings and monuments, and land covered with water, and in relation to Part 7 must be read in accordance with section 159;

'LNG facility' must be read in accordance with section 18(3);

'local planning authority' has the same meaning as in TCPA 1990 (see section 336(1) of that Act);

'monument' has the same meaning as in the Ancient Monuments and Archaeological Areas Act 1979 (c. 46) (see section 61 of that Act);

'nationally significant infrastructure project' has the meaning given by Part 3;

'national policy statement' has the meaning given by section 5(2);

'natural gas' means any gas derived from natural strata (including gas originating outside the United Kingdom);

'navigable watercourse' has the same meaning as in Part 6 of the Highways Act 1980 (see section 111(1) of that Act);

'non-navigable watercourse' means a watercourse that is not a navigable watercourse;

'pipe-line' has the meaning given by section 65 of the Pipe-lines Act 1962 (c. 58);

'planning permission' means permission under Part 3 of TCPA 1990;

'prescribed' means prescribed by regulations made by the Secretary of State (except in relation to matters authorised or required by this Act to be prescribed in another way);

'rail freight interchange' means a facility for the transfer of goods between railway and road, or between railway and another form of transport;

'railway' has the meaning given by section 67(1) of the Transport and Works Act 1992 (c. 42);

'renewable energy installation' has the same meaning as in Chapter 2 of Part 2 of the Energy Act 2004 (c. 20) (see section 104 of that Act);

'Renewable Energy Zone' has the meaning given by section 84(4) of the Energy Act 2004;

'special road' means a highway which is a special road in accordance with section 16 of the Highways Act 1980 or by virtue of an order granting development consent;

'standard', in relation to a volume of gas, means the volume of gas at a pressure of 101.325 kiloPascals and a temperature of 273 Kelvin;

'trunk road' means a highway which is a trunk road by virtue of—

(a) section 10(1) or 19 of the Highways Act 1980,

(b) an order or direction under section 10 of that Act, or

(c) an order granting development consent,

or under any other enactment;

'underground gas storage facilities' must be read in accordance with section 17(6);

'use' has the meaning given by section 336(1) of TCPA 1990.

(2) A reference in this Act to a right over land includes a reference to a right to do, or to place and maintain, anything in, on or under land or in the air-space above its surface.

(3) Subsection (4) applies to the question of which parts of waters up to the seaward limits of the territorial sea—

(a) are adjacent to Wales (and, in consequence, are not adjacent to England), or

(b) are not adjacent to Wales (and, in consequence, are adjacent to England).

(4) The question is to be determined by reference to an order or Order in Council made under or by virtue of section 158(3) or (4) of the Government of Wales Act 2006 (c. 32) (apportionment of sea areas) if, or to the extent that, the order or Order in Council is expressed to apply—

(a) by virtue of this subsection, for the purposes of this Act, or

(b) if no provision has been made by virtue of paragraph (a), for the general or residual purposes of that Act.

(5) Subsection (6) applies to the question of which parts of waters up to the seaward limits of the territorial sea—

(a) are adjacent to Scotland (and, in consequence, are not adjacent to England), or

(b) are not adjacent to Scotland (and, in consequence, are adjacent to England).

(6) The question is to be determined by reference to an Order in Council made under section 126(2) of the Scotland Act 1998 (c. 46) if, or to the extent that, the Order in Council is expressed to apply—

(a) by virtue of this subsection, for the purposes of this Act, or

(b) if no provision has been made by virtue of paragraph (a), for the general or residual purposes of that Act.

1 Definitions repealed by Localism Act 2011, ss 128(2), 237, Sch 13, paras 1, 69, Sch 25, Pt 20 (1 April 2012).

236 Application of Act to Scotland: modifications

The modifications set out in Schedule 12 have effect in the application of this Act to Scotland for the purpose mentioned in section 240(4).

237 Supplementary and consequential provision

(1) The Secretary of State may by order made by statutory instrument make—

(a) such supplementary, incidental or consequential provision, or

(b) such transitory, transitional or saving provision,

as the Secretary of State thinks appropriate for the general purposes, or any particular purpose, of this Act or in consequence of, or for giving full effect to, any provision made by this Act.

(2) The power conferred by subsection (1) includes power to make different provision for different purposes (including different areas).

(3) An order under subsection (1) may amend, repeal, revoke or otherwise modify—

(a) an Act passed on or before the last day of the Session in which this Act is passed, or

(b) an instrument made under an Act before the passing of this Act.

(4) An order under this section which amends or repeals any provision of an Act may not be made unless a draft of the instrument containing the order has been laid before, and approved by resolution of, each House of Parliament.

(5) A statutory instrument containing an order under this section which does not amend or repeal any provision of an Act is subject to annulment pursuant to a resolution of either House of Parliament.

(6) In this section any reference to an Act (other than this Act) includes a reference to an Act of the Scottish Parliament.

[237A Variation and replacement of section 33 consents: transitional provision

(1) This section applies where a section 33 consent ('the original consent') has been granted or made as a result of an application made before Part 4 came into force.

(2) Nothing in section 33 prevents the original consent, or a section 33 consent that replaces it, from being varied or replaced.

(3) If the original consent, or a section 33 consent that replaces it, is varied or replaced, section 31 does not apply to the development to which the consent as varied, or the replacement consent, relates (and so development consent is not required for that development).

(4) A section 33 consent replaces an earlier section 33 consent for the purposes of this section if (but only if)—

(a) it is granted or made on an application for consent for development without complying with conditions subject to which the earlier section 33 consent was granted or made, and

(b) it is granted subject to, or made on, different conditions, or unconditionally.

(5) In this section 'section 33 consent' means a consent, authorisation, order, notice or scheme mentioned in section 33(1), (2) or (4).][1]

1 Added by Growth and Infrastructure Act 2013, s 22(1) (1 March 2010: insertion deemed to have had effect from 1 March 2010).

238 Repeals

Schedule 13 contains repeals (including repeals of spent provisions).

239 Financial provisions

There is to be paid out of money provided by Parliament—

(a) any expenditure incurred under or by virtue of this Act by the Secretary of State, and

(b) any increase attributable to this Act in the sums payable under or by virtue of any other Act out of money so provided.

240 Extent

(1) The following provisions of this Act extend to England and Wales only—

(a) in Part 2, section 13;

(b) in Part 3, sections 15 to 20 and 22 to [30A][1];

(c) in Part 6, section 118;

(d) in Part 7, sections 133 and 139 to 149;

(e) in Part 9, sections 193 and 194;

(f) in Part 10, sections 203 and 204;

(g) Part 11.

(2) Section 178 extends to Scotland only.

(3) The following provisions of this Act extend to England and Wales and (subject to subsection (4)) to Scotland—

(a) Parts 1 to 8 (except the sections listed in paragraphs (a) to (d) of subsection (1));

(b) this Part.

(4) Those provisions extend to Scotland only so far as required for the purpose of the construction (other than by a gas transporter) of an oil or gas cross-country pipe-line—

(a) one end of which is in England or Wales, and

(b) the other end of which is in Scotland.

(5) Subsections (3) and (4) are subject to subsection (6).

(6) So far as it amends or repeals an enactment, this Act has the same extent as the enactment amended or repealed.

(7) An order under section 225(2) extends to each part of the United Kingdom.

1 Word substituted by Infrastructure Planning (Radioactive Waste Geological Disposal Facilities) Order 2015, SI 2015/949, art 2(1), (4) (27 March 2015).

241 Commencement

(1) The following provisions of this Act come into force on the day on which this Act is passed—

(a) the provisions of Parts 1 to 9 (except section 194(2) to (5) and paragraph 7 of Schedule 7) which—

(i) confer power to make orders (other than orders granting, or making changes to orders granting, development consent), regulations or rules, or

(ii) make provision about what is (or is not) permitted to be done, or what is required to be done, in the exercise of any such power;

(b) Part 11, except sections 206, 211(7), 224 and 225;

(c) this Part, except section 238.

(2) Nothing in subsection (1)(a) affects the operation of section 13 of the Interpretation Act 1978 (c. 30) in relation to this Act.

(3) Except as provided by subsection (1)(a), the provisions listed in subsection (4) come into force on such day as may be appointed by order made by—

(a) the Welsh Ministers, in relation to Wales;

(b) the Secretary of State, in relation to England.

(4) The provisions are—

(a) sections 183, 185, 187, 188, 191(1) and (3), 192, 193 and 197 to 200;

(b) paragraphs 1, 2(1) and (2), 3(1), (2) and (4) and 4 to 6 of Schedule 7;

(c) Schedules 8 and 11;

(d) the repeals in—

(i) TCPA 1990 (except those in Schedules 1 and 1A to that Act);

(ii) the Environmental Protection Act 1990 (c. 43);

(iii) the Planning and Compensation Act 1991 (c. 34);

(iv) sections 42(3) and 53 of PCPA 2004.

(5) Section 186 and the repeal in Schedule 1A to TCPA 1990 come into force on such day as the Welsh Ministers may by order appoint.

(6) Sections 194(2) to (5), 201, 202, 203 and 225 (together with related entries in Schedule 13), and paragraph 7 of Schedule 7, come into force at the end of two months beginning with the day on which this Act is passed.

(7) Section 204 comes into force in accordance with subsection (5) of that section.

(8) The other provisions of this Act come into force on such day as the Secretary of State may by order appoint.

(9) The powers conferred by this section are exercisable by statutory instrument.

(10) An order under this section may—

(a) appoint different days for different purposes (including different areas);

(b) contain transitional, transitory or saving provision in connection with the coming into force of this Act.

242 Short title

This Act may be cited as the Planning Act 2008.

Schedule 1 ...

Repealed by Localism Act 2011, ss 128(2), 237, Sch 13, paras 1, 2, Sch 25, Pt 20 as from 1 April 2012.

Schedule 2 ...

Amends Green Belt (London and Home Counties) Act 1938, Pipe-lines Act 1962, Harbours Act 1964, Gas Act 1965, Energy Act 1976, Ancient Monuments and Archaeological Areas Act 1979, Highways Act 1980, Electricity Act 1989, Town and Country Planning Act 1990, Planning (Listed Buildings and Conservation Areas) Act 1990, Planning (Hazardous

Substances) Act 1990, New Roads and Street Works Act 1991, Water Industry Act 1991, Transport and Works Act 1992, Town and Country Planning (Scotland) Act 1997, Planning (Hazardous Substances) (Scotland) Act 1997, Housing and Regeneration Act 2008, Crossrail Act 2008 (c. 18)

Schedule 3 ...

Repealed by Localism Act 2011, ss 128(2), 237, Sch 13, para 54, Sch 25, Pt 20 (1 April 2012).

Schedule 4 Correction of errors in development consent decisions

1 Correction of errors

(1) This paragraph applies if—

(a) the [Secretary of State][1] makes an order granting development consent, or refuses development consent, and

(b) the decision document contains a correctable error.

(2) The decision document is—

(a) in the case of an order granting development consent, the order;

(b) in the case of a refusal of development consent, the document recording the refusal.

(3) A correctable error is an error or omission which—

(a) is in a part of the decision document which records the decision, and

(b) is not part of the statement of reasons for the decision.

(4) The [Secretary of State][2] may correct the error or omission if (but only if) the conditions in sub-paragraphs (5) and (7) are met.

This is subject to sub-paragraph (11).

(5) The condition is that, before the end of the relevant period—

(a) the [Secretary of State][2] receives a written request to correct the error or omission from any person, or

(b) the [Secretary of State][2] sends a statement in writing to the applicant which explains the error or omission and states that the [Secretary of State][2] is considering making the correction.

(6) The relevant period is—

(a) if the decision document is an order granting development consent, the period specified in section 118(1)(b);

(b) if the decision document is the document recording a refusal of development consent, the period specified in section 118(2)(b).

(7) The condition is that the [Secretary of State][2] informs each relevant local planning authority that the request mentioned in sub-paragraph (5)(a) has been received or the statement mentioned in sub-paragraph (5)(b) has been sent (as the case may be).

(8) If—

(a) the decision document is an order granting development consent, and

(b) the order was required to be contained in a statutory instrument,

the power conferred by sub-paragraph (4) may be exercised only by order contained in a statutory instrument.

[...][3]

(10) As soon as practicable after the instrument [containing the order is made, the Secretary of State][4] must deposit a copy of it in the office of the Clerk of the Parliaments.

(11) The power conferred by sub-paragraph (4) may not be exercised in relation to provision included in an order granting development consent by virtue of [paragraph 30A or 30B of Schedule 5 (deemed marine licence under Marine and Coastal Access Act 2009)][5].

1 Words substituted by Localism Act 2011, s 128(2), Sch 13, paras 1, 70(1), (2) (1 April 2012).
2 Words substituted by Localism Act 2011, s 128(2), Sch 13, paras 1, 70(1), (3) (1 April 2012).
3 Repealed by Localism Act 2011, ss 128(2), 237, Sch 13, paras 1, 70(1), (4), Sch 25, Pt 20 (1 April 2012).
4 Words substituted by Localism Act 2011, s 128(2), Sch 13, paras 1, 70(1), (5) (1 April 2012).
5 Words substituted by Marine and Coastal Access Act 2009, s 112(1), Sch 8, para 4(1), (4) (6 April 2011).

2 Correction notice

(1) If paragraph 1(5)(a) or (b) applies the [Secretary of State][1] must issue a notice in writing (a 'correction notice') which—

(a) specifies the correction of the error or omission, or

(b) gives notice of the decision not to correct the error or omission.

(2) The [Secretary of State][1] must issue the correction notice as soon as practicable after making the correction or deciding not to make the correction.

(3) The [Secretary of State][1] must give the correction notice to—

(a) the applicant,

(b) each relevant local planning authority, and

(c) if the correction was requested by any other person, that person.

(4) The Secretary of State may [give the correction notice to persons other than those to whom sub-paragraph (3) requires it to be given.][2]

1 Words substituted by Localism Act 2011, s 128(2), Sch 13, paras 1, 70(1), (6) (1 April 2012).
2 Words substituted by Localism Act 2011, s 128(2), Sch 13, paras 1, 70(1), (7) (1 April 2012).

3 Effect of a correction

(1) If a correction is made in pursuance of paragraph 1—

(a) the original decision and the decision document containing it continue in force, and

(b) the decision document is treated as corrected as specified in the correction notice issued under paragraph 2 with effect from the date the correction notice is issued, or, if the correction is required to be made by order contained in a statutory instrument, the date specified in the order.

(2) If a correction is not made—

(a) the original decision continues to have full force and effect, and

(b) nothing in this Schedule affects anything done in pursuance of or in respect of the original decision.

(3) 'The original decision' means the decision to—

(a) make an order granting development consent, or

(b) refuse development consent.

4 Interpretation

In this Schedule—

'the applicant' means the person who made the application to which the decision relates;

[...][1]

'a relevant local planning authority' means a local planning authority for all or any part of the area in which the land to which the decision relates is situated.

1 Definition repealed by Localism Act 2011, ss 128(2), 237, Sch 13, paras 1, 70(1), (8), Sch 25, Pt 20 (1 April 2012).

Schedule 5 Provision relating to, or to matters ancillary to, development

Part 1 The matters

1

The acquisition of land, compulsorily or by agreement.

2

The creation, suspension or extinguishment of, or interference with, interests in or rights over land (including rights of navigation over water), compulsorily or by agreement.

3

The abrogation or modification of agreements relating to land.

4

Carrying out specified excavation, mining, quarrying or boring operations in a specified area.

5

The operation of a generating station.

6

Keeping electric lines installed above ground.

7

The use of underground gas storage facilities.

8

The sale, exchange or appropriation of Green Belt land.

9

Freeing land from any restriction imposed on it by or under the Green Belt (London and Home Counties) Act 1938 (c. xciii), or by a covenant or other agreement entered into for the purposes of that Act.

10

The protection of the property or interests of any person.

11

The imposition or exclusion of obligations or liability in respect of acts or omissions.

12

Carrying out surveys or taking soil samples.

13

Cutting down, uprooting, topping or lopping trees or shrubs or cutting back their roots.

14

The removal, disposal or re-siting of apparatus.

15

Carrying out civil engineering or other works.

16

The diversion of navigable or non-navigable watercourses.

17

The stopping up or diversion of highways.

18

Charging tolls, fares [(including penalty fares)][1] and other charges.

1 Words inserted by Localism Act 2011, s 128(2), Sch 13, paras 1, 71(1), (2) (1 April 2012).

19

The designation of a highway as a trunk road or special road.

20

The specification of the classes of traffic authorised to use a highway.

21

The appropriation of a highway for which the person proposing to construct or improve a highway is the highway authority.

22

The transfer to the person proposing to construct or improve a highway of a highway for which that person is not the highway authority.

23

The specification of the highway authority for a highway.

24

The operation and maintenance of a transport system.

25

Entering into an agreement for the provision of police services.

26

The discharge of water into inland waters or underground strata.

27–30 …

> Repealed by Marine and Coastal Access Act 2009, s 321, Sch 22, Pt 2 (6 April 2011).

[30A

Deeming a marine licence under Part 4 of the Marine and Coastal Access Act 2009 to have been given by the Secretary of State for activities specified in the order and subject to such conditions as may be specified in the order.][1]

1 Added by Marine and Coastal Access Act 2009, s 112(1), Sch 8, para 4(1), (5) (6 April 2011).

[30B

Deeming any such conditions to have been attached to the marine licence by the Secretary of State under that Part.][1]

1 Added by Marine and Coastal Access Act 2009, s 112(1), Sch 8, para 4(1), (5) (6 April 2011).

31

The creation of a harbour authority.

32

Changing the powers and duties of a harbour authority.

[32A

The making of byelaws by any person and their enforcement.][1]

1 Added by Localism Act 2011, s 128(2), Sch 13, paras 1, 71(1), (3) (1 April 2012).

[32B

(1) The creation of offences within sub-paragraph (2) in connection with—

(a) non-payment of tolls, fares or other charges,

(b) a person's failure to give the person's name or address in accordance with provision relating to penalty fares,

(c) enforcement of byelaws, or

(d) construction, improvement, maintenance or management of a harbour.

(2) An offence is within this sub-paragraph if—

(a) it is triable only summarily,

(b) a person guilty of the offence is not liable to imprisonment, and

(c) any fine to which a person guilty of the offence may be liable cannot be higher than level 3 on the standard scale.][1]

1 Added by Localism Act 2011, s 128(2), Sch 13, paras 1, 71(1), (3) (1 April 2012).

33

The transfer of property, rights, liabilities, or functions.

34

The transfer, leasing, suspension, discontinuance and revival of undertakings.

35

The payment of contributions.

36

The payment of compensation.

37

The submission of disputes to arbitration.

38

The alteration of borrowing limits.

Part 2 Interpretation

39

(1) This paragraph applies for the purposes of this Schedule.

(2) 'Transport system' means any of the following—

(a) a railway,

(b) a tramway,

(c) a trolley vehicle system,

(d) a system using a mode of guided transport prescribed by order under section 2 of the Transport and Works Act 1992 (c. 42).

(3) 'Maintenance', in relation to a transport system, includes the inspection, repair, adjustment, alteration, removal, reconstruction or replacement of the system.

(4) The following terms have the meanings given by section 67(1) (interpretation) of the Transport and Works Act 1992 (c. 42)—

'guided transport',

'tramway',

'trolley vehicle system'.

Schedule 6 Changes to, and revocation of, orders granting development consent

Preliminary

1

(1) This paragraph applies for the purposes of this Schedule.

(2) 'The applicant', in relation to a development consent order, means the person who applied for the order.

(3) 'A successor in title of the applicant' means a person who—

(a) derives title to the land from the applicant (whether directly or indirectly), and

(b) has an interest in the land.

[...][1]

(5) 'Development consent order' means an order granting development consent.

(6) 'The land', in relation to a development consent order, means the land to which the order relates or any part of that land.

1 Repealed by Localism Act 2011, ss 128(2), 237, Sch 13, paras 1, 72(1), (2), Sch 25, Pt 20 (1 April 2012).

Non-material changes

2

(1) The [Secretary of State][1] may make a change to a development consent order if [the Secretary of State][2] is satisfied that the change is not material.

This is subject to sub-paragraph (13).

(2) In deciding whether a change is material, the [Secretary of State][1] must have regard to the effect of the change, together with any previous changes made under this paragraph, on the development consent order as originally made.

(3) The power conferred by sub-paragraph (1) includes power—

(a) to impose new requirements in connection with the development for which consent is granted by the development consent order;

(b) to remove or alter existing requirements.

(4) The power conferred by sub-paragraph (1) may be exercised only on an application made to the [Secretary of State][3] by or on behalf of—

(a) the applicant or a successor in title of the applicant,

(b) a person with an interest in the land, or

(c) any other person for whose benefit the development consent order has effect.

(5) An application under sub-paragraph (4) must be made in the prescribed form and manner.

(6) Sub-paragraph (7) applies in relation to an application under sub-paragraph (4) made by or on behalf of a person with an interest in some, but not all, of the land to which the development consent order relates.

(7) The application may be made only in respect of so much of the order as affects the land in which the person has an interest.

(8) The [Secretary of State][1] [and the person who has made the application under subparagraph (4)][4] must comply with such requirements as may be prescribed as to consultation and publicity in relation to the exercise of the power conferred by sub-paragraph (1).

This is subject to sub-paragraphs (9) to (11).

[(8A) The power to make regulations under sub-paragraph (8) includes power to allow the Secretary of State or the person who has made the application under sub-paragraph (4) to exercise a discretion.][5]

(9) If the development consent order was required to be contained in a statutory instrument, the power conferred by sub-paragraph (1) may be exercised only by order contained in a statutory instrument.

[…][6]

(11) As soon as practicable after the instrument [containing the order][7] is made, the [Secretary of State][1] must deposit a copy of it in the office of the Clerk of the Parliaments.

(12) If a change is made to a development consent order under the power conferred by sub-paragraph (1)—

(a) the order continues in force,

(b) the [Secretary of State][1] must give notice of the change to the order to such persons as may be prescribed, and

(c) the change to the order takes effect from the date on which the notice is issued, or, if the change to the order is required to be made by order contained in a statutory instrument, the date specified in the order making the change.

(13) The power conferred by sub-paragraph (1) may not be exercised in relation to provision included in an order granting development consent by virtue of [paragraph 30A or 30B of Schedule 5 (deemed marine licence under Marine and Coastal Access Act 2009)][8].

1 Words substituted by Localism Act 2011, s 128(2), Sch 13, paras 1, 72(1), (3) (1 April 2012).
2 Word substituted by Localism Act 2011, s 128(2), Sch 13, paras 1, 72(1), (4) (1 April 2012).
3 Word substituted by Localism Act 2011, s 128(2), Sch 13, paras 1, 72(1), (5) (1 April 2012).
4 Words inserted by Infrastructure Act 2015, s 28(1), (2)(a) (12 February 2015).
5 Inserted by Infrastructure Act 2015, s 28(1), (2)(b) (12 February 2015).
6 Repealed by Localism Act 2011, ss 128(2), 237, Sch 13, paras 1, 72(1), (6), Sch 25, Pt 20 (1 April 2012).
7 Words inserted by Localism Act 2011, s 128(2), Sch 13, paras 1, 72(1), (7) (1 April 2012).
8 Words substituted by Marine and Coastal Access Act 2009, s 112(1), Sch 8, para 4(1), (6)(a) (1 October 2011: substitution came into force on 6 April 2011 but cannot take effect until the commencement of Planning Act 2008, Sch 6, para 2 on 1 October 2011).

Changes to, and revocation of, orders granting development consent

3

(1) The [Secretary of State][1] may by order make a change to, or revoke, a development consent order.

(2) The power conferred by sub-paragraph (1) may be exercised only in accordance with—

(a) the following provisions of this paragraph, and

(b) paragraphs 4 and 5.

(3) The power may be exercised without an application being made if the [Secretary of State][1] is satisfied that—

(a) the development consent order contains a significant error, and

(b) it would not be appropriate for the error to be corrected by means of the power conferred by paragraph 1 of Schedule 4 or paragraph 2 of this Schedule.

(4) The power may be exercised on an application made by or on behalf of—

(a) the applicant or a successor in title of the applicant,

(b) a person with an interest in the land, or

(c) any other person for whose benefit the development consent order has effect.

(5) The power may be exercised on an application made by a local planning authority if the [Secretary of State][1] is satisfied that—

(a) the development consent order grants development consent for development on land all or part of which is in the local planning authority's area,

(b) the development has begun but has been abandoned, and

(c) the amenity of other land in the local planning authority's area or an adjoining area is adversely affected by the condition of the land.

[(5A) The Secretary of State may refuse to exercise the power on an application made under sub-paragraph (4) or (5) if, in particular, the Secretary of State considers that the development that would be authorised as a result of the change should properly be the subject of an application under section 37 for a development consent order.][2]

[...][3]

(7) [The][4] power may be exercised without an application being made if the Secretary of State is satisfied that—

(a) if the development were carried out in accordance with the development consent order, there would be a contravention of [EU][5] law or any of the Convention rights, or

(b) there are other exceptional circumstances that make it appropriate to exercise the power.

(8) In this paragraph—

['EU law'][5] means—

(a) all the rights, powers, liabilities, obligations and restrictions from time to time created or arising by or under the [EU][6] Treaties, and

(b) all the remedies and procedures from time to time provided for by or under the [EU][6] Treaties;

'the Convention rights' has the same meaning as in the Human Rights Act 1998 (c. 42).

1 Words substituted by Localism Act 2011, s 128(2), Sch 13, paras 1, 72(1), (3) (1 April 2012).
2 Inserted by Infrastructure Act 2015, s 28(1), (3) (12 February 2015).
3 Repealed by Localism Act 2011, ss 128(2), 237, Sch 13, para 1, 72(1), (8), Sch 25, Pt 20 (1 April 2012).
4 Words substituted by Localism Act 2011, s 128(2), Sch 13, paras 1, 72(1), (9) (1 April 2012).

5 Word substituted by Treaty of Lisbon (Changes in Terminology) Order 2011, SI 2011/1043, art 6(2)(a) (1 October 2011: substitution came into force on 22 April 2011 but cannot take effect until the commencement of Planning Act 2008, Sch 6, para 3).

6 Word substituted by Treaty of Lisbon (Changes in Terminology) Order 2011, SI 2011/1043, art 6(1)(a) (1 October 2011: substitution came into force on 22 April 2011 but cannot take effect until the commencement of Planning Act 2008, Sch 6, para 3).

Changes to, and revocation of, orders: supplementary

4

(1) An application under paragraph 3 must be—

(a) made in the prescribed form and manner, and

(b) accompanied by information of a prescribed description.

(2) Sub-paragraph (3) applies in relation to an application under paragraph 3(4) made by or on behalf of a person with an interest in some, but not all, of the land to which the development consent order relates.

(3) The application may be made only in respect of so much of the order as affects the land in which the person has an interest.

(4) The Secretary of State may by regulations make provision about—

(a) the procedure to be followed before an application under paragraph 3 is made;

(b) the making of such an application;

(c) the decision-making process in relation to the exercise of the power conferred by paragraph 3(1);

(d) the making of the decision as to whether to exercise that power;

(e) the effect of a decision to exercise that power.

(5) Paragraphs (c) to (e) of sub-paragraph (4) apply in relation to the exercise of the power conferred by paragraph 3(1)—

(a) on an application under paragraph 3, or

(b) on the initiative of the [Secretary of State][1] under paragraph 3(3) or (7).

[(5A) The power to make regulations under sub-paragraph (4) includes power to allow a person to exercise a discretion.][2]

(6) If a development consent order is changed or revoked in the exercise of the power conferred by paragraph 3(1), the [Secretary of State][1] must give notice of the change or revocation to such persons as may be prescribed.

(7) If a development consent order was required to be contained in a statutory instrument, an order changing or revoking the development consent order made in the exercise of the power conferred by paragraph 3(1) must also be contained in a statutory instrument.

[…][3]

(9) As soon as practicable after the instrument [containing the order][4] is made, the [Secretary of State][1] must deposit a copy of it in the office of the Clerk of the Parliaments.

1 Words substituted by Localism Act 2011, s 128(2), Sch 13, paras 1, 72(1), (3) (1 April 2012).
2 Inserted by Infrastructure Act 2015, s 28(1), (4) (12 February 2015).
3 Repealed by Localism Act 2011, ss 128(2), 237, Sch 13, paras 1, 72(1), (10), Sch 25, Pt 20 (1 April 2012).
4 Words inserted by Localism Act 2011, s 128(2), Sch 13, paras 1, 72(1), (11) (1 April 2012).

5

(1) This paragraph applies in relation to the power conferred by paragraph 3(1) to make a change to, or revoke, a development consent order.

(2) The power may not be exercised after the end of the period of 4 years beginning with the date on which the relevant development was substantially completed.

(3) Sub-paragraph (2) does not prevent the exercise of the power—

(a) in relation to requirements imposed by the development consent order in connection with the relevant development, or

(b) to revoke the development consent order.

(4) The power includes power—

(a) to require the removal or alteration of buildings or works;

(b) to require the discontinuance of a use of land;

(c) to impose specified requirements in connection with the continuance of a use of land;

(d) to impose new requirements in connection with the relevant development;

(e) to remove or alter existing requirements.

(5) Subject to sub-paragraph (4)(a), the exercise of the power does not affect any building or other operations carried out in pursuance of the development consent order before the power is exercised.

(6) The power may not be exercised in relation to provision included in an order granting development consent by virtue of [paragraph 30A or 30B of Schedule 5 (deemed marine licence under Marine and Coastal Access Act 2009)][1].

(7) 'The relevant development' is the development for which consent is granted by the development consent order.

1 Words substituted by Marine and Coastal Access Act 2009, s 112(1), Sch 8, para 4(1), (6)(b) (1 October 2011: substitution came into force on 6 April 2011 but cannot take effect until the commencement of Planning Act 2008, Sch 6, para 5 on 1 October 2011).

Compensation

6

(1) This paragraph applies if—

(a) in exercise of the power conferred by paragraph 3, the [Secretary of State][1] makes a change to, or revokes, a development consent order,

(b) the case in which the power is exercised is one falling within sub-paragraph (3) […][2] or (7) of that paragraph,

(c) on a claim for compensation under this paragraph it is shown that a person with an interest in the land, or for whose benefit the development consent order has effect—

(i) has incurred expenditure in carrying out work which is rendered abortive by the change or revocation, or

(ii) has otherwise sustained loss or damage which is directly attributable to the change or revocation, and

(d) the claim is made to the [Secretary of State][1] in the prescribed manner and before the end of the prescribed period.

(2) Compensation in respect of the expenditure, loss or damage is payable to the person [by the Secretary of State.][3]

(3) The reference in sub-paragraph (1)(c)(i) to expenditure incurred in carrying out any work includes a reference to expenditure incurred—

(a) in the preparation of plans for the purposes of the work, or

(b) on other similar matters preparatory to carrying out the work.

(4) Subject to sub-paragraph (3), no compensation is to be paid under this paragraph—

(a) in respect of any work carried out before the development consent order was made, or

(b) in respect of any other loss or damage arising out of anything done or omitted to be done before the development consent order was made (other than loss or damage consisting of depreciation of the value of an interest in land).

(5) The Secretary of State may by regulations make provision about the assessment of compensation payable under this paragraph.

(6) The regulations may in particular include provision—

(a) for the reference of disputes about compensation for depreciation to, and the determination of such disputes by, […][4] the Lands Tribunal for Scotland, the First-tier Tribunal or the Upper Tribunal;

(b) applying, with or without modifications, a provision of or made under an Act.

1 Words substituted by Localism Act 2011, s 128(2), Sch 13, paras 1, 72(1), (3) (1 April 2012).
2 Word repealed by Localism Act 2011, s 237, Sch 25, Pt 20 (1 April 2012).
3 Words substituted for para 6(2)(a)-(b) and words by Localism Act 2011, s 128(2), Sch 13, paras 1, 72(1), (12) (1 April 2012).
4 Words repealed by Transfer of Tribunal Functions (Lands Tribunal and Miscellaneous Amendments) Order 2009, SI 2009/1307, art 5(1), (2), Sch 1, paras 291, 297 (1 June 2009).

7

(1) In this paragraph 'compensation for depreciation' means compensation payable under paragraph 6 in respect of loss or damage consisting of depreciation of the value of an interest in land.

(2) The Secretary of State may by regulations make provision about the apportionment of compensation for depreciation between different parts of the land to which the claim for the compensation relates.

(3) The regulations may in particular include provision about—

(a) who is to make an apportionment;

(b) the persons to whom notice of an apportionment is to be given;

(c) how an apportionment is to be made;

(d) the reference of disputes about an apportionment to, and the determination of such disputes by, [...][1] the Lands Tribunal for Scotland, the First-tier Tribunal or the Upper Tribunal.

(4) The Secretary of State may by regulations make provision for, and in connection with, the giving of notice of compensation for depreciation.

(5) The regulations may in particular include provision about—

(a) the persons to whom notice of compensation for depreciation is to be given;

(b) the status of such a notice;

(c) the registration of such a notice.

1 Words repealed by Transfer of Tribunal Functions (Lands Tribunal and Miscellaneous Amendments) Order 2009, SI 2009/1307, art 5(1), (2), Sch 1, paras 291, 297 (1 June 2009).

Schedule 7 ...

Amends Town and Country Planning Act 1990, Planning (Listed Buildings and Conservation Areas) Act 1990 and Planning and Compulsory Purchase Act 2004.

Schedule 8 ...

Amends Forestry Act 1967, Town and Country Planning Act 1990 and Planning and Compensation Act 1991.

Schedule 9 ...

Amends Local Government, Planning and Land Act 1980, New Towns Act 1981, Housing Act 1988, Town and Country Planning Act 1990 and Leasehold Reform, Housing and Urban Development Act 1993.

Schedule 10 ...

Amends Town and Country Planning Act 1990, Planning (Listed Buildings and Conservation Areas) Act 1990 and Planning (Hazardous Substances) Act 1990.

Schedule 11 ...

Amends Town and Country Planning Act 1990, Planning (Listed Buildings and Conservation Areas) Act 1990 and Planning (Hazardous Substances) Act 1990.

Schedule 12 ...

Modifies Town and Country Planning (Scotland) Act 1997,

Schedule 13 ...

Amends Forestry Act 1967, Town and Country Planning Act 1990, Environmental Protection Act 1990, Planning and Compensation Act 1991, Planning and Compulsory Purchase Act 2004 and Greater London Authority Act 2007.

Index